CHICAGO'S BATTERY BOYS

The Chicago Mercantile Battery
in the Civil War's Western Theater

Richard Brady Williams

D1414404

SB

Savas Beatie

New York and California

Cataloging-in-Publication Data is available from the Library of Congress.

ISBN 978-1-932714-38-8

First paperback edition, first printing

SB

Published by
Savas Beatie LLC
521 Fifth Avenue, Suite 3400
New York, NY 10175
Phone: 610-853-9131

Front cover: Death of Sergeant Dyer, engraved by J. J. Cade

Back cover: Chicago Mercantile Battery bugle, courtesy of Don Troiani

Cover design by Taylor J. Poole

Savas Beatie titles are available at special discounts for bulk purchases in the United States by corporations, institutions, and other organizations. For more details, please contact Special Sales, P.O. Box 4527, El Dorado Hills, CA 95762, or you may e-mail us at sales@savasbeatie.com, or click over and visit our website at www.savasbeatie.com for additional information.

— To Mary Jo, my wife and best friend for 31 wonderful years, who has supported my passion for preserving American Civil War stories, memorabilia, and battlefields;

— To my son Rick and daughter Elizabeth for their love and encouragement;

— And in memory of my avid-reading parents, Charles Brady and Josephine Nancy Williams, who are not here to join me in celebrating the publication of *Chicago's Battery Boys*

"WE DRAGGED ONE GUN UP."

Patrick H. White and his Chicago Mercantile Battery attacking
the 2nd Texas Lunette at Vicksburg, May 22, 1863.

Contents

Contents (continued)

[Note: This special reprint edition features the recent and remarkable discovery of dozens of previously unpublished images of men who served in the Chicago Mercantile Battery. These images, courtesy of the David Ray Private Collection, have been added to the book following the Index as Appendix 3.]

Maps, Photographs, and Illustrations

Maps, photographs, and illustrations are located throughout this work for the convenience of the reader.

Foreword

On September 28, 1955, I reported for duty at Vicksburg National Military Park to begin my 40-year career as a National Park Service historian. A long-time "Civil War buff," my focus had heretofore been on the War in the East and its associated personalities and commands. My first task would be to familiarize myself with the park and my responsibility to interpret the story of the Vicksburg Campaign to a diverse audience with varying degrees of interest in the Civil War—from the casual to the student. With the encouragement of Assistant Superintendent James Ford, I spent my first week on the job walking the park's roads, ridges, and ravines. I read the inscriptions and visited the sites of most of the park's hundreds of monuments and memorials.

It was then that I had my introduction to the Chicago Mercantile Battery and Captain Patrick White. The White portrait plaque was then located on Baldwin's Ferry Road. Nearby in the adjacent cemetery were and are iron War Department tablets describing the battery's role in the May 22, 1863, Union assault. The battery monument was on Union Avenue adjacent to what was called then Indiana Circle. Before the late 1960s and construction of the current visitor center, the Baldwin's Ferry

Road was a major access to the park's visitor center and Confederate Avenue. Also adjacent to the unit monument and White plaque, then as now, is Ansche Chesed Cemetery established in August 1863. The cemetery occupies the site of the 2nd Texas Lunette, a key Confederate work associated with the failed Union assault of May 22. In the ensuing Vicksburg siege, the lunette was the site of A. J. Smith's Approach—one of the most bitterly contested by the Confederates of the thirteen Union approaches.

Several other factors—besides closeness to the original visitor center and battle and siege actions at the 2nd Texas Lunette and Baldwin's Ferry Road—drew my attention to the Chicago Mercantile Battery's monument and White's portrait plaque. First, it was the unit's designation. At that time, being familiar with Chicago because of 1930s visits to my paternal grandparents who lived in the Windy City, I believed mistakenly that the battery was sponsored by the Merchandise Mart. After all, the Army of the Cumberland's Board of Trade Battery had been sponsored by the Chicago institution by that name. Second, why did Captain White merit a battlefield plaque? At Vicksburg there are 17 memorial statues, 63 memorial busts, and 95 memorial portrait plaques. Of the latter, only nine honor captains.

Finally, one of my vivid memories of my ten and one-half years at the Vicksburg park is associated with a late May 1956 visit to the park by Stephen Ambrose, who was at that time a young graduate of the University of Wisconsin. Steve was on the eve of entering the history graduate program at Louisiana State University. There, his major professor and mentor would be the articulate, much published, and beloved T. Harry Williams. Ambrose had bicycled from his home in Whitewater, Wisconsin, by way of Fort Donelson, Shiloh, and Corinth to Vicksburg. His purpose was to reconnoiter onsite Civil War battlefields to facilitate work on his thesis that was later published in 1962 by LSU Press under the title *Halleck: Lincoln's Chief of Staff*. After touring the Vicksburg park, Steve and I sat on the ground adjacent to Captain White's plaque, the Mercantile Battery's monument, and War Department tablets describing battle and siege actions at the 2nd Texas Lunette. We discussed the Vicksburg Campaign, U. S. Grant, General Halleck, and the "Battery Boys."

In subsequent years I expanded my Civil War horizons. In 1964, with the approach of the centennial of Nathaniel P. Banks' Red River

Campaign, I learned that both Captain White and his Chicagoans had had a bad day at Mansfield. My first visit to the Mansfield State Commemorative Area and other sites associated with Banks' failed campaign came in 1992 and was associated with my participation in the Congressionally mandated Civil War Sites Advisory Commission and its Baton Rouge public meeting. In the years since I have become increasingly familiar with that campaign and the Battle of Mansfield, having led a number of field trips to the region for such heritage interest groups as the Blue & Gray Education Society, Delta Queen Co., History America, and the Civil War Round Table Associates.

These trips and the people I met paid a worthwhile personal dividend in November 1998 when I led a tour of the Vicksburg Campaign for the Blue & Gray Education Society. Among the participants was Richard Brady Williams, a successful businessman with a keen interest in the Civil War. He told me of his desire to know more about and visit campaign sites associated with the Chicago Mercantile Battery and Captain White. In view of Rick's subject knowledge this added for both me and other battlefield aficionados a special dimension to this Vicksburg tour.

In November 2000, Williams joined me and others on a week-long tour of Louisiana Civil War sites sponsored by History America. This enabled him to retrace sites associated with the Chicago Mercantile Battery in the 1863 Teche Campaign and Banks' disastrous Red River expedition. Rick's presence on the tour and the insights he added on the experiences of the "Battery Boys," again as in 1998, enriched the tour.

At this time Rick informed me of his continuing research looking toward preparation and publication of a much needed and deserved Chicago Mercantile Battery unit history. He also told me about his "serendipitous" discovery of a treasure trove of Civil War correspondence—132 letters written by Quartermaster William L. Brown—archived in the Chicago Historical Society's collections but not available to the general public. Williams scored a coup by securing the Society's permission to edit and publish them. The Brown correspondence provided Williams an essential core around which to weave what proved to be a first-class unit history.

In 2002, Williams asked me to review and comment on the manuscript unit history he had researched and written titled *Chicago's Battery Boys: The Chicago Mercantile Battery in the Civil War's*

Western Theater. Twin factors—more than forty years of association with the Chicago battery, the Vicksburg Campaign, and Banks' Red River Expedition, and four years with Rick Williams as a frequent and knowledgeable tour participant—called for a positive response on my part.

A careful reading of the Williams typescript fired my enthusiasm for what I read. In masterful fashion Williams builds on the Brown correspondence incorporating other eyewitness accounts to tell the story of Captain White, Quartermaster Brown, and their comrades' wartime experiences. Thanks to his research and writing skills, Williams has provided a masterful unit history about "Chicago's Battery Boys."

Therefore, when Rick asked me to author his Foreword I felt honored because I do not accept this challenge lightly. I see a Foreword as constituting my imprimatur of a book. It has been a long time, but thanks to Rick, the Chicago Historical Society, cartographer George Skoch, and others, "Chicago's Battery Boys" finally get their due. As a unit history *Chicago's Battery Boys* measures up to the standard of excellence set for this genre by the late John J. Pullen back in 1957, when he authored *The Twentieth Maine: A Volunteer Regiment in the Civil War*.

Edwin C. Bearss
Chief Historian Emeritus
National Park Service

"It was a rich man's Battery with a poor man Captain."

Preface

As the jubilant members of the Chicago Mercantile Battery jumped off the train, they were disappointed to discover that few people were there to greet them. Passengers scurried past Captain Pat White and his returning artillerists into the station, rubbing the sleep and smoke out of their eyes as they prepared to enter the vibrant commercial center of the Old Northwest. What happened to the celebrations that other returning soldiers had experienced? Quartermaster Sergeant Will Brown, like many of his friends, was an avid reader of Chicago's newspapers and had followed the accounts of Civil War veterans on their way home to Wisconsin, Iowa, and Minnesota being hailed by flag-waving throngs, and then treated to festive dinners. He and his comrades did not expect a parade at 7:00 a.m. in the morning, but at least some of the city's leaders could have been there to welcome the returning hometown boys. But there was no cheering crowd, and the only whistling came from the steam locomotive of a departing train.[1]

Where were the Mercantile Association members who had sponsored and funded the company? Had the businessmen forgotten about their battery's Monday arrival on the Illinois Central Railroad? Or had they ignored the telegrams, which the artillerists had sent from Cairo after they disembarked from the *Brilliant*, upon completion of their journey up the Mississippi River?

The Mercantile Association (unrelated to today's Chicago Mercantile Exchange) had recruited some of the best and brightest young men in Chicago—including their own sons and employees—to become the first wave of "Battery Boys" in August 1862. At that time, the Mercantile Battery's sponsors made sure that the new "redlegs" were provided with glistening bronze cannon, up-to-date equipment, and, as the *Chicago Tribune* noted, "a handsome set of colors." The community leaders arranged for exhibition drills and dinner parties, held while the battery was training at Camp Doggett in South Chicago, to showcase the courageous young men who had responded to Lincoln's call for more troops. Upon mustering in, Will Brown told his father that the city's merchants "promise to take care of us and see that we are treated well."[2]

Were the mercantilists reneging on their promise because a majority of the original 153 Chicago Mercantile Battery recruits had already returned home? Most of them had mustered out early due to wounds or other disabilities. Eleven of the initial Battery Boys had died during the war. Another fifteen artillerists had returned to Chicago during the previous month, including John W. Arnold and four of his comrades, who had obtained permission to leave New Orleans so they could recover from their 18 months of captivity at Camp Ford in Texas. (Upon returning home, Arnold showed his family and friends the scrimshaw powder horn he carved as a memento of his ordeal at the Andersonville-like prison pen.) Some of the soldiers arriving on July 3, 1865, from both the first and second waves of recruits, may have wondered if Arnold and their other early-returning comrades had also faced an empty train station when they returned to Chicago.[3]

The war started off well for the Chicago merchants' battery. The affluent businessmen had been thrilled when the cannoneers received accolades for their courage and handiwork during the Vicksburg Campaign—Captain White and some of his men would later receive the Medal of Honor for their heroic actions during the May 22, 1863, assault on the 2nd Texas Lunette. After the war, their commander, Brigadier General A. J. Smith, noted, "White's battery was the only one that even for a moment gained possession of the enemy's line" during that day's attack against the left side of the Southerners' fortifications at Vicksburg. "The general never forgot White's bravery," recalled Smith's son.[4]

Garrison duty and drilling kept the unit from resuming combat until the spring of 1864, when the luck of the Battery Boys took a turn for the worse in the northwestern pine forests of Louisiana at Sabine Crossroads (Mansfield). Nathaniel Banks' Red River Campaign began with great promise, but quickly devolved due to the general's overconfidence and his battlefield mismanagement. The combat at Sabine Crossroads had a devastating effect on the Chicago organization. Four men were killed and several others wounded; many Mercantile Battery soldiers—including some of the company's highest-ranking officers—were herded like cattle past Shreveport to a Confederate prison camp in eastern Texas. Worst yet, the guns that had served the artillerists so well on different fields, along with most of their equipment and personal belongings, were snatched from them at the point of the bayonet. The unarmed survivors, dismayed by the defeat and in a state of shock, retreated with the rest of the army. The appalling experience of April 8, 1864, gripped each survivor and did not release its tentacles until the war's end.[5]

Letters sent home by the embittered redlegs, penned in the aftermath of the disastrous campaign, broke the Sabine Crossroads news blackout and created a political firestorm that swept across the country, thereby enraging the Mercantile Battery's commanding general and his staff. A whiff of high-level revenge lingered in the stifling, humid Louisiana air. For the Union cannoneers, the scent was not a pleasant one, and the weeks following the Red River fiasco were consumed with court-martials, embarrassing infantry duty, and accusations of mutiny. Only the Mercantile Association's extensive political network saved the Chicago battery from an even worse fate. The artillerists continued their service until the Confederate surrender, though they served as horse artillery rather than as a light field battery.[6]

Despite all that the Battery Boys had endured, none of their guardian angels were present to greet them when they arrived in Chicago on July 3, 1865. Were their Mercantile Association sponsors as forgiving about the mutiny fiasco as they had expressed in their letters the previous summer? The soldiers huddled together in small groups outside the train station, offering consolation to one another as they looked for their family and friends—some feeling like they were back in camp, agonizing, waiting for the sporadic mail service to bring news from home. The artillerists watched smoke drift back from departing trains. Memories of battlefield victories seemed to fade as the anxious men thought about past mistakes and their current predicament. Unbeknownst to them a telegraph problem prevented the Mercantile Association from knowing when the cannoneers had returned from Cairo. The business organization immediately rectified the situation upon receipt of the delayed dispatch.[7]

As the years passed, the thriving economy in the "New York City of the Midwest" provided ample opportunities for many of the men in White's Battery to accomplish as much in business as their Mercantile Association sponsors had—or, in Will Brown's case, to become even more successful. (Will Brown would become one of the wealthiest industrialists in the Midwest.) Members who stayed in the Chicago area sought to preserve their Civil War memories and friendships by forming a Chicago Mercantile Battery organization. Will served a stint as the group's president and Pat White, who moved to Albany after the war, sometimes took a train from his home to attend the battery's reunions.[8]

More than forty years after the war, a thin handful of the battery's survivors exercised their political and financial clout to make sure the unit was well represented at the new Vicksburg National Military Park. They wanted to be on hand when Illinois' $250,000 monument to its Civil War soldiers was dedicated in October 1906. Other monuments would follow, including one to Captain White. Unfortunately, the 2nd Texas Lunette was not preserved because the area had been converted into a civilian cemetery after the Confederate surrender. Park officials have historically played down the Union assault on the Rebel fort in an effort to prevent visitors to the Vicksburg battlefield from damaging the cemetery. This unlucky development ensured that the valor of Captain Patrick White and his brave Battery Boys has never been fully interpreted to park visitors.[9]

Despite the Chicago Mercantile Battery's stellar combat record and amazing journey through the Civil War, there has never been a comprehensive history written about White's company. No one stood to present a paper at a GAR or MOLLUS veterans' meeting; no one submitted an article to the *National Tribune*; none of the battery's soldiers published his diary, letters, or a reminiscence of the war. There is not a single known Mercantile Battery reunion or memorial keepsake. And this acclaimed Chicago artillery unit is rarely mentioned in books about the Civil War in the Western Theater, Medal of Honor recipients, or histories of Illinois troops.[10]

The 1871 Chicago Fire may have been one reason that nothing substantive was recorded by members of the Mercantile Battery. Many ex-soldiers lost their war mementos and personal documents (just as the Chicago Historical Society had), which made it difficult or impossible for them to chronicle their military experience. Thankfully, Mary Livermore had access to some of the Mercantile Battery's Civil War documents, including the diary of George Throop who, along with 33 other Battery Boys, had attended her husband's Church of the Redeemer in Chicago before the war. The famous women's suffragette featured Lt. Throop and his comrades in her 1887 book *My Story of the War*.[11]

It was not until almost a century after the Chicago Mercantile Battery disbanded that any major firsthand account appeared in print. In 1958, the diaries of Bugler Florison Pitts were featured in *Mid-America*, a regional Ohio publication. Sadly, only 40% of the diary was printed.[12]

Captain Pat White's posthumous memoir preceded the Pitts' article when it was published in the January 1923 issue of the *Journal of the Illinois Historical Society*. Only White's earlier service in Ezra Taylor's Battery B, 1st Illinois Light Artillery, however, was covered.[13]

The result of this dearth of published material leaves battery member Will Brown's comprehensive Civil War letter collection as one of the few primary sources covering the Chicago Mercantile Battery's service. Brown considered his record so valuable he paid to have each page of the 132 letters professionally mounted onto customized parchment papers. All 400 pages were bound in an ornately decorated blue-leather volume he presented to his father as a gift. The set of letters is now part of the Chicago Historical Society's collection. In the intervening years since Brown's volume was donated to the archives, it has been difficult for anyone to read his entire correspondence. Only a few of the letters have been copied for the general public to review. The complete letter collection forms the backbone of the book you are now reading.[14]

During his service in the Union army, Brown wrote a letter to his father almost every week, usually on Sundays. He also sent letters to his brothers Henry and Liberty (Lib) who, like Will, spent their military service in the Western Theater. The Battery Boy was often privy to undisclosed military information. For example, he once wrote his father that "The Captain is a good friend and takes me considerably into his confidence." Will was therefore in a good position to formulate opinions and make predictions about what was transpiring with his own unit as well as in the Western command overall.

Along with most of his fellow Battery Boys, Will Brown was well educated and a voracious reader. He often read multiple Northern and Southern newspapers in one sitting and provided his father with ongoing assessments of the war. As a leader in the state Republican Party, Hiram A. Brown kept his son informed of political events in Michigan. During the war they maintained a dialogue about national topics like the Copperhead peace movement, conscription policies, home guards, excessive bounties, fluctuating monetary rates, Lincoln's emancipation and amnesty proclamations, McClellan's Democratic candidacy, reconstruction controversies, and war-time elections.

Like Brown, many of the initial Mercantile Battery recruits came from influential Chicago families. Mary Livermore recalled how sixteen members of her Sunday School class became Battery Boys when the unit was formed. James H. Swan, the education superintendent at her husband's Universalist Church of the Redeemer, recruited almost three dozen young men to accompany him to muster into the Chicago Mercantile Battery in August 1862. The boys, Livermore noted, were "well-born, well-bred, well-educated. . . . Some were about to enter Harvard, Tufts, or Yale, and all were connected with good families." George Throop's mother wrote a letter to his sister Mattie at that time listing some of his Sunday School classmates who were "going in the Mercantile Association Battery which is to be a fine company they think. How our people are pouring out their money and men upon the altar of freedom." Prophetically, she added, "We shall not see them all again."[15]

The first wave of Mercantile Battery recruits characterized the backgrounds and occupations of Chicago's cosmopolitan population. All were living in the Garden City at the time of enlistment. Most of the initial members were originally from New England, New York, and Pennsylvania, having moved west to pursue greater economic opportunities either with their families or on their own. Although there had been a huge influx of immigrants into Chicago prior to the war, few joined the mercantile-sponsored battery at its formation in August 1862. Only four Irishmen mustered in: Michael Graham, Patrick McGuire (who would later receive a Medal of Honor), and Edward and Patrick Moran. Five of the redlegs were born in England. John Gruber and Charles Kellerman represented the large number of Germans moving to Chicago. There were also two Battery Boys from Canada, one from elsewhere in Europe, and Edwin Osgood from the British East Indies. The occupations of the recruits reflected Chicago's emerging role as the commercial hub of the Old Northwest. When the war began, many of the city's young men were working at railroads and lumber yards, in machine shops and meat-packing plants, and for printing companies, the Board of Trade, and wholesalers. Others were employed in positions such as bookkeepers, clerks, salesmen, and cashiers to support the fast-growing businesses. The battery also attracted a lawyer, a dentist, and two civil engineers, along with a policeman, newspaper editor, musician, and artist.[16]

Pat White, an Irish immigrant who worked as a butcher before the war, and later in low-level clerical positions in Albany, commented on the company's roots in his postwar memoir: "The Chicago Mercantile Battery was raised through the efforts of the Mercantile Association of Chicago . . . it was made up mostly of the merchants' sons." After White's death, one of his friends wrote, "It was a rich man's Battery with a poor man Captain, but those sons of the merchants of the Windy City took no heed of Pat White's earthly possessions, and he cared little about theirs, but, with his remarkable military ability made it one of the notable organizations of the Civil War." White's experience in the prewar Chicago Light Artillery was respected, especially by the first Mercantile Battery recruits who had read routinely about the militia unit in their hometown newspapers. However, White had more in common with the second wave of Battery Boys who, like their leader, were from other countries. After the initial enlistment, 40% of the 131 Mercantile Battery newcomers were immigrants (versus 10% of the original recruits) with 60% of them living in Illinois communities outside of Chicago.[17]

Although Will Brown came from a prominent family and fit in well with the elite orientation of the Chicago artillery unit, his roots extended fifty miles east to Michigan and his birthplace of St. Joseph. The town was perched high on the edge of a plateau above the bluish-green waters of Lake Michigan, into which flowed its namesake river. Will often discussed St. Joseph in his wartime letters and developed analogies based on landmarks in and around the town. His father was one of its founders.[18]

The year that Will's family arrived in Chicago was a critical one for the city's growth. As one historian aptly observed, "Modern Chicago was born in 1848." Incorporated in 1833, the Garden City rapidly developed into an economic powerhouse. Meat packing and lumbering were thriving businesses. Cyrus McCormick moved to Chicago in 1848 from the Shenandoah Valley and began to manufacture his innovative reapers. The formation of the Board of Trade in March transformed Chicagoans into preeminent middlemen between the wheat and corn farmers in the Old Northwest and markets on the East Coast and in Europe. Transportation and communication advances strengthened Chicago's position as a commercial focal point in the U.S. heartland. The year began with the first telegraph connection as well as the opening of the Illinois & Michigan Canal—creating a waterway passage between Lake Michigan and the Mississippi River—and the year ended with Chicago's first railroad (the Galena & Chicago Union) making its inaugural trip into the countryside and returning with a load of wheat. Soon, horse-drawn cars would also be carrying passengers down Chicago's new gas-lit, planked streets. A visitor to Chicago in 1848 wrote that it was "a small city in a big hurry, filled with a 'restless activity.'" The city's 1850 population was 30,000; just a decade later it was nearly four times that number.[19]

While Will and his brother Lib grew up in Chicago, their older stepbrother Henry remained in St. Joseph, where he captained ships on Lake Michigan. He was commissioned as a 1st lieutenant in the 19th Michigan Infantry at the beginning of August 1862. Will worked as a clerk at a grain commission house with the Board of Trade, where he had been employed since he was fifteen. When Lincoln made his second enlistment call Will enlisted in the Chicago Mercantile Battery several weeks later. Ironically, it was Lib, the youngest Brown sibling, who first joined the Union army in December 1861. He enlisted in Company B of the 12th Michigan Infantry at his St. Joseph birthplace, where few suspected he was underage.[20]

During the Civil War Will moved into a position in the battery that fit his educational background and administrative talents. Even in times of war men naturally gravitate toward duties that capitalize on their expertise and natural strengths. For some it was drilling raw recruits, constructing bridges or roads, or simply standing on the firing line. For Will Brown it was planning, organizing, and administrating the needs of the battery—skills he had learned well as a meticulous bookkeeper in Chicago's dynamic prewar economy.

Will served first in the No. 6 position, stationed behind a battery limber and watching over the ammunition chest. The comprehensive education he received at Garden City Academy in Chicago helped him calculate shell trajectories and estimate ranges. He was promoted to gunner in his platoon and actively participated in the actions that made up the complicated Vicksburg siege. His nostrils tingled with the smell of burning black powder and his ears were nearly deafened by the thunderous roar of the Mercantile Battery cannon.

Will became the battery's acting quartermaster after the Vicksburg campaign ended. In this capacity he devoted much of his time to meeting the outfit's complex logistical needs. He learned that managing the nearly overwhelming load of paperwork was almost as difficult as handling projectiles and cutting fuses in the midst of an artillery duel. Being better educated than his immigrant captain was, Will assumed more of the company's administrative duties than a quartermaster typically handled. Though demanding, his increased responsibilities helped him refine his writing skills, which he used to chronicle what life was like in a Western artillery battery.

From the date that the Battery Boys enlisted to their final mustering out in July 1865, Will took on the role of correspondent by providing regular "field reports" to his father. The young cannoneer delighted in interviewing Southerners with whom he came into contact: businessmen, townspeople, plantation owners, young women, slaves, contrabands, Rebel prisoners, and Union loyalists. He also kept his father apprised of the latest political maneuvering within the army and paid special attention to the controversial machinations of Generals John McClernand and Nathaniel Banks. Will not only commented on what he witnessed, but incorporated insights gleaned from comrades regarding the company and its military engagements and leaders.

From the celebrated Yankee victories at Champion Hill and the siege of Vicksburg to the oblivion following General Banks' April 1864 debacle along the Red River, Will Brown provided his father with a vivid summary of the Chicago Mercantile Battery's participation in key Western campaigns. His Chicago Historical Society letter volume offers the most exhaustive record of the battery's service.[21]

After the war, Captain Pat White moved to Albany, New York, where he lived for more than fifty years. Following his death in the early 20th century, White's Medals of Honor, frock coat, pistol, and scrapbook were placed in the New York State Museum. Also included with those memorabilia was White's sword, which was miraculously returned to him after the war by the daughter of a Texan who captured it at the Battle of Sabine Crossroads. John Boos, a young Civil War enthusiast, was intrigued with his hometown's Medal of Honor winner. So, he worked with White's family to preserve the captain's memoir and other important Mercantile Battery documents (including the original letter that the Rebel officer sent to his daughter along with White's sword).

Many years later, the author acquired the red-leather keepsake produced by Boos and embarked on a journey to track down other remaining pieces of the Battery Boys' puzzle. Besides uncovering the Brown letter collection at the Chicago Historical Society, he came across extensive firsthand accounts at that institution from Florison Pitts, Henry Roe, and James Sinclair. Other missing pieces of the Mercantile Battery story were found at history centers around the country, including the Abraham Lincoln Presidential Library in Springfield, Illinois (Pinckney Cone's diary), Library of Congress (George Throop's letters), National Archives and Records Administration in Washington, D.C. (records from the battery itself as well as for key members of the unit), U.S. Army Military History Institute (George Perry letters), Vicksburg National Military Park (personal correspondence between Captain White and Commissioner Rigby), and Wisconsin Historical Society Archives (Charles Haseltine's reminiscences).

In addition to hunting for eyewitness reports, the author played "history detective" and found Mercantile Battery memorabilia from John W. Arnold (the powder horn he carved at Camp Ford), Chase Dickinson (albumen image), John Q. Mason (carte de visite), Edmund E. Osgood (carte de visite), George Perry (discharge document), and Nelson Smith (enlistment papers) along with a gold postwar medal that included an engraving of each major battle in which Captain White's battery fought. David Ray, whose relative Michael Graham was a Battery Boy, provided letters from William Husted, and artist Don Troiani graciously furnished a photograph of Florison Pitts' bugle from his personal collection.

Counting Captain White, 286 men mustered into the Chicago Mercantile Battery during its three years of existence out of nearly three million men who served in the Union. It is amazing that so many personal accounts from so few Illinois soldiers have survived. For the first time, all of the pieces of the Battery Boys' puzzle have been assembled. Thanks especially to Will Brown and Pat White, their story can now be told.

Acknowledgments

During the writing of *Chicago's Battery Boys* I often felt like I was running a marathon. But researching, writing, and editing a Civil War history book is not a solitary journey. Perhaps it is more like the *Tour de France*. When Lance Armstrong crosses the finish line he knows he could not have reached his goal without the contributions of his team members who trained with him and provided assistance during the torturous 28-day competition.

Completing a Civil War book is also a team effort. I deeply appreciate the many people—historians, tour guides, archivists, curators, librarians, researchers, fellow Civil War enthusiasts, family, and friends—who helped me along the way. Thanks to their contributions and support, I made it across the finish line. I have no doubt that Captain Pat White, Quartermaster Will Brown, and their comrades would be grateful that the Chicago Mercantile Battery's achievements are finally being recognized.

When I started studying the Civil War more than a decade ago, I was intrigued by the idea of writing a book about some aspect of this American epic. In 1995, the Civil War Preservation Trust (then the APCWS) held its annual meeting in Tupelo, Mississippi, to celebrate the acquisition of land for the Brice's Cross Roads battlefield. I had the privilege of having dinner with Shelby Foote and was fortunate to meet other Civil War authors like James McPherson, Wiley Sword, and Larry Daniel. All of them encouraged me to pursue writing on my own, but recommended that I find some aspect of the Civil War that excited me.

My opportunity emerged in the summer of 1998 at a Gettysburg memorabilia and book show. I had been collecting "identified" Civil War antiques and documents, and my journey led me to Gettysburg, where I first encountered the Chicago Mercantile Battery when I purchased the memoir and document collection of Medal of Honor winner Captain Pat White from Civil War dealer Dave Zullo. I showed White's red leather-bound volume to Theodore P. Savas, a fellow Civil War enthusiast and friend from California who was exhibiting a superb collection of books he had published with Savas Publishing Company. Both Dave and Ted agreed that the Mercantile Battery story had potential as a book project.

During the early days of my research I went to Mansfield, Louisiana, where Captain White and his artillerists fell victim to General Nathaniel Banks' ill-conceived Red River Campaign. At the Mansfield State Historic Site I met Scott Dearman, interpretive ranger, and Steve Bounds, curator and historian.

Both men were thrilled that I was interested in developing a book on the Chicago Mercantile Battery, a unit they featured at their park.

From there it was on to Vicksburg, where I attended a three-day Blue Gray Education Society tour led by Ed Bearss, battlefield-guide extraordinaire and emeritus chief historian for the National Park Service, and Terry Winschel, Ed's replacement as historian at the Vicksburg National Military Park. It was an amazing experience. Ed showed me the Mercantile Battery's specific positions during Grant's campaign, and both historians informed me that no history had been written about Pat White and his battery from Chicago. They encouraged me to play "history detective" and conduct primary research on the unit.

After that first Vicksburg tour I spent two days with Terry Winschel, who generously opened up his archival files on the Mercantile Battery, which included Captain White's postwar correspondence with the park commissioner regarding his company's monuments and markers. Terry also allowed me to stray from the park's interpretive course and retrace the path that White and his men took as they hauled a 6-pounder Napoleon and carriage (together weighing a ton) up a steep slope to fire point-blank into the Confederates holding the 2nd Texas Lunette fort—a feat for which the Irish captain and five of his surviving artillerists received the Medal of Honor in 1895. Imagine my surprise when, upon reaching the apex of the Mercantile Battery's climb, I discovered a large portrait plaque of White at the base of the Rebel fort! I am grateful to Ed Bearss and everyone else who prompted me at this nascent stage to continue investigating the battery's story.

My next stop was the Chicago Historical Society, where I reviewed the diaries of Lieutenant Henry Roe, Sergeant James Sinclair, and Bugler Florison Pitts. Serendipitously, I also uncovered 132 letters from Quartermaster Will Brown that were kept in an archival storage vault and not available to the general public. These letters, along with my unpublished White memoir, form the core of this book. I added a succinct narrative so that readers can follow these eyewitness accounts within the context of what the battery was experiencing during the war.

I appreciate the cooperation and hospitality extended to me by the Chicago Historical Society staff during my trips there. Without their support this project would not have been possible. Unfortunately, the Brown collection was too fragile to be photocopied, which meant I had to read more than 400 pages of letters onsite into a portable recorder and return home to San Francisco to transcribe and edit them.

At the New York State Museum in Albany, I was also treated with great kindness by Bob Mulligan, a retired curator who spent the day showing me Pat

White's presentation sword, Medals of Honor, and other memorabilia that were in storage at the museum. When Bob was a child growing up in Albany he met John Boos, who had assembled the White collection that I later acquired.

Dr. B. D. "Buddy" Patterson and Peggy Fox of the Confederate Research Center in Hillsboro, Texas, also befriended me. To my surprise, Buddy had a personal interest in tracking down the Mercantile Battery guns that were captured at Mansfield by Walker's Texas Division and, as such, had the Chicago artillerists' entire descriptive list, morning reports, etc. from the National Archives on microfilm. Buddy graciously loaned me his microfilm to take back to San Francisco to make copies, which enabled me to have an invaluable foundation of information about Captain White, Will Brown, and their comrades. Art Bergeron tracked me down via the Internet and provided me with background information on the Mercantile Battery cannon. Art is now serving as historian at the U.S. Army Military History Institute, which is an excellent source of information about the Civil War (when visiting my son at nearby Dickinson College, I used to conduct research at this premier research center).

Besides visiting the history centers listed above, I have been in contact with numerous other archives and museums around the country. I am especially thankful for the support I received from the following institutions: Abraham Lincoln Presidential Library (thanks to Cheryl Schnirring for her assistance with the Pinckney S. Cone diaries), Berrien County Historical Association (Robert C. Myers, museum curator, shared his personal papers on Lib Brown's 12th Michigan Infantry Regiment as well as Henry Brown's accident with the *Hippocampus* after the war), Black River Historical Society, Boston Public Library, Center for American History at The University of Texas at Austin, Chicago Public Library, Evanston Historical Society, Drum Barracks Civil War Museum, Fayette Heritage Museum & Archives (Doretha Rapp at this LaGrange, Texas, center provided me with information on Captain Alex McDow who captured Captain White and preserved his sword), Fort Miami Heritage Center (at this research center in St. Joseph, Michigan, Ken Pott showed me his center's copy of the Atlas of Berrien County, Michigan, that belonged to Will Brown's brother Lib), Library of Congress, The Mariners' Museum, National Archives and Records Administration (especially Mike Pilgrim and Rick Peuser), the Museum of Historic Natchitoches (Daniel Graves), Northwestern State University of Louisiana, Old Court House Museum, Vicksburg, Mississippi, Pasadena Public Library, San Mateo Library (my local library in California that helped me to access about 150 interlibrary-loan books), Smith County Historical Society Archives, Swem

Library, College of William and Mary, Tulane University (Bill Meneray and Leon Miller allowed me to review the only extant copies of Banks' *Era* newspaper from New Orleans), USAMHI (Louise Friend), Victoria Regional History Center, Williamsburg Regional Library, Williams Research Center of The Historic New Orleans Collection, and Wisconsin Historical Society Archives.

Thanks to the many state and national park services, and the remarkable job done by James Lighthizer and the Civil War Preservation Trust, I have been able to visit the battlefields associated with the Chicago Mercantile Battery—as well as other key Civil War sites. The dozen Ed Bearss Civil War tours that I have attended in the past decade, along with those conducted by other noted history tour guides and authors such as Mark Bradley, Peter Carmichael, William C. "Jack" Davis, Gary Ecelberger, Chris Fonvielle, Gary Gallagher, A. Wilson Greene, Herman Hattaway, Gary Joiner, Parker Hills, Robert E. L. Krick, Robert K. Krick, Brooks Simpson, Wiley Sword, Joseph Whitehorne, and Terry Winschel have been inspirational and insightful. They have given me a broad perspective on both the Eastern and Western Theaters. In this era of instant information, there is still no substitute for actually walking in the footsteps of the soldiers about whom we write. By making stories like *Chicago's Battery Boys* available, our battlefields become more real.

Camp Ford in Tyler, Texas, was another historic site that had a significant effect upon my research. Attorney Randy Gilbert is one of the resident Camp Ford experts. He not only writes extensively on this Trans-Mississippi prison pen but has played a prominent role in restoring Camp Ford into a viable local site for history enthusiasts to visit (Randy started early in trying to preserve and interpret Camp Ford: his junior high school diorama of the prison stockade was still on display at the Smith County Historical Society Archives when I visited). Randy showed Southern hospitality to a stranger from California, gave me a private tour of Camp Ford, and welcomed me into his home to share his files with me.

The publication of *Chicago's Battery Boys* was also made possible because of the impeccable research conducted by Steve Zerbe and Rosanne Butler. Steve helped me launch the project by obtaining service and pension records. Rosanne, retired after 25 years of service at the National Archives, recently became my writing partner and technical editor. She also cross-checked references, handled archival permissions, and obtained photos, none of which is an easy task. Taylor Poole, Kelly Mihalcoe, George Skoch, and Laurie Brown did outstanding jobs in designing the dust jacket, producing photos, creating maps, and developing a web site, respectively, for this book. I am very grateful artist Don Troiani provided me with a photo of his Florison Pitts bugle to use.

I received ongoing encouragement from Civil War friends like Harriet Condon, Len Riedel, (founder of the Blue Gray Education Society), Sam and Wes Small (owners of Gettysburg's Horse Soldier shop), Ed Urban, Dave Van Doren, and Dave Zullo. David Ray, whose relative Michael Graham was a Battery Boy, has been a source of inspiration and surprised me last year with a unique Christmas gift—a letter written by William Husted from the Mercantile Battery. Dave Taylor, a Civil War dealer from Ohio, is someone else who played a pivotal role with *Chicago's Battery Boys*. Dave tracked down a rare scrimshaw-carved powder horn for me that Bugler John W. Arnold carved while at Camp Ford in Texas. The story I uncovered about Arnold and his memorabilia at the Smith County Historical Society Archives in nearby Tyler, Texas, greatly enriches this book. Dave also found a gold Mercantile Battery postwar reunion medal that lists each major battle that the Chicago artillerists fought in. Thanks also to my minister friends—Jeff Farrar, Bob Menges, and Mark Mitchell—who encouraged me to embark on a journey to combine my memorabilia-collecting and writing interests.

Friends in the medical-biotech field who were especially supportive of my Civil War research and writing pursuits over the years include Dave DeLong, Ken Gross, Robert Rosen, Mike Sperling, Dr. David Stump, Bill Torchiana, and Greg Vontz from my days at Genentech; Larry Black, Marsha Millonig, Randy Perry, and Kimberly Wiltz from the time I spent at Amerisource Bergen; and Dr. Naina Bhasin, Jeff Cook, James Coon, Dr. Geraldine Hamilton, and Dr. Ed LeCluyse at the cell-based biotech company I recently helped to launch. Louis Breton and Clay Feeter are two fellow entrepreneurs and history enthusiasts who pressured me to "close the book." Without their continual phone and email prodding, I may have abandoned this project along the way.

The medical treatment provided by Dr. Wolfgang Gilliar has also made this book possible. He is an osteopathic physiatrist in Palo Alto, CA, who literally changed my life by helping me to overcome a debilitating back problem and learn the value of daily stretching to maintain mobility. Dr. Gilliar also provided me with invaluable insights he learned from his scientific writing, including the exhortation to "Write with the reader in mind."

Ed Bearss is one of the most remarkable people I have ever met and a great source of inspiration. Not only is Ed an expert on anything related to the Civil War, but he is also knowledgeable about many other aspects of American history. He has done more than almost anyone else in the past 50 years to preserve and interpret historic sites around the country. Although Ed just celebrated his 82nd birthday, he is still traveling about 250 days a year lecturing and conducting onsite history tours. Ed is truly an American treasure and someone to be emulated. His boundless energy, joie de vivre, passion for knowledge, and consideration of others makes him an exemplary role model. I am deeply honored that Ed took the time to edit my entire manuscript and then write such a complimentary Foreword.

It is often said that "Life is timing." In this case, it was a major factor in my selection of a publisher for *Chicago's Battery Boys*. Although I had kept Ted Savas apprised of my book's progress over the years, he was not in a position to take on an unpublished business executive's niche-book project. Fortunately for me, as well as many current and future Civil War writers, Ted helped launch another military history publishing company based on the high standards upon which he built his first publishing house. Together with Russel "Cap" Beatie (who authored *Army of the Potomac: Birth of Command, November 1860 – September 1861*) Ted formed Savas Beatie LLC. When I contacted him in November 2003 for his advice about finding a publisher for my book, Ted told me he was interested in taking on my project. I am grateful for Ted's ongoing friendship, patience, and guidance as well as his commitment to publish well-crafted books based on in-depth research and sound scholarship. *Chicago's Battery Boys* would not have been possible without Ted's oversight.

I offer my apologies if I overlooked anyone who helped me along the way.

When I first came across Will Brown's collection at the Chicago Historical Society, I was intrigued by the quartermaster's commitment to communicate with his father every Sunday and how he created his keepsake leather volume with "Civil War Letters from William L. Brown to His Father" written in gilt on the spine. I could relate to Will since I had spoken by phone with my father almost every Sunday evening for 25 years. Charles Brady Williams and Hiram Brown were both risk takers and taught their sons valuable lessons about resourcefulness, continuous learning, integrity, judgment, persistence, and handling adversity. Will and I were both blessed to have such wise counsel.

While conducting research and developing my draft manuscript—neither of which I had ever done before—I received routine encouragement from my dad who enjoyed my stories about the Battery Boys and offered constructive feedback. While helping my father through several illnesses I spent a lot of time at his hospital bedside, often editing my manuscript while he lay sleeping. If my dad were still here, he would be pleased that the Battery Boys' stories have finally been published.

Despite the loss of my father, and my mother a year later, I am thankful that I can share the excitement of completing this Chicago Mercantile Battery project with my wife Mary Jo, son Rick, and daughter Elizabeth. They have been a great source of inspiration and fulfillment in my life. I am also thankful for the encouragement to research/write that I have received from other family members, including my sister Carol Castelli; sister-in-law Patti Tomashewski and her daughters Megan and Katie; and brother-in-law Louis Myers and his wife Karen (and her brother Gary Rauch who provided me with information on Pittsburgh's Allegheny Arsenal).

Most wives don't allow their husbands to expend significant time and resources to conduct Civil War research, collect rare memorabilia, purchase enough books for a small library, and take vacations alone to visit battlefields and historic sites. Very few would agree to move all the way across the country, from San Francisco to the East Coast, so their husband could take a two-year sabbatical to finalize his first book. I am grateful that Mary Jo has supported me throughout my quest to create a long-deserved written legacy of what Pat White, Will Brown, and their Mercantile Battery comrades achieved during the Civil War. Thanks!

Author's Note

In preparing to edit the Chicago's Battery Boys diaries, letters, and memoirs, I studied dozens of first-hand Civil War accounts and discovered that there was no uniform way of approaching a project like mine. After considerable thought I decided to only lightly edit the letters and firsthand accounts that appear in this book. I believe this will make it easier for readers to enjoy them without getting bogged down trying to decipher run-on sentences, inconsistent punctuation, and so on. My approach has been, "When in doubt, leave it alone."

I have preserved the original writings—including grammar, syntax, era-related misspellings, changes in tense, shifting points of view, etc., that are repeatedly wrong but reflect the writer's idiosyncrasies—while correcting blatant errors and adding consistency to punctuation and paragraph divisions. Hopefully this editorial process will make it easier for readers to move smoothly between my narrative and the eyewitness accounts. (Some of Will Brown's personal discussions about his family, along with non-Civil War topics about Chicago and St. Joseph, have been excised.)

Any criticism about this editing strategy should be aimed at me and not my publisher.

Chapter 1

On the Father of Waters

T he courthouse property was filled on Saturday, July 26, 1862, with 20,000 sweating Old Northwest patriots, crammed together to hear the rousing speeches of their city leaders. All businesses in Chicago had closed down at noon so everyone could attend "The Great War Meeting." President Abraham Lincoln, a fellow Illinoisan, had called for 300,000 more volunteers. Major General George B. McClellan had failed in his march on Richmond; and Major Generals Ulysses S. Grant, William S. Rosecrans, and Don Carlos Buell had not made much progress in the West. The flames of war must be rekindled and the Union restored.[1]

At this second war rally—the first "uprising" had been held five days ago—three platforms were set up around the perimeter of the public square. Chicago's most influential leaders were there. Politicians enjoyed the impromptu exposure. Members of the Board of Trade urged their families and friends to lend more financial support. Religious orators took the stage to pray for a speedy end to the war. Military officers on leave, like the colonel of the 8th Illinois Cavalry, were

Amos and
George Throop

Chicago Historical Society

suddenly pulled up to a podium to give a battlefield perspective. The city's leaders were unified in their call for volunteers. They took turns addressing the crowd. Stephen Douglas would have been proud of his legacy. The response to simultaneous speeches from three stages created a dizzying swirl of emotions, spinning faster and faster like a white-foam whirlpool in the path of a surging rapid.[2]

The crowd shifted and pressed closer to the center platform to hear Isaac N. Arnold, a United States Congressman and a close friend of Abraham Lincoln. His speech was interrupted with waves of applause that undulated across the throng. Arnold's deep voice boomed above the din: "Who shall pay the cost of this war? Let us quarter on the enemy, confiscate the property and free the slaves of rebels." The crowd responded with an ear-bursting cheer.[3]

Civil War rallies were held on the grounds of the Chicago Court House (photo circa 1860).

A band was seated behind Arnold on the platform. The musicians raised their instruments as a vocalist and his choir came on stage to sing a new war song. It had been written the day before by George F. Root, one of the United States' leading composers, who had been inspired while reading Lincoln's second call for volunteers. Two singers laureate had stopped by his store earlier to pick up something new to sing at today's rally. Jules G. Lumbard and his brother Frank practiced it once or twice and then took the music sheets with them to the meeting.[4]

The audience quieted. Jules Lumbard's bass voice trembled as he started the song: "Yes, we'll rally round the flag, boys, we'll rally once again, shouting the battle cry of freedom." Men raised their clenched fists in agreement. "We will rally from the hill side, we'll gather from the plain, shouting the battle cry of freedom." On stage, the choir, including Jules' brother Frank with his tenor voice, sang from their clean sheets of music, "The Union forever, hurrah, boys, hurrah! Down with the traitor, up with the star; while we rally 'round the flag, boys, rally once again, shouting the battle cry of freedom."

The band settled into the rhythm of this new song. Jules Lumbard grew confident as he started the second verse: "We are springing to the call for three hundred thousand more." Women began to dab at their eyes with white-lace kerchiefs. What would happen to their husbands, sons, grandsons, and nephews who were still home? A few people in the audience joined the second chorus.

Jules Lumbard's voice resonated throughout the Court House Square as he began to sing the third verse: "We will welcome to our numbers this loyal, true and brave." His last verse rose to a crescendo—"So we're springing to the call from the East and from the West"—and sent a chill that pulsated throughout the hot, steaming crowd. Immigrants saw an opportunity to connect with their new country; and to use the high bounties, though denounced by the *Chicago Tribune* as "utterly wrong in principle," to feed their families. Young hometown men like Will Brown, who previously hesitated to join the fray, furrowed their brows as they contemplated whether to answer this urgent plea. In frenzied unison, thousands of men and women shouted the last refrain: "The Union forever; hurrah, boys, hurrah! Down with the traitor, up with the star, while we rally round the flag, boys, rally once again; shouting the battle cry of freedom." The debut of a great American song reverberated through the streets as determined Chicagoans returned to their homes to think about how to respond to Lincoln's latest call. The popularity of Root's hastily penned song spread throughout the Union in the months that followed. After the Battle of Stones River, fought in December 1862, soldiers in the Army of the Cumberland began to sing it. "The Battle Cry of Freedom" was soon sung by Federal soldiers everywhere, "in camps, on the march, upon the battle field," and by their families and friends back home.[5]

The businessmen in the Mercantile Association held a special "War Meeting" on Monday evening, July 28. They met in their business office at the corner of Lake and State streets above the Hibbard & Co. store. John Farwell presided as chairman. After much discussion, and still stirred by Saturday's motivational rally, the members decided to follow the lead of the Board of Trade. In a week their business associates had successfully filled the ranks of an artillery battery and infantry regiment. Although the Mercantile Association was new—and thus did not have the clout or resources of the 10-year-old commodity exchange—its members believed it was important to show support for the war effort.[6]

The Mercantile Association voted to move forward with its new battery and, like the Board of Trade, pay for the company's equipment and additional bounties. Much discussion was given to arming their new artillerists with the "Coffee Mill Gun," a repeating rifle or early "machine gun" that had been demonstrated during the past few days at Michigan Park along the lake. It was doubtful, however, that enough of these innovative weapons could be procured in time. Charles G. Cooley was announced as the unit's captain. "Doggett Guards" was the tentative name given to his new battery.[7]

Another city rally was held on August 1. Chicago's leaders hoped that the response to these calls for volunteers would be as prolific as the initial 1861 outpouring of support for the war. After Fort Sumter, so many volunteers had shown up at the recruiting offices that the rolls for the Garden City's first Civil War units were immediately filled—leaving the governor to worry about having too many volunteers.[8]

Although Pat White was one of the most qualified men to join a Union battery in April 1861—he had been a member of the prestigious Chicago Light Artillery in which his relative Ezra Taylor served as a lieutenant—the young Irishman opted not to do so because his newlywed sister needed help to care for their two siblings. Their father, Bryan White, unexpectedly died in 1856 and mother Catherine had just passed away in January. Pat, a six-foot, broad-shouldered Irishman, was born in

Charles G. Cooley was the Chicago Mercantile Battery's first captain.
Chicago Historical Society

County Sligo in 1832. Five years later, he immigrated with his family to St. Johns, Nova Scotia. In 1850, the White family moved to Chicago during a time when there was a steady influx of Irish exiles. Like Ezra

Patrick H. White,
Chicago Mercantile Battery

Richard Brady Williams Private Collection

Taylor, Pat White worked in the meat-packing industry as the war opened.[9]

Voluntary militia organizations had been established in most major cities around the United States after the Mexican War. Elmer Ellsworth and his Zouaves, with their colorful uniforms patterned after those worn by France's elite North African troops, comprised the most famous Chicago unit before the Civil War. He and his infantrymen traveled around the country conducting exhibitions and bedazzling audiences with their drills and colorful attire. The Chicago Light Artillery was organized in 1854 under Captain James Smith as a successor to the Chicago Hussars and Light Artillery that had been formed seven years earlier. Ezra Taylor was the company's first lieutenant. Pat White joined in 1858. Despite having damaged fingers on his left hand (caused by a mishap while working in a Canadian sawmill), he earned "quite a reputation as 'A Number One'" with Smith's artillery militia, which was used to fire salutes at special occasions in the city (such as when the delegates for the Republican convention disembarked from trains on their way to nominate Abraham Lincoln to be president). In support of his sister, White kept his position as a butcher at Gordon S. Hubbard & Co. and resorted to taking the muddy back streets in Chicago to avoid answering questions about why he did not join his friends, who had left for Cairo in April 1861 as the Illinois Light Artillery, Battery A (also known as the Chicago Light Artillery, Company A).[10]

Frustrated with his decision to stay at home, White went by the armory one night and saw 100 young men drilling with a bronze cannon. Knowing some of them, White offered to teach the new recruits how to handle the 6-pounder. Unable to bear it any longer, he joined the artillery unit, which became known as the Illinois Light Artillery, Battery B or Taylor's Battery (in honor of its captain, Ezra Taylor). Lieutenant Pat

Edwin Osgood was one of the original "Battery Boys." He enlisted in August 1862.

Richard Brady Williams Private Collection

White "left for Cairo on the 4 of June, 1861," the day after Stephen A. Douglas died.[11]

Deployed by Brigadier General Ulysses Grant with a section of Taylor's Battery, White saw his first action at Fredericktown, Missouri, when his artillery section was engaged in pursuit of Southern partisan commander M. Jeff Thompson. After the engagement on October 21, 1861, the commander of the Union forces, Colonel J. B. Plummer, sent for White and told him that "I saw service in the Mexican War but I must say I never saw guns better handled." He also submitted a commendation to Grant, praising White's "effectiveness." From that point on, White steadily earned the respect of the future general-in-chief.[12]

On November 7, Taylor's Battery climbed off transports to assist Grant in driving Major General Leonidas Polk's Rebel troops out of Belmont, Missouri, across the Mississippi River from the Southern bastion at

John Q. Mason mustered into the Chicago Mercantile Battery with Will Brown.

Richard Brady Williams
Private Collection

Columbus, Kentucky. Pat White's artillery section was placed at the front of Grant's line, to the left of Colonel John A. Logan and his 31st Illinois Infantry regiment, as the attack began. He and his men dueled with a battery from New Orleans as Brigadier General John A. McClernand's troops drove the enemy from his entrenchments. After premature celebrating, led by McClernand, a former congressman who would soon become a thorn in Grant's side, the Union troops had to fall back to their transports. White and his cannoneers covered the retreat. "I was nearly the last getting out," the Irishman wrote after the war. "I knew the rebels were after us so I placed a gun to protect us while loading. . . . when all was aboard except this gun, the enemy came for us with a yell, so we gave them its contents and then ran it aboard and then used two guns on them from the bow of the boat. . . . We returned to camp at Bird's Point. It was quite a sight to see our limber chest riddled with bullet holes." Colonel W. H. L. Wallace credited the work of White and the rest of Taylor's Battery with "saving our broken forces at Belmont from utter destruction."[13]

Pat White remained in McClernand's division, which, as a part of Grant's command, advanced to Fort Donelson after the surrender of Fort Henry. On February 12, 1862, McClernand's Illinois troops were on the right of Grant's line. White participated in an artillery duel that day. During the ensuing darkness, the Union troops endured a frigid night without campfires, the novice soldiers now lamenting their decision to discard their heavy coats on the march from Fort Henry. Pat White recalled after the war that, "We could not build fires, as that would draw the enemy's attention, and to make matters worse, a driving storm of sleet set in toward morning. The enemy's pickets kept firing all night and the groans of the wounded, lying between the two armies, added to the terrors of that awful night." In the middle of the night, White "noticed some of the men who had blankets lying on the ground completely covered with snow and you would think they were dead if it was not for their breath like little puffs of steam." The next night was just as bad. McClernand's men, in retreating, had left their wounded comrades behind. White recalled, "We could here their cries all night and to make matters worse some were burned by the burning of the dead leaves and crust." The distraught lieutenant tried to sleep in a baggage wagon with Captain Ezra Taylor. However, "in a short time we had to get out as there was false alarm, caused by the icicles forming on the scrub oak trees trowing off by the wind, and the enemy thought we were chargeing their works so they opened fire all along their lines, in a short time our cloths were frozen on our backs."[14]

After the Fort Donelson victory, Taylor's Battery moved with the army down the Tennessee River to Pittsburg Landing, which was to serve as a base in the campaign to capture the strategic railway terminus at Corinth, Mississippi. Grant, who had been temporarily sidelined by his superior, Major General Henry W. Halleck, returned to command the forces at Pittsburg Landing on March 17. Pat White and his artillerists were encamped in an open field just behind the front lines near Shiloh Church, a local landmark, on Saturday, April 5. At dawn the next day, the "sun arose beautifully." Taylor's men were finishing their breakfasts and preparing for a 9:00 a.m. inspection when the Southerners interrupted their plans with a surprise attack. Since his horses were already harnessed for that morning's inspection, White was asked around 7:30 a.m. to advance immediately to the right of Shiloh Church. Brigadier General William T. Sherman was on hand to witness the bravery of Pat White and his redlegs as they engaged in a hot artillery duel with the Fifth Company from New Orleans' Washington Artillery. The Louisiana artillerists had turned their blue "jackets inside out so that the gray lining would be on the outside." Walter Scates, one of the artillerists in Taylor's Battery, wrote about the start of the Shiloh battle to his father, who was a prominent judge in Chicago. "Soon we could see bayonets glistening through the trees on the opposite side of the ravine & then the rebels came down the hill on the double quick," Scates recounted. "Give them cannister!" shouted the Union commanders. After repelling the onrushing grayclad soldiers, the men in Taylor's Battery cheered. "Every cap went up into the air & we danced about like madmen. Major Taylor (now chief of artillery for Sherman) rode up just then & shouted 'Boys' I'm proud of you. You're doing gloriously."[15]

Sherman—whom White described as "the coolest man I saw that day"—ordered Taylor's men to draw back at about 10:30 a.m., so they could replenish their ammunition chests. Scates wrote, "For over an hour we did some of the hardest work of our lives, our guns roaring incessantly & shot & shell plunging & bursting all over & around us." Falling back again, Taylor's Battery was showered with shot and shell for a half mile across an open field. Walter Scates recalled that "at one time I looked back & saw a shot strike the ground away from me & instantly I stooped just in time to save myself from being cut in two for it grazed my back." White would later count more than a dozen bullet holes in his powder-stained frock coat. His closest brush with death arrived in the form of a shell fragment that struck his side, shearing off his sword belt and ruining his sword.[16]

After the maelstrom of Shiloh, Pat White returned to Chicago on a 20-day leave to recruit for his battery and recuperate from the intense campaigning in Tennessee. When his sister opened the door of their house to greet him, she saw his bullet-ridden coat and pants. Neighbors were ushered in to inspect the evidence of White's close calls. The revitalized Irishman was soon ready to return to the field. But not before he received a special gift from some of the city's prominent citizens on May 1. On the front page of the next day's *Chicago Tribune*, it was noted that Pat White "was the recipient of a sword, sash and belt, at the hands of his friends in this city, last evening." The embarrassed lieutenant was taken aback and could only stammer, "Gentlemen, I do not deserve this compliment, I am serving my country, to the utmost of my feeble ability, because I love it. I promise you that no act of mine shall ever bring disgrace upon the sword you have given me, nor shall it ever be yielded to an inferior in rank of the enemy's line."[17]

White would keep his cherished sword throughout Grant's final, whirlwind drive against Vicksburg and during the town's ensuing siege. Two years after Shiloh, however, in a clearing carved out of the dense pine woods of Louisiana, Pat White would have a trying moment of truth in his new position as chief of artillery for Brigadier General Thomas E. G. Ransom's 13th Corps detachment: surrounded by Texas infantrymen, who held a gun to his chest and demanded the surrender of the Chicago presentation sword, White would have a split second to make a life-or-death decision about upholding the impromptu vow he had made.

After Shiloh, Henry Halleck pushed Grant aside so he could lead the next phase of the campaign against the Confederates, who had fallen back to Corinth. Halleck's advance was marked by excessive caution, with his troops entrenching at the end of each day. After taking nearly a month to march about 20 miles, Halleck captured Corinth but allowed the Southern army to retreat intact. Many soldiers from Chicago's leading families now languished in southwestern Tennessee. Grant made no further progress when he regained command after Halleck departed for

Washington to assume the position of general-in-chief, which had been vacated by Major General George B. McClellan in early March.[18]

Events moved even slower in the East, where Lincoln had been exasperated with the inactivity of McClellan's Army of the Potomac. Although the newspapers had dubbed him the "Young Napoleon," McClellan seemed reluctant to leave Washington and seek battle with Confederate General Joseph E. Johnston's army. The sight of Rebel campfires, glowing defiantly across the Potomac from Washington, disturbed the president. Lincoln's expectations for immediate action were tossed about like one of the general's errant hot-air observation balloons. Despite rebuilding the Army of the Potomac after its disaster at Bull Run and augmenting the defenses around the capital, McClellan frustrated Lincoln with his excessive planning. Worse yet, Republican firebrands in Congress were beginning to view McClellan's interminable hesitations as possible treason. The president desperately sought victories before his own political capital vanished like Johnston's army, which, unbeknownst to McClellan, had slipped away from northern Virginia.[19]

Propelled by a Machiavellian shove from Lincoln, the reluctant McClellan mobilized his men in mid-March 1862 and orchestrated an incredible military maneuver. In less than three weeks, McClellan used 389 vessels to transport approximately 122,000 men down the Potomac from Washington and Alexandria—along with the requisite supplies and materiel to accommodate his immense army—to the tip of the Virginia Peninsula, which poked out into Chesapeake Bay. Yet, after marching his amazing force up the Peninsula and coming within striking distance of the Confederate capital at Richmond, McClellan was beaten back by General Robert E. Lee, who had replaced the wounded Joe Johnston. (By August 16, the rear elements of McClellan's army would be retreating down the Peninsula toward Fort Monroe and Newport News.)[20]

In response to McClellan's defeat, which was exacerbated by the post-Shiloh standstill in the West, Lincoln and Secretary of War Edwin Stanton called for 300,000 additional three-year recruits to resuscitate the traumatized Union army. A month after the initial request the president issued a supplemental call for another 300,000 militia to serve out nine months. The combined quota from his home state of Illinois was 52,000 men.[21]

Young men like Will Brown had been immersed in helping to build Chicago's commercial empire, but they paused long enough to ponder the call from their state's rail-splitting hero. At the beginning of August, Will thought about his upcoming 20th birthday. Did he have time to interrupt his business career? He had been working in the Board of Trade network for about five years. Having started as a clerk, he advanced to an important bookkeeping position in Patrick & Company's commission-merchant business at 224 South Water Street. Will debated the virtues and disadvantages of military service with his friends, many of whom shared his dilemma. They had attended the rallies on July 21, July 26, and August 1. The young men felt more pressure to enlist as they read each day's front page of the Chicago newspapers and heard about another acquaintance joining the army. Or watched their employers in the Board of Trade and Mercantile Association continue to champion the Federal cause. On August 7, after much deliberation, Will decided to join in the Chicago Mercantile Battery. He was described as a 5'9" bookkeeper born in Berrien County, Michigan, with a light complexion, gray eyes, and brown hair.[22]

Will Brown and his new comrades mustered into the company on August 29 and began their military training on the outskirts of Chicago. Caught up in the euphoria of being recruits, they were oblivious to the dangers and hardships awaiting them. Learning how to fire cannon and handle artillery equipment was an adventure. Even the daily drills and camp life seemed to be tolerable. The Battery Boys especially enjoyed the attention they received from their influential Mercantile Association sponsors, who paraded them around at various Garden City exhibitions and took them to festive suppers.[23]

The Mercantile Battery soldiers started their war odyssey on November 8, 1862. They left Chicago on the Illinois Central Railroad but came to a premature halt the next day when their locomotive broke down past Centralia and had to be replaced. The Battery Boys finally reached Cairo at 11:00 p.m. and had to sleep in the train cars "with a stick of wood for a pillow." Cairo was a transportation hub located in southern Illinois on a triangle of land formed where the Ohio River flowed into the Mississippi River. That first stop, however, was a major disappointment for the Chicago artillerists. Cairo did not seem to have improved much from the "hard place" that Charles Dickens visited in 1842, or "the muddy, dirty, miasmatic regions of Cairo" described 18 months earlier by their friends in the Chicago Light Artillery, Company A. The inauspicious beginning settled upon the eager cannoneers like an early afternoon fog that suddenly drifted in from Lake Michigan, blocking out the sun. The young men from Cooley's company, with their new full-button jackets and dark-red-striped pants, began to be uneasy about what awaited them in the rural South.[24]

The artillerists' steamer, the *Diadem*, shoved off and stopped at Columbus, Kentucky, en route to Memphis. Pat White and Taylor's Battery had fought there a year ago. At the once formidable Confederate stronghold, Sergeant George Throop, a member of the Mercantile Battery, wrote home about the "monstrous chain, which was hung across the river by the rebels to prevent federal boats from passing. The chain & big cast iron torpedoes" were lying intact on the riverbank. After passing Island No. 10 and New Madrid, the *Diadem* got stuck on a Mississippi River sand bar, which some of the soldiers thought was a bad omen— especially to be stuck for a second time on the same trip. Dislodged from their predicament, the Chicagoans soon learned an elementary lesson about artillery. According to Florison Pitts, a bugler, the Boys decided to shoot several rounds from the stern-wheeler except that they "put 3 shell in wrong end foremost" and fired.[25]

Memphis was the next stop. The capital of the Delta had fallen prey to the Union's Anaconda Plan on June 6, 36 days after Major General Benjamin Butler and his troops occupied New Orleans. (Flag Officer David Glasgow Farragut and his squadron had rushed by Forts Jackson and St. Philip, thus forcing the city's stunned leaders to capitulate.) The Unionists now had a firm grasp on the Mississippi River "snake," holding the Memphis head in their right hand and the Crescent City tail in the left. Flag Officer Charles H. Davis took credit for the Union success at Memphis, but Colonel Charles Ellet and his converted-steamship "rams," sponsored by Stanton, played a pivotal role in the victory. Ellet's rams were designed for agility and rapid movement, not bombardments. Their primary weapon was a battering ram incorporated into the bow. Two of the rams—*Queen of the West* and *Monarch*—assisted Union gunboats in defeating the Confederates' River Defense Fleet (including the *Beauregard*, which the Battery Boys would soon use for target practice). In the aftermath of this naval battle, Charles Rivers Ellet, Jr.— the ram commander's son who just turned 19—took along three of the crew and rowed up to the Memphis bluffs to demand the city's surrender.

The younger Ellet raised the United States flag above the post office to signify that Memphis was no longer under Confederate control. He made a major contribution to the innovative Ram Fleet's victory and was promoted to become the youngest colonel in the Union army. (Will Brown later kept his father apprised of Ellet's ongoing daredevil exploits.) Vicksburg became the next naval target on the Mississippi. Farragut and Davis moved their warships and gunboats from New Orleans and Memphis, respectively, to converge on the Confederates' Gibraltar and probe its vaunted fortifications. The ironclad *Arkansas* was waiting there to extend a Southern welcome to Farragut and Davis.[26]

By November, when Will arrived in Memphis, the city had resumed its role as a leading business center in the Mississippi Delta. The young artilleryman provided his father with the first of many updates on Confederate commerce, which he would diligently continue during the next three years as he traversed the Deep South. This was a topic Will enjoyed discussing with his father. He explained to him that the Memphis cotton trade was again flourishing. After the Union occupation of Memphis, many of the city's business owners scrambled to resurrect their prewar trading relationships with the North.[27]

A journalist from *Harper's Weekly* wrote that there was minimal hostility toward Union soldiers at the beginning of the occupation. Yet, by the time Will arrived in Memphis, he was sensing an increase in tensions. He told his father that some of the young secessionist women in the city were very disrespectful to him and his friends. Those resentments likely intensified in response to the Union soldiers' destruction of local property. For example, when the first Mercantile Battery camp was set up outside of Memphis, Will mentioned, "Some of our troops are off down town to-night and they will probably set part of the town on fire before morning."

The blueclad pyromaniacs would get more opportunities to practice their new avocation during the upcoming Tallahatchie March.

* * *

Chicago Ill.
August 9th 1862[28]

Dear father

I am a soldier of the army of "Old Abe." Have been sworn in and am going into camp on Tuesday next. Am a member of the "Mercantile Battery" gotten up under the auspices of the "Merchants Association" who promise to take care of us and see that we are well treated.[29]

Billy Patrick, Charley Olcott and Dan Marble enlisted with me. The battery is made up of Chicago's finest men and I know nearly all of them. I have been thinking of enlisting for some time but wanted to go in the navy. This battery seemed to be the thing so I went into it.[30]

*   *   *

Camp Doggett
September 29th 1862

Dear father

I am very much obliged to you for the basket of peaches. I enjoyed them very much. I divided them around among my friends as far as possible and all said they were splendid peaches. Mr. Hayward very kindly brought them into camp. Mr. Patrick got his basket and is very much obliged. I will see that the baskets are returned as I explain they ought to be.[31]

There is nothing of consequence going on in camp. The boys are a little excited about going into Camp Douglas.[32] Col. [Joseph H.] Tucker is trying his best to get us in, but the boys say they won't submit and I don't think they will; at any rate not quietly.[33]

The paroled men from Harpers Ferry are nearly all here and a harder looking set of customers I never saw. Ragged, dirty and nasty with but few exceptions and most of them have only been in the field about five weeks. I have talked with several smart fellows and they say they were treated like dogs. They all say that Col. [Dixon] Miles was a traitor and was not killed soon enough.[34] I saw Lt. Col. W. Scott Stewart of the Scotch Regt yesterday. [35] He looks pretty well but rather seedy. The men do not say a great-deal about Gen. [Julius] White but evidently don't think a power of him.[36]

I have been expecting a letter from Henry for several days but it has not come yet. Tell him to write me in your next.[37]

We are looking for our guns daily and expect them this week sure soon. I understand that our horses are all ready for us when we get our guns. We expect to go down town this week on parade, exhibit ourselves to the citizens and afterwards take dinner at the Briggs House.

I wrote a letter to Lib yesterday. Tell sisters Delia and Belle that I will not forget to answer their letters. My love to all and excuse the shortness of this letter. I find that it is almost impossible to write letters with ink as my bottle is quite small and the ink don't last very long. Write soon.[38]

*   *   *

Camp Doggett
October 12th 1862

My dear father

I have been waiting very patiently for the past ten days to hear from you, but as yet have not had that pleasure. I wrote you several days since and presume that you have received the letter ere this.

We have our guns and are expecting our horses this week. Capt. Cooley told us this morning that he expected marching orders pretty soon now and wanted us to attend strictly to our drill. I am considerably disappointed in Capt. Cooley. He does not prove to be the man I supposed he would. Don't treat his men exactly right, not that he has ill-treated me. On the contrary, he has shown me a good many favors, but his general treatment of our boys don't suit me at all. He acts as if we were inferior beings over whom he had full sway and when he gives an order he is terribly exact in his style.

It won't do with our boys and, unless he changes his policy, we will have to change ours. I don't think it would be a very difficult matter to have him removed as our boys can, if they wish, exert a very strong influence. About the only thing we are waiting for at present is to find someone who is capable to take command; that matter is not a very difficult one, however, and we already have some good friends at work.[39]

I wish you could be here to see us go thro' our drill. It would make you laugh to see the boys mount and dismount. It puts me in mind of a flock of monkeys more than anything else. We are improving rapidly. Yesterday, we had an exhibition drill in the presence of the Mercantile Association and a large party of ladies and gentlemen. We did first-rate and were applauded by our audience. After [our] drill, we had a big supper gotten up under the auspices of the ladies and after supper we concluded our <u>time</u> with a dance.

We are having very fine weather during the day but at night it is not so nice. And we sometimes find it difficult to keep warm but we manage it in this way: Three of us first spread down our rubber blankets, then over-coats and two blankets with our jackets for pillows. And over us we spread one blanket and a shawl belonging to one of the boys. In this way we manage to sleep pretty comfortably.

I am commissary of our squad and draw rations for 24 men. I think it will be a good thing for me as I will learn something about rations, quartermaster stores &c. I have to hire and pay the cook and see that our rations are in good order and well-cooked. I find that it is pretty hard work for a man to eat his full rations and I expect our squad will make something in that way, tho' probably not a great-deal. For all the rations we save, we are paid in money [with the government] deducting ½ % from the contractors price. The boys in our squad forage some to-day. We are to have fourteen chickens for dinner. I am getting as healthy and hearty as a pig; getting heavy every day and as for eating, well, I won't attempt to tell you. I get down town quite often and generally call on Mr. Patrick and take a look at my books &c. Hayward has been up here to see me several times. Are you doing anything in the way of buying [railroad] ties for him at present?[40]

Have you heard from Henry lately and where is he? Was he in any of the late battles in Kentucky? I am anxious to hear from or about him. Tell me what you know. He has not answered a letter that I wrote him at Dowegiac [Michigan] and I presume he has not received it. Send me his address if you have it and I will write him.[41]

When I was at St. Jo., you had a petition asking the governor of Michigan to allow A. H. Morrison to make some appointments or something to that effect. Did or will the petition amount to anything? If so, do what you can for me. Write me soon and as often as you can as a letter is always gladly received. Love to one and all.[42]

*   *   *

Camp Doggett
October 19th 1862

Dear father

Well, we have got our horses at last and are kept pretty busy, so that at night we feel pretty tired. My position has been assigned to me. I am No. 6 on the gun. My duties are to deal out and prepare all the ammunition for the gun. The position is a responsible one and during a fight will keep me very busy. It is just the position I want. Charley Olcott and Dan Marble are postilions and ride horses.

On the march I ride on the limber of the guns, that is, on a seat on the front wheels of the gun carriage. There are two others on the seat with me. One is the first corporal (or gunner No.1); the other No. 5 or the "Powder monkey." Just behind us is the caisson drawn by six horses. On the caisson there are six men: No.'s 1, 7 and 2 on the front seat and No.'s 4, 8 and 3 on the rear seat. Bill Patrick is lead postilion on our gun and I think will make a good one.[43]

* * *

Chicago Ill.
October 28th 1862

Dear father

Our battery will probably be off some time during next week and I hope to see you over before we go. Our Capt. expects to receive marching orders to-day and we will then make preparations for immediate departure. I am down town to-day on duty for the company. We are fully equipped and ready to start at any time. The Adjutant General said yesterday that the first time he saw us he fell in love with us and now he likes us better and better. We went through our drill yesterday in his presence.

I saw John B. King this AM who told me that Bob was slightly wounded in the fight on the Hatchie. C.S. Bissell is dead. I suppose he will be a great loss to the regiment.[44]

* * *

On board steamer "Diadem"[45]
Mississippi River
November 13th 1862

My Dear father

Here I am on the "Father of rivers" bound for Memphis Tenn. We left Chicago on the IC RR last Saturday about 2 O'clock PM and did not arrive at Cairo 'till Sunday night 10 PM. Our train not being a regular one was what caused the principal delay. At some stations we had to wait nearly an hour. We were delayed at St. John's Station and I had an opportunity to see the coal mines there or rather a part of them. The mines are about 350 feet underground.[46]

The city of Cairo is a regular sand hole and has but one fine building in the place, the St. Charles Hotel where I took breakfast. There were several gunboats and lots of soldiers at and around the town. We left Cairo Monday night and arrived at Columbus [Kentucky] the same night; stopped there 'till the next day at 12 n.

Columbus is a very small place but better situated than Cairo. Its fortifications are immense and extend nearly, if not fully, ten miles. They are mostly on the hills that surround the place. I visited a few of them. At this place I found many of my old friends who are in the First Board of Trade—72nd Ill.—Regiment. They were very glad to see me and felt quite disappointed in not having me stay with them. Right opposite Columbus is Belmont. The only thing to be seen there was a couple of houses and a few trees. I was somewhat surprised to see the number of cannon and shot and shell that were lying around the banks of the river at Columbus, the most of them were from "Island No. 10." Our forces at this point have a good many guns mounted and keep a strong guard posted on the surrounding hills.[47]

After leaving Columbus, there is nothing to attract particular attention until you reach "Island No. 10." And but little even there, excepting its associations, as there [is] but little to be seen from the boat as she passes the island; tho' I presume if we had stopped and had gone over it we would have seen considerable. As it was, all we could see were a few dismantled gun carriages and several dismounted guns; tho' just before we reached the island we saw a lot of cannon piled up on the Missouri shore and presumed they were taken off the island. There were two gunboats at the island guarding it. Salutes were exchanged as we passed and the men on the boats gave us a cheer which we responded to with a tiger.[48]

We passed "Island No. 10" about 4 PM Tuesday and reached New Madrid about dusk; stopped at this point all night and started on again next morning. Got along finely 'till we got opposite Point Pleasant (Mo.) where we got on a sand bar in the middle of river and there we [were] stuck 'till that night about 8 O'clock PM. And lucky it was that we got off as we did, as the spar broke on account of the pressure and the shock seemed to send the boat forward. At any note we were off.

Point Pleasant is a very small place, now entirely deserted. It holds a place in the history of this river as being the point where Gen. Pope crossed the river and thereby cut off the retreat of the rebels from "Island No. 10." After getting off the sand bar, we only went a short distance and then anchored in the middle of the river for the night. Started on again this morning and so far am safe and sound. Have not seen anything of consequence so far with the exception of a gunboat that we passed a few moments since. We are now about twenty miles above "Fort Pillow" where we will probably stop all night. The boat is afraid to move during the night on account of the guerrillas that are all over the country. This boat was fired at about two weeks ago and they have been careful since that time. We have two guns stationed on the bow and we keep them loaded all the time so as to be ready in case of an attack. Last night, while on the sand bar, some of our boys feared an attack and we posted an extra guard for the night.[49]

I am somewhat disappointed in the aspect of the country along the river. It looks gloomy as a general thing and is very thinly settled, the houses being few and far between and, what few there are, of the poorest and meanest description. The inhabitants look sallow and sullen and are nearly all of the secesh stamp.[50]

For the first time in my life I have found out what it is to live on short rations and they [are] of the poorest kind viz: a piece of musty bread and half-cooked ham. When we left Chicago our friends supplied us with a lot of pretty good things but we "pitched" into them and finished them in short order, so that now we have to live as we do. Do not imagine that I am starving, however, as I am happy to state that I was thoughtful enough to take my haversack down town before leaving home; and having it well filled with provisions, they are not all gone yet. There are eight of us together in one state room and we fare pretty well by dividing around. Us eight filled our haversacks in Chicago.

I am very glad we are going to Memphis and we may have a chance to help take Vicksburg; tho' I hope we will be better drilled then than we are at present. There are eleven batteries in Memphis and ours will make the twelfth. Four regiments passed us bound for that place when we were on the sand bar.

"On coming up to the Tallahatchie river, we learned that they had burned their stores at Abbyville which is situated 2 miles on the other side and retreated."

Chapter 2

If the Rebels Had Not Retreated

On October 16, 1862, Ulysses S. Grant was given command of the Department of the Tennessee. The appointment ended what had been an exasperating field experience under the cautious Halleck, whose troops were immobilized in Tennessee and Mississippi. During the Corinth Campaign, Grant had been almost a spectator as Halleck took the lead and executed his inching-forward-and-entrenching strategy to avoid another Shiloh surprise attack. Grant's friend William T. Sherman had talked him out of resigning. Although still frustrated, Grant thought the situation would improve when he resumed command after Halleck was promoted to general-in-chief and left for Washington. Unfortunately, the Union war effort had bogged down not only in the West, but in the Eastern Theater as well.

A temporary surge of Federal optimism erupted, however, when the Confederate grand offensive in the late summer and early autumn of 1862 was beaten back. The Southerners had pushed north along a 1,000-mile line into Maryland, Kentucky, Tennessee, and Missouri, only to be stopped at Antietam, Perryville, Corinth (in northwestern Mississippi), and Newtonia. Nonetheless, Union commanders failed to capitalize on

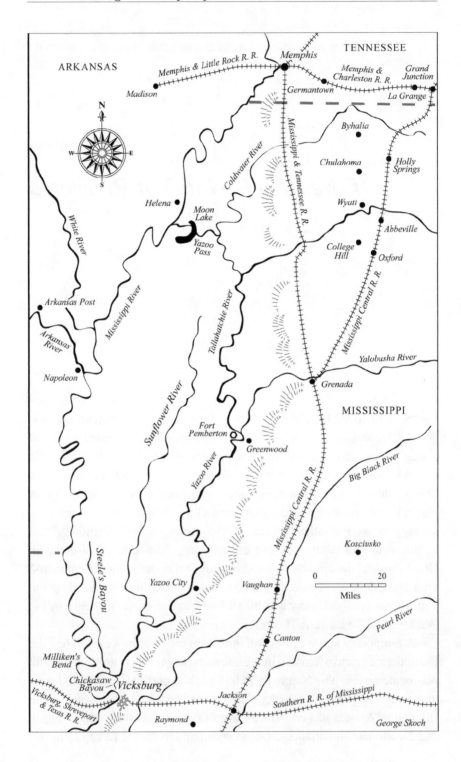

George Skoch

their victories by destroying their fleeing enemies. McClellan and Buell advanced so sluggishly that Lincoln relieved them both, though the president waited until after the November mid-term elections before firing the popular McClellan. For the moment, Rosecrans, who had beaten the Confederates at Corinth but allowed them to slip away, remained in Lincoln's favor, and he was promoted to Buell's former position in charge of the Army of the Cumberland. Meanwhile, Grant had no authorization from Halleck to strike out on his own for Vicksburg. In his memoir, Grant recalled, "The most anxious period of the war, to me, was during the time the Army of the Tennessee was guarding the territory acquired by the fall of Corinth and Memphis and before I was sufficiently reinforced to take the offensive."[1]

With Halleck's acquiescence, Grant commenced his Vicksburg Campaign on November 2 as he moved his armies from southern Tennessee towards Holly Springs and Grenada in Mississippi. His intelligence reports estimated the Confederates had about 30,000 troops, roughly the same number of men that he led. Halleck agreed to provide reinforcements—and the Chicago Mercantile Battery would be among them. In the interim, Grant organized his force into three wings, one each under Maj. Gens. James B. McPherson, Charles S. Hamilton, and William T. Sherman (the latter's troops stationed at Memphis). Grant planned to move his men overland through northern Mississippi and, with either a direct assault or a flanking maneuver, take Vicksburg. By entering the Confederate bastion's eastern back door, Grant would avoid the batteries along the river bluffs in its front yard. On the way, Grant would have to protect his railroad lifeline.[2]

Lieutenant General John C. Pemberton, a Pennsylvania-born Confederate who had taken command of the Department of Mississippi and East Louisiana in October, prepared to do battle with Grant. Hearing that Grant had massed his troops in West Tennessee for a strike into Mississippi, Pemberton edged his soldiers back from the "undefensible position" they held at Holly Springs and withdrew south of Tallahatchie River, covering Abbeville and Oxford on the Mississippi Central Railroad. This location was naturally formidable and enabled him to keep his grayclad army between Grant and Vicksburg, while the railroad afforded him excellent communications with his headquarters in Jackson. As he waited for Grant to move out of West Tennessee, the

Rebel commander ordered extensive entrenchments to be built—the imposing Tallahatchie Line.[3]

In mid-November, Grant asked Sherman, who had become his close friend and confidant, to bring the majority of his men from Memphis, leaving behind only a few regiments to protect the Federal garrison and supply depot. Grant planned to pound through Pemberton's defenses with as many of his troops as he could muster. Sherman's three divisions began the march out of Memphis on November 24 (two days later, the Chicago Mercantile Battery was among the last units to depart). The strong bond between Grant and Sherman had been established at Shiloh when together they turned back the unexpected Confederate onslaught. They also stood together in weathering a torrent of newspaper attacks that followed the blood- drenched battle. Now they were to fight enemies simultaneously in their front and rear. Ahead of them were Pemberton's Confederates. In their rear, the ambitious politician-turned-general John A. McClernand was plotting to lead an independent expedition down the Mississippi River into Grant's department. While Grant occupied the attention of Pemberton's army, McClernand planned to conquer an under-defended Vicksburg from a different direction.[4]

John McClernand had participated in the Black Hawk War and launched his political career in 1836, making his debut by winning election to the Illinois legislature at the age of 24. During these years when Illinois was the western frontier, McClernand became friends Abraham Lincoln, another self-made Springfield attorney and legislator who would emerge as McClernand's ally. In 1843, McClernand was elected to the U.S. House of Representatives, where he served with Stephen Douglas, and joined him in becoming Illinois' most powerful Democratic duo. Lincoln followed him to Washington three years later. Their camaraderie extended beyond politics as Mary Todd Lincoln became a friend of McClernand's wife. After Lincoln was inaugurated and secessionists ignited the Civil War, the new president exercised his clout and asked the secretary of war to select McClernand—33rd in seniority—in his first round of brigadier-general nominations. In addition to valuing his social connections with McClernand, Lincoln also knew the former legislator could help him, along with fellow political appointee John A. Logan, to neutralize Confederate sympathizers in southern Illinois. They were effective in influencing volunteers from the southern part of their home state to exceed the enlistment quotas.

Nathaniel Banks, a nationally recognized Republican politician from Massachusetts, was another of Lincoln's politically appointed generals. Banks had served as a state legislator, U.S. Congressman, Speaker of the House, and governor. Historian James McPherson hypothesized in his Pulitzer Prize-winning *Battle Cry of Freedom* that Lincoln's appointment of men like McClernand and Banks "was an essential part of the process by which a highly politicized society mobilized for war." In his book *The War within the Union High Command*, Thomas J. Goss attempted to defend Lincoln's selection of local and national leaders as generals due to a shortage of West Point graduates. Civilian commanders accounted for about one third of the 583 generals whom Lincoln appointed.[5]

Nevertheless, one could argue that the mistakes and miscalculations made by these amateur generals revealed the weakness of making military appointments based on political expediency. Sadly, McClernand and Banks would not be the sole victims of their own blundering. Their miscalculations on the battlefield would affect the lives of their soldiers, including the men of the Chicago Mercantile Battery, who would had the misfortune of serving under both generals. Starting with the Battle of Belmont on November 7, 1861, the fiery McClernand began to clash with his fellow Illinoisan, Ulysses S. Grant. McClernand disdained being anyone's subordinate, especially the unassuming Grant with his West Point pedigree. More importantly, McClernand viewed Grant as an obstacle in his quest to replicate the successes of George Washington, Andrew Jackson, and Zachary Taylor, whose war records catapulted them into the presidency. After displaying an aptitude for combat leadership at Fort Donelson and Shiloh, McClernand continued to complain to Lincoln and lobbied for equal status with Grant. McClernand believed that an independent command was the shortest distance between his current position and the White House. This obsession sparked numerous clashes with Grant, who often found out about McClernand's duplicitous moves from such people as General Halleck on the Washington scene. The deteriorating Grant-McClernand relationship would also have serious implications for McClernand's troops, such as the young men in the Chicago Mercantile Battery, who would experience its consequences at Vicksburg.[6]

In June 1862, John McClernand sent yet another letter to Lincoln, continuing his stealth campaign to undermine Grant. Two months later

Allan Pinkerton, President Abraham Lincoln, and Major General John
McClernand at McClellan's Antietam headquarters (October 1862).

he convinced Illinois Governor Richard Yates to procure a leave of
absence from the Army of the Tennessee. McClernand's persistence paid
off. The timing was conducive for Lincoln and Stanton to hear the Illinois
politician-general's proposal to mobilize an army in the West. Lincoln
arranged a meeting in Washington on the last day of September.
McClernand then accompanied him to the Antietam battlefield. With a
politician's aplomb, McClernand maneuvered himself into some of the
destined-to-become-famous photographs that Mathew Brady took on

October 3, depicting Lincoln, McClellan and other officers. The next day, McClernand inserted himself into a Brady photo session with Lincoln and detective Allan Pinkerton, who served as McClellan's intelligence chief. Before McClernand returned to the West, Lincoln and Stanton issued an order authorizing him to raise additional troops in Illinois, Indiana, and Iowa for an expedition down the Mississippi River. While Grant was busy keeping the main enemy force occupied in northern Mississippi, McClernand would assault those Southern troops who remained ensconced in the hills and hollows of Vicksburg. By breaking away from Grant, McClernand anticipated that his much-sought-after independent command would enable him to claim the military and political accolades he craved. With Lincoln's agreement, McClernand left Washington on October 21 and returned to Springfield, Illinois, where he successfully equipped and trained new recruits for Yates and the governors of adjoining states.[7]

Meanwhile, General Grant focused on redeeming his reputation, which had been tarnished by the near defeat at Shiloh. He realized nonetheless that it was going to be difficult to reach Vicksburg via the overland route. Though preoccupied with Pemberton's army in front of him, Grant was attentive to the rumors in his rear about John McClernand.[8]

When the Battery Boys left Memphis, they marched through the Tennessee countryside into northern Mississippi. Instead of dealing with black powder belching from red-hot cannon, Will Brown and the other young artillerists had to settle for "seeing the whole country in a smoke," which was caused by flames shooting up from Southern homes and barns lining the road in their wake. With the Confederates in retreat, Will and his comrades had an uneventful 70-mile march to the Tallahatchie River, near Grant's Mississippi supply depot at Holly Springs.[9]

Grant had outflanked Pemberton's fortified line on the Tallahatchie, but he had to halt his pursuit around Oxford to mend his frayed supply line. Locked in a stalemate with Pemberton, Grant had time to monitor McClernand's behind-the-scenes activities. "During the delay at Oxford in repairing railroads," Grant recollected, "I learned that an expedition down the Mississippi now was inevitable." With his own sleight of hand, and the blessing of Halleck, who did not approve of Lincoln's clandestine scheming with his Illinois politician chum, Grant decided to summon Sherman from his nearby headquarters. According to Sergeant George

Major General
William T. Sherman

NARA

Throop, a member of the
the Mercantile Battery:
"Captain   Cooley,   2
sergeants, 2 or 3 corp-
orals & 3 or 4 privates
and our orderly were
among the escorts" who
accompanied Sherman as
bodyguards to a meeting
with Grant on December 5 at Oxford. The generals held another meeting
on December 8 to plot their intricate chess moves against McClernand. It
was decided that Sherman should return to Memphis, where he would aid
Grant in hijacking McClernand's army-in-waiting. Grant planned to
augment this force with one of his divisions, led by Brigadier General
Morgan L. Smith, and sail it down the Mississippi under Sherman's
command. The expedition would land northeast of Vicksburg, cut its
communications, and capture the town.[10]

Since Will Brown and the Mercantile Battery served in Morgan L.
Smith's division, they were soon on their way back to Memphis. On
December 12, Sherman was pleased to find two McClernand divisions—
under Brigadier Generals Andrew Jackson Smith and George
Washington Morgan—equipped and ready to depart for Vicksburg. Once
Morgan L. Smith's division arrived the next day from northern
Mississippi, Sherman had a force of more than 20,000 men on hand.
Additional troops from the District of Eastern Arkansas would be added,
bringing the effective strength of Sherman's Vicksburg expedition to
more than 32,000. As he adjusted his organizational assignments,
Sherman transferred the Mercantile Battery to support A. J. "Whiskey"
Smith. A West Pointer and Mexican War veteran, Smith was a

Florison D. Pitts, a bugler with
the Chicago Mercantile Battery.

Chicago Historical Society

no-nonsense, tough fighter like
U. S. Grant and Sherman—and
all three would become Will
Brown's favorite generals.[11]

Will, in a letter written after
returning to Memphis, indicated
that he had sent a missive to his
father from Wyatt, a village on
the north side of the Tallahatchie River. Since this correspondence is
missing from Brown's postwar collection, an extensive letter written by
Florison D. Pitts, a bugler with the Mercantile Battery, has been added as
a replacement to cover the inaugural field experience gained by the
Chicago artillerists. Pitts described in detail to his parents what it was like
sleeping in muddy cornfields and trying to stay out of trouble. He also
mentioned how the Battery Boys were forced to scrounge for food
because Cooley had mismanaged the company's supplies. Back in
Memphis, the commissioned officers in the Mercantile Battery
unsuccessfully tried to get Cooley to resign. This topic would be
addressed again outside Vicksburg.[12]

*   *   *

In camp near Memphis Tenn.
November 25th 1862

My dear father

We are ordered to leave this place in the morning and have been
preparing our goods &c all day. We move with about 15.000 troops
among which [are] our Batteries A & B.[13] We are in Gen. Morgan
L. Smith's Division, Col. David Stuart's Brigade.[14]

Our Q.M. Sergeant has been sick for some time and did not leave Chicago with us. Since we have been here I have been acting in his place and it has kept me pretty busy particularly so for the past few days. But to-night I have got everything all straight and feel better. I do not know how long I will retain my position but probably 'till the Q.M. Sergeant returns.

I am very well and enjoying my new kind of life first-rate. Several of our boys are in the hospital quite sick and will not go along with us.

Memphis is quite a place but decidedly secesh. Some of our troops are off down town to-night and they will probably set part of the town on fire before morning. I am writing this letter in a very uncomfortable position viz: laying at full length on a blanket and for that reason you must excuse brevity. But one of the boys is writing and I thought I would just drop you a line. Love to all. Will write you again soon. Good night.

* * *

In camp 10 miles from Holly Springs Miss.
November 29th 1862

My dear father

I believe I mailed my last letter to you at Fort Pillow when I was on the river. Our battery arrived at Memphis two weeks ago yesterday and left that place last Wednesday, arriving at this point late last night where we expect to be encamped for the next day or two.

Memphis is a beautifully situated place and runs back gradually from the banks of the river. Its public buildings are of the finest kind and well-built public squares in different parts of the city. I saw some beautiful private residences tho' they don't look as well now as they would if the place was in a more prosperous condition. There are but few of its original inhabitants there at present; they all having left when the Federal army took possession. I saw several secesh <u>ladies</u> on the street and it made me laugh to see their actions holding their handkerchiefs over their faces, turning their pretty noses heavenward and in various other ways showing their <u>disgust</u> of us <u>Northern vandals</u>. But they are not all secesh by any means as the prettiest one I met while there waved her handkerchief as we passed her house. There are many Northern men in business in the place and of course Chicago is well-represented. . . . I saw considerable cotton on the levee but the dealers said it was a mere trifle to what they have in times of peace.[15]

I always had an idea that soldiering was pretty rough work but you have got to go thro' it to realize its beauties. The infantry service is awful as they are on foot all the time while we are riding. After getting in camp, say 9 PM, you have to pitch tents, make fires and get something to eat if you have it. If not, go without or forage. And I can assure you, if the Mercantile Battery don't get up a reputation for any thing else, they will for foraging. Taking to-day for instance: We got in camp early this afternoon and to-night we have in camp three steers all nearly butchered, about 25 bushel of sweet potatoes (nice ones), a lot of sugar house syrup, apples, hoe cake and many other things that I do not think of at present.

Our General (Morgan L. Smith) knows what we are fighting for and lets his men live on the enemy tho' he does not permit any shooting at all; and if you get anything you must get it quietly. Just after leaving Memphis our troops commenced setting fire to everything before them and kept it up for about thirty miles. As our battery was in the rear, I had an opportunity of seeing the whole country in a smoke and I assume it looked as if we were going in earnestly. And I think [our troops acted] justly as we must win and might just as well destroy now as to wait a little longer.

*   *   *

[Letter from Florison D. Pitts to His Parents][16]
Camp Wyatt
Dec 3/ 62

Dear Father & Mother

After we arrived at Memphis we camped for 2 or 3 days about four miles from town guarding a bridge near the last picket stationed outside of the city. We were then moved into the city close to the Charleston & Memphis rail road where we camped for several days. Thinking we would stop at Memphis during the winter we immediately sent to work building what we call shebangs, or in other words shanties. We went to a brick pile & took what brick we wanted. We then went up the track about a mile and tore down a house & barn that stood in the woods in rather a lonely spot. The owner was supposed to be with the secesh army. This served us for windows, doors & lumber. Generally we got well to work at our houses when we was ordered to be ready to march Wednesday morning at 8 o clock.

The troops in Memphis at the time numbered about 20,000. They were formed in three divisions; one under Genl [James W.] Denver, the second under Genl Smith & the third under Genl [Jacob]

Lauman. Our Division started at the appointed time Wednesday [November 26] morning. We made a march of 17 miles and went into camp at 10 o clock 2 miles beyond Germantown. Our Company was camped in a corn field. We did not pitch tents and was pretty cold laying in the open air. The next day we made about 15 miles with little of nothing to take note of except that at noon we camped for dinner on a plantation said to be owned by an Union man who said that the rebels had burnt 10 bales of cotton a few days before. But as his wife told some of the Co that they had it burned the year before we thought that his Unionism did not amount to much. So we took all the pigs, poultry & beef we wanted.[17]

We had an order read to us which was issued by Genl [M. L.] Smith saying that the Mercantile Battery had been stealing & threatening. If he heard of any more such tricks he would send us to the rear in disgrace. It seems that some of our boys had been into a hog pen some distance back and as the Genl Order read "Gallantly charged a hog pen. In the melee which occurred two hogs were killed & none <u>wounded</u>." They were imprudent enough to shoot twice. The consequence was that the infantry & cavalry came rushing to the front expecting that we are attacked. That night our Division went into camp at 10 o clock on a plantation said to [be] worth a million dollars. Here the army made general havoc burning all the houses in the neighborhood, killing everything that was fit to eat "and more to." Anybody that says that the Union army down this way don't live on the enemy when they can find anything that they can take, must be mistaken. That is as far as my experience extends, I can testify different. We are not allowed to forage on the enemy but all the Gold in Christendom can not stop it.[18]

Friday we started on our march about noon and made about 10 miles. Saturday we marched about 15 miles, the country into which we marched was very uneven with numberless hills & valleys covered with thick woods. In a great many places the trees had been felled across the road by the rebs which obstructed our march a great deal. We went into camp for the night about 3 miles from Ialia [Byhalia] in an everlasting corn field again. I believe they always mean to put us in corn fields. They are very convenient places for feeding our horses but most miserable places to sleep in. Sunday we took up our march again for the place where the Rebels were said to be posted in force. It being a very rainy day & Sunday to. We concluded that we would have a battle sure. Every one of the boys was in good spirits at the expectation of trying their guns before a live enemy. But when we got well on our way the cavalry brought us word that the rebels had evacuated as fast as they could leave.[19]

Our Division encamped on the ground used by the rebels for a camping ground the night before. Our orders were very strict for the day, no man being allowed to leave the ranks while on the march. At one place or plantation which we passed the cotton gin was set on fire. The General happened to pass at the time the fire broke out. He was terrible wrathy about it & laid it to the Mercantile Battery or the regiment of infantry in advance of our battery. But as the roll call proved <u>we</u> was there we [thus] got of free. He called a court martial & tried 2 or 3 men which they got on the premises. They finally pitched into a little fellow in the 55 Ill but they could not get anything out of him. They even put a rope around his neck & strung him up twice but he was as plucky as they were. At any rate they did not find out who set the building on fire though suspicion pointed to this man. So they put a placard on his back & a heavy ball & chain on his ankle. The last I see of him he was travelling towards his regiment under difficulties. I was glad of it because under the circumstances the Genl did not want the rebels to know where we were & besides that we had orders to build no fires on the road during the day.

They put us into another corn field to sleep. We got our horses taken care of & was just putting up our tents when it commenced to rain in torrents & blow a perfect hurricane. We had just got our tent up but not having it securely staked down over it went with all of us under it. There was considerable scrambling to get out from under it. I can tell you here we began to see something of the beauty of camp life. The rain coming down in torrents & wind blowing a perfect hurricane in a corn field with mud knee deep & no fire, it was not a very pleasant prospect I assure you.

Monday night we had everything fixed for a good nights rest out of the rain but at 12 o clock orders came to pack up and start. We turned out double quick, fed our horses, got our breakfast and got under way about half past two o clock. About 9 o clock it began to rain and continued to do so all day making the road awful for artillery & baggage wagons to pass along. The 54 Ohio was in the extreme advance. Our battery was next so if we had had a fight yesterday we would have had the post of honor, that is, the first to go into battle and the last to get out of it. If the rebels had not retreated we would have been at it about 4 o clock but, on coming up to the Tallahatchie river, we learned that they had burned their stores at Abbyville which is situated 2 miles on the other side and retreated…they had also burned the bridge over the river. So [we] were compelled to go into camp [at Wyatt] and have stayed here all night waiting for the men [mostly contrabands] to build another [bridge] over so we can go across. We will probably get over sometime tonight.[20]

We have news to day that [Maj. Gen. Samuel R.] Curtis has Grenada & with Grant on our left and the enemy near & our column in the centre we don't see how they are to get away. We heard heavy firing from Grants army all day yesterday and when our division get across the river you will have some stirring news. We are encamped in the town of Wyatt on the north side of the river. We have already taken all the fences of the town & all the out houses such as barns, sheds, corn cribs & fodder covers. The inhabitants had all left the place in great precipitation leaving everything there was even some good fires in some of the buildings showing with what haste they had fled. The Genl has already tore down some of the buildings especially the brick to get the sleepers for the bridge. The Genl wanted some nails when Turner went out about 2 miles from camp & got 210 lbs of 10[d] besides jerking a mule to bring them home on. He also got some sweet potatoes & lard, all of which stuff is mighty useful.[21]

Through the ignorance or inefficiency of our Captain we have nothing but hard crackers & we are put on ¼ rations at that. If it was not for the cattle & hogs we kill we would be in a pretty hard fix but at every stopping place we immediately start for the plantations and take whatever we can get. We generally find molasses sweet potatoes corn meal & honey so take it all round; we do not leave enough in the country which we pass through to feed an army of musquitoes much less . . . men. At our last encampment we got about 30 quarts of as good molasses as there is made. On another plantation where we camped we killed five beeves. So you see there is no danger of our starving. Then take an army of 30,000 men all living off the country in the same proportion you can form some estimate of what there is left. In our night marches when it is very cold the country for miles appears to be one mass of fire. The fences are all one mass of living fire which…[spread out] in all directions for miles presenting some of the grandest sights I ever saw.[22]

*   *   *

Concerned that he might not be able to hold off Grant's larger army, John Pemberton decided to avoid a pitched battle and instead rely upon cavalry raids to sever the Federal supply line and, hopefully, compel his enemy to retreat. He did not know that Grant had sent Sherman back to Memphis. Though weakened, Grant was still determined to oust Pemberton from his entrenched position behind the Yalobusha River and create a diversion behind Vicksburg while Sherman tried to kick in the front door.[23]

Will Brown, Florison Pitts, and their batterymates waited to be transported on a steamer down the Mississippi River, where they would "see the elephant" for the first time. It was during this time around Memphis that the Battery Boys were first exposed to the political battle that Grant and Sherman were waging against John McClernand. Sparks from the behind-the-scenes struggle would escalate and eventually produce a vicious internecine conflagration at Vicksburg. The repercussions of this feud—like the danger associated with a black-powder implosion in a poorly managed cannon—would harm innocent bystanders.

Since many of the Northerners at Memphis were new recruits, the pending battle above Vicksburg would be their first encounter with the enemy. They had missed the February fighting at Fort Donelson, where friends of the Mercantile Battery—such as Lieutenant Pat White and his Chicago comrades in Taylor's Battery—had fought and learned about combat first hand. Since then, the Illinois veterans had survived the April horrors at Shiloh and now better understood the harsh realities of war.

The latest batch of recruits were not the only ones oblivious to what awaited them; there were also untested soldiers like the Battery Boys, who had enlisted during the past summer. Together, the new and untried soldiers had been enjoying themselves in their camps above the Memphis bluffs. To them, war was still an adventure. They joked around the campfires. Entertained one another. Played pranks. Their chattering continued as they retired to their tents and huts to nestle in their hay-cushioned beds. The veterans in camp did not sleep as soundly. The sickening screams of friends being ripped apart by whistling minie balls haunted them. Lying in the dark, the veterans knew it would not be long before the greenhorns learned that warfare was more than pointless marches and foraging adventures. Worries about being trampled by "the elephant" would soon dampen their campfire merriment.

"I wish you could see these gunboats. They are powerful looking monsters and look so they could walk thro' the "jaws of death." . . . The prisoners we took at Arkansas Post told me that the gunboats were the only things they were afraid of."

Chapter 3

Jaws of Death

Although Sherman now commanded about 32,000 soldiers at Memphis, he was powerless to begin his move down the Mississippi until he amassed enough boats to carry his troops. Moreover, he needed those boats before McClernand could arrive on the scene and assume command of the expedition. Brigadier General Robert Allen, the chief quartermaster for the Department of Missouri, was charged with the daunting task of providing shipping for Sherman's men. On December 11, the day before Sherman arrived in Memphis, Allen, who was headquartered in Saint Louis, telegraphed Grant that he would not be able to meet his initial deadline. While the Battery Boys waited in Memphis along with the rest of the impatient Federals, Allen's men scrambled to find the transports that would carry them toward their first battles.[1]

Fortunately, Allen had a gifted subordinate in Colonel Lewis Baldwin Parsons. A graduate of Harvard Law School, the middle-aged Parsons was, like McClernand, a friend of Lincoln's and also a former Illinois attorney. But Parsons eschewed politics in favor of a business

Colonel Lewis B. Parsons

Chicago Historical Society

career. His civilian vocation, as chief executive officer of the Ohio & Mississippi Railroad, had given him experience in transportation and logistics that proved highly valuable to the Union cause. On December 15, Parsons wired Halleck from Cairo that 20 large steamboats were on the way to Memphis—with more to follow. Federal agents scoured every nearby river. Parsons performed a magic act, conjuring up a fleet of transports and supply boats. On the afternoon of December 19, he arrived in Memphis with the remainder of the 60 troop transports that were to be used in the initial expedition.[2]

McClernand's two divisions, plus the one that Morgan L. Smith had brought back from Grant's command near the Tallahatchie, began to board on December 20. In the meantime, Sherman decided to proceed down the Mississippi to meet Major General Frederick Steele and his soldiers, who awaited him at Helena, Arkansas. At Friars Point, just south of the town, the pieces of Sherman's patchwork army would come together for the amphibious expedition to Vicksburg. Sherman watched the Delta landscape pass by and reached Helena that evening. Meanwhile, Parsons continued to load Sherman's army. Based on Parsons' Memphis achievement, and similar logistical triumphs, he would eventually assume responsibility for all Union river and rail transportation by the end of the war and be promoted to brigadier general.[3]

On the same day (Saturday, December 20) that Sherman was en route to Helena to meet Steele, Confederate cavalry under Major General Earl

Van Dorn raided the vital Federal supply depot at Holly Springs, Mississippi. Grant initially estimated his losses at 1,500 men captured and $400,000 worth of materials taken or destroyed. This disaster did not end the litany of Grant's supply line troubles. Even as Van Dorn's troops were setting fire to Holly Springs, Brigadier General Nathan Bedford Forrest, leading some 2,500 Southern cavalrymen, had embarked on a raid behind Grant's lines. The intrepid and fearsome Forrest traversed some 300 miles in 15 days, uprooting railroad tracks, demolishing trestles and depots, and burning supplies that could not be carried away. For Grant and Sherman, the opportunity costs were incalculable. By crippling the flow of Grant's supplies, Van Dorn and Forrest hamstrung the Federal attack on Vicksburg. Grant would no longer be able to lend Sherman any support and, with the telegraph lines to Memphis severed, he was unable to notify him of the change in plans. Pemberton was now free to redeploy his troops from behind the Yalobusha River to the hills above the Yazoo swamps—and counter Sherman's upcoming attack.[4]

While Will Brown and his batterymates were at Memphis waiting for transportation, they amused themselves by shooting their cannon at one of the Confederate rams sunk by Ellet's *Monarch*. Sergeant George Throop wrote about the unusual practice session in a letter to his father, an influential businessman and politician in Chicago: "The target was the old gunboat *Beauregard* which is sunk in the river about a mile and a quarter from shore. The smooth bores carried a distance of about a mile and the rifled pieces about 2 miles." As part of Sherman's 1st Division—newly assigned to A. J. Smith and, therefore, among the last to leave Memphis—the impatient artillerists watched while their comrades loaded onto the seemingly endless line of boats. An infantryman in the 67th Indiana recalled that "it was a grand site to see this grand fleet loaded down to the guards with proud western troops, all in line; as it were, a flock of huge marine birds, all decorated with floating state banners and the flag of the Union proudly waving, while the great voices of brass bands were filling the air with sweet strains of patriotic music." After encountering some embarkation problems on Saturday, A. J. "Whiskey" Smith finally boarded his men on the 14 remaining troop transports the following day, December 21. Will and his friends hurried their cannon, limbers, caissons, equipment, and animals onto the *City of Louisiana,* a wearisome feat the Garden City redlegs would have to replicate many times on steamers during their service in Mississippi,

Louisiana, and Texas. They departed in an upbeat mood at 1:30 p.m. on Sunday, unaware that they were about to see a different aspect of soldiering from what they had experienced on their uneventful march to the Tallahatchie River.[5]

Cooley's Battery Boys celebrated as they steamed down the Mississippi River, acting as if they were taking part in a holiday parade. As the steamboats moved farther away from Memphis, the jubilant Chicagoans were oblivious to what awaited them just ahead in the swamps fronting the Chickasaw Bluffs. The neophytes and veterans of Sherman's army would soon be weaving through a watery, snake-filled labyrinth of cypress trees and impenetrable thickets. They would also get a bitter taste of what their colleagues in the Army of the Potomac had endured two weeks before, when they tried to storm Marye's Heights behind Fredericksburg, Virginia. There, a portion of Robert E. Lee's infantry, enjoying the protection of a stone wall and excellent artillery support, had shot down waves of Federal attackers. The Confederates outside Vicksburg waited behind their own impregnable fortifications, along the loessial Walnut Hills high above the twisting Yazoo River.

The men in Whiskey Smith's division steamed down the "Father of Waters" to rendezvous with the rest of Sherman's fleet. The convoy, which included 55 troop transports, five supply boats, and Rear Admiral David D. Porter's gunboats, set off for Vicksburg and neared Milliken's

Mary Livermore, *My Story of the War*

The Chicago Mercantile Battery during reveille at Chickasaw Bayou.

Bend on Christmas Eve. While Will and his batterymates ate their meager rations on board the *City of Louisiana*, they were unaware that Rebel officers in Vicksburg were enjoying a more elaborate repast at a gala holiday ball in Emma Balfour's home, which was prominently perched atop the Hill City. Southern leaders at the party were interrupted and notified about the Union flotilla coming down the river toward them. At 3:00 a.m., Rebel drummers awakened the men of Brigadier General Stephen D. Lee's brigade, hastening them toward their anticipated battleground near the Yazoo. Alerted to this new danger, Pemberton left Grenada, Mississippi, and arrived in Vicksburg the day after Christmas; he was no longer concerned about Grant, whose overland march had been stopped dead by Van Dorn and Forrest. Pemberton was now free to strip units from northern Mississippi and send them to strengthen the fortifications adorning the Walnut Hills, nine miles above Vicksburg. The Confederate general planned to thwart his numerically superior opponents by taking advantage of interior lines and the ruggedly formidable terrain.[6]

Will Brown and his Mercantile batterymates arrived at Chickasaw Bayou on December 28, among the last of Sherman's troops to land. The Chicago Mercantile Battery had shared its transportation with Brigadier General Stephen G. Burbridge's brigade, which was ordered to take a brief detour to Louisiana and destroy the 80-mile Vicksburg, Shreveport & Texas Railroad. Burbridge's troops landed at Milliken's Bend and marched on the railway. The brigade included the 60th Indiana, 67th Indiana, 83rd Ohio, 96th Ohio, and 23rd Wisconsin infantry regiments. The last four units would accompany the Mercantile Battery boys until after the ill-fated 1864 Red River Campaign. Burbridge's men straggled back from their brief mission, which caused A. J. Smith's transports to be late in departing for Chickasaw Bayou.[7]

On December 29, Sherman launched his main attack against the Confederate position on the Walnut Hills. The Mercantile Battery was positioned on Sherman's right to guard against a flank attack via the main road from Vicksburg. Although the marshy ground hampered the use of Federal artillery, infantrymen under Whiskey Smith's command were actively involved in the assault. They zigzagged through ribbons of swampland while dodging shots from the Southerners' unseen cannon and rifle-muskets; some even had to rush two-abreast across a sandbar tightrope "exposed to a double cross-fire" from the Confederate fortifications in the bluffs above them. In retrospect, the charge across the fields at Fort Donelson now seemed less daunting to the Illinois veterans. And the sight of the red-tinged waters of Chickasaw Bayou surely vied with memories of Shiloh's Bloody Pond. For newcomers like those in the nearby Mercantile Battery, "seeing the elephant" was much different than simply hearing about the beast.[8]

Sherman's assault was a disaster. During the limited daylight of late December, Sherman's men had attacked—and were slaughtered by the Rebels, who could not be dislodged from their formidable positions. According to a reporter from *Harper's Weekly*, "Our brave fellows had to scramble up bluffs under a terrible fire, positively working their way on their hands and knees, and pulling themselves up the smooth heights with their nails." Worse yet, during the nights, the beleaguered Northerners heard the unceasing clatter of railroad cars "constantly arriving in Vicksburg" and bringing more Confederate soldiers to the fray. Union losses for the Chickasaw Bayou Campaign came to 1,776, with 208 killed, 1,005 wounded and 563 missing. The vast majority of them had occurred in the December 29 assault. By contrast, the Confederate casualty list tallied a total of 187 men. It was one of the Confederacy's most one-sided triumphs. Although Will Brown's letter on the Battle of Chickasaw Bayou was lost—and his diary has never been located—he recalled after the war how despondent the Battery Boys had been at the end of December 1862, and believed then that "Genl W. T. Sherman was a d—d old fool."[9]

Lieutenant Pat White of Taylor's Battery, who would soon become captain of the Mercantile Battery, was also at Chickasaw Bayou and expressed his admiration for the 6th Missouri Infantry who "volunteered to cross the bayou, and charge the works, and lost 30 or 40 men in doing it. I have always thought that justice has never been done them, as it was as brave an [and] heroic a charge as was made during the war, as far as I know, and few regiments would have done it and none better than the 6th Missouri." Brigadier General Morgan L. Smith, in whose division the Battery Boys had formerly served, was wounded on Sunday, December 28, the day before the infantry charge of the 6th Missouri Infantry.[10]

To fill in the gap of Will Brown's missing correspondence, another unpublished letter is included from Florison Pitts, who wrote to his father about the Battle of Chickasaw Bayou and offered the same level of detail Brown typically provided, including a similar hand-drawn map. (Pitts

Don Troiani

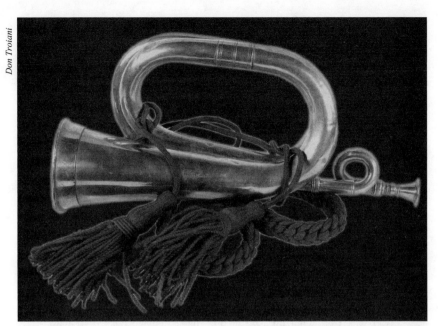

Florison Pitts' bugle

erred, though, in stating the 6th Missouri's charge took place on a Tuesday; it occurred on a Monday.)[11]

According to the young Mercantile Battery bugler, during a truce in the middle of the action, the Union retrieved their "dead & wounded that was lying thick on the sides of the swamps & thickets where the charge had been made" against the formidable Southern fortifications. Pitts also took note of the powdery flood lines visible high in the trees, and the gathering storm, which threatened to break loose and overwhelm the Union troops in the swampy terrain.[12]

*   *   *

On board steamer "City of Louisiana"
30 miles above Vicksburg Miss.
Dec. 25th—Christmas—1862

My dear father,

I have not the least idea where we are going or what we are going to do but, as we are so near Vicksburg, it would not surprise me if we attacked that point. Our fleet consisting of about 200 steamboats and from 60. to 100.000 troops (a wide margin) left Memphis on Saturday, Sunday and Monday and thus far have had an uninterrupted voyage; tho' I understand there was a slight skirmish somewhere below here early this morning. The boat I am on is in about the centre of the fleet so that all that takes place in the advance is not known to me. It is a grand glorious sight to see the whole fleet moving down stream. As far as the eye can see, a sea of boats meets your gaze. And when one boat passes another, a loud hurrah is heard from the boat that goes ahead and on the boat everything is busy noise and hubbub. Ah, there is much in soldier's life that those at home know little of.[13]

The country we are passing through does not resemble that [which] I saw above Memphis; the land is more even and the soil does not look so rich. What few towns I have seen look worn out and are entirely deserted. Napoleon at the mouth of the Arkansas river is quite a decent looking place but the only inhabitants to be seen while we were passing were one white, one negro and one mule and I presume the latter was the only one who was not afraid of us. I was somewhat amused at one place that we passed. It was situated on a high bank, but the joke of the thing was that all you could see from the boat was a large sign reading "MARIPOSA." I suppose the town was around some where.[14]

*   *   *

The following letter was written by Bugler Florison Pitts, and is used to replace Will Brown's lost letter on the Battle of Chickasaw Bayou.

On board steamer Adriatic
Jan 4th 1863

Dear Father

On the 20th of Dec we were ordered to move to the levee which we did in about two hours time. At the time we moved we expected the boat would be there to take our Battery on board. But we waited in vain all day & slept on the levee all night. Sunday about noon the Louisiana came down and we loaded our Battery on to her in a very short time [with] everything being ready; our Battery being about the last one that was loaded. Our Division consisting of 18 strs [steamers] started down the river in good style. The other two divisions had gone on ahead as they had got loaded first.

At Memphis before we moved down the river our Battery was transferred from the 2nd Division to the first. The expedition when we started from Memphis consisted of three divisions: the 1st under A. J. Smith of Kentucky, 2nd under Morgan L Smith of Mo. and the 3rd under [George W.] Morgan; the whole under command of GenL [William T.] Sherman. Nothing of note occurred on the river, until the next morning at Helena. Genl Steels [Frederick Steele's] Division took boats and proceeded down the river with us. At Helena about 300 of the 31st Iowa Infantry came on board of our boat which [made] it pretty tolerable crowded—besides being making it most intolerable dirty.

Thursday Dec 27th we found ourselves at Milligens [Milliken's] Bend which I believe is 22 miles above the mouth of the Yazoo on the La shore. Our Division was ordered to lay & the others went down the river. A part of our Division consisting of some 6000 Infantry were ordered out to destroy the Rail Road which leads from Vicksburg to Texas; which they accomplished successfully having tore up a mile of the track and bending the rails after heating them over a fire. They also destroyed 900 bales of cotton & 3 or 4 bridges. On Friday the Brigade came back and on Saturday the 27th at 3 o clock in the afternoon we got under way and soon after was making our way up the Yazoo, where we landed Saturday in the evening at the dotted marks.

Vicksburg is built on some very high bluffs; the bluffs extending along—as you will see by the drawing—to the Yazoo at which place is built a very strong fort. The bluffs, or as they are called Walnut Hills, descends to the swamps by what is called table lands that [have] a sharp descent & then a level or nearly level place; so continuing until they end in the cane brakes of the swamp. On the other side of this brake is the Bayou or ravines. On these hills and table lands the enemy had built their fortifications while at the foot of the hills they had dug rifle pits in which they put their sharpshooters & rifle men. The pits were made behind the thickets which lines the banks of the Bayou so that while they could see our men plainly our men could not see a hair of them.

Our line of battle was formed as you will see by the line at the edge of the woods—on the west side of the swamp—the Mercantile Battery forming the right of the line at the fortification ⟩ while the left of the line rested as near as I could find out on the bayou at the letter *L* [left]. The grounds and woods where our army was show signs of where the water has been 30 feet into the trees. So that at high water it would [be] rather an unhealthy place for an army of our size. The right of the army was under A. J. Smith, the right centre under Morgan L. Smith [and] the left centre under [George W.] Morgan; while the extreme left was under Genl Steel [Brig. Gen. Frederick Steele]. Our army numbered about 30,000 men.

With this little deviation to explain the situation I will continue the main part of my story. On Sunday morning [December 28] the Battery was turned out at 2 o clock & at 6 o clock got under way from the Bayou in the direction of the dotted line through the corn field into the woods. The roaring of artillery & the rattle of musketry was incessant & deafening. Our boys thought that the time for the Mercantile Battery to distinguish itself had arrived but although the fighting appeared to be directly in our front we pushed on until we arrived at ⅝ where they received orders to hold the road at any cost. On Sunday some very hard fighting occurred on the left. Col Wyman of the 13 Ill in charging across the swamps lost his life. Blair & DeCourceys Brigades [on the 29th] made some desperate charges on the left up the hills in face of the batteries and sharpshooters; and as a matter of course was driven back with extreme loss almost before their men had fired a shot. [15]

On Monday [December 29] the 6th & 8th Mo were ordered by Morgan L. Smith to charge across the sand bar in the Bayou when he immediately rode to the front and charged with his horse across the bar at the head of the men and held his position at the line—in front of Co. A [1st Ill. Light Artillery, Battery A]—in this charge he [M. L. Smith] was wounded on Tuesday. The firing in a great measure ceased Wednesday [December 31]. The armys agreed not to fire on one another so that our side could get the dead & wounded that was lying thick on the sides of the swamps & thickets where the charge had been made. Our men also traded buttons or anything they could get hold of for something from the enemy. [16]

On Thursday Jan 1st just as we was about getting ready to go to sleep the order was given for to harness as quickly and quitly as possible. In 20 minutes the guns & caissons was all ready. The caissons were ordered to move to the boats first while the guns were to remain behind until 2 o clock. The whole army were under orders to move to the boats as quickly as possible. In four hours after the order was issued the whole army had moved to the landing with the exceptions of our guns & 3 regiments of Infantry who were acting as pickets. At 2 o clock we were ordered to move with the 1st & 3rd section to move to the landing. The middle section was ordered to come in after all the pickets had come in. We arrived at the boats at about 3 o clock in the morning. The landing was crowded with teams, batteries & regiments, so that it was next to impossible to move around. But after a great deal of hard work & swearing, they got the whole army on board the boats about 6 oclock and in the afternoon took our way down the Yazoo as fast as steam would carry us.

I have tried to give you an idea of our weeks work but I am afraid I have made poor work at it. I hope you can understand some of it

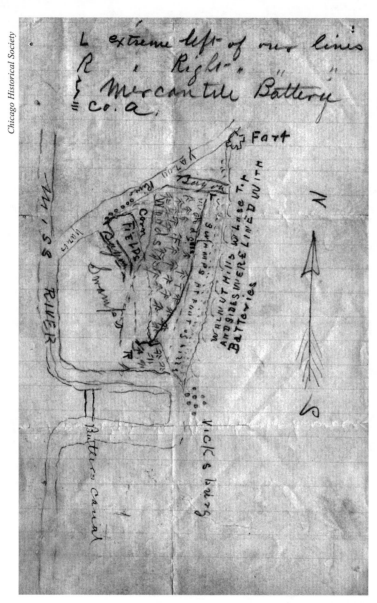

Florison Pitts' map of the Battle of Chickasaw Bayou.

anyway. The report is that on Sunday one of our gun boats engaged the fort up the Yazoo and that, after having 7 shots thrown clear through her and losing 17 men, she backed out and gave it up as a bad job in the fight. On Sunday & Monday the Rebels did not use any of their heavy guns on top of the hills but contented themselves with killing our men from their rifle pits & small fortifications on the side of the hills. We had only a very few if any guns that would do any harm to the batteries on top of the hills and our 6 pnds [pounders] would hardly reach ½ way there while all of their guns commanded our position. Completely added to all the rest they were constantly erecting new batteries & planting heavy siege guns on top of the hills.[17]

On Sunday & Monday nights the [Confederate railroad] cars were constantly arriving in Vicksburg with as we suppose reinforcements. It is thought that they must have brought in 40,000 troops from either Jackson or Mobile. The reason of our failure to take Vicksburg was the destruction of Grants immense provision train by the Rebel Cavalry at the time they recaptured Holly Springs; thus rendering it impossible for his army to move on Vicksburg by land. In the first place we was never shown into that swamp for the purpose of taking the place because the thing was perfectly impossible to take it from that side; even if we had had ten times as many men as they had. And if we had not got out of the place the right [moment when] we did, we would have never got off with anything [but] only ourselves.

It commenced to rain directly after we got started from the landing & rained 2 days and one night as hard as I ever saw it; which must have completely overflowed the swamp we was in. The roads were an awful condition the night we did retreat. So bad in fact that we could hardly get along. And I believe if we had laid there another day they would have opened all their batteries on us. And had they done so they would have blowed us into the Mississippi River and we could not have helped ourselves in the least. But as it is we have all our army safe on the Miss. Our loss in my opinion must be at least 1500 in killed, wounded & missing. So with the retreat of our army, the great destruction of property by the Rebels at Holly Springs and the defeat of Burnside [it] renders things a little blue amongst us.

Jennie tells me you sent a box to Memphis on the 21st. I hope I may get it. But if we do not go back there I do not see how it is possible for me to but I live in hopes. Give my love to all. Write soon.[18]

F. D. Pitts

*   *   *

Steaming back to the Mississippi, Sherman was unquestionably a disappointed man. He had hoped to redeem his December 29 assault with a move to outflank Pemberton. Brigadier General Frederick Steele's division, reinforced by a brigade from Morgan L. Smith's command, had been loaded onto transports and was poised to launch a surprise attack against the Confederate right at Snyder's Bluff. The plan had to be abandoned when a thick fog descended upon the area on New Year's Eve. The mist shrouded the bayou, with its makeshift Union graves, and made river navigation impossible. Then came the news of Grant's withdrawal to the Tallahatchie River alongside evidence of the gathering storm. With his latest plans frustrated, Sherman ordered his troops to reload their transports just after midnight. As Florison Pitts pointed out in his letter, however, the Mercantile Battery stayed behind to board last with the infantry pickets. In the morning, the boats were still moored at the Yazoo riverbank. Some of the Northern soldiers thought that, based on the delay and rumors of the flanking movement, the retreat must be a ruse—until they all steamed away in the afternoon. There was no New Year's Day revelry among members of the Mercantile Battery, or in any other Union unit. A somber silence instead reigned in their ranks.[19]

A torrential rainstorm erupted as Sherman's soldiers returned to the Mississippi, adding to their misery. Will Brown observed that his comrades were worried "they could never succeed [against] the South." Contrary to their sanguine hopes upon leaving Memphis, the Battery Boys had had a dismal holiday season.

For the men in Sherman's army, the defeat at Chickasaw Bayou would soon be offset by a relatively easy victory at Arkansas Post. Although the soldiers left behind the twisting bayous of the Chickasaw swamps, their top-ranking commanders remained entangled in political maneuvering. McClernand's suspicions of being duped by Grant and Sherman were confirmed when he arrived at Memphis on December 28. The Mississippi river-boat city had been converted into a Union supply depot; and McClernand discovered that the majority of his new recruits from Illinois, Indiana, and Iowa had vanished.[20]

With McClernand's anger rivaling the temperature in his steamboat's wood-stoked boiler room, he traveled down the Mississippi River, bringing with him orders to show that he was now in charge of the troops Sherman had been leading. He arrived at Milliken's Bend, which was located on the Louisiana shore on a prominent curve before the Mississippi briefly straightened out to accommodate the Yazoo River. The volatile political commander was ready to reclaim his stolen army.

In a vituperative meeting with Sherman and Porter that lasted into the early morning of January 4—aboard Porter's flagship, the *Black Hawk*— John McClernand learned firsthand about the defeat at Chickasaw Bayou. He also listened to a plan for launching a surprise attack against Arkansas Post (also known as Fort Hindman), a historic village on the Arkansas River. The Confederate stronghold appeared to be vulnerable and much less imposing than Vicksburg, especially since Grant's retreat had allowed Pemberton to divert a significant number of troops to protect the Hill City. Although Sherman was chagrined at McClernand's condescending attitude, he tried to collaborate with his new superior. They both yearned for a quick victory. For Sherman, it was an opportunity to redeem his failure in the Yazoo swamps. For McClernand, it presented the possibility of a victory to catapult him beyond Grant's reach. Now the two fierce-looking, stubble-bearded generals had something else in common: they both supported an attack against Arkansas Post. McClernand announced the next day that he would lead the amphibious assault himself, thus ensuring that Sherman would not abscond again with his army. He had already renamed his force the "Army of the Mississippi," further positioning it to become independent from Grant's Army of the Tennessee. The former politician, however, jeopardized his new partnership with Sherman by assigning him to command of one of the army's two corps. This put Sherman on equal status with Brigadier General George W. Morgan, whom he held responsible for much of the Chickasaw Bayou disaster.[21]

Five days later, a nervous Federal army approached Arkansas Post, still gun shy after its humiliating loss at Chickasaw Bayou. The small village and fort were located on the west bank of the Arkansas River, about 117 miles south of Little Rock—and within striking distance of Union transports and gunboats on the Mississippi. Brigadier General Thomas J. Churchill, the commander of the Confederate fort, was at a severe disadvantage against the combined forces of McClernand and Porter. Arkansas Post was known more for its historical significance as the first white settlement in the Lower Mississippi Valley than as an ideal location for an earthen fort. It had been hastily erected in three months and was built too low, with the same careless imprecision that had left Fort Henry susceptible to enemy gunboat fire from the Tennessee River. Besides worrying about the fort's poor design, Churchill also recognized the added danger presented by recent winter rains. The bloated Arkansas

River could give Northern gunboats a direct fire against his earthworks and hamper the plunging fire of heavy Southern guns. Additionally, Churchill's troops were too outnumbered to withstand the pending amphibious onslaught. Reinforcements were expected to arrive from western Arkansas but might not make it in time.[22]

Fort Hindman was built under the direction of Colonel John W. Dunnington, formerly a lieutenant in the Confederate Navy. He and his engineers built a square, full-bastioned earthen fort with sides approximately 100 yards long—and a slope of 18 feet—surrounded by a moat 20 feet across and eight feet deep. Around these walls was a 720-yard line of strong rifle pits. The fort was armed with 14 light guns and three heavy pieces (one 8-inch and two 9-inch Columbiads). In addition to the artillery, the fort possessed a garrison of about 4,900 troops.[23]

None of these extensive preparations, however, were likely to stop McClernand's 32,000-man army, whose artillery firepower was well supplemented by Porter's eight gunboats. The Union army was divided into Sherman's 15th Corps and Morgan's 13th Corps, each corps consisting of two divisions. A. J. Smith and Brigadier General Peter J. Osterhaus commanded Morgan's two divisions. The Battery Boys served with Osterhaus' men.[24]

Porter's gunboats, with their 66 guns, eased within range of Fort Hindman and at 1:00 p.m. on Sunday and unleashed a devastating close-range barrage. McClernand's field artillery joined the admiral in bombarding the Confederates while his infantry drove the Rebel ground force away from the rifle pits extending from the fort to Post Bayou back to Hindman's moat area. The overpowered Confederates also had to contend with Union field guns placed across the river. McClernand's battle plan specified that a detachment of infantry, cavalry, and artillery from Morgan's 13th Corps would debark on the river's opposite bank at Fletcher's Landing during the Friday evening deployment. This force marched across the peninsula and deployed on Saturday morning about three miles above the fort. Colonel Daniel W. Lindsey's detachment included 34 cannoneers from the Chicago Mercantile Battery led by Lieutenant Frank C. Wilson. (This was the right section in which Will Brown was serving.) They had been ordered to fill their knapsacks with three days of rations and take extra blankets and clothing with them. Besides the two 3-inch rifles from the Chicago Mercantile Battery, Lindsey also had two 20-pounder Parrotts manned by a section of the 1st

Wisconsin Light Artillery. Lindsey's detachment was ordered to open an enfilading fire upon Fort Hindman while preventing the Rebels from escaping or being reinforced.[25]

By January 11, McClernand's troops were in position to assault Fort Hindman. The brigade of Colonel Lionel A. Sheldon, from Osterhaus' division, tied the left flank of the army to the Arkansas River. Cooley was ordered to fire his smoothbore guns to support Sheldon's three regiments.[26]

Cooley and his four 6-pounders would be the first elements of the Chicago Mercantile Battery to engage the enemy at Arkansas Post. Osterhaus, who accompanied Sheldon's brigade, initially kept the Battery Boys in reserve, judging that the 800-yard range to Fort Hindman was too distant for the smoothbore artillery to be effective. Instead, the division commander opened fire with two 20-pound Parrott guns from the 1st Battery, Wisconsin Light Artillery. All across McClernand's line, Federal artillery pummeled the Southern fort, as did the guns of Porter's flotilla. At about 2 p.m., Osterhaus advanced Sheldon's infantry. In the general's phrase, Cooley had been "impatiently waiting for his share of strife" when he was ordered to go forward with the brigade. The Battery Boys took position behind a piece of rising ground within 200 yards of the enemy rifle pits and opened a devastating fire. To support the guns, Sheldon positioned the 118th Illinois to their right and the 120th Ohio on their left. He kept the 69th Indiana in reserve.[27]

The Confederate reply was comparatively feeble. William Gardner, a Chicago gunner who was hit in the right leg by a shell fragment, was the only member of the battery wounded that day. The gunner characterized the injury as "a severe flesh wound." The stricken artillerist was taken to the steamer *J. C. Snow*, a piece of the shell still stuck deep in his leg. Southern infantry fire also struck four of the battery's horses, rendering three unfit for further service.[28]

Cooley reported that his smoothbores expended 165 rounds during the battle. At the height of the fighting, he shifted two guns slightly to the left to enfilade the enemy fortifications. As Cooley noted, "My position enabled me to fire diagonally through the lines in rear of their earthworks, and also to observe quite accurately its effects." Osterhaus' report confirms the accuracy of this statement. Seeing the Southerners abandoning the parapet in his front, the general ordered the 120th Ohio to storm the fort. The terrain, however, offered a more formidable obstacle than had the fort's defenders, and the Ohioans found themselves pinned down in front of a yawning ravine. Osterhaus' assault had come to a standstill, but the Confederate defenses continued to crumble under the Federal barrage.[29]

Will Brown and his fellow artillerists in Wilson's section joined the fight at the last minute. They had spent the day concealed from the enemy's view, apparently waiting for the Rebels' relief force to make an appearance. Two 20-pound Parrott guns from Captain Jacob T. Foster's 1st Battery, Wisconsin Light Artillery, which had also been placed under Lindsey's command, had also been silent. As the day wore on, Foster noticed three gunboats pass the fort. One of the boats landed, and a naval officer debouched, telling Foster, "Now is your time to do something. Where is the officer in command?" Foster directed him to Lindsey, who soon ordered his artillery into action. The Battery Boys took position at a point opposite Fort Hindman, unlimbered their pieces to the left of Foster's guns, and began firing Hotchkiss shells with 3-second fuses. Wilson took aim at some log buildings in the rear of the fort and at the Confederate rifle pits. "We had only fired 4 rounds from each piece, and were just getting warmed up for work, when a white flag was shown," Wilson wrote in his report. A few minutes later, the Stars and Stripes was floating over the fort. In the words of Foster, who witnessed the scene, "we saw the flag for which we are ready to waste our last drop of blood proudly waving over the rebel Post Arkansas." Will mapped out the gun positions for his father and wrote that his section's two cannon on Sunday "were directly opposite the fort, all their [the Rebels'] guns pointing toward us had been disabled so that the only thing we had to stand was a few rifle balls." McClernand added in his battle report that Lindsey "opened an oblique fire from Foster's two twenty [pounders], and Lieutenant Wilson's two [Mercantile Battery] ten-pounder Parrott's, into the enemy's line of rifle-pits, carrying away his battle-flag and killing a number of his men."[30]

When the Union troops got closer to the fort, they saw the damage inflicted by Porter's gunboats as well as McClernand's field artillery. They understood why the enemy's resistance had vanished so abruptly. Besides taking 4,791 prisoners, the Unionists captured 17 cannon (seven of which were no longer operational), seven stands of colors, 3,000 small arms, and an assortment of war materiel.[31]

After razing Fort Hindman, the blueclad troops returned to their transports and headed back to the Mississippi. They huddled together, recounting their triumph. McClernand had won an impressive, if one-sided, victory. Lincoln would recognize this achievement by sending his congratulations to McClernand and his army. But the capture of Arkansas Post did not give the general sufficient clout to break free of Grant's authority, as he might have wished. The ambitious McClernand was soon to find himself a corps commander in Grant's army. With Halleck's consent, Grant was reinserting himself as "king" on the Union side of the Vicksburg chessboard.[32]

* * *

Arkansas Post
Arkansas river
Jan'y 12th 1863

My dear father,

I have been in a fight and come out all right. Our fleet left the Mississippi river last Thursday and on Saturday opened fire on the fort at this point. Did not do a great-deal on that day, but on yesterday—Sunday—we "pitched in" full force and at 4 O'clock PM the place surrendered. Of course, everything is in a mixture to-day and it is almost impossible to learn our loss or the amount of prisoners we have taken. From what I have seen I think we have at least 8.000 and probably more.[33]

The shortest way for me to give you an idea of our position will be to give you a sketch [reproduced on the facing page]:

(caption: by "our position" I mean the position of our two guns in our battery)

    xx Our position Saturday night
    ##   "   "   "   day time
    ### "   "   Sunday from 3 PM 'till the fort was taken.

I never saw anything as completely riddled as the fort. There don't seem to be a whole spot in it. The prisoners we have taken don't seem to feel very bad and all say they will keep the war up as long as possible. They are mostly from this state and Texas.

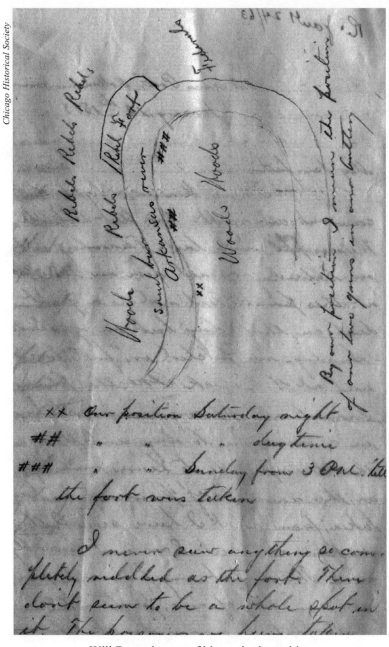

Will Brown's map of his section's position
at the Battle of Arkansas Post.

When we first got into position on Saturday, they fired at us and it would have amused you to see us dodge behind the big trees to get out of the way. But it was unnecessary to do this as all their shots fell short of us. Yesterday, when we were directly opposite the fort, all their guns pointing toward us had been disabled so that the only thing we had to stand was a few rifle balls. And as soon as we commenced firing this ceased so that in reality we were not in much danger.

Well, everything and everybody is excited to-day so that you must excuse the shortness and composition of this letter.

Chapter 4

Just the Man We Want

T he Battery Boys spent the next few months languishing along the
Mississippi River, a sojourn that quickly extinguished the
afterglow of the Union victory at Arkansas Post. Their frustration
rose as the river spilled over the levees during incessant rains, threatening
the Mercantile Battery camp. It was a miserable experience.

The inclement weather often forced Charles Cooley's waterlogged
redlegs to stay in their tents. Will Brown described to his father how he
ventured onto a military road "and got up to my knees in mud in a few
moments." The flood waters also threatened Grant's latest plan to open
the Mississippi River, which entailed the digging of a canal that would
allow Federal vessels to bypass Vicksburg and its river front guns. Will
was skeptical about whether the project—soon to be known as Grant's
Canal—would provide a solution to the Union's dilemma of getting past
the Confederate Gibraltar of the West.[1]

The canal project was the second of Grant's attempts to either
capture or neutralize Vicksburg. His first scheme had failed with
Sherman's assault at Chickasaw Bayou. By the end of February, the
persistent Grant had launched two other operations. His third project was

the Yazoo Pass Expedition, which began with Lieutenant Colonel James H. Wilson, a member of the general's staff, blowing up the levee at Moon Lake, located diagonally across from Helena on the eastern side of the Mississippi. Grant hoped that Wilson's efforts would ultimately enable Federal transports and gunboats to pass down the Coldwater and Tallahatchie rivers to the Yazoo River above Vicksburg. This would allow the Federals to roll up the right flank of the Confederate fortifications, located at Snyder's Bluff. Major General James B. McPherson was in charge of the fourth project, which sought to employ Lake Providence on the Mississippi's west side—above Milliken's Bend—as an avenue through the bayous. McPherson planned to flood Lake Providence and create a waterway passage to the Tensas, Ouachita, and Black rivers so Grant's boats could get below Vicksburg.[2]

When Ulysses Grant joined McClernand and Sherman after their detour to Arkansas Post, he notified Halleck, writing, "I found there was not sufficient confidence felt in General McClernand as a commander, either by the Army or Navy (viz., Porter)." With the issue of General Orders No. 13 on January 30, 1863, Grant assumed command of all Vicksburg tactical operations and reassigned McClernand to lead the 13th Corps, formerly the command of George W. Morgan.[3]

Grant's initial priority, after neutralizing his Illinois nemesis, was to complete the De Soto bypass canal. Brigadier General Thomas Williams' brigade had begun digging the waterway during the previous year under the orders of Major General Benjamin Butler. The project's goal was to cut a perpendicular swath across

General Ulysses S. Grant

NARA

the base of the De Soto Peninsula, thereby providing safe passage for a diverse collection of naval vessels to elude Vicksburg's guns. In addition to using his own troops, Williams had pressed 1,200 local contrabands into working on the canal project. It had been abandoned after encountering numerous challenges and setbacks, including the oppressive July heat and humidity, hard clay soil, falling water in the cut-off, and a surprise attack from the Confederate ram *Arkansas*. Now, Grant was attempting to resurrect Williams' project. One of his incentives was a terse telegram—"Direct your attention particularly to the canal proposed across the point. The President attaches much importance to this"—that Halleck sent to him on January 25.[4]

* * *

On board steamer "[City of] Louisiana"
Mississippi river
Jan'y 24th 1863

My dear father

Since I last wrote, we have again steamed down the river and reached this point (some 12 miles above Vicksburg) last Wednesday where we have been ever since. We are in profound ignorance in relation to our future movements and perhaps it is best it is so, tho' it would be more pleasant to know something about it. I have been informed to-day that our forces are at work on the canal commenced by Butler last Spring and it is hoped it can be made to operate successfully. Should it prove to [work], there would be little use in taking Vicksburg as it would then be an inland town and of but little consequence. I am told that good engineers have pronounced it perfectly practicable and very easily accomplished. I sincerely hope this is our plan as Vicksburg cannot be taken excepting by a good force and at a very heavy loss of life.[5]

I have been considerably amused by the newspaper accounts of our "Taking Vicksburg" and the part our battery sustained in the siege. Nearly every paper has a different [story] and not one as far as I have read is correct. Moral: Don't believe all you read.

The health of our boys is not very good at present. There are few very sick but nearly all are ailing. Thus far, I have been quite well and hope and trust I may remain so. I am quite anxious to hear from Henry and Liberty whom I fear were in the late fight between Rosecrans and Bragg. When you write me, let me known full particulars.[6]

I hardly know what to think of the people of the North. They do not seem to know which way to turn or what to do. All the Northern papers seem to be agitating the great question of the day but none seem able to solve the mystery. What will be the result of all this? It must strengthen the arm of the Southern people to see our people in such a mighty commotion. The so-called "Southern Cause" seems to brighten and the hope of our being successful daily decreases. Should the C.S.A. become a distinct government, I do not think it would be a lasting one as I cannot help but think of Lincoln's quotation "A house divided against itself must fall." It is not a very flattering prospect to think of; but one cannot help but think of it sometimes.

We have a report that the Illinois Legislature threatens to withdraw her troops from the field unless President Lincoln modifies his Emancipation Proclamation. Have you heard anything in relation to this matter and is there any truth in it? When you write I would like to have you give me all the political news as far as practicable. The newspapers we receive are generally all old dates and we only know from letters what is going on at present.[7]

I see by the papers that W. H. Wiley, of the Board of Trade Battery and formerly a member of our church in Chicago, was killed in the battle between Rosecrans and Bragg. I have not yet learned the particulars yet and sincerely hope the report may be a mere rumor.[8]

The Mississippi river is rising rapidly and the current is very strong indeed. Piles of driftwood come floating down and this afternoon I noticed a house rapidly travelling southward. We are having pretty fair weather at present. A little rain now and then but not very unpleasant. Write often. Love to all at home.

*   *   *

Chebang de Olcott & Brown
4 miles from Vicksburg
Feb'y 1st 1863

My dear father

My last to you written on board the steamer "[City of] Louisiana" was mailed on Jan'y 24th. Since that time we have gone into camp about two miles from the so-called "Butler's Canal" and are waiting for future movements. But how soon they will take place is still a mystery to all of us. We have a fine camping ground and now, for the first time since we left Chicago, we are enjoying real camp life. And I can assure [you], after tramping over the country for nearly three months, we are fully able to appreciate a few days of quiet. And altho' the enemy is not far distant, we work and act as if we were again in Camp Douglas and feel about as secure as we did there. As we are on the reserve at present, we are perfectly secure and in case of retreat would be out of all danger. Occasionally, we hear the <u>big guns</u> booming out telling us that the foe is on the alert and hatching every favorable opportunity to give us a shot. Our gunboats are around all the time too and they fire back quite often.[9]

Yesterday, I got a horse and rode down to the canal and took a look at it and also got a glimpse at Vicksburg. But as there was a light fog on the river, I could not see the place very distinctly; tho' I saw enough to convince that we will have a big fight there when we do take it. And take it we must as it will never do to have the rebels hold this river. And if a <u>Compromise</u> is made, I hope it will not be done 'till the Federal forces occupy every point on the river. The canal at present is about fifteen feet wide and from five to seven feet deep. There is a force at work making it wider but I do not think it will ever work. And judging from the way the force is at work on it I do not think our generals expect to make it work. There is some object in working at it but I do not [know] what it is.

There are seven or eight new-style gunboats here and I think they will help us greatly in taking the place. I wish you could see these gunboats. They are powerful looking monsters and look so they could walk thro' the "jaws of death." I have a great admiration for them and believe them to be the best thing ever invented. The prisoners we took at "Arkansas Post" told me that the gunboats were the only things they were afraid of.[10]

Nearly every paper that reaches us from the North are agitating the Compromise question and their opinions all seem to be divided. But the question seems to be up before the people and I think the ultimate result (humiliating as it may seem) will be a Compromise of some kind. I think the South are fully as tired of this war as we are. But they have an idea just present that they have the advantage of us at all points—and I think it will be necessary to give them one or two good sound thrashings before we talk of Compromise. I have about made up my mind, however, that we can never whip them outright and again restore this country to its old footing. There are many reasons for my thinking this way. In the first place there is a strong party in the North working against the government and I believe W<u>m</u> H. Seward heads that party. Seward is a politician and, if he can only gain his own ends, I don't think he cares a <u>Tinkers curse</u> where the country goes to. That is my opinion of the <u>Hon</u>. W. H. Seward. There is another party in the North called the Abolitionist. I wish a few leading ones could be hung up high as Haman.[11]

Again, in fighting the South, we have a great space of country to travel over and a great part of it is unknown to us. If we whip them at one point, they are off for another where they make a stand choosing their own ground and there we have to give it to them again. And so they keep it up and we can only follow them. Of course, when we take a place we have to leave a force to protect it. And probably our main army will not be gone but a few days when there will be a rebel guerrilla dash on the place; and our force will [be] captured, paroled and sent home. The place is then again in the hands of the rebels and our army will have to take the back track for fear of being surrounded.

This is the way the war has been managed so far and I see of no way to change it. Our many attempts to take Richmond have proved to be failures thus far and I do not think the place will ever be taken. Several of our states threaten to withdraw their men from the field and I think that, if this is done in a single instance, it will put an end to the war in short order. I do not know what to think exactly in relation to the whole matter. I would like to see the Union as it was and it seems hard to think we will have to give up. But at what a great sacrifice has the war been carried on thus far and how little very little have we gained. The army is rapidly falling into the hands of politicians and contractors and the result will be that the people will take the management of affairs in their own hands.

I am anxiously awaiting to hear from you and hope to soon. Have not heard from you in some time. Do not fail to write me often. Charley Olcott and myself have a tent together now a days. It is about ten feet square and six feet high. We live very comfortably in it. Considerable sickness among our boys. None very sick however. I am very well and feel first-rate. By the by, I was appointed Corporal today. Think of it. Corporal Brown. Do not hear from Henry or Lib. Were they well when you last heard from them?

Write often. Kind regards to all.[12]

* * *

Although discouraged with the Union army's predicament, Will Brown nevertheless tried to "Keep doing something." He believed routine exercise, such as regular horseback rides, was a major factor in a soldier's ability to avoid getting sick. The inquisitive corporal described a trip he made during the afternoon of February 2 to the eastern bank of De Soto Point—when there was a lull in the torrential rains, lightning bursts, and floods—to see the Vicksburg defenses up close. Will told his father how, earlier that morning, *Queen of the West*, the premier ram in

Harper's Pictorial History of the Great Rebellion

The *Queen of the West* ramming the *CSS Vicksburg*.

the Ellet family fleet, had stormed past the same place that he and his friends were standing. It was on its way to a successful running of the Confederate gauntlet at Vicksburg.

Although the *Queen of the West* had played a prominent role the previous June in vanquishing the Confederate rams at Memphis, she encountered a stronger opponent the following month. Confronted by the vaunted Southern ram *Arkansas* below the Vicksburg bluffs on July 15, 1862, the *Queen of the West* was forced to flee up the Mississippi River. A week later, the *Queen of the West* returned to attack the *Arkansas* but was badly damaged and taken out of action. (The Confederate ironclad would meet her end on August 6, 1862, above Baton Rouge.) Back in service for the Union's 1863 amphibious operations against Vicksburg, the *Queen of the West* ran past the Vicksburg batteries just as the sun was rising on February 2. On board was Colonel Charles Rivers Ellet, Jr., the energetic commander of the War Department's ram fleet that sailed with Porter. As noted by Will Brown, 300 water-soaked cotton bales covered the ram, positioned to protect the *Queen of the West's* machinery. Enduring shot and shell from the Vicksburg guns for about 50 minutes, Ellet's ram severely damaged the Confederate steamboat the *City of Vicksburg* and then slipped away. The Southerners had fired approximately 120 shots at the *Queen of the West*, but only a dozen found their target; none inflicted any major damage. Ellet descended the Mississippi, intent on disrupting river commerce below Vicksburg. That night, the *Queen of the West* tied up at Vidalia, opposite Natchez. She was then ready to prowl along the Red River. On February 3, Ellet seized three Confederate steamboats (the *A. W. Baker, Moro*, and *Berwick Bay*) and captured a large supply of commissary stores along with 60 prisoners, including several women. Seven Confederate officers jumped into the river and escaped. On his return upstream, Ellet discovered his prizes could not keep pace with the *Queen of the West* and he was forced to burn them and their cargo. He dropped off the captured Southern military personnel and sent them toward the Union lines under guard.[13]

On February 14, Ellet, during a second raid, took his ram and the *De Soto*, a small Army steamer, farther up the Red River. In the morning, they captured the enemy steamboat *Era No. 5* and continued on to Fort Taylor, an earthen Confederate fortification about 85 miles above the mouth of the Red River. While engaging Confederate batteries there, the *Queen of the West* ran aground. One of the shots from Fort Taylor severed the ram's steam pipe and Ellet had to abandon the boat. The Union commander escaped with some of his men, and they floated on cotton bales down to the *De Soto,* their support vessel. Ellet also decided to abandon that vessel, moving his men to the captured *Era No. 5* and burning the *De Soto*. On February 16, Ellet rendezvoused at Natchez with the ironclad *Indianola*, which Lieutenant Commander George W. Brown had brought down the Mississippi River. At nightfall on February 21, the colonel safely tied up *Era No. 5* at Biggs Landing, held by the Federals, below Vicksburg. In his report to Porter, Ellet placed the blame for the *Queen of the West* debacle on its pilot, whom he claimed had purposely grounded the ram. While the Chicago Mercantile Battery artillerists were intrigued with the *Queen of the West's* adventures, they preferred to go into battle—as they had at Arkansas Post—with Porter's "powerful looking monsters." Yet, many Union soldiers worried that even Porter's gunboats could not fare any better than Ellet's agile rams against the enemy firepower that guarded Vicksburg. The next two months would provide them with several opportunities to challenge that hypothesis.[14]

The Battery Boys had another diversion beside following the *Queen of the West's* exploits: they actively monitored the growing anti-war sentiment that was appearing in the Chicago newspapers, which they were routinely receiving due, in part, to Grant's stalled Vicksburg Campaign. The Union troops in the West were particularly angry at Confederate-appeasing Copperheads, whom they believed were emboldened to slither out from the shadows during the frustrating "Northern Winter of Discontent."[15]

Members of the Mercantile Battery were particularly irate about Wilbur F. Storey and his *Chicago Times*. Storey had purchased the newspaper from industrialist Cyrus McCormick in June 1861 so he could present a Democratic counterbalance to the Republican-leaning *Chicago Tribune*. His initial goal as editor had been to highlight Senator Stephen Douglas and his role in the Democratic Party. In his first newspaper issue, however, he had to cover Douglas' untimely death. As the Civil War progressed, Storey deviated from Douglas' "War Democrat" position and aggressively rallied support for the Northern "Peace Democrat" movement.[16]

As tensions escalated in the Northwest, the Board of Trade joined the Young Men's Christian Association in boycotting Storey's *Chicago Times*, which the business and religious leaders regarded as being egregiously damaging to the Union cause. An irate Major General Stephen A. Hurlbut, commanding the 16th Corps at Memphis, forbade the dissemination of Storey's newspaper among his troops. He was concerned that the *Chicago Times* had become a propaganda vehicle to foster desertion. Many of the Illinois troops were already uneasy about Lincoln's Emancipation Proclamation; they perceived it to be a "bait and switch" tactic to change the war's goal from restoration of the Union to the liberation of the slaves. By the end of the war, more than 13,000 Illinois troops would desert, with a large percentage occurring during this period. As Lincoln scholar Carl Sandburg noted, "Illinois had 2,001 deserters arrested in six months." Many of these discouraged soldiers came from southern Illinois, that precarious "triangle of land wedged between the Slave States of Kentucky and Missouri." On the home front, the Illinois state legislature's Democratic majority began preparing a series of bills to oppose Lincoln's policies. This, in Sandburg's words, led to "the first time in the history of Illinois [that] a governor prorogued the legislature, disbanded them, ordered them to go home."[17]

To combat the rising Copperhead movement, a group of Illinois officers met on January 30 in Corinth, Mississippi, to compose a reply from the state's soldiers in the field. They agreed upon "resolutions to show to Governor Yates and the other State officers of Illinois, and to all our friends at home, that we are still in favor of the vigorous prosecution of the war, and that we will uphold our President and Governor in all their efforts to put down this rebellion." Officers in the 7th, 8th, 12th, 50th, 52nd, 57th, 62nd, and 66th Illinois regiments threatened to take action against the Copperheads. "Beware of the terrible retribution that is falling upon your coadjutors at the South," they declared, "and that as your crime is tenfold blacker, it will swiftly smite you with tenfold more horror, should you persist in your damnable deeds of treason."[18]

The Battery Boys had their own challenges to deal with during this "Period of Despair." Two of the company's lieutenants, James H. Swan and David R. Crego, resigned—evidently due to problems with Charles Cooley. Many of the artillerists had begun to question Cooley's competence during the Tallahatchie march, and their concerns continued after they left Memphis. The battery's inactivity along the Mississippi gave Cooley's men time to compare him with more effective commanders. McClernand evidently shared some of their apprehensions. In Illinois, Brigadier General Allen C. Fuller, the state's adjutant general, had discussions about dismantling the Mercantile Battery and sending half of the artillerists to Illinois Light Artillery, Battery D, and the rest to Battery H. Fortuitously, representatives from the Mercantile Association arrived at Milliken's Bend to review the battery they were sponsoring. The business leaders were able to precipitate the Mercantile Battery's reorganization before it was dissolved.[19]

At the beginning of March, General McClernand announced that Patrick H. White was to become Cooley's replacement. As a first lieutenant in Taylor's Battery, White had earned Ulysses S. Grant's respect and endorsement, based upon his gallant work at Belmont, Fort

Lieutenant James H. Swan, Chicago Mercantile Battery

Chicago Historical Society

Lieutenant David R. Crego,
Chicago Mercantile Battery

Chicago Historical Society

Donelson, and Shiloh. Referring to his new captain, Will Brown wrote his father that White would "prove to be just the man we want."

Pat White was used to difficult situations. He had escaped the Irish Potato Famine and settled with his family in Nova Scotia. There, while working at a sawmill, White lost some fingers on his left hand in an accident. When his parents relocated to Chicago, he worked as a butcher at one of the unsanitary meat factories. During that time, White learned how to fire cannon in one of the city's prestigious militia organizations, the Chicago Light Artillery.[20]

What the Battery Boys did not know was that Grant and Sherman both paid personal attention to their new captain's promotion, though the two officers worked at cross purposes. In his postwar memoir, White wrote about the roles played by the prominent leaders in his assignment to the Mercantile Battery. "Early in February, Gen. Sherman called on me and said there was a scheme on foot to make me Captain of the Chicago Mercantile Battery, and for me not to accept it, as I would be captain of my own [Taylor's Battery] in a few weeks," remembered White. Sherman, he continued, "left with the understanding that I would remain where I was. About a half-hour after he left, I received an order from Gen. Grant, detailing me to take charge of the Mercantile Battery."[21]

*   *   *

In Louisiana near Vicksburg
Feb'y 8th 1863

My dear father

I manage to relieve the monotony of camp life in various ways and thus far have succeeded admirably. On last Monday [February 2], Charley Olcott, two members of Battery "B" and myself went thro' the woods and got directly opposite Vicksburg. We had an excellent look at the place and a good view of its fortifications, breastworks &c &c. The main part of the town is built on a side hill and, from our stand point, it looks as if it was built on an inclined plane. The city is neatly and compactly built and boasts some very fine buildings. Its large buildings stand out very distinctly and can be seen from a great distance. The right and left of the town is protected by very high bluffs and they can be covered with heavy guns. But after all, the guns are not so very dangerous as you will hear anon. Several seceshes in the place, seeing us, commenced to ask questions of us but the distance across the river was so great that we could not understand each other very well. And so the conversation was a very short one.

"When are you going to take Vicksburg?"
"How do you like the war?"
"How many gun boats have you got?"
"What are you doing at the canal?"
"You d__d yankees" and few other questions were all we heard and our replies were not very satisfactory I assure you. In fact, it would take a very strong imagination to believe anything we told them and I don't think their imagination is any stronger than the rest of mankinds. And now for the boasted strength and <u>terror</u> of their river batteries, breastworks and fortifications.[22]

Early on the morning of the day we <u>visited</u> the place one of our rams, the "Queen of the West," ran the blockade and only was hit eleven times; and these shots did not damage her in the least. She had but thirteen men on board and none of them were hurt. Considering that this ram is as large as any of the Mississippi steamers, her escape seems almost miraculous and her officers are entitled to all praise for their bravery and success. The object in running the blockade was to get a boat between Vicksburg and Port Hudson and thus destroy all rebel stores &c between these two points. I have just learned to-day the result of her trip down the river. She found and destroyed three rebel transports loaded with much provisions, clothing &c for army use and also captured a lot of rebels, paroled the privates and brought the officers back. So you see it paid to run a risk. These rams are great institutions. They are simply riverboats <u>attired</u> <u>for</u> <u>army</u> <u>use</u> with a ram at the bow. They are <u>iron-clad</u> with cotton bales and I tell you in this case "Cotton is King."

Nearly every pleasant day I take a horse back ride round among the different camps, works &c and in this way manage to pass away the time very pleasantly. There are four of us boys who mess together and we manage to live in pretty good style. There are plenty of sutlers and army pedlars around but everything they have tastes terribly of silver, or its equivalents rather, viz: <u>Greenbacks</u>. And as the most of us are not blessed with many dollars—not having recd <u>any red</u> from the government yet—we do not indulge in many of their luxury's. I find I can get along about as well with a little money in my pocket and live about as well as if I had plenty. The army is a great school and teaches one many things that he would not learn in private life. "Experience" after all "is the best teacher."

I meet many of my old friends here in the army and many are the <u>comforts</u> we have about matters and things at home. For the past month I have been striving to find or see an end to this war and, from the tone of many Northern speakers and papers, I think a settlement of our difficulties will be brought about ere many months have passed. But I am fearful that our great object will not be attained and that, if a settlement is brought about, it will result in the recognition of the Southern states as a separate Confederacy. And all our treasure and lives will have been spent for naught.

The so-called Democratic party of the North is again coming in power and they seem willing to do almost anything to end this war. The Chicago Times talks treason loudly and boldly and nothing is done about it. The editor of that paper would fare hard should he make his appearance amongst us and I fear he would get his neck stretched slightly—<u>if not more so</u>. What do you think of future prospects? Is <u>Honest</u> Old Abe able to wield the <u>mighty arm</u> or will he have to succumb? Two of our Lieuts—Swan and Crego—have resigned and start for home tomorrow. The cause of their resignation is sickness of Capt. Cooley and the service; and I think about as much [of] one as the other. I will send this letter as far as Chicago by one of them and then you will probably be sure to get it. Write often. I do not hear from Henry or Liberty. Love to all.

*   *   *

In Louisiana near Vicksburg
Feb'y 15th 1863

My dear father

During the past week there has been but little going on here. Nothing of consequence. An occasional arrival of a steamboat from the North, bringing us a supply of letters and papers, is about all that has tended to ward off the monotony. Night before last [Friday, February 13] very heavy firing was going on in this direction and yesterday we had a report in camp that one of our gunboats had run the blockade at Vicksburg. But the report has not been confirmed yet and I do not know how true it may prove to be. Would have found out about it yesterday but, as it was rainy, could not.[23]

I saw Generals Grant and Frank Blair the other day. Had a first-rate look at both of them. Grant is a man about your size, perhaps not quite so heavily built. He looks like a good-natured South Water St. merchant and is the last man I would take for a Chief. But we know that he <u>can</u> fight and has thus far proved himself to be a <u>winning man</u>. Blair is a large man with an <u>awful savage</u> look; probably made <u>more so</u> by a large heavy red moustache that he wears. I was not very favorably impressed with his appearance. I do not know how high he stands in army circles.[24]

What does all this hubbub and talk about Peace announcements [mean]? Is there any reliance to be placed in newspapers talk and in "Peace conventions," or is the whole thing a mere farce gotten up by a few to cause a stir among the many. The papers are all so partizan in their language that we hardly know what to think. Are the <u>people</u> asking for a peace or is it the so-called Democratic party. I am anxious to know what the <u>Peace convention</u> that proposes to meet at Louisville Ky. on the 22nd of this month intend to do and whether they act officially or as a party of individuals. Since this peace talk has come into existence, I find it is being favorably received by many, if not most, of our private soldiers. And they seem to think this war should be stopped. I do not think the proposition is so favorably received among our higher officers. Most of them are better situated now than ever before and they do not like to have a good big income "nipped in the bud." I do not think this is the feeling with all but by a decided majority.

There is one thing that looks very bad to me and that is the want of confidence in Greenbacks. I see that gold is quoted at 1.60 and in Richmond it only commands 2.20. 60¢ difference between money issued by the United States and that issued by an unrecognized government seems but little and does not look well for us. I see that Geo. F. Train is running around the country making peace speeches and, judging from Chicago letters, he was well-received at that place and gained a host of supporters. I read his speech in the Chicago Times and he said many things that would not be tolerated when I was there. This and many other things make me think that public opinion in the North has undergone a rapid change during the past three months and that a strong attempt is being made to settle our difficulties.

The river is still rising rapidly. Several new iron-clad gunboats have reached this place and more are looked for. Our friend Wm Chamberlain is still on the steamer "Polar Star." The steamer left for Memphis a few days since. A small force went up the river yesterday to a point called Greenville. Several of our boats have been fired on at this point and this force goes up to quiet things. Capt. Cooley is still quite unwell; not able to leave his room at the hospital. Many of our boys who were sick have gone to Chicago. I do not hear from Henry or Liberty. Hope to hear from you this week. Love to all at home.[25]

*   *   *

In Louisiana near Vicksburg
Feb'y 22nd 1863

My dear father,

During the past weeks our battery has received a lot of eatables and drinkables from the Mercantile Association and very gladly were they received. The principal articles received are a lot of butter, soda crackers, codfish, onions, green and dried apples; beside a lot of sanitary stores for the sick. There is not a great-deal but a little is gladly received now a days and tastes mighty good. Some of the boys at home have sent Charley Olcott and myself a box of sundries and I expect we will be nicely fixed before long.

Our new "Queen of the West" has fallen into rebel hands. The account as I hear it is about as follows: Somewhere near the Red river the ram was fired into by a land battery, the shot taking effect in her boilers and rendering her useless. Col. [Charles R.] Ellet, her commander, abandoned her. . . . throwing overboard several cotton bales, [he] got on them with his crew and floated down the river some distance where he knew there was a rebel transport. Arriving at or near this transport he boarded her, got up steam and before morning had her safely moored at the foot of the canal below Vicksburg. This Col. Ellet is a brave, daring fellow and always doing something unheard of.

I think the canal will be made to work after all. At any rate, our generals are making a considerable effort to make it successful. The roads have been so very muddy during the past week that I have not been able to go down to the canal and cannot tell how they are working at it. Intend going down as soon as the roads dry up. Talk about Chicago mud—there is not the least comparison between it

Colonel
Charles Rivers Ellet

*Harper's Pictorial History
of the Great Rebellion*

and this. I went out yesterday and got up to my knees in mud in a few moments and then concluded to return to camp as soon as possible.

Messrs. Munn and Willard of the Mercantile Association are here and are endeavoring to get our battery in good shape again. Capt. Cooley and our two lieutenants are to resign and a re-organization of our battery is to take place. I cannot write you full particulars in this letter but hope to be able to do so in my next.[26]

To-day [is] Washington's birth-day, a general salute [was] fired by all batteries and it made considerable noise . . . Our General—A. J. Smith—was with us when we fired and gave the orders. The General is a fine appearing man and considered a very good officer. I will send this letter by W. S. Wilson as far as Chicago. Wilson has got his discharge and starts for home early this week.[27]

From the papers I see that matters and things are more quiet at the North. Are the <u>Copperheads</u> getting quiet again or they afraid? Recd a letter from Lib the other day dated at Bolivar [Tennessee] Jan'y 26th. He was quite well. Love to all. Hoping that I may hear from you soon.[28]

*   *   *

In Louisiana near Vicksburg
March 2nd 1863

My dear father,

Your kind letter of Feb'y 15th reached me on the 25th. I am sorry to hear that Henry has been so very unlucky in being in a regiment governed by a dishonest colonel and I hope he may succeed in getting out of it if he can do so honorably. I can pretty [well] realize how very unpleasant his position is and am fully aware how very unpleasant it is to be under a man who is dishonest. Our former

Captain was a man of this stripe but went in too deep and was suddenly brought to a stand still. Of this more anon. I hope you will not worry on account of Henry. Hardly a day passes that I do not hear cases of this kind—or nearly like it—and I think there is where the great trouble exists. A secret history of this man would reveal many circumstances that you hardly realize. Speculation (no matter how dishonestly carried on) seems to be the ruling spirit with many of our higher officers. In fact, this war is fast tending to a vast speculation and I sometimes fear that contractors, officers and quartermasters will keep up this war as long as possible. However, so we go and there is little use in grumbling. The fact is, father, that I have about made up my mind to take things as they come and let the morrow take care of itself.[29]

French mediation is now the principal subject harped on by many of our Northern papers and some pretty strong reasons are put forth giving the grounds on which the French propose to put an end to our troubles. What do you learn in relation to this subject? I see by Chicago [newspaper] dates of the 23d Feb'y that there is to be another call for men for the army. I think we are getting war on the brain but I admire "Old Abe's" pluck and I would like to see our forces increased by about 600.000 more. Sometimes I think that I would not like to see any more of my friends in the army but still, if by their help we can crush out this rebellion, I say come along [and] let us do the work up sharply and then return home. I have recd several letters from my friends in Chicago and they are all "trembling in their boots" for fear they will have to go.[30]

Captain Cooley and our four lieutenants have resigned and Lieut. P. [Patrick] H. White of Taylor's Battery has taken our command. Our new lieuts. have not been appointed yet. Cooley has proved to be totally incompetent and Gen. McClernand, finding that our battery was becoming utterly demoralized, ordered that we should either re-organize or be put in other batteries. On this very strong hint our officers all resigned and we are now in a fair way to become a decent battery. Lieut. White is a fine fellow, a good officer and I think will prove to be just the man we want. I was acquainted with him before he took our command and always liked his appearance. We only have about 100 men now and an effort is to be made to recruit us our full number. I hope the attempt will prove successful as it is a great-deal easier to get along with our full quota. I do not know whether [we] will be permitted to elect our new lieuts. If we are, I think they will be [Pinckney] Cone, Adams, [George] Throop and [George] Bryant. The latter boy is my bedfellow and a first-rate chap. I hope he may get it.[31]

There is nothing new going on here; everything quiet. Our forces are still at work on the canal. There also [are] two dredges at work

New York State Museum, Albany, New York

Pat White in a mottled photograph. He became the Chicago Mercantile Battery's captain in February 1863. White received his presentation sword in Chicago after Shiloh, where he had served as a 1st lieutenant in Taylor's Battery.

on it. We have various rumors in camp in relation to the ram "Queen of the West" and the gunboat "Indianola." Fears are entertained that they have both fallen into rebel hands and I would not be surprised if such proved to be the case. However, nothing definite is known. New troops are coming here daily and our force is rapidly increased tho' no signs of a forward movement are yet manifest. Grant says that he intends taking Vicksburg with a very small loss of life. I hope he will.[32]

"The whole corps is moving forward. . . .
Our army is in the best of spirits and confident of success."

Chapter 5

On the Other Side of the River

B y early March, the Union campgrounds on Young's Point were being encroached upon—not by the enemy, but by water, which was coming from all directions. Spring rains poured down from the heavens like one continuous waterfall. On the Louisiana side of the Mississippi, the relentless storms filled the bayous, threatening to engulf the last vestige of dry land. Puddles and streams in the furrows nearby caused the Battery Boys to recall the rain-drenched cornfields where they camped three months ago during their Tallahatchie March, except that the rows of crops were now replaced by mounds of freshly dug Union graves.

East of the Mercantile Battery, walls of mud held back the swollen Mississippi River. The narrow levee looked as though it was about to burst and reminded some of the Chicagoans of the fragile lining of a defective Confederate cannon barrel, ready to explode at any moment. Will Brown and his friends wondered if their camp, as well as Grant's Canal, would be compromised when the Mississippi spilled its torrents of brown water over the river bank. Captain White and his lieutenants struggled to exercise new leadership in the midst of the deluge, fearful

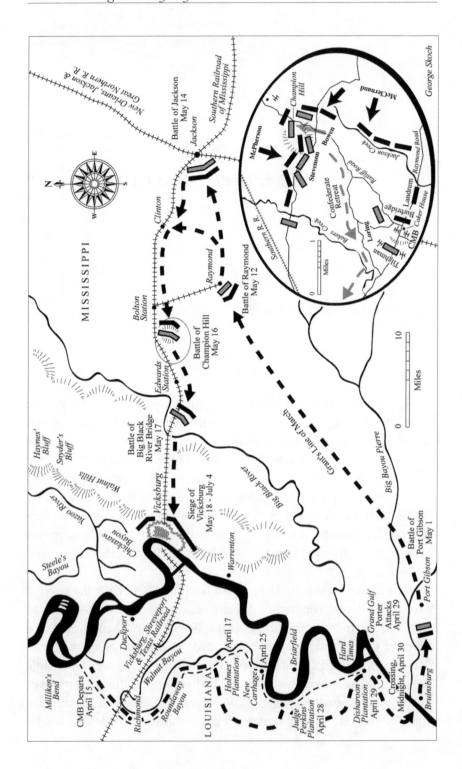

that the rapidly deteriorating living conditions would further jeopardize their artillerists' already fragile health.

Grant was also concerned about the bad weather and the failure of his De Soto Point operation to outflank Vicksburg. Still, he remained committed to completing it. Despite the prodigious efforts of Sherman's soldiers and the contraband diggers, augmented by two steam-powered dredges that Halleck had encouraged Grant to bring down from the north in mid-February, the canal project moved forward very slowly. The rising water table interfered with the Federals' work, the situation growing worse as the daily rain caused the Mississippi River to press harder against the levee along Young's Point. Finally, according to *Harper's Weekly* correspondents who were onsite, "the dam at this end gave way under a pressure of ten feet of Mississippi." The break caused the river to inundate the lower peninsula. McClernand's corps, which included the Battery Boys, received a frantic order to move upriver to Milliken's Bend.[1]

It was a difficult, frustrating time for Grant. In late March he was compelled to abandon the De Soto Point Canal. His promising Yazoo Pass expedition, under the leadership of Lieutenant Commander Watson Smith and Lieutenant Colonel James Wilson, encountered stiff resistance from the Rebels at Fort Pemberton, who blocked the way downstream to Haynes' Bluff. The Southerners thwarted this Union plan to connect the Mississippi, Coldwater, Tallahatchie, and Yazoo rivers and outflank Vicksburg's defenses from the north. On the opposite side of the Mississippi River at Lake Providence (almost midway between Cairo and New Orleans), the levee had been breached and the lake flooded. The high water created a navigable link to a series of bayous and rivers in eastern Louisiana. Grant, however, began questioning whether he could transport his troops via this Lake Providence "cut-off" to the Red River and thus enter the Mississippi well below the enemy's batteries. Other contingencies were explored. "There are many plans being made to circumvent the rebels at Vicksburg and I hope some of them may [be] successful," Will explained to his father. One such plan resulted in the Steele's Bayou Expedition, in which Porter tried to use a circuitous route to reach the Yazoo River beyond Pemberton's right flank. Natural and man-made obstructions hindered the admiral's progress, allowing the enemy time to block the Union flotilla. Worse yet, Porter found his gunboats in danger of being cut off, and Sherman had to dispatch a column to extricate him.[2]

While Grant labored to bypass Pemberton's troops, he was losing a battle of attrition against invisible enemies, some of which had also plagued George Washington's Continental Army. Many of the Union soldiers, especially the vulnerable new farm recruits, succumbed to dysentery, pneumonia, typhoid, small pox, and measles as they struggled with wretched living conditions. The health of young men from the Old Northwest, like the Battery Boys, had been steadily deteriorating since the Chickasaw Bayou Expedition, when they were first exposed to swamps. George Throop wrote his parents that many of the cannoneers had gotten sick at that time, attributing the problem to poor drinking water. Ironically, his solution was to drink from the muddy Mississippi instead of the more deadly Yazoo![3]

The battery's current problem transcended the quality of drinking water, as a civilian observer described: "The average depth of mud throughout the entire camp was not less than eighteen inches; in many places it was much deeper. In some cases the tents were surrounded by standing water." The pervasive mud made it difficult to dig sanitary drinking wells and latrines. Mosquitoes and bacteria proliferated in puddles of brackish water. Communicable diseases spread through the crowded camps faster than rumors. Hospital workers were overwhelmed by the number of soldiers who fell victim to the invisible invaders. One young small-pox-speckled man spent an entire day writhing and moaning on the levee in front of the Mercantile Battery's camp.[4]

One historian estimated that 85 men died during each of those spring days along the Young's Point levee. An Illinois infantryman in Burbridge's brigade wrote in his diary that "there was hardly an hour in the day but what we could hear the drums beating the dead march as some pour comrade was carried to his last resting place." Digging graves became a frequent duty for ambulatory soldiers—when the weather cooperated. Usually there was just enough dirt to cover the jacket buttons of the blueclad victims. Future floods would dislodge many of those bodies and send them, inside their coffins, floating down the Mississippi past Vicksburg. A minister from Chicago, who visited the Mississippi camps, was horrified at the conditions he found on the levee. "The most touching sight was that of the soldiers' graves in almost unbroken row for several miles along the levee . . . life was seen in such close proximity to death; for the tents were pitched close beside the graves." The Battery Boys did not want to alarm their families and, thus, they avoided mentioning the hazards of living in a Mississippi campsite during spring floods.[5]

* * *

In Louisiana near Vicksburg
March 8th 1863

My dear father,

During the past week, matters and things at this point have been a little more exciting than usual. Several new movements seem to be on foot and a general forward movement may be looked for ere many days. Perhaps I may be mistaken in my opinions, but I think not. The canal here is being rapidly pushed forward and is approaching completion. To-day the water has broken into it and may cause a slight delay but perhaps not as the dredges can work about as well now as they could before. I think our gunboats will be able to pass thro' the canal in a few days.

I have not heard from the "Lake Providence cut-off" for several days; but the last news from it was quite favorable and it was thought it would soon be in working order. If you can see a good map you can obtain a better idea of this "cut-off" than I can describe to you. By this cut-off, our fleet can get on the Red river and in that way take Vicksburg from below. There are many plans being made to <u>circumvent</u> the rebels at Vicksburg and I hope some of them may prove successful. To-day, we have a report that our forces are attempting to obtain possession of "Haines Bluffs" and in that way get on this high land above or north of Vicksburg.[6]

The situation of this bluff is about as follows [reproduced on the next page]:

This bottom land is now covered with water and our gunboats can run up to the foot of this hill and nearly all the way around it. I understand that the gunboats propose to shell the rebels off this bluff and, under cover of the gunboats, our land forces will take possession. And if we <u>do</u> get on it, I do not think we can be driven off by any force they can muster. Once on this hill we will be on almost an <u>equal</u> <u>footing</u> with the enemy and that is all Gen. Grant wants. We will see what we will see.[7]

Our present camping grounds is on a low piece of ground and there is considerable fear that we will have to <u>skedaddle</u> for higher land, as the river is rising rapidly and may break over the levee.

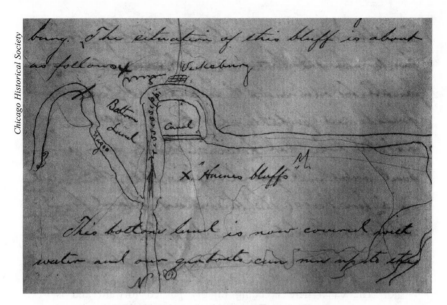

William Brown's sketch of Grant's Canal.

Many regiments have passed by our camp to-day bound for higher ground and probably our turn will come next. I hope not, however, as we are in very good order and have everything arranged nicely in fact (thanks to the efforts of our new captain). We have a model camp ground and it will compare favorably with any in this part of the army. We are very much pleased with our new Captain. I think he is just the man for us and, if we can only get a good set of lieutenants and recruit our Battery up to the standard number, we will yet become one of the best batteries in the service.

For about two months after leaving home I had the <u>blues</u> quite often. Now a days I am not troubled in that particular in the least. If I can only have my good health, I will be pretty well contented. And if care will keep me from being ill, I think I will be all right. I am very careful about keeping my body and under-clothing clean and, altho' it is very often the case that my outward appearance is rather muddy, underneath is all clean. To-day, I went down to the river, stripped and had a regular bath. Just imagine yourself taking a bath in Lake Michigan on the 8th of March. Rather <u>cool</u> comfort to say the least. The water here is rather cold but still I got along first-rate and had a good bath.[8]

Charley Olcott and myself have received a letter from our boy friends (chums) in Chicago saying they had sent us a box of sundries. Charley and myself are looking out for the box and hope to receive it in a few days. It will be gladly received I assure you.

There are several paymasters here and we have been mustered for pay (two months). Now, as we have already recd one months pay in advance and owe the government a small clothing bill, I do not think we will get much this time—and will have to wait three or four months longer before we receive any money of consequence. However, it don't make but little difference as the government is probably good for it; and when it does come there will be more of it.[9]

*   *   *

Milliken's Bend La.
20 miles above Vicksburg
March 14th 1863

My dear father

Your kind letters of Feb'y 27th and the 4th Instant reached me day before yesterday and were very welcome. They came with a pretty good lot of letters for our boys and were the first that we have received for several days. And as is usual—when we do not receive our mail regularly—we had lots of wild reports in regards to army movements on the Potomac and coast but the papers gave us the real accounts. And from them, we glean the intelligence that vigorous preparations are still being pushed forward and the time to strike well and deep not yet arrived. Our army and navy have been preparing all winter and I think, when active movements are again commenced, it will result in a series of Union victories that will put an entire new aspect on the look of affairs.[10]

As you say, victories are what we want now and I think we will chronicle several in the course of a few months. Altho' the country has been at war nearly two years, the people are just commencing to realize its extent and depth. And this is just what we want because, if the North says <u>must</u>, why then <u>must</u> will be the war cry and the result inevitable victory. If we can take Vicksburg, and there is little doubt in my mind about it, we will have accomplished a great-deal for our cause. As with its fall, the Mississippi will again be open and the products of our North-western states will again find a Southern market; truly "A consummation devoutly to be wished for."[11]

There is one thing I fear and that is foreign mediation. England and France are itching to have a hand in somewhere and, if they dared, would pitch in at once. I am anxiously waiting to hear what they will say and do when they hear of the recent <u>Copperhead</u> outbreak and I fear it will work against us. I tell you <u>Peace</u> (?) <u>Democrats</u> at home would fare <u>awfully</u> if they should visit this part of the army and I think there will be many a future knock-down when some of us return home. These peace men are looked on in a worse light by the army than the secesh and, if you at home do not keep them quiet, we will send up a few of our boys to do it in short order.[12]

You will notice by the heading of this letter that we have changed our camping grounds. The river was rising so rapidly that we were daily threatened with an overflow and so our division moved up to this point as the ground here is much higher. There is still a large force at the canal and they will probably stay there. Our new camping ground is delightfully situated and is the finest we have had since leaving home. It is right on the main bank and very desirable on that account as we are blessed with plenty of good cold water—and there is nothing that has bothered us as much as the want of this luxury. When at home I thought the Mississippi river water was very bad to drink but I have changed my mind now and like it first-rate.[13]

I hardly know what to say in regard to the canal below here. I sometimes think it is something like "The man who had the elephant" and about as much use. Its latest freak [development] was to break away the levee and, on the day we left, the water was rushing thro' it at a tremendous rate; and of course it put a stop to all digging. There are two dredges at work on it now and they may succeed in damming it up again, but it will be a difficult undertaking and take considerable time. It would not surprise me to hear the thing dubbed "Butler's folly" one of these days after the war is ended but still I hope it will work. Yet, I do not hear much about the Lake Providence cut-off but think it will be a success. I do not think the iron clad "Indianola" is in rebel hands. We have a report here that she has gone down past Port Hudson and joined the lower fleet. Hope the report may prove correct.[14]

I see that the 19th Mich. have been in fight and were defeated. The paper gives a mixed account of the affair. I am very anxious to hear if Henry is all right and trust your next letter will bring me news of his safety.[15]

We were paid off yesterday. I recd $23.80 and to-day I sent Orson Smith $12.00 by Dr. Bullack, our Battery physician, to remit the money to you and I trust you will receive it before this reaches you. We expect more pay before long.[16]

Recd a letter from Lib yesterday dated March 3d. He was well and in good spirits. Patriotic to the back bone.

*   *   *

Mary Livermore

My Story of the War

In October 1861, the Chicago Sanitary Commission, later renamed the Northwest Sanitary Commission, held its first official meeting as a branch of the United States Sanitary Commission, a national organization formed to foster good health among Union soldiers. Mssrs. Willard and Ira Y. Munn, both members of the Mercantile Association, were part of a delegation from the Chicago Sanitary Commission that was sent to Grant's encampments in February. During their visit, they documented the appallingly high rate of illness among Illinois troops. They also made note of the ever-lengthening line of Union graves that extended along the Mississippi. The delegation drew up recommendations for Grant and his commanders to improve the "truly awful" living conditions of their soldiers.[17]

Another delegation of the Chicago Sanitary Commission arrived in March to evaluate the army's progress in taking care of its young men. Will mentioned to his father that the delegation included Amos Gager Throop, A. M. Lewis, and Mary Livermore. Throop was one of Chicago's early political leaders, although he had been defeated in his mayoral bids, as a temperance candidate, in 1852 and 1854. A. M. Lewis was a commission merchant on South Water Street and involved with the Mercantile Association. Mary Livermore, one of the driving forces within the Sanitary Commission, wrote an extensive account of this humanitarian excursion in her book *My Story of the War*. Livermore would later draw on the experience she gained in organizing the Sanitary Commission to become a leader in the women's rights movement.[18]

In addition to the 3,500 boxes of sanitary supplies she helped bring down from Chicago, Livermore noted, "We also took down about five hundred 'private boxes,' forwarded by private parties for particular companies, or squads, or individuals, and committed to our care for safe transmission and delivery." The Battery Boys benefited from Livermore's deliveries, which Will took particular delight in describing to his father. Regarding the Mercantile Battery as her special hometown unit, Livermore socialized with her "Battery Boys" for two days and nights— sharing their hardships, eating army rations, and sleeping in a shebang that was made with rough planks. Years later she recalled how hard it was trying to sleep while "the incessant booming of the great guns at Vicksburg" echoed through the thin walls of her Milliken's Bend guest quarters.[19]

During one of the evenings before the Chicago gunners turned in for the night, George Throop, Mary Livermore's favorite Battery Boy, read from one of the New Testaments her congregation had given to each of their 34 soldiers who had enlisted in the Mercantile Battery. Throop asserted that he and his comrades had been reading their scriptures together almost every night. "We haven't failed but once or twice, and then we were on a forced march." Sergeant Leighton Dyer led the group in prayer that night. Livermore wrote years later about both of them, lamenting the fact that she never "saw again the young lieutenant who officiated as Bible reader, nor the sergeant who offered prayer."[20]

Jane Hoge, Livermore's associate in the Sanitary Commission and fellow organizer extraordinaire, also visited Vicksburg. The 51-year-old Hoge, mother of the Mercantile Battery's Holmes Hoge, spent two nights with her son and his comrades at Milliken's Bend. At the artillerists' camp, she stayed in the Battery Boys' "best shebang," with its rough-cut wood walls and floor, topped by a canvas roof. Hoge described the hut this way:

> Inside are two bunks, one built over the other, bedded with husks or hay, each large enough to accommodate two sleepers; a rough pantry with shelves, holding rations, odd crockery and cutlery, mostly 'jerked' from the secesh, a home-made table, and long bench, and these, with a bit of looking-glass, sundry pails and camp-kettles, and a drop-light extemporized from a glass bottle or broken bayonet, holding a candle suspended from the ridge-pole by a wire . . . the couch was of corn-husks, the covering a soldier's blanket, the pillow a soldier's overcoat." For her breakfast, the industrious cannoneers prepared "Hot biscuit, baked in ovens made

of Louisiana mud, ham deliciously fried, good sweetened coffee, to which we added condensed milk, potatoes and pickles.[21]

As the winter dragged on, the continuing reports of Copperhead activity, in both the newspapers and letters from home, infuriated the Chicago soldiers. Democrat leaders in Illinois, Indiana and Ohio, still riding the wave of political victory from the November 1862 elections, continued to agitate and threaten legislative intervention. Professor Mark Neely, Jr., in researching his book *The Union Divided*, found almost half of the Illinois troops were in favor of forcefully subduing the Copperhead politicians "if the governor or the president gave them the order." Threats of physical retaliation had been raised by Illinois soldiers at Corinth, Mississippi, and in camps in Tennessee and from as far away as Virginia and along the South Carolina coast. In analyzing this near-violent reaction to the Democrats' anti-war posturing, Neely commented that he had not found "similar threats from large numbers of organized military forces against civil power in all of United States history."[22]

While monitoring the potential anti-Copperhead insurrection, the Battery Boys were aware of another combustible situation smoldering along the banks of the Mississippi: the heated rivalry between Grant and McClernand. The predicament reminded the Chicagoans of the enemy torpedoes—the "infernal machines"—they first encountered on their way to the Chickasaw Bluffs. The torpedoes could still be seen, bobbing ominously on the surface of nearby waterways. Union soldiers and sailors knew it did not take much to precipitate an explosion, and wary river boat captains eased their way through the torpedo-infested waters. No one knew when a bomb would go off, how big the blast would be, or who would be hurt. The Army of the Tennessee had its own infernal device: on one side of the torpedo, the rope was attached to politician-turned-general John McClernand; on the other end, it was connected to Ulysses Grant, a no-nonsense military man. It was only a matter of time before one of them stumbled and detonated the bomb.

The Grant-McClernand feud was hardly a secret. Will Brown, for one, was aware of McClernand's autumn trip to lobby the president in person for an independent command. He also learned about the behind-the-scenes maneuvering that had taken place since some of the Battery Boys had accompanied Sherman to his first "planning" meeting with Grant at Oxford, Mississippi, on December 5, 1862. "Grant and

Sherman are both 'down on' Mc [McClernand]," Will confided to his father. In speculating on the potential ramifications of this internecine clash, Will used Lincoln's own words from his prewar debate with Stephen Douglas: "I wonder why 'Uncle Abe' don't bring his favorite mission home to roost. 'A house divided against itself cannot stand.'" About the only thing Grant, Sherman, and McClernand had agreed upon was the recent promotion of Pat White to become captain of the Mercantile Battery.[23]

* * *

Milliken's Bend La.
20 miles above Vicksburg
March 21st 1863

My dear father,

I have just received a box from my friends in Chicago containing a beautiful supply of goodies and I was very glad to receive it. Mr. [Amos G.] Throop, [Mr. A. M.] Lewis and Mrs. [Mary] Livermore are also here and have brought us potatoes, onions &c for the Battery. The truth is our friends in Chicago seem to think we have been shamefully ill-treated and are sending us a few reminders to show they have not forgotten us. Mr. Throop gave us a short speech this morning, congratulating us on our fine and healthy appearance and assuring us that our friends at home had not forgotten us by any means—and that they would look out for us and see that we were cared for. I think hereafter we will not find reason to complain but at one time I did not have much faith in the Mercantile Association. And Wm Farwell's speech made to us while we were at Chicago got to be quite a joke; particularly that part when he said "You shall be cared for." Now, however, we have good reason to think he was in earnest and I trust he will keep on so.[24]

I am looking for stirring times in this vicinity soon tho' I often times think the rebels will evacuate Vicksburg and not show fight at all. Everything around here is progressing favorably and rapidly approaching completion. Two of Farragut's iron clads are at the foot of the canal and bring the news that Banks is below Port Hudson ready to attack that point; and it is probable he has done so ere this. Grant has gone up the Yazoo with a large [force] and we have a report that he is in possession of Yazoo City. In fact, the whole grand plan has fairly started, I think, and a skedaddle by the rebs or a fight by us will soon be the order of the day. It is true we

Chicago Historical Society

Wilbur Storey's newspaper, the *Chicago Times*, was a strong supporter of the anti-war movement.

have been some time at it, but "Slow and sure" is often a good motto and generally wins sooner or later. I was very glad to hear that Banks faces us below as I have been quite anxious to know if he was going to have a hand in at this undertaking. Perhaps our generals would like all the honor of taking Vicksburg and Port Hudson themselves but, as for us, I can concede I am glad to hear that Banks is around as the more troops we have the better for us.[25]

I am glad, very glad indeed, to see the true loyal men at the North coming out boldly and strongly defending themselves from the stain the recent Copperhead outbreak caused. Let them keep on in their good work and if they would only clean out that dirty, low-lived secession sheet—"The Chicago Times"—our boys would bless them for it. I do not allow myself to get greatly excited over anything but I always get mad when I read that paper and I wonder why the people of Chicago allow it to be published.[26]

I presume you have often heard it said that even if President Lincoln did declare the slaves should be free, they would not leave home and their masters at any rate. I have often heard this idea expressed. But if any of these men could come down here and see the contrabands flocking in, I rather think they would change their opinions <u>somewhat</u>. Negroes, negroes—why that don't express it. More than half our camps are flooded with them; big and little, great and small—from the "pickininny" to the great stalwart field hand—all flocking into our lines and wanting something to do. I tell you Old Abe's proclamation is one of the most severe blows the <u>Confeds</u> have had to undergo and there are many more in store for them if they do not come to terms.[27]

*   *   *

Milliken's Bend La.
20 miles above Vicksburg
March 29th 1863

My dear father,

Inactivity still reigns supreme particularly in our Corps—the 13th. Rumors are rife but all lack confirmation. Sherman's Corps—the 15th—are spreading all over this part of the country. Carr's Division has arrived during the first week and are now at some point about twenty miles above us. More troops are looked for daily. On the morning of the 23d, two of our rams attempted to run by Vicksburg and only one of them succeeded; the other was sunk by the rebels and lost two men. The boat that succeeded in getting by is not very badly damaged and will be ready for work soon. I do not know what she is to do below. Perhaps her object may be to co-operate with Farragut against Port Hudson—however this is but my own opinion. The canal will probably prove a failure. So much for the digging ideas of our generals. I am told that Col. Bissell of the Engineer Corps has pronounced it to be a perfect failure.[28]

Col. Bissell is erecting a masked battery and, probably ere this reaches you, you will hear of some of the doings. I was down at Young's Point yesterday but did not have any news. Everything there seemed to be about as when we moved our camp. I presume you have read an account of our guerrilla boats. Five or six of them are down here. They are simply transports planked up on both sides and at the ends with loopholes pierced for musketry. I do not know how many men they have on them but, judging from outside appearances, I think they are pretty well supplied. Several new gunboats passed down yesterday towards Vicksburg.[29]

Quite a little piece of gossip is going the rounds here, the substance of which is about as follows: About the time our forces talked of making an attack on Vicksburg, Gen. McClernand went to Washington [and] saw "Old Abe" and the powers that be. At that point, and from them, [McClernand] got consent to take command of the forces when they started for Vicksburg. Mc started from Illinois and while on his way learned that Sherman had left Memphis with a large force bound for this point. On learning this, he at once started for this point and met Sherman just after his defeat and skedaddle [at Chickasaw Bayou]. McClernand at once assumed command, took our force up the [White] river as far as the Arkansas and up that river to Arkansas Post—it being his intention to keep on up that river and "Clean out the whole state." But after he had captured the Post, along comes Gen. Grant and he assumes command, censuring Gen. Mc for leaving Vicksburg or coming up the Arkansas. Grant and Sherman are both "down on" Mc and try to bother him as much as possible. Mc is sharp and I don't think they get the better of him in the least but, as long as this ill feeling—or hatred rather—exists just so long will we be at war. I wonder why "Uncle Abe" don't bring his favorite maxim home to roost: "A house divided against itself cannot stand."[30]

There are large quantities of cotton going up the river and I presume our Northern papers will come out with flurries saying that "The Union men of Louisiana are seeking the protection of our army and rapidly shipping their cotton to Northern ports." Gammon. Imported Union men, or cotton speculators rather. I cannot conceive why our government does not confiscate all cotton and, after the war is over, pay any man who proves himself to be a Union man for what cotton we take. We have already struck the root—the "negro"—then why not strike the branch viz: "Cotton" [31]

There is not a great amount of sickness among the troops. Small pox has been feared by many and there is a good-deal of it. I was vaccinated not long since and it worked on me first-rate so that I consider myself out of all danger in that respect. I think you would be somewhat astonished to see me. I am getting quite fleshy and my face presents the appearance of a full moon.[32]

*   *   *

Will Brown's father informed him that, while Grant's troops were stalled on the western bank of the Mississippi River, a portion of Rosecrans' army had been involved in a disastrous battle in Middle Tennessee. On March 5, Will's brother Henry and his regiment, the 19th Michigan, had been part of an undermanned infantry brigade led by Colonel John Coburn. The brigade had been sent from Franklin to reconnoiter south toward Columbia, Tennessee. A Federal cavalry brigade rode with the foot soldiers. At Thompson's Station, the Unionists clashed with Van Dorn's cavalry, two divisions under W. H. Jackson and Nathan B. Forrest. Although the sides were about evenly matched, the Union cavalry retreated from the field. Henry Brown and his fellow infantrymen, along with an Ohio battery, lacked the mobility to escape the Southern horsemen and were surrounded and captured. According to Van Dorn's report, the Federals succeeded in repulsing three Confederate assaults before Forrest got in their rear with two regiments, compelling the surrender.

Henry Brown's ordeal, however, did not end with Coburn's surrender. He was among the 19th Michigan's 345 men listed as captured or missing. (Another 113 had been killed in action.) After a march of several days, the prisoners reached Tullahoma, the headquarters of General Braxton Bragg. According to Coburn, Bragg's soldiers stripped their captives of overcoats, leggings, knapsacks, and other "extra clothing." Writing with discernible fury, the colonel recounted, "The men, shivering, half-starved, without sleep or rest, were then crowded into box cars, without a seat, and started for Chattanooga." The prisoners were ultimately bound for Libby Prison in Richmond, Virginia. Along the way their train stopped at Knoxville, Tennessee, where the townspeople tried to prevent the captured Union soldiers from receiving provisions. According to Coburn, some of his men were debilitated and "could go no farther, and were left." Finally, the train bearing Henry Brown and his surviving comrades reached Richmond. "From these cars they were marched to Libby Prison, and huddled, hundreds in a room, without fires or lights, like hogs in a slaughter-pen," Coburn reported. Many of Coburn's men succumbed to disease in the ensuing days.[33]

Back along the Mississippi River, Will Brown and his artillerist friends were among the thousands of mud-slicked, frustrated soldiers whose hopes of avoiding another frontal assault against Vicksburg were being swept away in the spring floods—like the secessionist house that Will had seen floating down the Mississippi River. There were soldiers, such as Will, who wanted to believe in Grant despite the disappointments of the De Soto Canal, Yazoo Pass Expedition, Lake Providence cut-off, and Steele's Bayou venture. But many thought that the new Duckport Canal was their last hope. Started on March 31, this project aimed to connect Duckport Landing with Walnut Bayou. If successful, the project would create a means for Grant to send flatboats and tugboats to New

Carthage, a village south of Vicksburg on the Mississippi's western bank, without subjecting them to enemy fire. Will sarcastically told his father that he would deem the latest canal to be successful "when I see some of our transports going through it." Will's criticism was far less caustic than that voiced by the newspapers and Copperheads.[34]

A year before, newsmen had hailed Grant as "The Hero of Fort Donelson" when he was featured on the cover of *Harper's Weekly*—in a fanciful, three-quarter-length pose that showcased a long, satiny beard and a uniform adorned with fine braids. Now, some reporters derided Grant for being a dullard; others accused him of being a drunkard. The press scoffed at the general's nondescript uniform coat and close-cropped beard. His military reputation, shaken by Shiloh, was being dismantled. The newspaper attacks grew more vicious with the failure of each of his Vicksburg expeditions. Even politician friends, like his Illinois sponsor Elihu Washburne, were worried. Yet Grant persevered. Like Will Brown, Grant sought solace in writing to his father. Reflecting on Vicksburg, he confided: "I am doing my best and am full of hope for complete success. Time has been consumed but it was absolutely impossible to avoid it. An attack upon the rebel works at any time since I arrived here must [have] inevitably resulted in the loss of a large portion of my army if not an entire defeat." But Grant was not going to be pressured into pursuing any movement that jeopardized his troops. "I have no idea of being driven to do a desperate or foolish act by the howlings of the press," he explained.[35]

On the *Magnolia*, Grant's steamboat headquarters on the Mississippi River, the general did his best to ignore the sniping of newspaper reporters and politicians. In the privacy of his office, Grant analyzed maps of the Vicksburg area while working his way through several boxes of cigars, developing a contingency plan to turn the Confederate position. On March 29, Grant ordered John McClernand to reconnoiter an overland route from Milliken's Bend to New Carthage, midway between the Confederate batteries at Warrenton and Grand Gulf. Grant wanted to use New Carthage as a base before he implemented a riskier maneuver: crossing the Mississippi and attacking Vicksburg from below.[36]

At Milliken's Bend, McClernand mobilized his troops and sent a column inland to Richmond, Louisiana, the seat of Madison Parish. The town was located on the western bank of Roundaway Bayou. A major Confederate supply line to Vicksburg passed through the area, where local planters had converted their farms from cotton to corn. McClernand learned the wagon road followed a natural levee that ran beside Roundaway Bayou—like a long, irregular, gopher ridge—until it stopped a couple of miles short of New Carthage. To make the route feasible for the army's use, Union engineers would need to build causeways and corduroy roads, which were created by laying tree trunks across the roadbed like railroad ties across iron rails. They would also have to manufacture makeshift boats for transporting the soldiers the final stretch of the way across flooded Bayou Vidal. Some historians regard this journey down to New Carthage as one of the most difficult attempted by a large army during the Civil War.[37]

According to Grant's Special Orders, No. 110, McClernand's 13th Corps would lead the way down the overland route, with McPherson's 17th Corps following immediately behind. Sherman's 15th Corps would follow, after part of it conducted a demonstration at the Yazoo bluffs to divert the Confederates' attention from the Federal flanking march. The Chicago Mercantile Battery was one of McClernand's last units to depart from Milliken's Bend. At 9:00 a.m. on April 15, the Battery Boys left with 10 days' rations, no tents, and minimal baggage. Drenched by more rain, they made their way down the broad, sweeping curves of the natural levees that together descended the bayous like a 25-mile muddy chute.

Harper's Pictorial History of the Great Rebellion

From Milliken's Bend, McClernand's 13th Corps marched south through the bogs along Roundabout Bayou.

The corduroyed roads were torn apart by the time they reached them. During the nights of the April 16 and 22, Pat White and his men heard cannonading from Vicksburg as the Union boats ran the city's gauntlet. On the first trip, Porter sent gunboats, barges, and transports; on the next he dispatched barges and transports alone. "The firing," Will Brown wrote his father, "was most horrific." Will was particularly impressed by the cacophonous noise of the artillery fire. "From our camp, the firing sounded like distant thunder and made the earth fairly tremble," he continued. "As we were about 25 miles from the place, you can perhaps form a faint idea of the noise."[38]

Grant now had enough gunboats, invasion barges, and troop transports to launch an attack on Grand Gulf, which he hoped to capture before driving toward Vicksburg. But the industrious Southerners, who were alert to the circuitous Federal march from Milliken's Bend, had been strengthening Grand Gulf's defenses for some six weeks. After sleeping with the rest of Burbridge's troops in damp, leaking transports, White's cannoneers awoke before dawn on Wednesday, April 29, ready to join in the attack on Grand Gulf. However, the Battery Boys spent the next five hours as spectators. While Porter's "jaws of death" ironclads were able to silence the enemy's heavy guns at Fort Wade, they failed against those at Fort Cobun, suffering substantial damage and casualties in the process. "Grand Gulf is the strongest place on the Mississippi," wrote a frustrated Porter, who lost 18 men killed and 57 wounded. Worse yet, Porter knew that his gunboats were stuck below Vicksburg—the steam engines in the bulky ironclads could not fight against the Mississippi's swift current to get back upriver to Young's Point. And Grant had two army corps below Vicksburg with another on the way. The Army and Navy had no choice but to implement their existing strategy.[39]

*   *   *

Milliken's Bend La.
April 7th 1863

Dear father,

Yours of March 23d enclosing one from sister Belle and a kind "PS" from Maria reached me on the 1st Inst. And since that time I have been anxiously waiting to learn full particulars in regard to Henry.

With your letter came one from Liberty and from it I <u>draw the inference</u> (the letter is not explicit) that Henry is all right bodily, tho' probably a paroled prisoner.[40]

Day before yesterday—Sunday—I succeeded in obtaining a pass outside our picket lines and with four of our boys had quite a ride in this part of "Dixie." The country is fine and well-cultivated, the plantations being quite large and <u>well-stocked</u>. Many of the planters have skedaddled, of course, but we visited one or two farms where they were going on in the even tenor of their way seemingly regardless of a war or anything pertaining thereto. All the plantations had a good supply of the "colored fraternity" and from them I learned many particulars in regard to how "Masser heard de big guns up de Yazoo and thought it time to leave right smart!" Nearly all these planters have taken their cotton, young negroes &c out in the interior. We visited several places however where our government had been and confiscated nearly everything. You would be surprised [if] could you visit a plantation. Everything has a careless look: Tools, farming implements &c—all of the primitive stamp—and one could about imagine himself in a country like Egypt. Invention and thriftiness do not seem to be characteristics of a Southerner and it is only occasionally you find a plantation looking neat and tidy. And I have never visited one of these latter yet that I did not find on inquiry that our "Yankees" had been there during times of peace.[41]

On our return home we saw a young alligator on a log in a bayou and as he was not far off I had a good look at him. He was the first live specimen I ever saw and of course excited my attention. We got back at camp about sunset after having traveled about thirty miles. I enjoyed the ride greatly and intend going again if we stay here. Love to all.[42]

* * *

Milliken's Bend La.
April 12th 1862 [1863]

My dear father,

I do not hear from you in regard to Henry yet but, from all I can learn, I am disposed to think him all right—tho' I am quite anxious to learn full particulars about him and his regiment.[43]

I am rather <u>hard up</u> for items this week as it has been a very quiet one; that is quiet as far as any movements are concerned. On Tuesday, our Battery was inspected by Gen. A. J. Smith who paid us several compliments. On Wednesday, we were out on general

Brigadier General
Andrew J. "Whiskey" Smith

Generals in Blue

inspection before Gen. McClernand and on Thursday out on Grand review before Gen. Grant. To a person who has never seen a review before it is quite interesting, and if ever one could [have] a favorable impression of soldiering, they would at that time. The review of Thursday did not embrace our whole army before Vicksburg—in fact it did not have half our Corps—but still it was sufficiently imposing. I have been at so many reviews that they do not interest me now but I would like to have you see one. We hear a great deal of the splendid appearance of the Potomac army but if you could see us you would think we ought to have our share of praise. We of the Western army have great ideas about Grant. We think Richmond will not be taken 'till he goes down that way and has a hand in. Some people have funny ideas you know.[44]

Gen. Grant is putting in force the cotton confiscation act and is picking up all the cotton he can find. On the levee, just below our camping grounds there, is piled up over $300.000 worth of it and the pile is rapidly accumulating. This is surely a strong blow at the rebellion and must be severely felt by the rebels. I am sorry the act was not passed long ago. Many are inclined to the opinion that the rebellion is on its last legs and cannot last much longer. Perhaps this may be so but I am not fully convinced of it yet. That the rebels are suffering for want of many articles I have not the least doubt. And I think they are fully as anxious for a settlement as we are, but still I think they will be able to resist for some time yet. If we can only gain entire possession of the Mississippi, I will then look for a speedy settlement; but as long as they can hold any part of it, so long will they fight.[45]

We have a report here that we have taken Charleston, SC. I hope it will prove true and that the gunboats at that place will join

Farragut in his attack on Port Hudson. The rebs are afraid of the iron clads and do not know how to manage them. By the by, it makes me laugh sometimes to read in our Northern papers of the "Dastardly conduct of the rebels in sinking torpedoes &c so as to blow up our iron clads." The papers seem to forget that "This is War" and that nearly anything one party can do to another is considered justifiable and according to the "Code de militaire."[46]

The [Duckport] canal across from a point about six miles above here to Carthage—a point below Vicksburg—is being rapidly pushed forward and it is believed will be a success. I will think so when I see some of our transports going through it. I am told that our forces are planting heavy guns down on the peninsula in front of Vicksburg but, if the Rebels have such guns as we hear about, I don't think they would allow us to plant those guns right in their faces. And for that reason I do not think we are trying to put any there. I see a report in the papers saying that some of the guns at Vicksburg are of the "Quaker pattern." I do not believe the report. "Quaker" guns were played out at Manassas.[47]

* * *

Milliken's Bend La.
April 17th 1863

My dear father,

On Wednesday last, our Battery moved from this point and are now encamped on rebel Gen. Holmes plantation about ten miles beyond Richmond [La.]. From there we expect to move to [New] Carthage. By looking at the map sent you some time since you will see the location of these places. Early this morning a squad of us returned to this point after our forge and Battery wagon. The roads were so muddy that we could not take them along when we left.[48]

Last night, seven iron clads and four transports ran the blockade at Vicksburg. The iron clads went thro' all right but one or two of the transports were badly damaged. From one of our boys who saw them go by, I learn that the sight was grand beyond description. Bonfires were made all along the Vicksburg shore and, of course, the river was perfectly lit up. Our camp was about 25 miles from Vicksburg and we heard the firing very plainly. I do not know what the object in moving by is, but I look for a movement now very soon. Our whole army corps is on the move.[49]

The country we passed thro' on our march is very fine and well-cultivated. But the rebels and our forces have cut the levees in so many different places that there is danger of an overflow and, should that be the case, it will be very bad for the plantations. Took dinner to-day on a plantation where there was a strong he and she ceshes. They gave us a good dinner and told us when we come back to bring them some flour. I picked a few ripe strawberries to-day. Peaches are about two inches in circumference. The Gen. Holmes plantation is a very large one and as fine a one as I ever saw, but it is rapidly going to rack and ruin. Cotton is still coming in rapidly. Over a million dollars worth has been brought in.

*   *   *

4 miles from [New] Carthage La.
April 25th 1863

My dear father,

Our whole Corps is moving forward and in a few days I think we will be on the other side of the river between Vicksburg and Port Hudson. There are at [New] Carthage now about eight transports and as much iron clads that have run the blockade at Vicksburg. Seven transports ran by on Wednesday night last [April 22] and the firing was most horrific. About 700 shots were fired but they only succeeded in sinking one of the boats. From our camp, the firing sounded like distant thunder and made the earth fairly tremble. As we were about 25 miles from the place, you can perhaps form a faint idea of the noise.[50]

We are all feeling first-rate and very glad to see a forward movement. I do not like the news from Charleston but hope we may get at them again soon. We must have Vicksburg and Charleston at all risks.[51]

*   *   *

Confronted with Porter's unsuccessful gunboat attack against Grand Gulf, Grant decided to move his Army of the Tennessee farther down the Mississippi and look for another place to cross over to the eastern shore. McClernand's men disembarked, marched across the base of Coffee Point, and headed for Disharoon's plantation, which was located about 10 miles below Grand Gulf on a high, natural levee. The plantation had acres of cleared fields that were suitable for campgrounds. In addition to possessing dry ground, the plantation was next to a bank where Porter's steam transports could tie up. Grant and McClernand arrived after dark. On their way downriver, they studied the Mississippi's eastern shore, looking for a safe landing spot and any signs of Pemberton having redeployed troops this far south. Some Union scouts returned from the Mississippi side of the river, bringing back a local slave. Wanting to be helpful to his Northern liberators, the slave told Grant about a road at Bruinsburg that went from the bluffs to Port Gibson. Grant finally had a viable landing site from which he could launch his amphibious operation to outflank Vicksburg. The element of surprise would also be on Grant's side. The Union general had sent Colonel Benjamin H. Grierson and some 1,700 cavalrymen on a decoy raid behind Southern lines. Utterly distracted, Pemberton sent his own horse soldiers (and some infantry) chasing after Grierson when, instead, they should have been watching the Mississippi shoreline for any sign of a crossing by Grant.[52]

On the morning of April 30, Grant's men began to board the transports. They cast off at approximately 8:00 a.m. and, with a band playing "Red, White, and Blue" to bolster the troops' confidence, the transports moved downstream to the Bruinsburg landing. Will Brown and the Mercantile Battery would not cross until the next day. Loading the infantry onto the transports was a priority—Grant wanted every available inch of the boats filled with combat soldiers. The good news for the Union army was that advance units of McClernand's 13th Corps, constituting the first wave, safely reached the other side of the Mississippi and established a beachhead by noon. The bad news was that the corps' supply wagons had mistakenly been left upriver, forcing the troops to wait four hours while rations were shuttled over to them. Since few of McClernand's units had horses or mules, many of the soldiers had to carry boxes of food on their shoulders. Others improvised, marching with hunks of meat impaled on the ends of their bayonets. Piles of unopened rations were lying on the eastern shore the next day, when the Mercantile Battery crossed over the Mississippi. Despite having to cope with challenges such as the 13th Corps' ration problem, Grant had had a successful day. As historian Edwin Bearss later summarized, "General Grant had transported 22,000 men across the Mississippi—the greatest amphibious operation in American history up to that time."[53]

Unfortunately, Will Brown's letter to his father about crossing the Mississippi River at Bruinsburg—and the ensuing battle and entrance into Port Gibson—is not part of the Chicago Historical Society's collection. This Port Gibson letter, along with several others, was likely lost in transit to his father. For this reason, an unpublished postwar

account written by Captain Pat White has been reproduced below to
provide a brief overview of the Mercantile Battery's crossing of the
Mississippi River and the beginning of Grant's swing through the Rebel
countryside to Vicksburg.

*   *   *

Captain Patrick H. White
Battle of Port Gibson[54]

April 29th, the whole of the XIII Corps arrived at Hardtimes
Landing opposite Grand Gulf. Admiral Porter, at 8 a.m.,
commenced bombarding Grand Gulf. The plan was for the naval
forces to silence the batteries, and immediately afterward the troops
were to land at the foot of the bluff and carry the place by storm. He
kept up a vigorous fire for five hours, running his vessels at times
almost within pistol shot of the batteries. The gunboats were
handled with skill and boldness, but the rebel batteries were too
much elevated for Porter to accomplish anything. He was not able to
dismount a solitary piece, and withdrew his fleet at 1:00 p.m. At
night the gunboats again engaged the batteries while the transports
ran by. That night the XIII Corps marched down the levee to
DeSchroon's, which was three miles below Hardtimes, and all day
of the . . . [30th] they were transported across the river at
Bruinsburg, which put us on the Vicksburg side.[55]

At daylight May 1st, I received an order from Gen. Smith, dated
near Port Gibson, to come to the front as fast as possible. The boat to
transport us lay a quarter of a mile below our camp. We found the
way blocked by two batteries of Logan's division, under Major
Stolebrand [C. J. Stohlbrand]. I requested the right of way, but he
refused it. I explained my orders, and that we only wanted room to
pass. He would not yield, so I went to Gen. [John A.] Logan, who
soon had the way open. We found lots of commissary stores
dumped on the levee and put a box of hardtack on each limber, but
wasted no time, as Gen. Smith had sent other orders for us to hasten
on. We made good time, halting but once for a short time to let the
horses breathe. We could tell by the sound that we were drawing
near the battlefield, but were delayed again by the 17th Ohio
Battery, which was scattered all over the road. I was furious, not
being in the best of temper anyway, because of an accident which
happened when we last stopped to rest. One of the leading drivers
thought we had rested long enough and moved without orders.

Before I got to my place, he was going up a hill. On his left was a
big bank, and out of this protruded an old tree which partly covered

the roadway. On his right was a deep gully. To avoid the tree he went too far to the right, when over went his carriage into the ravine.[56]

We reached the front at noon and went into action on the right of Gen. Smith's division, after traveling 12 miles from the landing. This battle was mostly fought by the XIII Corps, but at noon, Gen. Grant commanded in person. At the close of the day, everything was in our favor, and at night we slept by our guns with horses hitched. At dawn of May 2nd, we discovered the enemy had retreated in the night. We followed in hot haste through the town of Port Gibson to try and save the bridge at the other side of the town over [Little] Bayou Pierre, but we were too late.[57]

The army moved toward Raymond. Gen. Logan's division of the 17th Corps met and defeated the rebels there, and from that place pushed on to Jackson, the capital of Mississippi. Gen. Smith's division marched to Hawkin's [Hankinson's] Ferry on the Big Black and returned to old Auburn beyond Raymond, on the main road to Jackson. We camped here two days and nights. The cribs were filled with corn, and on the place was an old-fashioned mill, a primitive affair, with a long sweep to hitch a team to work it with. I detailed men to feed the mill, and other to pick out the best corn. It was not necessary to advertise the business. The whole army heard of it and we had lots of customers, who requested from a peck to a bushel of meal.[58]

"We attached a rope to the gun and between 50 and 75 men drew it to its position at the top of a terribly steep hill where we found a regiment of infantry at work and who cheered us lustily as we came up and opened fire."

Chapter 6

The Great Assault

For Mississippians, the months of April and May 1863 were difficult indeed. Events took a depressing turn for the Southerners on April 17 when Colonel Grierson's Federal cavalry cut through the countryside toward Baton Rouge, traversing much of the state's length. Grant was about to wreak even worse havoc as he crossed his army over the Mississippi River. Once on the east bank, he drove northeast across the state's torso, from Port Gibson to Raymond, and finally to the state capital at Jackson. Jefferson Davis' home state was quartered and hemorrhaging.

May 1863 only brought more bad news as secessionists across the South mourned the death of Lieutenant General Thomas J. "Stonewall" Jackson. The general's electrifying campaigns in the Shenandoah Valley and Northern Virginia had dominated headlines in Confederate newspapers for a year. He had been mortally wounded in early May in the battle of Chancellorsville after leading his corps in a spectacular flanking operation against the exposed right side of Joe Hooker's Army of the Potomac. Jackson's sudden attack crushed the 11th Corps, collapsed the Union army's wing, and set the stage for a general Union retreat from the battlefield. Grant was orchestrating a Jackson-like maneuver on a grand strategic scale against the Confederate defenders of Vicksburg. Unfortunately for the South, John Pemberton was no Stonewall Jackson. He was utterly ill-equipped to answer Grant even though the defender of Vicksburg was a West Point-trained artillerist and a veteran of the Mexican War. The Pennsylvania native, who was distrusted by many inside and outside the Confederate army, had never learned how to handle men in battle. While Jackson was at his best in combat, Pemberton was an administrator—a bureaucrat—and had no business leading an army.[1]

Pemberton's strategic position deteriorated further with each passing day in May. The indecisive general was being run by two masters. President Jefferson Davis had ordered him to protect Vicksburg at all costs. General Joseph E. Johnston, however, Pemberton's immediate superior and the region's theater commander, disagreed with this strategy (as did most of Pemberton's top subordinates). Johnston, who was gathering Confederate troops around the state capital at Jackson, urged Pemberton to leave his fortifications behind Big Black River and attack the Union invaders, who were even then rampaging through the countryside. He also suggested that he join forces with Johnston so together they could turn and face Grant. Above all else Johnston wanted Pemberton to preserve his army—even if it meant sacrificing Vicksburg.[2]

Acting on his own initiative, Brigadier General John Bowen, Pemberton's finest combat subordinate and a division commander, attempted to delay Grant by shifting men from Grand Gulf to Port Gibson, where the brushy ravine-strewn terrain offered good defensive possibilities. Bowen held out there for about 18 hours before being compelled to withdraw after heavy fighting. He simply lacked the manpower to stop the aggressive Federals. Once Bowen had been swept aside, Grant shifted direction and marched northeast across Mississippi, intent on smashing Vicksburg's railway communications in Jackson to isolate the Gibraltar of the West from the rest of the South. A victory at Jackson would cut off Pemberton's army and make it difficult for him to receive supplies or reinforcements. One of Pemberton's responses was to evacuate the hilltop defenses north of Vicksburg and spike any guns that could not be moved. Only a few days before, Sherman had feinted toward Snyder's Bluff while the rest of the Union troops crossed at Bruinsburg. Afterward, Sherman joined Grant's main force and was now himself on his way to Jackson. The formidable bluff fortifications above the Yazoo, which had once protected Vicksburg's right flank, were left to guard against rumors. Federal troops, including Will Brown's younger brother, occupied the position after the Battle of Champion Hill to ensure that a steady flow of supplies reached Grant's army. Pemberton's troops would later lament the loss of this viable escape route from Vicksburg.[3]

Grant's march toward Jackson was temporarily interrupted at Raymond on May 12 when part of his army was attacked and delayed in a sharp engagement. Grant, however, doggedly moved on. Unnerved, Johnston ordered the capital evacuated and left behind only a token force to delay the Unionists, who two days later drove into Jackson from the west and south, capturing the state capital and scattering Johnston's relief force. In order to ensure the logistical center could not be used as a springboard for the Confederates to relieve Vicksburg, Grant destroyed the railroad lines running into the city and burned tons of stores that could be useful to the enemy.

Leaving Sherman's corps behind to finish the job in Jackson, Grant turned his other two corps west just below the Southern Railroad of Mississippi toward Vicksburg. Pemberton debated whether he should remain on the defensive behind the Big Black or move out and challenge Grant to a pitched battle. The latter move seemed like a viable option, but it would expose the city to possible capture. The risk-averse Pemberton procrastinated. Johnston, however, convinced Pemberton he would move against Grant's rear to help him. This prompted the defender of Vicksburg to move out and meet the enemy. He did so too late and with too few troops, however, taking with him only about three-fifths of his Vicksburg army. After a grueling march that kept much of his army on its feet late into the early morning hours, Pemberton finally called a halt. May 16 was dawning, and with it the battle that would decide the entire Vicksburg campaign.[4]

Pemberton's 23,000 men were still in camp, or strung out on the roads around Champion Hill, early on May 16 when the head of Grant's southernmost wing marched west up Raymond Road and stumbled into a Confederate infantry outpost belonging to William Loring's Division. Two other Union columns were also probing westward, one up Middle Road and the other on Jackson Road just below the railroad. Grant with nearly 30,000 men was hunting for Pemberton in search of an opportunity to bring him to battle and crush him in the open field.

This 1937 photo provides a view of the Coker House as the postwar Gervin Plantation. Captain White's artillerists manned their guns nearby during the Battle of Champion Hill on May 16, 1863.

A. J. Smith's division of the 13th Corps held the advance position on the Raymond Road. Burbridge's brigade comprised the spearhead of the column. In the rear trailed Blair's division. Burbridge deployed his men and pressed Loring's infantry and associated cavalry backward onto the main Confederate line of battle atop the Coker House Ridge. For several hours the battle in the Raymond Road sector consisted of little more than desultory picket fire and a light artillery duel. Smith was under orders not to bring on a general engagement until ordered to do so. The battle's heavy fighting was about to unfold well to the north, where Grant's main attack with McPherson's corps was arcing south in a giant right hook to fall upon Pemberton's left and rear near Champion hill. As McPherson moved into position and then attacked, McClernand's corps eased its way up the Middle Road, threatening Pemberton's center.

It was about 4:30 in the afternoon when Smith finally mounted his attack against Pemberton's right flank. A bit more than one mile west of his position was one of the two fords across Bakers Creek. Its seizure would make it difficult, and perhaps impossible, for Pemberton to safely withdraw his troops from the field. Only a single brigade under Lloyd

Tilghman and two artillery batteries blocked the route, for Loring's other two Rebel brigades had been called north by Pemberton in an effort to shore up his crumbling left flank around Champion Hill. Burbridge's troops, reinforced by the 19th Kentucky and 77th Illinois infantry regiments, advanced just after Tilghman mistakenly evacuated the ridge in response to an order that had already been rescinded. The Union troops advanced quickly and took possession of the ridge where H. B. Coker's house stood.

"[Nestled] in a wilderness of flowers and shrubbery and large forest trees, stood the comfortable Coker house, with its large, airy hall running from end to end," recalled an Ohio infantryman. "It stood on brick pillars, some three feet or more above the ground, allowing a free circulation of air, a very necessary thing in that climate." Burbridge halted his line on the high ground, keeping the bulk of his regiments behind the ridge where enemy artillery fire could not directly reach them. A strong skirmish line was thrown forward toward Bakers Creek and quickly discovered Tilghman's new line about one-half mile distant. On the ridge itself Burbridge deployed Captain Pat White and his Mercantile Battery. White's task was to strike back at the Confederate field guns that were pounding the Federal position. Four 10-pound Parrott guns from the 17th Ohio Light Artillery unlimbered nearby and also commenced firing.

The furious duel engaged in by the Battery Boys pitted them against 10 guns manned by two Mississippi batteries. Tilghman's position was on a slight open rise, the last patch of decent defensible ground east of the lower crossing

Brigadier General Lloyd Tilghman was killed by a shell fired from one of the Chicago Mercantile Battery guns.

NARA

on Bakers Creek. If the Union gunners could weaken his line, the infantry might be able to pry his five regiments loose and turn Pemberton's right flank. Suddenly, Tilghman's position became the most important place on the field when bad news arrived: Pemberton's troops had been badly defeated around Champion Hill, the upper ford had been lost, and if Tilghman did not hold his ground the Confederate army would be trapped and annihilated.

Lloyd Tilghman had already witnessed Chicago's commitment to military readiness and strength. Before the war he had served as judge at a Garden City fair where the Ellsworth Zouave Cadets performed. More recently, he had commanded at Fort Henry, where Grant's forces, which included a large number of Chicago troops, had compelled his surrender in February 1862. Now, after his exchange, he was witnessing another demonstration of Chicago martial prowess.

Pat White later explained his role in the artillery duel with Tilghman: "I took four guns up the road [probably two 3-inch Ordnance Rifles and two 6-pounder smoothbores]. . . . We passed the line of infantry, who were lying down on either side of the road and went into battery on the left in front of a planter's [Coker's] house, which set back from the road about 300 feet. On the next ridge, which was about 330 yards from us, the rebel batteries and infantry were posted. Their batteries were plowing the ground around us. We unlimbered and ran the guns by hand nearly to the top of the ridge so as not to expose the horses."[5]

During the exchange of cannon fire, White relied on his two 3-inch rifles to pound the Confederates. "It was one of the hottest artillery fights I was ever in," he recalled. "I was deaf and dazed from the bursting of shells; I could hardly hear myself give an order and one of my ears bled. We used alternatively shell and canister, in order to disable them by killing their horses." As the Federal shells flew past him, Tilghman jokingly told his troops, "They are trying to spoil my new uniform." According to his Mississippi artillerymen, he leaned over an artillery piece to check its aim, stepped back, and was struck in the torso by a shell fired at 5:20 p.m. by one of White's guns. The fragment killed him instantaneously. As his body was carried off the field his embattled cannoneers continued to hold their ground as Southern infantry from other parts of the field arrived to take up positions and strengthen Pemberton's far right. For reasons that are still unclear, Smith's Union division did not aggressively attack off the Coker House Ridge, and most of Pemberton's troops managed to escape across Bakers Creek.

Loring's Division, however, holding the rearguard, was not able to cross the creek and was left on the wrong side of the river when darkness arrived. Unable to guide the guns over the plantation paths to avoid the victorious Unionists, the Rebels spiked and abandoned many of their guns, pitching the pieces into the creek. Some of the Mississippians were captured. According to the Mercantile Battery's Corporal Charles P. Haseltine, "We learned from these prisoners that the last shot we had fired had killed General Tilghman, the ball passing entirely through him, and killing his horse behind him." Separated from Pemberton's main force, Loring's three brigades made a circuitous and dangerous journey that carried them almost three days later to Jackson, where they rendezvoused with troops under Joe Johnston.[6]

Sergeant T. B. Marshall of the 83rd Ohio Infantry examined the Coker house after the artillery duel and saw that it had been hit many times: "One cannon shot went straight through the house...In the room nearest the battery was a piano, standing diagonally across the room, with the corner just in the right place in the path of the ball. Of course it was knocked off, but the tones were all left . . . on our road returning from [the Battle of Second] Jackson, we stopped a while on this hill, and Sergeant [David B.] Snow took the occasion to try the piano, and it furnished very good music as his fingers flew over the keys."[7]

The Federal victory at Champion Hill was overshadowed by the dual July triumphs of the Gettysburg battle and Vicksburg's surrender. There are Civil War experts, however, who contend Champion Hill was the pivotal Union victory of the war. Military historian J. F. C. Fuller considered Champion Hill "an amazing success, the greatest in Grant's life, and from a purely strategical point of view one of the greatest in military history." Other authorities on the Civil War's Western Theater, including historians Terrence Winschel, Timothy Smith, and Edwin C. Bearss, agree with Fuller. According to Winschel, "the Battle of Champion Hill was the decisive action of the campaign for Vicksburg, led to the fall of the Confederate bastion on the Mississippi River, and truly, sealed the fate of Richmond." Smith, who recently published the only full-length account of the battle, concluded that Champion Hill "had long-lasting repercussions on the course of the war by redirecting General Grant's career upward. He became commander-in-chief of the

Union armies, fought his historic duel with Robert E. Lee in Virginia, and eventually reached the White House in 1868." According to Bearss, "It can thus be argued that the battle of Champion Hill was the most important single engagement in the Civil War," and the late-afternoon confrontation between the Mercantile Battery and Tilghman's Rebel gunners was "one of the hottest artillery duels in the war."[8]

Unfortunately, either Will Brown never wrote a detailed account of his experiences during the Battle of Champion Hill—perhaps because Grant's army was on the move—or it was lost along with his Port Gibson letter. For this reason, an unpublished manuscript by Haseltine entitled "My Last Shot in the Siege of Vicksburg" is reproduced below. It provides a harrowing description of the artillery duel in front of the Coker house.[9]

*   *   *

Cpl. Charles P. Haseltine
Battle of Champion Hill
"My Last Shot in the Siege of Vicksburg"

Continuing its march towards Vicksburg, it [the Mercantile Battery] again encountered the enemy on the 16th of May at Champion Hills, where it had a fearful artillery duel with an eight gun battery belonging to the First Regiment of Mississippi Light Artillery. The fight occurred at the short range of three hundred yards. General Tilghman was killed by a well-directed shot from No 2 gun of this Battery. (Report of Adjutant General of Illinois, on Chicago Mercantile Battery)'[10]

That hole in my forehead? Oh, that's a little remainder the Rebs gave me of the Vicksburg campaign. I carried around the piece of shell that did it in my pocket for a long time, until I lost it. If I hadnt happened to be stooping over just at that moment—well, no matter, Im here anyway. Tell you about it?—Why sure,—I'm not much of a story teller, but I guess I can stand it if you can. You see, it was like this:

Our boys—the Chicago Mercantile Battery—after some fighting with Sherman's army north of Vicksburg in the winter of '62-'63, had spent several dreary, sloppy months trying to get past Vicksburg on the West bank of the Mississippi, and had dragged our guns miles and miles hub deep through mud and swamp, and finally on the night of April 30th 1863 we crossed the river at Bruinsberg with the 13th army corps under Gen [John] A.

Captain J. J. Cowan's 1st Mississippi Light Artillery Regiment, Company G, engaged in the Champion Hill artillery duel against the Chicago Mercantile Battery. This flag was produced according to the "Van Dorn Pattern" design.

McClernand, our battery forming a part of the tenth division under Gen A. J. Smith. There was a soldier for you; a commander after our own hearts: How he could fight—and swear—and drink whiskey; We called him <u>our</u> general, and I think we were his favorite battery.[11]

We crossed the Mississippi, and for the next few days had our hands full, driving the enemy in toward Vicksburg. There was something doing almost every minute, but the day I remember best was May 16th, for that is when I got my souvenir. Funny thing, too, for just the day before I had picked up an old black Reb straw hat in an abandoned house, and was wearing it, for the weather was hot, and I had said to the boys, as we went into action, "Well the Rebs won't shoot me to-day—I've got one of their hats on.

There had been fighting all day, and the Rebs had been driven back, but about four in the afternoon a Mississippi battery of eight guns and a New Orleans battery of five had taken a stand on Champion Hill in the edge of the woods, and partly concealed by an old rail fence. We brought up two guns against them, rifled Rodmans they were, and much better and more accurate weapons than the smooth bores we had started out with, taking a position in the door yard of the Champion [Coker] homestead under some magnificent live oak trees, and immediately the entire fire of the thirteen Confederate guns was concentrated on us, making things pretty lively, I can tell you. Around us were several regiments of Iowa infantry lying flat on the ground to escape the fire as best they could, and every little while a shell would burst above, and the fragments pin one of two of them to the earth. Almost the first thing a shell struck one of our guns, putting it entirely out of business, leaving only my gun, number two. We were just behind a little rise of ground, and we would load, roll the gun up until we could sight over, and fire,—the recoil kicking the gun back down the slope, ready to load again.[12]

It didn't take the Rebs long to find out that we had only the one gun, and they would wait until we had loaded, and when we rolled up again ready to fire they would let off about four or five at us. It was pretty hot work, but it [kept] up till nearly dark, when, just as I had aimed, and was raising my head, a piece of shell about the size of a walnut tore through the brim of my old straw hat, ploughed across my forehead, and laid the flesh down over my right eye…the shell of course knocked me unconscious, and the boys thought I was killed, and paid no further attention to me, for dead men were no novelty, and they had their hands full. They told me afterward that I partly regained consciousness and yelled out 'Captain, I'm killed,' and he called back, 'I guess not,—you're making too much noise for a dead man.'[13]

This was the last shot fired that day, for it was getting dusk, and the Rebs retired, dragging their guns after them, but found their retreat cut off by a section of our infantry which had surrounded them while the fighting was going on, and the two batteries and all their guns were captured. We learned from these prisoners that the last shot we had fired had killed General Tilgham [Tilghman], the ball passing entirely through him, and killing his horse behind him.[14]

In spite of the Captain's encouraging shout, he thought I was killed just the same, and when our battery had retired to camp they left me with the other dead on the field. Never will I forget the sensation I had when I woke up, and found myself alone on the field in the semi-darkness;—I thought I was dead. I remembered that a day or two before while peering through the chinks of a log cabin, some soldiers had brought the body of an officer and laid it down in front of me;—and I could see right through his head where the shot had torn its way, so I cautiously felt of the back of my head to see where the shot had come out.

I must have lain there for a long time, but after a while my brain cleared enough so that I realized that I was still alive, and that the boys had retired to camp, so getting painfully to my feet, with my hand to my forehead, I staggered back to where I knew camp lay.

Presently I heard voices, and my name, and I nearly ran into four of our boys who were coming with a stretcher to bring my body in.

Well, I wasn't much use for fighting during the rest of our siege. The Doc stitched my forehead back into place, but my right eye was swollen shut. And I had to content myself with carrying grub up to the men at the firing line. . . ."

*   *   *

The Mercantile Battery's bombardment of Tilghman's position helped complicate the Confederate retreat from Champion Hill. With the crossing at Bakers Creek inadequately protected, Pemberton's frantic soldiers had to squeeze through a bottleneck at a single bridge.

Despite the severe beating Pemberton's army suffered at Champion Hill, it survived to fight again. As the army stumbled toward the Vicksburg entrenchments the next day, Pemberton detailed Bowen and about 5,000 troops to defend a fortified line just east of the Big Black River. The Southern commander hoped to hold open a bridgehead for Loring, whom he wrongly believed was retreating toward Vicksburg with the Federals on his heels. Loring never made an appearance but McClernand's 13th Corps, accompanied by Grant, did. As fighting broke out, White and his Battery Boys unlimbered their pieces on the left side of the Jackson Road, where they provided artillery support. On the corps' right flank, Brigadier General Michael Lawler's Federal brigade sprang forward in a bayonet charge. Leading his troops on horseback, the overweight Lawler offered a prominent guide for his men and an easy target for the enemy. Lawler's Old Northwest troops followed him, converging on the Confederate center. Surprised, the exhausted and demoralized defenders broke and ran. When the rest of Pemberton's soldiers learned they had been outflanked, they turned and fled across a railroad bridge as well as a steamer (the *Dot*) that was moored lengthwise across the river to serve as a floating bridge. Many hundreds were cut off and taken prisoner. The Southerners, who had suffered embarrassing back-to-back losses, set fire to the railroad bridge as well as the *Dot*.[15]

Pemberton's fleeing soldiers left behind 1,751 prisoners, 18 cannon (two of which would end up in the hands of the Battery Boys), and an invaluable assortment of limbers, caissons, small arms, and ammunition. Vicksburg's vaunted river defense was easily breached and Grant moved rapidly toward the Hill City.[16]

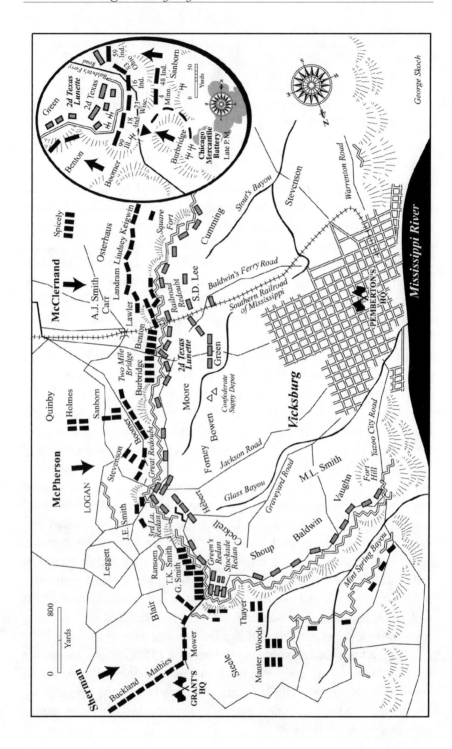

George Skoch

A. J. Smith's troops took the lead as McClernand's 13th Corps crossed Big Black River, heading down the Jackson road to Vicksburg. As White reported, "On the afternoon of May 18, 1863, we came in sight of the frowning heights of Vicksburg." He immediately ordered his artillerists to open fire on the Confederate skirmishers in the Vicksburg hills. The Battery Boys participated in Grant's first failed attack the next day, May 19, and in a more costly repulse three days later.[17]

In his unpublished memoir, White recounted his battery's role at Big Black River and in the first Union assault against Vicksburg. He also described its participation in the events of May 22. Will Brown was acting as a substitute quartermaster when the May 22 assault took place, and so did not witness the bloody fighting. He nonetheless gave his father a caustic comment on the Northern leadership that day: "Our Division made a charge but were driven back—or rather by some terrible mismanagement were nearly sacrificed." Will referred to the blundering of McClernand, who prodded his troops to keep up their May 22 attack on the Confederate right flank. The Illinois general caught up in another apparent surge of glory seeking, wrongly informed Grant that he had seized two key enemy fortifications, the Railroad Redoubt and the 2nd Texas Lunette. In fact, his troops had only captured part of the Railroad Redoubt. To ensure that the Confederates did not retake his alleged advance position, McClernand urged Grant to keep up pressure along the Rebel line. A skeptical Grant acquiesced, ordering Sherman and McPherson to renew their attacks, which only led to further useless bloodshed. Grant's tolerance of McClernand was about to end. In his battle report Grant accused his unruly subordinate of increasing the day's mortality rate by 50 percent—without gaining any additional advantage for the Federals.[18]

In the midst of the day's attack, Whiskey Smith ordered White to deploy, if possible, men and guns to support his embattled troops at the 2nd Texas Lunette. The men of Burbridge's and Brigadier General William P. Benton's brigades had begun the assault that morning—some carrying ladders and scaling tools along with their small arms—shouting "Vicksburg or hell." Enemy fire scythed the Northerners down, pinning the survivors in a ditch at the base of the fort. The fierce Texans hurled or rolled spherical shot—with fuses cut to five seconds—down at the Federals, who burrowed holes in the ground to shelter themselves from the exploding projectiles. White sent George Throop, his trusted lieutenant who been one of the first Battery Boys, to lead his section on a dangerous mission to help the beleaguered infantrymen on their right flank. Fifty men from the 23rd Wisconsin Infantry helped the Chicago artillerists tie a rope to the hitch of a 6-pounder smoothbore. They dragged the one-ton bronze piece through the brush and up a steep ravine to within 20 feet of the enemy's breastworks. The infantrymen also helped carry about 200 pounds of ammunition to the crest of the hill. Pat White instructed Throop and his cannoneers to fire point-blank into the enemy stronghold to batter down the walls or penetrate one of the embrasures.[19]

During the long hot afternoon of firing, the Chicago artillerists disabled a heavy cannon and "fired fourteen rounds of canister and spherical case into the embrasures" of Texas Lunette. As darkness set in, the exhausted Battery Boys needed to move back to safety, especially since most of their infantry support had retired. Getting the 6-pounder up the steep slope was hard enough, but who would help them to get it back down? Soldiers in Company C of the 4th Minnesota Infantry came to their rescue helping "to draw the piece from the ground . . . and down the ravine far enough for the battery men to hitch it." White, Throop, and their cannoneers were glad that they had not left any Battery Boys behind in the improvised shelters that their infantry comrades had dug into the

base of the lunette walls. Colonel Ashbel Smith, who commanded the 2nd Texas Lunette, made sure the holes were quickly filled up with "yankee carcasses." For 200 yards, Federal bodies coated the ground approaching the 2nd Texas Lunette.[20]

Colonel Ashbel Smith,
the commander of the
2nd Texas Lunette.

The Center for American History,
University of Texas at Austin

On June 9, George Throop wrote to his family in Chicago about the May 22 battle. By doing so he produced the only known (nearly) contemporaneous report of what he and his Mercantile Battery friends encountered at the 2nd Texas Lunette. If Throop had survived the war, he likely would have received the Medal of Honor in 1895 along with six other comrades who were recognized for their bravery in the fight for the 2nd Texas Lunette. Among the medal recipients, only White and Private William Stephens left accounts of the day's fiery ordeal. White praised the work of George Throop who, he wrote, "was as brave a man as ever lived." After the war, White labored hard to ensure accurately worded and sited markers were placed at Vicksburg National Military Park to honor the deeds of Throop and his men in the Mercantile Battery. Although the former artillery captain had provided a brief account of the Chicago Mercantile Battery's May 22 feat in a book on Medal of Honor winners (*Deeds of Valor*), he elaborated on the Vicksburg siege in his unpublished memoir, as reproduced below:[21]

*   *   *

Captain Patrick H. White
Big Black River Bridge to Vicksburg

Our next move was over Black River bridge. The next day I received an order from Gen. [Whiskey] Smith to report to Gen. [Albert] Lee, chief of cavalry. I thought this was rubbing it in. They were bound to have me earn my salary; but I obeyed. The rebels had burned the bridge and were in force on the bluffs overlooking the river. Lee wanted to lay pontoons over the stream, but the rebels were preventing him, by shooting at his men. When I reported, he said: 'I wish you would shell those fellows on the bluffs, so that my men can place the pontoons.' I went into battery behind a cane hedge for a screen as the place was low and flat. I gave the men instructions to fire high, to be careful of our men in front, and to shift the pieces to the right or left after each discharge to avoid the sharpshooters. Gen. Lee succeeded in laying the bridge and the next morning we passed over it.[22]

On the afternoon of May 18, 1863, we came in sight of the frowning heights of Vicksburg. We could locate our skirmishers far in advance, by the puffs of blue smoke from their guns. I went into battery on high ground, answering their fire, which we kept up for an hour. The position did not suit me, as it was too long range. I took two rifled pieces further in advance, halted the section in a valley and went on foot to find a place to suit me. There was a depression in the road as far front as I dared to go, and I chose this place for my guns. It was about 400 yards from the rebel trenches. The 1st U.S. Infantry was on my left, and with help, we leveled a place to plant the guns, with their muzzles pointing over the swell in the road. We had to hug mother earth pretty close as the sharpshooters got after us. We soon opened on them and kept pounding at their batteries till after dark.[23]

That night it was a grand sight to see their works to our right, which we could trace by their campfires. On the left, the ground was so broken we cold [could] see neither our own or the enemy's lines. The rebels kept up an artillery fire nearly all night. They had things all their own way, as our batteries were not all in position. I was awakened about 3 a.m., by an orderly from Gen. [Wm. P.] Benton of Carr's division. The orderly had to repeat his message before I could understand him, I was so tired and sleepy. The General wanted me to bring the guns down a gully, where they could be hauled up a hill to within 30 feet of, and partly overlooking, the rebel trenches. We brought forth the horses, and limbered up as the rebels would not see them in the dark. I examined the hill as best I could in the dark. It looked like an Indian mound, with an ascent of about 40 degrees. Finding no infantry to help us pull the guns up the hill, the guide went to look up the General, but being unable to find him, I ordered the men back to their old positions as fast as they could go, as day was breaking. The rebels saw us and opened on us. One musket ball grazed my ear. We dropped in our hole in the road and kept pretty close to the ground until they stopped firing.[24]

While in the ravine I saw the ridge would be a good position, as our guns would have a clean sweep of the two branches of the ravine and gully, as well as the rebel breastworks about 400 yards distant. I had a parapet thrown up here, and after dark on the 19th, placed four guns there, leaving two back at the first position under Sergeant Throop. This is the section that played an important part on the 22nd.

The morning of the 22nd, at 10:00 a.m., was set for the great assault. At 3a.m., the cannonading began from the land side. Every available gun was brought to bear on the works. It was the most terrible bombardment during the siege, and continued without intermission until nearly 11 o'clock, while our sharpshooters kept up such a galling fire that the rebel cannoneers could seldom rise to load their pieces. The artillery of McClernand's 13th Corps had succeeded in breaching several points of the enemy's works, silencing five or six guns and exploding four caissons. At ten a.m., the columns moved to the assault. About 12 o'clock I received a note from Gen. [A. J.] Smith, asking me to bring two guns down the

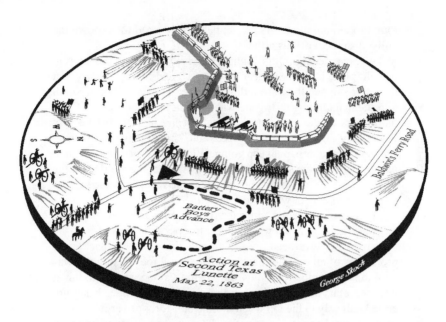

Action at
Second Texas
Lunette
May 22, 1863

George Skoch

ravine and get them close to the breastworks. I was to try and knock down one of their forts. I told my orderly to have Sergeant Throop bring up his section and report to Gen. Smith, and to show him the way we went down the ravine. In a short time the orderly returned, but did not come near me. I overheard him tell the cannoniers the boys would not go up with Throop. I stepped over the breastworks and found Gen. Smith, who said if we could get two guns up to the fort we would soon be inside the rebel works.[25]

I then went up the gully to look over the ground and the fort. It was a lunette in their works on the…[Baldwin's] Ferry Road, with a 24 pounder covering the road. Cotton bales were placed along the top, and in building it, they covered half the road with dirt, so there was only space enough for one gun…. we dragged the gun up to the breastworks with ropes. The infantry carried the ammunition in their arms. We used shrapnel, the fuse cut so close the shell exploded almost as soon as it left the gun. The first discharge was simultaneous with the rebels' and struck their gun in the muzzle, scattering death among their cannoniers. I never saw a gun loaded and fired so quickly, as every man was at his best. We disabled their gun, set the cotton bales on fire and they abandoned the fort for twenty minutes. That was the time for out infantry to pass in, but they did not do it. The rebels returned and commenced throwing water on the cotton, but our gun blew them to pieces. An Irishman of the . . . [23rd Wisconsin Infantry] detail called out: 'Begob, Captain, there's not a pound of him left, I'll go and get you another round of ammunition.' As he stepped off the road to go down the gully, a shot cut off his arm.[26]

The Seventeenth (Ohio Light Artillery) had taken a position in our old place in the road near the First United States Infantry, but the latter stopped them from doing further damage. General Smith told me that Quinby's Brigade was coming to support us, so I told the drivers of the guns and limbers that lay here, to get back to where they came from at full speed, and, should they meet with an accident, not to stop, but keep going. When part way up a hill a shell passed between the swing and wheel drivers, and exploded on the other side of them, throwing the swing driver on his face in the saddle; another shot went under the gun.

My four guns opened with a terrific fire from their position back on the ridge and they saw the troops fall back from the breast-works. Overhead in the ravine the air was black with projectiles of all descriptions from friend and foe. I thought it was time to see how the four guns were getting along, and to do this it was necessary to go back over the slope of the ridge. I had not gotten half way to the top when minnie balls dropped around me as thick as grasshoppers. I retraced my steps a short distance, and then obliqued around the ridge where it ended abruptly. When the men saw me they cheered.

After dark, Sergeant Throop brought the gun off safe and it was as hot as a live coal. Next day, the rebels closed the embrasure with dirt. The Sergeant was as brave a man as ever lived. He was nominated for a lieutenancy before I joined them and received the commission a few days after this affair. He was killed on the Red River, April 8, 1864. On the night of the 22nd, the troops were withdrawn from the most advanced positions reached during the assault, still retaining, however, the most important ground.[27]

On the 23rd, orders were given for the ax and shovel to support the bayonet. As we were in for a regular siege I thought it time to choose a camp, as our wagons had arrived from the rear. For one week after the assault, we slept by our guns, occasionally firing through the nights. For two weeks our horses did not have their harnesses off, and were kept close at hand, as we did not know, but that the enemy would try to escape from the city. Soon details opened roads and covered ways from one camp to another, while other details were cutting out fallen timber and constructing regular approaches. . . . About the 25th of May, I got a detail to build a fort on the Indian mound. The detail had to work nights, but when it was accomplished we had quite a fort within 50 feet of the rebel trenches, with embrasures for two guns. On top, I had cotton bales.

The embrasures were lined with gabions and facines. I cautioned my men to keep as much as possible from the front of the openings,

William Stephens was one of the
Battery Boys who received
the Medal of Honor.

Drum Barracks Civil War Museum,
Wilmington, California

but with all care they would forget
themselves, and two were mortally
wounded. To guard against any
more accidents of that kind, I had
regular trap doors made with
pulleys, swung from a timber across the top of the embrasure. The
shutter rested on the piece, and at the recoil would drop in front of
the opening. Then we would hear the bullets pattering against it.

Since writing these papers, I received a letter from W. G
Stephens, who was a member of the Mercantile Battery, and who
took part in the charge at Vicksburg. I will quote this letter in part:[28]

The place where the gun was to be used was so inaccessible that a
company of the 23rd Wisconsin was detailed to haul the gun up the
almost perpendicular wall. It was finally concluded that but one gun
could be worked to advantage, so the other gun remained in the
ravine, or was ordered back to the embrasure, I don't know which.
Finding my gun was not going into action, I went with you and
acted as No. 5, part of the time, and afterwards, as No. 4. While
acting as No. 5, we fired most of our canister in double rounds, and
when this was exhausted, I myself, under direction of Sergeant
Throop, cut the fuse of the round shell or spherical case shot at
half-second. . . . The flag of one of the infantry regiments was kept
on the earthwork all the afternoon, and Gen. McClernand, on the
strength of this, sent word to Gen. Grant that he had captured...[a]
part of the enemy's works. This flag was not more than 30 feet from
the mouth of our gun and I distinctly remember seeing it drop
several times. Each time it went down a dozen men rushed forward
to replace it.[29]

*   *   *

Lt. George Throop
June 9, 1863 Letter to His Sister Mattie

May 22 Assault on Vicksburg

At the commencement of the charge 2 guns (the right section) were on a hill between one and two hundred yards and the other guns (the centre and left sections) were several hundred yards from the scene of action in reserve & in my charge. Order came for me to report a section to Gen Burbridge for duty. I did so but in going had to pass down a side hill in front of the right section which exposed us to a galling fire from the rebels. I tell you the bullets flew.

We all dismounted and led our horses down the hill. One man said 4 bullets struck the wheel while he was locking it. We finally got into the ravine and I reported to Gen Burbridge. Wht [Capt. White] ordered me to take two companies of infantry & plant my guns within 50 ft of an embrasure where a big rebel gun had been firing.[30]

I went up under a shower of bullets to examine the position and found it impossible to get more than one gun up and not that until trees had been chopped away and a road prepared. This being done we attached a rope to the gun and between 50 and 75 men drew it to its position at the top of a terribly steep hill where we found a regiment of infantry at work and who cheered us lustily as we came up and opened fire [pouring canister, shell and shot into the embrasure]. We fired [2 hours & throwing about 150 rounds] until the gun became so hot that we could work with no safety and at the same time the enemy by a partial flank movement opened a cross fire of infantry & artillery [;] and at the same time our own batteries on the hills behind us opened and exploded shell around us cutting an infantryman's leg off near us & sending a piece half as large as one's hand onto the ground just in front of us & nearly killing some of our cannoneers.[31]

So you see we were fired upon from 3 directions but we kept up an occasional shot until one regiment had left entirely and the other leaving rapidly & instead of 60 only 6 were left to get our guns off. Some said leave it; said I, no we will get it as far as we can. So down we started, Denton and myself at the trail which was down & the other 4 at the wheels. When about 2/3 of the way down the gun got the start of us throwing Denton & myself headlong down the hill & we expecting the gun to come down upon us but instead it upset and tumbled bottom side up into the ravine below. By begging we got a few infantrymen to help us right it and on we went through the shower of bullets passing dead and wounded in all shapes and conditions & the infantry moving past us scared almost to death. We finally reached the horses and limbered up and went up the next hill under another shower of lead but how can I say or believe it no one was hurt.[32]

The Capt. was with us a short time while we were firing. But the charge was in my hands. Instead of me using hand grenades the rebels used them on us but did no harm. Instead of the battery [being at the original position] only 1 gun was there. Excuse the apparent egotism. Further details I will give at another time.

*   *   *

In the rear and within 2 miles of
Vicksburg May 25th 1863

My dear father,

Our success 'till we arrived here has been better than the most sanguine could expect. Here we find the army strongly fortified behind immense fortifications, breastworks and rifle pits. We have been here since last Tuesday noon and during that time have been constantly at work cannonading, building breastworks &c. On Friday, our Division made a charge but were driven back—or rather by some terrible mismanagement were nearly sacrificed. I did not witness this charge but am told, if it had been managed rightly, we could have held our position very easily. I have no doubt but what we can take the town in time and think it will be done ere long.[33]

Since crossing at Grand Gulf we have captured over 10.000 prisoners, 74 pieces of light artillery, burnt Jackson to the ground almost and destroyed the RR between Vicksburg and Jackson. Our army now surrounds Vicksburg—the right under Sherman resting on the Yazoo—the center under McPherson—and the left under McClernand resting on the Mississippi at Warrenton.[34]

"National salutes have been firing nearly all day. I wish I could describe to you
how our troops feel and act. All feel that we have done a big thing and
want to rejoice over it. Has ours not been a glorious fourth."

Chapter 7

Vicksburg has Fallen

In June, with the Battery Boys and much of Grant's army camped
outside Vicksburg's extensive fortifications, Pat White had time to
reflect on the events he and his men had experienced since crossing
the Mississippi River. The Irish captain was grateful his artillerists had
accepted him as their new commander. He had only been given a short
time to get them in shape, applying the experience he had gained in the
antebellum Chicago Light Artillery and during his wartime service with
Taylor's Battery. The "rich man's Battery" had responded to instructions
from its "poor man Captain," performing well during the battles of Port
Gibson, Champion Hill, and Big Black River Bridge.

At Vicksburg the "merchants' sons" had remained steadfast under
fire time after time, displaying steady nerves and brave hearts. They
calmly manned hot-barreled guns while shells exploded overhead and
riflemen's minie balls went whizzing by their ears. On the day after the
2nd Texas Lunette assault, a *Chicago Tribune* correspondent who had
accompanied Grant's army, devoted an article to the "Gallantry of the
Mercantile Battery." He noted White's artillerists were "gaining friends
in this army corps. It has a reputation for excellence, and the men have a

reputation for gallantry equal to that of the famous Companies A and B, of glorious memory."[1]

As the siege of Vicksburg wore on, the Battery Boys were pleased to contribute to the constant barrage that pounded against the Confederates' back door—their two rifled guns alone expending more than 1,200 rounds. The wheels of the Chicago battery's gun carriages rocked back and forth, forming deep grooves in the loamy Vicksburg soil. Cannon muzzles stayed hot. The heavy artillery from David Dixon Porter's gunboats battered the enemy fortifications from the opposite direction. Pemberton's soldiers were trapped in a crossfire, unable to break away to the south and join the Confederate garrison at Port Hudson or escape northeast along the Walnut Hills. At night, the Union heavy artillery launched shrieking "shooting stars" to keep the Rebels awake. During the day, the Confederates found it impossible to nap—the earthen walls of their entrenchments could not muffle the sound of thundering guns.[2]

* * *

In the field near Vicksburg Miss.
May 31st 1863

My dear father

If from hearing the report made from a six-pounder, smooth-bore gun charged with a blank cartridge only, you can form an idea of the noise made by say 300 guns of all sizes and calibres (from the three inch up to the thirteen)—and all going off at the same time—you will have a pretty fair idea of our present siege at this point. However, I doubt if you can form an idea from that. I imagine that the report of a six-pounder would not effect me much now. I did not used to like to get very near them when at home but the crack crack of guns all around me now a days has got to be an old story and I do not notice them but very little. Do not imagine from all of this, however, that I have got fully used to them. They do make me jump now and then right lively I assure you.

The siege thus far has been a big thing. We have the place completely surrounded and artillery bearing on it at every point. Heavy guns are being mounted daily and every preparation being made for a long and strong siege. If the place can not be taken soon, it can in time and I think we have time enough to do it. Our army can spend the summer here as well as in Vicksburg. There is not the least danger of having our supplies cut off and they have to be teamed eight miles only. The country here is high and hilly with plenty of springs of good cool water in the valleys. Our line of breastworks are now fully as strong as those of the rebels and are constantly being strengthened.

Our supply of ammunition is inexhaustible while that of the rebs is getting less every day. All their deserters say they are short of ammunition and provisions and, strange as it is may appear even tho' the Mississippi river runs at their feet, they are short of water. The gunboats command the river and woe to the poor reb that makes his appearance on the river bank. During the night, however, they must obtain some water tho' it probably gets very warm during the following day. I hear reports coming from various sources saying that we are undermining their forts at various points along their lines. If such is the case, you may expect to hear of the downfall of this stronghold at any time. So, I credit the report, think it perfectly practicable and think it easily accomplished.

I see by late Northern papers that fears are entertained [regarding] an attack in our rear by Joe Johnston. I think the fear all bosh. Even if he makes his appearance, he will get soundly whipped. I think Gen Grant knows exactly what he is about and did know it before crossing at Grand Gulf. Thus far, all his plans have worked admirably and he don't propose to be surprised now. At the Big Black, we have a heavy force. The side we occupy is hilly. The opposite side, where our enemy would have to show himself, low and open. It is laughable to read that Johnston has occupied Jackson. Supposing he has "Locked the barn door after the horse is stolen" is well illustrated if he has occupied this place. Probably Grant intended to have him occupy it after he (Grant) had left it. The fact is, in my opinion, Grant did not care anything about Jackson as a military point and only went there to destroy all its public property, stores &c. This he did pretty effectively and then left it. [3]

We have a rumor that our forces met Johnston a few days since and whipped him completely taking many prisoners and a large amount of ammunition. This is but a report, however, and not to be relied on. I don't believe it. Since the last "Taking of Richmond," I have [gotten] down on reports more than ever. Richmond was a bad thing indeed for us but it can and must be taken. I sincerely hope they will keep "Fighting Joe" [Hooker] in command. He may be a "right smart bragger" but I think he is the best fighter the Army of the Potomac ever had. It is this infernal constant changing of officers that plays the diaen [?] with soldiers. Some attention should be paid to the feelings of the men and not so much to the opinions of low-level demagogues who, not daring to face a bullet, stay at home and expound their principles. I look on the arrest of Vallandigham as the commencement of a good work and hope it may be carried on 'till all his kind are dealt with in a like manner. We must succeed and, if home traitors will not keep quiet, hang them to the first tree.[4]

Every available man in the C.S.A. is now in the army and, if we cannot whip them, we can outlive them in numbers. We have taken a big job in hand; let us finish it in the best possible manner. Nearly all the rebs I have seen say they don't expect to gain their independence now but are going to fight as long as they can and kill as many Yankees as possible. I hope they do not forget that it takes two to make a bargain.

I will write you again in a few days when I will try and give you a more detailed account of the bombardment of this place. Our Battery has two 12-pounder Napoleon bronze guns that were taken at the Big Black bridge. They are pretty pieces and look like English manufacture. We have not a supply of ammunition for them yet. Our two Rodman rifles do splendid work. We expend on them about 300 rounds daily.[5]

When did you hear from Henry? Lib writes me that he thinks he has been paroled. I hope he has. Love to all. Write me often.[6]

*   *   *

In the rear of Vicksburg
June 7, 1863

My dear father,

Our position is about the same as when I last wrote you; only that we are daily making it stronger and mounting more heavy artillery. Fourteen columbiads throwing a 64-pdr shot are being put in position near our Battery and several eleven inch guns (120-pounders) are on the way from the Yazoo river. It is very easy for us to throw up a good strong fortification. I will try to explain why. The surface of the country from the Big Black to the Mississippi is high and abounds in vast hills and valleys. Now the "situation" on our centre is about as follows:

— Rebel line of fortifications built on line of hill
— Valley filled with our rifle pits and sharpshooters
— Small hill where we have a few guns planted

Hills [are] fully as high as the rebels hills and on which nearly all of our artillery is planted. Our embrasures &c are made [by cutting into the hillside]. The muzzles of our guns is all that can be seen from the front. On both sides we have cotton bales thrown up so that we are well protected. Now you may imagine the rebels have fully as good and strong a line as ourselves. I think they have but do not think their artillery so heavy or nearly so great in number. Again, they have not so great a supply of ammunition as ourselves. We can pour in a heavy fire all day and then have plenty left.

All deserters say their only hope is assistance from Bragg or Johnston, and Grant is making preparations for these gentlemen should one or both appear with a force. Rosecrans will keep a good lookout for Bragg. We have reports now that Rosy is in full pursuit of Bragg and, even should Bragg get a several day start, we can easily keep him off 'till Rosy arrives with his men. I sometimes think that Grant has a particular purpose in not taking Vicksburg yet. He can receive reinforcements as fast if not faster than Johnston. We have the whole Mississippi to work on while nearly everything done by the rebels must be done on foot. Since Grierson's raid, they can not even use their poor RR lines. I tell you that raid of Grierson's was a <u>big</u> <u>thing</u> and has really done more damage to the C.S.A. than any other thing done during the rebellion. From stories that reach us, I imagine he is going to keep up the "raiding business" for some time.[7]

Banks is where Grant can call him in a few days and I think he will be with us before long, tho' I do not know anything about it. A rather good story is told about Grant but I was not there [and] cannot vouch for it . . . The other day he rode up to where one of our batteries was in position and watched the firing for a few moments. Just before riding off, one of the battery boys stepped up and said, "General, what will you do if Joe Johnston comes up in our rear?" "Young man," replied the General. "You just attend to my prisoners out over there (pointing towards Vicksburg) and I will attend to Johnston." Pretty good if true but it don't sound like Grant.[8]

Gen. [Admiral] Porter did some good work up the Yazoo. I presume you have read the account ere this. Thus far, the accounts given by Chicago papers of our proceedings at and around this place are about correct and may be depended on. Some of the minor details are not exactly correct but, as a general thing, they are well written. I have seen "Bod"—the Tribune correspondent—several times. He seems to be quite a favorite with all and, of course, understands how to keep on the right side.[9]

The grandest site of the siege is to see the mortar . . . shells thrown into town after nightfall. Away off toward the river you see a flash. Then up, up goes what appears to be a shooting star but now it turns slowly—then down faster, faster—when, just as it reaches the housetops, you see a great flash, then <u>BONG</u> and 220 pounds of iron is sent flying in all directions among the traitors. But these shells are not the only visitors the rebels have. At daylight, all along our lines a heavy firing is commenced and is usually kept up an hour. Shells are tossed in all directions and must do terrible execution. During the siege, our two rifled pieces have fired over 1.200 rounds, each round weighing twelve pounds. Now imagine 200 guns, mostly of heavier calibre than ours, throwing an equal amount of shot and shell.

Should Grant find himself hard pressed in our rear, he can mass his force at any given point and drive the rebels out of the place; but this is not his object. He wants to "bag them" and is bound to do it. I hear some reports that I do not like to write as some of my letters may miscarry or fall into rebel hands. Therefore, I do not like to write all I hear. But of this I think you may be assured and that is: We have nearly all of the advantages and in time will win—I do not think the siege will last much longer. No earthwork can stand against the shots of a 64-pounder columbiad and, if we once breach their earthworks, victory is easily won. I look for a speedy downfall of this great rebel stronghold and hope you may hear of it soon.

It has been some time since I have heard from you. Please write often as I am anxious to hear from you.[10]

*   *   *

In the June 14 letter to his father, Will again gave scant credence to the idea of General Joseph E. Johnston springing Pemberton loose from Vicksburg. A week later, he speculated whether Henry, his older brother who had been released from Libby Prison and was back in Tennessee, would be part of the reinforcements Grant was bringing to Vicksburg. Unbeknownst to Will, the reinforcements included his younger brother Lib, who was then camped only a few miles away at Snyder's Bluff.

Lib Brown's regiment—the 12th Michigan Infantry—was transported down the Mississippi River at the end of May, having spent the winter at Middleburg in southwestern Tennessee where it had been guarding the Mississippi Central Railroad. Grant had redeployed a large portion of Major General Stephen A. Hurlbut's 16th Corps from Tennessee to bolster his defense against a potential surprise assault from Joe Johnston. While Will Brown continued to downplay the possibility of a Confederate attack, Grant was acutely aware of the danger to his supply line on the northern bluffs above Vicksburg. Rumors abounded, indicating the Confederate general was going to deploy his Army of Relief from the Jackson area to Mechanicsburg. Johnston would then purportedly move down the corridor between the Yazoo and Big Black, and along the Vicksburg's northern bluffs to pop the cork that bottled up

Pemberton and his troops. Grant had already sent an expeditionary force at the end of May toward Mechanicsburg, but it quickly returned to the safety of the Union position fronting Vicksburg.[11]

On June 4, Brown's 12th Michigan disembarked at Satartia on the Yazoo River to join an expeditionary force led by Brigadier General Nathan Kimball, who had also arrived from Tennessee. Grant ordered him to take his division up through the Mechanicsburg Corridor and counter Johnston's anticipated move. The 12th Michigan marched with Kimball as his division drove toward Mechanicsburg, the advance units skirmishing with enemy cavalry along the way. After occupying Mechanicsburg, Kimball got nervous when a patrol returned from Yazoo City and reported the presence of a Confederate force with between 15,000 and 20,000 men. Kimball also learned the Yazoo River was rapidly falling, which left him in danger of being stranded, and he ordered the immediate withdrawal of his men back to Snyder's Bluff.[12]

On June 6, Will's younger brother and his fellow 12th Michigan comrades began a hasty 70-mile march to Haynes' Bluff and then to Snyder's Bluff. Lib's friend and company commander, Lieutenant Robert B. King, described the march as "about as hard a one as I have ever been on; over 50 of the regiment dropped down with sunstroke, and among the force, some six men died from the effects of heat. I started from Mechanicsburg with a company of 47 men . . . and on arriving at Haines Bluff had 5 left." Will's brother was one of the sunstroke victims and was carried by ambulance to Snyder's Bluff. By the time Will saw him three weeks later, Lib had recovered; but his eyes were permanently damaged, which would cause ongoing problems for him after the war.[13]

An artillerist, who was on the same "skedaddle" to Haynes' Bluff, remarked in his diary, "It is said that Gen. Kimball left Mechanicsburg out of fear, and without orders so criminally marched the troops because he was afraid of being gobbled."[14]

Private James A. Gray of the 4th Iowa Cavalry also commented on the Kimball incident. He believed the horrific heat was particularly hard on the men he traveled with, especially the 12th Michigan. Gray wrote on June 6 that Lib's regiment did not have enough of an opportunity to get acclimated to the oppressive Mississippi weather before the march:

> [Kimball's] infantry followed as fast as possible but that was very
> slow as the day was very warm and many of the troops fell in the

road sun struck. Out of the 12th Mich. Vol. 30 fell . . . 2 of which died. Other regiments suffered less severely as they were more used to the climate . . . While the 12th Mich. had but just come from Tennessee where they had been guarding the railroad and did not have to go on these long marches.[15]

*   *   *

In the rear of Vicksburg Miss.
June 14 1863

My dear father

The rebel line of fortifications are on the highest range of hills but still they are not high enough to overlook the valleys. The range of hills where the guns of our Battery are placed are about as follows:

1. Valley where our troops and ammunition supplies are;
2. Position of four of our guns;
3. Valley where two of our guns are masked to rake the valley in case the rebels attempt to break out;
4. Hill (little to the right of our four guns) where the pioneers are building embrasures for several heavy guns;
5. Our rifle pits;
6. Rebel fort;

The distance from [#] 2 to [#] 6 is about 800 yards; perhaps not quite so far. Our first line of rifle pits commence at [#] 2 and from there move in all directions thro' the valleys, up side hills, down cuts and in fact nearly everywhere. I wish I was able to sketch all the difficult positions but you know I am no sketcher. At the right and left of our guns, there are other batteries in position and all take turns in throwing shells into the rebel lines. For the past week, our orders have been to throw five shells an hour during the day and a round at 10 [O'clock], 1 [O'clock] &c 3 O'clock during the night.

During the night, the mortar boats are constantly playing shell on the city but we do not know what effect they have. It is very seldom the enemy reply to us with cannon but their sharpshooters are always on the alert and watch every opportunity to throw in a shot. Many reasons are given why the enemy does not use his cannon more, some think owing to the lack of ammunition. I think it owing to the splendid range our guns have on their embrasures and the almost certainty of our sharpshooters. Nearly every gun bearing on the rebel works can put two or three of their shots into the enemies embrasures and the rebs have not got any guns that they can spare. Our rifle pits are very close to the rebel forts and the sharpshooters have a novel way to protect themselves when they make a shot. They have a bag filled with sand and, thro' its middle, have a hole a little larger than the eye; thro' this hole they make a <u>bead</u> at the rebs without danger to themselves.[16]

I am glad to hear of the arrest and banishment of the traitor Vallandigham and I only hope "Old Abe" will keep on with his good work. I am sorry the order to suppress the [Chicago] Times was revoked. That paper talks secesh as much as it dares and is regarded as an advocate of Southern doctrines by all rebels. It has a large circulation throughout South. You would be surprised to hear how bitterly all our soldier boys talk of home traitors. We are down on them and, if the draft sends any of them down here, I am afraid they would not fare well.[17]

We had a heavy rainstorm here a few days ago and the valley was nearly all covered with water. My <u>baggage</u> got rather wet but as I have a good rubber overcoat I kept myself pretty dry. The valley is filled with tents and it was rather amusing to see everybody loaded down with their baggage, wading thro' the water and making for the hill side. Somewhere above us, a barrel of pork got loose and, as it came floating down by our camp, we picked it up and had a supply to put with what we had on hand.

The sanitary commission and our friends at home are sending a pretty good supply of vegetables and goodies and we are now living pretty well. We need vegetables very much. The weather is so very warm that we cannot eat much meat but have to eat some (too much perhaps) to <u>fill up</u>. Several new recruits from Chicago have reached us and most all of them are troubled with the "quick step."

Lib writes me that we are <u>uncles</u>. I congratulate sister Delia and hope the "little stranger" may flourish. Have you heard from Henry, and where and how is he? I am anxious to hear. Love to all at home. Write often.[18]

*   *   *

In the rear of Vicksburg Miss.
June 21st 1863

My dear father

Your welcome letter of the 1st Instant reached me on the 14th and relieved me of considerable anxiety, particularly in regard to Henry's welfare. I am very glad that he has returned safe and well and would very much like to hear of his many adventures "Mid flood and field." I would not be surprised if his regiment was ordered to report to us, as we are receiving reinforcements from all parts and probably need more.[19]

Gen. Logan is the nearest to the enemies fort . . . he is virtually inside their largest one. But I think he fears they will blow him up and therefore moves with the utmost caution. Logan is winning a big name, deservedly too I think. He is a gallant looking soldier and looks fight all over. I like his appearance and would like to be under him. Our right seems to be doing the main work. And if we take the town before it surrenders, I think it will be entered on the right.[20]

McClernand has been removed from command of our Corps and Gen. Ord takes his place. McClernand is not a favorite with those high in . . . this army. I have not learned the cause of his removal yet and don't expect to 'till I see late Northern [newspaper] dates.[21]

We have a report that a large force has gone out to attack Johnston in his rear and . . . you may expect to hear of a big fight soon. I hardly credit the report but still don't think Grant will allow Johnston to get a large force together in our rear. Grant has shown good generalship so far in this campaign and, if he should defeat Johnston and still keep the siege, it will cap the climax. The force inside of Vicksburg cannot hope of success unless they are reinforced by Johnston, and Grant is bound that this is not to be.[22]

Nothing new from Banks. I suppose his "situation" resembles ours in many particulars and like us he is taking his time. The contrabands are doing us a great-deal of good here and, by building all our fortifications &c, save our soldiers a good-deal of hard work. The negro regiments at Young's Point and Milliken's Bend are being put thro' the drill and learn pretty rapidly. I saw one of their officers the other day (he was formerly a sergeant in an Ill. regt.) and he gave a description of the recent fight at the Bend. He said the darkies did not know how to load their muskets when they were attacked and, after drawing them up in a line of battle and while the enemy were pouring in a heavy fire, the line officers went to each man and showed him how to use their guns. As soon as they found how to do it, they pitched in and gave the enemy an awful whipping.

The Southern papers say "Black flags for black men" and the darkies say they are willing but intend to return the [favor]. The darkies will fight when they are wanted. But I hope they will not have much of it 'till after the draft is enforced in the North, because "Old Abe" may think he can get enough of them without calling out any more of the "Loyal and patriotic men of the North."[23]

*   *   *

In the rear of Vicksburg Miss.
June 29th 1863

My dear father

The past week has been one of considerable excitement. Several movements have been made on the enemies fortifications. On Thursday about 4 PM, Gen. Logan sprung a mine under the centre of the rebel fort on his front and charged up on its outside—but feared to enter it, as he thinks the enemy have laid counter mines. He still holds his position but is constantly tossing hand grenades over among the enemy. He also has a large corps of sappers and miners at work under both ends of the fort and I think will blow it up before many days. This fort in front of Logan is the largest on the whole rebel lines and commands the town. Logan is bound to have it and . . . no one . . . can beat him in anything he undertakes.[24]

Logan says he killed and wounded 1.000 of the enemy. The earth, logs, barrels &c on the fort flew in all directions and completely filled the air fifty feet high. Large bodies of infantry were sent out in the rifle pits in front of our guns and were ordered to charge if they saw an opening. Yesterday, the rebels tried to blow up one of our rifle pits but the experiment proved a failure. The explosion did not hurt a man. On Friday, the gunner (J.H. White Jr.) of Squad One was hit by a rifle bullet. The bullet struck his left leg very close to the thigh bone and passed way thro'. He is now in the hospital and I think will recover, tho' the wound is considered a dangerous one.[25]

On Tuesday, we were awakened at 2 AM and had orders to be ready to move at daylight. Expected to reinforce Gen. Osterhaus at the Big Black. We kept prepared to move 'till Wednesday PM, when we were again ordered to take up our old position on the hills. Rumors and flying reports have been as plentiful as usual during the week. Among the rest is the story that Gen. Banks has taken and now occupies Port Hudson.[26]

I have not heard from Lib lately. I see by the papers that the troops have been withdrawn from Jackson and Bolivar [Tenn.] and gone to Grant. If this is so, perhaps Lib may be coming down here. I hope to hear from him soon and then will know something about his whereabouts. I wonder if he still has the gunboat fever?[27]

* * *

As the weeks dragged on, Vicksburg's defenders lost faith that Joe Johnston was coming to their relief. Placed on short rations and suffering from exhaustion, the soldiers grew weaker each day. On June 28, one group of demoralized Confederates wrote an "Appeal for help" under the pseudonym "Many Soldiers" and sent it to Pemberton. They advocated surrender unless their rations could be increased, observing that "one small biscuit and one or two mouthfuls of bacon per day" was not enough to sustain them. "This army is ripe for mutiny, unless it can be fed." Perhaps influenced by this document, Pemberton drafted a circular to his four division commanders, polling them on whether their troops were fit to break out of Vicksburg. Three of them doubted the enfeebled army could cut its way out of Vicksburg. Two recommended surrender.[28]

Major General John Bowen and one of Pemberton's staff officers, Lieutenant Colonel Louis M. Montgomery, approached the Union lines during the morning of July 3. They carried a white flag with them and passed near where Pat White and George Throop of the Chicago Mercantile Battery had positioned their 6-pounder to fire into the 2nd Texas Lunette on May 22. The men of Burbridge's brigade held this portion of the Union position. Burbridge himself was too ill to receive the Southerners, but A. J. Smith soon arrived on the scene. The two Confederate officers arranged for Grant to meet with Pemberton in the afternoon. During their ensuing discussion, Grant insisted that Pemberton surrender without conditions, just as he had demanded of the Rebels garrisoning Fort Donelson in early 1862. Pemberton refused the harsh terms. The two generals negotiated a compromise: Pemberton would surrender unconditionally, but Rebel soldiers would be paroled rather than shipped to prison camps. On Independence Day at 10:00 a.m.,

Cpl. John H. White, Jr., was killed
in the fighting at Vicksburg.

Al and Claudia Niemiec Private Collection

Major General John A. Logan—
a southern Illinois politician who
had worked with General Grant
instead of against him— led his
soldiers through the Rebel
fortifications and into the city of
Vicksburg. The Federals quickly
ran the Stars and Stripes up the
flagstaff on the Warren County
Court House—the same building
White's artillerists had targeted
during the long siege. The
flag-raising symbolized Pemberton's surrender. Vicksburg now
belonged to the United States of America.[29]

When the inquisitive Will Brown entered Vicksburg, he found
"Nearly every other house in the city has been struck by a shot or shell."
Most of the town's structures were still standing, some barely so, with
holes big enough to walk through; few buildings had any windows, most
having been shattered by concussions from the "visitors" Will had
previously described to his father.

Civilians and soldiers were in reasonably decent physical shape
despite their hardships. They had spent much of their 47-day ordeal
protected by Vicksburg's loess dirt, the noncombatants in caves and the
troops in ditches. The Northerners treated their prisoners well, as
described by a private from the 20th Wisconsin Infantry: "The Rebs have
been living pretty slim since they have been in here. ¼ lb flour and ¼ lb
bacon is their ration since they have been in the cage for the last three
days. They had no bread and was living on mule meat. You had ought to
see them pitch in to our crackers when we got over here. Evry Co in the
regt gave them a barrel of crackers when we come over here. They are a
very thin pole looking set." One of Ashbel Smith's men who had been on
the receiving end of the Battery Boys' May 22 barrage commented, "The

Grant's army took possession of Vicksburg on July 4, 1863.

Yankees appear quite civle [and] do not bost or appear to wish to give offense." The next day, he was gratified at the amount of food the Federals gave him, especially after eating "two meals of mule" on July 4: "I drew Rations for five days today from Gen Grants Commiessary & it really was astonishing to see the amount that was issued, it appeared to be…drawn for a month supply." Some of the Unionists took pity on the townspeople, breaking into the stores of greedy speculators to distribute hoarded goods. One Southerner noted the starving civilians and soldiers "felt as if a portion of their wrongs were avenged."[30]

Will enjoyed meeting the Confederate prisoners and sought their viewpoints on a host of topics, such as ending the war, the eating of mule meat, and the loss of Vicksburg. Many of the prisoners widely blamed their defeat on Pemberton, who was believed to have been in collusion with his Northern kinsmen and captors.

Will did not have much time to explore Vicksburg. He told his father the Battery Boys had orders to depart from the fallen Confederate bastion at dawn the next morning. The Mercantile Battery was going to join Sherman, who had been charged with bringing Johnston's Army of Relief to bay. Will predicted a short campaign, opining, "I do not think our movement toward the Big Black will amount to much as Johnston will probably skedaddle as soon as he hears of the fall of Vicksburg." Having served in the army for a year, Will understood a return to the field might be advantageous, thereby allowing him to avoid the work details that were busily cleaning up the Hill City. Consequently, he expected a speedy return to Vicksburg but hoped it would not be too soon.

*   *   *

Vicksburg
July 4, 1863

My dear father:

Vicksburg has fallen. Surrendered this morning and this PM—most of Gen. McPherson's Corps occupy the city. The first signs of surrender were made yesterday morning but the terms submitted were conditional. Gen. Grant, true to his nature, would not listen to anything but unconditional surrender. [T]he enemy, after debating the matter all last night, concluded to accept the terms. At 10 O'clock this morning, their men were marched out in front of their breastworks where they stacked arms and countermarched to the city where they were formally surrendered. All this took 'till about 1 O'clock PM and at this time we were allowed to enter the city.

I have been running round town ever since and to-night am completely tired out. Our victory is most complete. All the enemies artillery, ordnance, quartermasters, small arms &c are in tip-top order and we have the whole lot of them. Their force is variously estimated at from 15. to 25.000. I think it will reach the latter amount. Many of these are sick, however, beside a large number of wounded. Shot, shell and bullets are thicker than hailstones throughout the city. Nearly every other house in the city has been struck by a shot or shell. All the hills are filled with caves that were occupied by citizens and soldiers.[31]

Their artillery is of the finest kind. I noticed a Whitworth gun in particular. This gun throws a solid shot over five miles. They are very expensive and our army has but few of them.[32]

I have conversed with many rebs on all topics imaginable. The men are tired and sick of the war and most of them would willingly say quits, but their officers show good pluck and say they are bound to stick to the thing. They had but fifteen days full rations of provisions and I think they did well to make it last 48 days. They have been living on mule meat for the past five days. I saw some of it <u>dressed</u> <u>for</u> <u>the</u> <u>table</u>. It did not look bad. The rebs say it equals fresh beef only it is <u>more</u> <u>tender</u>.[33]

They have been looking for Johnston for some time but that individual <u>couldn't</u> <u>come</u> <u>in</u>. There seems to be but little for sale in the city. I saw some ladies but they appeared averse to military <u>strangers</u> so that I kept at a respectful distance. Many of the rebs swear that Pemberton sold the city to Grant for two million in gold. I tried to convince them to the contrary, but they firmly believe it. The mortar shells have not damaged the city so much as I imagined they would. The rebs say our bullets did a greater damage and <u>allow</u> that we have <u>right</u> <u>smart</u> sharpshooters. They willingly admit that ours is a great victory and find it will be more than the C.S.A. can stand. I captured (or confiscated) a very good sword belt and will send it home if a good opportunity offers.[34]

National salutes have been firing nearly all day. I wish I could describe to you how our troops feel and act. All feel that we have done a <u>big</u> <u>thing</u> and want to rejoice over it. Has ours not been a most <u>glorious</u> <u>fourth</u>. As I write this (10 PM), skyrockets and the fire works are being rapidly expended. Our Corps have orders to move toward Big Black in the morning. We are ordered to be ready to move at 5 AM. Do not know our destination but think it is to hunt up Joe Johnston—glory enough for one day.

On Wednesday, I received a letter from Lib saying that he was at Snyder's Bluffs on the Yazoo and, on Thursday, I rode out where he was—about 20 miles from here—and found him all right and well. Spent nearly all day with him and had a very pleasant time. Lib feels first-rate [and] is in good health, spirits and has grown to be quite a big fellow. Seems to be a universal favorite with both officers and men. He was very anxious to see Vicksburg and, now that it is taken, I think will have an opportunity to do so.[35]

Lieut. King feels and looks first-rate. He had just returned from a visit to Capt. F. A. Drake of the 7th Mo. Regt., at that time in the rifle pits with Gen. Logan's Division.[36]

I would like to see Drake and will do so if I can find him. Lib makes a good soldier. His gun looks splendidly and <u>speaks</u> well for him. His present position is first corporal but I think his chances for promotion are good. I wish you would write me where Henry is whenever you write and also write him where I addressed you from last.[37]

I do not think our movement toward the Big Black will amount to much as Johnston will probably skedaddle as soon as he hears of the fall of Vicksburg. I am glad we are going as we will thus avoid doing some pretty hard work in Vicksburg. I don't know if Lib will move into Vicksburg. Think not at present tho' I hope he will have an opportunity to visit the place. I daily expect to hear of the fall of Port Hudson and think this will soon come.[38]

"Gen. Sherman ordered the Rebel prisoners to dig out all the torpedoes sunk
by the Rebel force. A torpedo exploded while I was in the place."

Chapter 8

Capping the Climax

For the vast majority of men in Grant's army, July 4, 1863, must
have been the most memorable Independence Day of their lives.
After months of frustration and hardship, Vicksburg was finally in
their hands. A festive mood pervaded the Union ranks.

"This is a day of jubilee, a day of rejoicing to the faithful," William T.
Sherman declared in a letter to Grant. Will Brown and a number of his
Mercantile Battery comrades were fortunate in being able to join the
Fourth of July celebrations inside the fallen "Fortress on the
Mississippi." Many others in their corps had not lived to see the occasion.
The Battery Boys' respite from the war, though, was short lived. That
evening, Major General Edward O. C. Ord, who had replaced the
self-destructive McClernand three weeks before, received orders to join
an expeditionary force commanded by Sherman. Grant now wanted
Sherman to march east and strike Johnston's Army of Relief. Pat White
scrambled to get his Mercantile Battery ready to depart the next morning,
as did the rest of A. J. Smith's division, which also included eleven
infantry regiments and an Ohio battery. They were ordered to travel light
with five days of rations, no baggage or tents, and a minimum number of

Confederate ordnance captured at Vicksburg. *Old Court House Museum, Vicksburg, Mississippi*

wagons. The 13th Corps' marching orders specified, "Great attention must be paid to providing water."[1]

Sherman waited with about 30,000 soldiers east of Vicksburg. He had been there since June 23, prepared to repel Johnston Army of Relief should it attempt to cross the Big Black River in an effort to relieve Vicksburg's beleaguered defenders. Johnston had assembled about 32,000 effectives in the area east of the Big Black and, though his less than energetic attempt to rescue Pemberton had failed dismally, he still posed a considerable threat to the Federals. Sherman, worried the Confederates might steal a march on him, sought more troops. In the 16 months they had worked together, Grant had developed a partnership with Sherman and valued his keen insights. Their close relationship was underscored by Sherman's July 4 telegram warning him not to be deceived by the sudden rush of Vicksburg accolades: "Be natural and yourself, and this glittering flattery will be as a passing breeze of the sea on a warm summer day." Grant was accustomed to Sherman's cynicism and his volatile mood swings. He knew Johnston—as well as newspapermen and politicians— ought to be wary when Sherman lashed out. Grant did not hesitate and rushed his friend an additional 20,000 troops. He also gave Sherman a mandate "to drive Johnston from the Mississippi Central railroad; destroy bridges as far as Grenada with your cavalry, and do the enemy all the harm possible."[2]

Back in Richmond, Jefferson Davis read the telegram notifying him of Vicksburg's surrender. Joe Johnston had all but ignored his pleas to break through Grant's siege. For Davis, whose plantation home was near Vicksburg, the loss of the Hill City was a personal blow; for the Confederacy it was perhaps a fatal disaster. Davis blamed the debacle on Johnston, who had long acknowledged the danger to Pemberton and his army but had not responded fast enough to relieve the trapped defenders. Indeed, Johnston only seemed to move quickly when he sought to avoid battle, and his wartime career was marked by a succession of retreats. In March 1862, he had withdrawn his army from northern Virginia to take up a position behind the Rappahannock River. Two months later during the Peninsula Campaign, Johnston withdrew from Yorktown up the peninsula to the outskirts of Richmond, allowing McClellan's army to move within sight of the spires of the Confederate capital. More recently, as Grant's troops bore down on Jackson during the Vicksburg Campaign, the cautious Johnston had ordered the evacuation of the Mississippi state capital just one day after he arrived there from his Chattanooga headquarters. Johnston's order ensured that the Federals could easily take the capital and wreck what was left of its invaluable communication network. Now, large dust clouds were blowing across the 25 miles of farmland from east of Big Black River to Jackson: Johnston's Army of Relief was on the move. By July 7, after an efficient two-day retreat, it returned to the once-bustling town on the Pearl River. The next day Johnston's soldiers, along with impressed slaves, strengthened the same earthworks that some of them had briefly occupied during the May operations.[3]

The Battery Boys retraced the route they had taken into Vicksburg two months earlier from Champion Hill. The heat during their march was oppressive. First Lieutenant Pinckney Cone noted in his diary that it was so hot, "The sun fairly boiled the water in our canteens. The dust covered us so that we grew black and the Negroes white." When they reached the Big Black River on July 5, they halted while Federal engineers constructed a floating bridge. Heavy rains in northern Mississippi had caused the Big Black to rise four feet, slowing the engineers' work. While the Battery Boys waited, they set up camp with no shelter. Deciding to get some rest, Cone retired, lying "down with the clouds for a canopy."[4]

On July 7, the Mercantile Battery crossed the surging Big Black. In a strange twist of meteorological fate, while the northern part of Mississippi was drenched in rain, the central area was in the midst of a drought. If the oppressive heat and dust did not suffocate the cannoneers, the local water supply, which the Confederates had contaminated, might kill them. While pulling back to Jackson, Johnston had ordered his men to draw as much water as they could from the nearby wells, ponds, cisterns, and creeks. They were then to pollute what was not dried up or taken. The embittered Confederates dumped tar, turpentine, ashes, and even animal carcasses into the meager supply of water. As a member of the 67th Indiana recalled, the Federal troops had to "rake away the thick green scum and quench our thirst from these putrid waters."[5]

Given such wretched conditions, even a vigorous officer like Pinckney Cone was afflicted with headaches and stomachaches. As he waited near the Big Black River, Cone complained in his diary, "We were on the road 15 hours today. I say again it is cruel to march men in such weather." He had no choice but to persevere. The next day, Pat

White became incapacitated, leaving Cone in charge of the battery. The 13th Corps seems to have been especially hard hit by sickness. The corps' ambulances would subsequently make two trips to transport 3,200 sick soldiers—approximately 20 percent of Ord's 16,000-man command—from Jackson back to Vicksburg. About 15 percent of the Mercantile Battery redlegs were seriously ill in July and August; one of their sergeants, Joseph W. Hyde, got sick and died upon his return to Vicksburg. Will Brown was among the fortunate soldiers who remained healthy throughout the Jackson siege.[6]

The Chicago Mercantile Battery reached Clinton on July 9 and the outskirts of Jackson at 9:00 a.m. the following day. As part of 13th Corps, the Battery Boys were stationed on the Union right flank. Major General Frederick Steele's 15th Corps was in the center, and Major General John G. Parke's 9th Corps held the left. The Confederates had established a formidable perimeter of fortifications—their armaments including two rifled 32-pounders—and covered the approaches to Jackson west of Pearl River. Although Sherman had difficulty matching Johnston's heavy guns, he still invested the city and unleashed his light artillery to bombard it. On July 12, he notified Grant his trenches were completed. Starting at 7:00 a.m. that day he opened an intense hour-long cannonade. According to the Mercantile Battery's James Sinclair, the Chicago artillerists were ordered into position and fired 34 rounds into the enemy-infested woods to their right. Since he was traveling light, Sherman had not brought along enough artillery ammunition to keep up a constant fire on Jackson, and he now asked Grant to bolster his supply. On July 14, while still awaiting the ammunition train from Grant, Sherman ordered his four batteries to fire every five minutes, day and night.[7]

Sherman resisted launching a frontal assault—the experiences at Chickasaw Bayou plus the two failed assaults at Vicksburg were fresh in the Ohio general's mind—thus providing Johnston with time to evacuate Jackson and save his army. Under cover of darkness and using musicians to mask the noise of his retreat, Johnston successfully withdrew his troops and their equipment east of Pearl River on the night of July16-17. Will Brown and Pinckney Cone both heard an enemy band playing "Dixie" and "Bonnie Blue Flag," noting the serenade in their diaries. Johnston headed east. Parke's 9th Corps entered Jackson early the next morning, removing the enemy flag on top of the state house (one of the few major downtown buildings, along with the city hall and governor's

General
Joseph E. Johnston

NARA

mansion, still standing) and running up the United States flag. Many of the troops were relieved the Rebels had left without a big fight. Cone, for one, scrawled in his diary, "Another great agony over. Jackson [is] evacuated!"

Sherman set up his headquarters in the governor's mansion and dined with his generals that night, celebrating their victory over Johnston.[8]

Although the Confederates evacuated Jackson in a hurry, they found the time to leave a deadly surprise for the Federals. Johnston had buried land mines in the roads and among the rubble of the devastated city, much as he had done prior to his retreat from Yorktown. Sherman's troops first encountered the nefarious Mississippi River mines (which some referred to as "cannibals") in December of 1862. Southern torpedoes, also called "infernal machines" by the Unionists, had been submerged in the Yazoo River, where one sank Lieutenant Commander Thomas O. Selfridge's *USS Cairo*. Several days before Sherman's troops discovered the land mines in Jackson, another Federal ironclad, the *Baron de Kalb*, was sunk by torpedoes in the Yazoo River. When Union forces captured Yazoo City, they apprehended the men who positioned the mines nearby and gave them a choice to "be hung and have the town burnt or take every one of these things out of the river." Not surprisingly, the Yazoo Confederates chose the second alternative. Sherman followed a similar course at Jackson. As noted by Will Brown: "Gen. Sherman ordered the Rebel prisoners to dig out all the torpedoes sunk by the Rebel force."[9]

* * *

Lt. George Throop to his sister Mattie[10]

Front of Jackson, Miss.
Sat. July 11th 1863

My dear Mattie

This week's letter has been written & sent but this one can go to the next week's credit.

We reached Jackson yesterday but are not yet in the town, our host Joe Johnston not being quite ready for us. A shell just this minute from one of his guns struck quite near us making some of the boys jump & cautioning us to keep a little way off. It took a man's leg off about 200 ft from us. The sound is hardly out of my ears. Lieut. Barr says it came very nearly killing one of our teams.

1 Oclock P.M.

The firing became so severe in the position which I spoke of above that we were obliged to move the caissons back and afterwards to move our guns. I have just been far enough to the front to see the rebel fortifications....I saw a heavy cloud of dust arriving to our right which looks as if the enemy was performing a flank movement upon us. If this is the case, General Sherman undoubtedly knows it, or will know it.

The flow of operations seems to be something like the Arkansas Post affair. I think we are trying to surround them and then draw the lines closely upon them & compel them to do something.

Yesterday while our battery was halting in the road I took the notion to go to the front & see the town or the rebel works or something else. When about two thirds of the way a shell came thundering along and exploded between 50 and 100 ft directly in front of me sending the pieces in all directions around me & my horse, but fortunately nothing hit me except a little powder or dust or a very small fragment of shell upon the back of the hand producing a slight smarting sensation. How I escaped so easily is more than I can tell. . . . Willie Munn is in the hospital near Vicksburg and I am afraid he is not improving as fast as desirable. The Bracketts are improving....

4 Oclock P.M.

We are posted in the front with our guns & are within easy range of the rebel works. They have been pouring musketry into us. A man was wounded near me & one of our best horses (Hugh Wilson's) shot. Hugh has gone back after another horse. Bullets still continue to fly around us. We hear today that Port Hudson is ours with 5000 prisoners....[11]

*   *   *

Near Jackson Miss.
July 13th 1863

My dear father

Our army is here working away against Jackson. The enemy has a strong line of fortifications itself that are difficult to approach but time will do the work. I wrote you on the 4th in regard to the taking of Vicksburg and I trust the letter will reach you. We have glorious news from Port Hudson, Helena and the Potomac. I presume Lib with his regiment are near here somewhere probably in rear of the place.[12]

Excuse shortness but the mail leaves at once and I have no more time to write.

PS. This paper was captured in Vicksburg:

Oath of Allegiance[13]
Vicksburg, Mississippi, July 7th A. D. 1863

To All Whom it may Concern, Know Ye That: I, Wm Kelly, a private of Co. G 1st Reg't Lt Artillery Miss Vol., C.S.A., being a Prisoner of War, in the hands of the United States Forces, in virtue of the capitulation of the City of Vicksburg and its Garrison, by Lieut. Gen. John C. Pemberton, C. S. A., Commanding, on the 4th day of July, 1863, do in pursuance of the terms of said capitulation, give this my solemn parole under oath—

That I will not take up arms again against the United States, nor serve in any military, police, or constabulary force in any Fort, Garrison or field work, held by the Confederate States of America, against the United States of America, nor as guard of prison, depots or stores, nor discharge any duties usually performed by officers or soldiers against the United States of America until duly exchanged by the proper authorities.

Wm Kelly

Sworn to and subscribed before me at Vicksburg, Miss., this 7th day of July, 1863.

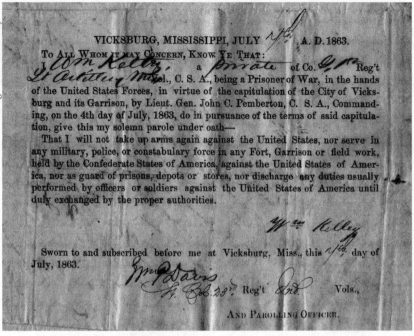

Oath of Allegiance for William Kelly, 1st Mississippi Light Artillery,
Company G (Cowan's Battery).

Wm P Davis
Lt. Col. 23d Reg't Ind. Vols.,
and Parolling Officer

*   *   *

Near Jackson Miss.
July 19th 1863

My dear father

We have capped the climax by entering Jackson and now for a while
I hope we may lay off on our honors—tho' if by pressing the enemy
any closer we can succeed in destroying him I am in for doing it.[14]

My last to you was written on the 13th and, to give you an
account of what I have been doing since that time, I extract from my
diary from July 14th to the 17th:

<u>14th</u> Rainy and cool. All pretty quiet. Several times during the day we were ordered to man the guns as it was expected the enemy would make a charge.

<u>15th</u> Cool. Glorious news from the Potomac. Lee whipped and driven from Penn. Meade in full pursuit. Potomac rising rapidly. Probably capture of the most of Lee's force. Official from corps head quarters says that Banks has taken and now holds Port Hudson and that Price has been severely whipped and lost many men at Helena Ark. Rosecrans occupies Tullahoma and is sharp after Bragg. The enemy have been shelling our batteries off on the left today but have been promptly responded to by our batteries. Most of the firing today has been on our left (We were in the centre).[15]

<u>16th</u> Clear and warm. Sharp firing on both sides commencing at day light. The enemy threw some shell and many bullets among us but without material damage (our Battery being masked and silent they could not get good range on us). About 2 PM Blair takes the enemies rifle pits on our left but is driven back with considerable loss. At 4 O'clock tries it again and at dark is in possession of them. Loss heavy on both sides. The Jackson band plays nightly, its favorite airs being "Dixie" and "Bonnie Blue Flag." At the time of writing this (9 PM) all is quiet on both sides.[16]

<u>17th</u> Evacuation of Jackson by the Confederates. Our forces in possession of the city. Several pieces of artillery and some prisoners taken. At 3 O'clock this morning was awakened by hearing the bells of Jackson ringing and alarm of fire. The city seemed all ablaze. At 5 O'clock heard loud cheering on our left and soon word reached us that <u>Jackson was evacuated</u>, and that the 9th Corps were then entering the city. Soon after this our guns were ordered back to the caissons and I was kept so busy during the balance of the day that I did not have time to visit the city or even see its line of earthworks and rifle pits. Several of the boys went into the city and did some tall <u>jerking</u>. The enemy destroyed large amounts of stores before leaving. They tried to destroy their shells by pouring the powder out of them but this defect can easily be remedied. Torpedoes were found in different places. Some of them exploded wounding some of our men. A greater part of the city is being fired by our troops. Houses in the city are riddled by our bullets. The enemy did not destroy the bridge crossing the Pearl river. Many prisoners were taken trying to destroy it. The enemy are being pursued by part of our force. Rebel papers printed at Jackson bearing date July 8th say that Vicksburg still holds out and that Meade had been whipped losing over 60.000 men and killed, wounded and prisoners. The citizens say however that later news has reached them to the effect that Lee has <u>retired</u> from Penn. and <u>is falling back</u> on Richmond. The citizens say their troops committed more depredations than our

Frank Leslie's Illustrated Newspaper

William T. Sherman made the Confederates remove torpedoes left buried in the roads when Joe Johnston's men retreated from Jackson. Sherman did this again at Fort McAllister, Georgia, in late 1864.

own troops. I doubt this however. At 3 PM are ordered to move toward Vicksburg and feel very glad to hear it as we are all anxious to return there. Marched about three miles and went into camp near a corn field in rear of our old rear picket guard line. Weather not too hot but roads very dusty indeed. More dust than I have seen before.[17]

Yesterday I expected we would again move forward but, as we did not, I got a pass and visited the city. Squads of prisoners from Johnston's retreating forces were coming in from all directions. We have the whole Jackson band. Gen. Sherman ordered the rebel prisoners to dig out all the torpedoes sunk by the rebel force. A torpedo exploded while I was in the place. The city has been a very pretty place and has some fine buildings but the war has ruined it and it is now but an example of ruin and desolation. Block after block of stores have been burned. Residences torn to pieces. Public buildings in ruins and all a blackened mass. The rail road depots, warehouses, rolling stock machine shops and such are being entirely destroyed by men detailed for that purpose. The rail road bridge crossing the Pearl is being blowed up by our troops.[18]

Nothing has been done to the earthworks as yet but I was told it was the intention to destroy them entirely. The line of works is pretty strong and most admirably situated. It would have taken us much longer to have approached them than it did at Vicksburg. I rode all along their works and saw several guns that the enemy could not take off. Altho' our success is not so great—as it would be had we bagged Johnston's force—yet I regard it a great victory for us and one we may be proud of.[19]

*   *   *

Camp in Vicksburg
July 28th 1863

My dear father

We left our camp near Jackson on the 21st and reached our old camp in rear of Vicksburg on the night of the 23d. We had a rough march. It was very warm indeed. Our horses suffered greatly but as the men could ride we did not suffer so much. On the 24th our Division entered Vicksburg. We now have a pretty nice camp in the southern part of the city, about half a mile from the central part of the city and very close to the bank of the river.[20]

I think our Corps will stay here and garrison the place 'till the Winter campaign. Furloughs are being granted to all troops. 5% allowed to go every ten days. I have not fully decided to go yet. Think I can if I want to. The expense is not very great. The Captain is anxious to let us all go. While I think of it, I must mention the Captain. He is one of the finest men it has ever been my fortune to be connected with. All the boys really love him. His sole aim seems to be to do everything he can for his men. There is nothing haughty or overbearing in his nature. He fully understands his business; is always kind and agreeable; pays great attention to his sick; sees that we have plenty to eat and that of the best kind the army affords. In fact, I regard him as a model officer and wish the army had many more like him. He intends starting for home soon for a twenty days leave. I wish you could be in Chicago to see him.

Vicksburg commences to look quite sprightly. Speculators from up the river are making their appearance and several good stocks of goods have come down. The streets are being cleaned up. Houses banged up by our shell during the siege are being repaired; saloons and barber shops are in great plenty, two express offices, post office re-opened &c &c. Down on the levee all is excitement and bustle but nearly everything arriving or departing belongs to government. A great amount of confiscated cotton is being shipped up the river. Occasionally, a boat arrives from New Orleans and vicinity but as yet the boats are few and far between. To-day, two transports passed up loaded with two-year discharged men from Banks' army.[21]

In one of your letters you asked me in regard to my position &c. When you wrote, I was chief of caisson with rank of corporal; since that time I have been promoted to gunner with still the same rank.

Chief of caisson and gunner both rank as corporals but a gunner is next to sergeant and the next step is to that position. The sergeant of my squad is at home on a sick leave and will not return 'till October. He left on July 1st and, since that time, I have been in command of squad as acting sergeant. While I fill this position, I have a horse of my own and have many other privileges not granted to the men. I regard the position of sergeant in a battery equal, if not more desirable, than that of a lieutenant in an infantry regiment.[22]

Where is Lib? I do not hear from him and as yet have not learned of his whereabouts. Let me know. I wish he was here to help me at my boxes. How and where was Henry when you last heard from him?[23]

*   *   *

Camp in Vicksburg Miss.
August 2d 1863

My dear father

The army is a good place to practice the motto "early to bed etc." We retire at 9 O'clock PM and rise at 5 O'clock AM. Our daily routine in camp is as follows: Reveille 5 AM. Roll call 5 15. Feed call at 5 20. Grooming horses from 5 30 to 6. Breakfast at 6. Guard mount 8. Water call 8 05. Physicians call 9 O'clock. Dinner 12. Water call 12 15. Feed call 12 30. Water call 5 O'clock. Feed call 5 30. Supper 6. Roll call and retreat 6 30. Feed call 7. Tattoo 8 30. Taps 9.

So you see, our mornings are pretty well taken care of but we have [more free time in] the afternoons and evenings. I have to attend to these calls pretty closely as the drivers and cannoneers in my squad have to be spoken to and their duties told them. The hardest part of camp life is the almost constant detail work that has to be done such as cleaning up camp, hunting feed for horses, cleaning stables and many other smaller things. I do not have this work to do. Eleven of our boys have gone home on thirty day furloughs and three or four more will go to-morrow or next day. Our Corps have orders to go to and garrison Natchez about 90 miles below here. One division left yesterday. Ours may leave this week but I think not 'till next. I have no objection to going; in fact rather like it. Natchez is a finer place than this and the war has not interfered with it but little. Another thing here [is that] we are with the whole army. There we would only have our Corps. Large armies are a good thing in the field but too many in camp or garrison are a nuisance. At Natchez, we would be under General E. O. C. Ord, our

Corps commander here. We are directly under him and Gen. Grant.[24]

Gen. Grant is doing all he can to put the city in good shape. In order [to accomplish that], contrabands in large numbers are busily engaged in cleaning and repairing the streets. Stores and houses partially destroyed by our shell are being repaired and many of them are already being occupied by different trades &c. As yet, no very large shipments are allowed to pass below Cairo but I think the day not far distant when free navigation on the entire length of the river will be permitted and encouraged.

I see by late papers that the business men have already started a petition having this object in view. The resumption of trade on the river will probably cause a fueling off of some of the business now going to Chicago. But still I do not think it will effect it materially. If business on the river opens again soon, why would not this or some other point along the river be a tip-top place to operate in?[25]

Our army never moves thro' the country now without burning or destroying near everything of value. Very few plantations are spared, none are left entirely unmolested. The negroes always follow us; we could not drive them back if we would. Many people at home say: Offer the people of the South their rights under the constitution and they will return and live under it now. I think they would myself, that is the majority would, but they have waited too long for this. After fighting against the constitution for two years and a half, they can hardly claim any privileges under it now. Before terms of peace can be made again we must have a new constitution.[26]

Reports favorable to our side come to us from both Rosecrans army and the army before Charleston but nothing definite reaches us yet. I hope we may take Charleston. It would be a glorious cap to our recent successes. Rosy will attend to Bragg. What could have been Morgan's idea when he made his recent raid into Indiana and Ohio? Did he expect aid from the Vallandinghams of those two states? He has been pretty well used up and I hope we will catch him personally.[27]

* * *

Camp at Vicksburg Miss.
August 9th 1863

My dear father
I have been out since early this morning looking at and examining the rebel lines of fortifications in the rear of this city. I have found that most of the guns captured by our forces have been removed

from the line of works. I wish you could see the works. All that science could do has been employed in their construction. The line is built so that, in case we took one fort or one line of rifle pits, the enemy could at once play on the points taken and would probably soon succeed in driving us out again. All the forts are built of earth, strengthened with bags filled with sand. What few guns that are left on the line are of secesh make and are of very poor material and finish.

You have probably heard of the gun called "Whistling Dick." This gun is a 20-pounder Parrott and very nicely finished. At the Big Black river fight, we captured two others just like it viz: "Lucky Price" and "Lucky Bowen." I believe "Dick" was at the Big Black but the rebs managed to carry it off when they retreated toward Vicksburg. The three guns belonging to a battery called "Bowen's Battery" named after Gen. [John] Bowen, a secesh general whom we captured there. I would [like] to see a list of the batteries we have taken since crossing the river below Grand Gulf. If you could see all of the artillery that we have here (our own and that captured), you would think we have had enough to blow up the whole of the so-called "C.S.A." Perhaps we have too. I incline to the opinion that the C.S.A. is pretty nearly played out; still I do not think the war ended yet. We have several more points to take. As yet, we have scarcely a foothold in the country between Hilton Head and New Orleans. I trust that Gillmore may yet be successful at Charleston but I do not know or understand the situation well enough to form an opinion. His charge on "Wagner" was disastrous and will, of course, encourage the enemy. But our charge here of May 22d was very disastrous also and, for a while, we all felt pretty blue but we soon rallied again and were more determined to win than ever.[28]

I see that Southern papers are trying to make their people believe that the loss of Vicksburg and [Port] Hudson don't amount to but very little. This seems foolish to me and I don't think the people of the South think as the papers try to make them. One thing is certain. If the loss of these places does not amount to anything, it seems very strange that they should make such desperate efforts to hold them. The South talk about "Dying in the last ditch." Well, if they are bound to hold out 'till every man is killed, I suppose we can't help it; and as we are in the majority, I suppose after we have killed them all, we will make our own terms. This is what I said to a reb not long since. He laughed and said he didn't think they would find the "Last ditch." By the by, Rosy is pushing Bragg pretty hard now and perhaps he may found <u>him</u> in the aforesaid ditch.

Have not heard from Lib lately. A friend of mine—Jack Vernon—saw him at the Big Black about three weeks ago. He was feeling first-rate.[29]

With this, I enclose you a copy of the Vicksburg Citizen printed on wallpaper. Read it and keep it as a curiosity. Tell me what you think of it. Love to one and all. Write often.[30]

*   *   *

Camp Mercantile Battery
Vicksburg Miss.
August 11th 1863

My dear brother

I don't think much of Vicksburg. The war has nearly used it up. We found it in awful state but, by the free use of Dixie and contrabands, it is assuming a more respectable state. And in time may become quite a place again. I wish you could visit the city, its line of fortifications and big guns. We have taken guns enough to man a young war on our own hook. And many of them are of the best material and make. English manufacture of course. The guns made by the secesh are poor things. The bore to some of them looks so it would be bully at shooting around corners but the great danger would be that they would burst in firing. Most of the guns in rear of the lines have been removed and put in [a public] park in the city. Some of the guns are very odd looking. I noticed several pieces of old Spanish make or, as they are called by the government, "Mexican trophies."[31]

I am glad to hear of your promotion. I find there is little use in being despondent or "having the blues." We are in for the war and may as well make the most of it. In many respects, I like the army but wish I held a better position in it; that is, a position that would pay me a little better. I think I am somewhat patriotic but still would like a little more pay for the patriotism. However, "If wishes were horses &c."[32]

Found Lieutenant Bob [King] and Captain Pearl. Feeling first-rate. Bob had just returned from a visit to your old friend Captain Drake of the Mo. 7th and assured me he had a high old time. He gave me a note of introduction to Drake but, three days after I saw Bob, we started for Jackson and as yet I have not had the pleasure of meeting him. Shall try and see him if he is here. Write me often and I will "Keep my end up." Hoping I hear from you often.[33]

*   *   *

Camp of Chicago Mercantile Battery
Vicksburg Miss.
August 16th 1863

My dear father

We will probably go to New Orleans soon at least from what we learn from head quarters. I infer that we are to go there. It is said we will be put in camp on Lake Ponchartrain six miles from New Orleans. The locality is said to be a very healthy one and where there is plenty of room for a large body of troops. I think that ultimately we will move against Mobile but not 'till the weather is cooler. Perhaps the movement may take place soon but I think not.[34]

I presume you have read accounts of how the people of Vicksburg are returning to their loyalty. Perhaps they are but I imagine, if it was not to get provisions to subsist on, that the loyalty of the many would come out "At the little end of the horn." It is said that all "Is fair in love and war" and I think the people of this place have adopted this as their motto. It would surprise you if you could be at the post commissaries and see the crowds of citizens awaiting their turn to present orders given them by the provost martial. Men who, before the war commenced, counted their families by hundreds of thousands; ladies who never before knew the difference between a hind quarter of mutton and hind quarter of beef; contrabands who have always trembled in the presence of their "massers;" "poor white trash" and last, but not least, Uncle Sam's own blue uniformed soldier—all mixed in a heavy mass, trying to be in first to have his or her order filled.[35]

I think there are men here who are true to the Union and who will exert a favorable influence over many of their wavering brethren. If we only get the Union feeling well started it will increase rapidly. People of the South-west are beginning to find out that we really mean fight and are bound to keep it up 'till we win. Once make this feeling general and it will not take long to settle the states bordering on the sea coast.

*   *   *

Vicksburg Miss.
August 23d

My father

I am a man to-day (in years) and, if I were a citizen, would have my taxes to pay and could vote.

Troops are moving to and fro nearly all the time. We still expect to go down the river soon, perhaps this week. Our destination is not positively known but presume it will be New Orleans. Hope so at least, as I would like to go there very much indeed and think it fully as healthy and cool a place as this. Everything there is much cheaper than here and we could probably obtain a greater variety than here. If we go there our camp will probably be at or near Lake Ponchartrain.

Last night, I recd a letter from Lib dated Helena Ark. August 6th. In it, he says that they expect to go up the river soon. Where was he when you last heard from him? Helena is the place where Charles Scammon has been stationed for over a year.[36]

There was a terrible explosion here last Tuesday. The "City of Madison" nearby loaded with ordnance burst her boilers wounding and killing over fifty men. The boat is a total wreck. One of our boys, who has a detail and was engaged on the boat, had a very narrow escape. He had just left the boat and was so close to her that he was knocked down by the concussion. Col. Mather—Chief of Ordnance 13th Corps—also had a very narrow escape. A horse that was on the boat was taken off after the explosion uninjured. The report of the explosion was terrific. For a few moments the air was filled with smoke and flying timbers. Many negroes engaged at that work on the boat were killed. Several were blown on the land and were uninjured. I have no idea what the loss will be. The explosion was caused by the careless handling of a box containing percussion shell. The box was tossed down causing the shells to explode and a piece entering the boiler caused its explosion.[37]

*   *   *

When the Battery Boys returned to Vicksburg, they discovered that their luck was taking a turn for the worse. Their corps was being transferred to the Department of the Gulf. McClernand's former command would eventually be sent on a major offensive operation up the Red River into northwestern Louisiana. McClernand himself was listed in *Harper's Weekly* as one of 11 Union major generals without a command. Most of them, including McClernand, were jockeying to be restored to service. From Illinois, he sent vociferous protests to Washington regarding his removal from command, attacking Grant in the process. While the president valued McClernand's friendship and political clout, he had come to place greater worth on Grant, his most successful general. After Vicksburg, Grant's value shot up like the

Union's celebratory fireworks bursting high above the Hill City. To McClernand's dismay, Lincoln ignored his protests.

The transfer of the 13th Corps created a dilemma for Will Brown and his comrades in the Chicago Mercantile Battery. They had earned the respect of Grant and Sherman. Their "bullet plugged flag," which would be displayed at the Sanitary Commission's Northwest Fair in October at Chicago, attested to the battery's gallantry displayed in the maelstrom of the Vicksburg battles. Leaving behind the undulating hills of Vicksburg meant the Illinois cannoneers would have to prove themselves again to officers in a new department. Still, they were veterans and determined to apply what they had learned in Mississippi to face whatever challenges awaited them. White and his men lamented their separation from Grant and Sherman, and would spend the balance of the war vicariously following their triumphs and setbacks.[38]

The battery's new Gulf department commander was Major General Nathaniel P. Banks, a former Massachusetts politician who had a lot in common with McClernand. Both generals were Lincoln's political appointees and had served in Congress before the war. Like McClernand, Banks was focused on gaining military laurels as a springboard to the White House. The two former politicians were known for their unwavering resolve to restore the Union, as well as their propensity for grandstanding. Unlike Banks, however, McClernand had displayed some competence on the battlefield. One thing the two generals shared in the summer of 1863 was a burning desire to rehabilitate their flagging reputations. McClernand had been outmaneuvered and banished by Grant, his rival and former superior. Banks' success in capturing Port Hudson had been overshadowed by Grant's much-acclaimed Vicksburg triumph. Banks still carried the stigma of his 1862 defeat in the Shenandoah Valley at the hands of Stonewall Jackson, who handed the Massachusetts politician another setback at the Battle of Cedar Mountain on August 9, 1862. Although Banks was more affable than McClernand, the Bay State general lacked his colleague's decisiveness and combat aggressiveness. In less than one year, Banks' weaknesses would yield tragic consequences in a pine-shrouded clearing in northwestern Louisiana.[39]

"There is considerable _feeling_ here between Eastern and Western troops. And from all I learn and see it is not all confined to the men; even the officers often times get into a broil on the subject."

Chapter 9

I Have Been to New Orleans

The past eight months had been a time of adventure and hardship for the Battery Boys. White's redlegs had enjoyed the excitement of their on-to-Vicksburg dash and had evolved from neophytes to veterans during the battles of Port Gibson, Champion Hill, Big Black River Bridge, and the long and difficult Vicksburg siege. These exploits had been sandwiched between three months of waterlogged camping on levees in the Louisiana swamps and Sherman's sun-baked campaign against Johnston's Army of Relief, experiences that brought sickness and death to many men in the Mercantile Battery. Having passed through these ordeals, the remaining Chicagoans were ready for a change of scenery. Exploring Vicksburg, in the wake of its fall, had initially been fun. But the restless artillerists became bored with it. Vicksburg—an agrarian city—was no substitute for bustling Chicago. By contrast, New Orleans' exotic reputation suggested it might be a more suitable substitute for their metropolitan hometown.

At 1:00 p.m. on August 26, the steamer _Atlantic_, carrying the Chicago Mercantile Battery, pulled away from the wharf at the foot of

Vicksburg's bluffs, wending its way through the crowd of commercial boats that flocked to take advantage of the rekindled cotton trade. At noon the next day, members of the battery got a look at Baton Rouge as their boat passed the city. None of them realized they would spend a lot of time in the Louisiana capital before the war ended. The men were impressed with the stately sugar plantation mansions crowning the Mississippi's shores. At 10:00 p.m., the *Atlantic* steamed up to the levee near Carrollton, a small town outside New Orleans. Although artillery-men like Will Brown and his friends had it better than their infantry comrades while campaigning (riding on caissons and limbers was easier than marching), they were much more encumbered when they had to take their equipment on and off transport boats. The Battery Boys were still struggling to get their cannon, limbers, and caissons ashore long after the infantrymen had grabbed their muskets and accoutrements and raced ahead in an effort to claim the best campsites.[1]

After unloading the battery, White and his cannoneers traveled a short distance from the dock to an encampment south of Carrollton. There, they set up their tents on one of the leftover campsites, quickly discovering the local mosquitoes were as much of a nuisance as the Confederates they had fought against in Mississippi. But the Battery Boys' mesh nets and shields, along with the waning of the yellow-fever season, offered them some opportunity of surviving the nights. Their only relief during the excruciatingly hot days was the increased availability of whiskey, beer, and wine. Two weeks after landing in Louisiana, Will Brown wrote his father the Chicagoans had "changed camp and now have a fine shady place." Florison Pitts, his bugler friend, approvingly described the new site as "a most lovely place in a grove of very large pecan trees. The moss hanging from each limb give the place a most unique appearance."[2]

Multi-ethnic New Orleans, with its cosmopolitan ambiance, mesmerized Will. Many of the letters he sent to his father on this trip, plus those he wrote during an extended visit in 1864, provided fascinating details about the Crescent City. In his first letter, he marveled, "The first thing you notice in walking thro' the streets is the perfect babel of languages. One would think that the four corners of the earth were here centered and were trying to argue which was the finest comer." For Will and his comrades, New Orleans offered a delightful break from warfare. They preferred riding on horse-drawn street cars to bouncing along on

Louisiana Division, New Orleans Public Library

Union generals used the luxurious St. Charles Hotel as their headquarters in New Orleans. This photograph of the hotel, which offers a grand view of its magnificent white pillars, first appeared in 1866. The original St. Charles Hotel burned down prior to the Civil War.

army limber chests and caissons; playing billiards and ten pins to dodging enemy sharpshooters; eating oysters, fish, crabs, and ice cream to hardtack and salt pork; drinking iced lemonade instead of tepid or, worse yet, contaminated water; attending performances at the St. Charles Theatre rather than listening to army bands in camp. They also enjoyed visiting tree-lined parks, outdoor statues of American heroes, and the city's unique aboveground cemeteries.[3]

Although the Chicagoans were pleased to trade Vicksburg for New Orleans, they would come to lament the day they had been transferred from the Department of the Tennessee to the Department of the Gulf. Pat White was already upset with his new assignment to Banks' command, largely because he had served under Grant from Belmont to Vicksburg. The rugged Irish captain might well have concurred with a *Harper's Weekly* comment on Banks, which noted the general had never "electrified the country by brilliant flashes of genius, by extraordinary exploits, or unusual triumphs." White wanted to return to one of the 1st Illinois Light Artillery companies. Pitts noted in his diary that the captain "sent in his resignation and then revoked it."[4]

The Battery Boys were surprised when they got another chance to see their hero, U. S. Grant, who was in New Orleans meeting with Banks. On September 4, the politician-turned-general from Massachusetts arranged a grand review for Grant. An Ohio infantryman wrote in his diary, "The customary salute was fired and General Grant rode into the field, and was greeted with loud cheers. He rode slowly along the front of each line and passing to the rear galloped back at racetrack speed. . . . The general had on his old brigadier coat and was in rather a marked contrast to the well formed and finely dressed General Banks." Unfortunately, as reported by Pitts, "Genl. Grant in turning a corner quite suddenly ran into a carriage that was coming the other way. Was thrown from his horse and hurt very bad." That was the last time members of the Mercantile Battery would see Grant during the war. Major General William B. Franklin, who had assumed command of Banks' 19th Corps on August 20, was also in New Orleans during Grant's visit. In a letter to his close friend, Major General William F. Smith, Franklin gossiped about Grant having been on a "bender" during the first two days of his New Orleans visit. Describing the September 4 review, Franklin commented that Grant's fall "stopped the frolic, for he could not walk, and was saved for the time." Franklin believed Grant would not have been drinking had his wife been present.[5]

For the Chicagoans, Banks' style of leadership, marked by east coast pomp and a higher regard for style than substance, replaced Grant's Western informality and aggressive drive. Tensions surfaced almost immediately in New Orleans. Will and his friends were unaware that the internecine conflict between Eastern and Western soldiers and their officers had already been smoldering. Prior to the transfer of the 13th Corps, the 6th Michigan Infantry, a unit recruited from near Will Brown's hometown, had been one of the few Western regiments in Louisiana. Immediately after the war, the colonel of the 6th Michigan recorded his regiment's experience in the Department of the Gulf. He reported his troops had been subjected to anti-Western slurs, claiming they had "been continually persecuted by the New England officials." The soldiers of the 6th Michigan closed ranks with other Western regiments against the New Englanders, whom they called "Nutmegs." The sectional friction between Banks' troops would later spark a roaring fire of interpersonal conflict in the pine woods along the Red River.[6]

*   *   *

New Orleans
Sept 1st 1863

Dear father

Your ever welcome letter of August 16th reached me on the 3d Instant and was gladly rec<u>d</u>. Am glad to hear that peaches are so plentiful with you and wish I could be with you to enjoy some of them. If you go into the warehouse business again, I trust you will meet with success and know of no reason why you will not. If you go into it write me full particulars.[7]

Since I last wrote you, I have been to New Orleans several times and have seen considerable that proved instructive as well as amusing. The streets of the city are very narrow and quite crooked but are all well paved and kept very clean. The first thing you notice in walking thro' the streets is the perfect babel of languages. One would think that the four corners of the earth were here centered and were trying to argue which was the finest comer. Nearly all the darkies in the place speak the French or Spanish language fluently and many of them can hardly speak English. The city is divided into two parts viz: the French and American—and one can easily discover either part both by the sign boards, style of architecture and many other ways. Horse rail roads run on nearly all the principal streets. The cars are different from any I ever saw before. They are about the length and breadth of the cars on State St. Chicago but are finished off like this [reproduced on the next page]:

1. The place for smokers
2. For negroes
3. For ladies
4. Non smokers

The driver sits up above with the smokers. No.'s 2, 3 and 4 are entered by doors at the side of the cars. No. 1 is entered by a flight of steps. I like the style of cars better than our own. New Orleans has many attractive sites to a stranger. Among the most noticeable are:

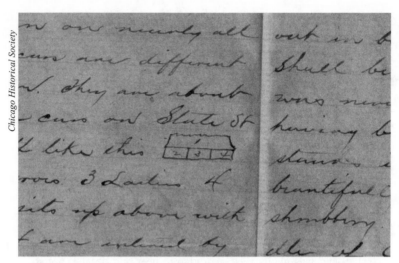

The capital; Clay statue; Jackson square and equestrian statue of that old hero; the French and American markets where one can find everything for sale; the new custom house (yet unfinished); the St. Charles hotel; the St. Charles theatre; French, American and soldiers cemeteries; the immense levees and our ships-of-the-line. French, English, Spanish and Russian men of wars, fine public buildings, public parks and a great-deal more . . .[8]

The Jackson statue pleased me greatly. It is a life size statue of [Andrew] Jackson and his horse done in bronze. On both sides of the pedestal, the following stands out in bold relief: "The Union must and Shall be preserved." It seems strange that this was never defaced but no traces of its even having been disturbed are visible. The statue stands in the centre of a large, fine park bountifully ornamented with trees, flowers and shrubbing.[9]

The Clay statue stands in the middle of Canal St. and near the business centre. It is larger than life but, as it is only raised about twelve feet above ground, does not look very well. The cemeteries are well worth visiting. They are filled with tombs of the finest descriptions all built above ground. In the French cemetery, I noticed the tombs decorated with fresh flowers, pictures, beads and various trinkets. The tombs in this country are washed off every other day by the servants of the family or friends of the deceased. The shipping was a great attraction to me. The harbor is filled with ships of all kinds from the little coasting logger and fishing smack to the full rigged brig and first-class passenger steamship. All in all, I enjoyed my visit to the city very much and shall go again.[10]

We hear some talk of a movement soon but am not certain where we are bound. Probably somewhere on the west side of the river. I have heard of the 75th NY but don't think they are here. Met a member the other day who said he was regimented with Hiram

Hoxie. If I can find him will write you all about it. Kind regards to all.[11]

*   *   *

Carrollton La.
Sept 13th 1863

My dear father

Owing to our having been running round in the field during the first six months, our quartermasters papers have got decidedly behind time and I am at work squaring them up. Our present Q.M. Sergeant is a stick at best and never does anything. He is at present at Chicago on a sick furlough. I like something to keep my mind and hand in play and, therefore, I am glad of this opportunity to do both.[12]

Yesterday, we changed camp and have a fine shady place in a large grove close to New Orleans and Lake Ponchartrain Rail Road track. There is a scarcity of North-western news here. The river is so low it takes boats a good while to reach us. Mails are very irregular.

I tried to find the 75th NY but learned they are at or near Brashear City. The 6th Michigan are at Port Hudson and have been made mounted infantry; I believe on "Jackass Cavalry" as Lib says.[13]

News and reports from Charleston reach us slowly but Gillmore seems to be pecking away and in time will "fetch things." Our last news was that Sumter and Wagner were ours and that we were shelling the city. Have you heard anything like the following: It is said that after Charleston falls, President Lincoln intends issuing a proclamation to the South offering them peace if they will lay down their arms [and] gradually emancipate what slaves they have left, allowing those already gone to be considered free; and I believe allowing him . . . to punish the leaders . . . of the rebellion. I may be mistaken in regard to the latter part but think not.[14]

The only hope the South can have now is Foreign intervention but this I do not greatly fear. England is waiting for France and France visa versa. It may look like bragging but I think France is afraid of us and will think a great while before she throws down the gauntlet. If England dared, she would interfere but now Johnny Bull has considerable to look after in the old country. All this time while the great Foreign debate is going on, Uncle Sam keeps winding round the South winning slowly but surely and keeping all he wins—and on looking round among his vast navy yards, you will find that something is on the stocks and everything launched has some improvement. Truly we are becoming a war-like nation.[15]

I have not heard from Lib for some time. Where was he when you last heard from him? Henry is I suppose . . . near . . . Chattanooga.[16]

*   *   *

Carrollton La.
September 20th 1863

My dear father

We have most glorious news from nearly every direction; in fact, so much that it is good that I am disposed to credit but little of it. Morris Island, Sumter, Wagner, and Gregg in our possession. Brave old Rosy in Chattanooga; Burnside at Knoxville and Steele in Little Rock Ark. All of which, if true, will send a thrill of hope thro' every loyal man almost equal to that of the fall of Vicksburg and Hudson. That we are daily becoming stronger and stronger all recent victories show. And with victory on our side, the soldier is still cheered on to renewed exertion.[17]

I have often thought of the despondent looks and dark ideas of our soldiers after our defeat under Sherman up the Yazoo river [at Chickasaw Bayou] near Vicksburg: We never could succeed; the South would whip and we might as well quit then as ever. How different the feeling three months afterwards when again we were marching toward that stronghold. Determination boldly stamped on each face thro' rain and mud, heat and cold; no matter where, all felt bright and sure of success. "Grand Gulf is ours" came along the route. Hurrah and faces bright became brighter.

Nothing could withstand such an army and now, when victories new and great almost daily reach our ear, have we not everything to be cheerful for? If we can believe even one fiftieth part, we hear the "Sunny South" is getting decidedly the worst for wear. Nearly all Southern papers talk as despondently as they dare and only wait to say more. Should Parson Brownlow go back to Knoxville, won't he just more than howl; tho' really I think it may be possible that he will do more harm than good. The Parson is a good man to talk to loyal men but his discourse to those who are "On the fence" may not be so pleasant.[18]

There is considerable feeling here between Eastern and Western troops. And from all I learn and see, it is not all confined to the men; even the officers often times get into a broil on the subject. The Eastern soldier is better disciplined than ours but has not done so much fighting. In camp, our boys think they should be allowed many privileges that the Eastern soldiers never think of. Many Eastern officers scarcely even speak to a soldier unless on business while our officers are most always among their men. Your Eastern officer conforms strictly to the U.S. Regulations while our officers have a Regulation of their own.[19]

*   *   *

Carrollton La.
September 29th 1863

My dear father

We have no news . . . since my last. Gillmore is still <u>pecking away</u> at Charleston and all accounts are favorable. A big battle seems impending between Rosecrans and Bragg. It is said that Bragg has rec<u>d</u> reinforcements from Johnston and Lee, and will give battle as soon as Rosy moves forward—or perhaps may endeavor to drive him from the present position. I do not fear for Rosy. He knows exactly what he can do and when the time comes will do it.[20]

There is a great-deal more <u>form</u> in this Department than in our old one. The reason is easy to explain. Grant's army has constantly been in the field and is on the move while this army has been in camp for nearly two years, and have had nothing else but <u>form</u> and <u>style</u> to think of. Whether this makes them better soldiers than ours is a question. I don't think it improves their fighting qualities . . . Two of my . . . friends have returned to the Battery. . . . Both were quite unwell when they left but are now pictures of health.

*   *   *

Carrollton
October 5th 1863

My dear father

For two days past, we have been under orders to leave for Brashear City immediately and would probably have been off before this, but we had some alterations to make in our artillery and could not get ready. We are to take but four guns on this expedition. The four to be the Rodman pattern and throwing a 3-inch, 10-pounder shell. We have always had two Rodmans and during the siege they did splendid work and won a big reputation.

Before we left Vicksburg, we obtained a Requisition on the Allegheny Arsenal pean [?] for four new guns of this pattern and a few days since rec<u>eived</u> notice that they have been forwarded. But Gen. Ord says that we cannot wait for them. So, we are to start with four guns from Vicksburg—we brought our two Rodmans and a couple of mongrel guns captured at that place. But since we have been here, we have found two more Rodmans [that are] considerably worn. But the Captain has so little confidence in the mongrels that he has concluded to take the Rodmans so we are to have four guns that we understand.[21]

I cannot tell certainly but I think our expedition is bound for Texas. At any rate, such is the general opinion and, from preparations that have been made, I see no reason particularly to doubt it. Tho' there is so little to be sure of in army movements that it would not greatly surprise me to see us start for a direction a good ways from Texas. However, as everybody talks Texas, I suppose we may take it for granted that Texas is the first in question.

I expect to see a good-deal in Texas; should we go to the Rio Grande, I expect we will have a grand time in general. The 19th Corps (Gen. Franklin's) and nearly all of our Corps have already moved from here and the advance are, I believe, en route toward the Texas line tho' I am not sure such is the case. Where we are going to strike—or where our destination is—is a mystery to me.[22]

Rosy got whaled pretty badly but it is his turn next. He is receiving heavy reinforcements from all points up river. Sherman's Corps are on their way and they don't know what defeat is. Rosy did big work even if he did get whaled and has lost but very little ground. One thing is certain, Bragg can not get a larger force without leaving other points open while Rosy can have all, if not more, men than he wants. It was unfortunate that the fight came off so soon but the End is not yet and we will yet gain the day.[23]

*   *   *

Franklin La.
October 11th 1863

My dear father

As I intimated in my last we have moved. Left Carrollton early Monday morning, crossing the river at New Orleans and taking the cars for Brashear City during the afternoon. We reached Brashear just after dark, crossed Berwick Bay during the night, went into camp next day (Tuesday) and on Wednesday morning early started towards Texas. Friday night, we had marched as far as New Iberia, a town 30 miles beyond this. But on that night, our Brigade received orders to return to this place as it needed a force here to protect baggage trains, boats passing up and down the bayou and supplies going forward to the advance.

We immediately started on the return trip and reached here this morning. So you see that we have done considerable marching since we started. I foot it up to about 75 miles and think the amount small enough. Don't know how long we are to remain here, perhaps a week and perhaps considerably longer. We may have this same country to travel over again but I hope not. Should the army move forward and take Sabine Pass, we may go there on transport via the Gulf of Mexico. Would like to take the trip first-rate.[24]

Have passed thro' several small towns and found them in pretty good condition tho' businesses seemed at a perfect stand still. This place is quite a pretty one and in peaceful times did a larger business. Many of its inhabitants profess a strong attachment to the Union but I have little confidence in what they say; in fact, it is almost impossible to tell who are true and who are not. . . . [M]any people in the South . . . would gladly avow a Union sentiment if they were sure of protection. But as soon as we leave the place, their enemies would pounce upon them and probably ruin them. If we can only get the Union sentiment well started throughout the South, it will not be long ere the war will receive its quietus.

Brashear City, of which you probably have heard so much about, is not much of a place. Before the rebellion, its principal business was receiving and forwarding cattle from Texas and sugar from plantations along Bayou Teche. By the by, this is called the Teche country and is probably the richest sugar growing country in the South. The word is pronounced as if spelled Tash. Every plantation has a large sugar house on it, but most of the darkies are non est. The fact is father the people of this country, that is this part of the country, lived too well and enjoyed too great a sway. They were becoming too great—had a great idea of themselves—and a very poor opinion of the rest of the world. Particularly that part of it 36° 30". I think this opinion changing and, in time, they may decide that they are not all the world.[25]

We do not get any particulars in regard to Rosecrans latest movements. A New Orleans paper of the 7th says that they have favorable news from him. And one of our boys, who just returned from furlough, says that he [Rosecrans] has whipped Bragg but did not learn any particulars. By paper received to-day, I see that Jack Hall was killed in the late fight at Rossville [Gap] and that Will Rice, son of J. B. Rice Esq of Chicago, was also killed. I was acquainted with both. We joined the army about the same time.[26]

Your letter of September 22nd reached me the night before we left Berwick and like all others was gladly recd. Was glad to hear about Lib and Henry. I am sorry to hear that Henry is so dissatisfied. Wish he could get out of it if he wants to. Hope you may succeed in getting your appointment for Lib as he certainly deserves it and I think would like it very much.[27]

Major General Nathaniel P. Banks

*"I would rather die the death of a dog and have one
minute's freedom, than to die a slave."*

Chapter 10

The Richest Sugar Growing Country

In July 1863, Nathaniel Banks was hoping to gain back some of the national respect he had held before the war and during its early months. He had been among the most effective Speakers in the history of the United States House of Representatives, having finessed and compromised his way to the top. His oratorical skills often drew thunderous applause from northeastern legislators, who sat shoulder to shoulder in support of his abolitionist views. But Banks was cautious not to cross the line too far and provoke his Southern colleagues as his friend Charles Sumner had done in 1856, when he was beaten senseless on the Senate floor by a cane-wielding South Carolina fire-eater.

After the war began, however, Banks was unable to translate his skill at parliamentary maneuvering into tangible military achievements on Virginia's battlefields. His bungled 1862 campaigns and tactical defeats at the hands of Stonewall Jackson deeply tarnished Banks' record. During the fighting in the Shenandoah Valley, Jackson captured huge quantities of supplies from Banks' army, prompting Southerners and Northerners alike to tar the general with the embarrassing nickname "Commissary Banks." The dismal record earned Banks a well-deserved exile to the Trans-Mississippi Theater. The transfer did not dampen his yearning to command the nation's attention, however, and likely increased it. In Louisiana in 1863, Banks hoped his victory at Port Hudson would erase his humiliating nickname and catapult him back into the national spotlight.[1]

To Banks' dismay, the Confederates surrendered at a most inopportune time: just after the Union triumphs at Gettysburg and Vicksburg had captured the public's attention. Banks' victory flashed on the front pages of newspapers and disappeared. The accolades he so deeply desired eluded him yet again. Undeterred, the persistent opportunist and keen observer of political trends believed that the route for redeeming his reputation and gaining the White House might pass through Louisiana and Texas.

In 1862, while Lincoln's military forces were preoccupied with suppressing the rebellion, Emperor Louis Napoleon invaded Mexico to secure a new colony for France. By June 1863, a 35,000-man French army captured Mexico City, ousting Benito Juarez's government. Napoleon installed his own puppet leader, Hapsburg Archduke Ferdinand Maximilian. Napoleon's audacious violation of the Monroe Doctrine was not the only challenge the French posed to Washington. After American diplomatic pressure thwarted a Confederate attempt to buy two ironclads in Great Britain, Southern procurement agents turned to France. The Confederates contracted for the building of four commerce raiders and two ironclads. Despite the South's waning fortunes, Napoleon flirted with the idea of recognizing the Confederacy. The leaders of the Federal government feared Napoleon would intervene and resuscitate the Southern states as an independent nation. Their apprehensions were grounded in the history lessons they learned in school. After all, the success of the American Revolution demonstrated how quickly power could shift during a war: without the cooperation of France's navy and army, George Washington would not have been able to defeat the British at Yorktown. The Lincoln administration determined that the French must be stopped before Napoleon could send troops and warships from Mexico into Texas.[2]

In August 1863, General Halleck gave Banks a new assignment. "The flag of the United States should be again raised [in Texas] and sustained somewhere," explained Halleck. The exact location was not that important. It was the permanent presence of Union troops anywhere on Texas soil that Lincoln was after, an achievement he believed would be sufficient to dampen Napoleon's growing ardor to recognize the Confederacy. To accomplish this goal, Banks advocated launching an attack on the Texas coast from his New Orleans base. Halleck preferred that the Federals enter the Lone Star State via southwest or northwest Louisiana. For logistical reasons, Banks disregarded Halleck's recommendation and pushed forward with his strategy for a coastal attack that faltered at Sabine Pass on September 8, 1863. Mortified, Banks acquiesced and moved to implement Halleck's strategy. A portion of his army would make the arduous march through the heartland of Louisiana and disperse Confederate Major General Richard Taylor's small army. During the Port Hudson Campaign, Banks had swatted aside Taylor's troops as if they were dried stalks of sugar cane stretched across his path. He was prepared to do it once more, but this time he would turn west toward Texas—and create a new opportunity to recapture the nation's attention.[3]

As part of a two-division 13th Corps detachment assigned to the overland expedition, the Chicago Mercantile Battery traveled north in September via boat, train, and horse on the Union army's circuitous route from New Orleans. The 13th Corps assumed a secondary role to a two-division contingent from the 19th Corps. Until recently, Banks had personally commanded the latter organization, a smaller formation than McClernand's former 13th Corps and one predominantly composed of Easterners. The Massachusetts general reorganized his troops prior to the campaign, turning over the 19th Corps to Major General William B. Franklin, who also commanded the expedition while Banks remained, for the time being, in New Orleans. The Mercantile Battery arrived at the town of Franklin, Louisiana, on October 8. The artillerists stayed there to protect the expedition's supply line from guerrilla attacks. From this vantage point, Will Brown complained to his father, "Our so-called 'Texas movement' wags slowly." By mid-October, the Federal column extended for miles as it inched along the meandering Bayou Teche.[4]

Although they were not pleased with their assignment, Will and the other artillerists appreciated the perquisites of being stationed at Franklin, a small community situated in the Acadian area. Henry Wadsworth Longfellow, in his epic poem "Evangeline," made Franklin famous with his story of a woman who lost her betrothed when he moved to Louisiana. Along with other French Acadians, he had been banished

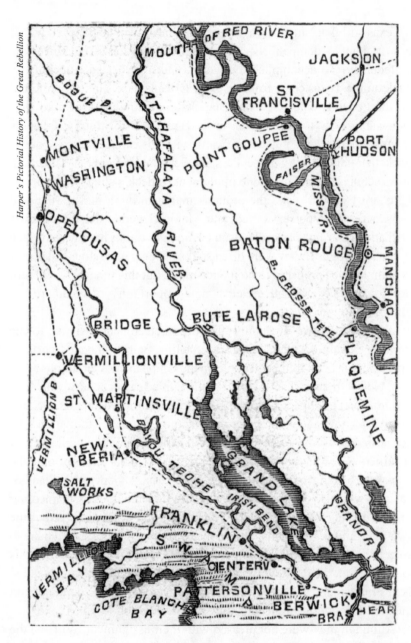

Harper's Pictorial History of the Great Rebellion

from his Canadian homeland in a vicious 18th century diaspora. Evangeline followed her exiled lover all the way to the Bayou Teche. In his verse, Longfellow described the beauties of the country through which Evangeline traveled:

Beautiful is the land, with its prairies and forests of fruit trees;
Under the feet a garden of flowers, and the bluest of heavens
Bending above, and resting its dome on the walls of the forest.
They who dwell there have named it the Eden of Louisiana![5]

Will and his friends made the most of their garrison duty "On the banks of the Teche." Outside of Franklin, they tore down a steam mill and used the boards to erect a comfortable shebang. Although the Chicagoans were in the Deep South, and surrounded by an intensely Pro-Confederate populace, they enjoyed Franklin's amenities. Will accompanied Pat White to visit some of the local plantation owners and their daughters who, though ardent secessionists, were hospitable to their Northern visitors. The young artillerists also benefited from the temperate climate and abundant farm produce. The Battery Boys were in "tip-top" shape.

During their stay in Franklin, White's men were pleased to have little interaction with Banks' Eastern troops—especially since the gunners resented their perceived coddling of local sugar planters and "the manner in which matters are conducted." Members of the Mercantile Battery preferred Grant's aggressive prosecution of the war, including his firm policies against civilian secessionists. In Banks' army, with the most important assignments monopolized by the favored 19th Corps, the Easterners treated their Western counterparts as outsiders. David C. Edmonds, the author of *Yankee Autumn in Acadiana*, found numerous examples of sectional antagonism between Banks' two corps. He commented that they were "Set apart by customs, mannerisms, attitudes, accents and sometimes even religion, it was inevitable that they would constantly be at each other's throats." A surgeon who had served in the 19th Corps explained the Easterners' bias in a postwar book: "The western men were strangers in this army, and attracted considerable attention from their peculiar habits in camp, and singular style of doing duty…they had a wonderful disregard of personal appearance, wearing all manner of dirty and outlandish costumes." The surgeon also claimed the 13th Corps troops were intent on "showing these paper collar and white glove gents how to fight."[6]

By mid-October, William Franklin moved his 19th Corps troops up the Teche, separating them from their Western tormentors. According to Edmonds, "So obnoxious were many of the jeering soldiers and so heated were the exchanges that at one point during the morning a guard had to be

posted on both sides of the road to keep the two army corps apart."
Tensions increased as Franklin foundered. Timid after his Sabine Pass
embarrassment, and still haunted by lingering blame for the Union's
Fredericksburg defeat, Franklin awaited direction from his superior
about whether to march west toward the Sabine River or north toward
Shreveport. With his supply situation worsening and no clear guidance
coming from Banks, Franklin decided to pull back to New Iberia, where
he could collect forage for his animals and stock provisions for his troops.
Brigadier General Stephen G. Burbridge covered the army's withdrawal
with a 1,250-man brigade from the 13th Corps, supplemented by some
500 cavalrymen and two batteries. On November 3, about 3,000
Confederates, predominantly from Brigadier General Thomas Green's
cavalry division, attacked Burbridge's men at what became known as the
Battle of Bayou Bourbeau or the Battle at Carrion Crow. Green's
onslaught routed the Northerners, but two divisions from the 13th Corps
arrived on the scene to halt the Confederate pursuit.[7]

Meanwhile, in his quest for a clear-cut victory in the Trans-
Mississippi, Nathaniel Banks had set out from New Orleans for the Texas
coast. Franklin's expedition had become a diversion by compelling the
Texas Confederates to protect their eastern flank while leaving the coast
vulnerable to Banks' amphibious assault. Banks' force, which included
some 4,000 soldiers, sailed for the mouth of the Rio Grande. The
Unionists landed unopposed at Brazos Island near Brownsville on
November 2. It took three days for Banks to unload his men, who

occupied Brownsville without a
battle. "Our enterprise," he
pompously announced, "has
been a complete success."[8]

Back at the Bayou Teche
town of Franklin, the Battery

Major General
William Franklin

Battles and Leaders of the Civil War

Boys were enjoying themselves. They played billiards, browsed the town's bookshop, bought cakes and pies from peddlers, attended church, and flirted with young secessionist girls. Some of the Federals—including Will Brown—thought the townspeople's professed loyalty to the Union a contrived facade. George Throop had a conversation that lent proof to such suspicions. One day, while walking through the town, Throop encountered a black woman in the backyard of a wealthy widow, a Mrs. Smith. She asked if the lieutenant was looking for her—the slave mistaking Throop for an official from the provost office. The slave wanted to return to New Orleans so she could join her mother, father, and sisters who lived there. George recorded the following conversation for his father, who was back home in Chicago:

> *Throop: "Isn't Mrs. Smith a good mistress?"*
> *Slave: "Yes, but I would rather be free if I have nothing but bread & water to live on."*
> *Throop: "Are you married?"*
> *Slave: "No."*
> *Throop: "Why not?"*
> *Slave: "Why? What is the use of getting married here? If I was as free as you I would be."*
> *Throop: "But isn't a slave better off married than single?"*
> *Slave: "No sir. If you master can't get money to pay his debts, then either the father or the mother or the children must be sold away and never see one another again. Why, I have seen mothers most killed by having their children taken from them. No, I never will be married here, but if I can get to N.O. I will be."*
> *Throop: "Are there any loyal people here?"*
> *Slave: "No, they would any of them cut your throat if they could. Yes, any of them, I won't make an exception. They talk one thing to you, and another to themselves. The ladies talk very nice, but they keep saying 'our folks will be here soon and catch these Yankees.' You had better be careful, they will come in on you some day and you won't know how they caught you. The citizens are all rebels and many have been . . . [or] are now in the rebel army. Yes, I would rather die the death of a dog and have one minute's freedom, than to die a slave."[9]*

*   *   *

Franklin La.
October 18th 1863

My dear father

As you will notice by the heading, we are still at Franklin and for aught I can see we are likely to remain here for some time yet, tho' I am not certain in regard to the matter.[10]

On Monday last, received letter from Lib at Little Rock. He was quite well and enjoying himself. Says he is having good living and is encamped on as fine a piece of ground as he ever saw. Ere this I presume you have heard from him. I do not hear a word from Henry but in all the papers I have seen there is no mention of the 19th Mich. And from this, I presume his regiment was not engaged in the late battle near Chattanooga. I also learn by the papers that the Board of Trade Battery were not engaged and this also relieves my mind of considerable anxiety, as I have many friends in that battery whose welfare I feel an interest in.[11]

Since I have been here, I have seen many new phases of the "Divine institution" and the more I see the less I think of it. I have conversed with planters and overseers and from them learned considerable. Not far from our camp, there is a very large sugar plantation in full blast, [with] negroes, planter, mistress, overseer, dogs, whipping stock and all. You would be surprised to see the light-colored and almost straight-haired appearance of some of the young darkies, or pickininnies as they are called.[12]

Some might wonder at the various shades of color seen but it would not take long to explain the reason. After visiting the negro quarters, call up to the plantation mansion. There you will probably find his wife and two or three daughters (the sons are about in the army). The family is very aristocratic of course. I wonder what the ladies would think if some one was bold enough to tell them that their fathers, brothers or husbands were negro breeders. Such a remark in their presence would be the climax of indecency and yet living on the plantations as they do, and seeing the various white faces among their slaves, can they help knowing where they [the people of mixed color] came from? I think not. Query: Who then are the real Abolitionists? I tell you father, that no sensible man would be long in the midst of slavery without fully making up his mind about it.

This place is quite a secesh hole. But as long as we stay here, I presume the people will conduct themselves in pretty good order. There are men here who profess a Union sentiment. Perhaps they are sincere in their professions. Hope they are; but I think they will bear watching.

Sugar is very plentiful here and we have all we can use. Pecan nuts (the darkies call them <u>puck-ons</u>) are also very plentiful and quite cheap. We have plenty of fine large sweet potatoes—or yams—and lots of fresh meat. The darkies also bring in eggs, butter, milk, onions &c. So, taking all in all we live very well indeed.[13]

*   *   *

Franklin La.
October 25th 1863

My dear father

The first week has been a quiet one with us. Our Lieut. Cone has returned from a brief furlough to Chicago bringing us news from friends at that place and his return was about all the excitement we have had.[14]

From our advance, we have a report that 2.000 rebel cavalry made a dash on part of the 19th Corps while they were in camp eating breakfast and created great confusion among them, driving them back some distance. But as soon as our Corps heard of it, they came to the rescue and drove the cavalry back with considerable loss. This story, according to my idea, partakes too much of the <u>cock and bull</u> order. Our Division (that part of it which is with the main force) has the advance and is now some distance [from] Opelousas.[15]

The longer I am in this Department, and the more I see of it, the less I like the manner in which matters are conducted. It seems useless to me to use half-way measures with traitors, whether in arms against the government or quietly staying at home—but rendering all possible assistance to the <u>Southern Cause</u>. Here in this part of the country—where there is sugar enough to supply our immense army for a long time and when it is known positively that this sugar belongs to men who have been, and are doing, all that they can against the government—it surprises me that part of it at least is not picked up and turned over to government. All the sugar we receive here comes from New Orleans and, of course, government pays a good round price for it. At this time, the government has all it can look after now. But should the powers that be in our Department call attention to this subject, perhaps we might see a change.[16]

In many things of this kind, the rebel government is far ahead of ours. They make use of all possible means while we have our set forms and pet ideas and no provision is made for particular cases.

We are getting war-wise every day, however, and as the war advances may become a great-deal more perfect.

From up river the news is interesting. Rosecrans position seems very dangerous but I think reinforcements will reach him in time and, if they do, he is safe and will yet decide the contest favorably [that was] so nearly fatal at one time. There is one thing about Rosy and his movements. He is always near the enemy and there is always an impending great battle. He is now so far down, however, that he can not move far without finding something to check him. But if he can get over the first barrier, I think him all right and would not wonder if he went as far as the Gulf.[17]

I have been and shall be busy for some time yet at Ordnance and Quartermaster papers belonging to the Battery. I am getting a very good idea of [this] Quartermaster business and like it for various reasons. The Captain leaves it all to me, even to writing the letters to the departments at Washington; and so you see I have some large correspondents.

*   *   *

Franklin La.
November 8th 1863

My dear Father

I returned from New Orleans yesterday morning having been absent from the Battery [for] six days. Our new guns are at Brashear and will be here tomorrow probably. I enjoyed the entire trip. At Brashear City, the base of supplies for our army business in connection with the army is very active. The base of supplies for a large [army] is always very active and it is quite interesting to see all that is going on.[18]

I found your letter of October 4th awaiting me and was happy to receive it. You wrote of Hiram Hoxie having received a commission in a negro regiment. I am glad to hear of it and hope he will like it. Such a commission can be obtained without great difficulty. A friend in New Orleans said he could get one for me if I wanted it. I do not [desire such a commission] for many reasons, some of which I will give you. In the first place, I do not like the infantry service. Again, if a man accepts position in a black regiment he has got to stay in the army for three years at least—as no resignations, unless for incapability, will be received. I think this reason itself almost a sufficient one. I do not want to be in the army three hours after the war has ended.[19]

I have no particular scruples because the regiments are composed of black men and think a man foolish who has. In my opinion, the day is not far distant when negro soldiers will be at a premium in our army. If, in time to come, I should see a good opportunity to obtain position in a negro battery of light or heavy artillery, I would endeavor to do so and think I would stand a good chance. I think batteries of this kind will be formed in time. If they are, I will look out for a chance. In the Battery, I am getting along very well; but better perhaps than the majority. The Captain is a good friend and takes me considerably into his confidence. There are some matters that I cannot explain to you through the medium of pen, ink and paper.[20]

It is just a year ago today that we left Chicago. At that time, our cause did not look nearly so bright as at present. Many people feared the result of Lincoln's proclamation of emancipation and built many dark ideas upon it. The subject was a dark one then.

The weather is delightful, the days being fine and pleasant and the nights cool enough to keep away musquitoes and sleep well. Remember me to all friends. Lon Jones writes us that he was at St. Jo not long since. Love to all. Will write Belle.[21]

*   *   *

Franklin La.
November 15th 1863

My Dear Father,

I have just returned from a very pleasant ride out about seven miles from camp. Went out with the Captain. We visited several plantations, but spent most of our time at Mrs. (or as she is called Madam) Porter's. This lady has a plantation of 7.000 acres, 350 negroes, three large sugar houses and as fine a mansion as I have ever seen in the South. She treated us very hospitably, made us feel perfectly at home and furnished us with a most sumptuous repast. She is, or pretends to be, a Union woman. [Madam Porter] has had one son in the rebel army but got him out in some way and immediately sent him off to Europe where he is at present. She has two daughters living in the North. The interior of the house is almost like a palace, her grounds abound in parks, statuary, groves, shrubbery, flowers &c &c. She has some of the finest blooded stock I ever saw. It far excels everything I ever saw on exhibition at any of our county or state fairs.[22]

During our stay, I was introduced to a young lady whose father owns a plantation near Madam Porter. Had quite a conversation with her. On the start, she avowed herself an unconquerable rebel—one of the Last ditch kind—I told her that I admired her frankness but thought, if she could only be in the army a couple of years, she might possibly change her opinion. She thought the South would never succumb 'till the last man in it was killed. I told her that we certainly would hold out forever and, if it comes to [sacrificing] man for man, we would in the end have several hundred thousands ahead—I came very nearly adding that, as we still had many men at home, our population was constantly increased while in the South all the men had gone to the war. But I did not for fear of consequence. I laughed at some of her notions and ideas and she laughed at some of mine. Neither of us got at all excited and on leaving she asked me to come out again and be sure to bring some newspapers, as it was very seldom she saw any. Think I will obtain a few copies of the Chicago Tribune, New York Ditto, New York Independent and Cincinnati Gazette and send to her. She would probably enjoy reading these, particularly the Independent.

The country does not show the effects of the war to any great extent. Most of the plantations still have plenty of negroes to work them and quite recently Gen. Banks has issued a circular offering very good terms and inducements to planters to ship their sugar, cotton and other produce to New Orleans. The planters are universally improving this offer; and sugar and cotton in very large quantities is being sent forward as rapidly as possible. Perhaps this offer is a good one and it may do much in starting a fresh good feeling between Feds and Confeds. Trade of course touches the pocket and, after all, the pocket is the true king and peacemaker. I cannot make head or tail to the present movement. Sometimes I think a big game of brag—again it looks like bluff and then again it looks like brag—and then again it looks like everything imaginable and still one can make nothing of it. Perhaps the best way to sum it up is to make use of the expression used by O. C. Kerr Esq. viz: "Strategy my boy."

To-day one section (two guns) of our Battery went up to New Iberia and another section will probably go to-morrow or next day. That will leave only one regiment and two guns here but from the situation of the place and position of our forces in front I think there is little danger of an attack here. We keep a good lookout, however, and if a force does come will give them a lively turn.[23]

* * *

Franklin La.
November 22nd 1863

My dear father

So little of interest has transpired since my last that I have but little material to write about; in fact, until this morning we have had no news at all. This morning a story reaches us by the way of New Orleans that Gen. Banks has succeeded in capturing Fort Isabel, a fort defending the mouth of the Rio Grande river. Cannot vouch for the truth of the report.[24]

Last night, about 150 rebel prisoners passed down the bayou. They were taken from a force that attacked us near New Iberia. The infantry of our Brigade are at work daily now throwing up a line of earthworks near our camp. As soon as the work is completed, we are to put our guns in position on it. From appearances, I imagine we will stay here some time, perhaps all Winter; and I will be satisfied if we do so, as the country is very healthy and well supplied with provisions. Would much rather stay here than take a tramp thro' Texas tho' would not care much if I did go; in fact, am bound to take everything as it comes whether Texas or an expedition to Japan. There is about as much use in trying to fly to the moon as there is in a soldier trying or thinking of settling down.[25]

Yesterday, our Lieut. Roe and one of the boys left for Chicago on recruiting service. I hope they will be successful. We need more men.[26]

We have just finished equipping the Battery with an entire new harness and four new guns and caissons and I assure you we look gay. The Battery is out on drill daily, and all are getting well posted in regard to the School. It is a grand site to see a battery going thro' the drill, particularly on the trot. I wish you could see us.

I see that Col. _____ has had quite a fight at Pine Bluffs Ark. and given the enemy a sound whipping. Suppose that Lib was not in the fight.[27]

*   *   *

Franklin La.
November 28th 1863

My dear brother Henry

Since we have been in the army, our letters like Angels visits "have been few and far between." The main reason is obvious. Distance from each other and the very poor management of army mails. Why something is not done to regulate army mails I cannot imagine. Certainly if anyone should receive his letters regularly that one should be the volunteer soldier. I hope to see somebody take hold of this matter before long and think it will be done.[28]

I little thought—when about a year ago at this time I was winding my way slowly over the hilly regions of northern Mississippi and with about 30.000 others trying to find an enemy along the banks of the Tallahatchie—that in a year from that time I would be way down here so close to the Gulf of Mexico. And in the midst of the richest sugar growing country in the South. But so it is and for aught I can see am likely to remain here for some time. I can't say that I am very favorably impressed with this Department. There is too much form and military etiquette to suit my Republican ideas.

I find everything here far different from what it was in Grant's Department. Here, it seems as if everybody was watching and trying to catch his neighbors either stealing or committing some grieve error; while in our old Department, every man attended to his own business. I think should both departments undergo a thorough investigation it would be found that one was fully as honest as the other.

As for the fighting part, you know as much about <u>that</u> as myself and no one claims to equal Grant as a winning man. You may imagine that I have got "<u>Grant</u> on the brain" but, had you been with him and seen as much of him as I have, you would probably excuse my praises. I congratulate you on having him over you and if he don't succeed I don't know who will.[29]

This parish (St. Mary's) is called a Union parish, and perhaps it is, but one must get up early in the morning to see it. I think, however, that there may be a few Union men in it. The feminines are very heavy on secesh and think the Yankees terrible creatures. Some of the young ladies, however, are very gay and very ladylike in their appearance and behavior. Nearly all the negroes speak the French or French-Creole language.[30]

For the past three months, I have been acting Quartermaster Sergeant of our Battery and this has given me a first-rate opportunity to improve myself in army accounts, as well as to keep my hand in, in writing. I have the position temporarily only as our Quartermaster Sergeant is absent on sick leave.[31]

I am in the enjoyment of the best of health and spirits and am getting as fat as a pig. Weigh the nice little sum of 163 pounds. I think the South agrees with me. Don't you? The 6th Michigan were at Port Hudson when we passed there last September on our way from Vicksburg to New Orleans but, as we only stopped long enough to report, I did not see any familiar faces or ever have time to make any inquiries.[32]

*   *   *

Franklin La
November 29th 1863
My dear father

Have you seen a copy of the circular lately issued by the rebel Gen.
Gantt of Arkansas? It is a very sensible circular and will, I think, be
of great benefit to our cause in that state. Gantt concedes that the
South must fail and that there is no use in holding out longer. I
presume the circular will be published in Northern papers and you
will see it.[33]

We kept Thanksgiving Day (26th) in regular style. Had our
turkies, chickens, ducks, pies, puddings etc. etc. So you see that
even soldiers can keep Thanksgiving.

The fort that I mentioned in my last is finished and is a pretty
good one. It is built in about the following shape:

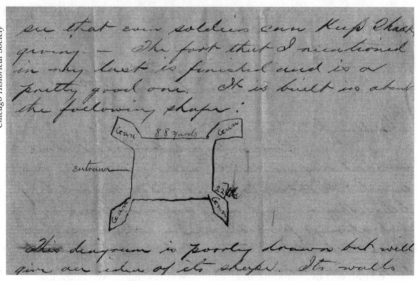

This diagram is poorly drawn but will give an idea of its shape.
Its walls are about six feet high and seven thick. I don't know
whether it is the intention of the commander of the post to put our
guns in the fort or whether he has built it simply for greater
protection in case we are attacked by a larger force. I think there is
little danger of an attack, however, as the larger part of the rebel
army has probably gone toward the Rio Grande where they will
attempt to keep back Banks and the forces under him.[34]

From the newspapers and last letters from Chicago, I learned that
the ladies North-western fair for the benefit of soldiers was in
everything a great success and netted a large amount. I see that the

[Chicago Mercantile Battery] flag we had at Vicksburg is on exhibition and incites considerable curiosity. The way it was "tattered and torn" is no joke but, had we had fifty others like [it], we could have had those looking as badly as it. Our flags being about the only thing the rebs could see to shoot at, they used to amuse themselves by <u>peppering</u> away at them nearly the whole time. It is a good thing to have a good reputation you know—and, of course, a <u>bullet-plugged</u> flag goes a great ways. This fair speaks well for the noble North-west. None of <u>her</u> soldiers can complain for want of attention and genuine regard.[35]

Two or three of us boys, wanting to keep ourselves employed part of the time, have purchased a few school books and are <u>brushing up</u> our old studies as well as taking up a few new ones. We have Rhetoric, Arithmetic and Physiology. I am reviving my old study of Rhetoric and find it quite interesting.

*   *   *

Franklin La
December 6th 1863

My dear father

We have most glorious news from Grant tho' as yet nothing official has been received. Our report says that he had met Bragg at or near Lookout mountain and had severely thrashed him, taking over sixty pieces of artillery and some 7.000 prisoners. We have another story that Meade was pushing forward towards Richmond and expected daily to engage the enemy. I hope to have particulars soon. If Grant has whipped Bragg, <u>well</u> I cannot imagine what the rebs will do next unless they <u>go</u> <u>for</u> that <u>Last</u> <u>ditch</u>.[36]

There is a greater feeling of antagonism existing between Eastern and Western troops than many would imagine. I don't think this feeling will ever amount to anything. Wherever we have been, the secesh have been hard on Eastern soldiers and admitted or tried to make us think that we were far superior to them [the Union's Eastern troops]. I think this may explain the cause of the feeling. A sensible man will soon see the policy of the rebs talking as they do. [I] am anxious to know if Henry was in the last fight but suppose he was not.

With a "Merry Christmas" and a "Happy New Year" to all at home.

"This afternoon the boys are amusing themselves throwing hard tack overboard and making the gulls that follow in our wake fight for the pieces. I cannot but think what gulls they are to fight for such thing as hard tack."

Chapter 11

Not Enough *Fight* in This Department

S pending autumn along Bayou Teche had been an enjoyable respite for the Mercantile Battery's men. Their garrison duty at Franklin enabled them to recuperate from eight hazardous months of campaigning, which began with the Chickasaw Bayou disaster and culminated in the Jackson siege with its heat-drenched, dust-filled marches. The Battery Boys appreciated the hospitality of Franklin's residents—who tended to be hostesses rather than hosts, since most of the area's younger men were dead, imprisoned, or serving in the Confederate army. But they were more disillusioned than ever about their assignment to the Department of the Gulf. When they departed New Orleans, the Chicagoans had been filled with hope for a swift, decisive campaign, such as they had grown accustomed to under Grant's leadership. Those hopes began to recede as they moved midway up Bayou Teche, ultimately drying up as the campaign stagnated around New Iberia.

Lieutenant George Throop and 33 men from the battery's center section had been detached to New Iberia in November. They were present when roughly 120 Confederate prisoners were paraded down its

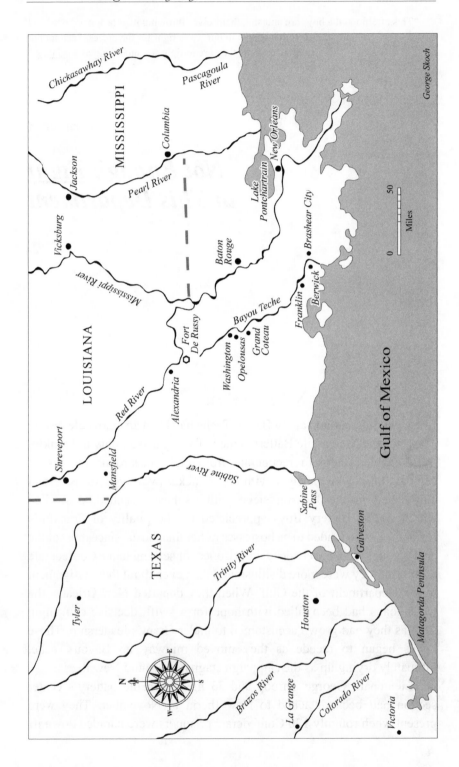

main street, accompanied by blaring Union bands. About 5,000 Federal troops, intent on settling the North's score for the humiliation heaped upon their comrades at the Battle of Carrion Crow, had captured the Rebels on November 20 at Spanish Lake. The Mercantile Battery veterans must have regarded this Department of the Gulf "victory" as paltry compared to the triumphs they had enjoyed under the hard-hitting leadership of Western generals such as Grant, Sherman, and Whiskey Smith.

Instead of advancing from Acadia, Nathaniel Banks, the Battery Boys' new departmental commander, focused his attention on Texas' 600-mile stretch of coastal islands and peninsulas. From the coast he hoped to push inland, perhaps taking Houston or marching up the Rio Grande valley to join with Union forces in New Mexico. To this end, Banks had already occupied Matagorda Island, near where the Mercantile Battery would soon be heading. Although the press was trying to pump up Banks' efforts, he had accomplished little with his attempts to reach the Texas heartland. William Franklin's overland expedition through Louisiana had failed to live up to expectations. Banks' much-trumpeted coastal assault was even less effective, resembling a cannon salute that boomed loudly but fired no shell. Despite Banks' optimism, the Lone Star State remained under enemy control. The Confederates continued to occupy the mainland along with Galveston and Sabine Pass on the northern coast.[1]

As the year drew to a close, the *St. Mary's* carried another contingent of Banks' troops, which included the Battery Boys, into Matagorda Bay. To reach the bay, the ship had to pass over a sandbar and then travel up Pass Cavallo, which linked Matagorda Bay to the Gulf of Mexico. The vessel was full of trusting soldiers who assumed their leaders would not send them to such a God-forsaken wasteland without providing them with the supplies they needed to survive. By this time, Banks himself was ensconced with his family in a New Orleans mansion (from which its secessionist owners had been ousted) enjoying dances, concerts, and receptions with prominent city residents. The festivities were part of an attempt to cultivate good will among the local Unionists. Surrounded by ostentatious luxury, Banks delegated to the quartermasters the responsibility of supplying his Texas-bound soldiers. Meanwhile, at 4:00 p.m. on December 27, the *St. Mary's* lurched across the Pass Cavallo sand bar, which lurked some 7-to-10 feet beneath the surface of the narrow channel, and fought its way into Matagorda Bay.[2]

First Lieutenant Pinckney Cone temporarily commanded the battery while Pat White remained in New Orleans. Chagrined at the bleakness of their new surroundings, the Battery Boys envied their captain's extended stay in the Crescent City. The abundant grass and leaves of the lush Teche country had been replaced by vistas of desolate sand. For most of the Mercantile Battery members, their only previous exposure to a sandy shore had been walking along the narrow strand surrounding Lake Michigan—or in Will Brown's case, a larger beach stretching along the base of the St. Joseph bluff.

In his diary, the usually upbeat Cone summed up the battery's initial response to the Matagorda Peninsula: "Good heavens! What a desolate cheerless sight met my eye. Nothing but a wild waste of sand & sand hills. Not a tree shrub or any green thing. It was the first time I regretted being a Soldier." The lack of trees and meager supply of coastal driftwood hindered the building of shelters and campfires. Keeping those campfires burning also proved to be a difficult task. The soldiers had to drop the few waterlogged chunks of wood they scavenged into sand holes so the wind would not blow out the sputtering flames. On January 5, as Pitts noted in his diary, some squads in the Mercantile Battery ran out of hardtack and had nothing to eat for two days. Pitts stayed in bed as much as possible to avoid the fate of a picket from the 23rd Wisconsin, who froze to death on duty. The Battery Boys' friends in the 77th Illinois were faring no better. After the war, one of the infantrymen recollected, "At night the cold northwesters would howl across the sandy waste, and it was no uncommon thing to see the whole encampment lying prostrate on the sand."[3]

The men in the Mercantile Battery were not the only ones appalled by their situation. Their corps commander, Major General Cadwallader Washburn, vociferously complained to Banks and his staff, telling them his men did not have an adequate supply of food at Matagorda Bay. "We are without a thing to eat except salt meat," wrote Washburn, whose command also suffered from a shortage of subsistence for its horses and mules. In New Orleans, the ineptitude of some of Banks' subordinates only exacerbated the problems at Matagorda Bay. One large steamer, the *Continental*, arrived carrying only a small number of troops. Washburn noted it "could also have brought from 700 to 1,000 tons of forage and

Lt. Pinckney S. Cone

Al and Claudia Niemiec Private Collection

commissary stores." Many of the supply vessels were too heavy to enter Pass Cavallo, and their cargo had to be transferred onto smaller craft. Once inside Matagorda Bay, Washburn reported, the "vessels cannot get near the shore." To address the landing problem, Washburn converted the broken down steamer *Warrior* into a makeshift wharf. Despite this ingenuity, food and other supplies only trickled in, further damaging morale.[4]

For two months, the young men in the Mercantile Battery adapted, as best they could, to living in a region where there was insufficient drinking water and, in the words of one soldier, "Nothing but wind and sand like an Arabian desert." They found scant produce available for purchase at nearby farms. The Federals resorted to confiscating sutler stores, but this desperate act could not compensate for their deplorable lack of food. After New Year's Eve—celebrated with raw pork, hardtack, and stale cheese—the battery's food situation improved somewhat when the hungry artillerists "charged" a flock of sheep near camp. Having gorged himself on mutton, Will Brown commented, "I am almost ashamed to look a sheep in the face." The cannoneers had a secret weapon in "capturing" sheep—their shepherd dog, Doggie Doggett. While encamped on Matagorda Peninsula, they proudly showcased the canine during a grand review. The fun-loving Chicagoans draped a blanket, secured with a red, white, and blue belt, on their mascot and had him walk at the head of a 13th Corps column.[5]

In mid-February, the supply of fresh meat disappeared when the battery's remaining sheep died during a merciless storm that swept across the unprotected peninsula. To alleviate their food shortage, some of the Battery Boys resorted to fishing, or took a wagon 18 miles up the coast to

NARA

Baseball game between Union prisoners at
Salisbury, North Carolina, 1863.

plunder oyster beds. Others searched for shore birds. One of the hunters shot a pelican and gave part of the wings to Will and his friends, who carved "a goodly number of pelican quill tooth-picks." Will also amused himself with a different kind of hunting—he scoured the seashore looking for "curiosities" such as sea horses, coral, and toadfish.[6]

The blueclad soldiers took advantage of the milder weather in mid-January to "play ball." During the Civil War, "base ball" became popular among some soldiers who faced extended periods of time in camp. (When the war's survivors returned home, they continued to play and formed local teams.) Florison Pitts penned multiple diary entries about playing in Texas. So did Cone, who scribbled that after drilling one Saturday his men "Clos[ed] up with a good grand game of base ball." The restless Mercantile Battery soldiers found other ways to keep busy. They attended revival meetings; played euchre and whist; read Shakespeare and Charles Dickens' *David Copperfield*; had a "stag dance;" and started a Mercantile Battery "Sons of Mars" club.[7]

Living like a shipwrecked Robinson Crusoe was bad enough, but Will's frustration grew when he realized his battery, though living under harsh circumstances, was serving no useful military purpose. While Banks' troops remained confined to the Texas coastline, the general's grand plans for an inland drive failed to materialize. Will scoffed at

Nathaniel Banks' inept efforts, especially in comparison to "Gen. Grant's successful campaign against Vicksburg." After six weeks of living among the "vast sand heaps," Will's criticism of Banks grew even more caustic.

During this period of their service, Will Brown and his colleagues got to know Brigadier General Thomas E. G. Ransom, who led the 4th Division of the 13th Corps. Their association with him was one of the few benefits the men of the Mercantile Battery gained during their stint on the Matagorda Peninsula. Ransom led some of the Battery Boys on a reconnaissance mission to Caney Creek en route to Indianola on the Texas mainland. They were excited when Ransom, a fellow Illinoisan whom Will recalled as being in the real estate business, had become one of the youngest and most promising commanders in the Union's Western armies. Grant considered assigning Ransom to command his cavalry, a vacancy that opened after Brigadier General James H. Wilson left to run the Cavalry Bureau in Washington. Although Grant regarded Ransom as "the best man I ever had to send on expeditions," he decided to leave the youthful general in the Trans-Mississippi to take part in Banks' upcoming Red River Campaign. [8]

Meanwhile, Nathaniel Banks and John McClernand remained obsessed with shoring up their military and political standing. In January 1864, they were thrown together. Lincoln and Stanton orchestrated McClernand's transfer to the Department of the Gulf. Banks immediately assigned the exiled general to resume command of the 13th Corps. [9]

McClernand longed to rebuild his reputation, which was so tarnished his political colleagues in Illinois rejected him as the Democratic candidate to replace Governor Richard Yates. Emerging from his obscurity—a horrible curse for someone with McClernand's craving for power and adulation—Lincoln's friend was eager to yank back command of the 13th Corps. But there were senior commanders who were loath to serve under him. Foremost among his detractors was Major General E. O. C. Ord, who had resumed command of the 13th Corps in early January. In a letter to Grant, Ord stated he would rather resign than serve under McClernand, as would Major General Napoleon J. T. Dana and Brigadier Generals Thomas Ransom and Michael Lawler. The protest failed. McClernand was reinstated as the 13th Corps' commander while Ord and Dana were transferred to other duties. Ransom soon left Texas with a detached division and joined up with his newly promoted chief of artillery—the Mercantile Battery's Pat White—in New Orleans, where Banks was preparing to enter Texas via the Red River valley. Of the former ranking Union generals in Texas, only Lawler was left to report to the returning politician-general. McClernand immediately vented his frustrations from the previous summer in another controversial Special Order: "That I was not permitted to share in the consummation of the Mississippi Campaign, by leading you into Vicksburg, is my misfortune rather than my fault. My non-participation in that deplorable event was involuntary and constrained, and is deeply deplored on my part."[10]

While senior officers may have decried the return of McClernand, many of the rank-and-file soldiers, including the Battery Boys, anticipated a renewed infusion of the bravado and aggressive leadership the general demonstrated during the Vicksburg Campaign. The Chicago redlegs were hopeful McClernand would rid his corps of the Eastern formalities that had been imposed since its transfer to the Department of the Gulf.

*   *   *

Algiers La.
December 20th 1863

My dear father

We got here (opposite New Orleans) on Thursday afternoon and are making preparations to leave for Texas. Don't know how soon we will get off but think some time during the week. From all I can learn, we will land at Matagorda Bay and from there move toward the interior. A part of our Corps are already at the bay.

Batteries and cavalry that have landed on the Texas shore have had great difficulty in landing their horses; in several cases losing more than half. The shore is so rough and the surf so troubled that the horses drown in trying to get to shore. Gen. Arnold, Chief of Artillery "Department of the Gulf," gave the Captain particular instructions yesterday in regard to this matter and I hope we will be able to land our horses safely.[11]

It would cheer the hearts of all earnest, true, Union-loving men to witness the embarkation of our troops on board the Gulf steamers. Standing on every conceivable object that will give them a fair view of the shore as the boat moves off, cheer after cheer loudly speaks how they feel and how glad they are to push forward wherever they are needed. Every American may be proud of his army and every

Western man cannot but speak with pride of our Western boys, in particular Western man <u>Grant</u>. I have all confidence in Grant and think he will yet bring the war to a close; that is, I think he will be the main instrument in closing it.

From our army in Texas, we have good news. Gen. Washburn of our Corps is moving forward and, as he passes thro' the country, finds a strong Union sentiment prevailing. I heard yesterday that a large shipment of muskets had been made to Texas to arm the Unionists there. These Union Texans are hot for revenge and will do all they can to assist our forces. The state of Texas is full of cotton, sugar and livestock and negroes; and I presume we will have plenty of all kinds of provisions to subsist on.[12]

*   *   *

On board Steamer "St Mary's"
New Orleans
December 26th 1863

My dear father

We are loaded on board transports and expect to leave for Texas to-night. The weather bids fair and I anticipate a pleasant journey. Our destination is Pass Cavallo on Matagorda Bay and, on reaching there, we expect to go in camp for the present. Nearly all our Corps is there at present.[13]

It has been considerable trouble to load our Battery as everything had to taken to pieces and lowered in the hold. Our steamer is a fine one; she is one of the New York and N.O. line of ocean packets. Yesterday—Christmas—passed off very quickly with us. I spent part of the day and evening in the city.

*   *   *

Pass Cavallo Texas
January 3d 1864

Dear father

I addressed you a short letter a few moments before our steamer left her wharf at New Orleans and trust the letter reached you in due time. We arrived here on the evening of December 30th all right. As an account of our trip may be interesting to you, I give the jottings down in my journal commencing from the day we left New Orleans:

Dec 26th All on board. Boat left her docks at noon and as I write we are rapidly steaming down the river toward the "delta." Am glad to be off. Could not get all of our horses on board so left about twenty head that will probably be sent forward by first boat. About dark was somewhat startled by the booming of the cannon across the water and on going on deck found we were approaching Forts Jackson and St. Philip. But owing to the increasing darkness could not get sight of either fort. Stopped boat only long enough to report. Noticed several signal rockets as we passed below the forts. The country on both sides of the river is well settled and has many fine plantations under a high state of cultivation. I [am] informed that they are all under government control at present. Owing to a heavy fog we will not run out to the Gulf 'till morning.[14]

Dec 27th Raining. Up early as I am anxious to view the surroundings as we pass out toward the Gulf. Steaming ahead at day light. Reaching the forks we take the one called "South-west Pass." Below the forks the aspect of the country changes entirely and now nothing is seen but a low marshy treeless country filled with bayous and lagunes. At noon are opposite Pilot-town, a small place consisting of a hotel for pilots and of course several rum-shops (I have not seen a town in the South yet that had more rum-shops than anything else) and now only have to pass over the bar when we will be fairly on the Gulf.

2 PM: In blue water and land rapidly disappearing from view. Sea running pretty high and the sickly pallor overspreading the countenances of many of our boys speaks louder than words of what is soon to follow. Now the fun—to me for as yet my digestive organs remain undisturbed—commences in earnest. Led off by "Doggett," our Battery dog, the uprising commences and a sicker crowd I never witnessed. Every available point where a man can get his head over the steamers side is engaged. And loud are the curses and deep the uprisings. I am standing on the wheel-house and laughing 'till my sides fairly ache. The worst part of it is the boys have only the deck to sleep on and at present the hold of the vessel is the only place they can go to lie down. Nearly every officer on board—Gen. Herron and staff are among the number—is sick and pitching up everything. I pity our horses as they are literally packed in and the rocking of the ship trembles them about greatly. Looking out on the water I notice several "Monsters of the deep" exhibiting themselves to our astonished western fresh-water visions. One of the sea-men informs me that most of the fish I see are "Porpoises" and "Dog-fish." Thro' kindness of Capt. White I have state-room and will therefore be quite comfortable.[15]

Dec 28th Clear and fine. "Water, water, everywhere." No land in sight. Sea more calm and as the boat moves gently along our boys venture about more freely, but such a lot of pale visages and so many earnest appeals to "Old Ocean" to keep quiet cannot but make one smile. I cannot imagine how often during the day I have been asked: "Have you been sea-sick?" This afternoon the boys are amusing themselves throwing hard tack overboard and making the gulls that follow in our wake fight for the pieces. I cannot but think what <u>gulls</u> they are to fight for such thing as <u>hard tack</u>.

<u>Dec 29th</u> Rainy. Last night was a beautiful one. Sea smooth as glass. At day light land in sight on our "Starboard bow." About noon noticed a blockading squadron and suppose it to be one stationed off Galveston. Steamed down the coast 'till 3 PM when we arrived off our landing point. From our steamer the land looks bleak and barren and were it not for the tents that line the shore everything would look desolate indeed. After waiting a half hour for a pilot to come aboard we steamed inward and in a few moments were safely over the bar on Matagorda Bay. Arrived at the pier (a very poor apology for one) about dark and commenced debarking immediately.[16]

So much for our trip. We are camped on a peninsula some sixty miles long and only two [miles] in width. Everything is <u>sand</u>—no trees, no shrubs—not even tuft of grass. Since we have been here, have not seen the sun but very little; tho' to-day it is doing very well and we are blessed with an occasional sunbeam. Have nothing but driftwood and have to go for five to seven miles for that. For fresh meat, we have any quantity of mutton and I have already eaten so much that I am almost ashamed to look a sheep in the face. The shore is lined with beautiful shells and I wish I could send a lot of them home.

In my next, will try to give you a more extended account of the country, our prospects, movements etc. etc. Love to all. Remember me to all friends.[17]

*   *   *

January 10th 1864

My dear father

As yet, nothing has transpired to give me an idea of our future destination. I think we will move toward the interior <u>one of these days</u> but have no idea how soon. Part of our forces are at Port Lavacca, a point some distance up the bay. I think from what I have seen thus far that nearly all movements are simply made as <u>feelers</u>. In army movements, however, there is always great chance for speculation. One is fully as apt to be wrong as right.[18]

There is said to be a larger force at Houston where the rebels have large supplies and direct rail way communication with Galveston. I have found many [who] express the opinion that, if we could take Houston, Galveston would fall by its own weight. I place little confidence in this opinion. All thro' the war, we have read of places falling in this way but, with the exception of Columbus Ky. and a few places on the Mississippi river, there has been nothing of this kind [that has] transpired. I hope that there is a strong Union feeling in the state and am inclined to think there is something of a feeling of this kind. Many Southern negro owners have brought their <u>stock</u> to this state thinking it a safe one from Federal encroachments. And now that we are here, if they find it will <u>pay</u> to be good Unionists, I have little doubt but what they will become. Many of the people of the South cannot but see the utter hopelessness of their cause and I imagine that many of them would [be] willing come back if they could.[19]

What is your opinion of the President's proclamation with his message? Do you think it will make many converts? I question if the time has yet come to offer any terms. We are doing well enough and can stand out as long as we wish, or longer if necessary. If all accounts are true, everything at home is in a flourishing condition and means are readily offered to supply our armies with men. The larger bounties now offered are enough to make most any man feel <u>patriotic</u>. Many men can do much better in the army than out of it; but still the chances for <u>living</u> at home are better and I presume have considerable influence.[20]

From our Lieut. Roe, who is in Chicago on recruiting service, we have encouraging news. On Dec. 20th he had fifteen recruits and good chances for more. We only need about thirty men and I think we will get them.[21]

*   *   *

Pass Cavallo Texas
January 17th 1864

My dear father

After all, it is not so very bad here when the weather is fine. [It is] true that sand is decidedly in the majority, but then we have a fine sea-shore to ramble on, pick up curiosities &c &c. It is quite interesting to walk along the beach, as it is covered with a great variety of shells, insects fish &c &c. I saw <u>something</u> the other day that had on it a perfect horse head in miniature. I wish it were possible to send some of these curiosities home—as they would, I have no doubt, be quite interesting to you—as well as an ornament for the centre table.

About eighteen miles up Matagorda Bay, there is an oyster bed but the distance is too great to attempt getting any of them. Beside [the distance], we have no apparatus for hauling the bivalves from their sandy bed. The other day one of our boys shot a pelican and brought him into camp. Some of us appropriated his wings for our own personal use and I now am possessed of a goodly number of pelican quill tooth-picks. The toad fish is another curiosity found the other day. The fish is about six inches long by four inches wide and his back is covered with warts.

There seems to be "Something rotten in Denmark" in our Corps. First, Gen. Ord takes command, issues a lot of orders in which he says this and that must be done. Then we move out on the Teche and Gen. Ord is taken sick, goes up the river and Gen. C. C. Washburn takes his place. Washburn, being a Western man, does very well and is well liked by all. He keeps command 'till the Corps is safely landed in Texas, when round comes Gen. N. J. T. Dana, a Potomac officer who succeeds Washburn—and of course issues more orders. But the play is not yet finished. For now it turns out that Gen. Ord assumes command and orders Head Quarters to New Orleans.[22]

So the play goes on. Surely we poor private soldiers are not the only sufferers of humanity that exist. Gen. Dana says in his last order "I propose to have my men fight on foot and not on wheels" but no sooner does this order come out than comes one from Gen. Ord saying "I command the 13th Corps and hereby order Head Quarters to New Orleans." Of all places for jealousies and red tape, the army caps the climax. When generals fail to agree, what cannot they expect of privates. So wags the world. But yesterday and McClellan was our demi-God; to-day he but an individual and by many looked on as mere demagogue.[23]

What is your opinion in regard to the coming presidential campaign? Will Lincoln again be nominated or are there other men who have a better show? Many people in the South have the wildest ideas in regard to Abe. They think he rules the North with an absolute despotism and that, when the time comes for the next presidential election arrives, he will issue a proclamation declaring it a necessity for him to remain in the presidential chair and that the people will have to submit. As ridiculous as this may appear to you, I have had it advanced several times and by men who pretended to be well educated. Many men in the South have great hopes that we will yet involve ourselves in a war with France and in this way have to recognize the C.S.A. The Southern press is continually starting some new theory or hope and many of the people placing implicit confidence in everything and all that is published are led astray.[24]

*   *   *

Pass Cavallo Texas
January 24th 1864

My dear father

On Wednesday, one gun of our Battery with twenty of our boys accompanied by the 1st Brigade of our Division—the whole [reconnaissance being] under command of Gen. Ransom—started up the peninsula to see the position of the enemy up toward the interior. The expedition has just returned and brings the news that a rebel force, variously estimated from six to ten thousand, is fortifying at the upper end of the peninsula and watching us from that point. From our present position, and my own idea in regard to the lay of the country near the upper end of the peninsula, I think the rebs will have to wait some time before we attack them in their present position.[25]

I am told that Gen. Ransom returns well satisfied with what he has seen. He praises our boys highly for their conduct during the scout. He tried to catch them doing something out of the way but did not succeed. One night, when several of our boys were out as advance picket, the General disguising himself rode out to see how faithfully his sentinels were doing their duty. At one post, he found an officer asleep and at once ordered him under arrest. After riding round and visiting several posts, he finally approached five of our boys who, seeing him incoming toward them, immediately deployed as skirmishers. Closer comes the General when out speaks Dick Powell, a young fellow about my age "Halt there." "All right," says the General. "Advance and give the counter sign," says Dick. "I am the General," says Ransom. "General be d____d. I'm on guard here and want the counter sign instantly or I'll shoot." And with this Dick cocks his musket. "Matagorda," speaks the General very quickly. "All right sir advance." The General then comes forward, asks Dick's name, tells him he is a good soldier and leaves. Next morning, that picket post receives a demi-john of whiskey with the General's compliments.

By the way, I think you may have seen the General. He [T. E. G. Ransom] was formerly connected with A. J. Galloway in the land-agent business. He is a young man, rather good looking, pleasant face and full of good humor. He is acquainted with several of our boys. Came into the army as adjutant of the 11th Ill. and has steadily advanced ever since. He is a univeral favorite among both officers and soldiers.

There seems to be a lack of interesting news at present. I suppose the holidays account for this as much as anything. From late home papers, I see that you are completely snowed in and are having very cold weather. Twenty to thirty degrees below zero be cold. Here we find it uncomfortable with our jackets on during the day. I presume there are many men in the North who would prefer freezing to death rather than to go [to a warm climate] for [duty as] a soldier. I cannot see why so many men are afraid of serving their country. It often makes me smile when I read in the papers how old So and so, who has several sons at home who would make good soldiers, has so very generously contributed $500 or even $1.000 for bounties for volunteers. After all father, riches are not the only blessings a man can enjoy. I am amused at some of the letters received by Charley Olcott from his father. Mr. O is sound on many subjects. In a letter not long since, he says "Every day I see a lot of little squirts running around town dressed to kill who would be much better off in the army and I hope they may yet be drafted."[26]

*   *   *

Pass Cavallo Texas
January 31st 1864

My dear father

Yours of Jan. 7th enclosing Henry's letter reached me on the 29th and was gladly received. I was very much pleased to hear from Henry. Last evening, I sat down and wrote him a good long letter one evening, six pages with a foolscap. He is evidently uneasy and not so well satisfied as I wish he might be. A man requires considerable Philosophy to be satisfied in the army. Even if his position is an easy one, and when is placed in a place like that which Henry occupies, he must exercise great patience and keep in the best of spirits.[27]

We are ordered to Indianola, a point on the opposite side of the bay and about forty miles distant from here. The 2d Division of our Corps is there. I am informed that most of our Division will be ordered there soon. Indianola is said to be a fine place and very healthy; much better for camping grounds than here. I do not anticipate a forward movement very soon. The policy seems to be to occupy the important points along the coast at present and then I would not be surprised if we concentrated at some given point in the interior.

As yet, I am unable to understand the movements at New Orleans. The impression prevails here that Mobile is to be attacked.

But it may be the policy to start such an impression and then suddenly pounce upon some place where we are the least expected. "Strategy my boy" prevails in this as well as the "Department of the Potomac."[28]

*   *   *

Pass Cavallo Texas
February 7th 1864

My father

When I wrote you last, I thought my next would be from Indianola. But the day after I wrote, our orders to move to that place were countermanded. We have also changed camp during the week and from this I do not think we will move very soon.

Yesterday, Gen. Ord arrived here from New Orleans and went thro' a very minute inspection of our Division. He complimented the appearance of our Battery very highly. Told the Captain that when he returned to New Orleans he intended to send out a lot of fishing nets and garden seed. Whether he will do so remains to be seen. If he does I think we will stay here for some time.

During the week, a rebel lieutenant, sergeant and one man have come into our lines from the rebel force at the other end of the peninsula. They say that whole companies will desert as soon as the opportunity offers. This lieutenant says that as soon as Lincoln's proclamation becomes known in this part of the Confederacy nearly all will stop fighting. He had not heard of the proclamation 'till he reached our lines and says that it is not known among soldiers. He expresses himself tired of the war and thinks that it will end soon. Of course, he tells a very plausible story as it is his policy to do so, but I have no great faith in these stories told by deserters.

Proclamation may do good and perhaps save the country, but I have much more faith in the power of powder and ball and a vigorous prosecution of the war. I think the integrity and valor of our troops, who so gallantly re-enlisting for three years longer, will do more toward ending the rebellion than all the proclamations issued or to be issued. If there is anything that should make our beautiful stay-at-homes and home guards bury their heads, it must be the noble manner in which nearly all of our troops are re-enlisting for the war. The patriotism among these veterans seems to be great as when they first joined the army. It is true that government pays large bounties, but government can better afford to do so than to recruit and equip new troops for the field. It takes a year to make a soldier and now Uncle Sam has his soldiers already made. So in this Department, nearly all the troops that can do so are re-enlisting and by the newspapers I see they are doing the same in all the departments.[29]

*   *   *

Pass Cavallo Texas
February 14th 1864

My dear father

Of war news and reports incident to the coming Spring campaign we have a goodly number. We have it that Grant is soon to, or has by this time, move forward; that the 15th Corps under the general order of Sherman is moving toward the Pearl river in Mississippi intending to cross it near Jackson and from there turn Hardee's right wing; that one or two other corps under the immediate command of Sherman are to move down the Mississippi to or near New Orleans and from there move across the country and make a demonstration against Mobile.[30]

All this looks quite plausible on paper but I question the veracity of it. I think . . . Sherman will soon be on the move . . . I form my opinion from a letter recently received by Captain White from Col. Ezra Taylor, Chief of Art'y on Sherman's staff. The Colonel writes from St. Louis. He says "General Sherman will soon make a big move, you will probably hear more of it soon." Grant has great confidence in Sherman and keeps him for his right hand man. We will see what we will see.[31]

I think I wrote you in a former letter that Gen. McClernand had resigned. I read such a story in a Springfield paper but it has

Major General
John A. McClernand

proved false as the General is now at New Orleans and, it is said, will soon take command of our Corps—his old one. I hope he will as no one ever looked more to our interests. And another thing, I prefer a Western man over all others. He may have blundered at Vicksburg but as yet there are two sides to the story and we cannot judge. One thing is certain, Mc- Clernand was always a favorite with the Corps and his probable return is hailed with pleasure by both officers and men.[32]

I recd a letter from Jack Vernon of Taylor's Chicago Battery the other day. He was with Sherman on his march from Memphis to Knoxville and a rough time he had, much worse than anything we have ever experienced. For several days, they lived on parched corn only and their horses would drop down in the road from starvation. It took them sixteen hours to march from Chattanooga to the river, a distance of fourteen miles. And while on this march, five out of six horses on Jack's caisson dropped dead. We have been down to a piece of cornbread and <u>sow belly</u> (i.e. bacon) but this only for a day or so, and we soon forgot it. But when it comes to parched corn, I think we will remember without having to refer to our diary's.[33]

*   *   *

Pass Cavallo Texas
February 20th 1864

My dear father

Yours of 31st Ult. reached me on the 18th. . . . I was . . . much pleased with the few <u>concluding remarks</u> by Maria and hope she will do the same thing often. Please assure her that her fears in regard to treating my good friend Mrs. Bigelow with indifference are entirely groundless as I have written that lady as regularly as usual —and will never forget her many many kindnesses to me. Katie has been like an older sister to me and I think of her as such.[34]

But for all this, garrison life at best is rather monotonous. Besides I cannot see we will do much there toward finishing the war. The fact is I think there is too much policy and not enough <u>fight</u> in this Department. Take our "Grand and overwhelming Texas campaign" for instance. We have "Occupied the coast" it is true, but the occupation was no more a difficulty than it would be to occupy Calumet at the present time.

I see Northern papers filled with the accounts of Gen. Banks glorious success in Texas but thus far I have failed to see it. The case is something like this: We will suppose the state of Michigan held by a large rebel force. We . . . concentrate a big force at Chicago, charter ships at big rates and cross part of the force over to St. Joseph, [from] which place the rebs leave as soon as our ships arrive in sight. From St. Jo., the force moves up the river and without any resistance on the part of the enemy occupy Niles. The balance of the force at St. Joseph move up the coast to Grand Rapids and several minor points along the Lake. The rebs leave as we advance. We now hold the entire coast with the exception of New Buffalo and here the rebs have strong works and a stronger position. After capturing these vast sand heaps all along the coast with the exception of the great point, we all at once receive orders to return to Chicago. Call Niles, Brownsville; New Buffalo, Galveston; and this place Grand Rapids and you have a fair idea of our great success in Texas.

It may be wrong for me to look at this matter as I do, and my opinion on this subject may be far from the correct one, but when I see so many brilliant newspaper accounts of this expedition I cannot but think "Something is rotten in Denmark." You know it is a soldier's privilege to grumble and you see I take advantage of it. Perhaps I am too anxious for our success. Sudden movements may not be the best plan for success. Yet Gen. Grant's successful campaign against Vicksburg was all a most glorious dash and how well he succeeded. Grant's strategy has . . . been successful. He did not move against Vicksburg 'till he was ready to go and when he started, no matter what the obstacles, he went all over. . . .[35]

I hardly know what to say on the subject of Lib's re-enlisting. I did not think he would do so, at least as a private soldier. I fully appreciate his feelings in regard to being exchanged into another regiment. I know that he has enough good sense to consider the step he has taken and with this I am . . . satisfied. From what he told me when I saw him at Vicksburg, and from the tone of his letters, I imagine he likes a soldier's life very well. And there is nothing like being satisfied with your fortune. If I thought the war would last three years longer I would be rather sorry he had re-enlisted. But I am strong in the hope that the war will end in the course of a year.[36]

*   *   *

Will Brown and his Mercantile Battery comrades survived their brief but harsh stint along the desolate Texas coast. They hoped to return to New Orleans for some rest and relaxation. Unfortunately, Banks' quest for glory and a possible run against Lincoln for the Republican presidential nomination would instead propel the Battery Boys into a campaign loaded with traumatic and gut-wrenching experiences. The hardships awaiting them along the Red River in Louisiana were going to make the trials of Grant's Vicksburg Campaign seem almost benign.

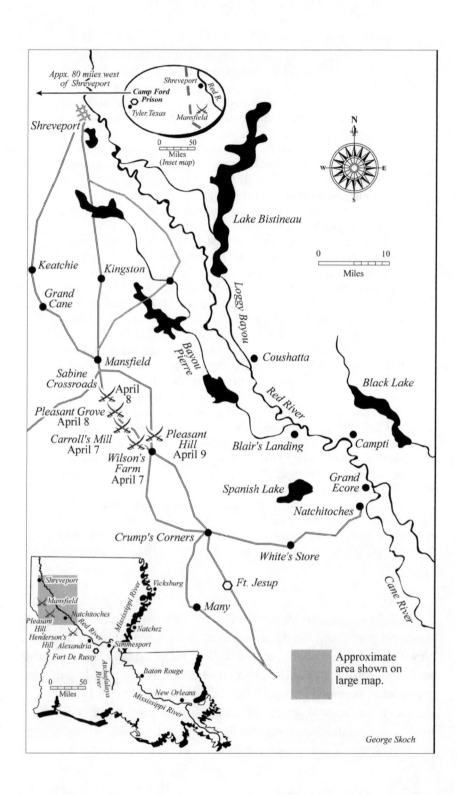

Appx. 80 miles west
of Shreveport

Shreveport

Camp Ford Prison

Tyler, Texas

Mansfield

Red R.

0   50
Miles
(Inset map)

Lake Bistineau

Loggy Bayou

N
W   E
S

0   10
Miles

Keatchie

Kingston

Grand Cane

Bayou Pierre

Coushatta

Black Lake

Mansfield

Red River

Sabine Crossroads

April 8

Pleasant Grove
April 8

Carroll's Mill
April 7

Pleasant Hill
April 9

Blair's Landing

Campti

Wilson's Farm
April 7

Grand Ecore

Spanish Lake

Natchitoches

Crump's Corners

White's Store

Cane River

Shreveport

Vicksburg

Ft. Jesup

Mansfield

Mississippi River

Natchitoches

Red River

Many

Pleasant Hill

Henderson's Hill

Natchez

Alexandria

Simmesport

Fort De Russy

Atchafalaya River

Baton Rouge

0   50
Miles

New Orleans

Mississippi River

Approximate
area shown on
large map.

George Skoch

"For if the N.O. papers can be relied on, Gen. Banks is not only the greatest general of ancient or modern times, but is also the greatest that ever will be. I think that the presidency <u>ails</u> Banks as much as anything. The desire is a peculiar one and troubles nearly all ambitious men."

Chapter 12

General Banks Commands the Expedition

As they sailed away from Matagorda Peninsula in the *Clinton*, the Battery Boys looked forward to being back in civilization. Instead of heading toward New Orleans, their ship steamed up Atchafalaya Bayou. Disappointed, the young Chicagoans thought about their previous trips to the Crescent City and regretted not being able to revisit its markets, restaurants, theaters, saloons, and landmarks. Late in the afternoon of February 27, 1864, the mood of the Mercantile Battery soldiers brightened as they spotted a lighthouse, built on piles of rock sunk into the sandbar guarding the entrance into Berwick Bay. If the soldiers were unable to return to festive New Orleans, they would gladly settle again for Longfellow's "Garden of Eden."[1]

As the *Clinton* pushed forward to Berwick Bay, the eager redlegs listened to the water splash off the churning paddle wheel. Without warning the wooden boat shuddered violently as it hit a sandbar, the blow nearly knocking Will Brown and his friends off their feet. The boat's engine kept pounding, belching out thick black smoke, but the steamer could not clear the sandbar blocking the bay's entrance. The pilot's cursing reminded some of the Mercantile Battery bystanders of their favorite general, Whiskey Smith, though the pilot's vocabulary of profanities was more limited. Once the vessel had been backed up, the pilot yanked the wheel and turned his ship around in a tight arc. With a full head of steam, the *Clinton* charged the sandbar only to groan to another grinding halt. Defeated, the pilot backed the steamer up again and ordered his crew to drop anchor.[2]

The Battery Boys grumbled about the delay. With the sun setting, and the light too scant for reading or card playing, Will joined his frowning comrades in turning in for the night. Some went to their crowded upper staterooms. The less fortunate went below deck, gagging from the putrid air—its foulness worsened by the horses and mules confined within the vessel. Despite the fetid atmosphere, these soldiers were nonetheless thankful the sea was calm. The lure of a cool night breeze led some of the troops, like Florison Pitts, to improvise their sleeping arrangements on deck. The night before, as Pitts noted in his diary, he had "Slept on a coil of rope [and] never rested better in my life."[3]

Early the next morning the *Clinton* weighed anchor and steamed over the sandbar into the bay. With a dull thud of wood against wood, the ship jerked to a stop in front of Berwick City. The men from the Mercantile Battery hurried to reach the dock, happy to once again be on Louisiana soil. They were thrilled to have escaped the barren Matagorda Peninsula. Moving to their new camp, the men were mesmerized by the white and pink blossoms bursting like fireworks from the early-blooming peach and cherry trees.[4]

The Battery Boys were also glad to see sutlers again, peddling their goods from New Orleans. Although they charged outrageous prices, the avaricious storekeepers at least provided a soldier's necessities—including items like butter, apples, soap, candles, paper, and ink. Up until their experience on Matagorda Peninsula, the Chicago artillerists had taken such commodities for granted. During that February 28 evening, Lieutenant Henry Roe arrived from Chicago with new recruits and packages from family and friends. After the hardships and near starvation they suffered in Texas, the veteran artillerists were ecstatic. In addition to the sutlers' goods, they had special treats to savor from home! When Will tried to write to his father the next day, he was so exhilarated he had to cut the letter short, commenting, "The whole Corps is in such a whirl of excitement over our recent arrivals from home." In addition to enjoying their replenished camp fare, the rejuvenated soldiers from the Mercantile Battery relaxed and played baseball. On March 4, Lieutenant Pinckney Cone recorded he was "engaged in a fascinating game of ball nearly all day. Head Qrs playing against the left section [and] defeating them."[5]

Will hoped John McClernand would lead the anticipated campaign up the Red River. But he discovered Nathaniel Banks planned to take personal command. He wondered what McClernand would do on the Texas coast, where sand dunes far outnumbered Union soldiers and opportunities for distinction. Will rightly surmised a desire for "the presidency ails Banks as much as anything." By relegating his former Congressional colleague, McClernand, to a backwater command, Banks may have been looking to ensure that a victorious Red River Campaign would boost only *his* own political capital. Just as he had done during the fall Bayou Teche expedition, Banks assigned responsibility for the tough overland march to Major General Franklin, a professional soldier who had no plans of running for office. McClernand was left behind in Texas, his consolation prize being the opportunity to dabble in international politics and continue his relentless pursuit of an independent command.[6]

Before rendezvousing with Franklin at Alexandria, Nathaniel Banks had to attend to some political business. First, he needed to fulfill Lincoln's request to establish a reconstructed government in Louisiana— and add more potential votes for the Republicans in the upcoming presidential election. As military governor, Banks was maneuvering to make certain his candidate, Michael Hahn, won the election as the first governor of the Free State of Louisiana.

General Sherman arrived on March 2 to discuss the Red River Campaign. Three objectives were on the table. The first was to meet and destroy Major General Richard Taylor's Confederate army, which the Union high command expected would do everything possible to disrupt Banks' march through Louisiana. Once Taylor was removed from the picture, Washington expected Banks to occupy East Texas. For its third objective, the Union army was to round up all the cotton it could find, confiscating the valuable commodity for Northern use. After their conference, Banks entreated Sherman to remain in New Orleans and take part in the March 4 inauguration festivities. Banks, recalled Sherman, "explained [the entertainments] would include the performance of the 'Anvil Chorus' by all the bands of his army and during the performance, church-bells were to be rung, and cannons were to be fired by electricity." With his distaste for politicians no doubt rising like a case of stinging indigestion, Sherman declined Banks' offer. There was also talk of Sherman accompanying Banks on the expedition. Banks, however, was senior to Sherman, and Grant's friend was not about to serve under the Massachusetts politician (perhaps finding the idea too reminiscent of his service under McClernand). After agreeing to loan Banks some of his troops, Sherman left New Orleans.[7]

Banks moved forward with his grand inaugural ceremony for Hahn, complete with floats, banners, fireworks and the melodies of some 300 musicians. On the speaker's platform—behind which was draped a banner honoring "Major General Banks, The Noble Citizen and the Dutiful Soldier"—the Gulf commander delivered the keynote address to a crowd of 20,000 people. Banks also took time to meet with Richard Yates, governor of Illinois, who had brought along some of his business acquaintances. Much of the time spent during these meetings with the Illinois delegation included discussions about how to capitalize on the Civil War's version of the California Gold Rush, i.e., the cotton trade. Northern brokers agonized over the severe shortage of cotton. The inflated profit margins on Red River cotton sales hovered between 300 percent to 600 percent—a phenomenal return on the traders' capital investment and an expedient solution for underutilized New England factories. In exchange for Banks' help in procuring cotton during his upcoming military campaign, the businessmen allegedly agreed to use some of their proceeds to help the general supplant Lincoln as the Republican Party's presidential nominee.[8]

After achieving his immediate political goals in New Orleans, Banks boarded the steamer *Black Hawk*, which was bound for Alexandria. Suspiciously, a large group of cotton speculators accompanied him aboard. The industrious businessmen were prepared for the journey that included some journalists who each paid $2,500 for an expedition pass. Business passengers with special permits to buy cotton had brought along a large quantity of accoutrements—bags and ropes, not military materiel—to package and ship their loot. Those speculators who did not obtain permits intended to tag cotton and pick up their precious bales later in New Orleans from a ring of illicit traders operating in Banks'

Department of the Gulf. Much of the cotton that was going to be procured in the Red River area was slated to rekindle the declining New England textile industry, the same industry that had helped launch and sustain Nathaniel Banks' political career.[9]

The Mercantile Battery was part of Ransom's 13th Corps detachment, which accompanied two divisions of the 19th Corps and Brigadier General Albert Lee's cavalry division through the Acadian bayous. Before the artillery company left Berwick City to join the troops at the Franklin staging area, Will Brown announced to his father that effective March 1, he had finally been promoted to quartermaster sergeant.

As they set out from Franklin on March 16, Chicago's Battery Boys were excited to see the sugar plantations again, or at least what was left of them after the Unionists' earlier marches through the area. In contrast to previous campaigns in the region, Federal generals ordered their soldiers to refrain from foraging and pillaging—Banks did not want to alienate the Acadian farmers who might, in turn, hinder his pre-planned transactions with Red River cotton planters. Ignoring their commanders' orders, Union troops took what they wanted from the local civilians and occasionally put their homes to the torch. Rising pillars of dirty gray smoke could be seen mixing with clouds of dust in the wake of Banks' advancing columns. Ahead, the lush bayous turned into vast rolling prairies that gave way to well-tended cotton fields. The soldiers, meanwhile, marched on. They passed through Alexandria on March 26 and camped four miles beyond the town.[10]

Perched on a bank high above the Red River, Alexandria was one of Louisiana's major cities. It was also a strategic target for Banks and his trading companions. If all went well, the miles of cotton fields surrounding the city would soon provide fuel for New England's factories and help oil Banks' political machine. The Union's army and naval forces were to converge at Alexandria and from there undertake a joint movement against Shreveport, where Confederate General Edmund Kirby Smith's Trans-Mississippi Department headquarters and the profit-generating Cotton Bureau were located. Once Shreveport was reached, the passageway was open into East Texas. After capturing Fort De Russy on their way up Red River, Rear Admiral David Dixon Porter and Brigadier General A. J. Smith arrived in time for their planned March 17 rendezvous. When Banks and the rest of the Union army failed to

Porter's fleet outside of Alexandria.

appear on schedule, however, Porter occupied his time rounding up cotton. He authorized his tars to confiscate the white commodity, and the eager sailors promptly broke into Alexandria's bulging warehouses where the Confederate government's 1863 cotton "taxes" (or produce tithes) were housed. Southern civilians had only recently paid their taxes to meet a March 1 deadline.[11]

In the aftermath of the failed Red River Campaign, Congress investigated the matter. Porter denied that his men had illegally confiscated cotton from plantations. Witnesses testified otherwise. They claimed some of the admiral's men, after emptying the enemy's governmental warehouses, took wagons from the townspeople and went several miles outside the city to plunder civilian-owned cotton. Complaints from the plantation owners were well justified. At the beginning of the year, the Federal Treasury Department had established a policy for its agents to buy produce from any Southerner who had taken the Union oath of allegiance. The planter would receive 25 percent of his produce's value along with a receipt for the balance, which was to be paid after the war, provided the seller remained loyal to the United States. Among other accusations, it was claimed Porter's seamen branded the logo "C.SA." on civilian cotton bales and then added their service's "U.S.N." imprimatur, thus falsely qualifying their spoil as a navy prize.[12]

By the time Banks belatedly arrived on March 24, bringing with him his boatload of speculators, Porter's sailors had already depleted much of the cotton in and around Alexandria. The confiscated cotton was bound for the navy's Western headquarters at Cairo, Illinois, not to New Orleans where it was supposed to benefit Banks. The civilian cotton traders were livid. They had risked their lives to enter enemy territory either to purchase their own cotton or to hand select bales to pick up later in New Orleans. Porter, however, had larger concerns than cotton on his mind: the admiral had to get his fleet up the Red River and, for the first spring since 1855, the winding stream was not rising.[13]

Porter's conversion of private cotton into government property had a serious, unintended consequence. Frantic plantation owners decided to hide their cotton rather than allow the Unionists to seize it. Worse yet, the confiscations enraged Richard Taylor, and the Confederate general had the power to retaliate. Taylor had been willing to ignore Red River planters who sold their personal supplies of cotton to Federal Treasury agents in compliance with the new remuneration policy. Taylor, however, would not countenance the taking of civilian cotton, which prevented farmers from using it to generate income for their suffering families. He responded to this Northern injustice by ordering the burning of thousands of bales. As one Texan wrote to his mother in a March 6 letter, many of the Southern soldiers were eager to carry out Taylor's orders and destroy the "brisk [cotton] trade carried on from this front with the feds . . . which is causing considerable dissatisfaction in the army. The men say they do not believe in fighting and trading with our enemies at the same time and that they derive no benefit from it and think the trade is carried on for the benefit of high officials . . . it has almost produced a mutiny in some regiments."[14]

*   *   *

Berwick La.
February 29th 1864

My dear father

I think the scene of our future operations will be in the Red river country, tho' I have no definite idea of the particular points to be operated against. The Red river country is of large extent and probably the richest west of the Mississippi river. From all accounts that I hear, there are immense stores of cotton and sugar there and, if we can only bring it out, it will of course be the source of a large revenue for our government. I am told that Gen. McClernand will command the expedition. If he does, and we only have a pretty force of cavalry, we will go thro' the country at a rate that will astonish that part of the so-called Confederacy.[15]

We have cheering news from Sherman. He treads the war-path with an iron foot and, if accounts are true, has already thrown the enemy into confusion. I hope to hear more particulars soon.[16]

Last night, just after we had got well fixed in camp, we were surprised and made glad by welcoming our Lieut. Roe with 32 recruits from Chicago. The Lieut. brought us a lot of packages from friends at home. I received a blouse and camel [?] journal that I wrote for some time ago.[17]

I may go to New Orleans in a few days as we are in want of horses and, at present, it is part of my business to drawing them. If I do go, I intend having some pictures taken and will send one home.

*   *   *

Berwick La
March 13th 1864

My dear father

Gen. Banks commands the expedition and is now at the front. I thought Gen. McClernand would be in command but he has gone to Texas and, I understand, intends staying there for the present—tho' I cannot see what he will do there at the present, as there [are] but few of our troops left in that state. And those few have two Maj. Gen.'s over them already.

I see by the papers that Senator Grimes of Iowa comes out pretty roughly on Banks and mentions his great success in Texas as a "Ridiculous Raid." Either Senator Grimes has failed to read the New Orleans newspapers or, if he has done so, he certainly cannot be influenced by newspaper gabble. For if the N.O. papers can be relied on, Gen. Banks is not only the greatest general of ancient or modern times, but is also the greatest that ever will be. I think that the presidency ails Banks as much as anything. The desire is a peculiar one and troubles nearly all ambitious men.[18]

I suppose that Lib has been with you and enjoyed his visit. I wish he could get something higher than his present position. I see by the paper that Lieut. King and Miss Abbott have been recently married. I suppose people will marry anyhow, war or no war. My compliments to the bride and bridegroom.[19]

I received the appointment of Quartermaster Sergeant of the Battery . . . to [date] . . . from March 1st. I have been acting in this capacity for some time and think I am fully competent to hold it. It places me as second on the list of non-commissioned officers and is quite a jump from my former position. I mess with our officers and therefore have very good fare. All in all, the position is nearly equal to that of a commissioned officer only I don't get nearly so much pay as one. My pay will be $17 per month. My duties are to draw all forage, wood, stationary, clothing, camp and garrison equipage, ordnance and ordnance stores, quarter- master stores &c &c for use of the Battery. I have a good many papers to make out and take care of but I have a very neat field desk for my own use and, therefore, get along very nicely. Have a good horse and equipment.[20]

Captain White has left us for the present and goes on the expedition as Chief of Artillery of our old Division. He will probably join us again as soon as the expedition returns. During his absence, Lieut. Cone takes command.[21]

My letter of 5th March had a newspaper enclosed giving a full account of the inaugural of Hahn, the first governor of the free state of Louisiana. I hope the letter will reach you safely. If you do not get it, write me and I will send to New Orleans for another copy . . .[22]

*   *   *

In the field
March 16th 1864

My dear father

I wrote you from Berwick Bay on the 12th Inst. and then thought we could go into camp at Brashear City. But next day we received orders to rejoin the Division and were off the same day. To-night, we are encamped between Franklin and New Iberia and to-morrow morning expect to move . . . past the latter point and, as that is the base of supplies, I may not have an opportunity to mail another letter for some time. I think we are bound for Alexandria on the Red river and from there may push forward some distance up the river.

There are about 25.000 men on this expedition, at least one half the number consisting of the finest cavalry force in our army. I think we will have a very pleasant trip, tho' of course we will see some rough life and may have to live on short rations. The weather feels fair, the roads are fine and plenty of water along the route. I am told that part of Sherman's army corps will co-operate with us at or near Alexandria. . . . I received a letter from Lib the other day, written from home.[23]

* * *

Alexandria La.
March 26th 1864

My dear father

We marched here to-day noon having marched from Berwick Bay to this place a distance of 180 miles in fourteen days. The march has been a good one for the troops, the weather being pleasant nearly all the time and the roads in good order. Individually, I have passed the most miserable two weeks that I have ever spent in the army and, at times, have been almost out of patience with myself and everything else. On the start, I was troubled with inflamed eyes. I soon cured them up and then took a very severe cold in my head. This I did not notice much but, in a day or so, the chills and fever commenced on me; commenced taking quinine, succeeding in checking it, then the cold got worse—throat sore and neck stiff—and so I have passed the entire journey.

We will probably stay here two or three days longer and then move forward toward Shreveport, where I think it likely we may burn some gunpowder. But as we are moving with a large force, the rebs may conclude that discretion is the better part of valor and skedaddle. The success of our forces so far has been as good as the most sanguine could expect. The best part of it is that Gen. [A. J.] Smith, after getting started, did not propose to wait for Gen. Banks and so has really come the upper cut at that gentleman. Smith is on the fight. Banks on the pomp and politics.[24]

About two thirds of the country along the route which we have just passed is wild, unbroken prairie, very sparsely settled and no improvements. But as we approached Alexandria, the change is very marked; the entire country being well settled and under the highest state of cultivation. On our route, we passed thro' the towns of Vermillionville, Opelousas, Washington and several small places the names of which I do not recollect. The towns like all others in the South look dilapidated, old and half in ruins. Saw a good many men at several of them, but presume the same chaps are now on the back of some poor horses that serve to make up the various parties of guerrillas that infest the country.[25]

*   *   *

After spending a much-appreciated day of rest outside Alexandria and finally getting paid, the Battery Boys set off at 6:00 a.m. on March 28 for a 66-mile march to Natchitoches. Shreveport was their distant goal. The Chicago artillerymen marched 21 miles and the next day headed inland. Lieutenant Pinckney Cone was commanding the battery in place of Pat White, who was now in charge of Ransom's artillery units.

Cone recorded the company's progress that night in his diary. "We soon left the Bayou Rapides to the right and struck off to the left across a rough pine country called 'Piney Woods.'" He added the redlegs, "Passed through Gen. Lee's Div of Cavalry 5000 in number, about evening, it was a fine sight. We camped on Cane River, quite a large stream, at sundown. Completely tired out."

The next day the Unionists discovered the enemy had burned the main bridge over the river, much as they had set fire to cotton bales along Banks' march route. Although Cane River looked benign, it was too deep to ford. The Chicago artillerymen took time to rest as Federal engineers constructed a pontoon bridge. Once it was completed, the Mercantile Battery took two hours crossing the makeshift bridge and establishing a new camp at Old Red River Ferry the next night. On April 1, the Northerners marched to within five miles of Natchitoches.[26]

The town of Natchitoches was the oldest permanent settlement in Louisiana, having been founded in 1714 as a port on Red River and a land junction between Mexico's El Camino Real and Natchez Trace to the east. After seeing Natchitoches, one of Franklin's soldiers reflected, "I must say that I was surprised to find such a place in rebeldom. . . . The houses are neat and clean, the folks at home, except the fighting portion, the negroes well clothed and the natives themselves quite respectable in appearance." Many of the town's prominent buildings, representing a quaint mix of French and Spanish cultures, lined the side of the spacious main street that faced the tranquil Cane River. The winding river had become a long oxbow lake when, approximately 25 years before the Civil War, its Red River mouth was plugged by a massive logjam. The blockage occurred just below Grand Ecore, a few miles above Natchitoches, which enabled it to remain intact as a key Red River port. As Cone led the Mercantile Battery along the Natchitoches roads, he noted the unusual international flavor of the area. "Passed a house today

Lieutenant George Throop and some of the other Battery Boys helped produce the April 1, 1864, issue of the *Natchitoches Union*.

from which were flying the flag of truce and the french flag," he wrote. "Had I been where I could have reached it I would have cut it down with my sabre. On the gate posts were these words: 'Dr. Burdin. Neutrality Here. Here live one foreign family which hope to receive protection from the honest officer and soldier of the Union Army according to International law & uses.'"[27]

On April 3 and 5, Lieutenant George Throop sent letters to his sister—the last he would ever write—and enclosed a copy of the *Natchitoches Union*. The newspaper was published impromptu "by our army while at this place and for which some of our boys are contributors." (One of the subheadings for the *Natchitoches Union* reflected the troops' awareness that Banks was jockeying to supplant Lincoln: "OUR TICKET FOR PRESIDENT, NATHANIEL P. BANKS, of Massachusetts, FOR VICE PRESIDENT, HON. B. F. WADE of Ohio.") Throop told his sister that the confident Battery Boys expected "soon to go to Grant's department after the enemy is whipped out in this region." A soldier in the 67th Indiana Infantry also wrote a last upbeat letter to his wife from Natchitoches, telling her, "we are all in the best of spirits and health and spirits and ready for all that is our duty to do as soldiers and hope to have the pleasure of seeing our homes, friends, and dear ones after our trials and deprivations are over and this cruel war is at an end." Like Throop, the Indianan would not survive the campaign.[28]

The Union army spent several days camped above Natchitoches, lured into a false sense of security by the calm Cane river-lake and picturesque town. On April 4, with the Confederate army nearby, Banks took time for a surprise review of the 13th Corps. In his diary, Cone described the review, to which he arrived late: "I heard loud cheering in our Div. I found the Regts and Batteries all drawn out in line and being informally reviewed by Banks. [Brigadier General Charles] Stone, [Brigadier General Thomas] Ransom, [Major General William] Franklin, [Brigadier General A. J.] Smith, and [Brigadier General Robert] Cameron with their respective staffs. The men received Gen Smith very enthusiastically but cared very little for Gen Banks or Franklin." Not surprisingly, Banks and Franklin drew a more enthusiastic reception at the next day's 19th Corps "nutmeg" review.[29]

Will Brown and his friends were surprised their Eastern commanders were not pursuing the enemy. Just as Banks had lingered in New Orleans to attend the recent gubernatorial inauguration, he was once again delaying military operations to suit a political agenda. Having set up temporary headquarters at nearby Grand Ecore, the state's military governor was overseeing the April 4 election he had mandated. Qualified Louisiana voters—those taking the Federal oath of allegiance—were casting ballots for delegates to the upcoming state constitutional convention. Instead of attending to his responsibilities as commander of the Red River Campaign, the politician-general was implementing the Union reconstruction policy to revise the Louisiana constitution and abolish slavery—and serving his own presidential ambitions.[30]

Once his political priorities were in order, Banks proceeded with his military plan. Porter, with Brigadier General Kilby Smith's troops accompanying his fleet, would steam up the Red River to Shreveport, while Banks led his army's main body along an inland route through the piney woods and past the towns of Pleasant Hill and Mansfield. Franklin established the order for the army's northward march, with A. J. Smith's divisions acting as the rear guard and the 13th Corps' undersized detachment leading the infantry. The 19th Corps—also known to the Western soldiers as Banks' "pets" or, less delicately, his "Headquarters' Pimps"—was sandwiched between them. Albert Lee and his cavalry division remained in front with the army's supply train.[31]

* * *

Natchitoches
April 2nd 1864

My dear father

We camped within 4 miles of this place last night and early this morning moved up to this place; will probably remain here 'till to-morrow morning and then move forward towards Shreveport, where I think we are bound. We are making good time, having good roads and fine weather. Have been troubled more by the dust than anything else.[32]

We struck Cane river several days ago and have marched along its banks ever since, so that we have been well supplied with water. At several crossings, the bridges were burnt and, at one place, we even delayed a day while the pontooniers built a bridge. This was the first regular pontoon bridge that I ever crossed, tho' I have crossed many a bridge built in a few hours and the material being formed of rail fences, stables, houses or anything else that could be picked up. A regular pontoon is a beauty and worth seeing. The one we crossed worked like a charm and the heaviest loads passed over it without displacing any part of it.

The country we are passing thro' appears well settled and cultivated, the principal staples being cotton and <u>negroes</u>. The latter, poor things, have <u>houses</u> of the most miserable description, much poorer than most people would use for pig pens. Many of the planters are foreigners but, fearing the terrible "Yankee," have run

Harper's Pictorial History of the Great Rebellion

Nathaniel Banks' Union troops crossing the Cane River.

many of their younger darkies, male and female off in the woods where they will be kept 'till we pass by. Some of these darkies have managed to elude the vigilance of their masters and overseers and come into our lines laden with a big bag of clothes. In reply to the question "Where you going darkey?" the universal answer is "We will goin wid you all Masser." The best of these negroes will be picked up by officers out with the expedition for that purpose and put in negro regiments where, after a due course of instruction, they will be sent to do battle for "Uncle Sam."

For the past week, I have noticed that, at nearly every plantation, the cotton was a smoldering mass of fire. And on many the cotton gins have shared the same fate. This is done by the rebel cavalry to keep the cotton from falling into our hands. I do not know why they destroy the gins unless they fear that we intend to occupy the country permanently and will . . . need them to gin the cotton.

Gen. [Albert] Lee's cavalry have the extreme advance and skirmish with the rebel cavalry nearly every day since leaving Alexandria. But so far the rebs have only made a very slight resistance and keep on the skedaddle as rapidly as possible. One or two days before we arrived at Alexandria—Col. Lucas comdg. a brigade of cavalry—came upon and captured an entire regiment of rebel cavalry. He did the thing in brilliant style and is deserving of high credit for it. There is a good deal of <u>strategy</u> going on and I would not be surprised if we bagged all and everything at Shreveport; but the future will tell all about it.[33]

I am again feeling as well as usual and that means "tip-top." My eyes cease to inflame, the ague "Nipped in the bud," has left—the cold has caught some other <u>feller.</u> And last, but not least, my neck is no longer <u>stiff</u> and now performs its regular duties in a manner equal to the majority of necks in general. I do not know if I can mail this here home but shall do so if possible and shall send it off as soon as opportunity offers. Let me know where Lib is and if he got that $200 bounty? With love to all.[34]

Brigadier General
Albert L. Lee

NARA

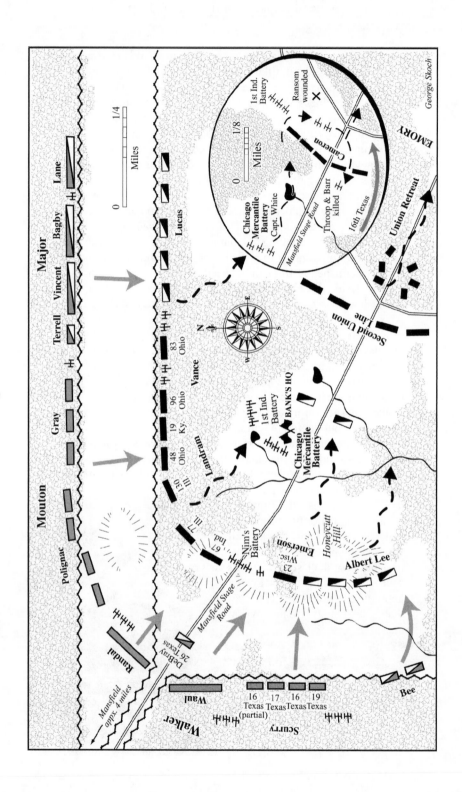

George Skoch

"The retreat soon became an utter rout and, before many moments, the road and woods were fairly filled with flying men, riderless horses, mules, ambulances, wagons &c. To write a description is impossible of this scene and even a verbal description would not do it justice. It was terrible."

Chapter 13

No Men Ever Displayed Better Courage

During the march from Alexandria to Natchitoches, Brigadier General Albert Lee's horse soldiers exchanged a frustrating fire with the rearguard of the enemy's cavalry. The Rebel horsemen repeated the same tactics over and over: dismount, skirmish, remount, and retreat. Lee grew more worried with each passing hour as his men probed the countryside for Confederate resistance while Banks' army remained camped along the placid Cane River. On April 4, Lee interrogated a Rebel deserter and passed along to his superiors a disturbing bit of intelligence: Richard Taylor's men, the man alleged, were preparing for battle and were determined to prevent the Federals from reaching Shreveport and entering Texas. Banks, however, remained nonchalant about the possible danger, choosing instead to review his troops and continue the sham election of state delegates at Grand Ecore. Franklin appeared only slightly more concerned. "It is my impression," he wrote his wife, "that the enemy does not wish to fight us and will keep out of our way, if possible, but then you know they may have other councils."[1]

Heavily outnumbered, Taylor's army had been steadily withdrawing in the face of the Federal advance, evacuating Alexandria and Natchitoches without a battle. Still, other Union officers, such as Major John B. Reid of the 130th Illinois Infantry, shared Lee's apprehension. Reid's regiment served with the Chicago Mercantile Battery under Colonel William Landram, who was now in charge of the 4th division, part of Thomas Ransom's 13th Corps detachment. From his camp near Natchitoches, the major wrote to his wife about the difficult time the cavalry was having in dislodging Taylor's troops from the area, and that it "looks very much as though we would [soon] have a severe battle." Reid also told her that enemy troops were still nearby and had captured three Union soldiers who had wandered away from camp, with one being killed. Reid added that he had spoken to a Confederate prisoner who told him that "the rebels were prepared to make a determined stand some place between here and Shreveport."[2]

While much of Banks' army marked time along the Cane River, Richard Taylor, the son of President Zachary Taylor, monitored his enemy's progress while gathering additional forces to prepare for battle. Included in Taylor's army was a Texas division led by Major General John G. Walker. The hardened frontiersmen were camped along the road to Mansfield. Their commander was a slight man, one who looked more like a professor than a military leader. He had received his major general's commission on November 8, 1862, after distinguishing himself as a division leader during Stonewall Jackson's masterful capture of Harpers Ferry and in the bloody fight that followed at Sharpsburg. Walker was transferred to the Trans-Mississippi that fall and placed in charge of a Texas infantry division.[3]

In January 1863, Walker led his division toward Arkansas Post in an attempt to reinforce Brigadier General Thomas Churchill's beleaguered troops. Unfortunately, the Lone Star men arrived too late: they were within five miles of their destination when they learned that Fort Hindman had surrendered to McClernand's troops. Walker's men had come close to meeting the Battery Boys on the field, as well as Pat White, who at that time was a member of the 1st Illinois Light Artillery, Battery B. The Texans and Chicagoans brushed past one another a second time during the Vicksburg Campaign when, in an effort to assist Pemberton's

Brigadier General
A. J. (Whiskey) Smith

NARA

embattled defenders, one of Walker's brigades attacked Union soldiers on the west bank of the Mississippi River at Milliken's Bend. In the Federal campaign along the Teche during the previous fall, three of Walker's regiments, detached from their brigades, took part in the Confederate victory at the Battle of Bayou Bourbeau (Carrion Crow). The Mercantile Battery's infantry comrades from the 23rd Wisconsin and 67th Indiana had not fared well in the fighting. The Battery Boys were garrisoned nearby at Franklin and thus missed the battle. This time, along the Red River, the men from Texas and Illinois would finally meet in a savage combat that would spin the entire campaign on a different course.[4]

The men in Walkers' command, which included the 16th Texas Infantry, were known as "Walker's Greyhounds," an apt moniker given that most of the men had spent substantially more time marching long distances than fighting. At the beginning of 1864, the 16th Texas was part of Brigadier General William Scurry's Brigade, which was helping to build fortifications at Yellow Bayou near Simmesport in preparation for the anticipated Union spring offensive up Red River. Federal transports carrying 10,000 troops moved down the Atchafalaya River and arrived at Simmesport on March 11. The Yankees were led by the hard-driving A. J. Smith, the Battery Boys' former commander who was known for his teamster-like vocabulary, fondness of whiskey, and penchant for piling up victories. When he learned of Smith's arrival, Walker left behind 350 men to garrison Fort DeRussy and rushed with his other brigades to reinforce Scurry. The Confederates joined forces and set up a line of battle in the prairie west of Marksville. Smith troops, however, ignored the Texans and marched three miles on March 14 to the Red River, overwhelming Fort DeRussy. Concerned about being cut off from the rest of Taylor's army, Walker ordered his men to burn the bridge over Yellow Bayou and retreat toward Shreveport, following an inland route that bypassed Alexandria and ran parallel to the river. The Texans held the enemy in disdain, regarding them as nothing more than barbarian invaders. Some recalled how the Romans had been caught off guard when Attila and his Huns swept in from the north and proceeded to terrorize and pillage their Mediterranean homeland.[5]

After Banks rejoined his troops, Lee and his cavalry led the Union army west away from Natchitoches on April 6. The army moved through White's Store and Crump's Corner and turned in a more northerly direction through Bellemont toward Pleasant Hill, where it camped for the night. Along the way the soldiers met fugitive blacks who reinforced the rumors that Taylor was planning to turn and fight the advancing Federals. On the afternoon of April 7, Lee and his troopers met stiff resistance a few miles beyond Pleasant Hill at Wilson's Farm, where Rebel horsemen began a running skirmish that culminated in a sharp evening engagement eight miles up the Mansfield-Pleasant Hill Road at Carroll's Mill. Lee tried to convince Franklin and his staff that the Confederates were showing signs that their retreat was ending. "I was laughed at for insisting that we would have a fight before we got to Shreveport," remembered Lee.[6]

Lee's claims did not seem to hold much credibility with Franklin and his staff. Perhaps this was because Banks and much of his Eastern officer corps had little respect for the Western troops (an allegation confirmed by the Battery Boys). Certainly the cavalry commander's lack of formal military training did not elevate his standing in a department where parades and pedigrees superseded battlefield toughness and laurels. Even the achievements Lee had attained during the Vicksburg Campaign may have been looked upon as a liability—especially by those who believed that Banks' Port Hudson victory had been overshadowed by the surrender of Vicksburg to Grant. According to one of Banks' staff officers, Franklin refused to send reinforcements into the Wilson's Farm engagement because he did not believe Lee was pushing his cavalry hard enough against the enemy. Franklin continued to believe that the heavy loss in Rebel cavalry three weeks earlier at Henderson Hill made it almost impossible for Richard Taylor to field much in the way of a cavalry force. After Wilson's Farm, however, Lee obtained more substantiation for his concerns when prisoners claimed that Brigadier General Thomas Green's brigade of veteran Rebel cavalry had arrived from Texas. Franklin remained convinced that the Yankee cavalry would hold its advantage all the way to Shreveport, where the Union troops would rendezvous with Porter's gunboats. So united, the Union amphibious force would seize General Kirby Smith's headquarters and his abundant supply of Trans-Mississippi cotton.[7]

In addition to being worried about the revitalized enemy in his front, Lee was concerned about his own overextended supply train. His wagons were lined up for several miles on what Banks described as "a narrow, crooked circuitous road; merely a country road through the dense forest." Lee reported that his provisions far exceeded a cavalry division's daily needs because he had "ten days' rations for my men, three days' forage for my animals, a large supply of ammunition, and some camp and garrison equipage." The wagons were too valuable to be exposed to capture or destruction, so Lee asked Franklin to relocate the train to the rear. He could keep daily supplies in a few wagons and draw from the train as needed. This move would also release about 1,000 Union horse soldiers from guard duty to join Lee's other 3,300 men at the front. Franklin denied the request. One of the major general's reasons was that he did not want Lee's supply train to interfere with his 19th Corps' camp grounds. The reluctance of Franklin and his staff to heed these warnings and take reasonably prudent measures while deep in enemy territory was so perplexing that Lee later told a Congressional committee, "The whole column was marching to the sound of my guns every day; still they would not believe there was fighting."[8]

Franklin could not have been more wrong. The rank-and-file Trans-Mississippi Rebel soldier relished the opportunity to strike back at the Yankees. As Banks pushed closer to Shreveport, the soldiers in Walker's Texas division grew more alarmed as they followed Kirby Smith's orders to retreat before the enemy. Each mile exposed large swaths of Southern land and family homes to the Northern horde, which most Rebel soldiers believed would terrorize the women and pillage civilian property. The foot soldiers and artillerymen became even more outraged when they heard from their cavalry comrades how the blueclad aggressors openly taunted the retreating Rebels. According to a member of the 32nd Texas

Major General
Richard Taylor

Battles and Leaders of the Civil War

Cavalry, the Yankees "jeer[ed] and hoot[ed] at our boys, shouting sooe! sooe! As though they were driving hogs."[9]

Banks' delays at Alexandria and Grand Ecore proved a blessing for Taylor, who had more time to plan his counter-attack as he awaited additional troops who were on the way from both Texas and Arkansas. It was time to punish the invaders and apply what he had learned studying his father's Mexican War victories. Though he lacked the training of a professional soldier, Taylor had not only learned warfare from his father but had benefited from serving under Stonewall Jackson in the 1862 Shenandoah Campaign. Taylor later wrote how Jackson had used rapid marches to concentrate his outnumbered troops, and then stealth and surprise to overcome Nathaniel Banks and several other Federal commanders. His retreat in the face of superior numbers had allowed Taylor to carefully husband his forces and study the terrain. He was convinced that the area around Mansfield offered outstanding possibilities for defeating the enemy. Banks' army was strung out more than 20 miles along a narrow, twisting country road. Taylor realized that he could mass his 8,800 soldiers on good ground and strike the vanguard of the Union column quickly and hard; Banks would only be able to draw upon a fraction of his approximately 25,000 soldiers to meet the assault. The Confederate retreat was over.[10]

A few days earlier, while Taylor was monitoring Banks' advance and calling in reinforcements, the Texas infantrymen in Walker's Division marched to the courthouse in Mansfield, which they reached on April 4. The infantry passed through the intersection and headed north on the Kingston Road. Four miles outside of town the Texans set up camp in a swampy bottom and awaited further instructions.[11]

One of Walker's officers was Captain Alex McDow of the 16th Texas Infantry. He was finally going to meet the Mercantile Battery's artillerists in person. Born in 1822, McDow had a successful cotton plantation in Sumter County, Alabama. In the late 1850s, the widower moved to Texas, where he settled with his teenage daughter Kate in the town of LaGrange. McDow purchased a mill there and a large tract of land along the Colorado River, where he built another profitable cotton-growing operation. The 40-year old planter remained at home during the war's first year, but on April 3, 1862, he decided it was time to join the Southern army to protect his adopted state. McDow enlisted in Company I, 16th Texas Infantry (Fournoy's Regiment) as a first lieutenant and was promoted to captain in 1863. His personal determination to resist Banks' army may have been strengthened by the recent death of his brother John, a Rebel army doctor who had died of pneumonia at Harrisonburg, Louisiana, just two months earlier.[12]

After the war, one of Walker's soldiers described the worries that plagued the Texans while camped outside of Mansfield. First and foremost in their minds was the horrifying prospect of their homes and families being overrun by Federal attackers: "Our wives and children were there, and as Texas had never seen the blazing torch, the burning towns and homes plundered by cruel hands, we felt we would rather die than retreat another step." (McDow's daughter was attending a woman's college in Gainesville, Alabama, where she was safe from Banks' invading army.) As one of Walker's Greyhounds recalled about the night of April 7, "There was much feeling manifested by the Texas boys as to what the morrow would bring. 'Fight, fight,' was the expression of the boys; 'if they don't stop and let us whip Banks, I am going home to protect my wife and children,' said another." While McDow likely detested the Unionists as much as any of his comrades did, the next day's events would also demonstrate the depth of his compassion.[13]

In addition to Walker's troops, Taylor's command included a small infantry division under Brigadier General Jean Jacques Alfred Alexander Mouton. A native Louisianan, Mouton had seen combat as a regimental commander at Shiloh, but had not yet proven himself at the head of a division. His command was composed of Colonel Henry Gray's Louisiana brigade and a Texas brigade led by the "Lafayette of the Confederacy," Brigadier General Camille Armand Jules Marie, Prince de Polignac. Around 2:00 a.m. on April 8, Mouton began mobilizing his brigades. As one of Gray's men recounted, Mouton directed his "troops forward on the road to Pleasant Hill, and the wagons to follow in the rear with the exception of the ammunition wagons and ambulances. That order showed clearly that some action was contemplated." At 6:30 a.m., Mouton's entire command was on the road running through Mansfield to Moss' plantation, about two and one-half miles beyond the town. Taylor placed Mouton's troops on the left of his new battle line. One of Gray's men wrote in his diary, "Our position was on a rather high hill at the edge of a forest behind a fence, with a large field before us, ending in a forest on a very high hill facing us."[14]

At 11:00 a.m., Taylor ordered John Walker to also move his men back south through Mansfield in the direction of Pleasant Hill. Walker's Texans eagerly marched ahead with "flying banners," the division's bands playing a raucous rendition of Dixie. The townspeople were surprised to see the troops return and pass through Mansfield. As one Confederate soldier recollected, the streets were "thronged with fair ladies—misses and matrons—who threw their bright garlands at our feet, and bade us, in God's name, to drive back the Yankees and save their cherished homes." The Texans marched past the courthouse and headed south toward Pleasant Hill. Noticing the Texans moving past him, a Confederate soldier observed, "General Walker's men are in a fine condition for fighting." After their long retreat, McDow and his comrades were at last headed for battle.[15]

Walker led his men forward, stopped at the edge of a woods, and ordered them to "Stack arms." He and his officers gathered for an early lunch. Infantry skirmishers pushed ahead to feel for the approaching enemy. Some of the men voiced a common sentiment as they awaited the arrival of bloody combat: "This calm before the storm . . . is more trying even than the battle itself." Meanwhile, at the edge of the next stand of timber Mouton's men looked up at the hill ahead of them. Halfway across the field was a rail fence. At the crest of the hill was a narrow cluster of tight-packed, towering pine trees providing cover for what looked like dismounted Union cavalry supported by infantry and horse artillery.[16]

Nathaniel Banks had arrived at Pleasant Hill from Grand Ecore the previous evening. When he learned that Franklin had denied Lee's request for infantry support, Banks authorized General Ransom to send Colonel William J. Landram, the commander of the 13th Corps' small 4th Division, forward with one of his brigades. Both were led by colonels, one under Frank Emerson and the other Joseph Vance. Landram reported to Lee at daylight and pushed his infantry ahead to support the cavalry. Near Sabine Crossroads, the Federals came across the largest clearing they had seen for some time, an elongated rectangular opening in the piney woods about 800 yards wide by 1,200 yards long. Lee ordered Landram to use his infantry and clear enemy skirmishers off a patch of high ground (Honeycutt Hill) in their front. That task was easily accomplished. However, the sight that greeted Landram from the top of Honeycutt Hill was an ominous one: Taylor's troops in order of battle were gathering on the opposite side of the field. He quickly aligned his troops, with Emerson's brigade on the left extending beyond the Mansfield-Pleasant Hill Road and Vance's brigade on the right. Dismounted cavalry from Lee's brigade held the Union left flank, while cavalry from Lucas' brigade held the far right. Four batteries of artillery, two near the road on the left front, and two more deployed on the right next to Lucas' troopers, bolstered the Union line of battle.[17]

About 2:00 p.m., the adjutant of the 96th Ohio Infantry climbed a tree to get a better look at the Confederates. The sun was high in a crisp and blue cloudless sky. The Ohioan balanced himself, pausing to wipe the forearm of the rough woolen uniform across his brow. He looked out over the open fields, where the ground gently sloped down to the woods. In the distance were dust clouds approaching from the north along the swath of country road. The slow-moving billows drew closer, like a steam-belching locomotive engine bearing down upon the Union army. Below and to the adjutant's left waited a Massachusetts horse soldier, who later remembered that "Cannoneers stood idly by and Troopers lounged lazily in the saddles—the calm that precedes a storm."[18]

Union soldiers on the crest of Honeycutt Hill noticed the glint of the late-afternoon sun reflecting off thousands of muskets and bayonets arrayed across their front. Much like the Union position at Gettysburg, the Confederate line at Sabine Crossroads resembled something of a fish hook. This Louisiana version, however, was pulled apart, with the short open end of the hook lying across the road facing the Union cavalry's left flank. Most of the Rebels, including Mouton's Division and Brigadier General James Major's Texas cavalry division, were drawn out along the hook's shank, which faced the long Federal right flank.

Banks and his staff had arrived on the battlefield about 1:00 p.m. The general and his entourage had commandeered a log house perched on a ridge on the right side of the wagon road where they enjoyed a commanding view of the field. After conferring with Lee, Banks seemed to realize for the first time that the head of his army was in a precarious situation. He immediately ordered Franklin to expedite the dispatch of reinforcements up the road. The Chicago Mercantile Battery was already on its way, having begun its march from Pleasant Hill that morning at 5:00 a.m. The guns had already rolled about 12 miles when orders arrived for the Battery Boys to proceed at the double quick. The Chicagoans rushed forward over the next three miles toward Honeycutt Hill, unaware of what to expect when they arrived there.[19]

By now it was 4:00 p.m. and time for Taylor to offer conclusive proof that he was no longer retreating to Shreveport. He had waited for some time for Banks to attack him so he could beat him back and counterattack his shallow front. When he did not, Taylor decided to go on the offensive. He ordered Mouton's troops, supported by a brigade detached from Walker's command, to attack the Union right front. Major's cavalry supported Mouton's left flank. An assortment of Rebel flags fluttered in the breeze above two lines of battle as the grayclad infantrymen began moving. Most were led by officers who rode into battle to inspire their troops, making themselves easy targets for the Yankee marksmen.[20]

After he got a chance to view the field, the last thing Thomas Ransom wanted to do was fight Taylor's army south of Mansfield. Upon receiving Franklin's order at 11:00 a.m. to accompany Landram's second brigade to the front, Thomas Ransom had ridden five miles at a trot and reached the large clearing about 1:30 p.m. What he found there surprised him. He spotted two Rebel batteries and a large number of infantrymen arrayed for battle. With his binoculars he watched as a steady stream of Southern soldiers eased their way through the towering pine trees beyond the Union right, stretching out the Confederate line eastward. The enemy was moving into position to attack. When someone told Ransom that Banks wanted him to order Landram's division forward, he muttered in reply, "that will finish me."[21]

Despite his reservations, Ransom obeyed his orders and instructed Landram to meet the advancing Louisianans and Texans. From left to right, the 77th Illinois, 130th Illinois, 48th Ohio, 19th Kentucky, 96th Ohio, and 83rd Ohio moved forward as they closed the distance with the Southerners, seeking, in Landram's words, "to meet them upon better ground and with a better effect." His division moved through a small stand of trees and took up a position along a fence at the perimeter of the meadow that offered them a wide open field of fire.[22]

They were in position only a short time when Taylor's infantry stepped out of the distant woods about 800 yards away and bore down on their position. Landram's troops enjoyed some initial success, their volleys driving Mouton's first line back upon the second. Although some of Mouton's men stopped to fire, most of the Confederate infantry continued attacking. While Landram's men held their ground and poured forth a storm of lead into the advancing enemy ranks, Ransom's artillery chief, Pat White, informed him that the Chicago Mercantile Battery had arrived on the field. The Battery Boys initially unlimbered their guns in a plowed field left of the Mansfield-Pleasant Hill Road. On Ransom's instructions, White ordered the Chicagoans to move to the right of Banks' makeshift headquarters on the opposite side of the road. The new position was near the edge of the woods where they could better support Landram's embattled line. Within minutes the Battery Boys were hurling shells at Mouton's advancing men.[23]

As Mouton's troops closed the distance against the Federal right, Taylor ordered Walker, with Scurry's and Brigadier General Thomas N. Waul's brigades, to attack and try to outflank the Union left stretching below the Mansfield-Pleasant Hill Road. Taylor also instructed two of Green's cavalry regiments, deployed on Walker's right, to strike the enemy. Behind the Confederate lines, John Walker shouted his imperious commands, beginning with "By companies, into line!" Walker looked through his field glass again before turning to yell, "Fix bayonets!" Scurry conveyed Walker's orders to Captain McDow and the other officers of his brigade: "Forward march!" The Texans advanced through a field and into some woods, where they could clearly hear the battle escalating into a deafening roar. As they walked through the trees and approached a distant rail fence, shells crashed through the limbs above them, showering the men with deadly wooden splinters and jagged iron fragments. Bullets began zipping through the leaves.[24]

Atop Honeycutt Hill were the gunners of Captain Ormand F. Nims' 2nd Massachusetts, Battery B. One gun was on the road to Mansfield, two unlimbered on its right, and three on its left. The Bay Staters loaded and fired as fast as they could into the advancing enemy infantry. When the enemy was only a short distance away, they fired double charges of canister that mowed down butternut and gray soldiers like a scythe

Captain Ormand F. Nims,
2nd Massachusetts
Light Artillery

U. S. Army Military History Institute

cutting through dry grain stalks. But for every Southern soldier who fell, another soldier took his spot and closed the ranks. Still they advanced, and the cacophony of battle edged its way toward a crescendo. The small arms and artillery were not going to stop the attack. Federal soldiers braced themselves for the worst.[25]

The Texans surged over the fence, in the words of the division's historian, "like an avalanche of fire" and drove up the hill. Walker's troops punctuated their attack with a loud yell as the order rang out to advance on the double quick. McDow's company rushed forward. Screams were followed by more screams as the Federals found their downhill range. The Texans leaned forward, dodging minie balls as they closed the final yards to the enemy line. About half way up the hill, McDow and his comrades encountered another rail fence. Clearing this hurdle, they propelled themselves toward the crest of Honeycutt Hill, hearts pounding and legs pumping.[26]

The men of the 3rd Massachusetts Cavalry, part of Colonel Nathan Dudley's brigade, anchored Banks' left flank. One of them remembered how "The rebels were literally swarming out of these woods. Then the battle began in real earnest: shell, canister, shrapnel, and lead were poured into the enemy's ranks, breaking them again and again; but only for an instant; for they would rally and press on, firing steadily, and defying us with that 'rebel yell' whose echo rang in our ears for so many days and disturbed our slumber for so many nights."[27]

The dismounted Federal cavalrymen tried to hold their ground. The commander of the 2nd Illinois Cavalry, also part of Dudley's brigade, cringed as each of his color bearers "was shot down the instant he raised the flag, until five were killed in succession." Dudley's cavalry melted away, exposing the left flank of the 23rd Wisconsin Infantry, which supported Nims' blazing battery straddling the main road. The sudden appearance of the enemy on their flank unraveled the Badger line almost as quickly. This, in turn triggered the hasty rearward flight of the 67th Indiana, which had also been supporting the Boston-based artillery unit.[28]

With the 23rd Wisconsin and 67th Indiana falling back, Nims' artillerists were suddenly in danger of being overrun. The gunners tried to withdraw their pieces, but there were not enough horses still alive to move them. Three cannon were wheeled away by hand, but the other three were abandoned and the screaming Confederates promptly turned them against the fleeing Northerners. The Texans cheered at the sight of the Union retreat. The cavalrymen on Walker's right—led by Colonel August Buchel and Colonel Alexander W. Terrell—plunged forward, wreaking more havoc on the fleeing enemy. After the sudden collapse of the Union left flank, the Confederates, in Ransom's words, "were in strong force on the hill and pouring a destructive fire into the batteries of the Fourth Division." Matters were no better on the army's right center, where Mouton's Louisiana troops had also reached and broken the main line a few hundred yards east of the road. Although Mouton and several high ranking Rebel officers had been killed, there was no stopping the Southern force as it moved up the hill and through the spearhead of Banks' army. Knowing there was no way he could hold his position, Ransom issued an order for the Battery Boys and the 1st Indiana Battery to take a position in the rear. He also attempted to withdraw Landram's regiments, but some were surrounded and forced to surrender.[29]

Overwhelmed, the Western infantrymen ducked and flinched as they headed away from the front in search of sanctuary. Ransom tried to reorganize his lines at the edge of the woods where the Mercantile Battery's 3-inch rifles were still blazing away, but it proved impossible to accomplish. A hail of minie balls was sweeping through the Union ranks;

some of the rounds whistled past the Yankee soldiers and into the woods beyond, while others stopped suddenly with a sickening thump followed by a groan or a scream. Ransom watched his soldiers continue flooding to the rear as the pincers of the Southern "V" enveloped his flanks and crushed them like a giant nutcracker. The stalwart Ransom waved his sword and urged his men to reform around the Federal guns. "For God's sake boys let us try and rally here!"[30]

About this time Federal reinforcements arrived in the form of Brigadier General Robert Cameron's Third Division, 13th Corps, accompanied by Franklin himself. Together with Colonel Landram, Ransom was working to reform his line as these troops were deploying when a Confederate bullet slammed into his knee, severely wounding him. Members of the Mercantile Battery shielded their fallen general and helped to carry him to the rear. Cameron's men prolonged the battle but could not stem the enemy attack. Outflanked like Landram's troops, they were likewise driven from the field. White and his men were among the last to leave the blood-soaked Sabine Crossroads clearing. Unfortunately for the Unionists, leaving the field was easier said than done. Banks' column was unable to execute an orderly withdrawal because there was no place for the large wagon train to quickly turn around. The result was a giant bottleneck of men, horses, guns, and wheeled vehicles.[31]

One month later Lieutenant Henry Roe summarized the Battery Boys' anger over the battle's outcome when he wrote in a letter home how "our once powerful battery as well as our noble little 4th Division was sacrificed that day through the ignorance of a political general." According to Roe, the battery fired about 250 rounds during the engagement and only retreated under orders to do so. "We succeeded in getting the pieces all off the field, but the road being blockaded by the wagons we were compelled to leave them," he lamented in his official report of the battle. The Southerners swarmed over the guns and one of the battery's commissioned officers apparently died after refusing to leave his piece. A soldier in the 77th Illinois wrote in his diary about seeing a lieutenant (most likely the Mercantile Battery's Joseph Barr, who stood over six feet tall) who was unable to move his cannon to safety because the horses had been shot. The valiant officer "refused to leave his battery and jumping onto one of his guns with a revolver in each hand fought until the rebels came up and killed him." Pat White almost shared a similar fate. After battering through the Union left flank, screaming

Confederates from the 16th Texas Infantry captured the Mercantile Battery captain. White, however, refused to surrender his sword, which had been presented to him by influential Chicagoans on May 1, 1862. As a lieutenant in Taylor's Battery, White had returned home after Shiloh on a recruiting mission. The numerous bullet holes in his dusty blue frock coat testified to his brave work at Shiloh, where he was stationed near William T. Sherman when the battle began. In that April maelstrom two years before a shell tore White's "sword, sash and belt from his body, and entirely destroyed them." When he was presented with a new sword in Chicago a month later, White vowed never to surrender it except to another officer. Fortunately for him, Captain Alex McDow rode up in time to accept White's surrender, and in doing so saved his life.[32]

Lieutenant George Throop was severely wounded when the Federal position collapsed. Orrin Nash and Chase Dickinson carried him off the field. "Leave me, boys," Throop told them, "for you can do nothing for me, but take care of yourselves." Except for his Sunday school friend Hugh Wilson, everyone else turned and ran. Wilson alone remained to help the injured lieutenant into an ambulance. As he later reported to his comrades, "A shell passed across his [Throop's] bowels and cut the bottom of his vest, but did not leave any mark on his skin. There was a lump on his side half as big as his head, caused by internal bleeding." The ambulance driver jumped out of the wagon, cut loose one of the mules, and fled. Hugh Wilson took his place and convinced the remaining mule to pull the ambulance through the woods. Confronted with an impassable stream he was forced to stop. A doctor who was in the ambulance ministering to Throop told Wilson his friend would not live. As the yelling Southerners closed in around them Wilson hesitated, unsure as to what to do next. Throop looked up at him and said, "Hugh! Raise my head up, and then run and save yourself; I am dying and you can do no good." Wilson followed his friend's advice. "I jerked out of my jacket and put it under his head and started for the rear," Wilson later wrote.[33]

Union soldiers flooded through the wooded shadows into the narrow one-lane road. The tangle of supply trains had become a dam blocking the path of a swift-running river. Retreating soldiers, realizing fully by this time that they would not be able to pass the train and escape, began to panic. Some later wrote that the stampede was eerily similar to the early war fiasco at Bull Run. After hiding in the underbrush and dodging enemy bullets, Hugh Wilson made it to the road where he was reunited

The Union retreat from Sabine Crossroads reminded many of the 1861 "stampede" from 1st Bull Run.

Library of Congress

with his Chicago comrades. Only the arrival of Brigadier General William H. Emory's division of William Franklin's well-rested 19th Corps—which was bigger than both of Ransom's undersized divisions combined—saved the 13th Corps soldiers and Lee's cavalrymen from complete annihilation. The fighting and pursuit only ended with the onset of darkness.[34]

The next day, April 9, Union troops stopped Taylor's stunning advance in a hard-fought defensive battle at Pleasant Hill. The Confederates came close to scoring another victory, but Whiskey Smith and his Western men stood firm and threw back Taylor's poorly delivered offensive, rescuing the army from what otherwise would have been a very serious disaster. Even Banks gratefully acknowledged Smith's efforts when he shook his hand and told him, "God bless you, general. You have saved the army."[35]

While Banks watched the Battle of Pleasant Hill being waged, he sent some of his demoralized troops back toward Grand Ecore on the Red River. The leaderless remnants of the Mercantile Battery, who had lost all their guns at Mansfield, joined this group and left the raging battle about noon. Extreme resentment pervaded the throng of marching soldiers, who grumbled and vehemently criticized Banks and Franklin for trying to "charge the enemy with a baggage-train." The men of Ormand Nims' battery had also lost their guns and equipment and, like their fellow Chicago artillerists, were reluctant participants in Banks' retreat. After the war, a veteran who served with Nims recalled, "we surely did get to Grand Ecore without any unnecessary delay." The cannoneer also remembered the Union soldiers singing, "In eighteen hundred and sixty four, we all skedaddled to Grand Ecore." At 3:00 p.m. on April 10, the Mercantile Battery men began arriving at the small village along the Red River. The demoralized Illinoisans collapsed that night in their makeshift camp, exhausted, embittered, and with few belongings.[36]

After a fitful sleep, Will Brown scribbled out a brief letter to his father on April 11 and had it shipped out on a hospital boat departing for New Orleans. Several of the other Battery Boys did likewise. In the confusion of the retreats and staggering turn of events, Banks and his staff overlooked these Mercantile Battery letters as they scrambled to protect the general's reputation from the consequences of his defeat at Sabine Crossroads. Unbeknownst to anyone, this Mercantile Battery correspondence—including part of Will Brown's letter—would soon be funneled into Chicago newspapers. Its publication would thwart Banks' efforts at damage control.[37]

Two days later while still in Grand Ecore, Will sent a more comprehensive letter, along with a detailed map, to Hiram Brown. By this time Will had recuperated somewhat from the strain of the past week and collect more information from his comrades about what had happened at Sabine Crossroads. Will excoriated Banks and Franklin for their abysmal management of the situation and blamed them for the capture of his comrades and the loss of the company's guns. He also wanted to ensure that his father understood the battery was not at fault for its plight. "Our brave Gen. Ransom has gone to New Orleans. It is feared he will lose his leg, but every effort will be made to save it," Will explained. "He paid our Battery a high compliment. Said they did all that men could do and no men ever displayed better courage."[38]

*   *   *

Grand Ecore La.
11th April 1864

My dear father

Ere this reaches you, I presume you will have heard of our most disastrous defeat of the 8th and I have no doubt you will be very anxious to hear from me. This [letter], however, will assure you of my safety.

I do not know what to write. The excitement of the last three days has kept nearly all my faculties hard at work and, now that we are safely under cover of our gunboats, I feel too tired to do hardly anything or write but a few words. We have lost our entire Battery but succeeded in saving our three baggage wagons. Capt. White, Lieuts. Cone, Throop and Barr and 22 men are missing. Lieut. Throop was left very badly wounded and is probably killed; of the others, we know nothing. Our boys stood by the guns 'till the last moment and got them off the field. And had the road not been blocked up by wagons, would have succeeded in getting them off all right.[39]

Our brave little Gen. Ransom stood by our guns 'till wounded badly. I saw him last night in the hospital. He said to me that our boys behaved nobly. I was not with the guns so did not see the fight. My place on the march is with the baggage wagons. It was only by the greatest exertion we succeeded in saving our wagons and, when we turned them around, the rebs were within a 1.000 yards of them. We were outnumbered five to one. Our little Division, numbering about 3.000 men, were the only men in the fight and most terribly were we whipped.[40]

The enemy took Nims Flying Batteries (six guns), Battery L [Battery G, 5th U.S.] Regulars (six guns), 1st Indiana (four guns) and our Battery (six guns)—in all 22 pieces. I never witnessed, never discussed or even thought of such a perfect rout as this fight proved to be and, if justice is done, some one will suffer. For a more miserably managed affair, I never thought of; but of this, more in a future letter. For I do assure you, my dear father, that as much as I would like to give all particulars now, I really cannot do so. I have been on the saddle nearly the whole time for three days and two nights and you will not wonder that I am tired and sleepy.[41]

I think that most of our men who are prisoners are all right otherwise. Charley Olcott and Dan Marble escaped uninjured. Charley was within ten feet of the Capt. when we was taken. All our Company papers are safe as they were in the wagons. Lieut. Roe is now the only officer we have with us. I think we will be ordered to New Orleans and there be re-equipped. Will write you again soon but, for to-day, please accept this very short letter. And be assured that, for the present at least, we are out of all danger. Love to all.[42]

*   *   *

Grand Ecore La.
April 13th 1864

My dear father

In my last, I told you where I was stationed during the fight and much of my information in regard to it has been derived from conversation with our boys. I was near enough to the front, however, to see a great-deal and was perfectly satisfied to get away as well as I did. Had our wagons not been faced to the rear at the moment they were, we would have lost them and, had they gone, I would have probably gone with them. And by this time, [I would have] been marching toward Texas as prisoner of war. But thanks to a kind Providence, I came out all right and only hope that I may fare as well in the future. But to give some account of the fight and its disastrous results:[43]

At 3 ½ O'clock on the morning of the 8th Inst., our Cavalry under Gen. Lee and the 1st Brigade of our Division (4th) started forward from Pleasant Hill. At day light, the 2nd Brigade, our Battery and the 1st Indiana Battery moved off and were followed by the 3d Div. [of the] 13th Army Corps under command of Gen. Cameron. After Gen. Cameron, came one Division of the 19th Corps under command of Gen. Emory and in the rear came the wagon trains of the 13th and 19th Corps. Gen Lee's train being in his (Lee's) immediate rear. To make the line of march more plain I give you the following:

| Supply and Ammunition Trains of 13th & 19th A.C. | 1st Division, 19th A. C. | 3rd Division, 13th A.C. | 2nd Brigade, 4th Div., 13th A.C. | 1st Brigade, 4th Div., 13th A.C. | Gen Lee's Supply Train | Gen Lee's Cavalry |

The road, after leaving Pleasant Hill, strikes into an immense stretch of timber country called the "Piney woods" and is so narrow that teams cannot pass each other. The woods are very dense and so filled with undergrowth that it is almost impossible for a man on horse back to make his way thro' them. As we advanced toward the front, we would come to an occasional clearing and, at each of these, the enemy had made a stand and showed fight.[44]

About 9 AM, both the Cavalry and the 1st Brigade commenced skirmishing and kept it up 'till the enemy finally made a decided stand about six miles from Mansfield and fifteen from Pleasant Hill. This was about 3 PM and Gen. Ransom, anticipating warm work, ordered our Battery, the 1st Indiana and 2nd Brigade up to support 1st Brigade. At this time, the 3d Division had gone into camp four miles from the fight and the 19th Corps seven miles from it. Our wagons passed these troops and moved on toward the front but, just after passing the 3d Div., were ordered to halt as it (the Division) had been ordered to the front. The Division passed us and we again moved forward.[45]

At this time, very heavy firing was going on ahead. Our wagons kept moving on and, not 'till we were within half or ¾ of a mile of the battlefield, were we ordered to halt. Had not halted but a few moments before a perfect stampede of negroes came rushing by us from the front and nearly all of them crying "The rebs is charging. The rebs is charging." And on they dashed toward the rear. This, of course, caused some confusion but was not considered of much moment as the negroes were officers servants and not of any use at the front.

No sooner, however, had the negroes fairly got past us than back, back, back came the cavalry dashing past in the greatest confusion and acting as if the enemy were at their heels. The retreat soon became an utter rout and, before many moments, the road and woods were fairly filled with flying men, riderless horses, mules, ambulances, wagons &c &c. To write a description is impossible of this scene and even a verbal description would not do it justice. It was terrible and I never want to see anything like it again.

As soon as it was possible to do so, I got our wagons turned round and moved backward with the mass as rapidly as possible. Kept the wagons on the road all night and, by daylight next morning, made Pleasant Hill. But now to go back to the Battery and give you an account of its fate. To make the matter plain as possible, I give you the following diagram:

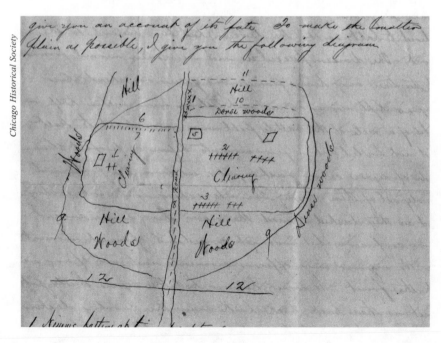

1. Nims Battery at time of capture
2. Our first position in Battery
3. " second "   "   "
4. Lieut. Throop's section at the time he was wounded
5. Our advance hospital (Farm house)
6. Rail fence across clearing
7. Our Cavalry in line
8.Head of wagon train
9. Line of the enemy when he flanked us
10. Our line of battle in the woods at the time we took our first position
11. Rebel line of battle

Nims Battery of six guns were with the cavalry and were taken to the position I have marked #1. # 2 is the position first taken by our Battery [and] was in the middle of the clearing. We did not commence firing 'till our line of battle at #10 had fallen back of the guns. Here, the Battery did good work 'till the enemy (who outnumbered us nearly ten to one) had advanced to the hospital (#5) when Gen. Ransom, seeing little use in waiting longer, ordered us to limber up and fall back. We did so and again took position at #3. Lieut. Throop's section was then ordered over to #4 and there he received a mortal wound.[46]

The cavalry at #7 were drawn up in line but, seeing the enemy coming up in great force, only stopped to fire one volley and then commenced running for the rear. At this time, Gen. Ransom, seeing all was hopeless and knowing that nearly his whole command was in the hands of the enemy, ordered us to get away if possible. It was while we were obeying his order that he fell from his horse—struck by a bullet—which entered him by some distance above the knee. [We] limbered up and started for the road, reached it and found it filled with Lee's train.

On came the enemy. There was no use in doing more and our brave boys, cutting loose as many horses as were not wounded, mounted them and started for the rear—many of them not leaving our guns 'till the enemy were on our (#6) immediately behind and shouting at them "Surrender you ***** ***** Yankees." How so many of our boys escaped unhurt seems almost a miracle. On came the enemy, flushed with victory and thinking he would carry all before him. But fortunately the 19th Corps had reached us at this time.[47]

Drawing themselves up in line at the position I have marked #12, they [the 19th Corps] waited 'till the enemy had approached within a few feet of them. And then pouring in a most deadly fire succeeded, not only in checking the enemy, but in driving him back in great confusion. The prompt manner in which the 19th Corps checked the enemy is what probably saved the balance of the army. And I have little doubt, if these troops had only been on hand at the commencement of the fight, the result would have been entirely different.[48]

Here, in my opinion, was the great fault and why they [the 19th Corps] were not with us remains to be told. I have heard the blame cast on several shoulders but forbear mentioning any names 'till something more definite is known. Darkness coming on, soon after the 19th Corps reached us, the firing ceased. And at midnight, the Corps commenced retreating toward Pleasant Hill, where they hoped to meet Gen. A. J. Smith with his force of 10,000 men.[49]

At this time, our wagons and quite a number of our boys who had escaped were moving toward Pleasant Hill and were about ten miles ahead of the 19th Corps. The road was filled with men going to the rear and many a poor wearied out soldier came to me begging permission to ride a little distance in the wagons. Poor fellows. I took as many as I could. As I have said before, we reached Point Pleasant at day light and then stopped to feed and breakfast.

Gen. [A.J. "Whiskey"] Smith and his force were here also, having made a forced march during the night in order to come to our aid. I cannot describe or even give you a poor description of the cheers that burst from our wearied out soldiers when they found that Gen. Smith had reached [us]. How I felt, I will attempt to tell you. Soon after we arrived, Gen. Smith commenced forming his troops in line of battle and I heard him remark that he was bound to win the day anyhow. After eating my breakfast (Hard tack and Coffee), I rode part way round his line and watched his troops moving up to their different positions. But we were soon ordered to move toward this place and by noon were again en route.[50]

[We] marched 'till after midnight, and then stopped 'till day break, so I had an opportunity for about four hours sleep—and I assume if ever I improved [in] four hours I did this. At day break, we were again on the road and about 3 PM were here safe under cover of our gunboats. Until this time I did not stop to think about being tired and worn out, but when we got in camp right gladly did I throw down my blankets, and lose myself in "Dreamy slumbers."[51]

We are now like Micawber "Waiting for something to turn up" [and] cannot do anything or find out what will be done with us. Don't know whether we will be re-equipped here or be sent somewhere else to refit. All we have left in the way of equipments is 46 horses, several parts of harness, 3 army wagons, 18 mules, several saddles and a few minor traps. Capt. White; Lieuts. Cone, Throop and Barr; and 22 men are missing. There is little doubt but what Lieut. Throop is killed. The doctor who was with him, just before the ambulance fell into rebel hands, says that it was impossible for him to live but a few moments. Brave, noble, high-minded soul, he was loved by all of us and it will be long ere we will see his equal. Of our other officers, we have no definite account but hope they are unhurt.[52]

Charley Olcott was within ten feet of the Captain when he was taken. Charley had several narrow escapes but managed to pick up a cavalry horse with equipments complete and came back all right. It hardly seems possible that our men, who are taken, all escaped uninjured; but I sincerely hope such is the case.

Nearly every man [in the Battery] lost everything he owned, except the clothing he had on his back. Some of the boys bought clothes for a dress suit not long since and, not wishing to spoil them, carried them in knapsack. All these clothes were lost, of course. Our Division . . .suffered terrible. [It] went in 2,400 strong and came out less than 1.200 men. The 48th Ohio Infantry has been commanded by an orderly sergeant for the past two days, but now has a Lieut. in command. Nearly every regiment is without a field officer. Our brave Gen. Ransom has gone to New Orleans. It is feared he will lose his leg, but every effort will be made to save it. He paid our Battery a very high compliment. Said they did all that men could do and no men ever displayed better courage.[53]

In the fight of the 9th Inst. at Pleasant Hill, Gen. Smith whipped the enemy, succeeded in driving him six miles and taking several pieces of artillery and between six hundred and a thousand prisoners. The fighting was terrible on both sides but Gen. Smith, having the advantage of position, carried the day. All his force have retired to near this point and are now in camp. What the next move on the board will be remains to be seen. Rumors of all kinds are flying around thickly. A report is current to-night that Gen. [Tom] Green—com-

Brigadier General
Thomas Ransom

Men from the Chicago Mercantile Battery carried the wounded general off the Sabine Crossroads field.

Harper's Pictorial History of the Great Rebellion

Captain Samuel Coulter,
96th Ohio Infantry

Coulter, one of the Battery
Boys' comrades, was killed
at Sabine Crossroads.

Richard Brady Williams

Private Collection

manding the rebel army here—
was killed this morning while
trying to board and capture a
gunboat.[54]

It will probably be several
days before I can mail this and,
if I think of anything else to
add to it, will do so before
mailing.

*   *   *

The following account is from Captain Patrick H. White's
unpublished memoir:[55]

On the morning of April 8, 1864, I was chief of artillery on the
staff of Gen. Ransom, commander of the 13th Corps. When I awoke
in the morning, I little thought that that day would deprive me of my
liberty for 14 months. The night of the 7th was a restless one, for the
reason that staff officers were coming and going all night, sending
regiments to the front to support the cavalry under Gen. Lee. We
had breakfast between 4 and 5 a.m., on the 8th. Nothing happened
until about 11 a.m., when I was ordered to ride back and put the
batteries in camp at St. Patrick's Bayou, as the scrimmage at the
front did not amount to much, and the generals were unanimous that
it was but the rear guard covering their retreat.[56]

After I had obeyed the order, I was returning to report, when I
met Capt. Dickey, A. A. G., to Gen. Ransom, who came back for the
infantry of the 13th Corps that had been left to guard the wagon
train. He told me the enemy had beaten us, and for me to help him
get these troops through the wagon train. They were a narrow old
wagon road through the forest and it was barely wide enough to let

the wagons pass. When we got within a half mile of the battle ground, we saw that our troops were in bad shape. When I reached the front, Gen. Ransom came toward me with sword drawn, and said; 'Captain help us or we will have a stampede here. Go to Gen. Lee and have him send an officer to put his wagon train to one side so you can get up the batteries.' The train, which was all of a mile long, was soon closed up on the side of the road.[57]

Two miles from the end of the wagon train, I met the 1st Indiana and Chicago Mercantile batteries. I told them what was wanted and they were soon on the move, the Mercantile in front. We soon came to a swamp a hundred feet wide, crossed by a corduroy bridge, in the middle of which stuck an ammunition wagon. The men dismounted and in a short time wagon and mules were out of the way, and we went into action just as our lines were broken.

The rebels had defeated our infantry and captured four of our batteries. I was assigned to a position on a hill to the right of the road. I had rarely got the guns planted, when our infantry line was broken. Some of the troops came pell mell on us. I told the men to double shot the guns, but they could not fire until the disorganized regiments got from out front. Then we opened on the rebels, and the way the men handled the guns was terrific. Gen. Ransom came to me and said; 'You have checked them in front, but we are flanked and nearly surrounded, as support is gone right and left.' I immediately limbered, and as there was a pond in my rear, I had no alternative but to go through it; to go round it was impossible and would mean capture. I rode into the pond myself and found the water would just reach my horses' girths. I called on the men to follow, which they did in fine style. I then told Lieut. P. S. Cone, who was in command of the battery, to take position under cover at the edge of the woods, about 600 yards to the rear, while I went to the 1st Indiana battery and ordered them to get to the rear as soon as possible, or we would all be lost. I then rejoined the Mercantile and found every man doing his best. I had just reached the battery and was ordering Lieut. Cone to limber up, when Gen. Ransom rode up and said; 'Captain, get farther into the woods for shelter.' With that he moved on about 20 feet and stopped to look back at the enemy, when a bullet struck me on the shoulder, between the shoulder strap and my neck, passed under my chin and struck the General in the leg. That was the last I ever saw of the gallant Gen. Ransom, as he died of disease near Atlanta, Ga., while in command of the 17th Corps.[58]

Lieut. Throop had taken his section across the road into a plowed field, about fifty yards in advance, to fight a rebel battery. I was surprised and angry when I discovered what he had done, but I had no alternative then to go through another ordeal of exposure and see what had happened to him. I followed a fence a short way, then dismounted, as I was very much exposed to the rebel sharpshooters and I had to cover myself as best I could. Finally I got to my last cover before I had to run across the road. There was an old post which one of our sharpshooters had just abandoned, and I got behind it for two or three seconds, the bullets whistling all around me. When I reached the section it was in bad shape, as I knew it would be before I reached it. They were making every shot count, and if I had not ordered them back, they would have fought on until every man and horse was killed. The enemy was pouring down on them; and it reminds me now of Rickett's Battery at Gettysburg, when the Louisiana troops charged them. Lieut. Throop was killed by a shell, and several horses were killed and wounded. I got them out of the place and told Sergeant Sinclair to get to the rear through the wagon train. I then joined the other part of the battery, knowing that if I did not retreat soon the battery would be lost. I told Lieut. Barr to take his section and get to the rear quietly. He had gone but a short way when he was sent back by a staff officer of Gen. Banks; so the section went into action again.

At this time an officer of Gen. Banks' staff came to me and asked what battery it was. I told him. I then noticed Gen. Banks and staff on my right and rear in the timber. In a short time the officer returned again and said; "The General says you are doing splendidly, and to hold the place you have, as the 19th Corps will be here in half an hour.' I learned afterwards that if the General had been promptly obeyed, the 19th Corps would have been on hand in a few minutes. But unfortunately, the commanding officer of the advanced brigade misunderstood, or received the order carelessly, and ordered his men to cook two days' rations. If they had come on time there would have been a different story. At this time, I sent Lieut. Throop's section to the rear, Gen. Cameron's brigade of the 13th Corps came up and went into position on the right and left of the road. This accounts for holding the enemy in check in front. But in the meantime, they were flanking in the shape of a letter 'V.' In a short time all was confusion. Our troops came back on us pell mell, as the enemy was closing in. I then limbered up the last section of the battery and started for the rear also. I had already sent the other two sections back and was pushing my way through the train, when Sergeant Hammett called; 'Captain, look behind you.' A rebel officer was holding a six shooter near the back of my head and it was lucky for me he did not shoot. I halted and dismounted. He then demanded my pistol, but I did not have it with me, having given it to my servant early in the day to lighten my load. He then took a fancy to my horse, and in particular to a new mackintosh overcoat on the pommel of my saddle.

I must say I was very much excited and angry at our officers for getting us in such a scrape, and I did not care whether I lived or died. I was soon surrounded by a troop of drunken rebel privates, whooping and yelling like Indians. 'Give up your sword,' they shouted. I unhooked it, but refused to hand it over to any but an officer. They all claimed to be officers. The cocked their pieces and said; 'Give up your sword or we will shoot.' I foolishly said; 'Shoot away.' The next moment an officer came along and spoke to the men, who hooted and jeered at him. I passed over my sword, which was a gift to me from the citizens of Chicago and was presented to me after the battle of Shiloh. The officer gave me his name and residence, but I have forgotten it.[59]

Just then Gen. Dick Taylor and staff came up, and he asked if I was a general officer. I said I did not have that honor, but that I was commandant of this battery. 'That is very nice,' he answered, 'We have both battery and captain. He was mistaken, as he had but one section, but the other four guns were afterward captured.

The boys got the four guns back to the corduroy bridge I spoke of, but found there a perfect jam of wagons, ambulances and horses. Some of the horses stuck in the middle of it with their riders on their backs and some looked as if they sprang from the bottom, like Cadmus armed men. Waiting as long as they dared to see if the road could be cleared, they were compelled to abandon their guns when the enemy began firing into them.

It was then that the 19th Corps came up in splendid order and called to the men to lie down and they would shoot over them. It was done as cooly as if on dress parade. They then opened their ranks and let the defeated troops pass through. No country ever saw the equal of such splendid troops and I wish my pen could do them justice. But history will do that for them, so I will confine myself to the squad that were taken prisoners with me.

The guards ordered us to fall in and as they were not inclined to let us have any of our tricks as they called our property on the guns and caissons, I tried to get a blanket. I managed to get two, and I gave one to Lieut. Cone. We were ordered to move, and about 8 p.m., we arrived at Mansfield, La., a few miles from Sabine Crossroads, the battleground. We were quartered in the Court House. Lieut. Cone and myself were ordered upstairs, and we thought we were going to have something extra. Not a bit of it. We were put in a large room and the door locked on us. The floor was packed with sleeping soldiers and the air in the room was terrible. By hard work we kicked and pushed the sleepers closer together and finally got room to spread our blankets.[60]

We were hustled out at daybreak next morning, the officers being formed into a separate squad. During the day I discovered our destination would be Tyler, Texas.

*   *   *

From Shreveport, Alex McDow sent a letter to his daughter Kate on April 16, 1863. In it, he described his capture of Ransom's chief of artillery. He also sent White's saber to her. After the war, McDow's daughter married John Brownson, a former member of Terry's Texas Rangers, and resided in Victoria, Texas (located across the channel from the Battery Boys' barren Matagorda Peninsula). After her father died, Kate ran an ad in an 1896 issue of the *National Tribune,* a Union veterans' publication, offering to return the sword McDow had captured at Sabine Crossroads. The section of Captain McDow's letter pertinent to the capture of White is included below:

> Not only ours beat the Feds also I captured a Capt. Of Bat. Capt. White, Chief of Ransom's Artillery, 1 Lt. & 5 or 6 privates, The Capt. Refused to Surrender to one of my men just ahead of me, said he wouldn't Surrender to anybody but an officer. My man (Cross) told him he would kill him, drew down his gun on him, was going to shoot him, I sprang in, presented my pistol to his breast, told him to surrender to me, I was an officer. He did so, give me his sword, pistol &c. It was a nice sword. I have sent it home. . . . [61]

*   *   *

Grand Ecore La.
April 17th 1864

My dear father

What will they do with us now is the universal cry in our Battery and all are anxious to know. Many seem to think we may possibly be sent to Chicago to refit but I have no idea that anything of that kind will be done, and question if it would pay the government to do so. It will probably be but a few days before something definite will be known.[62]

Many would think that, after our recent defeat, the men would feel sad and dejected but, could such people only be among our camps, how quickly would their opinions change. The enthusiasm among the troops is as great as when starting out on a campaign and all appear anxious to push forward. If our forces are only rightly managed, I think they will succeed yet. It is true the enemy feels confident over his recent success, but he feels too sure and on this depends much of our success.

I am of the opinion that Gen. Steele, with a large force of cavalry, infantry and artillery is not far from Shreveport and only waiting to hear from us. Steele cannot take Shreveport on account of the rebel gunboats there and, until he is heard from, our gunboats will not venture too near the place. Our gunboats have been within forty miles of Shreveport but, hearing of our defeat, started back towards this place. Had to run a perfect gauntlet of guerrilla parties &c &c. At one place, the rebs tried to board the gunboat "Lexington" but were repulsed with terrible slaughter; their Gen. Green being among the killed. This Gen. Green was one of the best officers in the rebel service and his loss will be severely felt. He commanded the force that whipped us on the 8th.[63]

We sent out a flag of truce to find our wounded and killed. Lieuts. Throop and Barr and Corporal Dyer of our Battery are killed. No other men's names of our Battery were on the list and we are strong in the hope that all the rest have escaped uninjured. We are told that an attempt to exchange will soon be made and, if it succeeds, we will soon have our boys with us again.[64]

*   *   *

New Orleans La.
April 27th 1864

My dear father

After a very hard tedious journey of five days, we have arrived here all safe and sound. Came down on a hospital boat from Grand Ecore to Alexandria, and from there took a regular old <u>tub</u> and "Slowly by degrees" made our way to this place. I reserve the incidents and <u>trials</u> of our journey for a future letter as I am very busy this morning and have only time to drop you a line to let you know how and where I am.[65]

We are here without anything but what we have on our backs and I am busily engaged in drawing supplies and clothing, cooking utensils, tents &c &c. Don't know how soon we will be <u>fixed out</u> with a new battery; am told that there is nothing here to equip us and, if that is the case, will probably have to stay here for some time. Do not hear anything from our boys who are prisoners and fear we will not for some time, as we already owe the enemy more men than we have to give. The prisoners taken by our Gen. A. J. Smith have all been exchanged and only paid for those [with men whom the] rebs took at Carion Crow Bayou last Fall.[66]

The city is very quiet, the army being all at the front and all soldiers arriving here sent immediately to their commands. On the levee, business looks pretty brisk but I think nearly everything is done on government account. At one time, our forces on the Red river were in possession of large quantities of cotton but, [during] the skedaddle, lost nearly all of it.

I will write again soon so, for the present, please accept this very short note and with love to all.

*   *   *

White, Cone, and their fellow prisoners from Banks' 13th Corps and 19th Corps were en route to Camp Ford, Texas. On April 9, the day after the Sabine Crossroads disaster, they began heading west by foot. The regimental historian of the 46th Indiana Infantry provided one of the only accounts of this torturous 16-day journey: "Chilled, hungry and weary, this band, numbering fifty commissioned officers and 1,200 men, was goaded forward between two lines of rebel cavalry, flushed with a temporary success. . . . The most insulting epithets were heaped on the defenseless men; and those who, from sickness or exhaustion, reeled in the ranks, were treated with a degree of barbarity almost beyond belief."[67]

White and his comrades trudged along, fatigued and suffering from a shortage of water. As they struggled forward, "many men were forced along by the bayonet and by threats of shooting." Most of the nights were passed trying to make dinner—using one frying pan per 100 prisoners—with musty corn meal, a minuscule amount of salted beef, and faltering fires. The Confederate guards added to the prisoners' misery by camping upstream and befouling their drinking water.

The Union soldiers marched during the day through a rural gauntlet of old men, women, and children, brandishing Confederate flags and hurling verbal abuse at the passing prisoners. Pat White and the other captives defiantly "drowned all shouts of exultation by the rebels with patriotic songs." There would not be much to sing about, however, when the Battery Boys reached Camp Ford, where they faced imprisonment for the next 14 months.

"The report of no regular correspondent has yet been permitted to see the light. The private letters that reached Chicago would doubtless have been detained by the officers who caused the [Sabine Crossroads] disaster had they suspected that those accounts would be published so promptly, as they described the disaster too plainly and laid the blame too freely on those who led the soldiers to defeat and destruction."

Chapter 14

Little Use in Disguising Defeat

T he Mercantile Battery survivors were still grieving over their Sabine Crossroads catastrophe when they reached New Orleans. The loss of their guns was embarrassing, but the loss of so many comrades killed, wounded, and captured was emotionally devastating.

Pat White's loss was especially difficult for the survivors. As Ransom's chief of artillery, Captain White would have known what to do to take care of the artillerists after their battlefield catastrophe. Unfortunately, there were no suitable senior commanders to replace him. Lieutenant Pinckney Cone had also been captured and was on his way with White to a Confederate prison. The highly respected Lieutenant George Throop had been killed, mortally struck in his abdomen during the battle. "I am dying but I am not afraid to die," he explained while massive internal bleeding drained away his life. "Tell my father and mother that I die willingly; my firm faith sustains me. I give my life for a glorious cause, and I do not regret it."[1]

Frank Leslie's Illustrated Newspaper

Nathaniel Banks' Grand Ecore fortifications

These losses were just the tip of the iceberg for White's battery. The survivors knew that two of their friends, a junior lieutenant and a sergeant, had died manning the guns. The fate of more than 20 other Mercantile Battery redlegs remained unknown. In all probability they were either in a Confederate hospital or prison—or buried in one of several mass Union graves on the Sabine Crossroads battlefield. As if these losses were not devastating enough, their favorite general and fellow Illinoisan, Thomas Ransom, had suffered a severe knee wound and had been sent downriver to New Orleans aboard the hospital transport *Laurel Hill*.[2]

The mismanagement of the Red River expedition by Nathaniel Banks and William Franklin was obvious to every Chicago artilleryman. Putting the wagons so close to the front of the column in the middle of enemy territory had been foolhardy, and had prevented an orderly withdrawal. For the Chicagoans, the most tangible result of this egregious blunder was the loss of the battery's six 3-inch rifled pieces and associated equipment. Most of the battery's survivors also lost their personal property, such as letters from loves ones and irreplaceable photographic images, which had been stored on the company wagons and caissons the enemy captured. "Nearly every man lost everything he owned, except the clothing he had on his back," Will Brown lamented to his father. Will and his friends had made their mad dash from the Sabine Crossroads battlefield in "shock"—the first stage of grieving—which anesthetized them sufficiently to endure the army's humiliating retreat.[3]

Banks was also shocked. His immediate fear in the aftermath of the April 8 battle was being overwhelmed again by Richard Taylor's victorious soldiers. Prior to the battle of Pleasant Hill, Banks sent Colonel William H. Dickey's Corps d'Afrique soldiers to lead his supply train back to Grand Ecore—and safety. Albert Lee's cavalry, along with the Mercantile Battery and the other mauled units of the 13th Corps, joined the retreating Union caravan, which arrived in Grand Ecore during the afternoon of April 10. There, the Mercantile Battery survivors entered the second stage of grieving, a "visceral emotional reaction." Many of the artillerists agonized over their predicament. The cry of "What will they do with us now?" echoed through the camp. Some of the battery members, including Will Brown and Private Chase Dickinson, vented their anger in letters.[4]

Brown and Dickinson jotted down hasty notes the next day, April 11, when they discovered the *Laurel Hill* was about to leave for New Orleans with 430 seriously wounded soldiers aboard. Dickinson, an attorney before the war, was asked to write to the Mercantile Association and explain to their sponsors that the artillerists were not responsible for their losses. "A deep gloom of despondency enshrouds the remnant of our once powerful battery," Dickinson lamented. "'Now is the winter of our discontent,' and the only vernal hint that breaks the gloom is the thought that we did our duty well, and that no one exertion of ours could have changed the result." The letters written by Chicago's Battery Boys during those first

Chase Dickinson

A graduate of Albany Law University, he practiced in Chicago before joining the Mercantile Battery in 1862.

Richard Brady Williams
Private Collection

two days in Grand Ecore would have a greater impact than anyone imagined. The spontaneous torrent of emotion unleashed by their pens provided the first unvarnished eyewitness accounts of Nathaniel Banks' Red River disaster, not only to their families and friends but also to the entire nation—including Lincoln, Stanton, and Grant. But it was only by accident that the Mercantile Battery letters made it into Chicago newspapers.[5]

Strengthened by A. J. Smith's leadership, Banks' senior commanders were left behind on April 9 to confront Taylor's army at Pleasant Hill. Strong infantry reinforcements under Brigadier General Thomas Churchill bolstered the advancing Confederates, who hoped to exceed their victory at Sabine Crossroads by destroying Banks' command. This time, however, Taylor's attack was thrown back with heavy losses in a clear tactical Union victory. Much of Churchill's command dissolved into rout as the sunlight faded over the battlefield.[6]

Banks spent most of the afternoon away from the battlefield in a structure known as "The Academy," which, along with a simple white church, was one of the few buildings comprising Pleasant Hill. It was there Banks perfected his plans for a full-scale retreat to Grand Ecore. The village, with its Red River landing, would be the expedition's next rendezvous point. Brigadier General Cuvier Grover's troops were ordered up from Alexandria. Porter and Brigadier General Thomas Kilby Smith would have to be notified of the change of plans, and a detachment of the 14th New York Cavalry was dispatched for that purpose. The horse soldiers found some of Smith's men on patrol near Loggy Bayou, where the Confederates had sunk a ship loaded with bricks and mud to arrest the progress of the Northern armada.[7]

That night, after the Union army had driven the Confederates from the Pleasant Hill battlefield, Banks held a council of war. Banks initially advocated resuming his advance against the Confederates, but Franklin and others convinced him to retreat. A. J. Smith was not present at the meeting, but Banks had assured him earlier that the army would take the offensive. Smith was livid when he found out about his commander's change of heart. His "ragged guerrillas," as his troops were called, had played a pivotal role that day in beating back Taylor's attack. Whiskey Smith argued that the army should move to meet Porter and Kilby Smith, not knowing that Banks had already sent couriers to inform them about his change of plans. Smith was so enraged that he tried to persuade

Admiral David Dixon Porter

Battles and Leaders
of the Civil War

Franklin, who was wounded but still second in command, to arrest Banks and take over the army's command. Already distressed by his own culpability for the loss at Sabine Crossroads, Franklin refused to support Smith's proposal. "Smith, don't you know this is mutiny?" Franklin had responded. The campaign was over and Banks' army would retreat; the wounded were to be abandoned; the dead would lie unburied.[8]

The journey to Grand Ecore was humiliating for Banks and his staff. Above the din of the retreating army, they heard catcalls from the ranks. Some soldiers shouted disparaging chants in unison. Banks and Franklin probably thought about their careers and reputations, both of which were on the verge of ruin. The soldiers' irreverence during the march was a foreshadowing of the inevitable public scorn that followed in the wake of their Sabine Crossroads mistakes and ensuing retrograde. When Banks and his men reached the temporary safety of Grand Ecore on April 11, they had to prepare for an alarming contingency: Taylor might attack them once again.[9]

Though demoralized, Banks issued a series of orders and dispatches. He directed his weary Union soldiers to throw up breastworks. They went to work with pickets posted in front and the Red River behind them. Within a few days, the Union soldiers had a two-mile, semicircular log and earthen barrier erected. Several navy gunboats, which had not accompanied Porter upstream, provided additional protection on their flanks. Knowing that Taylor had learned how to wage relentless warfare while serving under Stonewall Jackson, Banks may well have feared that his 1862 Shenandoah Valley fiasco was about to be reprised. His defensive precautions demonstrated that he believed the aggressive

Taylor would indeed pursue him—just as Jackson had done two years earlier. John McClernand, languishing in Texas, received orders to join Banks along with most of his 13th Corps troops at Pass Cavallo and take over the injured Ransom's responsibilities. Grover was pressed again to bring up as many of his 4,000 Alexandria reinforcements as he could spare. Still hoping to revive the expedition, Banks also urged Major General Frederick Steele to march his Arkansas column to Shreveport and join him in a renewed offensive. Meanwhile, Whiskey Smith and other officers awaited the return of Porter's flotilla and Kilby Smith's troops, worried that the Rebels may have already defeated them.[10]

Porter visited Banks when he returned to Grand Ecore. The general was resting in his cozy tent, "wearing a fine dressing gown, velvet cap, and comfortable slippers." Porter was irritated about the change of plans and abandonment of the advance against Shreveport. Banks tried to downplay the debacle at Sabine Crossroads and the retreat from Pleasant Hill, blaming the precipitous withdrawal on a shortage of water for his men. Always mindful of his political ambitions, Banks tried to convince Porter to proceed with their original plan. But the admiral was far from gullible and refused to be manipulated into extending the ill-fated Red River campaign. Porter considered it bizarre that, despite everything he was hearing from other officers, Banks was "under the delusion that he had won the battle of Mansfield [Sabine Crossroads]." Franklin had a more realistic view of what had transpired on April 8, but shared his thoughts only with his wife. "[W]e had a terrible fight yesterday [April 8]. . . . My men behaved admirably, but we were beaten nevertheless." After reaching Grand Ecore Franklin wrote to his wife again, explaining that Banks was to blame for the debacle by pushing the infantry blindly forward along the narrow wagon road to confront Taylor at Sabine Crossroads: "This induced putting forward another [infantry unit], and thus we were drawn into a genl engagement with most of our Infantry too far to the rear to bring up. It was disgraceful Generalship."[11]

Even if he knew Franklin's private thoughts, Banks was unconcerned about his subordinate's version of events. On April 13, the Department of the Gulf's commander fired his first official salvo in his plan to spin what had happened in Louisiana. In a brazen display of political gamesmanship designed to avoid responsibility for the bungled expedition, Banks sent his initial report to Henry Halleck. The onus of the defeat, explained Banks, belonged to his subordinates, including

Franklin and Lee. Banks knew his report would be forwarded to Grant, Stanton, and Lincoln. He fervently hoped his explanation would keep the president in his camp as friend and protector. The wily Banks trumpeted the Union's successes at Fort De Russy, Henderson's Hill, and Pleasant Grove while downplaying his April 8 defeat at Sabine Crossroads. "The rout of the enemy was complete," he explained, referring to the Pleasant Hill battle on April 9. Banks failed to credit A. J. Smith for the crucial role he played in the triumph. Through Halleck, Banks sought permission to renew the advance against Shreveport, which afforded him the only near-term opportunity to deflect attention from the Sabine Crossroads debacle.[12]

Aside from preparing to receive another potential assault from Taylor and, at the same time, trying to avoid a long-distance attack from Washington, Nathaniel Banks had another major impediment to face before resuming the Shreveport operation. Like sand slipping through an hour-glass, his 30-day period to use Sherman's 10,000 troops was nearly gone. The deadline for borrowing Sherman's battle-hardened soldiers was based on the original Alexandria rendezvous target in mid-March, and not the date of his arrival 10 days later. Banks was even more anxious when one of Sherman's generals showed up to remind him that only a few days remained; Whiskey Smith, Kilby Smith, and their troops were needed in Tennessee for the upcoming Atlanta Campaign.[13]

The beleaguered Red River commander realized he could not afford to lose the aggressive Western soldiers. In desperation, Banks contacted General-in-Chief Ulysses S. Grant, who was in Virginia preparing to launch his overland offensive against Robert E. Lee. Banks pleaded that he needed to retain Sherman's troops to advance against Shreveport and destroy the main body of the Confederacy's Trans-Mississippi army. "I regard that result as certain to be accomplished if our movement is not interrupted. . . . Its destruction is a work of certainty, requiring but a small force and a short time." Otherwise, Banks warned, the Confederates might capture Porter's gunboats and reach the Mississippi River, where they could interrupt Western river traffic. Banks failed to mention that the Red River's unseasonably low waters were now endangering Porter's fleet.[14]

Thus far, Banks reacted to his Red River situation with adept political dissembling. He "circled the wagons" to protect himself and preemptively disseminated his version of the campaign to key decision makers. The next phase of successful scandal management was to delay the emergence of the truth for as long as possible. Banks knew that if he could gain enough time to take Shreveport, earlier errors at Sabine Crossroads would be overshadowed by public celebrations of his Trans-Mississippi conquest, just as Grant's bloody May 19 and 22 assaults a year earlier at Vicksburg had been forgotten and forgiven when the stronghold surrendered on July 4. If he was successful, the former lawmaker would avoid the public beating he took in 1862 after his Shenandoah Valley and Cedar Mountain defeats. Banks' prospects of obtaining the Republican presidential nomination at his party's June 7 convention would be ruined if the press caught wind of his disastrous mistakes and once again ridiculed him as the Confederates' "best commissary" officer. Even if he did not win the 1864 nomination, Banks wanted to remain in good political favor, perhaps with an eye toward gaining the nomination at a later date. For all these reasons it was essential he control the public coverage of the Louisiana fiasco.[15]

The news of the Sabine Crossroads battle and retreat from Pleasant Hill was slow to reach the Northern press because the campaign took place far away from Northern media outlets. The editors of the *Chicago Tribune*, however, ascribed the delay to Banks, who had imposed one of the first news blackouts in American history. According to the paper, Banks restricted access to the military's telegraph and dispatch system— and their Cairo access point—so reporters, some of whom had paid an admission price to join the expedition, could not submit timely Red River battle reports to their editors. Banks also allegedly obstructed the delivery of Union mail. The result was that soldiers from the Department of the Gulf were unable to inform their families and friends about the defeat. Although not mentioned by the *Chicago Tribune*, another element of this information blackout pertained to New Orleans, where Banks' headquarters controlled local newspapers. "The papers here are under a strict military rule," Will Brown noted to his father upon his return to the Crescent City. Only sanitized accounts of the recent battles were permitted in the New Orleans papers—the only source of Red River information for the Northern press. Banks may have hoped that these whitewashed news stories, which downplayed the calamity at Sabine Crossroads and highlighted the victory at Pleasant Hill, would buy him time to move out again and capture Shreveport.[16]

In addition to managing the release of information, Banks tried to divert attention by shifting the blame for his defeat to someone else. His scapegoats included Albert Lee, his cavalry commander, and Charles Stone, his chief of staff. Stone made an ideal target because of his 1861 defeat at Ball's Bluff, which still cast a pall over his service. Brigadier General William Dwight replaced Stone. Dwight had performed well as a brigade commander in the 19th Corps. More importantly, he was also from Massachusetts and was the brother of a premier cotton trader who was working with the department's quartermaster. Banks dismissed Albert Lee and promoted Brigadier General Richard Arnold, his chief of artillery, to take charge of the cavalry.[17]

On April 21, Will Brown and the Mercantile Battery survivors left Grand Ecore on board the *William L. Ewing*. Bugler Florison Pitts recorded the battery's trip in his diary: "A lot of sick and wounded on her, but with one surgeon. He has no medicines. The boat has no rations for them. One man died in the night of <u>starvation</u>. Our boys offering their services as nurses, making tea and coffee for them from our own rations." Ten days before, a newspaper correspondent with the *New York Daily Tribune* had witnessed similar unnecessary sufferings among the first boatload of wounded soldiers sent from Grand Ecore on the *Laurel Hill*. The wounded General Ransom was also on board. Although the reporter did not accuse Banks specifically, he wrote that officials had jeopardized the health of the soldiers when the Red River expedition began by using hospital boats to transport speculators and cotton-packaging materials, rather than doctors and medical supplies. On April 23, a rainy and dreary day, the Battery Boys and other ambulatory passengers debarked two miles above Alexandria. With its load lightened, the *William L. Ewing* passed over the rapids. That evening the young men from Chicago buried three soldiers who had died during the trip.[18]

The sun darted in and out of the white clouds the next day as the Mercantile Battery departed on the *Kate Dale*. The Chicago redlegs were more troubled by the memories of their Red River ordeal than the vagaries of the weather. Reaching New Orleans was not going to be easy, especially on their dilapidated boat. There was good reason for them to be worried. Department of the Gulf quartermasters had been using the *Kate Dale,* a captured Confederate blockade runner, to haul coal from New Orleans up Red River. On the same day the anxious artillerymen arrived at Alexandria, Banks' assistant quartermaster sent a dispatch from there to his chief in New Orleans advising "that the *Kate Dale* not be sent up again, as she draws too much water." On her way down the Red River, the boat, Pitts noted, "ran into the river bank twice and broke both paddle wheels."[19]

The artillerists had to pass through an ominous gauntlet to reach New Orleans. Local Confederate bushwhackers converged upon the narrow twisting Red River to harass arriving and departing boats. The men of the Mercantile Battery were wary of possible attacks. Before they left Alexandria, the Chicagoans heard that enemy guerrillas had fired on the *Superior* at the mouth of the Red River, killing three men and wounding 17 others. "Passed Fort De Russy at sunset. River very crooked," wrote Florison Pitts in his diary about the battery's transport. "Our boys worked the two guns onboard, shelling the woods all the way down."[20]

The *Kate Dale* continued to struggle, careening along the Red River's hairpin turns like a driver-less wagon going through a mine tunnel. About four miles below Fort De Russy, the rickety boat ran into the riverbank and jerked to a stop. One of the steamer's wheels was severely damaged. Her passengers were stranded. The Battery Boys and their companions waited in darkness along the shore. Their two Dahlgren howitzers were silent. The Confederate deserters and contrabands on board remained quiet. The Yankees listened intently to the eerie cacophony of strange birds and insects, straining their ears for any evidence of enemy marauders. Will Brown recalled how they "[t]ried to call a gunboat by whistling but, receiving no reply, sent off a signal of men to hunt one up . . . at midnight the gunboat joined us." Lieutenant Roe and his men were fortunate to escape. One week later, Taylor slipped a noose around the Red River and, over the next five days, the Union lost three transports, two gunboats, and about 600 soldiers and sailors.[21]

Arriving in New Orleans on April 26, the relieved members of the Mercantile Battery began to enter into the third stage of grieving: "adjustment." This stage allowed them to move beyond the initial shock of the Sabine Crossroads losses and their subsequent emotional volatility. Will Brown spent his time trying to re-equip the battery. Some of the returning soldiers tracked down the company's mail, which provided them with both encouraging and discouraging information. The good news was the April 10 and 11 Grand Ecore letters had made it to Chicago unscathed, and had preempted Banks' attempts at damage control. The bad news was that a batch of their correspondence had apparently been lost. Their mood became more acerbic when they learned that Will had been forced to accept a shipment of infantry muskets someone had ordered to arm the battery.

*   *   *

Camp Parapet[22]
Defences of New Orleans
May 1st 1864

My dear father

As I sit writing this, I cannot but recall what we were doing one year ago to-day, i.e. moving forward on the <u>double quick</u> toward Port Gibson Miss. where, by noon, we were engaged in one of most successful fights of the Vicksburg campaign. To-day, how differently are we situated. Here am I comfortably quartered in a small brick house and as quietly engaged in writing as I could be were "Wars and rumors of wars" a thing long past. In walking thro' the streets of this great city, one cannot but reflect on the easy manner that we as a nation take the war. In the city, no one seems to think of war, yet only a two hour walk from it will bring one in the midst of the "Stern reality."[23]

All around the city, a strong line of works, forts, rifle pits &c &c are thrown up. And behind them are camped our troops. We are, for the present, camped near one of the forts but are of about as much use as a party of aborigines. A Battery without guns or horses is about as useful as a <u>second</u> tail to a dog. About all our boys have to do is to eat and <u>growl</u>; and in the latter line they can carry off the premium. It is a saying in the army that it is a soldier's special privilege to growl and complain. But everything can be carried to excess. The fact is our boys are generally dissatisfied but only time will cure them of the <u>disease</u>. I am kept very busy all the time; have not written hardly a letter and have at least a dozen to answer. I am kept running nearly all the time on business of some kind. Lieut. Roe depends on me for nearly everything the boys want and I have to get it. Will not be so busy in a few days, however, and then will write what letters I owe.

I dropped you a note on the second day after we arrived here and hope it will reach you in due time. Our trip from Alexandria was a pretty rough one. We, with a lot of rebel deserters, contrabands &c, were first on the "Kate Dale" a Mobile rebel blockade runner and about as fit for river navigation as "Little Mac" to command the Army of the Potomac. At nearly every bend of the river—and their

number is legion—part of our wheel-house would be knocked to
pieces. And just after dark of the first night out, and when a few
miles below Fort DeRussy, we broke completely down and had to
stop for the night. Tried to call a gunboat by whistling but, receiving
no reply, sent off a squad of men to hunt one up. This was about 8
PM and from that time 'till midnight kept out a strong guard; but
nary [a] guerrilla showed himself and at midnight the gunboat
joined us.

It is anything but a comfortable feeling to be in a country infested
with guerrillas, particularly in a country when the rascals have
every advantage. All along the river we expected to be fired into but
did not hear a rebel shot. We had on board one twelve and one
24-pounder rifled Dahlgren boat howitzer and I think their saucy
appearance had much to do toward keeping the enemy from firing
into us.

The morning we left Alexandria, a party of guerrillas dashed in
just across the river from the town and killed and wounded several
men. I was on the levee at Alexandria at the time and saw nearly the
whole affair. A few stray bullets were fired over where I was but did
no damage. A gunboat in the river waited 'till the rebs got close to
the bank and then commenced throwing shells among them. I never
saw such a lively movement as the rebs then made. The gunboat did
more than scatter them. As a general thing, the rebs have a perfect
horror of our gunboats and it is seldom they venture within shot of
one. Don't think they would have done so this time had they known
the boat was so close.

We do not receive any news from the Red river and are
profoundly ignorant in regard to its movements. The papers here are
under a strict military rule and dare not publish any war news 'till
they receive it from Northern papers. The news of our defeat was
recd in Chicago thro' letters from our boys. The "Journal" of the
20th of April has letters from our boys and I notice extracts from
Charley Olcott's and one of my own are among the number. Would
not be surprised if Gen. Banks gave us an order on this subject but,
for my part, I can see little use in disguising defeat when it was so
plain. Since I have been here, I have been asked about the fight by
more than a hundred persons, many of them occupying pretty high
official positions.[24]

Your letter giving an account of the death of little Willie did not
reach me 'till a few days ago. I deeply sympathize with brother and
sister in this, their hour of sorrow. Will write sister Delia in a few
days.[25]

* * *

Camp Parapet
Defences of N.O.
May 8th 1864

My dear father

Were one to credit half the news that are daily flying around New Orleans, he would not only think that the whole country was in a terrible bad way, but that our entire force in the Red river was surely lost as the sun [is] to shine. It is very easy to account for these rumors as it seems the policy of the Department [is] to keep everything in the dark as much as possible—and to throw a shade of mystery on all army movements. Here, outside of official quarters, nothing definite is known. One can only gain information on what is going on up the Red [river] by writing some acquaintance from there on business here. Yesterday, I saw an officer directly from Alexandria. He says that our army there is pretty strong and can get away all right but, if they leave, [will] lose many transports and gunboats.[26]

The guerrillas along the Red river are doing all in their power to obstruct navigation and are meeting with great success. They succeeded in capturing and sinking three transports and two tin clad gunboats during last week. Nearly every boat passing up or down is fired into and yesterday three boats returned here unable to run the gauntlet of rebel batteries on the river between Fort DeRussy and Alexandria. Had an acquaintance on one of the boats. He says their boat went within forty miles of Alexandria when the rebs opened on them with shot and shell, compelling them to come about as rapidly as possible and return to the Mississippi.[27]

From what I have seen of the Red river, I have no doubt but that small parties of the enemy, situated at different points, can most effectively blockade the navigation of it by unarmed transports. The river is so very crooked, and winds around in so many directions, that a boat moving fifteen or twenty miles only makes about six miles by land. And in consequence the enemy, after firing into her at one point, only have to move a few miles before they can take position and pour another fire into her. Prisoners taken pretend that this guerrilla mode of war-fare is not recognized by the C.S.A. but, it is evident from the way they are…[deployed] on the Red [river], the regular organized Confed. troops are engaged in this business.

It is impossible to form any definite opinion in regard to the ultimate result of the Red river expedition. I am fearful that we will lose several of our best upper Mississippi river gunboats and many transports also. The army can get away all right if they want, as they have only to cross the river at Alexandria and then take a bee-line for Natchez. Banks is evidently labored under a great mistake in regard to the enemies force in Western Louisiana. I do not think that anyone thought they had as large a force. Gens. [John A.] McClernand and [David] Hunter are with Banks at Alexandria and, as three heads are better than one, I think that everything will come out pretty well yet; but the taking of Shreveport will have to be postponed for the present.[28]

The enemy, knowing that a greater part of our force has been withdrawn from this vicinity, is again making demonstrations on the east side of the Mississippi between here and the mouth of the Red river. Plaquemine, Port Hudson and Baton Rouge have been threatened and at each place there are fears of an attack. There has been several sharp fights in rear of Baton Rouge and reinforcements from here have been sent up. The enemy is reported 10.000 strong in rear [of] Baton Rouge.

Yesterday, we received orders to draw infantry equipments and now have them in camp. But our boys say they will only use them to defend the city and, if an attempt is made to send us to the front with such arms, will not go. Gen. Reynolds assures Lieut. Roe that we are only to take these muskets temporarily and that as soon as possible we shall have a new battery.[29]

I do not think they can force us to take muskets as we are only known as an artillery company and cannot be put in any other branch of the service or be compelled to bear infantry arms. If it is necessary for defence of the city to take a musket, I don't think there is a man who would refuse. But to go in the field so equipped, not a man will do it. They cannot be blamed for this as they have had no practice with small arms and know but little of their use, or how to use them. It may seem rather odd that men who have been shot at time and again do not know how to shoot back in return. But I do not think there are ten men in the Company who ever fired a musket. I never did but once and then the thing kicked me like blazes. With our proper arm, and the one we enlisted to serve under, our boys will go anywhere they may be ordered and our past conduct will show whether we will fight or not.

I sincerely hope that no trouble will ensue from this order to draw muskets but, if they insist on our taking the field with them, the boys will not submit and I have no doubt that our friends at home will support us. A soldier's first duty is to obey all consistent orders and so far our boys have done so; but they will not be trampled upon by anybody. Fortunately, our Battery is not the only one that has the order to draw muskets. Captain Nims 2nd Mass. Battery has the same order and I think both batteries will act together in the matter. We are unfortunate in not having Captain White with us, as his cool head and good judgment would have greater influence toward coloring the minds of the boys than anything else. Lieut. Roe has very little experience as a commanding officer and does not know hardly what to do. In my present capacity, I am almost constantly in his society and I assure you that it keeps my mind constantly working to devise plans &c. But of all this, [and] more, one of these days. I hope the ultimate result will only be something to jest about in the future.[30]

*　　*　　*

After settling into Camp Parapet on April 29, Will Brown resumed writing his "weekly Sunday letter" to his father. He mentioned that an excerpt from one of his Grand Ecore letters was included in the Mercantile Battery letters that broke the news of Banks' Sabine Crossroads calamity. "The news of our defeat was recd in Chicago thro' letters from our boys," he wrote. "The 'Journal' of the 20th of April has letters from our boys and I notice extracts from Charley Olcott's and one of my own are among the number." Will also implied that Banks might retaliate against the battery.

As with most modern political scandals that trigger a vindictive response, Banks did not put anything in writing. If he was indeed behind any retaliation taken against the Chicago gunners, the general issued only verbal instructions to Major General Joseph Reynolds at his New Orleans headquarters.

In a more blatant case of retaliation, a reporter from the *New York World* who wrote a negative article about Banks on April 26 was kicked out of New Orleans. Banks denied any responsibility, but one historian who has written on the subject was not so sure. "It is entirely possible, however," wrote J. Cutler Andrews, "that the hostile criticisms, published in the *World*, of Banks' mismanagement of the campaign caused the *World* correspondent Philip Ripley to be expelled from New Orleans even before Banks returned from the Red River country." Tensions increased in early May when Brigadier General Thomas Sherman, in command of New Orleans' defenses, had a Boston reporter arrested and banned from writing an article about how Banks' Red River problems were making the city more vulnerable to enemy attack.[31]

The expulsion of reporters occurred around the same time Will Brown received the company's shipment of antiquated infantry muskets. The fear Will expressed to his father about reprisal if his disgruntled batterymates refused to take up arms except to defend against an attack on the city had materialized sooner than he expected. But were the young men provoked into the alleged mutiny because they had exposed the Sabine Crossroads disaster? Or was it simply a coincidence that they received such rough treatment?

The *Chicago Evening Journal* broke the news of Banks' defeat on April 19. That Tuesday morning, the newspaper received its first batch of Mercantile Battery letters sent from Grand Ecore. The letters likely arrived on board the *Luminary*, which docked in Cairo the day before, and were transported via the Illinois Central Railroad to Chicago. This meant the battery's correspondence left April 11 on board the *Laurel Hill* and was transferred to the *Luminary* while en route to New Orleans, likely at Port Hudson, Baton Rouge, or the mouth of the Red River. Two of the letters, along with an excerpt, were inserted into the *Evening Journal* under this heading: "The Chicago Mercantile Battery Lose their Guns, Four Officers and Twenty-two Men." The lead article began with this simple sentence: "We have met with a disaster." These letters from Grand Ecore provided the first accurate public account of the Battle of Sabine Crossroads.[32]

The next day, Wednesday, April 20, the *Evening Journal* published another lengthy letter and two more excerpts from the Mercantile Battery, including one written by Will Brown. In this issue, the *Evening Journal* had time to add its own editorial comments: "Chicago mourns. Some of her bravest and choicest sons have fallen in the fight. The noble Mercantile Battery has been captured....The Mercantile Battery was the pride of Chicago. Its officers and men came from some of our best and best-known families. . . . Last night more than one hearthstone in Chicago felt the bitterness and calamity of a vacant chair that never will be filled, of the absence of one who will never return." The issue of the *Evening Journal* also carried a wire report from New York. The nation's largest city had received its latest Red River information from New Orleans. It did not include any evidence of Banks' defeat at Sabine Crossroads. The article disputed the Battery Boys' reports, observing that "There is no news of the battle reported *via* Chicago."[33]

In its Wednesday edition, the *Chicago Tribune* printed the same Mercantile Battery letters its rival, the *Evening Journal*, had presented to the nation the previous day. The *Tribune* also ran a scathing editorial: "From Louisiana we have by mail intelligence of a disaster to the advance of our army near Shreveport. The telegraph is silent, but the letters published elsewhere tell the whole melancholy story. . . . The telegraph is under rigid censorship and silent. A day or two will, however, bring us full details of the affair." The articles appearing in the April 19 and April 20 issues of the *Chicago Evening Journal*, and in the April 20 issue of the *Chicago Tribune*, provided the country with firsthand accounts of Sabine Crossroads and the battle's mismanagement. All of this contradicted what Nathaniel Banks had been telling Halleck and Grant.[34]

Major Northern newspapers, especially those with correspondents accompanying Banks, remained skeptical and resented the Chicago Mercantile Battery articles being telegraphed around the country. The *St. Louis Missouri Republican*, for example, accused the Chicago newspapers of perpetrating a hoax. Without reports from their correspondents, who were restricted by the news blackout, Federal newspapers instead reprinted positive news from the Louisiana periodicals. Regarding Sabine Crossroads, New Orleans' *The Daily Picayune* opined, "Much credit is due Gen. Banks for gallantry upon the field." But the paper claimed its Pleasant Hill report was incomplete because "The steamer that brought the first news of the fight did not leave Grand Ecore until Monday the 11th"—which would have been the same steamer, the *Laurel Hill,* believed to be transporting the Battery Boys' letters. Banks' puppet New Orleans newspaper, *The Era,* produced the first sanctioned account of the Battle of Sabine Crossroads on April 15 and broadcast that Banks had "broken the main strength of the enemy in this Department." It took another 10 days before newspapers in other major Union cities presented their own full-length stories of the campaign, which confirmed the April 19 and April 20 accounts already published in Chicago and contradicted the versions released earlier from New Orleans.[35]

In its April 23 issue, the *Chicago Tribune* aggressively confronted Banks' manipulation of the press: "The New Orleans papers put the best face on the disaster possible, and cover up the blunder and dereliction of Banks artfully; but murder will out." The Chicago paper reaffirmed the veracity of the Mercantile Battery letters:

> Eastern papers are greatly puzzled to understand how the first accounts of the disaster to Banks' army appeared in the form of letters in the Chicago papers, instead of by dispatches from Cairo or

New Orleans. It happened simply in this way: That half a dozen letters were written by members of the Mercantile Battery to their friends in this city. As soon as received and read, the letters were given to the different newspapers for publication. They were all received here on Tuesday morning [April 19], and one or two of them handed to the evening paper in time for its edition; the others were inserted in the morning papers of the next morning [April 20]. Dispatches from Gen. Banks to Gen. Sherman came up the river by steamboat, but the reporters at Cairo were either kept in the dark, or not allowed to send anything to the press over the wires. We have a reporter with the expedition, but his letters have been delayed or suppressed by those who 'blundered.'

The report of no regular correspondent has yet been permitted to see the light. The private letters that reached Chicago would doubtless have been detained by the officers who caused the disaster had they suspected that those accounts would be published so promptly, as they described the disaster too plainly and laid the blame too freely on those who led the soldiers to defeat and destruction. Yesterday morning a dispatch was permitted to come from Cairo over the wires, announcing the termination of the battle, and claiming a partial success.[36]

On the same afternoon that the *Chicago Evening Journal* broke the Mercantile Battery story (on April 19) about Banks' Red River expedition, Edwin Stanton received a disturbing telegram from Illinois. Brigadier General Mason Brayman informed the secretary of war that Porter's Cairo headquarters had just obtained two damning letters— possibly from the same boat carrying the Mercantile Battery correspondence—written by naval officers who were stationed on Red River. The letters explained what the naval officers had heard about Sabine Crossroads. One of them noted that "the army under General Banks met with reverses on the 8th near Mansfield." Stanton sent an urgent telegram to Grant at Culpeper, Virginia, with additional information. "Detailed telegraphic reports from Chicago, which you will see in this morning's Chronicle, represent General Stone to have been in command of Banks' staff at the time of Banks' disaster, and that the operations were against the remonstrance of General Ransom, who is badly wounded," Stanton wrote.[37]

The "detailed telegraphic reports from Chicago" were the Mercantile Battery letters printed on April 19 and April 20 in the *Chicago Evening Journal* and the *Chicago Tribune*. Although newspapers mistakenly blamed Charles P. Stone for the Sabine Crossroads loss, they later exonerated Banks' chief of staff when additional details emerged that implicated his superior in the western Louisiana disaster.[38]

A few days later William T. Sherman, who was in Tennessee preparing to initiate his Atlanta Campaign, sent Halleck a copy of a letter from Porter that he wanted Stanton to forward to Grant. Major General John Corse, who Sherman had sent to Red River to meet personally with Banks, brought back the confidential letter from Porter. Sherman had no desire to personally attack Banks, but he informed Halleck that "The whole move has been too slow for complete success. Gen. Corse speaks of all the troops being demoralized except those of A. J. Smith."[39]

In his April 14 letter to Sherman from Grand Ecore, Porter was more critical in his comments about Banks:

> The army has been shamefully beaten by the rebels. There is no disguising the fact, notwithstanding [that] the general commanding and his staff try to make a victory. Armies victorious don't often go back as this one has done. . . . I cannot express to you my entire disappointment with this department. You know my opinion of political generals. It is a crying sin to put the lives of thousands in the hands of such men, and the time has come when there should a stop be put to it. This army is almost in a state of mutiny and not fit to go into a fight.[40]

After being apprised of Banks' mistakes via the Cairo naval letters, the Chicago Mercantile Battery eyewitness accounts, and Porter's message, Grant next received two private letters on April 25 from Louisiana—one sent anonymously from the 13th Corps along Red River. These letters had also eluded the Department of the Gulf's censors and reached Grant in Virginia. The general noted that they gave "deplorable accounts of General Banks' mismanagement." Grant had a difficult decision to make, and it was complicated by the fact that he knew he did not yet have enough political clout to overcome Banks' powerful allies in Washington—Lincoln among them. Should the Massachusetts general be removed from command? As general-in-chief of the Union army, Grant could neutralize Banks by removing him from field command while preparing for his ouster. Support arrived from Henry Halleck, who notified Banks on April 27 to leave his Red River expeditionary force and "return yourself immediately to New Orleans" until further notice.

Halleck was exasperated with having to deal with Lincoln's civilian generals. "Banks' operations in the West are about what should have been expected from a general so utterly destitute of military education and military capacity," Halleck confided to Sherman. "It seems but little better than murder to give important commands to such men as Banks, Butler, McClernand, Sigel, and Lew Wallace, and yet it seems impossible to prevent it."[41]

Major General David Hunter soon provided proof that validated Halleck's cynical views about Banks. Grant had sent Hunter across the country as his emissary to ascertain the truth of Banks' situation and ensure that the Boston politician abandoned his Texas campaign and refocused his attention on capturing Mobile. Hunter traveled by train to Cairo and down the Mississippi and Red rivers to Alexandria. The general was disgusted with what he found in Louisiana. Per Grant's request, he sent a confidential telegram about the plight of Porter's stranded vessels and told the general-in-chief that Banks had created a "complicated, perplexing, and precarious" situation for both the army and navy on the Red River. Hunter summarized his findings once he got to New Orleans in a May 2 telegram to Grant. "The Department of the Gulf is one great mass of corruption. Cotton and politics, instead of war, appear to have engrossed the army." Hunter, a noted abolitionist though not much of a field general himself, added, "The vital interest of the contest are laid aside and we are amused with sham State governments, which are a complete laughing-stock to the people, and the lives of our men are sacrificed in the interests of cotton speculators." Despite being charmed by Banks' "great politeness and kindness," Hunter recommended that Grant immediately replace him.[42]

Troublesome though these reports were, Grant had to gain Lincoln's consent before yanking Banks off the expedition. Disappointed by Banks' repeated failures, the president finally reorganized his Trans-Mississippi departments. On May 7, he placed Louisiana, Arkansas, and Missouri under Major General Edward S. Canby in the new Division of West Mississippi. The deft administrative move curtailed Banks' independence as a commander. Banks' control over the New Orleans newspapers allowed him to soften the impact of his demotion: "Gen. Banks continues in his command, but will report to Gen. Canby. . . . We cannot see from any intelligence that we have that the status of General Banks is affected in the slightest degree," was how one report read.[43]

Harper's Pictorial History of the Great Rebellion

Porter's fleet passing the dam at Alexandria.

Banks, meanwhile, remained in Alexandria to ensure the army and navy escaped from the enemy's trap. To free Porter's fleet, which was stranded on the Red River by low water, the Federals constructed a makeshift dam masterminded by Lieutenant Colonel Joseph Bailey. The structure helped raise the level of the water enough to allow the ships to pass the falls on May 13. With Porter's command no longer in danger of capture, the army continued its retreat to Simmesport. After engaging the enemy in a fierce artillery duel at Mansura on May 16, and fending off Taylor's last-ditch effort to destroy the Federal army at Yellow Bayou two days later, Banks' men began to cross the Atchafalaya River on May 20. They marched to Morganza on the Mississippi and boarded transports for their trip back to New Orleans. The Confederacy again controlled western Louisiana and its fertile cotton fields. A shaken Banks reentered New Orleans on May 21. The Department of the Gulf's commander had felt invincible when he left the Crescent City two months earlier and expected to return as a conquering hero. His hopes for a long-shot run at the presidency were rapidly fading.[44]

Once back at his headquarters, Banks had to contend with the growing allegations that his expedition had been little more than a giant cotton raid. The *Chicago Tribune* had been one of the first newspapers to call for an investigation that "should go deep enough to touch the very bottom . . . even if it be shown that it owed its inception to a ring of cotton speculators." That same day, the *New York Times* also advocated an investigation of Banks' campaign. Coincidentally, the *St. Louis Missouri Republican*, after accusing the Chicago papers of a hoax, was finally able to publish a belated April 13 report from its Grand Ecore correspondent. Banks, noted the reporter, had "lost the confidence of the entire army." The St. Louis reporter was no longer a staunch supporter of the former Massachusetts politician, writing, "General Banks has been engineering his department more to further his presidential aspirations than anything else. But if the [June 7] Baltimore Convention were composed of the army of the Gulf, his chances would be hopeless."[45]

The national clamor for a Red River inquiry continued to swell as newspapers compared the Red River debacle to the Federal disasters at Bull Run and Ball's Bluff. The public airing of Banks' laundry seemed to be heading toward a Congressional investigation. When Banks returned to New Orleans, Will Brown informed his father that the local military authorities had begun to retaliate against anyone who raised questions about Red River cotton speculation. "Several officers have been placed under arrest for saying so," Will told him. Those same department leaders were not about to be lenient with the artillerymen who broke the news of Banks's disaster and now balked at taking up muskets for fatigue and guard duty—even if the orders violated the soldiers' enlistment agreement that they remain cannoneers throughout the war.

*   *   *

Camp Parapet La.
May 15th 1864

My dear father

> I'm getting really anxious to hear from you, not having had that pleasure for some time. Have not heard from you acknowledging receipt of mine [in which I gave] an account of the engagement of April 8th and cannot understand why I do not. I presume you have written, of course, but the mail has not reached me.[46]
>
> Like myself, I presume you are anxiously looking for news from Liberty. I have a letter from him dated Little Rock, April 23d. In that letter, he says he expected to join Gen. Steele at Camden and would start in three or four days. The papers give accounts of a fight between Steele and Price near Camden and I am anxious to know if Lib was there. Let me know how late [are the] dates [of the letters] you have from him. The rebs have beaten us decidedly whenever we have met them this Spring on this west side of the Mississippi.

And probably when another move is made against them, our generals will proceed with more caution.[47]

Banks is still at Alexandria, but all news from him is suppressed here, so we hear very little and that not reliable. I heard last evening that two of the eight iron clads are above the rapids near Alexandria [and] had succeeded in getting below. If this is so, I think it will not be long before forces retire from that part of this loyal (?) state and again occupy the Teche country. I tell you father, the occupation of the Teche country is a "big thing" and furnishes "leaders" for the New Orleans papers every few days. I believe that Gen. Banks . . . has occupied] this part of the country 4 times since he has been in command.

All here awaiting tidings from Gen. Grant. It is impossible to describe to you the intense feeling that manifests itself here. The secessionists do not know what to say but have great confidence in their idol Gen. [Robert E.] Lee. All sorts of rumors are flying about; that which is most credited is that Lee was successful on the first day but that Grant drove him the second day—and that Burnside came up on the third day and the whole force were in pursuit of Lee. Butler was moving in two columns directly on Richmond and Sigel was on Lee's flank. What a mighty contest this will be and how important its results. I think Grant will succeed. He has thus far shown himself capable and now I think he will not be found wanting.[48]

From home we have news that the Mercantile Association have met, drafted a set of resolutions complimenting the Battery, resolving to aid us. [They] read a communication from Gen. Ransom in which he says of us all that one could say and pays us as high a compliment as general can. Rumor has it that we may be ordered to Chicago to refit but I have very little faith in this story. Many of the boys, however, have great faith in it and are building all kinds of castles about what they will do when we are there.[49]

The troubles about infantry equipments that I wrote you about in my last have not been settled yet. We have muskets in camp but the boys say they will not touch them, only in defence of the city. Yesterday, we received orders to make details for fatigue duty and I presume will have to obey if insisted upon. It sometimes seems to me, after doing all we have done, that now after our unfortunate loss we should be allowed a little resting spell. There are few troops that have seen more active service and none who have attended to their duties more promptly. A soldier who does his duty should have a few privileges, at least, but we are granted none. This, to say the least, is a very poor way to make veterans.

* * *

May 22nd 1864

My dear father

Gen. Banks arrived in the city yesterday and the general impression is that the army will be here very soon. The army, after getting the iron clads over the rapids, left Alexandria marching overland to Simmesport where, after three days hard fighting, they succeeded in chasing the enemy from his position near that place.

We have glorious news from Grant and if reports can be credited there is little doubt but what he is doing noble work for the cause. We also have good news from Sherman tho' no detailed accounts yet. The latest is that he was in possession of Dalton Ga. having captured 7.000 prisoners and ten pieces of artillery. One would be surprised to see the many long faces in the city over the news from Grant. "Secesh" sees the crushing effect a victory over Lee will have and now cannot but feel down in the mouth. The semi-reb papers try to cheer their hearts up by publishing the latest extracts from Mobile and Richmond papers but this seems of little use. Every boat's arrival is watched closely and I presume there are few in this city who do not know to a nicety just what time the next news will arrive.[50]

Gen. McClernand is here very sick. Has been considered in great danger but is now recovering. His loss would be deeply mourned by the 13th Corps. We all think there is no one like "Old Mc." In the city, very little of interest is transpiring. The levees look pretty busy but nearly everything is on government account. River steamers arrive and depart very regularly, navigation of the river being little interfered with. Occasionally, a boat is fired at but usually without much damage. The gunboats watch the banks closely and pounce down on all parties of the enemy found along the shore.[51]

The weather is getting very warm; in fact, hot. Here in camp, the shade of the large trees is much sought for and fortunately we have plenty of them. The nights are pretty cool but the musquitoes "Thicker than hair on a dog" and well versed in the singing and biting art.

From the surgeons who stayed with our wounded after the battle near Mansfield we learn that our wounded are well taken care, receiving the same treatment as the Confederate sick and wounded and occupying the same quarters.[52]

*   *   *

Camp Parapet La.
May 29th 1864

My dear father

From Henry or Liberty, I hear nothing excepting thro' your letter. As Henry is at the front with Sherman, I suppose he is seeing some pretty warm, hard work; but he has success with him and nothing cheers the soldier more than this. Sherman is rapidly pushing his way into the very heart of rebeldom and has, I think, force enough to carry out the full plan of his campaign. Judging from the papers, Steele is having an unpleasant—to say the least—time in Arkansas and will have some trouble to keep communications open. I will not be surprised if part of our forces were sent to him.[53]

General Canby [was] lately appointed to command of the trans-Mississippi Military Division. [He] seems to be up to something and time only will develop his plans. Have you noticed how Gen. Grant, since he has taken the head of affairs, has put in good positions several generals heretofore almost unknown. This looks to me like [his] work. He does not choose Major General So and So who has a big political and newspaper fame but quickly picks out men who, without pushing themselves forward, have nearly got more toward crushing the rebellion than many others. Canby and Baldy Smith are instances of this. Gen. Grant seemingly chooses men for their worth and not their political fame. The war has always been too much mixed up with politics and no sooner has a general succeeded in some skirmish, than his friends at home commence blowing [their horns] for some office.[54]

Sometimes, I think the war nothing but a big political undertaking and then I am disgusted. The South discards politics altogether. Read their newspapers—nothing about party. Talk with inhabitants—

Major General
Edward R. S. Canby

*Harper's Pictorial History
of the Great Rebellion*

nothing about this or that man; but all about the war. For it has been brought to their very doors and they cannot but feel it. But has it not been brought to many of our doors also and have not many felt it? The fact is the North is overrun by a set of political demagogues and, after we end this war, I hope we will give them a turn as they certainly need nearly as much as the people of the South.

We had a very destructive fire right here night before last. Eight river steamers and two small coasting schooners being entirely destroyed. All these boats were loaded with government stores and are a total loss. The fire is supposed to be the work of an incendiary; probably someone in the employ of Gen. Jefferson D. [Davis].

Our latest news from Grant is to the 21st which time a battle was momentarily expected on the South Anna river. We have news from our boys in secessia but the letter does not state how many are together. They are at Fort Tyler Texas [Camp Ford], are very kindly treated by the rebel authorities and expect soon to be exchanged. I do not learn anything further in regard to Augustus Chapman. His corps or corps commander has not arrived here yet and nothing can be found out at Department Head Quarters. Please say to Mr. Chapman that I will gladly aid him in anything connected with this matter. I think I can get a letter thro' the lines, should he wish to send one. Do not think he could aid Augustus by coming here and know he could not do anything toward effecting his exchange. From all we can learn, our sick and wounded in rebel hands are receiving the best of treatment.[55]

*   *   *

Post Parapet La.
June 5th 1864

My dear father

I find the dullness of camp life pretty heavy. Much more so than ever before. Two of my most intimate companions are with the rebs and I miss them greatly. The smiling face of Captain White is also missed. In my position, I was with him a great-deal. Whenever any Company business was transacted, I always went along. We have hopes to see all our boys soon. Col. Landram, our old Division commander, informed me a few days since that an exchange had recently been effected and that we might look for our officers and men before long. He also informed me that the killed among our Division is not nearly so large as was at first supposed. Many who were supposed to be killed have been heard from and will return as soon as exchanged.

We hear all kinds of stories about where our old Division will be stationed during the Summer; one day it is here and the next at Baton Rouge. I do not believe the question has been decided by anyone yet. The Red river expedition is over at last and its remnants are again on the Mississippi. Many people are of the opinion that it was really gotten up as a speculation. Several officers have been placed under arrest for saying so. In my own mind, I am fully convinced that it was more for cotton speculation than anything but I doubt if Gen. Banks had anything to do with it. Cotton speculation or not, there was no use in its resulting as it did and I hope to see whoever is to blame shown up. A soldier is punished for any petty offence he may commit and in justice the thing should be carried to those high in position as well as the soldier.

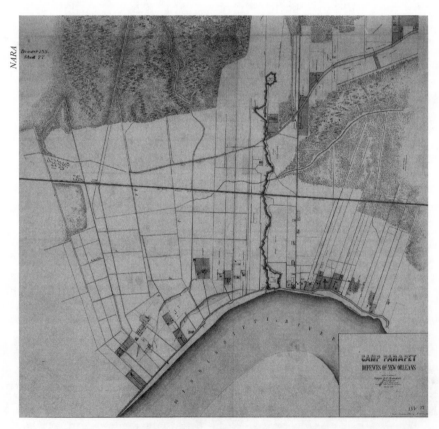

Camp Parapet was located near Carrollton, a town about eight miles upriver from New Orleans. The fort's line of fortifications was situated between the Mississippi River and Lake Pontchartrain.

"I am directed to inform you that no charges relative to the said Battery have been filed here nor is it known to the [War] Department under what circumstances it was ordered to perform Infantry duty on the embankments of New Orleans."

Chapter 15

Treated Like <u>Dogs</u>

The excessive amount of paperwork he had to process after the disaster at Sabine Crossroads nearly overwhelmed Will Brown. Like a prisoner in solitary confinement, Will spent most of his waking hours sequestered in his Camp Parapet tent, struggling to endure another day of unbearable heat and humidity. Regulations forced the meticulous sergeant to catalog his company's property that had been lost in the fighting near Mansfield. This was no easy task, for there were no forms to document the Battery Boys' extensive loss of personal belongings. Will did the best he could, filling out reams of quartermaster reports with names like "Abstract of Articles Expended, Lost, or Destroyed in the Public Service in the Field" and "Verification of Materials Abandoned." The "Monthly Reports" were perhaps the most frustrating of all.[1]

With four out of the battery's five commissioned officers either dead or captured, Lieutenant Henry Roe was the only one left to handle the official paperwork. The inexperienced commander was forced to chronicle the terrible circumstances that had left gaping holes in the ranks of the Mercantile Battery. The difficult paperwork was only a small part of the problem these men faced. Replacing the lost guns and equipment would prove to be tremendously difficult.

Banks' subordinates, meanwhile, had plenty of time to make the cannoneers' lives miserable. Will later commented to his father, "The powers that be here appear greatly incensed against us." When it learned that pressure was being applied against the survivors of the Mercantile Battery, the *Chicago Tribune* editorialized in favor of its hometown artillery outfit. The Battery Boys were characterized as being "under the spur of what we believe a great provocation." Many of the boys concurred, firmly believing that Banks was retaliating against them for breaking the news of his defeat to the outside world.[2]

The Mercantile Battery's problems began on April 28, when Roe received an order from Major General Joseph J. Reynolds, the commander in charge of the New Orleans defenses. While Banks remained in the field with the Red River expeditionary force, Reynolds ordered Roe to move his company from the Camp of Distribution way station and report to Colonel Robert Wilson, commanding the District of Carrollton. Roe assumed that he and his men were returning to the same camp where they stayed last August when they arrived from Vicksburg. Wilson's district was on the northern outskirts of New Orleans and included Carrollton and Camp Parapet. Most of the troops were stationed at the former camp, which Banks' chief engineer described as having "superior grounds for encampments." Camp Parapet constituted the Crescent City's outer defenses and served as the training area for Banks' black troops. After dinner the next day, Roe led his company's survivors toward the town of Carrollton, a small railroad hub with about 1,500 inhabitants. The Battery Boys were directed to bypass the camps housing white soldiers—their population being, in aggregate, three times larger than the size of the nearby town—and proceed up the road for another mile or so to Camp Parapet, which housed about 1,000 black troops.[3]

The Confederates had built Camp Parapet at the outbreak of the war. After New Orleans fell to Ben Butler and Admiral Farragut in April 1862, the Federals changed the fort's name from Fort John Morgan to Camp Parapet. Its line of defense started with a redoubt located near the Mississippi levee. The outer parapet extended at a right angle from the river eastward for one-and-one-half miles, zigzagging like a Virginia worm fence until it reached the impenetrable swamp that separated the fortifications from Lake Ponchartrain. Its walls, strengthened by the

Union army, extended another one-half mile. The fort's width was about
three-quarters of a mile. A New Hampshire infantryman who visited
Camp Parapet in February 1863 observed that the formidable fort was
"built ten feet above the level of the ground on the inside—about 5 feet up
it is flat & about four feet wide fore the men to stand & fire[.] while on the
out side there is a ditch dug eight feet deep & thirty wide in which there is
four or five feet of watter." With 20 heavy guns, some field pieces, and an
all-but-impregnable earthen fortification, Camp Parapet offered a
daunting deterrent to Taylor's victorious Confederates. Emboldened
after his recent defeat of Banks, Taylor contemplated moving against
New Orleans.[4]

During the previous year, while Will and his comrades were camped
at Carrollton, they spent most of their time drilling or taking the hourly
train into New Orleans to enjoy its cosmopolitan amenities. They did not
know much about Camp Parapet, other than it was used as the focal point
for training black troops (Banks had organized the Corps d'Afrique there
before the Chicago Mercantile Battery arrived). The black regiments
were formed, mustered, and subsequently sustained by a steady infusion
of contrabands from the Trans-Mississippi's sugar and cotton
plantations.

To assist the blacks in making the transition from slaves to soldiers,
Banks placed them in regiments half the size of standard organizations,
but possessing the same number of white officers. Rigorous drilling,
standing guard beside heavy guns, and performing fatigue duty—i.e.,
digging latrines, maintaining the earthworks, and handling supplies—
were primary responsibilities for the African soldiers at New Orleans'
outer fort. After Milliken's Bend and Port Hudson, some of the black
soldiers were given active combat duty. Most, however, continued to
receive defensive assignments like the one entrusted to the 11th U. S.
Colored Heavy Artillery (formerly the 14th Rhode Island Heavy
Artillery) stationed at Camp Parapet. This was the camp to which the
Battery Boys were ordered to report. They announced their arrival to the
post commander, Lieutenant Colonel Nelson Viall.[5]

Although Will Brown and his batterymates thought it was odd to be
moved to Camp Parapet, they tried to make the best of the situation.
Soon, grumbling in the Mercantile Battery tents at night rivaled the
nightly buzz of local mosquitoes. Why were they not being re-equipped?
Why were they always short of food? Florison Pitts alluded to the dearth

of victuals in one of his diary entries: "Rations gave out 2 days ago. Generally our rations for 10 days give out on the 8th day [and] 2 days we don't have any thing to eat." By contrast, Captain Ormand Nims' 2nd Massachusetts Light Artillery did not have any problems obtaining new supplies. Nims' unit, which had lost all its guns at Sabine Crossroads, seemed to be receiving better treatment down the road at Carrollton. Within a week of entering the Chicagoans' old campground, Nims' battery was informed its new guns "were on the way"—which was suspicious because many of the Bostonians were due to be mustered out. They had enlisted one year before the Mercantile Battery was formed, and their three-year obligation was about to expire. A report issued on June 12 noted the soldiers in Nims' command had been re-equipped with six 12-pounder bronze Napoleons, while their Mercantile Battery counterparts were still without any replacement guns.[6]

At Camp Parapet, the Battery Boys—"the only white troops who have had to do duty with the negroes"—learned that the Mercantile Association would meet on May 2 to ascertain how the influential businessmen could lobby to have their battery refit in Chicago. Instead of being notified his battery would return to the Windy City, however, Roe received a different order on May 6 from Colonel Robert Wilson, his district commander: "In obedience to instructions from headquarters defenses of New Orleans, you will without delay at all, make requisitions for infantry arms and equipments." Roe ordered Will Brown to complete the necessary forms. Will drew infantry arms the following day. No one was sure what was happening.[7]

Two days later Henry Roe and his quartermaster sergeant pried open one of the boxes. Instead of finding modern rifles inside, they discovered antiquated smoothbores that had been converted into rifle-muskets. When the rest of the Battery Boys learned about the shipment of muskets and the rearming of the organization, they voiced their suspicion that the battery was being transformed into an infantry unit. The Battery Boys had already heard rumors about heavy artillerymen being shoved into the Army of the Potomac's infantry ranks, even if they lacked appropriate training. "It may seem rather odd that men who have been shot at time and again do not know how to shoot back in return," Will related to his father, "but I don't think there are 10 men in the Company who ever fired a musket."

Lieutenant Henry Roe,
Chicago Mercantile Battery

Chicago Historical Society

Later that day (May 8) Roe left camp and visited headquarters for the District of Carrollton and the Department of the Gulf. According to Will Brown's June 12 letter, Roe was told at both places that the rifle-muskets had only been distributed as a contingency "in case of attack on the city, and that this was the only reason the muskets had been issued."

These assurances helped alleviate the Chicagoans' concerns, at least temporarily. On Sunday, May 15, Henry Roe was taken aback when a contradictory order was delivered to him: "Hereafter the following daily detail will be required from your command: For guard [duty] 21 Privates 1 Corporal. For fatigue [duty] 25 Privates 1 Corporal 1 Sergt." Roe met with his sergeants and instructed them to form the appropriate details for the next morning. While the Chicago artillerists were unfamiliar with muskets, they nevertheless knew what constituted fatigue and guard duty. The young men in the Mercantile Battery, as noted in one of their company reports, were about to be "employed in running as Guards on Rail Road trains, digging ditches, building targets for other batteries to shoot at, guarding Negro Colonels Head Quarters, loading and unloading hay, handling lumber, wheeling dirt and similar 'Light Artillery duties.'"[8]

The news outraged the Battery Boys, who gathered together that night to draft a polite, but firm, protest. The cannoneers acknowledged a "willingness to lend our aid in any capacity in case of emergency or attack by the enemy" but argued, according to army regulations, none of the artillerists could be forced to transfer "from one branch of the service to another without his consent." At dawn on the morning of May 16, several of the soldiers thrust the written protest—signed by 119 of the 123 members present with the battery—into the hands of the inexperienced Roe, who immediately passed it to his commander, Lieutenant Colonel Viall of the 11th U.S. Colored Heavy Artillery. Viall was a Mexican War veteran who had served in various Rhode Island militia units. He was also a strict taskmaster with a volatile personality, hot temper, and a history of angry outbursts. After a series of commendations for his performance in the Army of the Potomac, in which he had served from First Bull Run to Fredericksburg, Viall was offered the colonelcy of the 2nd Rhode Island Infantry. Unfortunately for his career, he rejected the position because he was outraged over the simultaneous (and what he believed to be the undeserved) promotion of the regimental chaplain. Instead of assuming a new command Viall stormed off to Rhode Island. He had spent the last year trying to rebuild his army career, to little avail.[9]

Roe met Viall coming down the back steps of his headquarters. The lieutenant told Viall that his "men refused to obey the order," but before he could elicit advice from the commander about how to handle the situation, Viall "immediately flew into a passion," wrote Roe, "saying 'Damn them I will have them up here by 8 o'clock if it takes every man in the Parapet' and at once placed me in arrest, giving me no time to say anything else."[10]

Informed about Viall's furious response to their resolution, the Battery Boys hurriedly sent lawyer Chase Dickinson to New Orleans to discuss their situation with several senior officers. Dickinson, as Will explained to his father, checked with "good military men and was told that we had done wrong." The officers said the Battery Boys should have obeyed the order first—and then filed a protest. Worried about the ramifications of the impetuous declaration, the artillerists established a committee to speak with Viall about the matter. Viall was unavailable to meet with them, however, so the impromptu Mercantile Battery committee sought out Wilson, Viall's immediate superior, who accepted their retraction. In Will Brown's words, Wilson said there would be "little trouble in getting the paper returned from Gen. Reynolds Head Quarters and further proceedings dropped."[11]

Despite Wilson's assurances, the battery's resolution remained with Reynolds, who was at that time the highest-ranking officer in New

Orleans. Banks was still struggling to extricate his troops from the Louisiana countryside, and Porter's flotilla from the shallow Red River. To demonstrate their repentance, the battery members rushed to take up their infantry arms. "As an earnest of our return to obedience," Will reported, "the muskets and equipments, which had not before been unpacked, were issued out to the men during the afternoon of the 16th." The Boys' effort to recuperate from their mistake was too late. That same day Reynolds sent a telegram to Wilson ordering him to arrest and confine Roe and all non-commissioned officers except two sergeants and two corporals of his choosing.[12]

On May 17, a captain in Wilson's 14th New Hampshire regiment was ordered "to proceed to the camp of the Chicago Mercantile Battery with a guard of one Sergt. [and] twenty men and arrest Lieut Roe and all the non-commissioned officers of the Chicago Mercantile Battery except 1st Sergt. F. B. Meacham, Q. M. Sergt. William Brown, Corporal John A. Gilbert and [Corporal] Warren Gilmore and proceed with them to Capt. Twining, Provost Marshal, 48 Baronne Street New Orleans for confinement." No formal accusation was lodged against them, however, thus violating the 79th Article of War (which stipulated that an officer could not be confined more than eight days without being charged). That night Florison Pitts recorded in his diary that the "Day [was] very sultry. A heavy thunder storm came up at dark."[13]

*   *   *

Defences of New Orleans, La.
June 12th 1864

My dear father

In a former letter, I wrote you about our having been furnished with muskets and that I thought trouble would follow. Subsequent events have proved that my surmises were correct. I have not written in regard to the matter for the reason I thought it best to keep the matter quiet 'till something definite was known. Both the Orderly Sgt. [Florus Meacham] and myself requested the boys not to write about the matter and many of them promised they would not. But [they] did not pay the least regard to their promises and nearly all have written about it. Perhaps it is just as well that they have done so but, as they have nothing definite to write about, I fear that many have excited causeless fires among their friends at home. But let me give you a history of the case.[14]

About May 8th, Lieut. Roe received orders to draw infantry arms and equipments for his entire command. He obeyed the order and kept the muskets in their boxes in camp. Our boys did not like the order and requested Roe to find out why it was issued. He did so and received assurances from several officers at District and Department Head Quarters that it was only done so that we could give aid in case of attack on the city, and that this was the only reason the muskets had been issued to us. All felt better on hearing this and expressed their entire willingness to do all they could in case of an attack.

On Sunday [the 15th of] May, came an order from the Comdt. of this Post ordering a daily detail of 25 men for guards and picket duty and 25 for fatigue, thus putting nearly one half the Company on daily active duty. All were mad at this order and said they would not do picket duty anyhow as they were mustered and sworn in as artillerymen. And therefore could not be made to perform that branch of service usually assigned to infantrymen. Immediately a set of resolutions—gentlemanly in language and carefully written—were drafted and signed by every soldier and non-commissioned officer of the Company. The resolutions set forth that we always had [been], and were, perfectly willing to do our duty in the branch of the service under which we had enlisted.

But that the handling of muskets and duty appertaining to that branch we could not and would not perform and that, in our opinions, the Regulations governing the army of the U.S. would sustain us in our decision. (In this, I still think we are right but we did not go at the matter in the right way. Of this more).

Lieutenant Colonel
Nelson Viall,
11th New Hampshire
Heavy Artillery

U.S. Army Military History Institute

Early on the morning of the . . . [16th], the resolutions were handed to Lieut. Roe and he took them over to Col. [Nelson] Viall Comdg. Post—Lieut. Col. of a regiment of negroes from Rhode Island. The Col. got exceedingly wrathy and ordered Roe under arrest. (Cannot see or find his authority for doing this) As soon as we heard this, one of the boys [Chase Dickinson] went to the city, consulted as good military men and was told that we had done wrong. He then returned to camp, gave us the result of his inquiries and we immediately appointed a committee to wait on Col. Viall and retract the paper if possible. [Our] committee did as instructed but Col. Viall was absent. They then went to Carrollton, where the paper had been forwarded, and called on Col. [Robert] Wilson, Comdg. [our] District. He—Wilson—said the paper had reached him and that he had forwarded it to Gen. [Joseph J.] Reynolds Hd. Qrs. for instruction. Our committee talked with him [for] some time and convinced him that we had no intention to disregard military law and that we had acted hastily, and while laboring under a mistaken impression. Col. [Wilson] expressed his satisfaction, was glad we had retracted so soon and thought he would have little trouble in getting the paper returned from Gen. Reynolds Hd. Qrs. and further proceedings dropped. Promised to attend to immediately.

Next morning . . . [on May 17th] up came a guard with orders direct from Gen. Reynolds to arrest and take to the city Lieut. Roe and all the non-commissioned officers but the Orderly, two Corporals and myself. Things looked serious and for a few days I felt particularly <u>blue</u>. Roe and the non-commissioned [officers] were taken to the city and have been in confinement since. At first, I feared the thing would result seriously to all but we have good strong influential friends at work in our favor and so will not suffer much, in my opinion, tho' as yet I know nothing definite. The great trouble is we committed a blunder on the start. Had we obeyed the order, and then sent in a protest, we would have been doing the thing according to the strict military code. In all probability, no attention would have been paid to our request as the ideas and notions of private soldiers are as little regarded as the barking of a nasty cur. Morally, we are right in the stand we took. When joining the service, we were assured that our arms would be artillery and that nothing else could be forced upon us. The question was [raised] in Chicago before we left home and there decided.[15]

The Mercantile Association are highly indignant at the way we have been treated and will, I think, see us thro' it. All friends write us that they admire our pluck and hope we will stick [it] out. This is all very romantic but, inasmuch as "Military necessity knows no law," I think our best plan will be to get out of the difficulty the best way possible. We have really been treated like <u>dogs</u> ever since the "Sabine Cross Road" affair. [We] have been camped alongside several regiments of "American citizens of African descent" and, for the last three weeks, have been about the only white troops who have had to do duty with the <u>negroes</u>. This <u>may</u> be all right and just, but <u>we</u> do not look at in that way—and think it a poor recompense for past services and duties—always ready when wanted, nearly always in the field [during the entire time] we have been in the army. We have never failed to do our duty no matter how hard or where required. The experience of the last two months will not tend to make many of us Veterans, I assure you. I will keep you posted about this affair. Do not feel troubled about it as I have little doubt but that it will come out all right. Even if we are punished, we can bear it with as good grace and with the inward consolation that we have done nothing morally wrong.

Did you read Gen. Blunt's speech made to the Chicago Board of Trade? It just suits me and expresses my ideas exactly; that is, as far as he goes. I would like to hear his opinion of the negro and what he thinks of the policy of the government in regard to them. At one time, I thought the idea of arming the negro a good one but I am getting over it. You may be surprised at this. I am glad that slavery is dead, in fact totally killed, but I think there are better plans for the negro than to make him a soldier. Of this more in some future letter.[16]

I do not hear from Henry or Liberty direct. Am looking for a letter from the latter but suppose Henry does not know my address.[17]

*   *   *

Defences in New Orleans
June 19th 1864

My dear Father,

I am high in the hope "Tho' clouds which lower round our house will soon be in deep bosom of ocean buried." At any rate, the "clouds" are breaking a little and gleams of sunshine come through, making all smile and feel <u>comfortable</u>. The rainbow don't show itself just yet, but Maj. Gen. Reynolds comes in with the following <u>bow</u> and shows that he still <u>reigns</u> and otherwise lives:

Special Orders #142
Headquarters Defence of New Orleans
New Orleans June 15, 1864

The following non-commissioned officers of the Chicago Mercantile Battery are hereby reduced to the ranks for mutinousconduct on the 15th day of May 1864 at Camp Parapet near Carrollton La. vis:

W. A. Prior, Sergeant
E. J. Thomas, Sergeant
J. [James] C. Sinclair, Sergeant
H. [Hiram] Arnick, Corpl
H. [Henry] L. Bush, Corpl
D. [Danforth] Marble, Corpl.
W. [William] H. Monroe, Corpl.
A. [Albert] G. Mather, Corpl.
S. [Sidney] G. Higby, Corpl.
L. [Leonard] S. Hudson, Corpl.

The above non-commissioned officers in common with the entire command (excepting four), including [one] commissioned officer, Lieut. Roe, have been guilty of conduct which merits the severest punishment known to Military laws.

The Major General Commanding Defences of New Orleans, with whose painful duty it is to take cognizance of this conduct, is thus lenient because of the distinguished reputation which this Battery has established for itself on various occasions in the face of the enemy, and he indulges the hope that the company will in future sustain its high character and add new laurels to those already won.

The case of Lieut. Roe will be investigated by Court Martial. By command of Maj. Gen. J. J. Reynolds. Signed John Levering Maj. and A. A. Genl.

You will notice that neither the Orderly's or my name occur among the list of non-commissioned. Why, I

Major General
Joseph J. Reynolds

NARA

do not know. Lieut. Roe has been court martialed but his sentence not made public. I have been told, however, that it is a very light one and that he will come out all right.

In regard to the whole matter, I think Gen. Reynolds has found that the <u>pressure</u> in our favor was greater than he could well <u>kick</u> against. I have been told that he also received letters from Washington inquiring into the alleged abuses in the Mercantile Battery. The fact is we have brought big influence in our favor and you know that it is a big help in military as well as civil life. I think the whole matter will be settled in a few days now. Will keep you posted in regard to it.

Sgt. Gardner of our Battery, who was taken in "Sabine Cross Roads," has just returned on parole. He was slightly wounded and sent to hospital in Mansfield, so that he has not seen any of our boys [as] prisoners. He was with Lieut. Barr and Corp. Dyer when they died and buried them. He also attended [to] Capt. Dickey of Gen. Ransom's staff and helped bury him. He was well treated by everybody; has heard Dick Taylor's congratulatory address and was around the reb camps as much as he pleased. After recovering from his wounds—end of his thumb and light scratch on the side—he was made [a] nurse in the hospital and given the freedom of Mansfield. [He] says the country is filled with Union men and that they felt terribly [bad] over our defeat. The ladies did everything they could to relieve our suffering soldiers and many of them volunteered as nurses. Our money passes readily, its value being $1<u>00</u> for $10<u>00</u> of theirs. Gardner is a sharp, shrewd fellow—very observing and what he says one can depend upon. He looks pretty ragged but feels well and [is] glad to get back. I think the rest of our boys will be here in a few days as it certainly [is] known that a parole has been effected.[18]

You will no doubt laugh when I tell you that we have an officer [Lieutenant Daniel J. Viall] of negro troops temporarily in command of our Battery. He is from the 14th Regt. of Rhode Island Heavy Artillery and is really a <u>bully fellow</u>. We all like him. I am in a tent with him and I like him first-rate. Of course, he will be with us but a few days. He was sent here because, in order to obtain supplies &c, we had to have the signature of a commissioned officer and, not having [one] of our own, he was ordered here. It makes me laugh to think what Capt. White and Lieut. Cone will say when they return.[19]

Your letter of 2nd Inst. reached me on the 15th. I was pained to hear that Henry was wounded but very glad his wound is so light. Although I suppose he is very anxious to return to his regiment, yet I almost hope he will not be able to do so 'till the campaign is over. One wound is enough for one campaign and there is little use in running the chances of another. I suppose that one should think that every soldier ought to be doing his duty as much as possible. Well, I suppose I feel that way, particularly where the soldier is not my brother. But when he is, I would a little rather see him where it isn't quite so healthy as an on active campaign. I will write him in a few days. I have a letter from Lib being dated 10th Inst.

Was quite well and has just returned from a wild goose chase after somebody.

*   *   *

For the residents of New Orleans, the month of June marked the beginning of sweltering temperatures. As the Department of the Gulf's titular head, Banks was being subjected to intense political and military heat from which he wanted to hide. High-ranking officials in Washington like Secretary of the Navy Gideon Welles—who was not duped by Banks' recent manipulation of the Red River news "to convert this reverse into a victory"—continued to urge Lincoln to get rid of his friend. Federal newspapers clamored for a Congressional inquiry into the Red River cotton scandal. Meanwhile, Banks' new superior, Major General Edward Canby, launched his own investigation into the Department of the Gulf's supply departments and announced he was bringing in his own chief quartermaster for the Division of West Mississippi.[20]

Chicago's Battery Boys squirmed as New Orleans' summer heat intensified—and many wondered if Banks was responsible for their latest man-made discomfort. Roe and 10 of his non-commissioned officers were still in prison. They had been "put in an awful hard hole full of grey backs," but an officer in the 97th Illinois Infantry arranged for them to move to a room by themselves. After ignoring three requests made by Henry Roe, who sought information about why he was being "kept in confinement without a trial," Reynolds issued Special Orders No. 142, after doing nothing for four weeks. He claimed the battery's officers were "guilty of conduct which merits the severist punishment known to military law" but, instead of being punished further, the imprisoned officers—excluding Roe—were being "reduced to the ranks." The major general ended his special order by declaring that Roe would still have to face a court martial—his trial would start that very day (June 15) at 10:00 a.m.—but added a cryptic comment about how the battery would be given a chance to redeem its reputation.[21]

Will Brown believed the battery's powerful civilian friends had forced Banks' second-in-command into this odd reversal, writing, "Gen. Reynolds has found that the <u>pressure</u> in our favor was greater than he could well <u>kick</u> against." Confronted with an attack as seemingly hostile as any they had encountered on battlefields east and west of the Mississippi, the men of the Battery Boys had summoned all of their collective influence among family, friends, the Mercantile Association, Governor Richard Yates, the Northwest Sanitary Commission, and the United States Congress. Chicagoan Isaac Newton Arnold was one of their most formidable allies. In addition to being an influential member of the House of Representatives, Arnold was also Lincoln's personal friend. In response to Arnold's intervention, the War Department notified the Mercantile Association on June 3 that "no charges relative to the said Battery have been filed here. . . . The Department will protect the men fully in all their rights, and, as requested by you, a full investigation and report has been ordered."[22]

Reynolds probably received the War Department request on or about June 8. Having avoided collateral damage during his Chickamauga association with Rosecrans, Reynolds apparently did not want to become entangled in dangerous Washington investigations. He probably wanted to sever any connection with Banks and escape from New Orleans to a field assignment. Therefore, when he discovered the War Department intended to delve into the Mercantile Battery case, the major general moved forward to proceed with Roe's court martial and bring the matter to a close. The Battery Boys did not look upon Reynolds' newfound cooperation as a coincidence. In a letter to the *Chicago Tribune* describing the battery's mistreatment since the Red River Campaign, one of the cannoneers observed that the War Department's unexpected involvement was "the reason the authorities [in New Orleans] have so suddenly taken our case in hand. If this be true, I am inclined to think Lieut. Roe will get off easily."[23]

Roe's court martial began on June 15. Judge Advocate G. B. Russell, captain of the 38th Massachusetts Infantry, presided over the court martial, with seven other officers, including five from Western regiments, serving on it. Roe was charged with "conduct to the prejudice of good order and military discipline" and that, after his men had refused to obey an order, the Mercantile Battery commander "did fail to use proper endeavors to prevent, check or suppress such mutiny, but did encourage and sustain the men of his command in their mutinous conduct." Because of Reynolds' quick announcement of the court martial, Roe and his counsel lacked adequate time for preparing a response to the prosecution's allegations.[24]

After the Mercantile Battery's commander pleaded innocent to the charges, his immediate superior, Lieutenant Colonel Nelson Viall, was called to testify as a witness for the prosecution. He informed the court that Roe openly supported the battery's rebellion before handing over the written resolution. Under cross-examination, Viall denied he had lost his temper when Roe presented the resolution to him. Viall reluctantly acknowledged Roe had acted in a "gentlemanly" manner toward him. When pressed further, Viall admitted Roe had conformed to his instructions to form fatigue details, but it was the battery's soldiers who refused to perform the duty. It was finally established that Roe "did not refuse to obey any order." The court adjourned until the next morning so Roe could "confer with his counsel and arrange his defence."[25]

The next morning, Sergeant Florus Meacham was called as a witness for the defense. Meacham testified that Roe, in following Viall's order, asked his sergeants in the evening to form details for fatigue and guard duty the next day. It was the soldiers themselves, without any input from Roe, who lodged the protest first thing in the morning. According to the sergeant, the Mercantile Battery's lieutenant acted during the entire episode as if he fully intended to carry out Viall's order.[26]

The judge advocate called another Mercantile Battery sergeant to testify. He corroborated Meacham's testimony that Roe did not play a role in inciting a mutiny, but had only taken the protest to Viall as soon as he received it. After clearing the room, the court deliberated for a short time before determining that Roe was "Guilty, but without criminal intent," and should be acquitted. That afternoon Reynolds ordered the judge advocate to "allow Lt Roe the limits of the city hereafter until further orders."[27]

That same day, June 16, Brigadier General Thomas Sherman assumed command of the New Orleans' defenses. Reynolds had accepted a field assignment to lead Banks' 19th Corps and had left to report directly to Canby in his campaign to capture Mobile. Sherman was angry that Roe and the Mercantile Battery non-commissioned officers had been acquitted. He denounced the court's findings, asking Lincoln to intercede and dismiss Roe from the army. However, in deference to the War

Department, which was looking over his shoulder, Sherman concluded his remarks by writing, "The one hundred and nineteen men of the Mercantile Battery, who have conceived the highest degree of insubordination, will be furnished an opportunity to retrieve their former standing in the army of the United States." Lincoln upheld the Mercantile Battery acquittals, championed by his friend Congressman Isaac Arnold, and ignored Sherman's request to punish Roe.[28]

Henry Roe was reinstated after the Battery Boys were moved from Camp Parapet and Viall to the campground at Carrollton. In a bizarre example of military irony, Roe participated in another court martial a month later—this time as a member of the tribunal sitting in judgment of other accused soldiers. On September 1, Roe was promoted to 1st lieutenant.[29]

The Chicago newspapers' Red River ink was barely dry when they turned to the Mercantile Battery arrests in New Orleans. They were aware of possible connections between the Battery Boys' current plight and their breech of Banks' apparent news blackout. When the *Chicago Evening Journal* first learned about the arrest of the battery's leaders, its editor, aware the Mercantile Association was simultaneously trying to re-equip its namesake unit, saw a suspicious pattern in the order to arm the artillerists with muskets.[30]

On June 30, the *Chicago Tribune* printed extensive front-page coverage of the entire episode, including documents passed from Lieutenant Colonel Reuben B. Hatch, a colleague of Will Brown's in the Gulf quartermaster department, to an agent in the Illinois Sanitary Commission. The agent had written the *Chicago Tribune* on June 11, stating Hatch had taken substantial personal risk to intervene: "In consequence of the peculiar position occupied by these men [the Mercantile Battery], no one at this place can interfere in their behalf, without a certainty of his efforts not only proving abortive, but absolutely damaging to himself." As Will Brown informed his father, "We have a good, true friend in Lieut. Col. R. B. Hatch, Chief Quartermaster 13th Corps. He has shown his kindness in many particulars and is now on his way up river [on his way to Washington] with all the papers and the various statements in regard to our case." The *Chicago Tribune* editors thought the Battery Boys had been mistreated, and someone had "entrapped these Chicago boys into a real and serious offence, by a no less real and serious provocation. The War Department should go to the bottom of the affair."[31]

The Chicago newspapers never specifically implicated Banks in his department's peculiar administration of the cases against Henry Roe and the Mercantile Battery's non-commissioned officers. The Massachusetts general had cause to retaliate against the battery, however, and enough influence to carry out any such vendetta. Banks returned from the Red River Campaign to New Orleans on May 21, five days after the battery's officers were imprisoned, and was the ranking officer in the Crescent City. He could easily have given direction to Reynolds, Wilson, and Viall regarding the Mercantile Battery's situation. During that same time, seven other Battery Boys—Privates Chase Dickinson, Charles Haseltine, Isiah Hill, Andrew Howell, Everett Hudson, John Kitt, and James McNaught—were arrested for being "Absent without Leave." The men had returned from an officially approved leave only to discover the rest of the Boys had moved from Camp Parapet. They, too, were exonerated.[32]

Not surprisingly, there has never been any tangible evidence to link Nathaniel Banks to the mistreatment of the Mercantile Battery. Neither was there proof the Chicagoans were purposely treated worse than their counterparts in Nims' battery. Yet the available facts strongly suggest that was the case. Both batteries, after having lost their guns and vital equipment at the Battle of Sabine Crossroads, arrived in New Orleans on the same day. Chicago's Battery Boys were assigned to serve at Camp Parapet—and ordered to work as "Guards on Rail Road trains, digging ditches, building targets for other batteries to shoot at, guarding Negro Colonels Head Quarters, loading and unloading hay, handling lumber, [and] wheeling dirt." On the other hand, Nims' Battery "was transported to Carrollton [on May 10], where an outfit of light guns and horses was furnished them to be used in defense of New Orleans." Nims' veterans drilled with their six bronze Napoleons until the end of July, when they returned to Boston to muster out of the army.[33]

Will Brown was convinced Banks and his officers were persecuting the Chicagoans, despite lacking concrete evidence to prove his suspicions. "I want to see the thing pushed now," he wrote his father, so the Mercantile Battery's tormentors could be exposed. If not, he figured "the balance of our time in the Dept. of the Gulf will not be at all pleasant. We have won the ill will of those high in command and they, having the power, will probably exercise it."

*   *   *

Carrollton La.
June 26th 1864

My dear father,

Our non-commissioned officers, [who were] under arrest, have been released from "Durance" and are again with us. I think they will be reinstated as soon as Captain White returns. Lieut. Roe's sentence has not been made public yet but I have it from good authority that he will come out all right. I sincerely hope so, as he did only what he thought was right. Perhaps those officers who think they know a little bit more than everything will "Draw in their horns" when they see the following letter I have just received by us:

U.S. War Department
Adjutant General's Office
Washington DC
June 3d 1864

Honorable I. N. Arnold M.C.
Washington DC

Sir,

I have the honor to acknowledge the receipt through you of a letter from Mr. [Merrill] Ladd of Chicago and a newspaper extract, relative to the Mercantile Battery, Ills. Vols. In reply, I am directed to inform you that no charges relative to the said Battery have been filed here nor is it known to the [War]Department under what circumstances it was ordered to perform Infantry duty on the embankments of New Orleans.

It is proper to add that a department or army commander has the power to assign artillerists to temporary duty as Infantry if, in his opinion, the public interest should so demand, and it may be that said authority is now being exercised—temporarily—in the case of the Mercantile Battery.

The Department will protect the men fully in all their rights, and, as requested by you, a full investigation and report has been ordered. When the report shall have been received, you will be duly informed of the result.
I have the honor to remain

Very Resptly Your Obdt Svt,

Congressman Isaac Arnold
used his influence with the War
Department to exonerate the
Battery Boys.

Frederick F. Cook,

Bygone Days in Chicago

Thomas M. Vincent
Asst. Adj. Gen.

You know, Father, this letter is addressed to Hon. I. N. [Isaac Newton] Arnold. He forwarded it to the Merc. Assoc. and they sent it to us. I cannot see how the public [interest] demanded the transfer.

There were plenty of troops here and many of them doing no duty excepting in camp. I want to see the <u>thing</u> pushed now. [There is] scarcely an officer in this Department but who is [not] overbearing and acting as if they knew it all. Soldiers may not have any rights that an officer is bound to respect, but we propose to try it on anyhow. Because we happen to be thrown under such officers, we don't intend to be kicked by them; nor will we be. Many officers think, because a man is a private soldier, he don't know anything and will take abuse with impunity. Fortunately, we are not of this class and beside we have "tip-top" backers at home. We have lately received repeated assurances from the Mercantile Association that they will see us through and they have also <u>spoken</u> in a very substantial manner, i.e. sending us $500 to buy vegetables and such other commodities as we may need. They also are still at work trying to have us sent home to refit and recruit.[34]

We have been removed from Camp Parapet and are now doing duty as infantry guard. The duty is easier than that at Parapet and much more agreeable as we don't have anything to do with the "Africans."[35]

The old 13th Corps is no more. Less than a year ago it came into this Department 20.000 strong. Today, it is broken up because it . . . [does] not [have] men enough to form a corps. It does not number more than half its former strength. Gen. Canby is evidently a worker. He issues few orders and those few [are] models of conciseness. I think he is preparing an expedition for <u>somewhere</u>

and where it is yet a question. I hear whispers and rumors pointing all the way from Mobile to Shreveport. The sutlers are watching and buying in a stock. This is generally a pretty good sign of a movement but not always a sure one. These sutlers are as much a clique as any body of men I ever saw.[36]

*   *   *

Carrollton La.
July 3d 1864

My dear father

Since I last wrote, I have had the pleasure of meeting Hiram Hoxie who, being down here on business, <u>hunted me up</u>. Altho' really an entire stranger, he seemed like an old acquaintance and, of course, both had many questions to ask and answer. He is a fine, caring young man, about Henry's age I should think, and a little heavier built. He enquired particularly about friends at home and said he wished he could visit you. Says he has written you several times but never received an answer. I gave him your address and think he will write you soon. His address is Care 88th Regt. U.S.C. Inft'y Port Hudson. His regiment is not there—he is stationed there and has something to do with the steamer clearances &c—a kind of military port overseer. I suppose it is much better than being with his regiment. I notice all these "Corps de Afrique" fellows like to get on detached service if possible. He gave me cousin Augusta's address and I have written her.

I have yours announcing Henry's return on furlough and am very glad to hear of it. Home cares and comforts are <u>everything</u> to a sick or wounded soldier and I wish many more of them could go home. Cousin Val Hurd writes me that his regiment has been in another engagement in which the major was killed. One here only learns of the actual business Sherman is doing by hearing from some friend with him. The newspapers say but little and that little quite indefinite.

The rebs are making demonstrations in this vicinity again. They feel very confident on the strength of their success in the Red river country and, in consequence, are getting <u>brash</u>. I am told that Dick Taylor has promised his friends here that they should hear the thunder of his artillery ere many days. I imagine if he only comes close enough that the echo of our guns may have a tendency to curb his spirit. Gen. Canby assumes command of the military wheel here and he, I think, knows how to deal with rebel traitors. I look for a movement from here soon but can hardly guess where. A few

knowing ones point very significantly over toward Lake Ponchartrain thereby indicating a movement against Mobile.[37]

To-morrow being the glorious 4th, preparations are going
forward in the city to celebrate the day in a becoming manner.
Among the attractions will be an oration by Gen. Sickles and I shall
try to see him; more out of curiosity to see the individual than care to
hear his speech. I suppose like nearly all other 4th of July orations,
his will be much about the eagle and negro, two individuals now
very closely connected and, if anything, the latter is ahead. I do
hope that these negro shriekers will have a chance to exercise their
opinions one of these days. I don't like the negro policy at all and
would like to see a change.[38]

We are still doing infantry duty but don't have to work very hard.
I think it will not be long before we will be furnished with a new
battery.

*   *   *

Carrollton La.
July 10th 1864

My dear father

The C.M.B. seems in a fair way to gain all the notoriety usually
given to a body of troops, if not a little more. The latest sensation is
an article published in the Chicago Times and not only gives a most
amusing—to me—account of how our boys have been treated but
makes a ten strike against the administration, Old Abe and nearly
everyone else. Fortunately, the foundation of this article does not
rest on our shoulders. We have enough on hand already. The
"powers that be" here appear greatly incensed against us,
particularly against Lieut. Roe. Sometimes, I think they show "petty
malice" in what they do but such thoughts as these are not safe
particularly from a soldier. We have a good, true friend in Lieut.
Col. R. B. Hatch, Chief Quartermaster 13th Corps. He has shown
his kindness in many particulars and is now on his way up river with
all the papers and the various statements in regard to our case.[39]

The punishments have all been carried out as I wrote you in a
former letter, that is, ten of our non-commissioned officers have
been reduced and Lieut. Roe has been tried by Court martial. In the
cases of the Orderly and myself, nothing has been done nor do I
think anything will be. Altho' those high in command can do nearly
what they please with those under them, there are certain influences
that even the highest will submit to.

To-day our Orderly has received a commission as lieut., from Gov. Yates, and will probably be mustered in to-morrow. I am glad of this appointment as the Orderly is a tip-top good fellow and a universal favorite. My position don't go any higher. As QM Sgt., I am out of the line of promotion so cannot look for promotion. But even were this not the case, there are one or two men in our command who really ought to have the other vacancy and I hope one of them may get it. Of course, I would like promotion but I will not do anything to throw myself in where I think others more deserving. The men I speak of are our oldest Sergeants and really deserve the position. One of them in particular, James C. Sinclair, son of your old acquaintance James Sinclair. Tinnes [?] is a fine fellow and I hope will get the position as none deserve it more. There is one fellow who has been on detached service at 13th Corps Head Quarters who has been figuring for the appointment for some time; but I doubt if he gets it and sincerely hope not.[40]

My great consolation is that the original members of the C.M.B. have only about fourteen months longer to serve. I do not get dissatisfied, however, nor do I allow myself to have the blues. I can stand pretty nearly everything, am possessed of a good conscience, health, the usual flow of animal spirits and in fact don't care much anyhow. [I] don't feel particularly reckless and have little fear but that all will come out all right in the end. I write you just as I feel.[41]

We are still at infantry duty and get along with it very well. I hope and think we will soon be relieved. With love to all.

*   *   *

Post Parapet La
July 17th 1864

My dear father

I enclose herewith a copy of the Court martial in the case of Lieut. Roe. You will notice that the Gen. [Thomas] Sherman is as hard on the court as he is on the Lieut., but evidently hopes the President will dismiss him from the service. A countercheck to the Gen.'s movement has already taken place. In fact, a force is moving on both his flanks and on his rear—we still boldly holding the front. Our right flank movement is composed of Col. Hatch, Chief Q.M. 13th Corps who is on his way to Washington with all papers necessary to explain matters. Our force composing the left flank movement consists of Gov. Yates who not only knows the Battery but is always ready to see his own troops well taken care of. The rear, composed of the Mercantile Association, will do good work.

We also have a good many scouts, among whom may be mentioned Dr. Long, agent of the Illinois State Sanitary Commission and a working man.[42]

With such a combination, I think we may look for success. But I am pretty well satisfied that, whatever the decision of the President may be, the balance of our time in the Dept. of the Gulf will not be at all pleasant. We have won the ill will of those high in command and they, having the power, will probably exercise it. I think, however, we can now undergo most anything and live thro' it. In my letters # 7 and # 8, I sent you copy of Gen. Reynolds order reducing part of our non-commissioned officers and I thought that order final. But it would seem that Gen. Sherman proposes giving them the same chances to retrieve as the rest of us. We are again at Parapet but do not have the same duties to perform as when here before. About one fourth of the Company are on duty as guards; the balance having to drill about three hours. We hear nothing of a new battery, nor do I think we will 'till the return of Capt. White. Lieut. Hunt of the 17th Ohio Battery is in command. All of the officers from the colored regiments have left us. Lieut. Hunt is a pretty good officer. His battery was formerly in our old Division (4th) but, like us, has been detached and are now in camp at N.O.[43]

The rebel report of the capture of Little Rock proves false but Steele seems to have his hands full. The capture of the far-famed rebel privateer "Alabama" is hailed with delight by all soldiers and the name of the "Kearsarge" will be long remembered. It was a gallant exploit and gallantly carried out. I hope we will get Semmes.[44]

*   *   *

Parapet La.
July 24th 1864

My dear father

The week has been one of startling rumors and wild ones. The capture of the New York Mail S.S. "Electric Spark" by the rebel privateer "Florida" has been the great topic of street conversation. At one time, we had a dispatch from the Balize saying that the "Evening Star" had also been taken. This has since proved false. Until yesterday, we have not received a mail per ocean steamer for nearly three weeks. The "Electric Spark" had 65 bags of mail on board.[45]

Yesterday, very favorable news came from Grant and Sherman tho' very little of it official. Washington is again safe. If the rebs did not make an occasional raid on Washington I don't know what the newspapers would do. One of these <u>raids</u> is worth a small mint to the newspapers and newsboys. "Grapevines" are plentiful, particularly from Mobile and Woodville Miss. I do not think the rebs are on their last legs yet, but I do think they feel pretty gloomy and wish we had fewer men like Sherman, Grant, Hooker, Meade and Smith.[46]

By the way, what a worker Smith is. I mean Gen. A. J. Smith, our old Division commander during the Vicksburg campaign. He is nearly always in the field and never so happy as when well filled with whiskey and at the head of his command. I have been more amused at him and his doings than any other officer I have ever seen. His favorite speech to his men is "Go in boys, go in, and send them to H__l a Kiting, yes a Kiting." He always <u>jerks</u> his words out.

I see that Maj. Gen. Franklin was taken prisoner near Baltimore and managed to escape. The papers talk a good-deal about his good fortune. But I have heard several say that the rebels would rather not have him as he can do more damage to our cause by having command of our forces in the field. I have heard whispers not at all flattering to Gen. Franklin's loyalty. It seems rather strange that the enemy allowed him to escape so easily. The most absurd rumors reach us on days when there are no arrivals [of mail or newspapers] from the North. Sometimes, one would think the whole country had gone to <u>smash</u>, and then again the rebellion is surely on its last legs.[47]

I sent you a copy of the New Orleans Times of 22nd Inst. and hope it will reach you as I would like you to see the account of the <u>Constitutional</u> conventions proceeding. I marked that article. The <u>convention</u> has got up an awful howl about Mr. May, the editor of the Times, and proposed to <u>chain him up</u>; but I rather think he will survive it. The fact is [that] this <u>convention</u> is a simple farce and many of its numbers, I am informed, cannot even write their names. Each member is paid $8 per day and, of course, there is no hurry to adjourn. I would be surprised if, just before they adjourn, they passed an act allowing each member $500 for <u>contingent expenses</u>. Something like the Chicago council under the Boone administration, who voted for a painting of each Alderman composing that body—the same to be paid for out of the public funds. Much has been, and will be, said about this convention. I fear its proceedings will do much more damage than good to the Federal cause in this state.[48]

Troops are gradually leaving here, bound for the Potomac. I think nothing but infantry and cavalry have gone as yet. I suppose Grant has plenty of artillery.

The weather has been comfortable. The past two days have been quite cool. I do not think the difference in heat is much greater than further North, tho' the hot season is much longer. I do not notice the heat nearly as much as I did at Vicksburg last year. I have not heard from Lib very lately. I suppose Henry has again joined his regiment. I wrote Belle yesterday.[49]

*   *   *

Post Parapet
July 31st 1864

My dear father

During the past week, we have received reliable intelligence of Captain White and our boys [who are still] prisoners of Camp Ford near Tyler Texas. A lot of officers and soldiers have arrived directly from there and several of the former have called upon us. I had the pleasure of meeting a Lieut. who had been in the same mess with Capt. White and Lieut. Cone. He says [they] are well treated, that is, as well as the Confeds can afford. For food, they have ¾ lbs of corn-meal and 1 lb of fresh meat daily. If any are fortunate enough to have money, they can buy flour at about the rate of $1—greenbacks—per pound. They can also purchase vegetables at the same living rates.

This lieut. says we can use them (the rebels) up if we only work right. He has been a prisoner for thirteen months and, during that time, has had a very fair opportunity to observe the working of the institution. He thinks their whole system of government is a false one. The army is distrustful of its leaders; the people inwardly pray for peace; the soldier only fights because he fears to give up and, altho' a strong Union feeling prevails throughout both army and civil life, each individual faces fears to trust his sentiments to another. This, in itself, will end the contest.

All our boys [who are prisoners] are hopeful but, of course, cannot tell when they will be exchanged. I hear rumors in regard to an exchange soon but, as a rumor, I place little faith in it.

What do you think of the "Peace Proposition" at Niagara Falls? I am almost inclined to think it a political dodge, but do not know enough of the antecedents of the rebel commissioners to decide. The letter of Clay and Holcomb about the South "Submitting to terms of peace at the expense of liberty and happiness" is a played out tirade and one used by all Southerners and their Copperhead friends in the North. I think Grant and Sherman are pursuing the shortest course towards "peace" and the one that will finally succeed. If the South will fight, let them. We are getting pretty well posted in that line of business. I think [we] can make a pretty good show. I am not particularly blood-thirsty, nor do I wish to see the war prolonged, but I believe in the motto "No compromise with traitors in arms." Did you read Gen. Sherman's letter of instruction to Gen. Burbridge? I think it one of the best letters he ever wrote and you know he has written many good ones.[50]

Grant's campaign in Virginia seems much like that of Vicksburg. He is hanging on with his usual tenacity and pluck and will, I think, succeed in accomplishing his object. Dick Taylor is making some demonstrations on our line between here and the mouth of the Red river. But I imagine he is only doing it to effect the crossing of his force to join the rebel army near Atlanta. I don't think he cares about getting possession of this place, nor do I think he would take it even if he should try; he certainly could not hold it long.

Our commanding officer (Lieut. Rice of the 17th Ohio Battery) is trying to have us relieved from present duty and ordered to the Camp of Artillery Instruction now forming. Whether he will succeed in this is a question and I suppose Brig. Gen. [Thomas] Sherman will be the one to answer it. If so, I <u>don't</u> think the effort [of Lieut. Rice] will prove a success as the General is <u>down</u> on us and knows that nothing would please us better than to again have a battery. We can stand it, however, whatever the results.[51]

"Gen. Banks has <u>really</u> gone home and Gen. Hurlbut is in command of the Dept."

Chapter 16

A Shot Thro' the Bull's Eye

Lieutenant Henry Roe and his non-commissioned officers emerged from the shadows of the oppressive building on Baronne Street and stepped out into the daylight. They left the Federal prison jubilant about regaining their freedom, just as the Union loyalists at Vicksburg had celebrated one year earlier when they were released from confinement. The liberated townspeople had cheered when the Stars and Stripes were raised once again above the majestic Warren County courthouse. The Mercantile Battery leaders were grateful to be returning to their camp instead of being sent off to Ship Island, as Banks' officials had threatened. They were more than willing to fulfill Lieutenant Colonel Viall's order to handle infantry and fatigue duties.[1]

Roe and his officers enjoyed being back on the horse-drawn train, which ran hourly between downtown and Carrollton and passed some of the area's finest homes and most colorful, lush gardens. It reminded them of the Hyde Park train in Chicago. Savoring their renewed freedom, the Battery Boys were not bothered by the frequent stops to drop off passengers. The ride gave them time to reflect on how much had happened since their first glimpse of the St. Charles Street train cars.

Last August, White's men had arrived on the steamer *Atlantic* from Vicksburg, unaware of how quickly the sterling record they had developed under Grant and Sherman would be tarnished. They had not gotten off to a good start in the Department of the Gulf. The captain himself had tried to get transferred from Banks' command. In September, William Husted had written his family in Chicago to express his frustration. He wished that Grant "could be put in command here, and send Banks and his Eastern troops to Charleston or some where else." The private also commented that he and his comrades could not afford the ten-cent fare to ride the St. Charles Street train "for the simple reason that we have got no money, and there is no prospect of Uncle Sam's coming around with any at present." In retrospect, the Battery Boys' initial frustrations were minor in comparison to the ordeals they had passed through since that time.[2]

The Mercantile Battery's luck, however, was finally changing. Lieutenant Roe had been exonerated and the unit had been ordered to transfer out of Camp Parapet and return to its old Carrollton campground. Brigadier General Richard Arnold, the Department of the Gulf's chief of artillery, had rescued the Mercantile Battery from performing what he called "duties entirely foreign to its Arm of the Service," and reestablished the unit in "its legitimate branch." Despite some resistance from Thomas Sherman, who was still in command of New Orleans' defenses, Arnold succeeded in relocating the Chicagoans to his Camp of Instruction for Reserve Artillery at nearby Greenville. The Battery Boys embraced their artillery duties and even enjoyed their four daily hours of drilling, which reminded them of their carefree basic-training days at Camp Doggett two years ago.[3]

There had been other occasions for Will Brown and his comrades to rejoice since the mutiny allegations were dropped. First and foremost, Nathaniel Banks departed for Washington—probably to solicit a new political assignment from Lincoln—and was no longer in a position to influence the destiny of the Chicago Mercantile Battery. He had headed the Department of the Gulf for a year and a half, but was now replaced by Major General Stephen Hurlbut, a Western commander. Will informed his father that "Gen. Banks has really gone home" and hoped for "his permanent absence." Thomas Sherman was rumored to be on his way out as well, and General Reynolds and Colonel Robert Wilson had both left the area to participate in Canby's campaign to capture Mobile.

Lieutenant Colonel Viall—or "Lieutenant Colonel Vile" as some called him—stayed behind at Camp Parapet to oversee the training of more contraband troops.[4]

Unfortunately, the Battery Boys did not know the true character of fellow Illinoisan Stephen Hurlbut, who was as crafty a politician as his predecessor had been—and perhaps even more so. Jeffrey Lash, Hurlbut's biographer, researched and documented the major general's involvement in corrupt schemes during his tenure in New Orleans. Hurlbut had been accused of similar chicanery earlier in the war when he served as commander of the garrison at Memphis. While overseeing both cities he conjured up an image of himself as a strict military leader in the occupied South. In Memphis, he banned the Copperhead-leaning *Chicago Times*. Now, in the Crescent City, he imposed restrictions on gambling and Sunday entertainment venues while extorting money from cotton speculators. This explained why the local cotton ring, described by Will Brown in letters to his father, was not exposed and punished. "The harsh truth," summarized Lash, "was that in both Memphis and New Orleans Hurlbut had masterfully concealed a clear pattern of official misconduct under the façade of strict and efficient administration."[5]

After Hurlbut took over Banks' former command, he continued to keep the Department of the Gulf's headquarters in the luxurious St. Charles Hotel. He also retained some of Banks' unsavory staff members, such as the provost marshal, Lieutenant Colonel Harai Robinson. Because he was preoccupied with his Mobile operation, Canby did not pay enough attention to the thriving cotton ring. In late July, however, Lincoln informed Canby about the complaints he was receiving regarding the corruption surrounding the cotton traders. Men like Harai Robinson were allegedly shaking down the cotton traders.[6]

Hurlbut was also involved in counteracting Reconstruction measures (which Banks had implemented in New Orleans for Lincoln), interfered with newly elected Governor Michael Hahn, and concocted a scheme to convert contrabands into a "contract-labor system." By that fall Hurlbut would also tangle with the editor of the *New Orleans Tribune*, the first daily newspaper in the country owned and run by blacks. Hurlbut's activities escalated tensions and interfered with the new state government. He retaliated when the governor complained to the president. Hurlbut, claiming Hahn was sheltering an active Confederate sympathizer, ordered his dishonest henchman Harai Robinson to search the governor's mansion while Hahn was away. Lincoln sent a letter to Hurlbut expressing disappointment over the general's clashes with Louisiana's civil government and his wrongful treatment of blacks.[7]

It can be argued that Lincoln himself was partially to blame for creating the conditions leading to the unconscionable abuse of power in New Orleans. The president had pressured Banks, Canby, and Hurlbut to allow Northern businessmen to acquire cotton from Louisiana's Confederate plantation owners. Although a case could be made that Banks misused the situation for political gain, both nationally and for his Massachusetts' constituents, Lincoln wanted Union-sanctioned cotton traders to facilitate the exchange of Northern agricultural and manufacturing goods for enemy cotton. This, in turn, would weaken the Confederacy's ability to purchase foreign war material while relieving the shortage of cotton and gold in the North. Hurlbut took further advantage of Lincoln's national objectives for his own self-aggrandizement. The president's impatience, however, led him to appoint an independent commission to investigate the cotton ring operating in the Department of the Gulf, an inquiry he had expected Canby to undertake.[8]

In addition to being rid of their Department of the Gulf tormentors, the Mercantile Battery soldiers had another reason to rejoice. Arnold, their miracle-working chief of artillery, had not only freed them from the grasp of Thomas Sherman, but had somehow arranged for Battery G of the United States Artillery to relinquish its cannon. The Mercantile Battery trained with their new guns to join a cavalry division led by Brigadier General John Davidson, a stern-looking horseman whose face was accentuated by a long mustache drooping down over a wispy goatee. Amazed and elated, the Chicagoans understood it was a privilege and rare honor for a unit of volunteer soldiers to become horse artillerymen. Instead of digging ditches and serving as guards, they would be "Battery Boys" again. In their new capacity as a horse artillery unit, most of the rejuvenated artillerists found themselves mounted on horses, though a few were forced to ride on caissons or the limbers that pulled their 3-inch rifled guns.[9]

In the training camp, Will Brown was responsible for making sure that his friends had everything they needed to engage in "practical artillery." Sometimes, Will took a break from his quartermaster paperwork to watch target practice, and to smell black powder again.

Although the Illinois cannoneers had not fired a gun since April 8, they were remarkably accurate—"Striking a target at a distance of nearly 1 ½ miles"—with their four new rifled guns.

* * *

Camp of Reserve Artillery
Greenville
August 7th 1864

My dear father

We again bloom out in our colors; the flower opens gradually, however, and it will be several days before it comes out in all its beauty's. But to come down from simile to fact: We have left Parapet.

[We have] done away with our smooth-bores of 69 calibre and during this week hope to have four pieces of our legitimate arm viz: 3-inch rifled guns. This change has been brought about by repeated efforts on the part of our Commanding Officer [Brig. Gen. Richard Arnold]. Gen. [Thomas] Sherman, who has appeared to take especial delight in doing everything for us that we did not want, was not consulted in this matter. We are no longer under his control, nor do we have anything to do with officers of colored regiments.[10]

The object of the present camp is to instruct both officers and men in both practical and theoretical artillery. There are eight batteries in the camp, all of them belonging to the 13th Corps. There are three principal Schools namely: the School of the Piece (gun), School of the Battery and School of the Battalion. We have four hours [of] drill

Chief of Artillery Richard Arnold rescued the Chicago Battery from infantry duty.

Rhode Island State Archives

daily. I think the form of instruction very good and imagine that it will benefit us. We are very good practically, but many of us know but little about Theory. The camp is under charge of Capt. Jacob Foster of the 1st Wis. Battery. The batteries are divided into two battalions, four in each. Our camp is right out in the sun but we are going to erect shade houses in front of quarters. We camped at nearly the same place we were [last year] when we arrived here from Vicksburg.[11]

This morning's "Times" has pretty good news from Mobile. Our gunboats have succeeded in silencing and passing Forts Johnston [Gaines], Powell and Morgan, and the paper says they now have Mobile at their mercy. I don't hardly believe <u>all</u> this, particularly the latter part. Still, I am inclined to the opinion that we will take the place before many days as there is a big force there, or near there. Admiral Farragut and Gen. Morgan [Major General Gordon Granger] are the field and sea operators against Mobile, tho' I suppose Gen. Canby is prince mover. [Major] Gen. [Francis Jay] Herron's Division (2nd Div. 13th Corps) arrived here from Brownsville last week and to-day were embarking on ocean transports, their supposed destination being Mobile.[12]

*   *   *

Carrollton La.
September 4th 1864

My dear father

I wish it were possible for Grant to gain a signal victory during the next six weeks. I think it would do more toward putting a <u>quietus</u> to peace talk than anything else. I believe that he is working—working hard too—and I hope with success. What we need now is more men in the field. Instead of figuring on bounties and things of that kind, I wish they would enforce the draft and <u>make</u> the men come out. This has been the policy of the South for the two past years and, notwithstanding Northern newspaper accounts of desertions of rebel conscripts, I notice the rebs manage to get fight out of these men and good fight too. It is all very well for men to say they want [to] fight. But when it comes to it, and they find an enemy popping away where they are and the bullets uncomfortably playing round their ears, they naturally shoot back again and of personal revenge. Conscripts will not fight as veterans but still they will do some work and help the rest.[13]

Did you see General [William. T.] Sherman's letter to a Massachusetts commissioner? I think it one of the best letters ever written and one that hits the nail fairly and squarely on the head. After the war, I would like to collect Sherman war letters, frame them and hang them up in a conspicuous place; they are too good to be lost. Sherman is an [astute] observer. He knows the feeling of his army and has the right mode of expressing his opinion.[14]

Indications look as if an "On to Mobile" [campaign] were not intended at present. Why I do not know, but suppose there are good and sufficient reasons. Probably a small force will be left at the forts for garrison purposes and the balance withdrawn to some point where they are more needed.[15]

* * *

Carrollton La.
September 11th 1864
My dear father

I have been very busy during the past week and probably will be for the coming week. Lieut. Hunt is about to leave us and Lieut. Roe will again take command. Roe depends on me to see that his papers &c are kept all right and this in itself is no easy job, but my mind is occupied all the time and business won't hurt me.

The news of the fall of Atlanta was rec<u>d</u> here with the greatest rejoicing; and the cannons boomed out merrily with their bong, bong, bong. Secesh bangs his head and watches the proceedings of the Chicago convention, which rumor says has nominated "Little Mac" for the White House. We have no particulars from Atlanta yet but am looking for them by every boat.[16]

I wish I could hear from Henry. When you write him, please tell him that I have written twice since having rec<u>d</u> any of his favors. I am daily looking for a letter from Lib.[17]

* * *

Carrollton La.
September 18th 1864

My dear father

I have been so busy during the week that I have hardly looked at the newspapers—have just kept well enough posted to know that the war still goes on notwithstanding the peace effort to the contrary. It seems that "Little Mac" accepted the Chicago nomination but makes his own platform. And if he means what he says, I cannot see where the peace howlers can find any comfort. In the army, I think the great majority are for Lincoln. They have tried him and know his plan of operations. I think there may be better men than Lincoln but present events require his presence in the Presidential chair and there hope he will stay. After the war is over, I hope to see some good military man nominated and I will give him my vote. I suppose McClellan will now resign his position in the army, so "It's an ill wind that blows nobody good."[18]

[William T.] Sherman's recent success, and Grant's gradually tightening his lines, will do more towards peace than forty such conventions as that recently held in Chicago. The rebs say they can easily lose the Weldon RR and still they are doing all in their power to re-take it; and so far without success. The news from Arkansas is not good—a large reb force are cowering round our lines in that quarter and "gobbling up" whatever they can find. I think that Gen. Canby sees the danger and will make ample preparations for it. It takes a man with a good head to watch the whole Mississippi river.[19]

The rebel [Brigadier] Gen. [Richard L.] Page, who destroyed considerable ordnance after he had raised the white flag over Fort Morgan, is on trial before a military commission. But I presume nothing will be done with him as it will probably be a difficult matter to convict him. Page is a fine looking man but a big rebel; in fact, it is among such men as he that the rebellion has its ablest supporters.[20]

* * *

Carrollton La.
September 25th 1864

My dear father

"Gen. Banks is going home on a twenty days leave with permission to ask for an extension at the War Department." This is the latest and I think it is true. Gen. Hurlbut of Ill. succeeds and takes possession in the morning. Canby has played smash with the "Red tape" while he has been here. One would be surprised to see the difference between his and Banks head quarters. A stranger would think that Banks commanded the army while Gen. Canby only had charge of a brigade. I hope to see this made a decidedly Western department and think it rapidly verging in that direction. We of the North-west should control the Mississippi so that, in case of future troubles, we may hold a strong hand. I think that Brig. Gen. [Thomas] Sherman will soon be relieved from command of the Defences; rumor says so now, tho' it may not be so.[21]

I have a letter from Henry bearing the date Atlanta 8th. He complains of continued illness and hopes to go home soon. I sincerely hope that he will succeed not only in that, but in getting out of the army as I feel confident that it is no place for him.[22]

* * *

Carrollton La.
October 2nd 1864

My dear father

We have <u>lots</u> of good news this week and at least three times have the cannon in the city belched forth their thunder tones, with their bong, bong, shout with joy—Grant's flanks plays pranks with Jeff's ranks, so give thanks—Victory! Victory! Victory!![23]

How pleasantly sound the "Big guns" when we know they mean success. How they stir the heart and how many a wish goes up that they may one day be the symbols of peace as they have been the leaders of war. Such victories as Sheridan's are greater "Aids and comfort" to the Administration party than all the newspaper clack and political harangues that have taken or will take place between this and election day.

I commence to think that Maj. Gen. [William T.] Sherman really understands "The situation" better than any man in the country. He does not think of individuals, or of sections, but goes in for the whole country and just as much <u>war</u> as the South wants. I presume you have read his letters to Hood and the mayor of Atlanta. No chance to misunderstand his meaning there, and no handling the enemy with kid gloves.[24]

Gen. Banks has <u>really</u> gone home and Gen. Hurlbut is in command of the Dept. I do not know if Banks has left for good, but think that fewer tears will be shed for his permanent absence than joyful ones for his return. He is a favorite with the <u>loyal citizens</u> and that don't speak well for him. You would be amused to hear some of the ladies of New Orleans "Pitch in" to Ben Butler. One only has to mention his name to see their pretty nasal appendages and "Quickly upward turning" in their eyes speak volumes. Old Ben would stand a poor show among a colony of Southern women. The poorer class liked him and to-day wished that he would return.[25]

I have seen the captured rebel ram "Tennessee" and she is a formidable looking craft and, when again in order, will be quite an addition to our naval power. I think she looks saucy and one can hardly believe that a "Wooden wall" ever dared approach her.[26]

I have a letter from Lib from DeValls Bluff in which he says that he has received the appointment of regimental QM sergeant. This will increase his pay and is, in fact, a much better position than his old one. He says that quite a number of troops are arriving at the Bluff. I think this looks like work in Arkansas and would not be surprised to hear stirring news from that quarter soon.[27]

* * *

Carrollton La.
October 9th 1864

My dear father

Appearances indicate a change. The generals are looking around among us and seeing how we are "fixed" and if we look fit for active service. Gen. Totten, Chief of Artillery, went thro' camp the other day and made the remark that our caissons were too heavy for the soil and that he would have to move them. We have been transferred to command of Gen. Davidson, Chief of Cavalry, Mil. Div. West Miss.—and when we do move will probably be under his orders. We find it [a] difficult matter to obtain what horses we require. With [the Battery's] present strength, we should have 150 horses and as yet we have only 100. We expect to obtain the requisite number soon.[28]

A battery of horse artillery makes quite a show when drawn up in line or marching in column. We are out on drill nearly every day and are getting pretty well posted. By <u>we</u>, I do not include myself, as my duties are such that I have nothing to do with the drill. A QM Sergeant is quite a personage when a battery is fitting out and usually has his hands full. As we have only two commissioned officers with us, I have much more to attend to than I would otherwise. Another thing, our commanding officer [Lieutenant Henry Roe], tho' a tip-top good fellow, knows scarcely anything about the minor details and usually leaves it all to me. It is impossible for me to explain to you fully what my duties are but I think I <u>earn my pay</u>.

If we move, I think we will go to Baton Rouge; there join [Albert] Lee's Cavalry Division and then move when he does.[29]

* * *

Carrollton La.
October 16th 1864

My dear father

Another week has rolled its length around and in it the unconquerable hosts of Grant have steadily braved the perils of many a fight and are pushing for the hot bed of treason—Richmond. What great majorities is Sheridan making for the Union cause; and what a thrill of hope runs thro' ones veins when he reads of the successes in the Shenandoah. And thro' it all, how plainly the master hand of Grant stands forth. He seems to be everywhere and always at the right time. He dispatches to Stanton—short and only facts; no bombast, no ideas as to the future. I think the final fall of Richmond as sure as the rising of the sun and Grant will take it.[30]

From [William T.] Sherman and his army we hear very little. The fact that Jeff [Confederate President Jefferson Davis] has lately visited that part of rebeldom is almost enough to convince one of the tiny thread on which hangs that part of the Confederacy. I don't believe that Sherman fears Hood. In fact, I believe that he is watching Hood closely so that he will not have opportunity to send a part of his force to help [Robert E.] Lee.[31]

I suppose that the [presidential] election during the coming month is the all absorbing topic with you and I hope the majority [of people in St. Joseph] are with the administration. Here, the political talk is almost <u>nix</u>. The civil population is made up of so mixed a class. And military authority is so very <u>sudden</u>, pouncing down on a man when he least expects it, that men are careful how they express themselves. We have lately had a McClellan mutiny and it tells the whole history when I say that it was made up of men noted for their disloyalty to the government in "<u>Blockade Times</u>" i.e. the time when the rebs held the city. There were also a few <u>sore</u> heads, men who were defeated from office during the last state election. The mutiny was a tame affair and like the Chicago convention did not account to much.

All of our flags lost on the Red river campaign have lately been recaptured while [the Confederates were] attempting to take them across the Mississippi river. Gen. Canby is out with a congratulatory order about it. According to the Ancients, I believe a thing of this kind was considered a very good omen.

*   *   *

Carrollton La.
October 23d 1864

My dear father

Really, I wish you could visit the French markets. New Orleans boasts many fine buildings but they do not show off well. The city is built as if there was very little room to spare and, in consequence, the streets are very narrow. It takes time to find the fine buildings. There are many of them but they appear to be shut out and only time will develop them. The great Custom house that we used to read so much about is yet unfinished and probably it will be a great while before it will be. When we first came here, there was no roof on it. But during the past year, a common one has been put on and the lower part of the building is occupied by the Post Office and government officials. One corner of the building has a store in it which contains the name of G. T. [Pierre Gustave Toutant] Beauregard, Architect.[32]

The shell road leading to Lake Ponchartrain is one of the institutions of the city. It leads to the race course, drilling grounds and the Lake. It is a great drive for the "fast boys" and otherwise, and on race days is usually filled with gay turn outs &c &c. In the summer, [going] to the lake is a favorite drive and there one finds bath houses and all the fixins attached to a fashionable watering place. While Gen. Banks was doing the successful [expedition] up the Red river this Spring, the Mrs. Major Gen. gave a private dinner party to about fifteen ladies at the Lake. The party cost the neat little sum of $1.500, or nearly four bales of cotton—phew.[33]

We have it from pretty reliable authority that Captain White and our boys are on their way down the Red river; the cartel of exchange having been arranged and nothing to keep them from joining us as soon as the boats can bring them here. Col. Cowan of the 19th Ky. Inf'y told me this yesterday and I hope it will prove true. The Col. was a prisoner with our boys but was exchanged a couple of months since…. His regiment formerly belonged to the old 4th Div.[34]

We still have rumors that we will be move[d] soon, but I can so see nothing that indicates what point we will move toward; still I think we will go somewhere soon. Have not had much new news during the week. I see that Hood is trying the flank business but I imagine he will find it a poor speculation. Love to all.[35]

* * *

Contrary to Will Brown's prediction, his Mercantile Battery comrades were not released from Camp Ford. Captain Patrick White and

Lieutenant Pinckney Cone still languished in captivity, along with Sergeant Joseph Day, Sergeant George Bryant, Corporal Samuel Hammett, Corporal Henry Brackett, and nine privates (including Bugler John Arnold.)[36]

During 1863, Camp Ford was established in East Texas as the Rebels' primary prison camp for the Trans-Mississippi region. It was located four miles outside of Tyler, an active commercial center in northeastern Texas, which included a major Confederate ordnance factory and two salt mines in the surrounding area. The six-acre prison was built on the side of a hill, gently sloping down to Rays Creek, which ran along the southern side of the enclosure. The Camp Ford stockade consisted of 12-foot logs buried four feet in the ground. They were split in half lengthwise—with the smooth side facing inward to discourage prisoners from getting a foothold to climb over the fence. Dirt was piled up outside the walls to create platforms, along which the guards patrolled.[37]

There was an active spring at the upper, northwestern end of the compound, which the prisoners cherished as a life-preserving gift. It ran perpendicular to the creek and flowed into it. The prisoners designed wooden reservoirs for drinking and bathing. As a sanitary safeguard, each sluice was kept separate from the latrines at the lower end of the hill. After the war, a veteran of the 120th Ohio Infantry who had been imprisoned at Camp Ford returned to visit the site and found the spring still flowing. He recalled how the fresh water had been a blessing to the Union prisoners: "with tears falling from my eyes, I picked up an old gourd and drank deep, of the pure, cool water, that was verily as the water of life, to us poor fellows, thirty years ago."[38]

Like the Confederate prison camps at Andersonville, Florence, and Salisbury in the Southeast, Camp Ford was an open-air compound, which meant the inmates had minimal protection against the oppressive summer sun, cool evenings, and winter weather. Prisoners at Camp Ford were allowed to visit a nearby forest, under heavy guard, to chop trees for building shebangs. However, according to Mary Livermore, when her Boys arrived at Camp Ford, they discovered "there were but six axes for the entire seven thousand men." White and his cannoneers had to haul logs about a half mile to construct their huts because the trees closest to the prison had already been cut down. Due to the shortage of axes, as well as the limited number of supervised work parties allowed out of the

An officer's hut (a "shebang") at
Camp Ford in Tyler, Texas.

Richard Brady Williams Private Collection

compound, some rank-and-file soldiers were forced to dig caves into the sides of the hill and live like "woodchucks," with rodents and maggots for neighbors. Others improvised and created "a wigwam metropolis" with lean-tos, covering them with branches and underbrush. The prisoners lamented no longer having army-issue shelters to keep out the scorpions and snakes. Leaping, furry tarantulas—some as big as a man's clenched fist—worried them the most. One of the massive spiders had already bitten and killed a fellow prisoner.[39]

A correspondent from the local Tyler newspaper was astonished when he saw the inside of Camp Ford. He reported that the prison was "filled with huts and shanties of almost every imaginable shape, and constructed of every available material." To create some semblance of order, the prisoners arranged their makeshift shelters in a grid of streets. Fifth Avenue, lined with brush-covered verandahs, was the central thoroughfare. Camp Ford also had a park area and a market place. The prisoners decided their urban milieu and burgeoning population—with 5,000 inhabitants the prison approximated the size of a major Southern city such as Vicksburg or Baton Rouge—warranted the compound's "Ford City" nickname.[40]

The captured Battery Boys tried to make the best of a difficult situation. In July, when they had only been in Camp Ford for three months, Cone wrote to Roe, noting, "The boys are all doing well and in good spirits for prisoners—all except [Walter H.] Felter who is low with dysentery." The prolonged effects of Camp Ford's living conditions took an increasing toll on the Mercantile Battery prisoners' health. In October, their batterymates in Louisiana—themselves recently liberated from Camp Parapet—witnessed the more severe effects of Confederate imprisonment when they welcomed back a "motley crowd" of Camp Ford parolees, who arrived with "armless shirts and legless trousers [and] bits of blanket tied about the loins." Daily boiling of the former inmates' clothes, a measure meant to kill lice, had accelerated the deterioration of their scant garments. Due to their clothes' condition, some of the former prisoners recalled, the soldiers were kept from public view when they first returned from captivity: "After disembarking, we were sent to the parole camp, by way of the back streets and alleys, being too ragged to be seen."[41]

The clothing shortage at the East Texas prison, plus the lack of medicine, compelled the Union officers there to send an impassioned plea to Banks in June 1864, asking him to address their lack of basic necessities. In September, after Banks was gone, the Department of the Gulf finally sent clothing and medicine. Unfortunately, only 1,200 articles of clothing—those that survived Confederate pilferage en route—were meted out to the frustrated prisoners.[42]

Beside the dearth of shelter and clothing, Union prisoners had to deal with an ongoing shortage of food. The lack of fresh or desiccated vegetables was serious—scurvy causing some of the prisoners to return home with teeth "in their pockets instead of in their mouths." Some of the prisoners tried to ward off scurvy by cultivating a vegetable garden outside the stockade. At least the prisoners had an adequate supply of Texas cattle, which they were allowed to butcher for themselves. In his July 31 letter, Will Brown informed his father the Mercantile Battery prisoners were getting ¾ pound of corn meal and a pound of beef per day. The amount was often decreased, based on available supply.[43]

The soldiers tried as best they could to pass the time while they waited for their exchange or an end to the war. Their work-related activities at Ford City reflected the gamut of interests, professions, and skills existing in a typical American town. Artisans plied their trades. The prison community had its own tailor, shoemaker, watchmaker, and baker. Several mechanically inclined men engineered "crude, primitive turning-lathes" and crafted tools, table legs, chessmen, and checkers. Others

Captain May sewed three issues of *The Old Flag* beneath his shoulder straps and smuggled them out of Camp Ford. This carte de visite depicts how May, barefoot and in tattered clothes, left the East Texas prison with his violin case.

Richard Brady Williams
Private Collection

manufactured stools, chairs, and musical instruments; or used the prison's red clay to make dinnerware and pipes. Because some of the men in the Mercantile Battery were helping to butcher the cattle, they had access to horns. They made the horns into combs, which they sold. White also had a hat business and Cone sold homemade butter. With some of their earnings, the Boys bought vegetables from local farmers to combat scurvy.[44]

There also existed a wide variety of leisure activities to occupy the prisoners' time. Keno was popular and gambling institutions flourished in the camp's public square. The daily church service was well attended, and there were also chess matches, baseball games, gymnastics, wrestling, and concerts. Even singing performances were provided by Cone's Mercantile Battery glee club. A 100-yard walking track circled around the upper compound, and "the steady tramp of the prisoners was heard from early morn until late at night." Since books were scarce, the prisoners enjoyed renting and reading the homemade newspapers produced at Camp Ford. One of the officers captured before Sabine Crossroads, Captain William May from the 23rd Connecticut Infantry, had been a newspaper editor prior to the war. With a steel pen and Rebel ink he produced a four-page publication entitled *The Old Flag*. When he was released from Camp Ford, May smuggled out the three editions of *The Old Flag* by sewing them under his shoulder straps.[45]

Captain William May, from the 23rd Connecticut Infantry,
was the editor of Camp Ford's *The Old Flag* newspaper.

The Ford City Herald and *The Camp Ford News* succeeded William May's newspaper. The May 1, 1865, issue of the *Camp Ford News*, which includes information about Pat White and some of his men, survived the war. One of the newspaper articles mentioned that White "seems to be quite successful in taming his collection of wild animals." There was also the following ad: "Wanted: The Undersigned is desirous of procuring a few more squirrels for which the highest price will be paid. Capt. P. H. White, No. 7, Myrtle Av."[46]

Although living conditions at Camp Ford were not as abominable as those existing at more infamous prisons like Andersonville and Elmira, they were bad enough. Andersonville was much more crowded and held seven times as many prisoners at its peak as did Camp Ford. As dangerously unhealthy as Andersonville was for prisoners, the Federal prison pen at Elmira, New York, had an even higher percentage of deaths. While conditions slowly worsened at Camp Ford, many of the prisoners grew impatient with the haphazard exchange system. The exchange cartel broke down in May 1863 over the problem of how to handle black troops and their white officers. The Federals suspended it in late October of that year. Local commanders could exercise their own discretion to parole or exchange prisoners, but officers were not motivated to challenge Stanton and Grant, who discouraged the practice based on their previous experiences. Grant believed such magnanimity enabled the Confederates to use the system to replenish their depleted ranks. As Will Brown noted after the fighting at Pleasant Hill, A. J. Smith readily exchanged captured Confederates for Federal prisoners. Most Union commanders did not share Whiskey Smith's assertiveness.[47]

On July 22, 1864, Union and Confederate officials exchanged 856 Red River survivors from Banks' 13th and 19th Corps. They constituted the first wave of Camp Ford prisoners to be released. The following October, 1,000 more prisoners returned to their armies. Members of the 48th Ohio Infantry, who had fought alongside the Mercantile Battery at Sabine Crossroads, numbered among the second group. Will told his father how those gallant Western soldiers "saved and brought their regimental flag back with them," which they had preserved at Camp Ford despite much risk and travail. The men in the 48th Ohio at first had kept the regimental flag buried, but fearing it would be damaged, they sewed it inside the blouse of one of their captains. The Ohioans only brought out the cherished flag for special occasions, such as the 4th of July. Will related how, during those festivities, "they raised it in their camp, jerking it down again as rapidly as possible." After their exchange, the men in the 48th Ohio boarded the *St. Mary's* and immediately pulled their silk flag from its hiding place. As the banner fluttered in the wind, a Federal band struck up the "Star-Spangled Banner" while the newly released prisoners cheered and a group of Union officers' wives waved their handkerchiefs.[48]

Exasperated with the exchange delays, some Camp Ford prisoners sought ways to escape. Only a few of the soldiers were desperate enough to climb over the stockade wall and risk being shot by their guards. Many decided it was safer to dig tunnels under the walls. This was especially true after word reached them that more than 100 Union officers under Colonel Thomas E. Rose had dug their way out of Richmond's infamous Libby Prison in early February 1864. Another escape technique, one that required an especially strong stomach, involved hiding in the prison's refuse cart until it was wheeled outside the stockade each day to be emptied. Once beyond the confines of Camp Ford, the begrimed escapees would don replacement clothing hidden in the weeds and make a dash through the woods. Rebel guards aggressively tracked down fleeing inmates, often with the help of bloodhounds trained for that purpose. Successful escapes were very rare. Most Union accounts of life at Camp Ford include some mention of the canine trackers. One prisoner who later returned to New Hampshire commented how he could not forget the "wolf-like yelp and long hyena-howl of these trained man-hunters." Even if escapees eluded the dogs and guards, they still had to travel through enemy territory at least 300 miles to reach either Little Rock or Natchez; Baton Rouge or the Gulf of Mexico were even farther away.[49]

Will wrote to his father on October 30 about a failed escape attempt by some of the Battery Boys earlier that summer: "Two of the boys escaped but, after journeying 10 days, were compelled to give themselves up as they could not obtain enough to live on." John Kennedy, a soldier in the 77th Illinois Regiment who also had been captured at Sabine Crossroads, was part of the escape attempt Will mentioned. Two of Kennedy's associates in the endeavor were Battery Boys Private John W. Arnold, a bugler, and Corporal Samuel Hammett. Kennedy described their exploits in his diary on Tuesday, August 16, 1864: "John Arnold, Sam Hadlock, Sam Hamlet [Hammett] and myself made escape today from Tyler Prison, had several narrow escapes, the guards past within 10 feet of us twice. Hid in woods all day and traveled by night, met no one." The men managed to reach the Sabine River. On August 27, Kennedy recorded, the escapees approached a local black man for food, but he turned the Northerners in to Confederate authorities. The two Mercantile

Battery escapees were returned to Camp Ford where they were isolated in a jail called the "wolf pen."[50]

Back in prison, Arnold memorialized his attempted escape by carving the scene onto a horn from one of the prison's butchered cattle. Arnold apparently depicted himself and one of his fleeing companions running from the Camp Ford stockade with two bloodhounds nipping at their heels. The pursuit also includes a mounted Confederate guard waving a sword in his outstretched hand. Like similar scenes etched by ancient Egyptians inside pyramids and by American Indians on cave walls, this rare horn, with its own unique scrimshaw picture story, has survived and provides a reminder of the hardships suffered by John Arnold and the other Mercantile Battery prisoners at Camp Ford.[51]

The combination of fresh water, adequate food, makeshift shelters, temperate weather, and a modest prison population enabled Camp Ford to have one of the lowest mortality rates among Civil War prisons. Most of the deaths there occurred from May to October 1864, between the conclusion of the Red River Campaign and the subsequent large-scale prisoner exchanges. The mortality rate among the camp's prisoners was about five percent, as compared to an average of 15.5 percent at all Rebel prisons and 12 percent for those operated by the Union. During the war, the highest mortality rates were at places such as Andersonville in the South and Camp Douglas and Elmira in the North, with rates approaching 33 percent. Even though the Illinoisans were in the Tyler prison for one of the longest periods of time, only one of the Mercantile Battery soldiers, a man named Walter Felter, died at Camp Ford.[52]

* * *

Carrollton La.
October 30th 1864

My dear father

    We have been testing the accuracy of our guns and yesterday were out on target practice having Brig. Gen. [Benjamin] Roberts—Chief of Cav'y, Dept. of the Gulf; Gen. Totten—Chief of Art'y to Canby; Gen. Davidson—Chief of Cav'y to Canby and a host of smaller straps as witnesses. Our first shooting was at a distance of 400 yards from the target and we put a shot thro' the Bull's Eye nearly every time. We then tried it at 800 and 1.300 yards and were nearly as successful; and finally took range at 2.300 yards and hit the target every time. The size of the target was 12 x 26 feet; diameter of Bull's Eye fifteen inches. Striking a target at a distance of nearly 1 ½ miles is, in my opinion, pretty fair shooting. I think that our guns will throw a solid shot fully four miles, and perhaps further.[53]

"Wild Phil" Sheridan still canvasses the Shenandoah and, altho' the rebs have got up Early and paraded their Long-street, they have not succeeded in driving him back and I don't think they will. His last success first came to us thro' rebel sources and, of course, he had been terribly whipped. The reb jaw dropped when the steamer brought the official account of the affair.[54]

What a poor, miserable-feeling lot of whelps the great unwashed must be when they see how Indiana, Ohio and Penn. have spoken. Their confidence in "Little Mac" must certainly be on the wane.[55]

In my last, I wrote that I thought our boys [who are] prisoners in Texas would be with us during the week. About 800 were exchanged but none of ours among the number. Some of those exchanged brought letters from Capt. White, Lieut. Cone and many of the boys. One man has died since they have been there and another is quite sick. Capt. writes cheerfully, says all are very well with the exception of the one I have mentioned. Lieut. Cone writes that the Captain is likely to be exchanged in place of a rebel captain now in prison at Rock Island Ill. Cone says all the boys are ragged but have pretty good shelter. They have built log huts. Two of the boys escaped but, after journeying 10 days, were compelled to give themselves up as they could not obtain enough to live on. They hope to be exchanged with the next lot as they are now the oldest

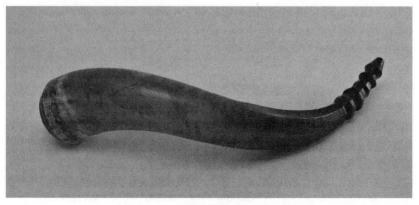

Powder horn carved by the Battery Boys' John Arnold
while he was a prisoner at Camp Ford.

Richard Brady Williams Private Collection; Kelly Mihalcoe, photography

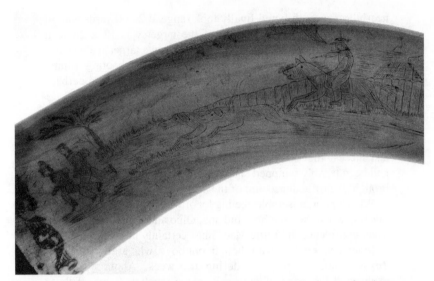

John Arnold likely carved this scene onto his powder horn after he was recaptured. The scene shows two Union prisoners (probably Arnold and Samuel Hammett, his fellow Battery Boy) escaping from Camp Ford.

Richard Brady Williams Private Collection; Kelly Mihalcoe, photography

prisoners there. The letters from them are written on all kinds of paper. I notice one that was written between the lines of an old letter.[56]

The men exchanged [from Camp Ford] were a motley crowd and were dressed in nearly every conceivable shape. Several had great white hats with various mottoes written on them such as "Texas rough" "Texas pal" "Hunky boy" and many other titles equally <u>high flown</u>. They all feel first-rate; many of them had served out their time some months ago.

The 48th Ohio Infantry, a regiment of our old Division, saved and brought their regimental flag back with them. They kept it buried while at Tyler. On the 4th of July, they raised it in their camp, jerked it down again as rapidly as possible. And altho' the rebel commandant did everything in his power to find it, he did not succeed. He then offered $500 for it but money would not buy it there. The boys feel very proud over their success in saving it.[57]

* * *

Carrollton La.
November 6th 1864

My dear father

Last week—the 1st Inst.—All Saints' Day was celebrated in the city. I say "celebrated" as the word really expresses the fact. While one reading an account of the day would hardly think it a fitting one. The people of New Orleans apparently do not think by "halves" and, when they undertake a thing, <u>do it all</u>. On the 1st, I went to the city early and there found everybody out in holiday costume. Nearly every lady and child I met had a boquet, cross, rosette or emblem of some description. I followed the crowd and soon found myself at one of the many cemeteries situated in the heart of the city. The gates and interior of the cemetery were decked with flowers and every tomb told that the living had not forgotten those passed away.

The custom is a beautiful one but the manner of its performance was what surprised me. The people did not seem to come there to mourn. Men strolled thro' the avenues with cigar in mouth, evidently more intent on the flavor of their Havana than on the beauty of the scene. Ladies bedecked in the latest styles were admiring the little cherubs and every bijous that decorated the tombs and probably thinking "How very sweet." I must confess that I left the cemetery with rather an odd idea of humanity, particularly that phase of [it] exhibited on All Saints Day. About the origin of this day, I presume you know so much if not more than myself. I never heard of it being observed in the North and doubt if it is.

The day after to-morrow decides the great question and all eyes are looking forward for the result. I think Lincoln has a sure thing. Many here—the natives—say they believe his reelection is certain continuation of the war for four years longer. Possibly they are right, but I think not. They forget that we are just as able to fight as ever. And in reality, have never brought forward but few of our real sources and are but just becoming a fighting nation.

Future movements are still in the hands of Madam Rumor and we know nothing definite. Now that Price has been whipped and driven out of Missouri I suppose he will commence operations here again and we may [be] wanted.[58]

*　*　*

Carrollton La.
November 13th 1864

My dear father

I do not [know] when I have received more pleasant news than that announcing Henry's safe arrival home and resignation from the army. I have always felt pretty patriotic but not quite enough so to think it just right for three of us to be in the army. Hank has been in long enough to fully understand [the] <u>many beauties</u> of soldiering and perhaps the knowledge will naturally benefit him hereafter.

Well, the election is over. And altho' I am very confident of the success of the Union ticket, still I am quite anxious to see the returns and "Make assurance doubly sure." No one that I have conversed with has an idea that McClellan will be successful, but many think every possible effort will be made by the Peace party to have the Union majority as small as possible.[59]

Seventeen recruits reached us last week. All of these recruits are in it for a year only and received large bounties, much more than some of them could earn at home. I have a <u>sore spot</u> about these big bounties paid to men who know nothing about soldiering; perhaps will write to you more about the matter in some future letter.[60]

The newspapers give us an account of the death of Gen. T. [Thomas] E. G. Ransom, that [officer who] formerly commanded our old Division of the 13th Corps. I never saw an officer more beloved by the men under his command and it will be long before his loss will be replaced by so worthy a man. He was nearly the youngest brig. gen. in the army. I believe there were only two younger.[61]

Gen. Canby was lately wounded while ascending the White river; was shot by a guerrilla. He—the Gen.—is now in the city and rapidly recovering. He received a severe flesh wound in the upper part of his leg.[62]

*   *   *

Carrollton La.
November 19th 1864

My dear father

We are under marching orders and are expected to leave as soon as [our] transport arrives from the city. We will probably leave sometime to-morrow but perhaps not 'till next day. We go up river and <u>where</u> "The papers don't state." I will write when we get <u>there</u>. The move appears sudden, [and I] have only had a half day for preparation; and of course it had to work. You would smile could you could see me. I have been out in the mud and rain—it always rains on the eve of a move—and am completely covered with a mixture of Louisiana soil. Have been in camp so long that I am getting quite fastidious; field service will probably take the <u>kinks</u> out.

The election news is glorious, far better than the most sanguine could expect. As yet we have not full particulars.

*   *   *

West Baton Rouge La.
November 24th 1864

My dear father

We soon leave here bound westward <u>somewhere</u>. From the tenor of orders, think we will be gone from fifteen to twenty days. We move very light; no tents and all baggage carried on horses. Speed seems to be the main object. Nothing but cavalry, artillery and a pontoon train along. There will be quite a force, how large I am not able to state nor would it be best to do so. Brig. Gen. Davidson, Chf. of Cavalry to Gen. Canby, commands the expedition. He has the reputation of being one of the best cavalry officers in the West.

"We have endeavored to 'Retrieve our former standing in the armies of the United States' and I think have succeeded."

Chapter 17

"I Have Been on a Raid"

O n November 16, 1864, General William T. Sherman left Atlanta with about 60,000 troops on his "March to the Sea." His troops would live off the land all the way to Savannah and the Atlantic coast. At least part of Sherman's intent was to expose the privations of war to Georgia farmers who, for the past three years, had only read about them in newspapers. Five days later, Confederate General John Bell Hood moved his army in the opposite direction into northern Georgia and Alabama in the hope that Sherman would follow him out of Georgia. When Sherman did not take the bait, Hood decided to drive his army into Tennessee by way of Nashville and perhaps into Kentucky, where he hoped to win a decisive victory and turn the tide of the war in the West back in favor of the Confederacy. Hood did not expect to find many provisions along the way, especially since much of Tennessee had been one large battleground for more than two long years.[1]

To accomplish his mission, Hood had to rely on a deteriorating railroad system to support his troops. Confederate quartermasters planned to send supplies from Mobile on a zigzag path up the Mobile & Ohio Railroad; through the rehabilitated hubs at Meridian and Corinth; east on the Memphis & Charleston to Tuscumbia, Alabama; and north up

Major General
William T. Sherman

NARA

the Tennessee & Alabama Railroad behind Hood's advance. But
Hood's Army of Tennessee had to
wait three exasperating weeks in
northern Alabama while the
Mobile & Ohio and Memphis &
Charleston railroad lines were
repaired. Persistent rainstorms
only made the situation worse. In the meantime, Hood carried on a
running feud with his superior, General P. G. T. Beauregard, over both
Hood's strategy and how long it was taking him to move the Army of
Tennessee against Nashville. Beauregard sent messages from Corinth
pleading with Hood to move faster because Major General George
Thomas, whom Sherman had left behind to deal with Hood, was
assembling a formidable force to confront him.[2]

Hood's delay also allowed the Union high command to organize
cavalry raids into Mississippi against key railroad lines. John Davidson,
chief of cavalry in Canby's Military Division of West Mississippi,
commanded one of the Union expeditions, some 4,000-men strong.
Brigadier General Edmund Davis, former colonel of the 1st Texas
Cavalry, commanded one of Canby's two divisions. The Chicago
Mercantile Battery, recently converted to horse artillery, was part of
Davis' command. Davidson's plan was to lead his men through eastern
Louisiana and across southern Mississippi to where the Mobile & Ohio
paralleled the Alabama state line. He hoped to wreck a large railroad
section and cut off the flow of supplies to Hood's Army of Tennessee.[3]

Davidson and his troops left their training camps outside New
Orleans and rendezvoused at Baton Rouge. On November 23, he issued
General Orders No. 2, which specified the supplies, rations,
accoutrements, and transport his troops should take on the expedition.
The cavalry commander emphasized that only a few wagons were
permitted with the column. Davidson also instructed quartermasters,

such as Will Brown, to take along only mess kits, ammunition, haversacks, a few blank record books, a small amount of food (17 days of salt, coffee, and sugar but only ¼ rations of bacon and ½ rations of hardtack), and subsistence, nose bags, spare shoes, and nails for the horses. Davidson ordered that "every superfluous article of baggage" was to be left behind. Speed, mobility, and the ability to wage close combat were critical to the operation's success. "The Sabre is the weapon to be used when mounted, and the Carbine dismounted," he declared.[4]

On November 27, Davidson and his troops departed from Baton Rouge and rode east toward Mississippi. For Will and his Mercantile Battery comrades, the demanding journey proceeded at a dizzying pace. Although the Illinois cannoneers had participated in Grant's whirlwind march through Mississippi on the way to Vicksburg, they quickly discovered cavalrymen, when not hampered by infantry, moved at an even faster pace. The Battery Boys rushed along with the frenetic horse soldiers for 17 days with but little sleep. Despite the hardships they endured, most agreed that serving as horse artillery was preferable to performing fatigue and guard duty at Camp Parapet.

Davidson's men cut across numerous swamps and waterways in eastern Louisiana, destroying Camp Moore, a Confederate training facility at Tangipahoa. Will Brown wrote his father that pine trees were plentiful but food was scarce. The blueclad raiders had to scrounge from local farms to supplement the short rations they packed on their horses. Soldiers from the 12th Illinois Cavalry called it the "sweet potato raid because they ate sweet potatoes instead of bread." Although Davidson permitted the cavalrymen to forage from the countryside, he prohibited them from touching civilian homes. When the Federals crossed Pearl River into Mississippi, Davidson issued an order against plundering. Will thought the order appropriate because, based on his first few days of his cavalry experience, there was a high probability the horse soldiers would "steal anything but a red hot stove"—and that might not be enough of a deterrent if they could "pick up a mule to carry it along."[5]

Edmund J. Davis was a Texas politician and judge who had recruited a regiment for the Union in 1862. Now he led the division with which the Battery Boys rode. Davis' 1st Texas Cavalry consisted primarily of Mexicans who lived on either side of the Rio Grande River, though some of the cavalrymen were European immigrants. A few were Indians. A year after Davis mustered his regiment he was kidnapped by local Rebels who nearly hanged him for his Unionist loyalties. In June 1864, after Banks' aborted Red River incursion into East Texas, Davis was ordered to take his horse soldiers to Louisiana, where he was promoted to brigadier general just before John Davidson's raid into Mississippi.[6]

According to Will Brown, the men he met in Davis' 1st Texas Cavalry excelled at "bush whacking and skirmishing." Always inquisitive, Will took the opportunity to learn more about their culture. He later told his father how the Texas cavalrymen cooked "meat on the end of a stick," rode bareback, and sang raucously around the campfire. During the raid, the Texans "captured a keg of red ochre and had a regular Indian time." From these unorthodox soldiers, Will also learned how to make "chiroots . . . using corn husks for wrappers" that he could smoke on the run.

The autumn rains flooded the rivers and slowed Davidson's advance. "Only a small federal detachment threatened the [Mobile and Ohio] rail line," explained Louisiana historian Art Bergeron. On December 10, Confederate soldiers pushed back this Federal contingent. "Unable to cross the Pascagoula River and fearing the Confederate forces gathering against him, Davidson decided to take his men to West Pascagoula," Bergeron continued. The cavalrymen halted at the rundown resort town

on the Gulf of Mexico until they had a means of crossing the Pascagoula River. Davidson had brought along 300 feet of bridging material to span the river, but it was not enough to reach the far bank. He waited for Federal authorities to send him barges and lighters to cross his men into East Pascagoula, which provided an easier approach to the Mobile & Ohio.[7]

Brigadier General
John W. Davidson

U.S. Army Military History Institute

While Davidson and his men were regrouping, they learned that Federal Brigadier General Benjamin Grierson had launched a series of cavalry raids from Memphis during the last week of December and Thomas had decisively defeated Hood outside Nashville. Grierson succeeded in wrecking a key section of the Mobile & Ohio, which hindered the remnants of Hood army as it limped south after its humiliating defeats at Franklin and Nashville. A. J. Smith—the Battery Boys' hero who, in Will's words, showed up "always 'In the nick of time' and ever ready"—was pursuing the Confederates after garnering new laurels in the Nashville combat. Only about one-third of the 38,000 Rebels who had embarked on the campaign remained with the army. They soon found themselves trapped against the Tennessee River. The ragged soldiers huddled together in somber clusters on Christmas Day, their anxieties heightened by Union gunboats that had ascended the river to Muscle Shoals. A. J. Smith and his troops were intent on bagging the survivors, but cold weather mixed with sleet and rain hampered the pursuit, and the last elements of the Confederate army crossed the river on December 28.[8]

Since June of 1864, the feisty Smith and his wandering "Lost Tribes of Israel," as the general referred to his peripatetic command, had run circles around the Confederates. After returning to Memphis from Banks' failed Red River Campaign, Whiskey Smith marched his 16th Corps to confront Lieutenant General Stephen D. Lee's and Major General Nathan Bedford Forrest's Confederates at Tupelo. On July 14, Smith, in the words of a Union cavalry officer who took part in the engagement, "defeated Forrest as he had never been defeated before." After marching to Oxford and sacking the Mississippi university town, Smith rushed his victorious men to Missouri to thwart Sterling Price's invasion. Then it was on to Nashville to assist in stopping Hood's advance. To rub salt into Southern wounds, Smith and his men hounded Hood's retreating army as far as Pulaski. They seemed about to complete the Army of Tennessee's destruction as Hood's engineers threw up the pontoon bridge that carried his surviving troops to safety. During the bridge's construction, the shivering men dressed in ragged uniforms of faded grays and browns could see the south bank of the river, where they had camped just one month earlier. For them there was no longer much doubt whether or not the Confederacy would survive, but only how long the nightmare of war and suffering would continue.[9]

Meanwhile, the Mercantile Association's artillerists spent a joyless Christmas Day on Mississippi's gulf coast. They were isolated in West Pascagoula far from their Chicago homes. Will Brown and his friends ate a meager dinner of "Hard tack, Meat and Coffee," and surely thought about their friends who remained imprisoned at Camp Ford.

The artillerists were tired of miserable holidays. For the third time in a row they suffered through a dreary New Year. The Battery Boys recalled how they had spent their first New Year's Eve in the army, loading guns, horses, and equipment onto transports in the wake of Sherman's Chickasaw Bayou disaster, steaming down the Yazoo River while crouching together on a cold deck as a rainstorm lashed their boat. The start of January 1864 had not been much better. Will and his comrades departed from New Orleans after Christmas only to endure a harrowing trip across the Gulf of Mexico. They had barely made it to Decrow's Point on the desolate Matagorda peninsula. There, they celebrated New Year's Eve amidst the sand dunes eating nearly rancid pork, stale cheese, and "Lincoln biscuits" (hardtack crackers). A sense of melancholy overwhelmed Lieutenant Pinckney Cone after that somber holiday. "May I never see such a New Year again," he wrote in his diary. He had no way of knowing that confinement in Camp Ford would make this year the worst one yet.[10]

The Illinois cannoneers were therefore disappointed when they kicked off 1865 with yet another unappetizing holiday meal while aboard yet another gulf steamer. Just like their previous voyage to the Texas coast, they were tossed around by tumultuous waves that delayed their return voyage to New Orleans. The Battery Boys hoped and prayed they would celebrate their next New Year at home rocking by the family fireplace instead of riding on drafty transports; eating sumptuous meals instead of government-issued staples; and drinking champagne instead of bitter army coffee. White, Cone, and their fellow prisoners, meanwhile, suffered through the New Year in a Confederate prison.

On January 13, 1865, after briefly revisiting their Crescent City haunts, the young men in the Mercantile Battery marched to Baton Rouge. Four years before, on January 10, 1861, Governor Thomas O. Moore had taken over the United States barracks and arsenal in the city after the Southern states seceded. Moore's action netted the Confederacy 47,372 small arms plus a large supply of gunpowder. When the Battery Boys reached the former Louisiana capital, they learned (if they did not already know) that the Confederates and Federals had each twice controlled the vital Mississippi port.[11]

The Yankees initially wrested control of Baton Rouge from the Southerners in May 1862 after Farragut and Butler cracked the defenses of New Orleans and turned their attention 130 miles upriver. Unlike New Orleans, which was built on low ground, Baton Rouge was perched atop loess bluffs. The town's Union garrison of Brigadier General Thomas Williams' brigade left in late June 1862 to accompany Farragut to Vicksburg. Across the river from the Hill City, Williams and his troops attempted to bypass the Confederate stronghold by digging a canal across De Soto Peninsula.[12]

Williams returned to Baton Rouge on July 26, 1862, but only about 800 men of the roughly 3,200 he had taken north were in any condition to perform their duties. The men had been exposed to the same diseases that would later sicken and kill many of Grant's troops when they camped across from Vicksburg in the winter and spring of 1863. When he heard that Williams and his weakened soldiers had returned to Baton Rouge, Confederate Major General John Breckinridge moved his men west from nearby Camp Moore (the same Tangipahoa training facility Davidson's Union troopers had destroyed on their recent raid). Breckinridge launched a dawn attack on August 5, 1862. Supported by their blue-water navy, the outnumbered Northerners gave ground but eventually held and threw back the Confederates. Will Brown's friends in Nims' battery and the 6th Michigan Infantry played prominent roles in repulsing the attack.[13]

In late August 1862, while the Confederates occupied nearby Port Hudson (but before they had converted the Mississippi River defenses into the fortress it would become), Ben Butler ordered the Union army to evacuate Baton Rouge. Although the Confederates reclaimed the city, they were dismayed by what was left of Baton Rouge. Many of the 5,000 inhabitants had fled, and the Unionists had looted and destroyed many buildings both inside the city limits and out in the surrounding countryside. Solidifying his place in history as one of America's premier plunderers, Butler had even ordered his men to remove the state library's books and the city's public statue of George Washington.[14]

In June 1862, a Massachusetts soldier serving at Baton Rouge wrote home, describing how his regiment wantonly destroyed homes and farms for a distance up to 15 miles outside of the city:

I immediately proceeded to the hen roast [roost] where I began to separate the heads of geese and turkey's from their bodies with my sabre [and] over a hundred or two fowls fell beneath the blade[.] that morning hogs were bayoneted and orchard of small trees were cut down close to the root by us, then the white females were allowed a small shanty to stop in[.] we then set fire to all the houses about 20 including negro shanties cotton mills store houses &c and in 15 min. all was in a blaze. . . . We then proceeded to another seceshes but he had also fled [so] we destroyed every thing on his place[.] I with another one happened to be in his mansion [and] was ordered to fire it[.] I tore down all the pictures there was on the walls including a large oil picture of a lady [and] threw them into a corner [with the] frames on top[.] took of the blinds those also on [top.] knocked a hole in the plastering for vent then ignited it and in 15 min. the largest house around in a blaze . . . reached camp that night[. It was] a big days work for Sunday the 8 June.[15]

The Union army left Baton Rouge in shambles on August 21, but returned four months later after Nathaniel Banks replaced Butler. Before the end of 1862, the spiteful Yankees attained their crowning glory (or infamy), in the former capital of Louisiana. In an effort to subdue Baton Rouge's remaining secessionist populace once and for all, someone burned the white Gothic Revival state capital building. At the time Will Brown and his batterymates joined the city's garrison, only the charred walls of this once-grand architectural masterpiece remained standing. The mood of the residents seemed to match the gloominess of their desolate surroundings. Vengeance-seeking Federals, many of whom were enraged New England abolitionists, had broken their will to resist. As Will pointed out in a letter to his father, the civilians left in Baton Rouge at the beginning of 1865 seemed docile: "In the city, the natives are very quiet [while] attending to their business and seldom complaining."[16]

*   *   *

West Pascagoula Miss.
December 14th 1864

My dear father

I have been on a raid. Think I now know what raids are and don't think much of them. Seventeen days sleepless nights and marching all day. Thro' swamps and streams, sometimes with little to eat and again [not] with any quantity. The route has been mostly thro' pine woods and, in consequence, our faces have assumed the appearance of tar barrels. Hog and sweet potatoes have formed the chief staple in the commissary line and I may be regarded as a travelling potato patch and hog pen.

I don't know what the raid has accomplished but rumor says much. We saw lots of country but nary [a] reb. The cavalry with us saw a few but scarcely fired a gun. The entire distance [of the] march was something over 300 miles. We passed thro' the towns of Tangipahoa, Franklinton, and touched [New] Augusta on the Leaf river, from there travelling southward. I have not seen a map and have a very informal idea of our directions.[17]

One day and night we got stuck in the mud and had to leave a wagon behind. It would have amused you to see me that day. Wet and muddy, dirty and hungry, I like all others was doing my utmost to move forward. As I write I cannot but laugh at the many ludicrous incidents of the campaign.

I think part of our force succeeded in destroying part of the Mobile and Ohio RR but I am not certain of this. It has been three weeks since I have seen a newspaper and so I know nothing of the outside world. Hope to have a mail soon and think it will be a good one.

Our present situation is on Pascagoula Bay about fifty miles from Mobile and 100 from New Orleans. Communication with N. O. is by way of Ponchartrain Lake and the time about twelve hours. Where we will go next is a question. Rumor says we will remain here a month and I think it is very probable we will. This place has been quite a resort as a watering place and boasts a fine hotel; about the only building here. It is possible that I may have to go to Baton Rouge after our Company property &c left behind.

The weather has been warm and with the exception of some rain all would have been merry. Swimming horses thro' streams is the worst part of raids. You are liable to wet your horse. During the march, we crossed on pontoons the following rivers: Amite, Comite, Pearl, Black and Yellow. I would give you a description of the pontoon but space forbids. We passed thro' the pine and pitch district of Miss. and I saw where they got it but not how it was prepared for market. Judging from what I have seen, I think Gen. Grant's remark very true when he says the Confederacy "Have robbed the cradle and the grave." There were no men in the country thro' which we passed. The plantations along our route will long have reason to remember us as we had to subsist almost entirely on the country; wherever we went we left no corn or forage. I am told that a large force tried to catch us but this is probably mere rumor.[18]

* * *

West Pascagoula Miss.
December 19th 1864

My dear father

I wrote you several days giving a <u>mixed</u> account of our late expedition. I will now endeavor to give you an account more in detail. We left Baton Rouge on Nov. 27th our Battery being assigned to the 2nd Cavalry Division under command of Col. [Brigadier General Edmund] Davis of the 1st Texas Cavalry; 1st Division under command of Brig. Gen. Bailey of Red river fame; the whole under command of Brig. Gen. [John] Davidson, Chief of Cavalry to Gen. Canby. The pontoon train accompanied the expedition. From Baton Rouge, we moved toward the East crossing the Amite, Comite and Tangipahoa rivers and passing thro' several small towns almost too small to own a name. The road was in the Pine woods and civilization very sensibly left that part of the country to be settled by future generations.[19]

We came across very few plantations and, in consequence, food and forage was not very plentiful. However, we managed to do very well and as we approached the Pearl river everything became quite plentiful. I forgot to state that we started from Baton Rouge with only half rations for fourteen days for the run; and one day's forage for animals. All our baggage and extra men were left behind and were ordered to carry all their blankets on their horses.

On Dec. 4th, we reached and crossed the Pearl going into camp that night near Columbia, Miss. (you will find it on the map). Here, Gen. Davidson issued an order of which the following forms a part: "On crossing the Pearl river and advancing into that portion of the enemy's country where at any time they can concentrate a force equal to ours in cavalry, and superior in artillery, the Chief of Cavalry finds it necessary, and for the last time, to announce the principles upon which this expedition shall be conducted. They are: no straggling and no plundering. These are not rules of my own creation—they are from the Articles of War by which the armies of the U.S. are governed. By following them, I will have that confidence in you which a General should have in his soldiers, and you, when you lay aside the garb of the soldier, will the better put on that of the law abiding citizen. All supplies of subsistence, forage, horses and mules necessary and convenient for this command, will be taken with a free hand by Division commanders and distributed without stint to the troops."

I thought the order a good one and liked its tone. But written orders will not keep cavalry in order and I believe of all the <u>cusses</u> to plunder they cap the climax. They will steal anything but a red hot stove and I believe some would even steal that if he could pick up a mule to carry it along.

From Dec. 5th to 10th, we did all kinds of marching and saw all kinds of weather. I think the real game was played during these six days and I am not certain who won. The rain and mud was <u>awful</u> and many a time did my horse have to swim while crossing a ravine. Of course, I was wet and muddy but every one around looked so glum and swore so much that I could not but to keep in good humor and laugh at their discomfort. I find it is well to take things easy, particularly where one can't help it or make matters better.

The cavalry in crossing streams would form a picture for Punch. Sometimes a horse would flounder and horse, rider and all would go under. Many were the ludicrous scenes while en route. One night, we got the Battery in the road and the mud was so thick that by day light we had not moved a half mile. On the 10th, we reached higher ground and were then at the cross roads; the one leading toward Mobile, the other here. I have heard many rumors about what was to have been done at these cross roads but space does not permit room for rumors. What was accomplished, or what the object of the expedition, I still know nothing about nor do I expect to at present. I find that nearly all are as ignorant as myself and I give the Gen. full credit for one thing—and that is knowing how to keep his own affairs to himself.

We reached here on the 12th very glad to get here both on account of rest and supplies from Uncle Sam. On the march, we had plenty of fresh meat and sweet potatoes and brought a good supply of the latter in camp with us. Our forces show the effect of hard travel and need a good rest. I don't know where we go next—rumor says first to New Orleans and then <u>somewhere</u> else. Part of the command are now loading on transports, bound for New Orleans; we may follow and may not. Uncle Sam's <u>big guns</u> gave the orders and like good soldiers we obey.[20]

*   *   *

Chicago Mercantile Battery
December 25th 1864

My dear father

A merry, merry Christmas to all and [may you all] do my part of the enjoyment also as "The situation" will not allow me to participate.

My Christmas dinner, just eaten, consisted of Hard tack, Meat and Coffee. I can eat and live on such a food for some time but to-day would certainly have enjoyed a dinner of different material. However, "What's the odds as long as you're happy."

Since I last wrote, the troops have gradually become less, slowly embarking for N. O. We are to remain 'till nearly all are gone and it will probably be some time before we get away. The facilities for embarking are very poor and transportation quite limited.

From a late N. O. paper, I have learned something in regard to our expedition and what was proposed to accomplish. It seems we were [to move] across the Leaf river somewhere near [New] Augusta and from there make an effort to destroy part of the Mobile and Ohio RR. On reaching the Leaf, the General found it too wide for his pontoons and at once decided to make for the coast in order to obtain supplies &c. This is the story as given by N. O. papers. How true it is I can only conjecture. If true, we certainly did not accomplish the object of the expedition.[21]

Since we have been here, a force under Gen. Granger has landed on the other side of the bay—East Pascagoula. Various rumors have reached us in regard to their doings but nothing definite.[22]

Like all others I am very anxious to hear from Sherman's army [in Georgia]. I think he will succeed in his undertaking. I hope we may hear from him soon.

*   *   *

Carrollton La.
January 2nd 1865

My dear father

Civilization is again graced with our presence. We have been somewhere, accomplished any amount of strategy, burnt up any quantity of fine woods, destroyed several pigs and sweet potatoes, eaten an oyster bed dry, showed the Confederacy that we were bound to win, used up a lot of government horses and done I don't know what. But to use a Southern expression: "I allow we have done right smart." To-night I feel more civilized than usual, Company Head Quarters having been kindly furnished with a good room, fire place and plenty of room to make a comfortable bed on the floor (Hank will probably understand how well I appreciate the latter comfort).

We commenced loading on the steamer "Belvedere"—Gulf boat—on Dec. 30th and we are only 36 hours in accomplishing the object; up two nights nearly all night. The tide was what bothered us. The trip from Pascagoula to N. O. was quite pleasant. We came by way of the Gulf and I had a good opportunity to see Ship Island, a place made quite notorious in the war, and particularly this Department, as being where disloyal citizens and unruly soldiers are incarcerated. It don't look like a very desirable place and I shall endeavor to keep away from it. We heard a good-deal about the Island last Spring during our celebrated "Mutiny time."[23]

The war news is glorious, better than I expected to hear. We seem to be after them with a firm hand and hit them where they feel it. Such "Christmas presents" as the one Sherman sent to Old Abe are what we all wish for and Thomas mode of drawing artillery is good. I see that Lincoln means work and kindly asks for 300.000 to help us. I wish he would punch up his Secretary of the Treasury and have him put his Greenback machine in good order as we all really need a little, not having received any for the past six months.[24]

To-day the mail brought a letter from Lib from DeVall's Bluff, Dec. 18th. He was quite well. I wish <u>that</u> letter from Henry would come. I presume we have a mail at Baton Rouge and hope it may be with it.[25]

*   *   *

Carrollton La.
January 8th 1865

My dear father

We are still here awaiting orders for upriver. Rumor says we <u>are</u> going to Baton Rouge but written orders have not arrived yet and so we wait.

I see the papers are determined to make our raid a great and gallant affair and I have <u>read</u> so many accounts of it that I commence to believe it must have been huge. I think we did succeed in drawing a force from Hood's army but our part of the expedition did not see the Mobile and Ohio RR. I think a movement will take place from here soon but I do not know what part the cavalry will take; probably go on a raid <u>somewhere</u>.[26]

Sherman's success is all the talk here and I see papers from abroad are speculating on its results. The Confeds are really frightened and Southern papers talk gloomy. It is amusing to read extracts from Richmond papers. How they do howl at Jeff and Hood. In time to come, Jefferson D.'s sins will be felt all over the Confederacy. The very sanguine now look for a speedy peace but I think the war far from being ended. Lee and his army must be well whipped before the tide will really turn; and I think the coming

Spring will see great work at and near Richmond. Sherman will not remain idle and his army will keep going for points along the coast. Sherman is bound to win wherever he goes.

In the city, nearly everybody is enjoying the holidays and the display of presents &c is great. N. O. has been a great place for such things and the people still keep it up. It has been the custom here to keep places of amusement &c open on Sunday but Gen. [Thomas] Sherman has stopped it. I sent you the "Times" yesterday; in it you will see the order. I do not uphold these Sunday amusements but I think that a general assumes too much when he orders them discontinued. This morning's paper contains an order from Gen. Canby ordering a draft to take place next month. This will cause a great stir among the <u>loyal Southerners</u> and I think the population will rapidly decrease.[27]

*   *   *

Baton Rouge La.
January 15th 1865

My dear father

We left here well-equipped in every particular having everything necessary to complete field organization. We have returned with a lot of <u>harness racks</u> in the shape of horses and everything else is in like order. All of our boys fared first-rate and got fat while on the raid and <u>we</u> look better than we did. But the appearance of the Battery shows that the expedition was a very hard one. It is part of my duty to find out what is out of order and to draw necessary supplies when needed. I have got my hands full and will have plenty to do now for some time.

We marched here from New Orleans on the morning of the 13th and immediately went into camp on a nice, high piece of ground near the river bank and close to the city. Company Head Quarters were furnished a house and so I have a good bed to sleep in and a room with a fire place to use during the day time.

You have mentioned something in regard to obtaining higher position in the army than I hold at present. I have now only about seven months more to serve and then I want to quit the army for good. I think I will then have done my share and, if more men are wanted, let those who are still at home come out and do some of the "Crushing." For the past year, I have had all the privileges of an officer [but] without the pay. Since Lieut. Roe has been in command, I have all his Returns to look after as he does not pretend to know anything about them. I have never desired commission in the Battery and now would not take one even if offered. Since I have been in the army, I have never shoved my claims and don't know if it would have resulted in any good had I done so. Capt. White made me his QM Sgt. because I was useful in that position and could do the work connected with the office. It was an easy position and so I took it.

Since I have been in the army, I have always felt pretty independent and have always done my duty. If I could get the position of captain and assistant quartermaster of Vols., I would take it but it takes considerable influence to obtain the position and I have not that influence. I have had several offers for positions in negro regiments but I did not accept for the reason that I don't like that branch of the service.[28]

I hope you succeed in obtaining a position for Lib as he certainly deserves it. I think he makes a good soldier and likes it better than either Henry or myself. I hear from him pretty regularly and he writes in the best of spirits. Gen. Reynolds, who commands his department, is the one who hauled us over the coals last Spring. Since then, we have endeavored "To retrieve our former standing in the armies of the United States" and I think have succeeded. Gen. Davidson compliments us on our good behavior during the raid.[29]

* * *

Baton Rouge La.
January 19th 1865

My dear Maria

I laugh at your description of old Chicago faces, particularly that of my so-called old flame (It is an amusing word to look at). How easily we revive from such old fancies, our desperation seldom goes beyond rhyme and mine never got that far. I wouldn't wonder if I never found the one just to suit—would you? My best and truest friend has been Kate Seymour (Mrs. Bigelow). She is a true friend and looks after Will now as much as she did when he was at C. [Chicago].[30]

I was glad to hear of Henry's return home and hope that you will now keep him there. It must be much more pleasant for father and I know Delia likes it better.

* * *

Baton Rouge La.
January 22nd 1865

My dear father

As yet I have seen very little of the city, most of my time being occupied in <u>squaring up</u> Company papers that necessarily ran behind during the <u>raid</u>. The heads of departments at Washington are very particular about Returns &c and if they are not forwarded on time there is a general fuss all around.

The State house is the finest building here and the grounds surrounding it are beautiful and kept in complete order. From the river, it has the appearance of a castle as seen in many pictures of the banks of the river Rhine. It cost a goodly sum; I have heard the amount but have forgotten it.[31]

We have had several rumors lately in regard to a "Peace party" gone from Richmond to Washington. I have heard the story from several sources but have seen no newspaper account of it and think it must be something started for mere effect. I do not think the South yet ready for peace, particularly on terms offered by the President in his last message. They say they care nothing for slavery and still they talk about it, discussing it pro and con. The fact is the negro has been the great element in the South and without his aid they do not know how to improve their land. In times of peace, the planter and his family know nothing about work; they spend the warm weather in the North and the Winter in pleasure and enjoyment. Knowing they [the Southerners] had plenty, they distributed with a free hand and gave themselves the name of "The most hospitable people in the world." Possessing the balance of power, they controlled the state government and were ambitious to control all. Not satisfied with every enjoyment that man could wish for, they thought the whole world should be theirs. And so they fell. It is this fall that hurts them and many will give life in all before they will submit.[32]

There is considerable cotton coming in. I believe a special permit to bring the produce of the country inside our lines has been granted. But it takes a great-deal of figuring to get anything out, that is, in the legitimate line. I am told that considerable smuggling is done and I suppose it is so, as it pays a great percentage and the risk is not very great. I have seen several cases of officers tried by Courts martial for taking part in smuggling operations and I suppose that <u>all</u> of them have not been caught.[33]

I enclose with this a circular recently issued by the Chief of Cavalry, Dept. of the Gulf. Gen. Roberts is of the Regular army and fine-appearing old gentleman. Of his abilities in the field I know nothing. We are now attached to the 2nd Cavalry Brigade, Col.

[John G.] Fonda [of the] 118th Ill. Mounted Infantry comdg. Bvt.
Brig. Gen. [Joseph] Bailey of Red river fame commands the Div.
and Post. He is a very unassuming officer and one who looks to the
welfare of his men. Our Brigade consists of 118th Ill. Mtd. Inf'y,
12th Ill. Cav'y, 4th Wis. Cav'y and 11th NY Cav'y. So you see we
have plenty of Western men. I have found several acquaintances in
the 12th.[34]

*   *   *

Baton Rouge La.
January 29th 1865

My dear father,

The past week has brought us the news of the capture of Fort Fisher
by our land and naval forces. This is quite a step toward the
occupation of Wilmington and I think will be of great benefit to
[William T.] Sherman if he moves on that place. The rebs seem to
be in a quandary as regards Sherman and his army. They make
attempts to frighten him with loud-mouthed newspaper talk but he
is used to such talk and probably never notices it.[35]

Northern papers give indefinite accounts of the Blair mission to
Richmond and say nothing to its results. I am down on these
"missions." They show a weakness that the soldier does not feel. If
President Lincoln means what he says in his messages, why the
terms for peace are plain enough and need no explanation. It is time
that "Blair goes to Richmond in the character of a private individual
on business of a private nature." Still he requests and has an
interview with Davis and the latter gives him permission to have
that interview published. We have had enough of these private
missions. I think they do no good. Gen. Grant's mission to
Richmond will probably do more toward peace than would fifty
Blairs; and Grant's plan is certainly the most honorable one.[36]

Baton Rouge is the head quarters of the celebrated "Grapevine
route" and every day brings something from the Confederacy. As a
general thing its dispatches are very unreliable and seldom prove
correct. In the city, the natives are very quiet [while] attending to
their business and seldom complaining. As far as I can learn, they
are preparing for the draft ordered by Gen. Canby and will quickly
submit to it. The fact is there is very little choice about this matter. If
they don't want to serve they can go outside the lines. And then they
will certainly be conscripted into the reb army, as parties of scouts
are running all over the country picking up every able-bodied man
they can find. I was talking with a German [Southerner] the other

day who had just come inside our lines. He had been chased all over the country and was greatly rejoiced at his escape. "Dey is tyfels [teufels: devils]" said he. "And will hunt you mit de dogs 'till you are shust dead."[37]

There are a number of cotton speculators here. I think they figure with both sides and make a good profit. It is dangerous business, however, and they often fail.

Have you read Gov. Yates last message? I think it a fine thing and in the true spirit particularly as regards to the war. Illinois has been very fortunate in having a man like him and will never find a better one. He has studied the comfort and care of the soldier and all speak of him in the highest terms. I think that nearly every Illinois soldier is glad that he has been sent to Congress.[38]

We hope to see Captain White and our boys soon. A lot of reb officers in New Orleans are to be sent forward for exchange and our boys may be among the fortunate few that are exchanged for them. They have now been held nearly ten months and are the oldest prisoners at Tyler. We really need Capt. White. He understands us and studies our interests. We have always felt his loss and it has been the hope of his ultimate return that has kept the organization up to the standard. It is impossible for us to write you fully in regard to this matter as the story is quite a lengthy one.

*   *   *

Baton Rouge La.
February 5th 1865

My dear father

Outside of the many rumors that are constantly flying round, and the few "grapevines" coming in daily, there is very little news. At New Orleans, preparations are going forward for a movement and the "Outer circles" say Mobile is the objective point. I don't know why we particularly want Mobile. The capture of Forts Gaines and Morgan put an effectual check to blockade runners and, if we take the place, it will take quite a garrison to hold it.[39]

Peace parties seem plentiful as flies in Summer and will probably amount to about as much. The Blairs are flitting between Washington and Richmond and the unquenchable Horace [Greeley] shines out in the light of the peace maker. Like the "Cat and chestnuts," somebody may get burnt.

Since we have been here, several of our boys concluded to give a "Burnt-cork opera" and last week they made their first appearance, playing for three nights to crowded houses. The concerts were gotten up in good style and everybody seemed well pleased.[40]

Recruits still arrive and we really have more men than we want, particularly for a 4-gun battery. All who come are in for one year only and think of nothing but the bounty. They already count their time by weeks and appear very anxious to have the expiration of their term of service arrive.

*   *   *

Baton Rouge La.
February 12th 1865

My dear father

We had quite an excitement yesterday morning. About 4 O'clock, a gun at the fort opened quite briskly and soon after an orderly rode into camp with orders for us to "Hitch up" immediately, as our picket line had been driven in and an attack was expected. I, of course, popped out of bed with the rest and walked out a little ways to hear the firing at the picket line but could hear nary shot. About daybreak the Battery moved out toward the picket line where all the troops were drawn up in line. Only stayed a few moments when it returned to camp.

During the day, I heard an account of the scare. It seems Gen. [Joseph] Bailey had been contemplating something of this kind in order to see how quickly his command could get out and be formed, ready to repel attack. His plan was well-executed and I think resulted satisfactorily. It frightened the natives. They thinking a fight sure. These scares are common in the army and generally result as did this one, tho' they are not always started under the same circumstances.

New Orleans papers contain conflicting accounts of the peace movement. They probably know nothing about but wish to get up an excitement in order to have their papers sell well. I think there must be something in the movement but do not think it will result in peace, tho' I can only judge from my own observation. I think the end is coming near but it will take some hard fighting yet to bring the enemy to terms.[41]

I hear nothing new in regard to movements in the Department. All commands here are making preparations for field service but this is always the case whether a move is on foot or not. Rumor says that Gen. Canby is taking command of the force at Kennerville and will soon attack Mobile. I don't know how much truth there is in this report but I would not be surprised at any time to hear that

Mobile had been attacked. Northern papers say considerable about Sherman's coming campaign and, if he moves as they say he will, I think he will occupy the entire Eastern coast before commencement of Summer. Sherman's part of the <u>anaconda</u> almost deserves a separate animile as he seems to be doing the grand work of the war.[42]

The Butler <u>fuss</u> appears to stir up parties at Washington and some of them act as if they feared an "expose." The unwritten history of the war would make a large volume and would contain some interesting facts. "Old Ben" has played a conspicuous part in the war and probably will not be willing to be placed on the shelf at the present time. I wonder what these fellows would do should Abe and the Confeds come to terms. What a host of <u>warriors</u> we will have after the close of the present war. It will take a majority of the privates of the Regular army to act as orderlies to the "Big stripes."[43]

*   *   *

Baton Rouge La.
February 19th 1865

My dear father

A change in commanders has taken place during the week; and with the change, a new military name is given to this portion of the state.

Maj. Gen. [Francis J.] Herron takes command of the "Northern Division of Louisiana" with Head Quarters at this place. He has reorganized the cavalry, taking our Battery from it and ordering it to report direct to Gen. Bailey, commanding Post. I do not know if this is only a temporary matter, but

Major General
Francis J. Herron

*Harper's Pictorial History
of the Great Rebellion*

presume it is as we will probably be wanted somewhere before a great while.[44]

Maj. Gen. A. J. Smith was here a few days since and I believe went down the river. How he does keep on the move and where he goes there is sure to be work on hand: now up Red river, soon in Missouri, then with Thomas, again scouting in Mississippi, down the river, up again and no one knows where—but always "In the nick of time" and ever ready. I little thought, when he commanded our Division in the rear of Vicksburg, that he would ever become quite so famous as he is. And by the way, how many of those Vicksburg heroes have since occupied high places in the army? Vicksburg was the turning point for many of our Western generals and, since then, how many have won a name?[45]

The peace confab resulted about as I thought it would, tho' I now think the enemy is more ready to give up than I did before the conference. We have nearly every advantage and telling blows will soon end the struggle. I do not think this Department will remain idle. There seems to be a general getting ready all around and orders have a tone of active field service. Gen. Baldy Smith has been in New Orleans for some time investigating the QM and other depts. The result is the arrest of several officers and I presume a general Court martial will be the next step. It is such an easy thing for men in the army to take things that many cannot resist the temptation.[46]

* * *

Baton Rouge La.
February 26th 1865

My dear father

A fleet of about fifty transports passed down river early in the week. They were loaded with Gen. [A.J.] Smith's force and I suppose will join the expedition against Mobile. Everything betokens preparation for an active campaign in the Department. Gen. Smith's force is organized as the 16th Army Corps and the old 13th Corps is re-organized with Gen. Gordon Granger in command. Gen. Canby has lately issued strong war-like orders and seems to be perfecting all organizations. New Orleans papers say Canby will act in conjunction with Thomas in that Alabama and Georgia will soon see plenty of the Union army.[47]

I think Capt. White and our boys will soon be with us as a flag of truce boat loaded with rebel prisoners passed upriver a few days since and is now probably at the mouth of Red river.[48]

Will Brown's letter about the assassination of Lincoln, written on April 23, 1864, describes the reaction of the Union forces stationed at Baton Rouge and New Orleans.

"The news of the terrible death of President Lincoln reached us early on the morning of the 19th . . . I cannot describe to you the universal gloom felt by all. Men felt as if they had lost a near and dear friend."

Chapter 18

The Terrible Death of President Lincoln

lthough there were many pivotal events left to be played out in the Trans-Mississippi region, Davidson's cavalry raid against the Mobile & Ohio Railroad marked the end of the Battery Boys' field service. Will Brown and the rest of his comrades in Baton Rouge faced the boredom of garrison duty, but appreciated the luxury of having a bed and fireplace, and the time to scour newspapers from around the country. Will was excited about the North's war prospects, even if he had to monitor the escalating victories from a distance. "Babylon Is Falling" he wrote his father in early March.[1]

General Grant also realized the war was drawing to a close. After driving General Robert E. Lee's Army of Northern Virginia from the Rapidan River in May 1864 to the outskirts of Richmond and Petersburg in June, he held his main army there inside a ring of fortifications while Sherman approached Atlanta and other engagements were fought across the South. Grant determined to move hard against Lee and other Rebel forces as soon as the roads were dry enough to do so—weeks earlier than any other major Spring offensive to date. To launch his multifaceted strategy, he relied upon Phil Sheridan, William T. Sherman, George H. Thomas, and Edward R. S. Canby.[2]

While Grant extended his left flank at Petersburg (simultaneously forcing Lee to thin his own lines to meet the threat), Phil Sheridan broke apart the last pocket of Confederate resistance in the Shenandoah Valley. After pulverizing Jubal Early's remnant at Waynesboro on March 2, Sheridan headed toward Petersburg to join the Army of the Potomac in time to participate in its offensive. "The Valley was dead," observed historian Bruce Catton. Just over one month later, Sheridan and his men would slice through Lee's overextended defenses at Five Forks, triggering the collapse of his Richmond-Petersburg position and final retreat toward Appomattox. Sherman, meanwhile, wielded the second hammer in Grant's strategy. He continued to pound South Carolina mercilessly, gathering supplies, burning stores, and sending sparks flying throughout the heart of secession. Columbia, the state capital, was engulfed in flames. Disregarding Charleston, which was now more of a nuisance to the Federals than a strategic prize, Sherman headed into North Carolina, where he planned to break one of Lee's last supply lifelines and eventually join up with Grant outside Richmond. The Confederates evacuated Charleston, the Cradle of the Confederacy, during the night of February 17. Only Joe Johnston's small army, cobbled together from several sources, stood in his way. [3]

Grant's third hammer was George Thomas' detached cavalry. On March 20, Major General George Stoneman took his horse soldiers into western North Carolina as a decoy to distract Joe Johnston from concentrating against Sherman. Meanwhile, Major General James H. Wilson led his 14,000-man cavalry force southeast from Eastport, Mississippi, on March 22 into the Alabama heartland. Wielding another of Grant's spring hammers, Wilson was tasked with smashing much of the Confederacy's remaining industrial capability.[4]

Canby was poised to strike the last of the major Union blows. His hammer would fall along the coast of Alabama, where he moved his 45,000 troops against Spanish Fort and Fort Blakely defending Mobile. After battering down those fortifications, Canby was supposed to turn on Mobile or, if he could not expeditiously beat the Confederate stronghold into submission, move his troops north and assist Wilson. Canby was slow, even sluggish, in starting his amphibious assault on Mobile Bay.

By contrast, James Wilson moved with lightning speed into central Alabama where, on April 2, he defeated Nathan Bedford Forrest's cavalry at Selma. Wilson paused for a week to destroy the city's arsenal, naval foundry, factories, warehouses, and other industrial facilities. He next took his cavalry force to Montgomery, occupying the former Confederate capital on April 12. Wilson then led his horse soldiers swiftly into Georgia where, south of Macon, some of them would later apprehend Jefferson Davis. The Confederate president was caught while fleeing to Florida, hoping to find a boat there to take him to Texas.[5]

Lieutenant Henry Roe's artillerists stayed behind as part of the Baton Rouge garrison and remained largely idle except for some assorted messenger duties and false alarms. Many of their old 13th Corps friends, however, moved out with Canby's army to take Mobile. The young men in the Mercantile Battery would never have another opportunity to reunite with the soldiers who had tramped alongside them for so long. On February 18, 1865, many of their old comrades were reorganized under the command of Major General Gordon Granger, who was promoted by Canby against Grant's recommendation. This reconstituted 13th Corps included units from Landram's former division: the 77th Illinois, 83rd Ohio, 96th Ohio, and 23rd Wisconsin infantry regiments. The 48th Ohio and 130th Illinois infantry regiments, which had not recovered from the Sabine Crossroads disaster, were consolidated into the 83rd Ohio and 77th Illinois, respectively. Soldiers in the 19th Kentucky did not join the Mobile campaign; their unit was so depleted it had mustered out early.[6]

With only about 9,000 Confederate troops at Mobile, Major General Dabney H. Maury was gravely outnumbered. For

Major General
Gordon Granger

Battles and Leaders
of the Civil War

more than 18 months the well-bred Virginian had been strengthening his Mobile defenses, capitalizing on the combat lessons he had learned at Pea Ridge, Corinth, Iuka, and Vicksburg. The loss of Forts Morgan, Gaines, and Powell during the Battle of Mobile Bay the past summer had made further strengthening of the land fortifications imperative. They were laid out in a triple-ringed semicircle around the western approaches to the city. Maury believed this formidable defense system could withstand an attack launched from the west. Canby had other plans. In December, he had learned more about the strength of Maury's western perimeter after Granger, who led an expedition from East Pascagoula, Mississippi, probed the defenses. Canby decided to approach Mobile from the east. The Union commander focused on investing the two major forts situated opposite the city. After capturing Spanish Fort and Fort Blakely on the eastern side of Mobile Bay, Canby planned to transport his troops across the upper bay, disable the enemy's floating batteries, and assault Mobile—or circle around and attack overland from above the city where its fortifications were the weakest.[7]

On March 17, Canby landed 32,000 men on Mobile Point. They moved immediately toward Spanish Fort. A. J. Smith's 16th Corps comprised two-thirds of the main attack force. His "Lost Tribes of Israel" were transported from Fort Gaines on Dauphin Island while Granger's 13th Corps traveled overland from Mobile Point. Frederick Steele left Pensacola on March 20 with his 13,000 men and 270 wagons, marching through the muddy swamp roads to Fort Blakely, Mobile's northeastern stronghold.[8]

Brigadier General Randall Lee Gibson, a dashing veteran officer from the Army of Tennessee, was in charge of defending Spanish Fort. He had a mere 1,800 men for the job. His artillery consisted of six heavy pieces, 14 field guns, and 12 Coehorn mortars. More than one mile of well-constructed breastworks, deep ditches, and dense abatis protected the bastion. Brigadier General St. John Richardson Liddell defended Fort Blakely. Liddell, an experienced but volatile officer, had been assigned to Mobile in September 1864. He had expected to be rid of Richard Taylor, with whom Liddell had clashed in the Trans-Mississippi region. Aside from confronting many of the same Yankees he had fought during the Red River Campaign—the 13th Corps and A. J. Smith's troops— Liddell had to cope with Taylor, who was once again watching over his shoulder. Military politics paled in comparison to his latest challenge:

how could he defend Fort Blakely—a three-mile crescent-shaped fortification—with only 2,700 troops against a Union force of 32,000 men? Liddell's force was slightly larger than Gibson's command, but even if the Confederate commanders united their troops, they still faced overwhelming odds, and Canby had more than enough soldiers to conduct two simultaneous sieges.[9]

Desperate to hold Mobile, Maury, Gibson, and Liddell attempted to address their numerical disadvantage by supplementing their defenses with explosive devices. Their engineers buried landmine "cannibals" around the forts and hid stationary torpedoes along the shores of numerous waterways. In addition to these fixed explosives, mines floated and bobbed on top of the water like half-submerged alligators waiting to lunge. Rear Admiral Henry K. Thatcher, who provided Canby's naval support, eased his squadron of six ironclads and an assortment of 15 gunboats, tinclads, and wooden vessels up the Mobile waterways. A. J. Smith and Gordon Granger focused their attention on Spanish Fort; Frederick Steele moved on Fort Blakely. Before the campaign was over, Thatcher's flotilla would feel the power of the infernal Rebel machines.[10]

During the first week of April, the Unionists edged up to the besieged forts. Chief of Artillery Richard Arnold, who had liberated the Chicago Mercantile Battery from New Orleans guard duty, positioned about 100 siege and field guns preparatory to the Union land assault on Spanish Fort. Federal minesweepers opened the waters for gunboats, ensuring they would add the weight of their artillery to the Federal cannonade. Canby opened a deafening bombardment at 5:30 p.m. on April 8 (the first anniversary of the Sabine Crossroads catastrophe). As one Southerner inside Spanish Fort lamented, "There was no shelter from these bombs— no defense from that fire." Overwhelmed, Gibson and many of his men retreated during the night across a "wooden treadway" that had been recently built across the wetlands behind the fort. Some of the Rebels were shifted to reinforce Fort Blakely, which was still undermanned and unable to withstand the heavy onslaught everyone expected the next day. Although he relished a good fight, Liddell gave up.[11]

The Union army suffered about the same number of casualties (roughly 1,200 men) during the sieges as the defeated Confederates. Canby and Steele captured almost 4,000 prisoners in addition to a large number of light and heavy artillery pieces. Their victories forced Dabney Maury to abandon Mobile. Three days later, on April 12, his 4,500 troops evacuated the area, traveling north on the Mobile & Ohio Railroad. The remaining Southern naval vessels steamed up the Mobile and Tombigbee rivers, dropping more torpedoes in their wake to slow any Union pursuit. The mayor of Mobile stayed behind to surrender his city. Fort Blakely had been the penultimate infantry battle of the war, and Mobile was the final Union key to unlocking and penetrating the Deep South.[12]

By the time Canby struck the Mobile anvil, the rest of Grant's hammer strokes had already deafened the country with the sound of their blows: Fayetteville, Bentonville, Goldsboro, Petersburg, Richmond, Selma, and Montgomery had all fallen. Troops from Meade's Army of the Potomac made the loudest noise when they broke through the Petersburg defenses at dawn on April 2. Led by the aggressive Sheridan and Brigadier General George Armstrong Custer, the Federals pursued Lee and his reeling Army of Northern Virginia. His hungry and demoralized soldiers tried to link up with Joe Johnston's troops in North Carolina but were unsuccessful. Lee surrendered his army at Appomattox Court House on April 9—the same date Fort Blakely fell and three days before the surrender of Mobile. With 40,000 inhabitants, Mobile became the last major Confederate city to fall to Union arms.[13]

Will Brown was ecstatic about the South's rapid dismemberment, and expressed his joy in an April 9 letter. "All the day yesterday, everybody was rejoicing. . . . At noon, a salute of 100 guns was fired from the Fort and the echo from up the river [indicated] that the Navy and Port Hudson were also celebrating," he wrote. During the evening of the April 2 Petersburg breakthrough, Jefferson Davis and his cabinet, along with other government officials, took what they could carry and fled Richmond on trains to Danville, Virginia. Davis and his party left behind a stunned Richmond populace who watched in horror as buildings and bridges disappeared after fires spread from the War Department and some key warehouses. Explosions from the armory and arsenal, combined with a brisk breeze, intensified the inferno and destroyed a major portion of Richmond's lower west end. At about 5:00 a.m. on April 3, the last vessels in the Confederates' James River fleet, including the ironclad *Virginia II*, were blown up. The explosions, noted a witness, "sent shock waves rolling over Richmond. Mirrors and windowpanes rattled for miles." The next day thousands of blacks celebrated amidst the charred ruins as blueclad soldiers—many of whom were freed slaves—marched into the former Confederate capital. On April 4,

Lincoln arrived to tour Richmond. John Beauchamp Jones, who had witnessed the birth, growth, and decline of the Confederacy while working in its War Department, watched the smiling Union president travel under escort through cheering throngs. Jones noted in his diary that the scene reminded him of the "royal parties" he had seen "ride in Europe." A week later, with the final death of the secession movement hovering near, the depressed clerk made a simple notation in his diary: "I never thought it would end this way." His feelings reflected the agony and resignation felt by many Southerners.[14]

Impromptu parades erupted in Northern cities. Chicagoans poured into the streets of the northwest commercial hub to celebrate. Families and friends of the Mercantile Battery rejoiced: their Battery Boys would soon be coming home! Newspaper headlines charted the destruction of the Confederacy. Lee's once-vaunted army had surrendered. It was only a matter of time before the armies of Joe Johnston and Kirby Smith in North Carolina and in the Trans-Mississippi region, respectively, did the same.

Northern soldiers suspected that recalcitrant secessionists would soon see the futility of dying in what Will Brown called the "Last ditch." In a letter to his father, Will expressed his personal satisfaction in helping to restore the Union. He also passed along a prediction that he and his Chicago comrades hoped would soon be realized: "The majority think we will be home by the 4th of July."

*   *   *

Baton Rouge La.
March 5th 1865

My dear father

"Babylon is falling" and at a rapid rate. The war cloud brightens and tints of sunshine break thro' in many places. Wilmington and Charleston no longer boast the rebel flag and the "great work" goes on. I am at a loss to think where [Wm. T.] Sherman will make a halt. If a victory on victory will make an army invincible, his must be so. When the news of the occupation of Charleston first reached here I could hardly believe it. I thought they would fight there no matter how great the odds. "Southern chivalry" along the Atlantic coast seems much like that along the Mississippi—they are all willing to die in that "Last ditch" but are in no hurry to find it.[15]

The movement in this Department is not yet fairly started tho' I think the advance are moving. Outwardly, Mobile seems the objective point, but it would not surprise [me] if Selma Ala. was the point. The possession of that place would render Mobile useless and [the city] would fall by its own weight. One thing is pretty certain: Gen. Canby stands well as a military man and he is bringing together a force that [is] all fight. On the 1st Inst., nearly all of the cavalry here started on expedition moving eastward of this place. I do not know the object of the move. I am informed that over 150.000 men move from different points along and near the river on the same day. Troops will not be idle this Spring. Strong blows, dispatch and little baggage will be the motto.[16]

Yesterday morning at day-light, 25 of our boys—mounted and with carbines—left here as escort to dispatch bearer, with dispatches for Gen. Bailey in command of the expedition that left on the 1st. They found him 24 miles from here, dispatches were delivered and all returned about 8 PM last evening. 48 miles over very muddy roads was a pretty good trip for one day. 25 more of the boys have gone on a similar journey to-day.[17]

We are again disappointed in not seeing our officers and men [who have been] prisoners of war [at Camp Ford]. 1.200 exchanged men passed down the river earlier in the week but none of our boys were with them. Letters from Captain White, Lieut. Cone and several of the boys were received. All were well and hopeful. Cone is in charge of the commissary dept. of the "Bull Pen" and says he manages to live pretty well; and of course our boys share with him. Capt. White writes a characteristic letter. He says: "I wish to God I was with you again and it will be the happiest moment of my life when I again can be. Tell Brown to have my papers all right." His papers have always been a source of trouble to him and he is never satisfied 'till he knows they have been forwarded.[18]

The natives had a holiday on the 1st. They called it "Madi Gras" pronounced Marde-I-Graw-Day. It is kept something like the last day of the Carnival in Italy and I noticed several masked faces on the streets. In the evening, a grand "Bal du Masque" took place in the city hall and I presume the elite were there of course. In New Orleans, the day is a regular holiday and kept by nearly everyone. I am not certain about its origin but I believe "Madi Gras" was the patron saint of France and like "St Patrick" has a day of his own. There are so many French-Creole holidays in this country that one can hardly keep pace with them. Nearly all of the negroes here speak French; in fact, many of them cannot talk a word of English. It used to sound odd to me but I have got used to it.

The rebs have been firing into several boats lately and it is reported that Kirby Smith is near the Atchafalaya river with a reb force; number not stated. It may be that he is trying to cross the river and is making a demonstration at one point while he crosses at another.[19]

*   *   *

Baton Rouge La.
March 12th 1865

My dear father

The week closes with the usual batch of good news from both Sherman and Grant. Northern dates of 6th received this morning give accounts of another brilliant victory by Sheridan in which he completely <u>used up</u> Early's entire command.[20]

The cavalry that left here ten days ago returned yesterday. They only went thirty miles east. They saw quite a number of rebs but all were in small forces and would not stand a fight. Bush whacking and skirmishing was about all that was done. The rebs captured one of our trains consisting of thirteen wagons and one ambulance. This was quite a loss and gave them the advantage. The reb force outnumbered ours considerably, they having a force estimated 3.000 while we had but about 1.200. I am told that the object of the expedition was fully accomplished; it being only intended as a <u>demonstration</u> to draw off and occupy the attention of certain forces that would otherwise help to impede progress of our forces operating around Mobile. The reb force was under command of Gen. [George Baird] Hodge and it is thought part of Forrest's command is with him.[21]

Yesterday, I saw a deserter just arrived from Hood's army—has been a soldier 25 months and thinks he has seen the elephant. Says Hood's entire force would desert if they could and nearly the entire Southern army would do the same thing if good opportunity would offer. He is very bitter on Hood and Davis but thinks there are a few good leaders left; thinks the war will end in the next six months. Says Forrest is in Mississippi with about 10.000 men and will move toward some point along the river to attempt the crossing of Kirby Smith's forces now on the west side of the river. This fellow seems sharp and shrewd and is bound for Illinois.[22]

By the way, I have been considerably surprised lately to see the number of refugees who are "Going up to <u>Illinois</u> to settle." Nearly every boat going upriver takes one or more families bound for the land of promise. It is sad to see many of them: they are nearly destitute and have little idea what they will do. Their tale is a hard one and the determination in the eyes of most of the men show they have a long account to settle with the South. Many of them say they will go into the army when they get their families settled and, when such men <u>do</u> go in, they fight with a vengeance. They are all <u>down on</u> the negro, think him a pest and want to see him dropped entirely. It is strange what a diversity of opinion exists in regard to the negro.[23]

Gen. Bailey has been relieved from command here and goes to Mobile. Gen. [Edmund] Davis takes his place. Davis was formerly Col. of 1st Texas Cavalry and commanded our Brigade on <u>that raid</u>. I do not think much of his merit as an officer tho' for all that he may be a good one.[24]

By the way, did I ever write you of the 1st Texas Cavalry? The regiment is made up of Texas Mexicans—regular <u>greasers</u>—and Indians. They are perfect devils at bush whacking and skirmishing. On the last expedition, they captured a keg of red ochre and had a regular <u>Indian time</u>. In camp and on the march, they are a jovial crowd and full of sly tricks. I wish you could hear a <u>greaser</u> sing. His song is a cross between the bray of a jackass and the note of [a] turkey buzzard, and far excels either in melody.[25]

They [Texas Mexicans] are great smokers, making their own <u>chiroots</u> and generally using corn husks for wrappers. It is quite a knack to put these wrappers on right and I got one to teach me the "<u>modus operandi</u>." I can make a <u>kind</u> of one but haven't the real <u>knack</u>. They are great beef eaters, usually cooking the meat on the end of a stick and eating it without seasoning of any kind. I don't know that I ever saw one use any salt and I have watched them purposely to see if they did. Round a camp fire they are like a lot of jack-daws, chattering along all the time. Their complexion is quite dark but features quite regular, showing Castillian stock. All are good horsemen and ride bareback as well as in saddle.

* * *

Baton Rouge La.
March 19th 1865

My dear father

To-day's mail brought me letters from Lib and Hiram Hoxie. Lib's, dated 28th Ult., says he is well and enjoying life as well as possible. He thinks they will stay at the "Bluff"—I write this word as he sends it—'till the war ends which he <u>allows</u> will be along some time next Fall. I like Lib's letters. They sound just like him and have a sort of twang peculiar to himself. Hiram Hoxie writes from home and still talks of going out West. I think you will see him out there one of these days. Says the snow is getting so reduced that they can again see the fences. This to me sounds "Decidedly cold."[26]

Military movements and changes in the Department are quite numerous. Gen. Canby has left New Orleans and I suppose he is in command of the force near Mobile. No published accounts of movements in that vicinity have been received. But from one of our boys who came up from New Orleans to-day, I learned that a lot of wounded have arrived at that place from near Mobile; and so it is quite probably that some fighting has been done. From the same source, I learned that we have captured three rebel batteries. If anything is going on there, I presume you will hear of it thro' the newspapers ere this reaches you. Gen. [Edmund] Davis, in command of this Post, has been relieved and ordered to Brownsville Texas. This story is a rumor only and, as we have no force at that place, I think it must be a canard.[27]

We had a report this week that [since] we had been assigned to this Post, our horses would not be necessary for us. And as horses are short in the Dept., ours would probably be wanted for batteries doing active field duty. I do not credit this report tho' it looks quite plausible. I hope it will not prove correct as it looks much better to be fully equipped than the "half-horse style." However, the "Powers that be" must be obeyed no matter what one thinks.[28]

Sherman's movements are as much a mystery as ever and no one pretends to know of his whereabouts, what he is doing or what he will do. To-day, the "Grapevine" brings a report that he and Johnston have had a great battle in which both were killed. Rather an unlikely story that; still it fully illustrates the majority of "Grapevine reliables."[29]

* * *

Baton Rouge La.
26 March 1865

My dear father

There is nothing of particular interest going on here, everything being as quiet as usual. Passengers by the boat from New Orleans say fighting has commenced in Mobile but that is all they know. I presume the New Orleans press is prohibited from publishing anything from that quarter and probably the first news that we get will be from Northern papers. A number of transports loaded with troops have passed down river during the week and will, I suppose, go to Mobile. Some of these troops are from Arkansas. I saw one man who was well acquainted with Lib's regiment. Many of these regiments are very strong, some of them having as many men as our brigades. Among the regiments [that] passed this week was the 3d Mich. Cavalry. I have seen very few Michigan troops since I have been in the service.[30]

Had another change of commanders here this week. Davis relieved and Gen. Lawler took his place. Lawler is about such a shaped man as Frank Barber only shorter, wears a hickory shirt, an old white hat and otherwise <u>odd</u>. I don't know who will be in command next week but suppose there will [be] a change, no one man staying over two weeks.[31]

*   *   *

Baton Rouge La.
April 2nd 1865

My dear father

"Quiet reigns supreme" in these parts—hardly enough transpiring to form an item—and the <u>item</u> once formed don't contain any news. Baton Rouge does not present many varied phases of humanity or, rather, I have not seen many since we have been here. Occasionally, we have a negro riot and some of the many colored ones hereabout get hurt. Now and then a bush whacker is caught and brought inside the lines. Every day there are a number of arrivals of steamers from up and down river, but there is nothing like excitement here and even a newspaper reporter would starve. Some little time ago there was considerable cotton coming inside the lines. But the decline in gold has stopped it and I suppose parties are holding on for another rise.[32]

Nearly everybody is speculating on Sherman's campaign and trying to form some idea of his ultimate object. It surprises me to see how rapidly he moves thro' a part of the country that the enemy have always boasted so much about. I imagine the <u>climax</u> rapidly approaching, particularly if Lee attempts to hold Richmond. And even if he retreats, I cannot see where he can hope to do better. With the fall of Richmond, I look for the fall of the Confederacy and I believe the enemy will hold it or lose all. If Canby is successful at Mobile—and there is little doubt but he will be—the real war will be brought down to a small circumference; so small perhaps that the reb joke on the fall of Atlanta will be realized i.e. "Our big guns will be able to shoot clean across the Confederacy." [33]

*   *   *

Baton Rouge La.
April 9th 1865

My dear father

We are all in excitement over the glorious news from Grant and his army. The first official account of the occupation of Richmond reached here at midnight of the 7th and our camp was soon awakened by the artillery at the fort. Kept up a lively noise 'till nearly 2 O'clock AM on yesterday. All the day yesterday, everybody was rejoicing, paying no attention to anything but the war, Richmond and Old Abe—whom it seems is paying particular attention to Richmond just at present. At noon, a salute of 100 guns was fired from the fort and the echo from up the river showed that the navy and Port Hudson were also celebrating. It would have amused you to have heard the various rumors of yesterday: "Lee and Davis taken, Mobile ours, Johnston's army surrendered to Sherman" and any number of others equally as absurd. Everybody was bound to feel good and so everyone had a good report to tell his neighbor.[34]

We have news up to the 5th and look for better [information] by the next boat. For if Lee could not cope with Grant behind fortifications, it does not look probable that he will be able to make a very successful resistance in open field or behind inferior fortifications. It is probable that Sherman is also on the move by this time and knows where to strike. One thing is pretty certain: the Confederacy is killed to all intent and purposes and the prospects for speedy peace very bright.[35]

The movement against Mobile seems to progress quite slowly but is probably being pushed forward as rapidly as possible under the circumstances. The siege of Fort Spanish progresses slowly and newspaper correspondents say it must soon fall. Two of our gunboats have been destroyed, one by torpedoes and one by explosion of boiler. The roads leading towards the city are filled with torpedoes and many have had narrow escapes tho' no lives have been lost as yet. Our killed and wounded in front of Fort Spanish amount to 500. I think Steele's army is moving to the rear of the city. Our force there is estimated at about 80.000. A Mobile paper dated 4th Inst. says: "Gen. [James H.] Wilson has captured Selma, taking 23 pieces of artillery and large quantities of government stores." We have no news of this kind from the North yet. I suppose the Gen. Wilson spoken of is the one who left Eastport Miss. not long since with 15.000 cavalry. As Selma is one of the main supply depots for the South, its loss will be severely felt and may do much toward the fall of Mobile.[36]

We have a fine band here. They have been at Port Hudson, but as Gen. Herron has his Head Quarters here, I suppose he thought he would have the Division muses here also. The band consists of 28 pieces and play in the public square or "Boulevard"—we are all French here—every other night. Nearly all Baton Rouge turns out to see and hear them and everything has a lively appearance.[37]

* * *

Baton Rouge La.
April 16th 1865

My dear father

Yours of 4th Inst. giving account of your celebration over the fall of Richmond came to hand a few days since and was gladly received. In it, you speak of a letter written the day before that has not yet reached me.

We have had a week of glorious news and yesterday a holiday in accordance with orders from Department Head Quarters. The artillery in the fort fired 200 guns and the gunboats on the river also fired a number of rounds. I presume you have heard of the occupation of Mobile. I have not seen the particulars of its capture nor do I expect to 'till I see a Northern paper.[38]

Yesterday, a dispatch from Memphis stated that Johnston had surrendered to Sherman. This is not official but is generally believed. We have plenty of rumors. Among the most prominent the following: Kirby Smith in New Orleans offering to surrender Texas; "Old Pap Price" [Sterling Price] coming from Arkansas to surrender that state; Forrest in Memphis trying to make terms with Gen. [Cadwallader C.] Washburn and the governors of all Southern states at, or on their way, to Richmond where they go to meet President Lincoln and arrange terms of peace.[39]

I hardly know how to rejoice over recent successes. It seems too grand for common talk and the inward satisfaction felt by every soldier is too great to find expression in words. We have always felt sure of the ultimate result but war and war talk has been so much in vogue that one can hardly bring his mind down to peace. A restored country, right upheld, the laws sustained, the knowledge that we <u>are</u> the strongest nation in the world—and, best of all, the satisfaction of feeling <u>you took part in the contest</u>—almost repays the soldier for the many hardships and trials he has endured.

> When the war is over, I think there will be few soldiers who will
> not be proud to say: "I was one of Uncle Sam's boys." It would
> amuse you to hear our speculations in regard to peace. The majority
> think we will be home by the 4th of July. I think a good-deal on the
> subject but can't tell much about it.

*   *   *

The news of Lincoln's assassination shattered Will Brown's revelry.
Dreams about starting the next phase of his life were put on hold. As Will
mourned the loss of Lincoln, he communicated to his father how the
Union army in Baton Rouge was handling the president's death: "I
cannot describe to you the universal gloom felt by all. Men felt as if they
had lost a near and dear friend." Will accurately predicted that Lincoln's
assassination would have dire consequences for the South.[40]

In New Orleans, drama aficionados recalled having seen John
Wilkes Booth appear in Shakespeare's *Richard III* at the St. Charles
Theatre. He had opened the previous year on March 14 and, despite
suffering from a hoarse throat, performed there until April 3, 1864. Loyal
secessionists in the Crescent City, like their allies in other parts of
Louisiana, shared Booth's passion for Southern independence. While not
endorsing the actor's murderous attempt to salvage their cause—or at
least not as publicly as some Texas newspapers had done—many
Louisianans empathized with Booth and the anguish he felt over the
Confederacy's collapse. Though they yearned to turn back the tide of the
North's victory, most with secessionist sympathies remained bystanders
in the unfolding drama.[41]

Like other Union soldiers who had spent a lot of time in Louisiana,
the Battery Boys enjoyed the Southerners' discomfort. No more cocky
proclamations were heard from their neighbors about defeating the
Union. Most secessionists seemed ambivalent about the South's current
situation. They were relieved the war was ending, but fearful of what the
future held for them. Jefferson Davis and his cabinet were even then
fleeing through North Carolina like common criminals. Lee's army was
part of history, and Joe Johnston and Richard Taylor were on the verge of
surrender. The last unoccupied Confederate cities were strangled by
blockade, and Federal cavalrymen swarmed the countryside. Instead of
offering resistance, many Confederate soldiers elbowed one another

aside in their hurry to return home. How much longer could the Confederate forces in the Trans-Mississippi region survive?

Louisiana secessionists brooded like displeased patrons in a dark theater. They gazed straight ahead, queasy but braced for the war's final curtain. But no one clamored for a Booth encore. He had done enough damage already. Booth's reported shout of "Sic semper tyrannis" at Ford's Theater—his voice no longer hoarse since he had spent more time conspiring than acting in the past year—and the gruesome death of Lincoln had silenced Northern pleas for postwar benevolence. The murder of Abraham Lincoln allowed Andrew Johnson, the new president, and the Radical Republicans in Congress to cast aside Lincoln's policy of a merciful national reunification and replace it with an iron-fisted reconstruction. Few civilians in the Pelican State would have disagreed with Will Brown's observation that Lincoln's assassination would "do more to awaken the spirit of revenge than anything else that could be done."

A remnant of staunch Confederates under Kirby Smith remained in the field, hoping perhaps for a happy ending to this morbid play entitled *The War Between the States*. He and his army lingered, hoping somehow that Jefferson Davis could perform a miracle or the Trans-Mississippi Confederacy might prevail alone. A few "last ditch" Confederates made the mistake of openly rejoicing about Lincoln's assassination. Will informed his father that a man in Baton Rouge "who expressed joy over the death of the President was arrested and put in irons." In New Orleans, the Union response had been more severe. "Some colored soldiers bayoneted two citizens for expressing delight," wrote Will. "And all the negroes had to be kept in quarters that day for fear that they would raise a regular row."

In Confederate-occupied areas of Louisiana, primarily the western half of the state, responses to the uncertain future were mixed. Residents of Opelousas, who had once supported making their city the interim state capital after Baton Rouge fell, now recognized their cause was lost. They gathered along the Teche to celebrate the news of Richmond's fall, to cheer for the U.S. flag, and recommit their allegiance to the Union. In Shreveport, the current Confederate state capital as well as headquarters for the Department of the Trans-Mississippi, Governor Henry Watkins Allen and Kirby Smith tried to sustain morale. They announced that Jefferson Davis and his cabinet were en route and planned to direct the

Confederacy from Texas. Smith reminded everyone that he still had some 50,000 men under arms. He was also hopeful that the *Missouri*, an ironclad nearing completion in Shreveport, would soon be available to harass the Federal's brown-water ships. Meanwhile, Smith decided to unleash Lieutenant Charles W. "Savez" Read, an intrepid naval officer and the South's version of Charles Rivers Ellet, Jr. Read was ordered to test the Union's Western blockade and generate some victories to motivate his demoralized troops.

* * *

Baton Rouge La.
April 23d 1865

My dear father

Your welcome letter of the 12th Inst. has reached me and like all others was gladly received. The news of the terrible death of President Lincoln reached us early on the morning of the 19th. The story, as at first received, seemed too improbable for belief but the arrival of the "Pauline Carroll" (with Gen. Banks on board) gave us full particulars and there could no longer be even a doubt. I cannot describe to you the universal gloom felt by all. Men felt as if they had lost a near and dear friend. On the reception of the news, Gen. Herron issued an order, a copy of which I enclose with this. As a touching tribute to departed [people that I regard as] worth[while], I have read nothing that equals it.[42]

Business of all kinds was suspended, flags were displayed at half mast and draped in mourning. The different Head Quarters were also draped and everything that could show respect was done. On the 20th, a military and civic procession formed at 2 Rue and marched thro' the principal streets of the city. All day guns were fired every half hour—and, while the procession was moving, one [gun fired] every minute. After conclusion of the procession, speeches were made by several officers.

It seems impossible to conceive the ideas of the man who committed the deed. It will do more to awaken the spirit of revenge than anything else that could be done. I presume high Southern authority will deny any foreknowledge of deed; still I would not trust them. I hope the thing will be sifted to the bottom. And altho' the lives of the culprits are as nothing when compared with that of the late President, it will be well to know that such men cannot live.[43]

The first news received said that Sec'y Seward was killed but later accounts have it that he is better and hope for his recovery. One man here who expressed joy over the death of the President was arrested and put in irons. In New Orleans, some colored soldiers bayoneted two citizens for expressing delight. And all the negroes had to be kept in quarters that day for fear they would raise a regular row.[44]

I have confidence in the loyalty of Johnson but do not think he has the ability of the late President. His address on taking the oath of office as President, partly foreshadows his policy. I think the South will find it more difficult to make terms with him than if they could have had the late President to deal with.[45]

The real war seems virtually ended. Lee cannot expect, and I doubt if he desires, to again take up arms. Sherman probably has Johnston by this time or, if he has not, the combinations moving against him will probably not fail to whip him. Wilson is moving toward him with a great force of cavalry. A. J. Smith has already left Mobile for the interior and part of Grant's force can now be spared to co-operate with Sherman, provided he wants them; and I doubt if such is the case as Sherman has a great army of his own. I think the great difficulty we have to contend against now is: How to settle the trouble and keep the dignity of the government intact. Of course, we can afford to be liberal as we have gained everything. We have got good men at the head of affairs, men who have done well thus far, and it is to be hoped they will not err now.[46]

Gen. Banks has again assumed command of this Department. I am told Gen. Hurlbut will go to Mobile and take command of the 13th Corps now doing garrison duty there; also that Head Quarters [for the] Mil. Div. West Miss. will soon remove to that place. The 16th Corps under A.J. Smith are moving toward the interior.[47]

Quite a fleet of gunboats are off [the coast of] Galveston. This may mean a move in that direction. The capture of Mobile makes this place way out of the Confederacy and, if the war keeps on, I would not be surprised if a new line of occupation was formed. A small body of cavalry went out the other day. They only found eleven bush whackers; three of these brought in as prisoners; the balance shot. They tried to ambush our forces but were not successful. I have [a recent] letter from Lib dated 5th Inst. He gives an account of the "earthquake," also what their Inspector Gen. had to say to them. These Inspector Gen.'s are the terror of both officers and men. Love to all.[48]

* * *

Head Quarters Northern Division of Louisiana
Baton Rouge, La.

April 19th 1865

General Orders No. 14[49]

The nation mourns! ABRAHAM LINCOLN, late President of the United States, is dead! He fell by the ruthless hand of an assassin, just as his labors were being crowned with success. The whole civilized world will mourn his loss. Like Israel's great leader, he was shown the deliverance of his people, and then the light went out from his eyes forever. But he lives in the memory of all who love their Country, and will be named with reverence by the good and great in all time to come. In consequence of this deplorable event, no public business will be transacted this day, at any of the public offices in this Division, and the Major General Commanding requests all good citizens to take such measures to show their respect for the memory of the late President as they may deem fitting and proper.

By command of Major General Herron: Wm. H. Clapp, Captain and Assistant Adjutant General

Official: W. H. Gladwin, 1st Lt., 1st Texas Cav., A.A. A. General

Headquarters, Military Division of West Mississippi,

New Orleans, La., June 5" 1865.

I Certify, that P. H. White Captain of

Company _____ of the Chicago Regiment of Batty

Merc.

Volunteers, captured by the enemy on the 8" day of April

1864, was exchanged as a prisoner of war at Red River Landing, La.,

on the Twenty-seventh day of May 1865.

Wm W E Dye

Colonel and Agent of Exchange,
Military Div. West Miss.

Captain Pat White's parole document. White was exchanged
at Red River Landing on May 27, 1865.

"The fact is the rebs west of the river have never got over their victory's of last Spring. . . . We have lots of troops who would like to get after them and the C.M.B. is among the number."

Chapter 19

A Sinking Confederacy

C harles W. "Savez" Read was preparing to take the Confederate ram *Webb* down the Red River, elude gunboats and ships of the Federal deep-water navy on the Mississippi, and steam past New Orleans into the Gulf of Mexico. At Shreveport, the daring seaman equipped the 206-foot warship with a 30-pound Parrott rifle and two 12-pound boat howitzers. His crew consisted of 16 officers and 51 other adventurous men. They lined the ram's exterior bulwarks with 190 bales of cotton, which had two uses: it would act as a cushion against artillery projectiles and serve as "white gold"—currency to trade for supplies in Cuba. Packed with one-month's provisions and a load of pine knots for fuel, the *Webb* left for Alexandria on April 16. One week later Read was ready to embark on his mission. Only a year earlier the Chicago Mercantile Battery had been in Alexandria preparing to make a dangerous journey down the Red River to New Orleans aboard the rickety *Kate Dale*.[1]

From his Trans-Mississippi headquarters, Kirby Smith issued an address to boost the morale of his troops stating, "With you rests the hopes of our nation, and upon your action depends the fate of our people." He planned to hold a major rally at Shreveport on April 29 to demonstrate his commitment to prolong the fight despite the collapse of the entire Eastern Theater. Major General John B. Magruder, still convinced theatrics would give the Confederates an edge, tried to motivate his soldiers in the District of Texas. A mass meeting was also held in Houston to display public support, and the governor of the Lone Star State called for his constituents to "rally around the battle scarred and well known flag of the Confederacy."[2]

Despite witnessing the flag-waving bravado of their leaders, rank-and-file soldiers doubted the dissolving Confederacy had enough money, food, and materiel left to sustain the fight west of the Mississippi. No one seemed to care that the troops had been paid sporadically over the past two years and could not send money home to their families, who had suffered unbearable hardships. Their plight would only worsen if the war dragged on. Many of the Southern troops knew about Canby's March 3 announcement promising favorable treatment to Confederate deserters. Skeptical veterans were enticed, weighing the dangers of desertion against continued service in the field. Confederate troops caught deserting were usually executed on Fridays in an ongoing ceremony that Smith and his officers had been overseeing on a weekly basis since January. If the Rebels remained for the next act in this extended Trans-Mississippi play, however, they might be killed for a cause that was so clearly lost. Many soldiers decided to ignore Kirby Smith's plea to "Stand by your colors." Bypassing their guards, the weary soldiers left for home.[3]

Meanwhile, Jefferson Davis learned that Joe Johnston had signed an armistice with Sherman in North Carolina, meaning that only the Trans-Mississippi was left to sustain the fleeing Confederate government. Davis and his cabinet decided to work their way west along the lower half of the Confederacy, where they could cross the Mississippi and regroup in Texas. Their progress was slowed by a trainload of government documents and about one-third of a million dollars from the Confederate Treasury. Suspecting Davis and his entourage were heading overland, Edwin Stanton notified Union commanders in New Orleans and Baton Rouge to be on the lookout for the fleeing Rebels leaders.[4]

Under a foggy, moonless sky on the night of April 23, Savez Read and his men eased the *Webb* ahead toward the Mississippi. Only surprise and luck would enable the desperate Southerners to take their side-wheel steamer 300 miles to the Gulf of Mexico. Union gunboats anchored at the mouth of the Red River were their major obstacles. Read was certain his cotton-clad ram could withstand just about anything except a shot from a 15-inch Dahlgren gun. As a contingency, Read brought with him torpedo spars that could be strapped to the *Webb's* bow to ram his way through a blockade. Instead of attacking the Union vessels ahead, Read decided to outrun them. At full steam the Confederate craft rushed past the enemy vessels, somehow avoiding damaging hits from the enemy artillery. Safely downstream, Read stopped the *Webb*. On the east shore of the Mississippi near Morganza, he sent out a crew to cut the telegraph wires that connected the mouth of the Red River to Baton Rouge and New Orleans. He repeated his defensive precautions beyond St. Francisville.[5]

Read conned his ram past Port Hudson to Baton Rouge, where the Battery Boys were part of the sleeping garrison. All along the Mississippi, blueclad guards continued to mistake the *Webb* for a Union boat. At Baton Rouge, the Union gunboat *Ouachita* approached and Read raised some captured Union signal flags. The deception worked. Read, who still had the element of surprise on his side, continued to believe he could steam his way past New Orleans. With a United States flag flying at half-mast to give the impression of honoring the slain Lincoln, the *Webb* passed Camp Parapet, the site of the Mercantile Battery's travails a year earlier. Unbeknownst to Read, an inland telegraph transmitted a message at 9:20 a.m. to Nathaniel Banks, who was back in charge of the Department of the Gulf, informing him that a Confederate ram was heading his way.[6]

Because he was not expecting an enemy vessel to sail past, Thomas Sherman (the Battery Boys' old nemesis who was in charge of New Orleans' defenses) did not have any shore guns positioned to deal with the threat. Both Banks and Sherman ordered all Union ships tied up at the Crescent City docks to be ready to fire on the oncoming enemy ram. To reduce confusion, they issued a detailed description of the *Webb*: "She is a small vessel, painted white, one smoke stack, two upright engines, and one small foremast." The generals also contacted commanding officers below the city to alert them to be ready with their huge 15-inch Dahlgrens and 100-pounder Parrotts in case the ram reached the forts.[7]

At 1:00 p.m. on April 24, the *Webb* picked up steam as Read and his audacious crew, disguised in blue, looked at the New Orleans buildings fading behind them. Two final obstacles stood between the Confederate sailors and freedom: Forts St. Philip and Jackson. Telegrams between the

Union leaders in Banks' department hummed over the wires faster than the *Webb* was moving toward the gulf. When a sudden artillery shot ripped through the ram's bow, Read knew his ruse was over. He ordered the vessel's United States flag replaced with the Stars and Bars and he proceeded ahead at full speed. [8]

Read and his men pondered the response of the enemy as they drew closer to the Union forts guarding the Mississippi River below New Orleans. Their apprehension grew when they saw a powerful enemy warship bearing down on them. It was the formidable sloop-of-war *Richmond,* a ship Read had encountered in the past. The small cotton-clad could never win against such odds. Read decided to abandon the *Webb*, for the safety of his men superseded the bold Rebel's plan to escape to Cuba. According to Will Brown, "Thirty miles below the city she was set on fire, run ashore and abandoned [with] only three men being caught on her. A party of Marines were soon ashore and captured nearly all those who had escaped from the boat."[9]

During the *Webb's* escapade, wild rumors circulated among Union troops in the Military Division of West Mississippi. The Battery Boys heard several theories espoused about the occupants and cargo of the renegade ram: (1) Jefferson Davis had boarded *Webb* somewhere between Vicksburg and New Orleans, (2) Kirby Smith was accompanying Davis to Texas where they would set up the new Confederate government, and (3) the Southern Treasury was being smuggled out of the country to fund plans to sustain the Confederacy. In New Orleans, Federal soldiers and Unionist residents alike were especially eager to find Davis; Andrew Johnson had announced a $100,000 reward for the capture of the Confederate president. There were

Burning of the *CSS Webb* below New Orleans on April 24, 1865.

U.S. Naval Historical Center

also those who believed that John Wilkes Booth might be on board the *Webb*. Although diehard secessionists interpreted the *Webb* incident as a sign the Confederacy was not entirely moribund, most settled back into their deathwatch.[10]

As May progressed, the plight of the Confederate Trans-Mississippi only worsened. Lincoln's assassination strengthened Federal resolve to overcome the last vestiges of the rebellion. There would be no help from Taylor's soldiers because they had taken the Union oath of allegiance and were returning to their homes in Alabama, Tennessee, Mississippi, Louisiana, and Texas. Davis and most of his cabinet, Treasury, and documents had been captured. There was no Confederate government to reestablish. Joe Johnston was about to finalize his surrender. Reading the writing on the wall, Kirby Smith offered the services of his army—more than 50,000 men—to the Emperor of Mexico. He was turned down.[11]

On May 8, Union Lieutenant Colonel J. T. Sprague, Major General John Pope's chief of staff, traveled to Shreveport under a flag of truce to try to broker the surrender of the Confederate Trans-Mississippi Department. Kirby Smith left the next day to present the terms at an emergency meeting with the governors in his department. They met in Marshall, the third largest city in Texas, on May 13. Subsequently, Smith returned to Shreveport bearing a counterproposal that sought more liberal terms than Lee, Johnston, and Taylor had recently been granted. Sprague carried the demands back for his superiors to review. The exchange bought Kirby Smith what he really wanted: more time. On May 18, he began moving his headquarters to Houston. If there was to be a last Confederate stand, the men of the Trans-Mississippi Department would make it in Texas.[12]

Will Brown and his comrades in the Mercantile Battery received orders on May 4 to return to New Orleans so they could prepare for "immediate field service." The Chicagoans soon learned that meant they were going to Texas in pursuit of Kirby Smith's army. Their friends in the 13th Corps, stationed in Mobile, were also being "held in readiness for the movement against Galveston." With Texas shaping up as the last battlefield of the war, Grant sent his cavalry chieftain Philip Sheridan— whom Will described as "Wild Phil" to Hiram Brown—to take charge of operations west of the Mississippi. The next day, May 18, the Union general-in-chief also ordered Canby to "fit Steele out with a force of not less than 6,000 men immediately for the Rio Grande." Waiting in New

General
Kirby Smith

Generals in Gray

Orleans, Will predicted to his father that if the Trans-Mississippi Rebels continued resisting, the Battery Boys would seek to avenge the company's fortunes, which had never been fully recovered since the Sabine Crossroads debacle.[13]

Kirby Smith's plan to keep fighting fell apart when his troops began deserting in droves. By the time Smith reached Houston on May 24 much of his field army had melted away. Except for a sprinkling of garrison troops in Texas and West Louisiana and Brigadier General Joseph O. Shelby's Missouri brigade, he had nothing left to command.[14]

At Camp Ford, the Rebel guards and their officers deserted on May 15. According to Mary Livermore, Captain Pat White and his cannoneers "had been preparing to leave for some time, and, as they earned money, had bought supplies of crackers, and sewed them in their clothing." This was fortuitous, Livermore continued, because the released Battery Boys now had a "meager supply" of rations for their long journey back to Union lines. The Mercantile Battery redlegs and about 1,200 additional prisoners started for Shreveport two days later accompanied by some "Good Samaritan" Southern cavalrymen who escorted them to ensure that they made it safely back to the Mississippi River. On their 40-mile journey, the weak soldiers passed through Marshall, where Kirby Smith and the western governors had met a few days before to discuss surrender terms. At Shreveport, one of the liberated Northern prisoners observed that "[t]he rebel soldiers had attempted to burn the city the night previous to our arrival, in which they had partly succeeded." Lieutenant General Simon Buckner and Major General Sterling Price were also trying to reach New Orleans, intending to discuss surrender terms with Canby.[15]

On May 26, Buckner accepted a preliminary Appomattox-like agreement on behalf of Kirby Smith for the Trans-Mississippi command. The surrender ceremony was conducted at the St. Charles Hotel, where Banks and Hurlbut kept their headquarters and where the Battery Boys had spent so many enjoyable times during their stops in the Crescent City. Richard Taylor, who was asked to be a witness to the surrender, recalled how he had been present at the Confederacy's beginning and its end, having "sat by its cradle and followed its hearse."[16]

Two days later, Captain White and his men reached New Orleans after being formally released at the mouth of the Red River. In his diary, Bugler Florison Pitts noted the momentousness of the occasion: "Sunday, May 28: A Day to be remembered. The men who were taken prisoners at the Battle of Mansfield the 8th of April 1864 came back to-day." The reunited Battery Boys celebrated in the Crescent City. With the return of Captain White and Lieutenant Pinckney Cone, the Chicago artillerists were confident there would not be any recurrences of the indignities they had been subjected to during the previous year at Camp Parapet.[17]

President Andrew Johnson put a nail in the Trans-Mississippi coffin on May 29 when he issued an amnesty proclamation for Confederate soldiers who continued to hold out. Kirby Smith had no choice but to approve the surrender document signed by Buckner and Price. He went aboard the Union steamer *Fort Jackson* in Galveston Harbor on June 2 and added the final surrender signature. In his farewell address, Smith scolded those soldiers of his department who had already forsaken the Confederate cause and deserted. "I am a Commander without an army—a general without troops. You have made your choice. It was unwise and unpatriotic, but it is final. I pray you will not live to regret it." Governor Watkins Allen chose instead to deliver an uplifting speech in which he encouraged his fellow Louisianans to "begin life anew . . . not talk of despair, nor whine about our misfortunes." Allen said he was going into exile not "to lead back foreign armies against my native land—but rather to avoid persecution."[18]

Smith and Allen joined as many as 2,000 unwilling-to-be-reconstructed Rebels fleeing the United States; most ended up in Mexico, Central America, Cuba, or South America. Phil Sheridan voiced suspicion over the closing of the war's Trans-Mississippi chapter. About a month later, the savvy general informed Grant that the Confederate surrender was "a swindle on the part of Kirby Smith and Company, as all the Texas troops had disbanded or had been discharged and gone home before the commissioners were sent to General Canby." Sheridan had missed the Grand Review in Washington, D.C., and lamented the fact that there was no Trans-Mississippi opposition to crush. "Kirby Smith, Magruder, Shelby, Slaughter, Walker, and others of military rank have gone to Mexico," he wrote. "Everything on wheels—artillery, horses, mules, &c—have been run over to Mexico."[19]

* * *

Baton Rouge La.
April 30th 1865

My dear father

We have had a sensation of our own this week. Early last Monday morning, <u>everybody</u> said the rebel ram "Webb" had run past here during the night. The story seemed too improbable for belief. The wires to New Orleans were down so we could get no news from below. About noon, [a] report had [reached us and said] that she had been sunk while entering Bayou Laforche. Tuesday's boat from New Orleans brought the news that she had run by New Orleans and Wednesday's gave the particulars of her capture etc. etc.[20]

It seems she left Shreveport loaded with 250 bales cotton, six guns and a crew of thirty men, steamed down Red river and got into the Mississippi all right (this a joke on the navy as they have been <u>blockading</u> the mouth of the Red river for some time). On reaching the river, she raised the Stars and Stripes and so I suppose did not excite suspicion. She passed…Port Hudson and this place in the night. I do not know why they did not fire at her here as every boat passing is under orders to stop. Perhaps they thought she might shoot back and there is only one gun bearing on the river.

She [the *Webb*] reached N. O. about noon, got about two thirds past the city and then hoisted the Stars and Bars. The "Lackawana" opened on her and gave her two 100-pdr. shots. This injured but did not stop her and she kept on [going] down [the Mississippi River]. Dispatches were telegraphed to Forts Jackson and St. Philip and a tugboat with one gun started in pursuit. Thirty five miles below the city she was set on fire, run ashore and abandoned; only three men being caught on her. A party of marines were soon ashore and captured nearly all those who had escaped from the boat.[21]

It is laughable to think of the rumors we had here [the] first day [we heard about the incident]. Among the rest were: "Jeff Davis on board, $300.000 in gold, Kirby Smith" and any number of others. Secesh rejoiced as much as he dared and <u>allowed</u> she would escape and perhaps become a <u>pirat</u> on the high seas. They were afraid to say much but they <u>looked</u> a great-deal. As yet, we have no information of the object of this daring attempt but I presume the prime movers see a sinking Confederacy and, loading their boat with cotton, attempted to make their way to the Gulf.[22]

There seems to be some trouble between Gen. [William T.] Sherman and President Johnson. I cannot believe that Sherman has fallen into error—his past does not look like it—and that he will make too gentle terms with those he is fighting against, I cannot believe. It is unfortunate that we should have even a whisper [of conflict between Sherman and President Johnson] at present and I hope the thing will be cleared up. It is pretty genuinely credited that Kirby Smith is negotiating for the surrender of the Trans-Mississippi Department. Nothing official in regard to it has been published.[23]

I hear that a Brig. Gen. [Joseph Farmer] Knipe will soon be here, where he will organize a force of cavalry to operate somewhere; probably in Mississippi.[24]

*   *   *

Baton Rouge La.
May 7th 1865

My dear father,

Yesterday evening came an order from Department Head Quarters ordering us to proceed to New Orleans, there to report to Gen. Weis [Joseph R. West] and immediately prepare for active field service. We will probably leave here to-morrow or next day. We were rather surprised on receiving this order. [We] have been here so long that we imagined we had a kind of <u>contract</u> to stay here 'till we had served out our time or were mustered out of service. Mr. Secretary Stanton's late orders had also aroused our hopes and we didn't know but we might spend the coming [July] 4th north of Mason and Dixon's. The hardest part of <u>my</u> moving is giving up that feather bed and good cozy quarters. Still, <u>such is fate</u> and the General's orders and as [such] I submit.[25]

I have not heard what expedition is on foot. Do not think we are wanted east of the Mississippi as Dick Taylor has surrendered to Canby and there is now no armed force of consequence east of the river. I can only think of Texas and it is more than probable that will be the objective point; <u>where</u> I cannot tell. I hope we will first go to Brownsville as I would like first-rate to get a sight of the "Max domains." It will take us several days to fit out before we can leave New Orleans and from there perhaps I can send you particulars.[26]

Kirby Smith, who has his head quarters at Alexandria La. at present, has lately issued a <u>Manifesto</u> that would do justice to some of Beauregard's <u>flowers</u>. He proposes <u>redeeming</u> the Confederacy and, of course, <u>talks</u> loudly. It is probable we will <u>go for him</u> and, as we now have plenty of men, I think we go in force sufficient to fully accomplish what we undertake. The fact is the rebs west of the river have never got over their victory's of last Spring and have an idea they can fight a <u>leetle</u> better than the rest of <u>our Southern brethren</u>. We have lots of troops who would like to get after them and the C.M.B. is among the number. We have a rumor that Gen. "Phil" Sheridan will take command of the forces moving against Texas. I hope so as everyone has confidence in his ability.

We have news of the surrender of Johnston on the same terms as granted to Lee, the shooting of the assassin Booth by a squad of our cavalry and the surrender of Dick Taylor to Canby. The town is filled with <u>Johnnies</u> paroled and on their way home. I have talked with several. Most of them think the war nearly over but a few are ashamed to acknowledge they are whipped. Most of them have good uniforms and look fully as healthy as our boys. Of course, it is hard for them to give up but they can see there is little use in attempting to hold out.[27]

Orders from the War Department look as if the authorities at Washington regard the war as virtually closed, and I think a part of the volunteer force will soon be mustered out. Should we go to Texas, we probably will not be among the number. But our term is only a little over three months longer and I guess we can stand it out; at any rate we will try.[28]

*   *   *

While all this was going on, life in New Orleans during May 1865 was more frenetic than usual for Chicago's Battery Boys—and far more confusing. The company was "camped at the Apollo Stables corner [of] 8th & St. Charles" and, being near the downtown, its members carefully monitored the local Union war machine for signs of activity that might herald another campaign. Will Brown and his companions thought the army's engine was groaning to a halt. Some decided to relax and went swimming in Lake Ponchartrain, but the motor began to rev faster after

Confederate Colonel John S. Ford led his troops to their small victory at Palmito Ranch, and Kirby Smith threatened to make a last stand in Texas. White, Cone, and the other 18 prisoners from the Chicago battery returned on May 28. Unfortunately, they had to walk around in their Camp Ford rags, for few had returned with their "redlegs" intact. It took four days before army officials issued them new clothing. The cannoneers hoped Banks' quartermaster department was not still bearing a grudge against them.[29]

On June 4, Will and the rest of the battery's original recruits thought they were going home. As Florison Pitts wrote in his diary, "the old members expect to be mustered out of the service under the order discharging the men whose time expires before the first of October." Except for Lieutenant Cone, who had somehow already finagled a leave to Chicago, the officers scrambled to update the unit's muster rolls. When White and his officers showed up to submit the battery's final mustering-out paperwork, however, they were told that the War Department had put all discharges on hold until further notice. In the midst of these daily emotional gyrations, one question remained: would the Mercantile Battery be ordered to Texas or sent home to Chicago? Each day brought a different, and equally frustrating, answer.[30]

Will, meanwhile, was so busy that after he wrote his hurried May 7 letter he did not send any more correspondence home from New Orleans. The battery's quartermaster filled out stacks of government forms during the day and tried to relax with his friends at night. The diary entries for Pitts and Lieutenant James Sinclair illustrate how the Battery Boys spent their leisure time. Pitts wrote about horseback riding and visiting the Academy of Music, minstrel shows, and the French Market. Sinclair spent a lot of time with Pat White (with Will Brown accompanying them during some of those outings). They attended Sunday church services, strolled downtown, took advantage of public baths, played billiards at the St. Charles Hotel, visited the above-ground cemeteries, and went to the market for ice cream. Sinclair also "wrote letter No. 146," which he planned to send home in the event he was transferred to Texas.[31]

Some of the boys had girlfriends in New Orleans and needed to make a decision about whether or not to continue their romances. One of these paramours named Billy Munroe, explained Pitts, decided to stay in Louisiana. When his Chicago comrades finally steamed away, they "passed him standing on the bank of the river at Carrollton with his girl."[32]

Lieutenant Roe had his own dilemma. His girlfriend Jimmie was applying pressure for him to stay. She gave him the following love poem on June 20, her Southern drawl reflected in the rhymes:

> Hard by there is a Battery,
> We call the Mercantile.
> Tis commanded by Lt. Roe,
> A Soldier true as steel.
>
> But he forgot his duty,
> To his country and its cause.
> And laid aside his uniform,
> To indulge in Cupid's wars.
>
> A maiden living near the Park,
> This young Lieutenant saw.
> And vowed that she would have his heart,
> Before the close of war.
>
> One Summer's eve she set her trap,
> As only woman can.
> And as the spider would a fly,
> She gently drew him in.
>
> And very soon, he desperate got,
> And went and bought a ring.
> To bind his fair dulcinea,
> In a matrimonial bin.
>
> And now if you pass the Park,
> This maiden fair you'll see.
> Waiting that he be mustered out,
> That they may married be.[33]

With so many forms to fill out, Will Brown had no time for romance. The overworked quartermaster sergeant was more interested in news that Kirby Smith had finally surrendered. While Phil Sheridan (Brown's new senior commander) may have regretted missing a Trans-Mississippi altercation, Will was relieved he would not have to return to Texas. His previous trips to the Lone Star State had not exactly been a stroll along the Teche.[34]

On June 22, Canby issued Special Order No. 166, stating "the horses, ordnance and ordnance stores of the Chicago Mercantile Battery, will be turned over to the proper departments in this city. The Company will proceed without delay to the State rendezvous at Chicago, Illinois, for muster-out of service." Will Brown and his friends were going home! Florison Pitts reacted to Canby's order with pleasure, noting it was "very good news and relieves my mind vastly." Over the next two days, Sinclair began to close out his war diary: "Turned over our Battery and Ordnance Stores . . . Camp and Garrison Equipage, also our horses." Before the Battery Boys left it started to rain, but the ebullient cannoneers ignored the minor inconvenience and focused instead on their pending departure.[35]

As the soldiers prepared to leave New Orleans, they discovered, "amid the confusion of regiments hastening homeward," that their mascot, Doggie Doggett, had been mistakenly left with another battery. Mary Livermore wrote that the Battery Boys' little shepherd dog had been adept at tracking down sheep and had accompanied the Chicago cannoneers across the South. He was an honorary member of A. J. Smith's foraging "guerrillas." The disappointed artillerists heard a rumor that Doggie Doggett had gone to Brashear City. They obtained a pass for a batterymate to track down their pet. He returned empty handed. On June 25, Pat White received the Quartermaster Department's order to depart: "The Steamer 'Brilliant' is now ready to load your command for Cairo. Please load to day as she is ready to leave to night." Members of the battery walked aboard at 5:00 p.m. There was still no sign of their mascot. Two hours later, the *Brilliant* slipped away from the docks, with many of the Battery Boys hoping that the loss of Doggie Doggett was not a bad omen for their return trip.[36]

On their way up the Mississippi River, Will and his friends retraced their war journey back to November 1862, when they had left Chicago with high hopes and innocent thoughts of war. The battery was departing New Orleans for the last time. No one was unhappy about it.

The Battery Boys passed Baton Rouge, where thoughts of their long year of garrison duty flooded back. Their time there had prevented them from participating in the Mobile Campaign. To the east was the route of

Davidson's pell-mell cavalry raid to West Pascagoula. To the west lay the Teche and Red River regions. Will and his batterymates had enjoyed visiting Longfellow's Acadian Louisiana. Still, they had no fond memories of Mansfield and nearby Sabine Crossroads, where Nathaniel Banks had sacrificed tens of hundreds of soldiers on the altar of his presidential aspirations. The irreplaceable personal belongings the Chicagoans had lost near the battlefield were never found. At Grand Ecore, the Illinois artillerists had innocently broken Banks' alleged news blackout—and suffered as a consequence. The battery's boat steamed beyond Port Hudson. At the mouth of Red River, the homeward-bound soldiers cheered when they passed the site of Captain White's recent parole; the nightmares of Red River and Camp Ford were finally behind them.[37]

The cannoneers reminisced about the Vicksburg Campaign as the *Brilliant* continued steaming northward. Grant's unpredictable campaign had swept them to victories at Port Gibson, Champion Hill, Big Black Bridge, and Vicksburg. Will Brown may have remembered writing to his father on July 19, 1863, about how the battery had "capped the climax" at Jackson against Joe Johnston—not knowing at that time that the victory would be the "high-water mark" of the Mercantile Battery's war history.[38]

And now it was over. No more dealings with Banks, Joseph Reynolds, Thomas Sherman, or Nelson Viall. No more tormentors. No more Rebels to fight. Will Brown preferred to remember his Vicksburg heroes—Ulysses S. Grant, William Sherman, A. J. Smith—and the jubilation he witnessed at the city's fall. The quartermaster looked forward to an even more momentous 4th of July celebration in Chicago.

Passing Vicksburg reminded Will of the "Winter of Northern Discontent" and his comrades who were listed in the battery's documents under "Discharges" and "Deaths." During the war, 286 men had served as Battery Boys. Only 130 were returning home to muster out. From the first wave of recruits who left with Will Brown for Memphis on November 8, 1862, only 34 were with him still. The remainder of the returning soldiers had joined the Mercantile Battery after the initial enlistment phase. Of the missing soldiers, 50 had mustered out early because of some disability. Many of them suffered from serious morbidity, among them George Kretsinger, whose eventual Medal of Honor would in no way compensate him for contracting small pox in

New Orleans, which would blind him in the right eye. Fifteen of Will's friends were among those previously discharged—bright and promising men like Chase Dickinson, Charlie Haseltine, Holmes Hoge, and Billy Patrick. They had received promotions and orders to report to other units.[39]

Another 15 Mercantile Battery soldiers had died serving their country. Lieutenant George Throop, Lieutenant Joseph Barr, Corporal Leighton Dyer, and Private Isaac Carpenter had been killed or suffered fatal injuries at Sabine Crossroads on April 8, 1864. Private Walter Felter died while in prison at Camp Ford. Corporal John White, Jr., suffered a mortal wound during the Vicksburg siege and a sergeant drowned on his way back to Vicksburg after a furlough. One of the Battery Boys perished in an insane asylum, possibly the victim of a particularly virulent strain of venereal disease he contracted at a New Orleans brothel. Others died of dysentery, small pox, typhoid fever, or measles.[40]

The battery's boat departed from Vicksburg and paused at Young's Point to pick up 1,500 bushels of coal. Will may have thought about the Chickasaw Bayou disaster, which would have been much worse if Sherman had not decided against a frontal assault on the Walnut Hills as 1862 ended. It was after that, while encamped along the opposite bank of the Mississippi River, when the demoralized battery members learned Charles Cooley had been forced to resign as their commander and Pat White of Taylor's Battery would serve in his place. White promoted Pinckney Cone, Joseph Barr, George Throop, and Henry Roe to serve as his lieutenants. White and his officers earned the respect of their troops. On May 22, 1863, White and Throop won acclaim for the Mercantile Battery with their gallant leadership in front of the 2nd Texas Lunette.[41]

Some of the battery's survivors wondered how George Throop's parents were handling the loss of their son, who had died during the rout of Banks' army at Sabine Crossroads. Amos Throop, a member of the Mercantile Association and the Board of Trade, had been a staunch supporter of the battery. The influential Chicagoan had visited the cannoneers near Vicksburg, along with Jane Hoge and Mary Livermore, as part of the Northwest Sanitary Commission delegation. Mrs. Hoge was happy her son Holmes, a former member of the battery, had survived the war. Mary Livermore, however, was still grieving over the younger Throop's death. George had attended her Sunday School class before joining 33 other young men from their church who enlisted in the new artillery company. Livermore had enjoyed the two days she spent in the field with George Throop and "her Battery Boys." Throop's sustained commitment to his faith, even in the midst of the miasmic conditions above Vicksburg, moved her deeply. Only eight Mercantile Battery artillerists from Mary Livermore's church were returning to Chicago.[42]

The Mercantile Battery boat headed north again, back to the beginning of the artillerists' war journey. It bypassed White River. Two and one-half years earlier in early January 1862, Will and his comrades had journeyed up that waterway to claim their first battlefield victory at Arkansas Post. Their steamer's next stop was Memphis, which they reached on June 29. The first chapter of the company's story was covered in the extensive letters Will and his friends had sent home from there. The young quartermaster hoped to preserve those letters for posterity.

From Memphis the boys had embarked on their first military campaign, the uneventful Tallahatchie march. It was during that expedition that the Chicagoans were introduced to William T. Sherman. The cannoneers had naively chanted war songs as they marched down the narrow northern Mississippi roads. Their ardor was irrepressible, even when they were compelled to camp among shriveled cornstalks with streams of muddy rainwater flooding their tent grounds at night. Everything was new and stimulating. They experimented with foraging and learned about "jerking" and "spontaneous combustion"— justifiable forms of looting and arson, respectively—and discovered that wreaking havoc on defenseless secessionist plantations was rarely punished. Now, as they made their way home past that same blighted countryside, they wanted nothing more than to forgot the depredations and suffering that war carried with it to everyone's doorstep.[43]

The *Brilliant* broke a wheel en route to Cairo and the steamer had to be repaired. Perhaps the damage took the artillerists back to the time they were caught on a sandbar on their way down the Mississippi, and how they had wondered whether it was an unlucky sign to break down before they reached the war zone. After arriving at Cairo on July 1 at 9:00 p.m., the Battery Boys entered the St. Charles Hotel, where many had stayed in November 1862. The lodging was still an oasis in the middle of a desolate landscape—though nowhere near as luxurious as its New Orleans namesake. From there, they sent a telegram to notify their benefactors— the influential businessmen in the Mercantile Association—that they were due to arrive in Chicago at 7:00 a.m. on Monday, July 3. The boys looked forward to a joyous reception, and their expectations were heightened by news that the city's residents had routinely lavished special treatment on returning soldiers.[44]

Chicagoans had begun preparing for the end of the war as early as April 3, when they learned that Grant had broken through Lee's lines at Petersburg and that Richmond had fallen. The news that "Babylon is fallen" united residents across the political spectrum. Republicans, War Democrats, and Copperheads all participated in the raucous citywide revelry, relieved that the long and agonizing war was nearly at an end. The celebrations were reignited less than one week later on the evening of April 9, which was Palm Sunday. Chicago's churchgoers returned home to spend a quiet evening with their families. The tranquility was shattered by clanging bells: Lee's army had surrendered! People spilled out into the streets and formed a four-mile-long procession through the streets of Chicago, preempting the politicians and community leaders who ordinarily set up citywide rallies. Bonfires and bursting fireworks underscored the collective jubilation. The 100-round salute of the Dearborn Light Artillery at midnight "capped the climax," as Will Brown might have said.[45]

For the moment, nearly everyone had forgotten the past four years of grief and sacrifice. The people of Chicago had made an extraordinary commitment to the war effort. By the end of the conflict, the city and surrounding Cook County had contributed $58,000,000 to the national government's prosecution of the war and another $4,000,000 locally. The Board of Trade and Mercantile Association had emerged as leaders in the prolonged struggle. In addition to providing significant funds to defer the general costs of the war, the two business organizations paid for the units they sponsored—including the Mercantile and Board of Trade batteries. They also contributed $295,000 to ease the war-related hardships of needy families, an amount that exceeded the war charity spent by the city and the county *combined*.[46]

But the people of Chicago and Cook County provided more than money. Fifteen thousand of their sons had joined the Union army—a substantial recruitment since the city had less than 20,000 total registered voters at that time. Approximately 25 percent of the Chicago recruits, or 4,000, died during the war. Many homes were adorned with black crepe, testifying to the death of family members. But on this evening of merrymaking, mourners such as the parents of Lieutenant George

Throop tried hard to ignore their personal loss and rejoice with their neighbors, all of whom looked forward to being reunited with their sons, husbands, nephews, fathers, and friends.[47]

Mary Livermore, who had witnessed so much of Chicago's suffering during the war, was thrilled to discover that April 10 brought with it another wave of celebrations. "[T]he rejoicing was renewed with more *abandon* than ever," she later wrote. Thousands of United States flags appeared; the Stars and Stripes were everywhere, flying from steeples and pinned to buttonholes. The city was awash in red, white, and blue. Businesses and schools were closed. Chicagoans pressed into the streets to form a milling mass of jubilation. An impromptu procession wound its way through the city. Livermore recalled the carnival April 10 atmosphere:

> On they came—men on horseback, men a-foot, six abreast, led by the Veteran Reserve Corps Band....The great multitude—tens of thousands of men, women, and children—caught up the refrain, and joined the glorious chorus, singing, with heart and soul and might, "GLORY, GLORY, HALLELUJAH! Still they came. All the drays in the city; all the steam fire-engines, with the red-costumed firemen; all the express wagons; all the post-office wagons; all the omnibuses, loaded with men, and boys, and soldiers, ringing bells, beating drums, blowing trumpets, and fifes, and every manner of instrument that make a joyful sound; blossoming with flags, vocal with hurrahs, bearing banners with eloquent mottoes, firing guns and pistols into the air, and in every conceivable manner testifying their unbounded gladness."[48]

For the next two months, most of the trains pulling into Chicago brought Illinois soldiers, as well as those who were stopping on their way home to Michigan, Wisconsin, Iowa, and Minnesota. The men stayed at Camp Douglas and Camp Fry until they could turn in their uniforms, equipment, and firearms and sign the mustering-out documents. Livermore and her devoted associates took every opportunity to show their hospitality and gratitude to the returning Western soldiers. As she recalled, "Addresses were made to them, and dinner furnished at the Soldiers' Home, where the ladies were always in readiness to feed two hundred men."[49]

Livermore, together with her collaborator Jane Hoge, also organized the second Northwest Sanitary Fair, which was held from May 30 to June

24. This fundraiser was even more festive than the one conducted in the fall of 1863. Soldiers who returned that week, such as those from the Second Board of Trade Regiment (88th Illinois), the Railroad Regiment (89th Illinois), and the Irish Legion (90th Illinois), enjoyed a hearty welcome and a modified version of Washington's Grand Review. Grant and Sherman attended the fair. Lincoln had planned to attend. Chicago was special to him. It was there he had been nominated as the Republican presidential candidate in 1860.

At 11:00 a.m. on May 1, Lincoln returned to the Garden City in a coffin. The Funeral Train stopped short of Great Central Station, halting instead at a temporary platform a mile to the south. Bells rang and guns boomed to alert Chicagoans their president had arrived. At 11:15 a.m., eight members of the Veteran Reserve Guard took Lincoln's coffin from the Funeral Train car to a specially built dais and arch. Mourners gathered around the remains of the slain healer of the Union. "The Lincoln Requiem" played as the assassinated president's body was placed in a hearse and escorted to the courthouse for public viewing. It was estimated that more than 120,000 people lined the streets or stood in line to pay their final respects. At the first Sanitary Fair in Chicago, Lincoln's manuscript copy of the Emancipation Proclamation had been auctioned off to raise funds for the well-being of Union soldiers. At the second fair, which was held after his funeral, all that was left of the Illinois hero were his words of liberation and national unity that echoed in the hearts of his admirers.[50]

When Will Brown and his fellow Mercantile Battery members jumped onto the platform at the Illinois Central Railroad station at 7:00 a.m. on Monday, July 3, disappointment washed over them. Few Chicagoans were there to greet them. Hardly anyone knew they were coming, and the emotional homecoming they had dreamed of for years sputtered and died. The telegram the Battery Boys had sent before leaving Cairo did not reach the Mercantile Association until *after* Captain White and his cannoneers arrived.

Fortunately, the Mercantile Association was holding a meeting that evening and the returning artillerists were formally received at the gathering. Vice President H. W. King acted as chair while Merrill Ladd was secretary. Apologies were made about the confusion that morning and the Battery Boys were invited to a dinner at the Union Hall the next day at 4:00 p.m. on July 4. The early dinner would allow them time to enjoy the Independence Day display of fireworks with their family and friends. A ceremonial banquet was planned for the battery at the prestigious Tremont House on Thursday, and the Association agreed to cover the cost of the celebration.[51]

Will Brown scribbled a quick note to his father but downplayed the lack of fanfare at the train station. He was still preoccupied with handling the company's final paperwork. The quicker Will's battery could muster out, the sooner he would be back in St. Joseph with his family. It was the last letter of the war penned by the Mercantile Battery's quartermaster.[52]

*   *   *

Chicago Ill.
July 3d 1865

My dear father

We arrived here this morning all right. As yet, we do not know what will be done before [we] muster out, but shall find out as soon as possible. And if I can get away before that time, shall be with you. I think I can get away for a day or so and, if so, will be over. Have not been able to see Capt. White since morning so cannot write anything definite. I am quite anxious to see you and will be over as soon as possible. We received a very cordial reception by our friends this morning, all of whom appeared glad to see us. Love to all.[53]

Hastily yours, W. L. Brown

*   *   *

Neither Will Brown nor his comrades took the time to write about their return to Chicago. They mustered out on Monday, July 10, and separated for home. It was time for them to move on and build successful new lives as civilians.

On the previous day (July 9), congregations in the Battery Boys' hometown churches gave thanks for the safe return of their soldiers. George Throop's mother and father were among the churchgoers. Later that day, Mrs. Throop described the service in a letter to her daughter Mattie. It was a time of both celebration and sorrow. Chicagoans rejoiced for the artillerists who had made it back safely, including Captain White,

Lieutenants Cone, Roe, Meacham, and Sinclair, Quartermaster Will Brown, and Buglers Pitts and Arnold. They also wept for the missing Battery Boys including George Throop, who lay in an unmarked Louisiana grave.

*   *   *

Letter from George Throop's mother to her daughter Mattie

Chicago
July 9, 1865

Dear Mattie,

I have just returned from Church feeling rather sad as we had a sermon appropriate to the occasion of the boys coming home. He [the minister] alluded to our case with much feeling which completely broke me down. The day is a rainy one consequently but few were at Church but the Soldiers were there, rain would not be likely to keep them away. I looked for Fred Sampson but did not see him. We had an excellent sermon & we thought it a pity there were not more present. Oh how hard it is that our dear boy is missing when around us are so many rejoicing, but I do not forget there are many whose homes are sad as well as our own. How much we need the faith that sustained George to carry us through this trial. It must be all for the best, also why was it permitted. [According to Mary Livermore, as George Throop was dying at Sabine Crossroads on April 8, 1864, he said "Tell my father and mother that I die willingly; my faith sustains me."] Capt White called to see us the other day, how much I was reminded of the time when he was here before & George was home....The Mercantile Association gave a banquet to the Battery last Thursday evening at the Tremont House, your father was there and said they had a splendid time, only one thing to mar the whole and that was the thought of those they left behind. They have gone before not left behind." [54]

(Top) Captain Pat White's original Medal of Honor; (right) White's updated Medal of Honor.

Epilogue

After mustering out on July 10, 1865, the men in the Chicago Mercantile Battery headed for their respective homes. They were ambivalent about the war's end. Although thrilled to be reunited with their families and friends, the Battery Boys were also sad about having to say farewell to the comrades with whom they had camped, waged war, and shared their lives. The artillerists had traveled side by side on horseback, caissons, and limbers, riding along the dusty back roads of the Trans-Mississippi South. Together they had "seen the elephant." And now it was all at an end.

Pat White returned to one of the shabby Irish neighborhoods in Chicago, "broken in health" because of the lingering effects of his thirteen-month ordeal at Camp Ford Prison. Friends may have noticed that his countenance was as dark as his complexion. His once-powerful six-foot frame was weakened now, his broad shoulders bowed by years of war. As fellow immigrants, his friends understood White's lack of optimism about building a postwar career. Although the "poor man captain" had succeeded in leading "a rich man's battery," White did not have the same civilian opportunities that were available to his well-educated soldiers like Will Brown, who were better equipped to take advantage of the ongoing Industrial Revolution. White returned to his deceased parents' home to help his sister raise their siblings. There, he contemplated his future in Chicago as an unskilled laborer in a technologically advancing economy.[1]

Restless and unsatisfied with his new life in Chicago, White moved to Albany, New York, where he met a widow named Annie Owens. They married on May 10, 1866. In November, he declined a commission as second lieutenant in the U.S. Army's 41st Infantry Regiment. The following year he became involved in a fish and oyster business. As the years passed the memories of his effective leadership on a variety of Civil War battlefields faded. The Irishman settled for a series of clerical jobs. He spent the last 20 years of his life working as a night watchman in the state controller's office.[2]

Although White never earned much money, he somehow found the means and the time to travel extensively. He made the long, arduous train trip from Albany to Chicago to attend battery reunions for both Taylor's Battery and the Chicago Mercantile Battery. He traveled twice to Vicksburg, where he helped place monuments and markers to highlight his battery's service during Grant's siege. Another example of White's hard work to preserve the accomplishments and sacrifices of soldiers during the war occurred around 1890, when the ex-captain spent two years lecturing at the Battle of Gettysburg panorama (one of the 360-degree Cyclorama paintings produced in 1883 by the French artist Paul Philopoteaux). Most likely he made his presentations at the exhibit in Chicago.[3]

After he mustered out, Will Brown returned to St. Joseph, Michigan, to visit his father and older brother Henry. He had not seen either one since enlisting in the Mercantile Battery three years earlier. His younger brother Lib was still in Arkansas, where he was still serving as quartermaster in the 12th Michigan Infantry.[4]

The elder Brown had been involved in the shipping trade for most of his adult life, having moved at the age of 30 from New York to Lake Michigan to manage a wholesale shipping business and construct boats used to navigate the St. Joseph River. He made the first trans-Lake Michigan shipment of wheat to Chicago. When the local economy plummeted, however, Hiram Brown was forced to move his family to Chicago, where he operated a line of boats on the Illinois & Michigan Canal. On returning to Michigan in 1862, the same year Will joined the

Chicago Mercantile Battery, Hiram obtained a position as Deputy Collector of Customs for the port of St. Joseph. Henry followed in his father's footsteps, working his way up from sailor, a job he took before the war at the age of 15. After recovering from his Resaca wounds, he became a captain in the Great Lakes shipping trade.[5]

Like his father, Will started his business career in the wholesale commission field. He was intrigued with the process of reselling bulk goods, which arrived at Chicago on Lake Michigan vessels, to retailers throughout the Midwest. Shipping was in Will's blood, and he, too, would seek an opportunity to work in that field.

After returning from the war to Chicago, the hearty former quartermaster took a job as a bookkeeper for Arthur B. Meeker & Company. Working for this iron foundry, Will was able to learn about steelmaking, a new business destined to transform the United States into a global economic power. He learned his lessons well. Five years later Brown became Meeker's partner. The pig iron the firm manufactured was essential in producing high-quality steel. Made in coal-heated furnaces, which smelted iron ore with coke and limestone, pig iron was at that time predominantly imported from Glasgow, Scotland. Arriving in New Orleans, the pig iron was transported on the same path the returning Mercantile Battery cannoneers had taken on their way back to Chicago after the war. From New Orleans, the pig iron was transferred to riverboats that hauled the raw material up the Mississippi River past Vicksburg and Memphis to Cairo, where it was transferred to railroad cars and taken to Chicago. To someone like Will Brown, who had learned logistics firsthand in the Civil War, this seemed to be sluggish and unprofitable. Ever resourceful, Will hired chemists whose subsequent experiments optimized the manufacture and shipment of pig iron from Great Lakes ore.[6]

Chicago was poised to play a pivotal role in the manufacture of American iron. Eber B. Ward established the Chicago Rolling Mill Company in 1857. By the end of the Civil War it was producing about 100 tons of iron rails each day. The Chicago Iron Ore Company began producing pig iron for the city's factories in 1868. As new mines opened in southern Illinois, increasing the availability of bituminous coal, more companies became involved in the business of smelting pig iron. The railroads transported the bituminous coal from those mines to foundries like Arthur B. Meeker & Company, which used the mineral in their blast furnaces. A decade later, more than ten Chicago companies employing almost 3,000 men were manufacturing approximately 400,000 tons of pig iron each year.[7]

With the increasing demand for iron ore, Will Brown decided to focus on solving some of the supply problems of this nascent industry. He decided to control his own destiny by gaining direct access to the Menominee Range, where a major deposit of iron ore had been discovered. In the area between Michigan and Wisconsin, Will met other entrepreneurs with the same plan. He collaborated with former Civil War soldiers James Pickands, Henry Pickands, and Jay C. Morse, along with their Cleveland friend Samuel Mather and Brown's partner Arthur B. Meeker, to form the Menominee Iron Company in 1872. Henry Pickands had been a major in the 103rd Ohio Infantry while his brother James had risen to command the 124th Ohio Infantry. Both had been toughened by their time in the Civil War's Western Theater. They were excited to meet another independent, ambitious veteran, welcoming Will Brown to join their other ventures. It was an association that would dramatically alter the course of his life.[8]

Another major life-changing event had occurred the previous year on September 27, 1871, when Brown married Mrs. Catherine (Kate) E. Seymour Bigelow—the "Mrs. Bigelow" pen pal from the Civil War. Kate was a widow and the daughter of Dr. Stephen Seymour, a progressive well-respected local physician. Dr. Seymour was also one of the founders of Hahnemann Medical College of Chicago. Will and Kate Brown would share many happy years together in Chicago and nearby Evanston.[9]

Brown's postwar career simulated the trajectory of a long-range shot from a Mercantile Battery rifled gun. In 1875 he bought out Meeker and assumed control of the Chicago iron foundry. With Henry Pickands, Brown formed Pickands, Brown & Company in 1883 (the same year his father, Hiram, died). The firm's other partners included James Pickands, Samuel Mather, and Jay C. Morse. Years later a newspaper article proclaimed that this five-member partnership was "destined to be one of the largest and most successful iron-and-steel operating groups in the trade." Will Brown retained a life-long equity position in Pickands, Mather & Company, which was headquartered in Cleveland. (After Brown's death, the company acquired his iron business.) Will also maintained a long-term friendship with Morse.[10]

On May 24, 1865—the final day of Grant's grand review in Washington, D.C.—Eber Ward's Chicago Rolling Mill Company manufactured its first steel rail. A unique pool of mechanically oriented managers and unskilled immigrant laborers, along with the transportation advantages afforded by shipping on the Great Lakes and the Chicago area's railroad network, would support the Windy City's auspicious debut in the steel industry. Limestone, a key ingredient in the manufacture of steel, was available near Chicago. Coal was shipped on railroad cars from mines in southern Illinois and the Appalachian range. Chicago was poised to become a world leader in steel production.[11]

It would take another 15 years, however, for iron ore to be transported from Lake Superior to Lake Michigan in sufficient quantities to feed the ravenous steel industry. With their increased access to the Menominee Range iron ore, Brown and Pickands were well positioned to take advantage of this explosive growth. Pickands, Brown & Company became one of the "leading iron merchants on Lake Michigan," especially as iron ore from the Lake Superior area became the industry standard in the 1880s. On May 1, 1889, Will's friend Jay Morse became the first president of the Illinois Steel Company, which was formed by merging the North Chicago Rolling Mill with the Joliet Steel Company and the Union Iron and Steel Company. Morse subsequently employed Pickands, Brown & Company to acquire pig iron for the new steel enterprise, whose grounds began to sprawl across 260 acres along the shores of Lake Michigan. Morse's company would become a major part of the United States Steel Corporation in 1901.[12]

In the next decade, vast iron ore deposits were discovered in the Mesabi Range between Lake Superior and Lake Winnipeg in northern Minnesota. The steel industry was ready to exploit what author Walter Havighurst called the "greatest reservoir of iron ore then known, a bed of iron formation a hundred miles long and up to two miles wide with many pockets of deep, rich hematite ore." During the financial panic of 1893, a wily corporate warrior entered the fray to exert his influence over the Mesabi Range. John D. Rockefeller had used his Standard Oil fortune and cash liquidity amidst the ensuing depression to bail out some floundering amateur businessmen in Minnesota. When they defaulted on their loans, Rockefeller took possession of the rich ore fields. Rockefeller became, in Havighurst's words, the "chief landlord of the Mesabi Range." Once steel makers adjusted their furnaces to accommodate

Mesabi fine-dust iron ore, the Rockefeller management team dropped their prices to gain a dominant position with key mills situated along Lake Michigan and Pittsburgh's three-pronged rivers.[13]

In 1890, Will combined his lifelong passion for shipping with his interest in steel by founding the Chicago Ship Building Company. He was in the right place at the right time. As author Richard J. Wright wrote in his history of the industry, Brown's company rode the "tremendous surge in steel shipbuilding that swept the lakes during 1890-1891." Brown purchased 23 acres on the east bank of the Calumet River at 101st street in South Chicago, about one mile from the river's entrance into Lake Michigan, and near his strategic neighbor, the Illinois Steel Company.[14]

Will also invested in his new shipbuilding company's future by hiring as his chief engineer Washington Irving Babcock, a graduate of Brooklyn Polytechnic Institute and Rensselaer. As chairman of the Board, Brown put together the necessary capital so Babcock could implement a series of innovative technological advancements in ship construction (many of which are still in use today). Among other accomplishments, Babcock automated the shipyard's production work via pneumatic tools and steam-driven equipment. As Wright observed, "W. I. Babcock proved to be one of the most talented marine engineers to emerge from the lake region. His bold concepts in yard management and naval architecture revolutionized the cost and design of bulk freighters on the lakes."[15]

The Chicago Ship Building Company began to build the *Marina* for the Minnesota Steamship Company in July 1890, launching it in March 1891. It was an historic occasion. Wright noted that the *Marina* was "the first steel-hulled ship built on Lake Michigan." When the president of his company unexpectedly died (35-year-old Emmons Blaine, eldest son of politician James G. Blaine), Will took over day-to-day operations. He continued to apply the same intensity and perspicacity in dealing with business challenges that had helped make him a successful manager of Civil War logistics.[16]

Both of Brown's companies were inextricably linked to the iron-ore industry. Pickands, Brown & Company remained a prominent sales broker of pig iron, while the Chicago Ship Building Company became a leader in the construction of steel-hulled ships to haul iron ore from Lake Superior to eastern furnaces controlled by industrialists such as Andrew

Carnegie. Wright observed that the Chicago Ship Building Company's "meteoric rise was due to the originality and daring practicality displayed by W. I. Babcock . . . and to the progressive forethought displayed by the board of directors under the able leadership of William L. Brown." He added, "By 1899, the Chicago Ship Building Company was the most progressive and productive shipyard on the Great Lakes."[17]

John D. Rockefeller, knowing the economic value of dominating an industry's primary mode of transportation, now applied this principle in what would become his last major business venture, that of maximizing his return on his Mesabi Range investment. Unleashing his aggressive management team—and using William Brown's friend Samuel Mather—Rockefeller acquired 56 steel vessels, establishing the largest ore-shipping fleet on the Great Lakes. Rockefeller's rapid control of the iron ore industry, combined with the pressure on America's entrepreneurial industrial ventures to remain profitable in the throes of price wars, led to a wave of major consolidation in the shipping and production of steel.[18]

In December 1898, seven companies involved in the Great Lakes shipping trade held a secret meeting at the Waldorf Astoria Hotel in New York City. Attorney James H. Hoyt from the American Steel Barge Company took part in the clandestine gathering. (Ironically, Hoyt was affiliated with Rockefeller's Standard Oil.) Will attended on behalf of his Chicago Ship Building Company. Brown's firm was one of the two strongest businesses represented, the other being the Detroit Dry Dock Company. The seven companies agreed to merge, and the new American Ship Building Company was incorporated in New Jersey the following month, with a capitalization of approximately $30 million. At the April shareholders meeting, Will became the first president; Hoyt was its chief counsel. An onsite superintendent ran each of the business units, with executives from the parent companies sitting on the new Board of Directors. As president, Brown commuted to the new headquarters in Cleveland, where his chief engineer, chief counsel, and other key staff were stationed.[19]

In 1895, while William Brown was scaling up the Chicago Ship Building Company enterprise, his dear old friend Pat White received a letter that electrified him:

> I have the honor to inform you that, by direction of the President and in accordance with the act of Congress approved March 3, 1863, providing for the presentation of medals of honor to such officers, non-commissioned officers and privates as have most distinguished themselves in action, the Acting Secretary of War has awarded you a medal of honor for most distinguished gallantry with the storming party at the assault on the enemy's works at Vicksburg, Mississippi, May 22, 1863.[20]

White sent a reply to the War Department three days later to acknowledge he had received his medal, an award that he cherished deeply. White's Medal of Honor provided a wonderful reminder that he had achieved something of lasting importance more than thirty years earlier when, as a young man on battlefields in Tennessee, Mississippi, and Louisiana, he had been the valiant commander of the Chicago Mercantile Battery:

> Sir: I have the honor to inform you that I have recd the medal of honor that the president and congress has awarded me. I thank you personally very much and I feel very proud of the same. I assure you I would not feel any more pleased if I had [learned] that I was to get a present of ten thousand dollars and am a poor man at that.[21]

White was not the only member of his battery awarded the Medal of Honor for supporting the Union assault against the 2nd Texas Lunette. Corporal James Dunne and Privates Charles Kloth, George Kretsinger, Patrick McGuire, and William Stephens also received the decoration as the other surviving Mercantile Battery members who had "Carried with others by hand a cannon up to and fired it through an embrasure of the enemy's works." Ninety-nine surviving members of Grant's army received the Medal of Honor for their bravery on May 22, 1863, at Vicksburg. In contrast, 62 surviving veterans from the Army of the Potomac were awarded the decoration for Gettysburg's "3 days of inferno."[22]

White and his five Mercantile Battery veterans were thrilled to receive the prestigious Medal of Honor in recognition for their gallant response to A. J. Smith, who requested artillery support for the Federal infantrymen stranded in front of the 2nd Texas Lunette. In his correspondence with the War Department, White recalled the incident: "Gen Smith called on several batteries but the officers of each emphatically refused, declaring it to be impossible to haul the guns up the perpendicular hill and that it was simply murderous to expose the men to certain death." Despite the ignominy of their New Orleans mutiny troubles and disastrous Red River losses, the Battery Boys had finally gained the recognition they deserved for their meritorious service. Surviving comrades like Will Brown rejoiced that White and their former batterymates were honored with "the highest military award for bravery that can be given to any individual in the United States of America."[23]

Pat White had another surprise the following year when his special sword, taken by a Texan at the Battle of Sabine Crossroads, was returned to him. White had surrendered the weapon to Alex McDow, a captain in Walker's 16th Texas Infantry. McDow, in turn, had sent the sword home to his daughter Kate in Texas and reclaimed it after returning from the war.[24]

White had risked death when he refused to surrender his sword to anyone but another officer—this in deference to the commitment he made to the Chicagoans who had presented the saber to him after his first sword was destroyed by a cannon shell fragment at the Battle of Shiloh. An Albany newspaper recounted the day White received his new saber, belt, and sash in a January 11, 1896, article:

> On the evening of May 1, 1862, in the city of Chicago, a number of its most prominent citizens called upon a young man who had just returned from war on a brief furlough and presented him with a handsome sword. It was given to him, they said, in recognition of valor already shown and with the hope that it would inspire him to further patriotic achievements. The young man, frail in health and weak in speech, overcome by surprise and his own emotions, could barely reply to the address of the committee. He could say but few words, and they were: 'Gentlemen, I do not deserve this compliment, I am serving my country, to the utmost of my feeble ability, because I love it. I promise you that no act of mine shall ever bring disgrace upon the sword you have given me, nor shall it ever be yielded to an inferior in rank of the enemy's line.'[25]

Captain Alex McDow surrendered his Company I, 16th Texas Infantry, part of Kirby Smith's army of the Trans-Mississippi Department, at Houston, Texas, on July 26, 1865. After his parole, McDow returned home to LaGrange, Texas, where he resumed farming. He was one of the wealthiest landowners in the community, and when he

Kate McDow Brownson

Photographic Collection,
Victoria Regional History Center,
Victoria College / UH-Victoria Library

retired, McDow moved to Victoria, Texas, to live with his daughter Kate. In 1870, she had married John Brownson, a former member of Terry's Texas Rangers, who became a successful businessman and banker in Victoria. Kate herself was a forceful woman who was active in community affairs, having helped start the Bronte Literary Club—one of the oldest women's organizations in the country. She also became "probably the only woman member of the Chamber of Commerce of Victoria." Additionally, Kate helped found the Victoria chapter of the United Daughters of the Confederacy. She received national recognition for her work with the philanthropic organization, which was started in 1890 to support aging Confederate veterans and build memorials commemorating their Civil War service. Her father Alex died on February 5, 1891, at the age of 69. Almost five years later, she wrote to the *National Tribune*, a publication for Union veterans, seeking to return her father's captured Federal sword to its rightful owner. Her brief notice appeared in the January 2, 1896, issue of the *National Tribune*.[26]

> I have an old saber, captured by my father from an officer in Gen. Banks' army in Louisiana. The inscription is much defaced, but I can make out: 'Lieutenant P. H. (?) White, Later's [Taylor's] Battery. From his Chicago friend, May 1, 1862.' I would be glad to return it to any of his family. Mrs. J. M. Brownson. Victoria, Texas.[27]

Pat White was living in Albany when he read the small notice, which was buried in the back pages of the newspaper. He immediately responded to Kate Brownson:

My dear Madam,

It would be impossible for you to imagine how deeply the newspaper note in the National Tribune affected me. It was like a message from a dear friend. Mourned as irrevocably lost in our last awful fratricidal contest. The sword is hallowed in my memory.... The possibility of the recovery of the old sword that clung so faithfully to my side during my service in the field after its presentation thrills me with a pleasure and gratification that mere words are inadequate to express. You can not realize how grateful I am to you for the thoughtfulness that caused the publication of the fact that you are the possessor of my old sword, and are willing to return it to me. I wish you would forward it by express to my address, and I will pay the charges thereon. When the old relic comes into my possession, I shall be the happiest man in existence, and I shall forever preserve it in my family as a token of the love that has now sealed by its indissoluble bonds the hearts of all patriotic Americans into a union of fraternal peace and good will, which, God grant, may endure to the end of time.[28]

Before White's letter reached Brownson, however, a veteran from Missouri tried to claim the sword for himself. Fortunately, she was able to prevent the sword from falling into the wrong hands. Kate was thrilled to have tracked down Captain White, which allowed her to fulfill a

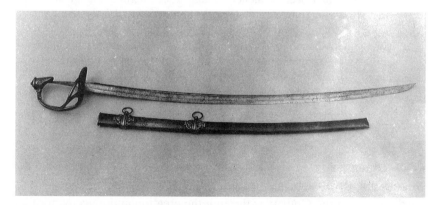

Captain Pat White was thrilled to receive his sword, albeit 32 years after he surrendered it to Captain Alex McDow, of the 16th Texas Infantry, during the Battle of Sabine Crossroads. *New York State Museum, Albany, New York*

promise she made to her father to return the saber. She recalled how Alex McDow had repeatedly told her "that he would have liked to learn the fate of the gallant Captain, for he said he was brave to the heart's core." McDow added that he "would be glad to have the 'old sword hang in its place.' It was worthly worn, and surrendered as gallantly as by any knight of yore."[29]

On January 16, 1896, Kate sent the following letter to White:

My Dear Captain,

I am in receipt of your letter of the 11th. My husband will take pleasure in packing the sword and sending it per express to you. . . . My father told me he gave Capt White his name, went to the rear and bespoke kind treatment as there were no accommodations, and the Captain looked frail, but he never saw him again, his command being ordered forward.

You probably have confused the two men. My father was 6 ft high—The private named Cross had his gun on you and was ready to shoot when Captain McDow sprang in put his pistol to your heart and told you to surrender to him. You had said you would rather die before you would give your sword to a non commissioned officer. Fortunately I have two of my father's letters to confirm all I know.

The sword since my marriage 1870 has held the place of honor in our home. It was damaged, as you see, by an overflow in the Colorado river in 1870, which swept away our household goods and was recovered in a field after the water subsided. I deeply regret not being able to return it in good condition. (The leather on the sword's hilt was missing as was part of the scabbard; the presentation inscription had been scratched though it was legible enough for Mrs. Brownson to quote it in her note to the *National Tribune*.)

Probably there is no heart made more happy than mine—next to yours—over the return of the sword. I feel a personal interest in one, around whose name hangs the halo of gallant bravery, in defense of his sword, and who wore it as truly as any knight of old, who surrendered it with courtly grace at the risk of his own life's blood.[30]

White received another vivid reminder of his Civil War days when the 1,283-acre Vicksburg National Military Park was formed in February 1899. Illinoisans played a key role in establishing the park near the Mississippi River and, at the same time, memorializing their state's participation in the Civil War through the creation and placement of 79 regimental monuments and 85 markers. The latter were "erected in honor of commands that served in the investment line [such as the Chicago Mercantile Battery]. These are placed on the exact spots where the events they commemorated occurred." Influential businessmen like the Mercantile Battery's Will Brown and Florus Meacham provided financial support while other veterans like Pat White contributed their time and effort to advance the cause. White worked closely with Iowa Captain William T. Rigby who, along with Lieutenant General Stephen D. Lee of Mississippi and Captain James G. Everest of Illinois, served as one of the original Vicksburg National Military Park commissioners appointed by the secretary of war in March 1899. Congress also approved the development of military parks at Gettysburg, Chickamauga–Missionary Ridge, and Shiloh. The parks were created as a legacy in honor of both the Union and Confederate men who fought and died on the preserved battlefields.[31]

"If I am alive in 1903 [for the 40th anniversary of Grant's siege], White wrote in April 1902, "I intend to go to Vicksburg to visit the old ground." The aging captain did not have to wait that long. He journeyed to the Hill City in the summer of 1902. According to a Chicago newspaper article, "the government asked the battery to name a representative to go to Vicksburg and mark the spot where [the Mercantile Battery] guns stood. . . . the choice fell unanimously to their old commander. To show once more the respect in which all his former comrades in arms regard him, Captain White was persuaded to go south by way of Chicago and stay a few days as their guest [to celebrate the 40th reunion of the battery's formation]." There were only about 25 of the original 150 first-wave Battery Boys left. Describing the reunion dinner, the newspaper article further stated, "Most of them were there last night and told reminiscences of their youthful fighting days and the glorious part Captain White played in the struggle . . . now many [such as Will Brown and Florus Meacham] are millionaires and leaders in the commercial and financial world."[32]

White headed for Vicksburg, likely with the financial support of his more prosperous soldiers. In Mississippi, he positioned his unit's monuments and markers. In 1902, the *Vicksburg Evening Post* recorded that White "spent the day [September 8] with Captain Rigby, the Engineer of the Commission, in locating the position of the Battery camp and the several guns [used] during the siege. . . . The old veteran returned Sunday delighted with his visit saying, 'I will be back again.'" White

New York State Museum, Albany, New York

The Chicago Mercantile Battery survivors visited Vicksburg in 1906 for the dedication of the Illinois monument. Captain White (standing, far left) placed this photo in his scrapbook and labeled it: "The Boys—'63." Will Brown appears to be the third man from the left, standing next to White.

would get his wish. On December 13, 1906, he attended the dedication of the massive Illinois monument at Vicksburg, where he posed for photographs with other Chicago veterans (including one titled "The Boys—63," which appears to have Will Brown in it).[33]

Nine years later, Patrick White died on Thanksgiving Day. He was 83 years old. The Irish immigrant who had been honored by his adopted country with its highest military decoration had lived a full life, loved and admired by his family and friends in Albany and Chicago. He was pleased to have taken the lead role in honoring his Battery Boys with monuments and markers at Vicksburg National Military Park. After his death, battery survivors like Will Brown reciprocated by erecting a monument to their beloved captain at the base of what was once the 2nd Texas Lunette. In contrast to many of his Civil War comrades who were buried in Chicago's Rosehill Cemetery, however, White chose a grave site in Albany, where he had spent his last fifty years.[34]

(Right) Pat White, photo circa 1900, and his portrait plaque (below) at Vicksburg National Military Park.

Richard Brady Williams
Private Collection

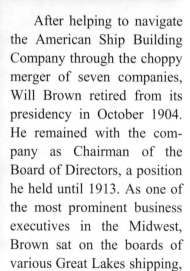

CAPT. PATRICK H. WHITE
CHICAGO MERCANTILE BATTERY
FOR GALLANT ACTION
ASSAULT, MAY 22 1863

After helping to navigate the American Ship Building Company through the choppy merger of seven companies, Will Brown retired from its presidency in October 1904. He remained with the company as Chairman of the Board of Directors, a position he held until 1913. As one of the most prominent business executives in the Midwest, Brown sat on the boards of various Great Lakes shipping, pig iron, and iron-ore companies, as well as several banks in Chicago. He often provided business insights to his friends. During his entire career, Brown maintained an office in the Rookery Building in downtown Chicago, which he visited for the last time two weeks before his death at age 87.[35]

Throughout his life, Brown was involved with a wide variety of civic and philanthropic activities. For example, he served the Chicago and Evanston communities by applying his organizational expertise in co-founding the Chicago Orchestral Association and Chicago Art Institute. He also helped to guide Northwestern University as a trustee. In addition, the affluent industrialist generously contributed to local Chicago hospitals and other worthy causes.[36]

Will Brown retired from active business life in his late 70s and moved to Pasadena, California, where he had previously vacationed. Much as he had done in Chicago, Brown took part in Pasadena's civic activities and became so well known that his death, which occurred on November 1, 1929, was covered in major front-page articles. A typical comment from one of these articles proclaimed, "Every one who knew Mr. Brown called him 'Uncle Billy' because of his lovable nature and kindly manner."[37]

The headlines and sub-headings of the Pasadena newspapers summarized Will Brown's accomplishments and generosity:

A gold postwar medal featuring the major battles in which the Chicago Mercantile Battery participated. *Richard Brady Williams Private Collection; Kelly Mihalcoe, photography*

The Mariners' Museum, Newport News, Virginia

William Liston Brown (circa 1900).

William L. Brown, Chicago Shipbuilding Magnate, Financier, Dies Here: Steel Firm Founder Is Summoned

'Uncle Billy' Brown's Death Ends Career Filled With Deeds of Kindness

Uncle Billy Brown Dies Here Today: Death Ends Fine Career of Steel Company Founder and Philanthropist

Steel Trade Pioneer Is Mourned: William Liston Brown Is Dead at Home Here

HE BLAZED WAY IN PIG-IRON FIELD: Developed Methods Which Stopped Importation[38]

One of the greatest highlights of Will Brown's life was being a Battery Boy. His service as president of the Chicago Mercantile Battery Association enabled him to collaborate with his comrades to sustain the memories of their Civil War service. And it was his letter collection, so carefully written and saved, that made it possible to preserve a record of the battery's service forever.

Appendix 1

Walking Vicksburg with the Chicago Mercantile Battery

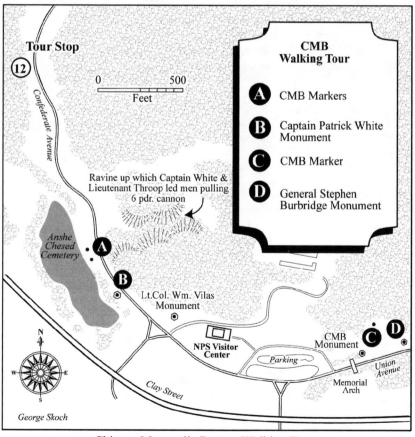

Chicago Mercantile Battery Walking Tour,
Vicksburg National Military Park

Appendix 2

Chicago Mercantile Battery Roster

Below is a roster for the Chicago Mercantile Battery. The information comes from the compiled service records of its members and a smattering of other sources, including pension records. These records include, as information allows, each soldier's: name, date of muster, age, birth place, residence, occupation, muster out date, and additional comments of interest.

Captains

Cooley, Charles G. 8/29/1862. Chicago. Resigned 2/24/1863.
White, Patrick H. 3/1/1863. Ireland. Chicago. Meat packer. 7/10/1865. Camp Ford POW.

First Lieutenants

Wilson, Frank C. 8/29/1862. Chicago. Resigned 2/22/1863.
Swan, James H. 8/29/1862. Chicago. Resigned 2/6/1863.
Throop, George 3/1/1863. 23. MI. Chicago. Bookkeeper. KIA at Mansfield on 4/8/1864.
Cone, Pinckney, S. 2/22/1863. 25. AL. Chicago. Bookkeeper. 7/10/1865. Camp Ford POW.
Roe, Henry 9/1/1864. 24. NY. Chicago Express messenger. 7/10/1865. Commanded CMB from 4/1864 to 5/1865.

Second Lieutenants

Crego, David R. 8/29/1862. Chicago. Resigned 2/6/1863.
Bickford, Frederick B. 8/29/1862. Chicago. Resigned. 2/22/1863.
Barr, Joseph W. 5/1/1863. 31. PA. Chicago. Bookkeeper. KIA Mansfield on 4/8/1864.
Roe, Henry 5/1/1863. 24. NY. Chicago Express messenger. Promoted to 1st lieutenant in 6/1864.
Meacham, Florus D. 7/9/1864. 20. NY. Chicago Clerk. 7/10/1865.
Sinclair, James C. 10/26/1864. 26. IL. Chicago. Clerk. 7/10/1865.

Privates: Original Battery Boys

Adams, Orla E. 8/29/1862. 21. NY. Chicago. Clerk. 7/10/1865.

Adams, Oliver M. 8/29/1862. 26. NH. Chicago. Clerk. Discharged 8/29/1863, disability.

Addicks, Charles H. 8/29/1862. 19. PA. Chicago. Bookkeeper. Discharged 11/5/1862, promotion.

Akerman, William F. 8/29/1862. 25. ME. Chicago. RR Employee. Discharged 1/13/1864, promotion.

Allen, Charles S. 8/29/1862. 20. NY. Chicago. Clerk. Discharged 12/4/1864, disability.

Allen, Sidney G. 8/29/1862. 21. NY. Chicago. Clerk. Absent at muster out due to sickness.

Amick, Hiram 8/29/1862 25. IL. Chicago. Conductor. 7/10/1865. Mustered out as a sergeant.

Arnold, John W. 8/29/1862. 21. NY. Chicago. Soldier. 6/16/1865. Camp Ford POW; bugler.

Barker, Alfred C. 8/29/1862. 24. England. Chicago. 7/10/1865. Mustered out as artificer.

Bartlett, Andrew J. 8/29/1862. 28. NY. Chicago. Printer. 7/9/1865.

Brackett, Francis E. 8/29/1862. 24. MA. Chicago. RR employee. 7/10/1865.

Brackett, Henry C. 8/29/1862. 31. MA. Chicago. RR employee. 6/16/1865. Mustered out as sergeant; Camp Ford POW.

Brewster, George H. 8/29/1862. 27. CT. Chicago. Clerk. Deserted 11/15/1862.

Briggs, Harvey D. 8/29/1862. 22. NY. Chicago. Clerk. Discharged 4/12/1863, disability.

Brown, William L. 8/29/1862. 20. MI. Chicago. Bookkeeper. 7/10/1865. Mustered out as quartermaster sergeant.

Bryant, George E. 8/29/1862. 24. MA. Chicago. Clerk. 6/16/1865. Sergeant. Camp Ford POW; MOH recipient.

Butler, Thomas B. 8/29/1862. 27. England. Chicago. Butcher. Absent at muster out due to sickness.

Bush, Henry L. 8/29/1862. 20. IL. Chicago. Clerk. 7/10/1865. Mustered out as sergeant.

Carder, Charles H. 8/29/1862. 21. RI. Chicago. Driver. 7/10/1865.

Carey, William C. 8/29/1862. 29. OH. Chicago. Absent at muster out due to sickness.

Cleary, George H. 8/29/1862. 24. MD. Chicago. Gas fitter. 6/22/1865.

Cleveland, William H. 8/29/1862. 23. IL. Chicago. Lumber work. Deserted 10/28/1862.

Cone, Pinckney S. 8/29/1862. 25. AL. Chicago. Bookkeeper. Promoted 1st sergeant; 1st lieutenant 2/1863.

Cotes, William R. 8/29/1862. 31. OH. Chicago. Clerk. 6/7/1865.

Cozens, Charles B. 8/29/1862. 20. CT. Chicago. Engineer. 7/10/1865. Mustered out as corporal.

Crandell, Edwin J. 8/29/1862. 27. NY. Chicago. Cashier. Discharged 2/1863 & 1/1865; quartermaster sergeant.

Day, Joseph L. 8/29/1862. 24. CT. Chicago. 6/16/1865. Mustered out as sergeant; Camp Ford POW.

DeGraff, William. 8/29/1862. 20. NY. Chicago. Clerk. Discharged 2/17/1863, disability.

Denton, Solomon F. 8/29/1862. 31. IN. Chicago. Student. Discharged 2/29/1864, promotion.

Dickinson, Chase H. 8/29/1862. 25. VT. Chicago. Lawyer. Discharged 6/29/1864, promotion.

Dickinson, Seymour R. 8/29/1862. 22. NY. Chicago. Clerk. 6/10/1865.

Diven, Alexander. 8/29/1862. 22. NY. Chicago. Bookkeeper. Discharged 12/11/1862, promotion.

Dodge, Lewis. 8/29/1862. 24. NY. Chicago. Clerk. 6/10/1865.

Doron, Hugh. 8/29/1862. 22. NY. Chicago. Blacksmith. Discharged 4/7/1863, disability.

Dunne, James. 8/29/1862. 21. MI. Chicago. Brakeman. 710/1865. Mustered out as corporal; MOH recipient.

Dyer, Leighton W. 8/29/1862. 36. VT. Chicago. Express Messenger. Corporal; KIA at Mansfield on 4/8/1864.

Ely, John P. 8/29/1862. 22. NY. Chicago. Bookkeeper. Discharged 4/27/1863, disability.

Fay, Ezra S. 8/29/1862. 23. OH. Chicago. Clerk. Discharged 5/6/1863, disability.

Fishburn, Eugene H. 8/29/1862. 22. IL. Chicago. Bookkeeper. Discharged 3/16/1863, disability.

Gardner, William 8/29/1862. 27. NY. Chicago. Driver. 6/17/1865. WIA at Mansfield. Mustered out as a sergeant.

Gates, Ralph J. 8/29/1862. 33. NY. Chicago. Molder. Discharged 11/15/1862, disability.

George, Hiram. 8/29/1862. 25. NH. Chicago. Mechanic. 7/10/1865.

Gilbert, Eugene H. 8/29/1862. 21. IL. Chicago. Salesman. 8/29/1865.

Gilbert, John N. 8/29/1862. 23. NY. Chicago. Clerk. Sergeant. Discharged 1/2/1865, promotion.

Gilmore, Warren. 8/29/1862. 28. PA. Chicago. Painter. WIA Arkansas Post. Discharged 6/19/1865; corporal.

Gooding, Edward L. 8/29/1862. 20. IL. Chicago. Bookkeeper. Discharged 8/23/63, promotion.

Goodrich, Edward B. 8/29/1862. 24. NY. Chicago. Clerk. 7/10/1865.

Goodrich, Sidney E. 8/29/1862. 18. NY. Chicago. Clerk. Discharged 2/7/1863, disability.

Graham, Michael. 8/29/1862. 24. Ireland. Chicago. Conductor. 7/10/1865.

Gray, Henry C. 8/29/1862. 21. IA. Chicago. Clerk. 7/10/1865.

Gruber, John F. 8/29/1862. 22. Germany. Chicago. Hotel worker. 7/10/1865. Mustered out as corporal.

Gunlock, John C. 8/29/1862. 24. PA. Chicago. Jeweler. 7/10/1865.

Gunlock, Philip. 8/29/1862. 21. PA. Chicago. Brakeman. 7/10/1865. Mustered out as corporal.

Haight, Charles H. 8/29/1862. 28. MI. Chicago. Cashier. Absent at muster out due to sickness.

Hall, Olin. 8/29/1862. 21. NY. Chicago. Brakeman. Discharged 3/13/1863, disability.

Hallenbeck, Peter. 8/29/1862. 29. NY. Chicago. Clerk. Discharged 6/16/1863, disability.

Hamblin, John J. 8/29/1862. 27. NJ. Chicago. Plumber. 7/10/1865. Mustered out as corporal.

Hammett, Samuel. 8/29/1862. 29. PA. Chicago. Clerk. 7/10/1865. Mustered out as corporal. Camp Ford POW.

Hanford, Charles C. 8/29/1862. 23. IL. Chicago. Farmer. 7/10/1865.

Harper, George W. 8/29/1862. 19. IL. Chicago. Clerk. Discharged 3/28/1863, disability.

Harris, Abraham. 8/29/1862. 29. England. Chicago. Painter. Discharged 10/12/1863, disability.

Haseltine, Charles P. 8/29/1862. 26. NY. Chicago. Civil Engineer. Discharged 8/6/1864, lieutenant in 97th USCT.

Higby, Sidney C. 8/29/1862 27. NY. Chicago. Machinist. 7/10/1865. Mustered out as corporal.

Hoge, Holmes. 8/29/1862. 21. PA. Chicago. Clerk. Discharged. 5/24/1863, promotion.

Hollingsworth, Hogarth. 8/29/1862. 20. DE. Chicago. Clerk. 7/6/1865. Transferred to Vet. Res. Corps 9/3/1863.

Howell, Andrew J. 8/29/1862. 29. NY. Chicago. Engineer. 7/10/1865.

Hudson, Everett E. 8/29/1862. 24. OH. Chicago. Grocer. 7/10/1865.

Hudson, Leonard S. 8/29/1862. 25. MA. Chicago. Butcher. 7/10/1865. Mustered out as sergeant.

Husted, William H. 8/29/1862. 18. IL. Chicago. Clerk. 7/10/1865.

Hutchinson, Thomas, M. 8/29/1862. 29. PA. Chicago. Salesman. Discharged 6/23/1863 as corporal.

Hyde, Joseph W. 8/29/1862. 26. VT. Chicago. Bookkeeper. Sergeant; died at Vicksburg 7/25/1863 of dysentery.

Imus, Nelson 8/29/1862. 23. MI. Chicago. Brakeman. Died at Grand Gulf, MS, 5/14/1864, of typhoid fever.

Johnson, William T. 8/29/1862. 22. ME. Chicago. Clerk. 7/10/1865.

Kellerman, Charles. 8/29/1862. 26. Germany. Chicago. Harness man. 7/10/1865.

Kenyon, John W. 8/29/1862. 22. NY. Chicago. Molder. 7/10/1865. Mustered out as corporal.

King, Hudson B. 8/29/1862. 26. NY. Chicago. Molder. Discharged 10/7/1863, disability.

Kitt, John B. 8/29/1862. 30. England. Chicago. Painter. 7/10/1865.

Kloth, Charles H. 8/29/1862. 22. Europe. Chicago. Clerk. 6/17/1865. MOH recipient.

Knight, Don C. 8/29/1862. 20. IL. Chicago. Driver. 7/10/1865.

Knight, William M. 8/29/1862. 21. MI. Chicago. Brakeman. Sergeant; discharged 1/1/1863, disability.

Kretsinger, George. 8/29/1862. 20. NY. Chicago. Clerk. Discharged 5/3/1865, disability. MOH recipient.

Lee, John C. 8/29/1862. 33. OH. Chicago. Grainer. 7/10/1865.

Leet, George K. 8/29/1862. 27. PA. Chicago. Clerk. Discharged 10/29/1863, promotion.

Lewis, Charles R. 8/29/1862. 18. NY. Chicago. Nursery. Died 1/25/1863, at Young's Pt., LA., due to dysentery.

Lunt, John. 8/29/1862. 30. VA. Chicago. Artist. Discharged, disability.

Maguire, Patrick. 8/29/1862. 22. Ireland. Chicago. Driver. 7/10/1865. MOH recipient.

Marble, Danforth. 8/29/1862. 21. NY. Chicago. Printer. 7/10/1865. Mustered out as sergeant.

Mason, John Q. 8/29/1862. 20. IL. Chicago. 8/2/1865.

Mather, Albert G. 8/29/1862. 21. NY. Chicago. Clerk. 7/10/1865. Mustered out as sergeant.

McLean, Edward C. 8/29/1862. 19. PA. Chicago. Machinist. 7/10/1865. Mustered out as corporal.

McNaught, James. 8/29/1862. 29. NY. Chicago. Driver. 7/10/1865.

Meacham, Florus D. Jr. 8/29/1862. 20. NY. Chicago. Clerk. 7/10/1865. Promoted to ordnance sergeant & 2nd lieutenant.

Mendsen, George H. 8/29/1862. 23. PA. Chicago. Clerk. 7/10/1865.

Montgomery, George W. 8/29/1862. 21. NY. Chicago. Bookkeeper. Discharged 2/9/1863, disability.

Moran, Edward. 8/29/1862. 22. Ireland. Chicago. Driver. 7/10/1865.

Moran, Patrick. 8/29/1862. 35. Ireland. Chicago. Driver. Discharged 4/15/1863, disability.

Mortimer, John. 8/29/1862. 20. England. Chicago. Clerk. Died 1/1/1864 at Cairo, IL. from dysentery.

Munn, William. 8/29/1862. 22. IL. Chicago. Grain machinist. 6/16/1865. Camp Ford POW.

Munroe, William H. 8/29/1862. 20. CT. Chicago. Carpenter. 7/10/1865. Mustered out as sergeant.

Nash, Orrin W. 8/29/1862. 20. MA. Chicago. Clerk. 7/10/1865. Mustered out as corporal.

Olcott, Charles E. 8/29/1862. 22. NY. Chicago. Carpenter. 7/10/1865.

Osgood, Edwin S. 8/29/1862. 20. British East India. Chicago. Clerk. 7/10/1865. Mustered out as corporal.

Parker, Fletcher A. 8/29/1862. 20. OH. Chicago. Music. Discharged 2/29/1864, promotion.

Parker, Sanford L. 8/29/1862. 23. NY. Chicago. Policeman. 6/16/1865. Camp Ford POW.

Parsons, John L. 8/29/1862. 24. NJ. Chicago. Clerk. Discharged 8/25/1864, disability.

Patrick, J. Lewis 8/29/1862. 18. OH. Chicago. Printer. Died 1/1/1863 in Memphis due to measles.

Patrick, William. 8/29/1862. 19. PA. Chicago. Clerk. Discharge 11/1/1862, promotion.

Pitts, Florison D. 8/29/1862. 24. ME. Chicago. Bookkeeper. 7/10/1865. Mustered out as bugler.

Pratt, Albert H. 8/29/1862. 27. VT. Chicago. Clerk. Discharged 3/27/1864, disability.

Pratt, Horatio. 8/29/1862. 25. CT. Chicago. Miner. Discharged 2/29/1864, promotion.

Pride, Charles G. 8/29/1862. 28. NY. Chicago. Farmer. Discharged 2/16/1863, disability.

Pride, John C., Jr. 8/29/1862. 37. NY. Chicago. Dentist. Died. Wash., DC asylum 2/4/1865.

Prior, William A. 8/29/1862. 26. Canada. Chicago. Clerk.

Putman, William H. 8/29/1862. 21. MA. Chicago. Clerk. 5/29/1865.

Queal, Orrin H. 8/29/1862. 26. NY. Chicago. Livery dealer. Discharged 3/13/1863, disability.

Ransom, Dick 8/29/1862. 21. VT. Chicago. Printer. Discharged 3/24/1863, disability.

Remington, Stephen J. 8/29/1862. 25. NY. Chicago. Horseman. Discharged 10/17/1862, disability.

Roe, Henry. 8/29/1862. 24. NY. Chicago. Express messenger. Promoted to 2nd lieutenant.

Rogers, Charles A. D. 8/29/1862. 22. NY. Chicago. Clerk. 7/10/1865.

Sampson, Frederick A. 8/29/1862. 27. IL. Chicago. Land agent. 7/10/1865.

Sampson, Joseph A. 8/29/1862. 25. NY. Chicago. RR employee. Discharged 10/18/1862, disability.

Sherman, William W. 8/29/1862. 24. NY. Chicago. Clerk. 7/10/1865.

Sickles, Thomas N. 8/29/1862. 23. IN. Chicago. Editor. Discharged 1/4/1864, promotion.

Simons, Edward, Jr. 8/29/1862. 20. IL. Chicago. Farmer. Discharged 3/2/1863, disability.

Sinclair, James C. 8/29/1862 26. IL. Chicago. Clerk. Promoted to 1st sergeant & 2nd lieutenant.

Squier, Henry. 8/29/1862. 19. IL. Chicago. Driver. Discharged 2/24/1863, disability.

Stees, Gilbert. 8/29/1862. 22. IL. Chicago. Drug industry. 7/10/1865.

Stephens, William G. 8/29/1862. 19. NY. Chicago. Clerk. 7/10/1865. MOH recipient.

Stone, Charles L. 8/29/1862. 21. CT. Chicago. Clerk. 7/10/1865.

Tallmadge, Samuel H. 8/29/1862. 23. IL. Chicago. Salesman 7/10/1865.

Thomas, Edward J. 8/29/1862. 31. NY. Chicago. Express messenger. Sergeant. Discharged 12/5/1864, disability.

Throop, George. 8/29/1862. 23. MI. Chicago. Bookkeeper. Promoted to sergeant & 1st lieutenant. Mortally wounded at Mansfield on 4/8/1864.

Toland, Cornelius H. 8/29/1862. 33. OH. Chicago. Mechanic. Sergeant. Drowned 9/26/1863 while on furlough.

Tripp, Gideon W. 8/29/1862. Age unk. CT. Chicago. Sailor. 6/24/1865.

Turner, Lowell D. 8/29/1862. 24. NY. Chicago. Bookkeeper. Discharged 4/22/1863, disability.

Wadsworth, Elisha L. 8/29/1862. 20. MA. Chicago. Bookkeeper. Discharged 4/10/1864, promotion.

Walton, Lewis M. 8/29/1862. 24. PA. Chicago. Clerk. Discharged 2/16/1865, promotion.

Waters, William H. 8/29/1862. 19. NY. Chicago. Printer. 7/10/1865.

Weeks, Harvey 8/29/1862. 20. IL. Chicago. Clerk. 7/10/1865. Mustered out as wagoner.

Wells, Charles F. 8/29/1862. 20. CT. Chicago. Clerk. Discharged 2/9/1863, disability.

Westbrook, Ira. 8/29/1862. 25. Canada. Chicago. Livery dealer. 7/10/1865. Mustered out as corporal.

White, John H. 8/29/1862. 27. POB unknown. Chicago. Clerk. Corporal. MWIA at Vicksburg, died on 7/5/1863.

Whitney, P. Warren. 8/29/1862. 30. MA. Chicago. RR employee. Sergeant. Discharged 3/2/1863, disability.

Wisenbourne, Joseph. 8/29/1862. Age unk. POB unknown. Chicago. Profession unknown. Deserted 9/8/1862 in Chicago.

Willard, Gardner G. 8/29/1862. 18. IL. Chicago. Clerk. Discharged 2/24/1863, promotion.

Wilson, Hugh G. 8/29/1862. 17. NY. Chicago. Clerk. 7/10/1865.

Wilson, William S. 8/29/1862. 19. MA. Chicago. Student. Discharged 2/16/1863, disability.

Wolcott, Charles W. 8/29/1862. 26. NY. Chicago. Bookkeeper. Discharged 3/11/1864, promotion.

Recruits

Ackersook, Cornelius. 12/31/1863. 38. Holland. Chicago. Farmer. 7/10/1865.

Amish, Frank. 10/12/1864. 19. Germany. Chicago. Clerk. 7/10/1865.

Arnes, Peter. 1/31/1861. 25. Germany. Ford Co. Clerk. 7/10/1865.

Ash, Walter. 5/14/1863. 24. England. Chicago. Clerk. 5/23/1865.

Avery, James E. 10/3/1864. 22. OH. Chicago. Clerk. 7/10/1865.

Ball, Samuel E. ¼/1864. 20. NY. Lockport. Boatman. 7/10/1865.

Barr, Joseph W. 11/6/1862. Chicago. Promoted to 2nd lieutenant.

Barrows, Dennis C. 11/6/1862. 46. NY. Chicago. Farmer. Deserted 7/1/1863.

Bell, John D. 1/31/1864. 45. England. Ford Co. Farmer. 7/10/1865.

Bell, Joshua 1/31/1864. 20. IN. Chicago. Harness work. 7/10/1865. Mustered out Vet. Res. Corps.

Bell, Samuel 1/31/1864. 36. England. Chicago. Farmer. 7/10/1865. Camp Ford POW.

Bennett, Malcom O. 1/31/1864. 22 IL Bloomington. Painter. 7/10/1865.

Benson, Abram H. 8/31/1863. 35 NY Chicago. Merchant. With detachment at muster out.

Binckley, Ohio H. 5/29/1863. 22. OH. Chicago. Soldier. Discharged 1/12/1864, promotion.

Bishop, John. 9/30/1864. 19. Germany. Chicago. Laborer. 7/10/1865.

Bools, Joseph. 1/4/1864. 29. England. Lockport. Laborer. 7/10/1865.

Borgus, Arthur. 9/16/1864. 20. England. Lemont. Laborer. 7/10/1865.

Bostwick, Samuel E. 8/16/1864. Chicago. 8/16/1864. Substitute; assigned to 45th IL.

Bowe, Walter S. 9/29/1864. 44. NY. Chicago. 7/10/1865.

Brainard, George. 1/4/1864. 45. NY. Lockport. Farmer. 7/10/1865.

Brownell, James. 9/22/1864. 22. WI. Lake View. Laborer. 7/10/1865.

Brownell, Otis. 9/22/1864. 19. WI. Lake View. Laborer. 7/10/1865.

Buckley, Benjamin F. 10/4/1864. 20. NY. Chicago. Laborer 7/10/1865.

Buckley, John M. 10/4/1864. Chicago.

Buckwalter, Daniel 12/31/1863. 37. PA. Chicago. Discharged 9/5/1864, disability.

Bugh, John 10/4/1864. 22. Germany. Chicago. Cooper. 7/10/1865.

Burdick, Amos L. 1/4/1864. 19. IL. Lockport. Printer. 7/10/1865. Camp Ford POW.

Carpenter, Isaac T. 12/31/1863. 30. NY. Chicago. Carpenter. KIA 4/8/1864 at Mansfield.

Catin, Thomas. 1/31/1864. 25. NJ. Ford Co. Teacher. 7/10/1865.

Chilson, Erastus C. 12/7/1863. 23. OH. Chicago. Laborer. 7/10/1865.

Coe, William. 2/17/1864. 43. NY. Joliet. Machinist. 7/10/1865.

Colvin, Horace. 8/31/1863. 19. MI. Chicago. Butcher. 7/10/1865.

Cowan, John J. 1/31/1864. 30. Scotland. Chicago. Carpenter. 7/10/1865.

Cranson, John 1/4/1864. 38. MI. Lockport. Farmer. 7/10/1865.

Crosby, John F. 5/28/1863. Springfield.

Cummins, Michael. 10/19/1864. Chicago.

Cutting, John T. 1/31/1864. 20. NY. Ford Co. Clerk. 7/10/1865.

Dale, Peter W. 1/31/1864. 25. PA. Ford Co. Farmer. 6/23/1865.

Derscheid, Christian. 10/7/1864. 32. Germany. Chicago. Baker. 7/10/1865.

Durkin, William. 12/30/1864. Proviso. Deserted 6/21/1865.

Eddleman, Michael. 10/1/1864. Chicago.

Edmonds, George. 10/4/1864. Chicago.

Egan, Thomas. 5/14/1863. 21. NY. Chicago. Clerk. 7/10/1865.

Ensign, Hiland. 5/8/1863. Chicago.

Fay, Ezra S. 12/31/1863. OH. Chicago. Clerk. 7/10/1865.

Fenn, William R. 1/4/1864. 31. England. Lockport. Boatman. 7/10/1865.

Felter, Walter H. 1/4/1864. 18. IL. Lockport. Farmer. Died 7/13/1864 at Camp Ford.

Finland, Michael. 2/29/1864. 40. Ireland. Lemont. Farmer. 7/10/1865.

Fisk, Henry E. 10/29/1862. 21. MA. Chicago. Clerk. 7/10/1865.

Francis, Richard J. 5/1/1863. 44. NY. Chicago. Bookkeeper. Discharged. 7/5/1863.

Gilbert, John A. 12/31/1863. 26. NY. Chicago. Upholsterer. 5/22/1865.

Giles, Thomas. 1/31/1864. 39. Denmark. Chicago. Upholsterer. 7/10/1865.

Gooding, William. 2/29/1864. 19. IL. Lemont. Clerk. 7/10/1865.

Grace, Michael. 8/25/1864. Chicago. Substitute.

Green, Peleg. 12/31/1863. 23. IL. Chicago. Farmer. 7/10/1865. Camp Ford POW.

Hall, Hiland W. 12/31/1863. 28. NY. Chicago. Drover. 7/10/1865. Camp Ford POW.

Halligan, William B. 5/29/1863. 23. IL. Chicago. Engineer. Absent at muster out due to sickness.

Hammersham, James. 1/4/1864. 31. England. Homer. Farmer. 7/10/1865.

Hansbury, Lewis. 1/31/1864. 19. PA. Chicago. Farmer. 7/10/1865.

Harrigan, Michael. 12/31/1863. 26. IN. Chicago. Blacksmith. Discharged 6/16/1865, disability.

Harrup, Thomas. 10/18/1864. 37. England. Chicago. Laborer. 7/10/1865.

Henning, Henry. 10/12/1864. 18. Germany. Chicago. Laborer. 7/10/1865.

Hohn, Christopher. 10/14/1864. 32. Germany. Chicago. Laborer. 7/10/1865.

Hunt, Edmond. 2/29/1864. 28. Ireland. Chicago. Laborer. 7/10/1865.

Immendorf, Daniel. 9/29/1864. 28. Germany. Chicago. Bartender. 7/10/1865.

Ingalls, John. 10/5/1864. 28. Germany. Chicago. Farmer. 7/10/1865.

Jerrold, William. 5/20/1863. Chicago.

Jors, Charles. 9/30/1864. 19. Germany. Chicago. Laborer. 7/10/1865.

Judson, Walter C. 5/14/1863. 22. VT. Chicago. Lawyer. Discharged. 6/3/1865, disability.

Kaegens, Matthew. 9/30/1864. 19. IL. Chicago. Miller. 7/10/1865.

Kent, Benjamin R. 10/10/1864. Chicago.

Kent, Frederick H. 10/8/1864. Chicago.

King, John. 12/31/1863. Chicago. Deserted.

Krewer, John. 9/30/1864. 17. Germany. Chicago. Lawyer. 7/10/1865.

Launneyhall, Frank W. 9/30/1864. 18. Saxony. Chicago. 7/10/1865.

Mann, Flavius C. 3/3/1864. 18. IA. Chicago. Clerk. 7/10/1865.

Mann, Lewis. 10/5/1863. 18. IL. Farmer. 7/10/1865. Camp Ford POW.

Maynard, Harry. 1/6/1865. Thornton.

Maynard, Smith B. 10/4/1864. 26. NY. Chicago. Clerk. 7/10/1865.

McCluggage, Hugh. 5/29/1863. 35. Ireland. Chicago. Accountant. Tr. to Inv. Corps 1/18/1864.

McDonald, Patrick. 9/16/1864. 19. MD. Lemont. Laborer. 7/10/1865.

McHenry, James. 5/15/1863. Chicago.

Miller, Martin S. 1/4/1864. 17. PA. Lockport. Farmer. 7/10/1865.

Mowry, Daniel S. 10/6/1864. Chicago. 5/23/1865.

Nash, James H. 1/31/1864. 37. MA. Ford Co. Farmer. Died 3/2/1864 at New Orleans due to small pox.

Norris, William E. 10/19/1862. 26. MA. Chicago. Merchant. Absent at muster out due to sickness.

Payne, John 5/14/1863. 22. Ireland. Chicago. Carpenter. 7/10/1865.

Perry, George 10/4/1864. 22. England. Chicago. Clerk. 7/10/1865.

Pitts, Nicholas. 1/4/1864. 16. Germany. Lockport. Watchmaker. 7/10/1865.

Powell, Richard. 10/5/1863. 19. Ireland. Bookkeeper. Discharged 6/17/1865, disability.

Reaker, John. 1/31/1864. Chicago.

Redington, Robert. 10/5/1864. 22. MA. Chicago. Druggist. 7/10/1865.

Reed, William. 8/31/1863. 30. Ireland. Laborer. 7/10/1865.

Richardson, William S. 4/8/1864. 17. IL. Bloomington. Clerk. 7/10/1865.

Robb, Alexander G. 5/29/1863. 20. PA. Chicago. Soldier. 7/10/1865.

Roe, Albert J. 2/17/1864. 17. IL. Bloomington. Clerk. 7/10/1865.

Roe, Charles A. 10/21/1864. 20. NH. Chicago. Printer. 7/10/1865.

Rumsey, Arthur W. 5/14/1863. 20. NY. Chicago. Farmer. 7/10/1865. Camp Ford POW.

Ryan, James. 5/14/1863. 23. England. Chicago. Clerk. Discharged 12/2/1863, disability.

Ryan, Philip E. 10/29/1862. 21. OH. Chicago. Bookkeeper. 5/13/1865. Deserted 11/23/1862 to C.S.A.

Sampson, Walter D. 9/29/1862. 24. IL. Chicago. Bookkeeper. Discharged 2/9/1863, disability.

Sheath, John. 12/24/1864. 19. NY. Orland. Farmer. 7/10/1865.

Sheldon, Charles W. 1/4/1864. 16. NY. Lockport. Farmer. 7/10/1865.

Simmons, Henry. 10/11/1864. 20. England. Chicago. Clerk. Discharged 6/5/1865, disability.

Simon, William. 10/12/1864. 18. Germany. Chicago. Laborer. 7/10/1865.

Smith, Albert S. 1/31/1864. 37. MA. Ford Co. 7/9/1865.

Smith, Nelson. 1/31/1864. 37. Canada. Ford Co. Farmer. 7/10/1865.

Snow, Henry H. 10/12/1864. Florence.

Snyder, John. 10/24/1864. Momence.

Standley, George. 10/4/1864. 22. England. Chicago. Machinist. 7/10/1865.

Stanley, Edward B. 1/31/1864. 36. PA. Chicago. Mill worker. 7/10/1865.

Stanton, John. 5/1/1863. Chicago.

Stevens, Thomas H. W. 5/29/1863. 25. MD. Chicago. Farmer. Died 1/1/1865 in New Orleans due to dysentery.

Stone, Elijah. 10/29/1862. 25. PA. Chicago. Cook. 7/10/1865.

Swain, George. 10/5/1864. Northville.

Tanner, Cornelius B. 1/31/1864. 25. RI. Ford Co. Engineer. 7/10/1865.

Tickle, Robert. 9/29/1862. 29. England. Chicago. Blacksmith. 7/10/1865. Mustered out as artificer.

Trambley, David. 1/31/1864. 25. Canada. Ford Co. Laborer. 7/10/1865.

Van Buren, Charles H. 1/4/1864. 15. NY. Lockport. Farmer. 7/10/1865.

Vollman, Jacob. 10/7/1864. 25. NY. Chicago. Machinist. 7/10/1865.

Ward, Waldo. 10/5/1863. 21. IL. Chicago. Farmer. 7/10/1865.

Warner, Matthew. 9/16/1864. 18. NY. Lemont. Druggist. 7/10/1865.

Waterhouse, George E. 5/14/1863. 22. ME. Chicago. Soldier. 7/10/1865.

White, Sedgwick. 10/21/1864. 21. NY. Chicago. Jeweler. 7/10/1865.

White, Thomas. 2/2/1864. 36. Ireland. Waukegan. Shoemaker. 7/10/1865.

Williams, Joseph H. 9/24/1864. Chicago. 7/10/1865.

Wismond, John. 10/12/1864. Florence. 7/10/1865.

Witt, Christ. 10/11/1864. 18. Germany. Chicago. Laborer. 7/10/1865.

Worst, Frederick. 12/29/1864. 18. Prussia. Palatine. Varnisher. 7/10/1865.

Wyman, Franklin C. 10/4/1864. 29. VT. Chicago. Shoemaker. 7/10/1865.

Zenner, Phillip M. 10/6/1864. Chicago. 7/10/1865.

Notes

1. The *Chicago Tribune* covered the confusion surrounding the Chicago Mercantile Battery's (CMB) arrival in its July 4, 1865 issue. The Battery Boys' disappointment seemed justified. One historian who studied Chicago's role in the Civil War wrote, "Although they returned victorious, the boys in blue were cheered more lustily when they went off to war than when they came marching home." The celebrations that the soldiers in the had been reading about while in Louisiana had more to do with veterans who returned at a more favorable time, e.g., during the second Northwest Sanitary Commission Fair. "Mercantile Association," *Chicago Tribune*, July 4, 1865; Theodore J. Karaminski, *Rally 'Round the Flag: Chicago and the Civil War* (Chicago, IL, 1993), xi-xiv.

2. Mary Livermore was actively involved with many community affairs in Chicago and, after the Civil War, would become a prominent postwar leader in the fight for women's rights. She had a long association with the young men in the Mercantile Battery, whom she called "Our Battery Boys." This nickname was also used by others when referring to the Mercantile Association's battery. Regarding Chicago's Civil War artillery batteries, some people assume that if today's Board of Trade funded the Board of Trade Battery, then the Chicago Mercantile Exchange must have supported the Mercantile Battery. The Mercantile Association, however, was unrelated to today's Mercantile Exchange. While the Chicago Board of Trade was a formal organization formed in 1848 to handle the trading of commodities, its counterpart, the Mercantile Association, was more akin to a local group of small-business owners. Many people continue to confuse the Mercantile Battery with the Board of Trade Battery.

At the beginning of the Civil War, it was not uncommon for influential businessmen in major cities to sponsor military units, such as Philadelphia's Corn Regiment. Other examples of special units sponsored in Chicago include the Board of Trade's infantry regiments and the Sturgis Rifles. These business-sponsored military units would be analogous to the sports teams today that are owned by affluent business people and whose stadiums and arenas bear the names of corporations. Cannoneers were often referred to as "redlegs" because of the red stripe on their uniform trousers. Mary Livermore, *My Story of the War: A Woman's Narrative of Four Years Personal Experience* (Hartford, CT, 1889), 374; Karaminski, *Rally 'Round the Flag*, 76; J. W. Vance, *Report of the Adjutant General of the State of Illinois*, vol. 8 (Springfield, IL, 1886), 739-743; *Chicago Evening Journal*, October 14, 1862.

3. During the year that the Civil War began, there was an association of merchants who met to deal with issues related to wholesale products like dry goods (e.g., Cooley, Farwell & Co.), boots and shoes (e.g., Doggett, Bassett & Hills), grocers (e.g., Ladd & Williams), drugs (e.g., B. Mann & Co.), hardware (e.g., Tuttle, Hibbard & Co.), and agricultural tools (e.g., W. H. Kretsinger) rather than wheat and corn commodities that were under the purview of the Board of Trade. Among the members

were also commission merchants like Dickinson & Hosmer, H. B. & A. M. Lewis, Patrick & Co., and Willard Bros. & Co. as well as a grain elevator operator (Ira Y. Munn) and hotelier (Harvey Day). They met at the Tremont Hotel, which is where the Board of Trade met (to make matters more confusing, some of the businessmen belonged to both organizations and many of their places of business were along Water Street). On March 19, 1861, the merchants' group assumed the name of the Mercantile Association of Chicago. (Today's Mercantile Exchange emanated from the 1874 Chicago Produce Exchange and the 1898 Butter and Egg Board rather than from the Civil War-era association of small-business owners.)

Key founding members for the Mercantile Association were George C. Cook, William E. Doggett, Merrill Ladd, W. G. Thompson, and Frederick Tuttle. Article II of their bylaws stated that "This Corporation is for the purpose of concentrating, as far as practicable, the mercantile influence of the community, giving to business a solid and secure basis, and considering and doing all matters affecting mercantile interests." The Mercantile Association and the Board of Trade collaborated on many key issues related to Chicago's future business success such as developing a waterway connection between the Mississippi River and Lake Michigan —and on to the Atlantic Ocean. John W. Arnold's Camp Ford powder horn is part of the author's private collection. I. D. Guyer, *History of Chicago: Commercial and Manufacturing Interests and Industry* (Chicago, IL, 1862), 85, 168-169; Bob Tamarkin, *The Merc: The Emergence of a Global Financial Powerhouse* (Chicago, IL, 1993), 24, 29; Chicago Mercantile Association Bylaws, 1861, Chicago Historical Society (hereafter cited as CHS); *Map of the Business Portion of Chicago* (Chicago, IL, 1862); *The Necessity of a Ship Canal between East and West: Report of the Proceedings of the Board of Trade, The Mercantile Association, and the Business Men of Chicago, February 24, 1863* (Chicago, IL, 1863).

4. The Mercantile Battery's participation in the Vicksburg Campaign is extensively covered in Chapter 6 of this book and includes Lieutenant George Throop's letter—the only known contemporaneous war-time report of his battery's valiant work on May 22 at the Second Texas Lunette—and postwar accounts from Pat White and Will Stephens. Contrary to the report provided by A. J. Smith's son, no Union troops, except those who were prisoners, entered the 2nd Texas Lunette during the May 22 assault. Chicago Mercantile Battery Files, "Capt. White's Bravery," Vicksburg National Military Park (hereafter referred to as VNMP).

5. For details about the Mercantile Battery's Sabine Crossroads casualties, as well as the prisoners who were held at Camp Ford, please see the CMB roster in the Appendix 2.

6. An editorial in the *Chicago Tribune* on June 30, 1864, summarized how Chicago's leaders reacted to what they perceived as mistreatment of their Battery Boys: "'some one has blundered' at New Orleans, and so entrapped these Chicago boys into a real and serious offence, by no less real and serious provocation. The War Department should get to the bottom of the affair." "Chicago Mercantile Battery," *Chicago Tribune*, June 30, 1864.

7. "Mercantile Association," *Chicago Tribune*, July 4, 1865.

8. After the war, members of Taylor's Battery routinely convened as did their counterparts in the Mercantile Battery. They met for anniversary celebrations and also published reminiscences of their company's service at Belmont and Fort Donelson. Pat White attended some of those Taylor's Battery reunions, such as the 1900 meeting at the Union League in Chicago. A Chicago newspaper article, covering the 1902 CMB reunion, chronicled the postwar success of Battery Boys like Will Brown, stating that ". . . many are millionaires and leaders in the commercial and financial world. Among those present last night were: F. D. Meacham, Harvey T. Weeks, W. L. Brown of Pickands, Brown, & Co., Henry C. Gray, Henry L. Bush of the Board of Trade, Joseph Dunne of the Chicago and Northwestern railroad, E. S. Osgood." (The 1902 article reported that only about 25 of the original 153 Battery Boys were still living.) "Last Night's Society," *Chicago Inter-Ocean*, February 11, 1882, 4; Chicago Mercantile Battery Files, "Captain Patrick H. White Is the Guest of Old Comrades," VNMP; Patrick H. White, "Civil War Diary of Patrick H. White. Contributed by J. E. Boos," *Journal of the Illinois Historical Society,* October 1922-January 1923, vol. 15, nos. 3-4, 640-63; Charles Pierce, *Reunions of Taylor's Battery: 18th Anniversary of the Battle of Fort Donelson, February 14, 1880, 25th Anniversary of the Battle of Belmont, November 6, 1886*

(Chicago, IL, 1890); Taylor's Battery reunion document, August 29, 1900, at the Union League in Chicago, Richard Brady Williams Private Collection (RBWPC).

9. The article on the 1902 CMB reunion mentioned that in the early 1890s White acted as a lecturer for two years telling the story of Gettysburg at the Cyclorama exhibit (most likely the one at Chicago). Captain White also had been selected by his surviving soldiers to represent them in working with Captain W. T. Rigby to position the CMB monuments and markers at Vicksburg National Military Park. For information on the Illinois monument at Vicksburg National Military Park, please see *Illinois at Vicksburg* (Chicago, IL, 1907). Chicago Mercantile Battery Files, "Captain Patrick H. White Is the Guest of Old Comrades," VNMP; "Capt. White: Famous Artillery Veteran Visits Scenes of Carnage in '63," *Vicksburg Evening Post*, September 8, 1902; CMB Files, White Correspondence with Rigby, VNMP.

10. The Grand Army of the Republic (GAR), was a formidable socio-political organization that became the largest lobbying group for Union veterans. It was started in Illinois after the war by Dr. Benjamin F. Stephenson—who had served in the 14th Illinois as a surgeon—along with a former governor (Richard J. Oglesby) and General John Logan. For a broad overview of the GAR and its impact on postwar America, please see Stuart McConnell, *Glorious Contentment: The Grand Army of the Republic, 1865-1900* (Chapel Hill, NC, 1992). The Military Order of the Loyal Legion of the United States (MOLLUS) was the second largest veterans' organization in the North. W. F. Beyer and O. F. Keydel, ed., *Deeds of Valor: How America's Civil War Heroes Won the Congressional Medal of Honor* (New York, NY, 2000), 188-190; Mary Dearing, *Veterans in Politics: The Story of the G.A.R.* (Baton Rouge, LA, 1952), 80-85; Robert Girard Carroon and Dana B. Shoaf, *Union Blue: The History of the Military Order of the Loyal Legion of the United States* (Shippensburg, PA, 2001).

11. Israel P. Rumsey, who had been a comrade of Pat White's when they served together in Taylor's Battery, wrote a letter in June 1911 lamenting the loss of Civil War memorabilia at the Chicago Historical Society when "some of its greatest treasures were destroyed in the great conflagration of 1871." The Chicago Historical Society's loss included Abraham Lincoln's original draft of the Emancipation Proclamation, which had been kept in the archives after it was sent to the October 1863 Northwestern Sanitary Commission Fair and used to raise funds for disabled soldiers. Mary Livermore's colleague in the Northwest Sanitary Commission, Jane Hoge, also wrote about the Mercantile Battery in *The Boys in Blue*. Hoge had a personal interest in White's unit: her son, Holmes, was one of the original Battery Boys. Most Civil War enthusiasts and historians, however, do not expect to find details about an artillery company in books written by leaders of the Northwest Sanitary Commission. The absence of indexes in the Livermore and Hoge books has made it difficult for researchers to track down information on the battery. J. Henry Haynie, *The Nineteenth Illinois* (Chicago, IL, 1912), 62; Livermore, *My Story of the War*, 401-402, 430; Jane Hoge, *The Boys in Blue* (New York, NY, 1867), 271-274.

12. Florison D. Pitts, "The Civil War Diary of Florison D. Pitts," *Mid-America xl* (Chicago 1958), 22-63.

13. Patrick H. White, "Civil War Diary of Patrick H. White. Contributed by J. E. Boos," *JIHS xv* (1923), 640-643.

14. Except where otherwise noted, all contemporary accounts used in this book are from the letters of Will Brown of the Chicago Mercantile Battery. William Liston Brown Letters, Chicago Historical Society (CHS).

15. Besides George Throop, among the other 32 Battery Boys who attended Mrs. Livermore's Church of the Redeemer were Francis E. Brackett, Henry O. Brackett, George W. Montgomery, William Munn, Orrin Nash, Florison Pitts, Fred Sampson, Lowell D. Turner, Gardner G. Willard, and Hugh G. Wilson. Additionally, there were at least four young men from the Church of the Redeemer who joined the Board of Trade Battery and more than a half dozen who entered infantry regiments. Livermore, *My Story of the War*, 225-227, 304, 369-374, 387; "A Patriotic Sunday School," *Chicago Tribune*, July 29, 1862; August 29, 1862 letter from George Throop's mother to his sister Mattie, Library of Congress (hereafter LOC).

16. Analysis of 1862-1865 Descriptive Rolls, Descriptive List and Order Book for the Chicago Mercantile Battery, Regimental Bound Volumes and Descriptive Books of Volunteer Organizations, Records of the Adjutant General's Office, 1780s–1917, Record Group 94 (Descriptive List and Order Book for the CMB), National Archives and Records Administration (hereafter NARA).

17. Patrick H. White Collection, RBWPC; White, "Civil War Diary of Patrick H. White," *JIHS xv* (1923), 640; Descriptive List and Order Book for the CMB, Analysis of Descriptive Rolls, NARA; Vance, *Report of the Adjutant General of the State of Illinois,* vol. 8, 739-743.

18. St. Joseph was located on Lake Michigan's strategic shipping route between Chicago and Detroit. It benefited from being a major stop on the stagecoach road linking these gateways to the emerging Northwest, and thus provided a conduit to the farming and lumber region of southwestern Michigan and northern Indiana. Will Brown's father had been one of St. Joseph's founders and wrote about making the pioneering move from New York to Michigan in a manuscript entitled "Incidents of the Life of Hiram A. Brown," which was passed on to his sons. Reflecting on the small village where he set up a successful shipping business, the elder Brown stated, "I arrived in St. Joseph on the fourth day of July, 1834. . . . There was a small population and less comfort....The buildings consisted of two warehouses on the bank of the river, one of which I accepted." After a decision was made for the major railroad to bypass the town, Will's father decided to move his family to Chicago in 1848. Hiram's fears about St. Joseph materialized as the town plunged into an economic depression and its population dwindled to seven hundred people. He did not return to the city until fourteen years later when it was being resurrected as the "Great Fruit Belt of Michigan. Orville W. Coolidge, *A Twentieth Century History of Berrien County, Michigan* (Chicago, IL, 1906), 176-180; J. S. Morton, *Reminiscences of the Lower St. Joseph River Valley* (Benton Harbor, MI, n.d.), 30-31; *Historical Sketch of St. Joseph* (1896), 11; *History of Berrien and Van Buren Counties, Michigan* (Philadelphia, PA, 1880), 312, 315; "Obituary: Hiram Brown," *St. Joseph Herald,* August 25, 1883; Harry Ellsworth Cole, *Stagecoach and Tavern Tales of the Old Northwest* (Cleveland, OH, 1930).

19. Donald L. Miller, *City of the Century: The Epic of Chicago and the Making of America* (New York, NY, 1997), 89-91; Bessie Louise Pierce, *A History of Chicago,* vol. 2 (New York, NY, 1940), 3-5, 35-37; Frederic William Bond, *A Little History of a Great City* (Chicago, IL, 1930).

20. Henry M. Brown and Hiram Liberty Brown Pension Files, Pension and Bounty and Application Files Based Upon Service in the Civil War and Spanish-American War ("Civil War and Later"), Records of the Department of Veteran Affairs, 1773-1985, Record Group 15, NARA; George H. Brown, *Record of Service of Michigan Volunteers in the Civil War, 1861-1865,* vol. 12 (Kalamazoo, MI, nd), 1-2; George H. Brown, *Record of Service of Michigan Volunteers in the Civil War, 1861-1865,* vol. 19 (Kalamazoo, MI, nd), 1-3, 17.

21. For an overview of the Chicago Mercantile Battery's service in the Civil War, please see T. M. Eddy, *The Patriotism of Illinois: A Record of the Civil and Military History of the State in the War for the Union,* vol. 2 (Chicago, IL, 1866), 670-672.

CHAPTER 1

1. "The Great War Meeting," *Chicago Tribune,* July 28, 1862; Karamanski, *Rally 'Round the Flag,* 108-109.

2. "The Great War Meeting," *Chicago Tribune,* July 28, 1863.

3. *Ibid.*

4. Frederick Frances Cook, *Bygone Days in Chicago: Recollections of the "Garden City" of the Sixties* (Chicago, IL, 1910), 120.

5. Early in 1862, the Cook County Board of Supervisors levied a special tax to create funding for $60 bounties to entice new enlistees into the army. The Board of Trade raised $200,000 for bounties, which were used to sponsor artillery battery and infantry regiments. "The Great War Meeting," *Chicago Tribune,* July 28, 1862; "The Bounties," *Chicago Tribune,* July 30, 1862; Karamanski, *Rally 'Round the Flag,* 109-110; James M. McPherson, *Battle Cry of Freedom: The Civil War Era* (New York, NY, 1988), vi; Pierce, *A History of Chicago,* vol. 2, 273-274.

6. A special meeting of the Mercantile Association was held at 9:00 a.m. on Monday to develop a strategy to recruit troops, capitalizing on the excess funds collected by the Board of Trade. In preparation, an advertisement had been run on Saturday, July 26, in the *Chicago Tribune* announcing the Association's intention to sponsor a regiment. A businessman named Tyrell was the program chair (from Wright & Tyrell real estate/notary). The merchants initially planned to support an entire infantry regiment, "The Mercantile Association Regiment," much as the Board of Trade was doing. Walter B. Scates, F. H. Bowen, and W. H. Hinsdale were selected to represent the Mercantile Association in discussions with the Board of Trade, which had a surplus of recruitment funds (the donors' names and amounts given were listed in the *Chicago Tribune*). The Board of Trade had generated more than $20,000 in donations in 24 hours—and was well on its way to raising over $50,000 by August 4. That evening, the Association held a full meeting, discussing their prospective military unit in more detail. They considered creating an infantry unit with six companies, which would be led by a man named Sloan. This idea was eventually rejected due to concerns about the proposed leader. It was decided, instead, to form an artillery battery. Because both the Mercantile Association and Board of Trade formed batteries at the same time, there has always been confusion about the two business-sponsored units. While the boys in the Mercantile Battery served primarily in Mississippi and Louisiana, their friends in the Board of Trade Battery fought in Tennessee and Georgia. The Board of Trade's list of major engagements included Stones River, Chickamauga (their battery fired the first and last cannon shot in the battle), Chattanooga, and Nashville. They also took part in the Atlanta Campaign and Major General James H. Wilson's Alabama raid. "Mercantile Association War Meeting," *Chicago Tribune*, July 26, 1863; "Mercantile Association: Special War Meeting," *Chicago Tribune*, July 29, 1862; "Board of Trade Subscriptions," *Chicago Tribune*, August 1, 1862; *Historical Sketch of the Chicago Board of Trade* (Chicago, IL, 1902), 44-48; *Chicago Tribune*, August 4, 1862.

7. "The 'Coffee Mill' Gun," *Chicago Tribune*, July 30, 1862; "Military Notices," *Chicago Tribune*, August 1, 1862.

8. Karaminski, *Rally 'Round the Flag*, 109.

9. Patrick H. White Civil War Pension File, NARA.

10. *Ibid.*; White, "Civil War Diary of Patrick H. White," *JIHS*, 641; Charles B. Kimball, *History of Battery "A" First Illinois Light Artillery Volunteers* (Chicago, IL, 1899), 9-10; *Chicago Tribune*, May 14, 1860.

11. Stephen Douglas died at his home in Springfield, Illinois, on June 3, 1861. White, "Civil War Diary of Patrick H. White," *JIHS*, 641-642; Patricia Faust, ed., *Historical Times Illustrated Encyclopedia of the Civil War* (New York, NY, 1986), 225.

12. *Ibid.*, 643-645; Eddy, *The Patriotism of Illinois*, 171-172; Jerry Ponder, *The Civil War Battle of Fredericktown, Missouri* (Independence, MO, 1995), 87-92.

13. White, "Civil War Diary of Patrick H. White," *JIHS*, 646-648; Nathaniel Cheairs Hughes, Jr., *The Battle of Belmont: Grant Strikes South* (Chapel Hill, NC, 1991), 125-126, 202.

14. White, "Civil War Diary of Patrick H. White," *JIHS*, 649-651. For a comprehensive review of the Union victories at Forts Henry and Donelson, see Benjamin Franklin Cooling, *Forts Henry and Donelson: The Key to the Confederate Heartland* (Knoxville, TN, 1987).

15. Walter Scates, April 9, 1862 letter, RBWPC; Wiley Sword, *Shiloh: Bloody April* (Dayton, OH, 2001), 131, 192, 193, 206-208; Nathaniel Cheairs Hughes, Jr., *The Pride of the Confederate Artillery: The Washington Artillery in the Army of Tennessee* (Baton Rouge, LA, 1997), 24-29.

16. Sword, *Shiloh*, 210; Walter Scates, April 9, 1862 letter, RBWPC.

17. White, "Civil War Diary of Patrick H. White," *JIHS*, 655; "Presentation," *Chicago Tribune*, May 3, 1862.

18. Karamanski, *'Rally Round the Flag,* 86-89; Ulysses S. Grant, *Personal Memoirs,* vol. 1 (New York, NY 1885), 376-377, 392-396.

19. Shelby Foote, *The Civil War, A Narrative: Fort Sumter to Perryville* (New York, 1958), 247-253, 262-269; Stephen W. Sears, *To the Gates of Richmond: The Peninsula Campaign* (New York, NY, 1992), 3-5, 9.

20. *Ibid.*, 23, 343-355.

21. Cook, *Bygone Days in Chicago*, 23-25.

22. Descriptive List and Order Book, Chicago Mercantile Battery, Descriptive Roll, NARA.

23. The Mercantile Battery trained outside the Camp Douglas complex, calling their area "Camp Doggett" in honor of William E. Doggett, one of their Mercantile Association benefactors. The merchants presented Lieutenant David R. Crego with a "sword, sash, belt, and pistol, the gift of the Mercantile Association. The company was drawn up in a hollow square, and a final presentation of the articles was made by Captain Charles G. Cooley." The ceremony was listed in the newspaper as occurring at "Camp Doggett." "Presentation," *Chicago Evening Journal*, October 8, 1862.

24. The *Union Picket Guard* was a hand-made bulletin designed in a newspaper format and produced by soldiers in the Chicago Light Artillery and 9th Illinois Infantry for their families and friends in Chicago; they were two of the first Illinois regiments to travel through Cairo. Pitts Diary, 24; John McMurray Lansden, *A History of the City of Cairo* (Chicago, IL, 1910), 106; *The Union Picket Guard,* vol.1, no. 1 (September 14, 1861), Paducah, Kentucky, Boston Public Library (hereafter cited as BPL).

25. Amos G. Throop Collection, November 11, 1862 letter from son George to his friends, LOC; Pitts Diary, 25.

26. Lieutenant General Winfield Scott, who was the Union general-in-chief when the Civil War broke out, developed the Anaconda Plan in the spring of 1861, named after the South American snake that crushes its victims. Blockading western rivers—especially the Mississippi River—was a key element of Scott's plan to cut off the Confederacy's trade. According to historian Edwin C. Bearss, "The military history of the Vicksburg Campaign, I discovered, began with the mid-May 1862 advance up the Mississippi from New Orleans by Flag-Officer David G. Farragut's ocean-going squadron and the downriver thrust from Memphis by Flag-Officer Charles H. Davis' river gunboats following the June 6 surrender of Memphis." Charles Dana Gibson, *Assault and Logistics: Union Army Coastal and River Operations, 1861-1866* (Camden, ME, 1995), xx-xxi; Frances H. Kennedy, ed., *The Civil War Battlefield Guide, 2nd edition* (Boston, 1998), 56-58; Chester G. Hearn, *Ellet's Brigade: The Strangest Outfit of All* (Baton Rouge, LA, 2000), 2-38; Edwin Cole Bearss, *The Campaign for Vicksburg,* vol. 1 (Dayton, OH, 1985), 5-6.

27. "Affairs at Memphis," *Harper's Weekly*, June 28, 1862, 403.

28. Charles G. Cooley became the first captain of the CMB when it was mustered into service. The battery was also known as the "Mercantile Battery, Chicago," "Cooley's Battery," "Cooley's Independent Battery Light Artillery," "Independent Battery, 4th," and "Doggett's Guards." Will Brown was part of the initial group of recruits in the summer of 1862. This letter is the first installment in a series of 132 weekly letters Will would send during the war to his father, Hiram A. Brown, who had moved from Chicago back home to St. Joseph, Michigan. Based on his letter, Will thought he was going to be mustered in on Saturday, August 23. Though already enlisted, he did not muster in until Friday, August 29. With his extensive background in import/export businesses, coupled with local political clout, Hiram Brown was working in 1862 as the Deputy Collector of Customs for the port of St. Joseph. Either in that role or in a separate business, Hiram was also involved with the shipping of railroad ties. St. Joseph had become one of the leading railroad-tie producers in the nation. By 1868, some 70,000 railroad ties had been exported from Will's hometown. *Illinois Military Units in the Civil War* (Springfield, IL, 1962), 43-48; J. W. Vance, *Report of the Adjutant General of the State of Illinois,* vol. 8 (Springfield, IL, 1886), 739, 744; "Obituary: Hiram Brown," *St. Joseph Herald,* August 25, 1883; Morton, *Reminiscences of the Lower St. Joseph River Valley*, 28-29.

29. The Mercantile Association of Chicago was an organization of prominent merchants who met regularly to address commercial issues. The group of small businessmen had previously been known

as the Merchants' Association. On March 19, 1861, the new organization was officially formed as the Mercantile Association. Members of the Mercantile Association were closely aligned with their counterparts in the Board of Trade—one of the most powerful and affluent business groups in the nation—and they worked together to sponsor prestigious military units. Both groups helped to pay for soldiers' equipment and supplemental bounties. There were 153 young men in the first wave of Mercantile Battery recruits. Mercantile Association of Chicago Bylaws, March 19, 1861, CHS; Eddy, *The Patriotism of Illinois,* vol. 2, 670.

30. Many of the Mercantile Battery's first soldiers were from prominent families, a fact Pat White notes in his memoirs. William Patrick, Charles E. Olcott, and Danforth (Dan) Marble were three of the young men who enlisted alongside 20-year-old Will Brown in August 1862 for a three-year stint in the CMB. Patrick is noted in the battery's Descriptive Roll as having enlisted at the age of 19. He had been a clerk and appears to have worked with Will Brown at the Patrick & Co. commission-merchant business on 224 S. Water Street. Olcott was 22 years old and originally from Utica, New York, where he had worked as a carpenter. Marble was also from New York (Buffalo) and enlisted at the age of 21, having worked as a printer. Chicago had a population of about 100,000 when the war started and approximately 15,000 of its male residents would fight for the Union. Patrick H. White Collection, RBWPC; Descriptive List and Order Book for the CMB, Descriptive Roll, NARA; Cook, *Bygone Days in Chicago*, 30; *Map of the Business Portion of Chicago* (Chicago, IL, 1862).

31. Two days after Will sent this letter to his father, the *St. Joseph Traveler* newspaper carried an article about the town's newest export. The article noted that even though "the wheat of this country is celebrated for its good quality and [is] much sought after by millers," peaches were emerging as the most valuable crop in St. Joseph. Farmers had discovered that the area's soil and temperate climate were especially well suited for growing fruit; approximately $500 was being realized for each peach-orchard acre around St. Joseph. The writer also forecast in his October 1, 1862, story that about 20,000 baskets of peaches would be shipped from St. Joseph during Will's first year in the army. In 1868, the export of peaches had grown to more than half a million packages. "St. Joseph and Its Fruit Orchards," *St. Joseph Traveler*, October 1, 1862; "Gazetteer and Business Directory of the State of Michigan," *St. Joseph Traveler,* January 15, 1863; Morton, *Reminiscences of the Lower St. Joseph River Valley,* 28-29

32. When the battery members left Chicago, they took with them a Newfoundland and a small shepherd as mascots, the latter named "Doggie Doggett" in honor of their training camp set up in the fall of 1861, south of Chicago and outside Camp Douglas. The camps were built on 60 acres donated by the estate of Stephen A. Douglas—the adversary of Abraham Lincoln in the 1858 Illinois senatorial election and its famed debates—and located in an area near today's University of Chicago. Camp Douglas was bounded by 31st Street on the north, 33rd Street on the south, Cottage Grove Avenue on the east, and Giles Avenue on the west. Livermore, *My Story of the War*, 390; Karaminski, *Rally 'Round the Flag*, 83.

33. Colonel Joseph H. Tucker helped to establish Camp Douglas as a formal training installation for Chicago recruits. Illinois Governor Richard Yates appointed Tucker to be its first commandant; he managed the camp's eventual transformation into a prison for Southern troops. Camp Douglas initially housed Union soldiers who, having been captured by the Confederates, were now on parole and waiting to be exchanged. In the early days of the war, Union and Confederate authorities created a cartel to handle the prisoner-exchange process. Privates were exchanged "one for one" while officers had a higher replacement value, e.g., up to 60 privates for a general. As the parole process became more stringent, Camp Douglas became a prison primarily for Confederate soldiers captured in Western battles. By the end of 1862, Brigadier General Jacob Ammen had replaced Tucker as the prison commandant. *Ibid.*, 83-83, 142-144.

34. Colonel Dixon Miles was accused of drunkenness during the First Battle of Bull Run, but a court of inquiry attributed his inebriation to a doctor's prescription. Miles was relegated to a non-combat position as the commander at Harpers Ferry and of the Railroad Brigade, where his political gamesmanship would prove disastrous for him. He initially reported to Major General John

Wool. Both Miles and Wool belonged to the Regular Army, an association Miles used as leverage with Wool to undercut the authority of his immediate commander, Brigadier General Julius White, a citizen soldier. Wool decided to leave Dixon Miles in charge of Harpers Ferry and sent White to nearby Martinsburg. Julius White, whose brigade remained at Harpers Ferry under Miles' command, complained about his assignment to Major General Henry Halleck, the Federal general-in-chief. Halleck, however, ordered him to let Miles handle the situation at Harpers Ferry, which was then vulnerable to a Confederate attack. On September 13-15, Miles mismanaged the town's defense, allowing Confederate Major General Thomas "Stonewall" Jackson to orchestrate a major strategic victory on his way to Antietam by capturing Harpers Ferry and about 11,000 Union soldiers. As Miles attempted to end the siege by raising a white flag of surrender, a fluke cannon shot mortally wounded him. Miles botched the defense of Harpers Ferry so badly that an unconfirmed rumor claimed he had been killed by one of his own troops, a notion that explains Will's comment "all say that Col. Miles was a traitor and not killed soon enough." The Union prisoners were sent from Harpers Ferry to Camp Douglas in Chicago to await exchange. Chester G. Hearn, *Six Years of Hell: Harpers Ferry During the Civil War* (Baton Rouge, LA, 1996), 110-112, 126-129, 186-189.

35. Born in May 1825 in Scotland, William Scott Stewart became a commission merchant and specialized in produce (Stewart's office was at the Board of Trade building). After joining the Union army in 1862, he was promoted twice before the CMB was mustered in. His first promotion was to that of major in the 65th Illinois Infantry—the "Scotch Regiment"—on March 15, 1862. Immediately thereafter, he became the regiment's lieutenant colonel. The 65th Illinois had the misfortune of being sent to Harpers Ferry in 1862, where it served under Colonel Dixon Miles. Stewart and his men were captured when Stonewall Jackson forced Miles to surrender. The regiment recovered from this dubious start, and Stewart was promoted to brevet brigadier general on March 13, 1865. Having survived the perils of the Civil War, Stewart entered a seemingly benign profession—becoming a schoolteacher—but was accidentally killed in a freak railroad accident on December 6, 1895. *Chicago Tribune*, May 11, 1861; Roger D. Hunt & Jack R. Brown, *Brevet Brigadier Generals in Blue* (Gaithersburg, MD, 1990), 588.

36. After Abraham Lincoln was elected president, he appointed Julius White collector of customs in Chicago. After the defeat of the Union army at First Bull Run in July 1861, White organized the 37th Illinois Infantry and served as its colonel. White's effective handling of his men at the Battle of Pea Ridge in Arkansas brought him a promotion to brigadier general on June 9, 1862. Assigned to supersede Dixon Miles at Harpers Ferry, Julius White fell victim to political wrangling and ended up inappropriately stationed at Martinsburg, without his brigade. He rejoined his command at Harpers Ferry, where he was captured after Miles bungled the town's defense. As a result of that catastrophe, White, who was technically Miles' superior, was arrested. When an examining commission reviewed the facts, White was exonerated and assigned to command a division at Knoxville, Tennessee, under Major General Ambrose E. Burnside. White's friendship with Lincoln undoubtedly helped him to escape the backlash from the Harpers Ferry fiasco. Hearn, *Six Years of Hell*, 126-129; Ezra J. Warner, *Generals in Blue: Lives of the Union Commanders* (Baton Rouge, LA, 1964), 556-557.

37. Will's older brother Henry was in Cincinnati with his comrades from the 19th Michigan Infantry. They did not participate in the Battle of Perryville, the pivotal engagement of Confederate General Braxton Bragg's invasion of Kentucky. After the battle, which took place on October 8, 1862, Bragg withdrew to Tennessee. While these events were transpiring, the 19th Michigan was in Ohio, preparing to defend Cincinnati in case the Union army was unable to halt the Confederate advance through Kentucky. William M. Anderson, *They Died to Make Men Free: A History of the 19th Michigan Infantry in the Civil War* (Dayton, OH, 1994), 66-67.

38. Delia, a school teacher, was Will's sister-in-law and the wife of Henry Brown. Belle was Will's younger sister. *History of Berrien and Van Buren Counties, Michigan*, 322.

39. Will expressed the Battery Boys' initial displeasure with Cooley as captain. In Memphis, after the Tallahatchie March, they would begin discussing how to get rid of him. In his October 12, 1862 letter, Will alluded to the perceived power the battery members could exert by contacting their

sponsors in Chicago to make a change in leadership. This same attitude eventually created an extremely difficult situation for the artillerists who, after refusing to shoulder infantry arms in New Orleans in May 1864, were accused of mutiny.

40. A typical Union light artillery battery like the CMB possessed six guns, 120 men, 120 horses, 12 limbers, six caissons, a traveling forge, a battery wagon, and two supply wagons. The captain of the battery would divide the unit into three sections: the right section, center section, and left section. Each section, commanded by a lieutenant, had two guns. Each gun—with its accompanying men, equipment, materiel, animals, etc.—constituted a squad or platoon led by a sergeant. Will's organizational and administrative skills, developed as a clerk for the Board of Trade, enabled him to assume a position of responsibility in his platoon. Ross M. Kimmel, "A Well-drilled Artillery Battery. . . ", *America's Civil War*, July 2001, 12.

41. Will did not know Henry's regiment had left its training camp in Dowegiac, Michigan, and was in Ohio. As noted earlier, the 19th Michigan Infantry did not participate in the Battle of Perryville.

42. Alexander Hamilton Morrison was a successful businessman and politician in St. Joseph. In 1861, Lincoln offered him a position as commissary of subsistence in the army, but Morrison declined. The following year he became Collector of Internal Revenue for the second district of Michigan. In this role, Morrison selected Hiram A. Brown—a fellow staunch Republican—as his customs collector for the port of St. Joseph, a position Will's father would hold for many years. *History of Berrien and Van Buren Counties, Michigan*, 314a.

43. Each platoon with its single cannon was commanded by a sergeant, or "chief of the piece," who typically had two corporals as his assistants. His crew was comprised of a gunner and eight cannoneers. Will was assigned to the No. 6 position, which meant, during combat, he was stationed behind the limber containing the ammunition chest. Will's job was to select the rounds his gunner requested, calculate distances, prepare the charges, and set the fuses on case shot and shells. He would then place the rounds in the haversack of the man assigned to the No. 5 position, who took them back to the cannon to be fired. The soldier assigned to the No. 7 position stood at the rear of the caisson and assisted Will while the No. 8 man stayed nearby to help, too. The soldier in the No. 1 position was the sponger, who cleaned the gun's barrel and rammed the charge (cartridge) to the back of the tube. The artillerist in the No. 2 position took a finished charge from the No. 5 man and placed it in the muzzle of the gun. The soldier assigned to the No. 3 position pressed his leather thumbstall over the gun's vent during sponging and ramming; he also pricked a hole in the projectile's powder bag with a priming wire. The gunner (sometimes a noncommissioned officer) ordered the man in the No. 6 position, such as Will Brown, to bring the charges and fuses he needed from the ammunition chest. The gunner also told the man in the No. 4 position when to fire the cannon.

When the gun was ready to be fired, the No. 4 man attached the primer to a lanyard (a wooden handle attached to a 12-foot cord and a hook), which he then pulled, causing the primer to explode down the vent and ignite the powder. The gunner also issued the following commands: "From Battery—Load—In Battery—Point—Ready—Fire" with the sequence continuing until the officer in charge shouted "Cease Firing." Rates of artillery fire varied with the type of cannon used and the cartridges being fired. Properly trained, the Mercantile Battery would be able to fire 1-2 rounds per minute. Postilions such as Charley Olcott and Dan Marble rode the lead horse of each team, which pulled the limbers and caissons. Dean S. Thomas, *Cannons: An Introduction to Civil War Artillery* (Arendtsville, PA, 1985), 3; Arthur W. Bergeron, Jr. and Lawrence L. Hewitt, *Boone's Louisiana Battery: A History and Roster* (Baton Rouge, LA, 1986), 47-49; Warren Ripley, *Artillery and Ammunition of The Civil War* (Charleston, SC, 1984), 223-228.

44. The Battle of Davis Bridge occurred on October 5 along the border between Tennessee and Mississippi. Federal troops under major generals Stephen Hurlbut and Edward O. C. Ord engaged the lead elements of Major General Earl Van Dorn's Confederate army, which was retreating from its defeat at the Battle of Corinth (October 3-4, 1862). Will's younger brother, Lib, was in the 12th Michigan Infantry, which took part in the action. The Unionists suffered some 500 casualties in the battle. Among them was Charles L. Bissel, who had enlisted in the 12th Michigan a month after Lib.

Bissel died of disease at Bolivar, Tennessee, on October 26, 1862. Peter Cozzens, *The Darkness of War: The Battles of Iuka and Corinth* (Chapel Hill, NC, 1997), 280-290; The American Civil War Research Database, Historical Data Systems, Inc.

45. The *Diadem* was one of the earliest steamboats on the Mississippi River to transport Union army troops such as the CMB. It was not used in Sherman's massive flotilla from Memphis to the Chickasaw Bayou. The *Diadem* would reappear on the Mercantile Battery's Civil War journey during April 1864 when it was being used to transport Maj. Gen. Nathaniel Banks' troops on the Red River. Charles Dana Gibson, *Assault and Logistics*, 368.

46. The Illinois Central Railway ["the IC"] offered the only major access by land from Chicago to Cairo. The railroad bisected the swamp that locked in the town on a sliver of land jutting between the confluence of the Mississippi and Ohio rivers. "The Camp at Cairo, Illinois," *Harper's Weekly*, June 1, 1861, 350.

47. The 72nd Illinois was an infantry regiment sponsored by the Chicago Board of Trade. Although its men mustered in at the same time as the CMB, they were immediately ordered to Paducah on September 6, 1862—one year after Brigadier General Ulysses S. Grant led a bloodless takeover of that Kentucky city. From there, the 72nd Illinois moved on to Columbus, Kentucky, where they were stationed when Will and the rest of the Battery Boys arrived in November 1862 from Cairo. Across the river was Belmont, Missouri, where, a year earlier (on November 7, 1861), Grant obtained his first significant Civil War combat experience in a confused battle against Confederate troops under Major General Leonidas Polk and Brigadier General Gideon Pillow. The American Civil War Research Database, Historical Data Systems, Inc. For a comprehensive study of the engagement at Belmont, see Hughes, *The Battle of Belmont.*

48. In February 1862, Federal Brigadier General John Pope led his Army of the Mississippi south through Missouri. Their objective was to attack New Madrid, a town on the Mississippi River where some of the Confederates had fled after Columbus was abandoned. On March 13, the Confederates evacuated New Madrid and its three forts, which Pope had invested for almost two weeks. Pope's next target was Island No. 10, which was the "tenth island" south of the confluence of the Mississippi and Ohio rivers at Cairo. It was a Confederate stronghold and was strategically situated at a hairpin turn on the Mississippi River. Flag Officer Andrew H. Foote, after playing a pivotal role in the recent capture of Fort Henry and a lesser role in the surrender of Fort Donelson, attacked with his gunboats from the north while Pope's men advanced up along the Missouri shore from New Madrid. On April 4, Foote sent some steamboats through a canal—built by Pope's engineers to bypass the Confederate fort. In addition, two gunboats ran down the Mississippi River, under cover of a storm, to assist the Union army. The aggressive Pope used the steamboats to transport his men across the river to attack the Confederate position while Foote's gunboats lent support to the attack. On April 7, Confederate Brigadier General William W. Mackall agreed to a formal surrender of some 7,000 men plus approximately 52 pieces of heavy artillery and numerous field guns. John Pope's successful investment of Island No. 10 was accomplished without a single combat loss to the Union side. Pope had already been promoted to major general for his success at New Madrid. Pope joined Grant as a Federal general whose early Western victories catapulted him to national prominence; his aggressiveness, however, would eventually transmute into recklessness and subsequent embarrassment at the Battle of Second Bull Run. McPherson, *Battle Cry of Freedom*, 415; E. B. Long, *The Civil War Day by Day: An Almanac, 1861-1865* (New York, NY, 1971*)*, 176-178, 185, 196; Foote, *The Civil War, A Narrative: Fort Sumter to Perryville*, 307-314; Kennedy, *The Civil War Battlefield Guide*, 56-57.

49. After Shiloh, while Pope's army was diverted to help Major General Henry Halleck pursue the retreating Confederates in Mississippi, Captain Charles H. Davis spearheaded the ongoing Union naval effort to reopen the "Father of Waters." Davis had replaced Flag Officer Andrew H. Foote, who had not fully recovered from the serious wound he received during the February 14 assault on Fort Donelson. Consequently, Foote, on May 9, relinquished control of his "brown-water navy" to Davis, who was to receive assistance from a somewhat unorthodox source. The Ram Fleet joined the Union effort to win control of the Mississippi River. Charles Ellet was a prominent engineer prior to

the Civil War, noted for his work in designing suspension bridges. After the battle between *Monitor* and *Virginia* [formerly *Merrimac*] on March 9, 1862, Ellet convinced Secretary of War Edwin Stanton to allow him to buy steamboats, convert them into "battering rams," and assist the Union navy on the Mississippi River. He had developed his concept based on the ancient warfare practice of mounting rams on the prows of oar-driven galleys. Ellet wanted to reapply the technique to modern steamships.

With Stanton's permission, and his independent War Department resources, Ellet purchased three large side-wheeler steamers and one smaller one, converting all of them into "rams." His Ram Fleet also included smaller support vessels. The first of the large steamers he acquired—the *Queen of the West*—would become famous during the campaign against Vicksburg, and Will Brown would tell his father about her exploits. In designing his rams, Ellet implemented protective measures that included barricading the boiler rooms on each of the side-wheeler steamers and encasing the pilothouses in iron. To streamline the boats, the upper decks of the rams were cleared away. Speed was an important part of Ellet's design, since his boats carried no cannon and were meant to destroy enemy vessels by outmaneuvering and ramming them. On June 5, Ellet raced ahead of Captain Davis' gunboats to try his rams out against the Confederate river fleet at Fort Pillow. He was surprised to discover the enemy warships had moved farther south to Memphis. Hearn, *Ellet's Brigade*, 2-38; Long, *The Civil War Day by Day*, 484.

50. "Secesh" was a slang word that Union loyalists pejoratively used to deride secessionists. Web Garrison, *The Encyclopedia of Civil War Usage: An Illustrated Compendium of the Everyday Language of Soldiers and Civilians* (Nashville, TN, 2001), 222.

CHAPTER 2

1. As historian Edwin C. Bearss noted, "Never again would the South be this close to victory." Grant, *Personal Memoirs of U. S. Grant,* vol. 1, 395, 421; Bearss, *The Campaign for Vicksburg,* vol.1, 21.

2. Grant had more than 56,000 troops in his three major districts—Corinth, Jackson (Tennessee), and Memphis. They were organized into what became known as the Army of the Tennessee. He could only mobilize about 30,000 effectives for an attack against Pemberton because his department was so spread out and he had many miles of railroad tracks to protect and maintain. Governor Richard Yates of Illinois followed through with his commitment to send more troops. As Bearss noted, "During the period November 6-15, these infantry units reached Memphis: the 93d, 113th, 114th, 116th, 117th, 120th, 127th, 130th Illinois Infantry Regiments...and the Chicago Mercantile Battery [which left Chicago on November 8]." Grant, *Personal Memoirs of U. S. Grant*, vol.1, 423; Bearss, *The Campaign for Vicksburg,* vol.1, 22, 25, 32, 59.

3. Major General Earl Van Dorn had gotten into trouble with the governor of Mississippi when, as Bearss wrote, "he had declared martial law in a number of counties." Pressed to replace him, Jefferson Davis chose John C. Pemberton, a Northerner who commanded the Department of South Carolina and Georgia. Headquartered at Charleston, Pemberton had also been having problems with South Carolina's Governor Francis W. Pickens. Davis promoted Pemberton to lieutenant general, sending him west while transferring General P. G. T. Beauregard to Charleston. Pemberton arrived in the middle of October to take charge of his new Department of Mississippi and East Louisiana. He found his troops demoralized by Van Dorn's recent defeat at Corinth. Immediately after arriving at his Jackson headquarters, Pemberton was told that Grant was preparing to march Federal troops into northern Mississippi. Major Samuel H. Lockett was his military engineer who had accomplished, in the words of historians William L. Shea and Terrence J. Winschel, the "task of constructing a semicircular line of earthworks around Vicksburg." This was a considerable achievement. As Shea and Winschel wrote, "The terrain was rugged beyond description; hillsides were covered by dense forests, and ravines were choked with canebrakes." Pemberton likely summoned Lockett to develop his new defensive line behind the Tallahatchie River. With the assistance of local slave labor, rapid

progress was made in fortifying the Confederates' new position. *Ibid.*, 43-45, 51-52; William L. Shea and Terrence J. Winschel, *Vicksburg Is the Key: The Struggle for the Mississippi River* (Lincoln, NE, 2003), 37.

4. William Tecumseh Sherman, *Memoirs of General W. T. Sherman,* vol. 1 (New York, 1892), 307-309; Sword, *Shiloh,* 432-439; Bearss, *The Campaign for Vicksburg,* vol.1, 26-28.

5. Richard L. Kiper, *Major General John Alexander McClernand: Politician in Uniform* (Kent, OH, 1999), 2-25; McPherson, *Battle Cry of Freedom,* 329; Thomas J. Goss, *The War within the Union High Command: Politics and Generalship during the Civil War* (Lawrence, KS, 2003), 18, 25, 41-42.

6. Kiper, *Major General John Alexander McClernand,* 47-49, 89, 110-115.

7. *Ibid,* 124-140; Shelby Foote, *The Civil War: A Narrative, Fredericksburg to Meridian* (New York, NY, 1963), 60-61.

8. Kiper, *Major General John Alexander McClernand,* 141-143; Grant, *Personal Memoirs of U. S. Grant,* vol.1, 426.

9. Grant selected Holly Springs as his depot since it was located on the Mississippi Central Railroad close to the Tennessee line. All of Grant's supplies and munitions were coming down by rail from Columbus, Kentucky. *Ibid.,* 427.

10. Florison Pitts, Mercantile Battery, noted in his diary: "Dec.4/62. Capt. and some of the boys went to Oxford with Sherman as a bodyguard." In his memoir, Sherman noted, "...on the 5th of December my whole command was at College Hill, ten miles from Oxford, whence I reported to General Grant in Oxford." Sherman also wrote about this "pre-meeting" with Grant to his brother on December 6: "The day before yesterday I rode forward to Oxford where I found Grant & received further orders to cross and occupy College Hill, 4 miles to his Right." Based on all of these notations, Sherman indeed met with Grant prior to their pivotal December 8 meeting (the latter occurred when Grant received support from Halleck to preempt McClernand and summoned Sherman back from College Hill). *Ibid.,* 428-431; Amos G. Throop Collection, December 4, 1862 letter from son George, LOC; Pitts Diary, 22 (hereafter referred to as Pitts Diary); Brooks D. Simpson and Jean V. Berlin, ed., *Sherman's Civil War: Selected Correspondence of William T. Sherman, 1860-1865* (Chapel Hill, NC, 1999), vol. 1, 329-331.

11. Sherman, *Memoirs of General W. T. Sherman,* vol.1, 309-314; Kiper, *Major General John Alexander McClernand,* 145; Foote, *The Civil War: A Narrative, Fredericksburg to Meridian,* 63-64; Bearss, *The Campaign for Vicksburg,* vol. 1, 113-128.

12. On December 18, Pitts wrote: "All the Lieuts. waited on captain, requesting him to resign. Commissioned and non-commissioned officers had a meeting in the evening about it." Pitts Diary, 28.

13. Many of Will Brown's friends from Chicago served in Batteries A and B. The former was known at various times during the course of the war as the 1st Illinois Light Artillery, Battery A; 1st Illinois Light Artillery, Company A; Chicago Light Artillery Company A; Smith's Battery; Morgan's Battery; Wood's Battery; Willard's Battery; and Wilcox's Battery. Battery A would be with the Mercantile Battery during the Vicksburg Campaign. When the CMB was transferred to serve under Banks in New Orleans, Battery A remained with Sherman and accompanied him to Atlanta. The names Battery B was known by included: 1st Illinois Light Artillery, Battery B; 1st Illinois Light Artillery, Company B; Chicago Light Artillery, Company B; Taylor's Battery; Barrett's Battery; White's Battery; Bridges' Battery; and Rumsey's Battery. At a postwar reunion, a member of Taylor's Battery stated that the Mercantile Battery had ended up with two of his unit's guns. *Illinois Military Units in the Civil War,* 42-52; Pierce, *Reunion of Taylor's Battery,* 21.

14. Morgan Lewis Smith was promoted to brigadier general on July 16, 1862, after rendering distinguished service at Fort Donelson and Shiloh. As colonel of the 55th Illinois, David Stuart commanded a brigade in Sherman's division at Shiloh and was wounded while defending the Federal left flank. He was promoted to brigadier general four days after Will mentioned him in his November 25, 1862 letter to his father. Ezra J. Warner, *Generals in Blue,* 460, 484-485.

15. Memphis was a major cotton and commercial center for the South. Its loss brought dire economic consequences for the Southerners, while reopening more of the upper Mississippi River to Federal military and commercial shipping. The June 28 issue of *Harper's Weekly* stated that, within three weeks of the fall of Memphis, merchants submitted applications to the Union authorities to ship 6,000 bales of cotton. The *Harper's* reporter who wrote the article also observed the townspeople's apparent change in attitude toward the North: "The people of Memphis treat our soldiers with kindness and cordiality." "Affairs at Memphis," *Harper's Weekly*, June 28, 1862, 403.

16. Florison D. Pitts Letter, December 3, 1862, CHS.

17. Halleck cooperated with Grant in assembling a force to reinforce McPherson and Hamilton against Pemberton. His initial plan called for Sherman to leave Memphis on Wednesday, November 26, and, in Bearss' words, "rendezvous with Grant's columns south of Holly Springs on Sunday, November 30. General Steele was to send a column from Helena to threaten Grenada, and Admiral David D. Porter had ordered Captain Walke's flotilla down the Mississippi to reconnoiter the lower Yazoo." Sherman's troops marched out of Memphis in three columns led by Brigadier Generals James W. Denver, Jacob Lauman, and Morgan L. Smith. The Mercantile Battery was part of M.L. Smith's column, marching, as Bearrs wrote, " out Poplar Street and State Line road to Germantown." The CMB's march was supposed to take them to Byhalia on the second day and then down the Chulahoma road for a November 29 rendezvous with the rest of Sherman's force. In his diary, Pitts noted on November 26, 1862: "Broke camp at daybreak and took up line of march for the sunny south. . . . Arrived at Germantown [Tennessee] at dusk. A hundred Rebel cavalry had passed through the town the night before towards Memphis. Went into camp two miles beyond at 9 o'clock. Slept without tents under the gun cover." Bearss, *The Campaign for Vicksburg*, vol. 1, 70-72; Pitts Diary, 26.

18. On Thursday, November 27, the Battery Boys "Went into camp 2 miles from Coldwater, Miss. Supper off of hard bread and coffee. Lodging under a log." *Ibid.*

19. On Friday, November 28, the battery "Broke camp near Coldwater at 12 o'clock M. passed many burning fences, 'houses,' also barns, out-houses, and everything that would burn was on fire." Pitts also wrote that the cornfield in which the battery camped on Sunday, November 30, was at Chullahoma, Mississippi. *Ibid.*

20. According to Pitts, the CMB got to the Tallahatchie on Tuesday, December 2. "Reached Wyat [Wyatt] on the east bank of the Tallahatchie at 12 o'clock in a drenching rain. The 'rebs' had cut the ferry, stopping our progress. Took up my quarters with Squad 1 in a fodder shed. Slept up in the rafters. The men were marched to the river to help build a bridge. Sent back; services not required." The day before, Grant's cavalry discovered that Pemberton's army had evacuated their Tallahatchie Line—but not before the Confederates destroyed the floating and railroad bridges. As noted by Pitts, Sherman's engineers had to build a new bridge, which caused a couple days of delay (the Mercantile Battery Boys used the extra time to write letters home). Grant wanted to pursue Pemberton's army but first had to build bridges, reconstruct railroad tracks, and contend with torrential rains, which wreaked havoc with the roads. Bearss, *The Campaign for Vicksburg*, vol. 1, 57-97; Pitts Diary, 27.

21. On December 3, the railroad was open to Holly Springs but the bridge across the Tallahatchie was not finished. The next day, Grant moved his headquarters from Abbeville south on the Mississippi Central to Oxford (site of the University of Mississippi). Sherman was somehow able to cross the Tallahatchie River on December 4 when, with Captain Cooley and some of the Battery Boys, he went over to Oxford to meet with Grant the next day. Sherman moved his troops from Wyatt and, according to Pitts, they went into camp that night at College Hill "on the brow of the hill. First rate place to camp. We were opposite a large plantation." Bearss, *The Campaign for Vicksburg*, vol. 1, 108-109; Pitts Diary, 27.

22. Cooley's "ignorance or inefficiency" may not have been the sole cause of the Battery Boys' scant rations. According to Bearss, "A 100-wagon train had been sent to the Coldwater depot to pick up rations." Perhaps the food problem was more widespread than the Chicago artillerists realized. Grant would learn from this otherwise fruitless Tallahatchie March that his troops could live off the

land as they marched through it, and he applied this lesson when his army crossed the Mississippi River at Bruinsburg six months later. Bearss, *The Campaign for Vicksburg,* vol. 1, 98.

23. Long, *The Civil War Day by Day,* 279; Sherman, *Memoirs of General W. T. Sherman,* vol. 1, 307-309.

CHAPTER 3

1. Bearss, *The Campaign for Vicksburg,* vol. 1, 114-124; *The War of the Rebellion: A Compilation of the Official Records of the Union and Confederate Armies,* 128 vols. (Washington D.C., 1880-1901), Series 1, vol. 17, pt. 2, 399, 409 (hereafter cited as *OR*). All references are to Series 1 unless otherwise noted.

2. Parsons picked up another 11 boats that were held for later use. *Ibid.,* 125-129; Gibson, *Assault and Logistics,* 151-152; Warner, *Generals in Blue,* 360-361; John H. and David J. Eicher, *Civil War High Commands* (Stanford, CA, 2001), 417.

3. Bearss, *The Campaign for Vicksburg,* vol. 1, 130-133.

4. *OR* 17, pt. 1, 477-478; Bearss, *The Campaign for Vicksburg,* vol. 1, 272-273; Foote, *The Civil War: A Narrative, Fredericksburg to Meridian,* 65-73.

5. Under pressure from his officers regarding mismanagement of supplies during the recent Tallahatchie March, Cooley replaced quartermaster J. Crandall with J. H. Tallmadge on December 9 (dated from December 1). Tallmadge would not perform much better and Will Brown would eventually take over his duties. Amos Throop Collection, December 16, 1862 letter from son George, LOC; Hearn, *Ellet's Brigade,* 34-35; Bearss, *The Campaign for Vicksburg,* vol.1, 121, 131-132; Descriptive List and Order Book for the CMB, December 1862 Morning Report, NARA; Reuben B. Scott, *The History of the 67th Regiment Indiana Infantry Volunteers, War of the Rebellion* (Bedford, IN, 1892), 14.

6. Lewis Parsons' miracle-working also included providing medical transports that Sherman had ordered. "These hospital boats were to stay in the field until filled and were then to act as medical evacuation vessels carrying the wounded and sick back to Saint Louis [and Memphis]." The special hospital boats were what Amos Throop (Lieutenant George Throop's father), Jane Hoge, and Mary Livermore inspected as part of their Sanitary Commission responsibilities. Bearss, *The Campaign for Vicksburg,* vol. 1, 149-154; Gibson, *Assault and Logistics,* 152-154; Herman Hattaway, *General Stephen D. Lee* (Jackson, MS, 1976), 68.

7. *OR* 17, pt. 1, 629-630; Bearss, *The Campaign for Vicksburg,* vol. 1, 155-157; Scott, *The History of the 67th Regiment Indiana Infantry Volunteers,* 15.

8. "General Sherman's Expedition," Frank J. Moore, ed., *The Rebellion Record: A Diary of American Events,* vol. 6 (New York, NY, 1871), 314-315; Bearss, *The Campaign for Vicksburg,* vol.1, 186-187, 205-207; George W. Morgan, "The Assault on Chickasaw Bluffs," Robert U. Johnson, ed., *Battles and Leaders of the Civil War,* vol. 3 (New York, NY, 1888), 462-470.

9. Bearss, *The Campaign for Vicksburg,* vol. 1, 220-222; Foote, *The Civil War: A Narrative, Fredericksburg to Meridian,* 76-77; "The Battle of Vicksburg," *Harper's Weekly,* May 7, 1863, 164; Gibson, *Assault and Logistics,* 156; Florison D. Pitts Collection, March 4, 1896 letter to W. J. Chalmers from W. L. Brown, CHS.

10. White, "Civil War Diary of Patrick H. White," 658.

11. Florison D. Pitts Collection, January 4, 1863 letter, CHS.

12. *Ibid.*

13. On Saturday, December 20, 1862, the men of Brigadier General Morgan L. Smith's 2nd Division were the first to leave Memphis. Next, Brigadier General George W. Morgan boarded his 3rd Division onto transports provided by Lewis Parsons. Will and the Mercantile Battery left the next day (December 21) on the steamer *City of Louisiana* with the 131st Illinois Infantry. There were 14 troop transports, a commissary boat, and an ordnance boat transporting Whiskey Smith's 1st Division. Will's exuberance about being a part of this massive flotilla led him to inflate his estimate

about the number of boats and soldiers involved. When Colonel Parsons initially received the order to furnish transportation for Sherman's troops, he only had access to eight steamers. He eventually procured a total of 71 boats. This was far less than the 200 boats Will Brown mentioned. At Helena, the first high point on the Arkansas side of the Mississippi, Brigadier General Frederick Steele's 4th Division joined the armada. Porter's gunboats took the lead and were interspersed throughout the convoy, protecting the flanks and rear of the column. In his memoir, Sherman corroborated Will Brown's observations about what the troops had encountered on the shore while obtaining wood to fuel the boats: "What few inhabitants remained at the plantations on the river-bank were unfriendly, except the slaves." Slightly varying estimates exist for the size of the force under Sherman's command. Edwin C. Bearss, while stationed at Vicksburg National Military Park in 1955-1966, conducted a study that concluded Sherman led a total of 32,000 Union soldiers (definitely not the 60,000 to 100,000 suggested by Will Brown). Gibson, *Assault and Logistics*, 151-153; Sherman, *Memoirs of General William T. Sherman*, vol. 1, 314-317; Kennedy, *The Civil War Battlefield Guide*, 154; Edwin C. Bearss' Chickasaw Bayou Analysis, on file, VNMP.

14. Sherman's fleet passed Napoleon at noon on Tuesday, December 23, and stopped 30 miles south below the mouth of the Arkansas River at Gaines Landing. In between Helena and Napoleon, the Federals destroyed many plantations as retaliation against Confederate bushwhackers who fired on Union transports. Napoleon was also the site where McClernand, Sherman, and Porter rendezvoused after their victory at Arkansas Post. There, McClernand received a letter from Grant expressing his disapproval of the Arkansas Post "wild goose chase." Much to Sherman's chagrin, Union soldiers later destroyed the town of Napoleon. Bearss, *The Campaign for Vicksburg*, vol.1, 134; Sherman, *Memoirs of General William T. Sherman*, vol.1, 330.

15. On December 28, Colonel J. B. Wyman led his 13th Illinois Regiment across a newly constructed bridge next to Mrs. Annie E. Lake's house as part of a Union attack commanded by Brigadier General Frank P. Blair, Jr. (who led part of Brigadier General Frederick Steele's 4th Division from Arkansas). An enemy sniper killed Wyman. Bearss, *The Campaign for Vicksburg*, vol.1, 185-186.

16. According to a reporter from the *Missouri Democrat*, Morgan L. Smith was reconnoitering to determine if his troops could use a sandbar to cross over the bayou and "as he was in the act of turning his horse to return to his command, a volley of about seventy shots was fired at him from a force concealed in an adjacent canebrake." A bullet hit Smith in the hip and lodged in his spine. The reporter was impressed with Smith's valor and added, "He then rode on for half a mile as if nothing had happened, hoping to get to the rear without his men knowing that he was wounded, fearing its demoralizing effect on them." At Sherman's order, Brigadier General David Stuart took battlefield command of Morgan L. Smith's division. "General Sherman's Expedition," Moore, *The Rebellion Record*, vol. 6, 314; Bearss, *The Campaign for Vicksburg*, vol.1, 186-187, 205-207.

17. Pitts was evidently referring to the naval episode that occurred on Saturday, December 27. Commander William Gwin was sent up Yazoo River to create a diversion at Snyder's Bluff, north of Chickasaw Bayou. His lead gunboat—the cumbersome *Benton* which had been Andrew Foote's flagship during the Island No. 10 campaign—was accompanied by three other gunboats and the *Queen of the West*. Commander Gwin was on board the *Benton* and was killed during the ensuing action, along with several of his sailors. Over two dozen enemy projectiles hit the ironclad. Some plunged through the deck, damaging two Union guns. The gunboat *Cincinnati* was hit hard, too. The Confederate defenders, however, suffered minimal damage in thwarting the Union naval diversion. *Ibid.*, 172-175; Foote, *The Civil War: A Narrative, Fredericksburg to Meridian*, 75-76.

18. Mary Livermore discussed Florison Pitts in her Civil War memoir, writing, "Pitts had just taken to his heart and home a beautiful bride, a fair young girl, who shrank in an agony of apprehension from the prospect of his leaving her for the dangers of the tented field." The bride referred to in Livermore's book was "Jennie," whom Pitts mentioned at the end of this Chickasaw Bayou letter to his parents. Mary Livermore also included an engraving of the Chicago Mercantile Battery in her book: "Our Battery at the Front—Reveille after an Anxious Night." It depicted the unit at Chickasaw Bayou. Livermore, *My Story of the War*, 369-374.

19. Bearss, *The Campaign for Vicksburg,* vol.1, 216-224; "General Sherman's Expedition," Moore, *The Rebellion Record,* vol. 6, 317; David J. Eicher, *The Longest Night: A Military History of the Civil War* (New York, NY, 2001), 390-392.

20. Bearss, *The Campaign for Vicksburg,* vol. 1, 359-360; Kiper, *Major General John Alexander McClernand,* 153-155; Foote, *The Civil War: A Narrative, Fredericksburg to Meridian,* 65.

21. Kiper, *Major General John Alexander McClernand,* 156-161; Bearss, *The Campaign for Vicksburg,* vol.1, 360-363.

22. *Ibid.,* 349-350; John D. Milligan, *Gunboats Down the Mississippi* (Annapolis, MD, 1965), 114.

23. Bearss, *The Campaign for Vicksburg,* vol. 1, 349-351, 378; Foote, *The Civil War: A Narrative, Fredericksburg to Meridian,* 134-135; "Capture of the Post of Arkansas," *Harper's Weekly,* February 7, 1863, 94.

24. Bearss, *The Campaign for Vicksburg,* vol. 1, 378; *OR* 17, pt. 1, 700-701, 745-747; D. Eicher, *The Longest Night,* 430.

25. Besides the right section of the Mercantile Battery, Lindsey's brigade also consisted of a section of the 1st Wisconsin Light Artillery under Captain Jacob T. Foster, the 7th Kentucky, 49th Indiana, and 114th Ohio infantry regiments, and Captain Andrew B. Kirkbride's company of the 3d Illinois Cavalry. Charles D. Spurlin, ed., *The Civil War Diary of Charles A. Leuschner* (Austin, TX, 1992), 11; Francis Vinton Greene, *The Mississippi: Campaigns of the Civil War,* vol. 8 (New York, NY, 1882), 86; Edwin Bearss, "The Battle of the Post of Arkansas, *Arkansas Historical Quarterly,* vol. 18, Autumn 1959, no. 3, 250, 263-264; "Battle of Arkansas Post: Report of Major-General McClernand," Moore, *The Rebellion Record,* vol. 6, 363-365; Descriptive List and Order Book for the CMB, January 9, 1863, Special Order No. 19, NARA; *OR* 17, pt. 1, 753.

26. *OR* 17, pt. 1, 728, 745-746.

27. *OR* 17, pt. 1, 746-747.

28. *Ibid.,* 716, 728.

29. *Ibid.,* 728, 747; Bearss, *The Campaign for Vicksburg,* vol. 1, 401-402.

30. *OR* 17, pt. 1, 708, 748-749, 753.

31. Bearss, *The Campaign for Vicksburg,* vol. 1, 405; Milligan, *Gunboats Down the Mississippi,* 117-118.

32. *OR* 17, pt. 1, 710; *OR* 24, pt. 1, 11; Foote, *The Civil War: A Narrative, Fredericksburg to Meridian,* 143-145.

33. Union losses during the Battle of Arkansas Post were minimal: 134 killed, 898 wounded, and 29 missing. An incomplete return for the Confederates listed 60 killed and 80 wounded, in addition to the 4,791 prisoners taken by the Federals. Bearss, *The Campaign for Vicksburg,* vol.1, 405.

CHAPTER 4

1. For a modern comprehensive single-volume treatment of the Vicksburg campaign, see Michael B. Ballard, *Vicksburg: The Campaign that Opened the Mississippi* (Chapel Hill, NC, 2004); Bearss, *The Campaign for Vicksburg,* vol. 1, 436-437; David F. Bastian, *Grant's Canal: The Union's Attempt to Bypass Vicksburg* (Shippensburg, PA, 1995), 41.

2. After Flag Officer David G. Farragut compelled the surrender of New Orleans on April 25, 1862, he cruised north along the Mississippi River. Baton Rouge and Natchez—other major Confederate commercial centers—surrendered without Farragut having to fire a shot. By May 19, some of his ships were below Vicksburg. When the fortified Confederate city did not succumb as easily, Farragut withdrew to New Orleans and conferred with Major General Benjamin Butler. The egomaniacal Butler had been placed in charge of New Orleans after its fall. With the approval of Secretary of War Edwin M. Stanton, Farragut and Butler proceeded with their plan to build a canal across the peninsula at De Soto Point. If successful, the waterway would enable their gunboats and troop transports to bypass Vicksburg. This would also permit Union vessels to ascend and descend

the Mississippi River beyond the range of enemy guns. In a report to the Assistant Adjutant General on February 4, Grant summarized four of his "Amphibious Operations to Defeat Vicksburg": Grant's Canal, Yazoo Pass, Lake Providence, and Steele's Bayou (the latter project would not be activated until March); *OR* 24, pt. 1, 14; Bearss, *The Campaign for Vicksburg*, vol. 1, 467, 482, 486.

3. Halleck supported Grant's attempts to remove McClernand from command of the Vicksburg expedition. The general-in-chief had also persuaded Lincoln to renege on his surreptitious order of October 1862, which had enabled McClernand to embark on his independent Vicksburg expedition in the first place. One wonders if political expediency had motivated Lincoln to issue the order in the first place and if, after the November elections, he found the troublesome McClernand less valuable. *OR* 24, pt. 1, 8, 11.

4. Lincoln was familiar with the natural bypasses created by the rambunctious Mississippi River since, as a young man, he had spent two "round-trips" working on the river. His interest in the De Soto canal was evinced by the message that Halleck relayed on his behalf to Grant. Bearss, *The Campaign for Vicksburg*, vol. 1, 436-437; Bastian, *Grant's Canal*: 8-11; *OR* 24, pt. 1, 10; Shea and Winschel, *Vicksburg Is the Key*, 22-28.

5. On June 25, 1862, Brigadier General Thomas Williams and his 3,000 troops arrived on the Louisiana side of the Mississippi across from Vicksburg. A large fleet comprised of Porter's 17 mortar boats and steamers, Farragut's 12 gunboats and three sloops, and Lieutenant Colonel Alfred W. Ellet's Ram Fleet, including the *Queen of the West* (Ellet and his youthful nephew—Colonel Charles R. Ellet, Jr.—were riding the crest of their acclaimed work at Memphis, performed earlier in the month), supported Williams. Flag Officer Charles H. Davis arrived from Memphis with four more gunboats and six mortar boats. Despite hard work on the part of Williams' soldiers and contrabands, they were only able to dig a "ditch" less than four feet deep. Williams was ordered to abandon the project on July 21 and returned to Baton Rouge. Now, six months later, Major General Ulysses S. Grant intended to complete "Williams' ditch." Bastian, *Grant's Canal*, 1-21.

6. Will and the other young men in the Chicago Mercantile Battery were still aboard the *City of Louisiana*. Their health was starting to suffer as they made the transition from benign conditions in the Tallahatchie Campaign to the battles of Chickasaw Bayou and Arkansas Post. Plus, they were on the verge of having to endure three months of camp life along the levees and swamps of the Mississippi River. Interestingly, the day after Will wrote his father—assuring him everyone's health was good—his comrade, Charles L. Lewis, died on board the boat. The Battle of Stones River took place from December 31, 1862, to January 2, 1863, in Rutherford County, Tennessee, outside of Murfreesboro. Major General William S. Rosecrans led the Union forces. Will Brown held a favorable opinion of Rosecrans and often discussed him in letters to his father. General Braxton Bragg, against whom Rosecrans won a questionable victory, led the Confederates. Neither Henry Brown nor Lib Brown participated in the battle, which was among the war's bloodiest. Descriptive List and Order Book for the CMB, January 1863 Morning Report, NARA; McPherson, *Battle Cry of Freedom*, 579-583; Kennedy, *The Civil War Battlefield Guide, Second Edition*, 150-154. For a comprehensive account of Stones River, see Peter Cozzens, *No Better Place to Die: The Battle of Stones River* (Urbana, IL, 1990).

7. On New Year's Day, Lincoln signed into law his Emancipation Proclamation, affecting the country's areas still engaged in rebellion: "I do order and declare that all persons held as slaves within said designated States and parts of States are and henceforward shall be free." *Harper's Weekly* noted the proclamation did nothing to abolish slavery in western Virginia; New Orleans and various Union-controlled parishes of Louisiana; and the Virginia cities of Norfolk and Portsmouth, along with Union-controlled counties in Virginia. According to historian James McPherson, "Lincoln acted under his war powers to seize enemy resources; he had no constitutional power to act against slavery in areas loyal to the United States...[the Emancipation Proclamation] also sanctioned the enlistment of black soldiers and sailors in Union forces." While abolitionists in the New England states were pleased that Lincoln's proclamation advanced their cause—albeit as an evolution and not a revolution—there were many in the Northwest states, such as Illinois (as noted by Will Brown), who objected to making the end of slavery a major goal of the war effort. They believed the conflict

should be fought predominantly to restore the Union. McPherson, *Battle Cry of Freedom*, 567-567; "A Proclamation," *Harper's Weekly*, January 17, 1863.

8. William H. Wiley from Chicago mustered into the Board of Trade Battery in the midst of the August 1862 rallies in Chicago—during the same time his friend Will Brown joined the Mercantile Battery. Hiram Brown and his family attended the Swedenborgian church in Chicago. William Wiley apparently attended the same house of worship. Wiley was one of the three men from the Board of Trade Battery killed at Stones River. He died on December 31, 1862. The American Civil War Research Database, Historical Data Systems, Inc.

9. Grant's troops were strung out for up to 50 or 60 miles along the levees lining the overflowing Mississippi River. Although members of the Mercantile Battery camped on relatively high ground, they would have to cope with the flooding Mississippi over the next couple of months. Spring flooding became such a problem that Union soldiers had a difficult time finding dry land in which to bury their comrades, who were dying from disease at an increasing rate. H. Allen Gosnell, *Guns on the Western Waters: The Story of River Gunboats in the Civil War* (Baton Rouge, LA, 1949), 146.

10. The decision to build Porter's "jaws of death" had initially come from Lieutenant General Winfield Scott while developing his Anaconda Plan. In June 1861, Scott recommended 16 ironclad gunboats be constructed. On August 7, businessman and entrepreneur James B. Eads finalized his contract to construct seven ironclads for proposed actions on Western rivers. He would build them at the Carondelet shipyard near St. Louis and at Mound City, Illinois, and deliver them to the Union naval base at Cairo. Each vessel was to be covered by 75 tons of iron plating, intended to protect its machinery and deflect enemy projectiles. Commander John Rodgers initially worked with the army on these gunboat projects and acted as the construction supervisor. From the beginning, there was significant political friction with the building and managing of the gunboats. The army was in overall charge and provided some of the men for the crews. The navy furnished the commanders and armaments. On October 12, 1861, the first of the Eads ironclads was launched—fittingly named the *Carondelet*. One year later, after much interdepartmental wrangling, the navy took over the Western Gunboat Flotilla.

Many of the early gunboats were commercial freight and passenger steamers converted for warfare. The side-wheel and stern-wheel paddleboats were ideal for navigating the sometimes shallow Western waters. Some of these first gunboats were woodclad, e.g., *Tyler*, *Lexington*, and *Conestoga*. The first four of Eads' ironclads—the *Carondelet*, *Cincinnati*, *Essex* (ironclad ram/gunboat), *Pittsburg*, and *St. Louis* (later renamed *Baron de Kalb*) played pivotal roles in reducing Fort Henry and attacking Fort Donelson. Other ironclads listed in the Western Gunboat Flotilla, when it was transferred to the Navy on September 30, 1862, included the *Cairo* (blown up by Confederate torpedoes outside Vicksburg in December 1862), *Benton*, *Eastport* (a captured Southern ironclad ram/gunboat), *Louisville*, *Mound City*, and *Pittsburg*. Porter's gunboats played a vital role throughout Grant's Vicksburg Campaign. The gunboat *Indianola* emerged as an important Vicksburg topic for Will Brown to share with his father. Edwin C. Bearss, *Hardluck Ironclad: The Sinking and Salvage of the CAIRO* (Baton Rouge, LA, 1966), 10-26; Gibson, *Assault and Logistics*, 58-69, 555-558; Gosnell, *Guns on the Western Waters*, 1-6.

11. A Republican like his father Hiram, Will was concerned about the rising clamor in the North for some kind of peaceful settlement with the Confederacy. He worried that foreign powers might insist on mediating an end to the war, leading to recognition for the South's independence. When Lincoln issued the Emancipation Proclamation, he made it more difficult for European countries to openly assist the Confederacy. For example, while Charles Francis Adams had struggled in 1861 and 1862 as Lincoln's minister to Great Britain, he reported that formally freeing the slaves in 1863 made a significant difference there. Despite taking effect only in areas under Confederate control, Lincoln's proclamation had precipitated a tangible ground swell of British support. Adams' son, who was his assistant, summed up the impact of the New Year's Day announcement: "The Emancipation Proclamation has done more for us here than all our former victories and all our diplomacy." Despite neutralizing Great Britain, the United States still had to contend with France's devious emperor, Louis Napoleon, who had directed his minister in America to approach Secretary of State William

Seward about brokering some kind of "compromise" between the North and South. Although Louis Napoleon was not prepared to offer the Confederacy official diplomatic recognition, he did provide financial support for the Confederates through a special French loan. Additionally, he had been scheming to install a puppet government in Mexico, which would also facilitate easier trade with the South. McPherson, *Battle Cry of Freedom*, 567; Bruce Catton, *The Civil War* (Boston, MA, 1987), 107-108.

12. Will humorously referred to his Young's Point camp dwelling as a "Chebang," which most soldiers spelled with the Americanized "shebang." Shebang was a general term for any kind of military shack or lean-to, such as those that the Union soldiers built as prisoners of war. In a future letter, Will told his father that he and Charley Olcott were really living in a tent. From the dimensions—10 feet square by six feet high—Will's tent was likely a smaller version of the Sibley tent, a bell-shaped or conical tent with the top being held up by a center pole (like a wigwam). The Sibley tent was not used for mobile operations because of its 18- by 12-foot size. Union soldiers used a pup tent in the field. Florison Pitts noted on April 11, 1863, "Turned over our Sibley tents and got 18 Bell tents." Pitts also mentioned the Mercantile Battery's bell-shaped tents in a letter to his father a few days later while still at Milliken's Bend. "We have been getting some new tents, called the Bell tent. They are intended to accommodate 10 men but our Capt drew 18 tents which will give us 3 tents to a squad and in the present reduced state of our Co we have only four in a tent which gives a plenty of room for dining and sleeping apartments." As acting quartermaster, Will might have been issued one of the new "bell" tents two months earlier so he and Charly Olcott could evaluate it for the entire battery. The Sibley tents that the battery turned in were evidently of much larger dimension than the one Will described to his father. Francis A. Lord, *Civil War Collector's Encyclopedia,* vol. 1 (Edison, NJ, 1995), 280; Pitts Diary, CHS.

13. Bearss, *The Campaign for Vicksburg*, vol. 1, 619-627; "The Ram 'Queen of the West,'" *Harper's Weekly*, February 21, 1863, 115; "The 'Queen of the West,'" *Harper's Weekly*, February 28, 1863, 139; *OR* 24, pt. 1, 17; Faust, ed., *Historical Times Illustrated Encyclopedia of the Civil War*, 607; Long, *The Civil War Day by Day*, 318; Hearn, *Ellet's Brigade*, 96-97.

14. Bearss, *The Campaign for Vicksburg*, vol. 1, 639-645; Hearns, *Ellet's Brigade*, 104-115; "Reported Capture of the 'Queen of the West,'" *Harper's Weekly*, March 7, 1863, 147.

15. The "Period of Despair" occurred in the North during the winter of 1862-1863. Historian James McPherson also referred to that time as the "Northern Winter of Discontent." During that bleak mid-point of the war, Democrats rebounded to victory in the November elections; Burnside presided over a Federal bloodbath at Marye's Heights behind Fredericksburg, and then led his troops on a ludicrous Mud March; Grant retreated from northern Mississippi; Sherman suffered defeat at the base of the Walnut Hills; Rosecrans celebrated a questionable victory at Stones River over Bragg and erred in not pursuing him; Lincoln emboldened Peace Democrats with his suspension of the writ of habeas corpus and issuance of the final Emancipation Proclamation; and, after the Arkansas Post win, Grant's Army of the Tennessee was stalled in the Mississippi mire above Vicksburg. As hopes for a Union victory diminished, emotions ran high in the South with an expectation that some kind of compromise would be struck. Wood Gray, *The Hidden Civil War: The Story of the Copperheads* (New York, NY, 1964), 118; McPherson, *Battle Cry of Freedom*, 558-593.

16. Cook, *Bygone Days in Chicago*, 331-333.

17. Carl Sandburg, *Abraham Lincoln: The War Years,* vol. 2 (New York, NY, 1939), 129-130, 157; Victor Hicken, *Illinois in the Civil War* (Urbana, IL, 1966), 139.

18. *The Echo from the Army: What Our Soldiers Say about the Copperheads* (New York, 1863), 3-7.

19. 1st Lieutenant James H. Swan and 2nd Lieutenant David R. Crego resigned on February 6, 1863. Mary Livermore, in her book on the Civil War, discussed James Swan at length. Prior to the war, he was Superintendent of Sunday School for approximately 400 children at her husband's Church of the Redeemer. According to Livermore, Swan led 33 other young men from the church to join the Chicago Mercantile Battery during its first wave of enlistment in August 1862. Livermore stated the highly respected Swan "was forced to resign because of circumstances that he could not

control"—likely referring to problems he had with the soon-to-be-deposed Captain Charles Cooley. Livermore, *My Story of the War*, 372, 387; Vance, *Report of the Adjutant General of the State of Illinois*, vol. 8, 739; Descriptive List and Order Book for the CMB, correspondence on March 9, 1863, between Springfield and Memphis, NARA.

20. Patrick H. White Civil War Pension Records, NARA.

21. Sherman probably wanted White to command the battery in which he was already serving (Taylor's Battery/1st Illinois Light Artillery B). Sherman knew the position would soon be vacant since he was in the process of promoting Captain Ezra Taylor to become his chief of artillery! Some postwar accounts indicate Ezra Taylor was White's brother-in-law. However, one of Taylor's men, Schuyler P. Coe, made a note about this in an October 23, 1861 letter. Referring to the section of Taylor's Battery that fought under White's command at Fredericktown, Missouri, Coe mentioned "our 2nd Lieutenant White—the Capt' nephew. Who is a tip top officer." Patrick H. White Collection, RBWPC; Schuyler P. Coe Letter Collection, Civil War Miscellaneous Collection, Box 1, U.S. Army Military History Institute (hereafter cited as USAMHI).

22. The city of Vicksburg was incorporated in 1825. It became a major Southern commercial center because of its location next to the Mississippi River and near the Delta's cotton crops. In 1860, prior to the outbreak of the Civil War, Vicksburg was a bustling river town with a population of 4,591 people, 30 percent of whom were slaves. Observing Vicksburg from near De Soto Point, Will Brown had a panoramic view of the "inclined-plane" city, from the riverside up to the cupola of its grand, hilltop courthouse. The first of the "tiers" along Vicksburg's hillside—across from Will's position in the woods—was the warehouse district with its long, low buildings, steamboat wharves, and immigrant's shacks stretching for about a mile. Along the waterfront, there were also seedy "Vicksburg-under-the-hill" establishments. Two blocks above the riverfront was Washington Street, which was lined with stores and shops. The Greek Revival-style homes of Vicksburg's affluent citizens constituted the third tier, progressing to the top of the bluffs. Along the Vicksburg bluffs, the Confederates' heavy guns watched over the city, along with the courthouse cupola and the spire of St. Paul's Church. The day after Will scouted Vicksburg, two soldiers from Taylor's Battery went down near the river to view the city themselves. One of them had a spyglass and they "could read the signs and see the people walking about very plainly" and "could see the Sentry on the Courthouse; the latter is a very fine building seemingly of white marble and stands so as to command a fine view of the river. All along the bluffs are beautiful residences surrounded by evergreens and other shrubbery." Peter F. Walker, *Vicksburg: A People at War, 1860-1865* (Chapel Hill, NC, 1960), 6-18; Schuyler P. Coe Letter Collection, February 6, 1863 letter from "Camp on Butlers Canal, La.," USAMHI.

23. The ironclad gunboat *Indianola* ran the Confederate blockade at Vicksburg on Friday, January 28. Will heard the "very heavy firing" but *Indianola* escaped unscathed along with her two accompanying barges. Long, *The Civil War Day by Day*, 320.

24. Shelby Foote, in his epic Civil War trilogy, recounted the observation of a journalist who concurred with Will's view that Grant looked like a nondescript merchant rather than one of the Federal army's highest ranking officers. Francis P. Blair, Jr., whom Will Brown saw with Grant, was a brigadier general and brigade commander in the Army of the Tennessee. His brother Montgomery was Lincoln's first postmaster general and his father was influential in the Republican Party—and later in the war would play a prominent role in trying to facilitate behind-the-scenes mediation with the South. Francis P. Blair, Jr. had previously served as a congressman from Missouri and, in historian Ezra Warner's words, was "instrumental in saving Missouri for the Union." During the war, he became Sherman's close friend. Foote, *The Civil War: A Narrative, Fredericksburg to Meridian*, 218-219; Warner, *Generals in Blue*, 35-36.

25. On February 14, 1863, Brigadier General Stephen Burbridge and his 1,600-man brigade departed from Young's Point on steamboats "to quiet things." They headed to Greenville, Mississippi, which was on the other side of the river. A. J. Smith had given Burbridge the assignment of halting the Confederate guerrilla attacks—some of which had been accompanied by cannonading—that were harassing unarmed Union vessels on the Mississippi River. Burbridge and

his men returned to their Young's Point camps on February 27, carrying with them, as Bearss wrote, "some 200 mules, 100 cattle, and 25 horses...having been out 14 days on 3 days' rations." They had successfully driven away the Confederate partisans, while living off secessionist farms. The Mercantile Battery did not take part in the expedition (probably because the Chicago battery was in the process of being reorganized), which had been supported by the 17th Ohio Light Artillery. Bearss, *The Campaign for Vicksburg,* vol.1, 709-713.

26. As previously noted, a number of the Mercantile Battery redlegs—especially those from the first wave of enlistment—were sons of their Mercantile Association sponsors. Many of the other early recruits had been employees of the same Chicago merchants. Thus, it is not surprising that members of the Mercantile Association made a special trip to Grant's camps above Vicksburg to evaluate what was going on in the supposedly elite Chicago battery. Beside being worried about rumors of mismanagement in the unit, the organization's members would also have had personal concerns about the health and well being of the soldiers during this "Period of Despair." Ira Y. Munn was probably the father of Private William Munn. The senior Munn arrived in Chicago around 1850 and was one of its early commercial leaders. He was in the grain elevator business. In addition to his responsibilities with the Mercantile Association and its small-business interests, Ira Munn was actively involved with the Board of Trade, having helped to raise its units. The younger Munn enlisted in the Mercantile Battery with Will Brown. The Willard about whom Will spoke was probably P. H. Willard (E. W. Willard was his brother and a member, at the Civil War's outbreak, of the powerful Union Defence Committee). Willard Bros. & Co. was a prominent commission merchant business on South Water Street. P. H. Willard later attended the first reunion of the Mercantile Battery with Private Gardner Willard, who had joined the battery with the first wave of recruits in 1862. It is interesting to note that Gardner Willard was discharged for disability on February 24, 1863, two days after Will Brown wrote the letter to his father describing the visit of Ira Munn and a Mr. Willard. The businessmen were therefore visiting the Mercantile Battery's camp for two reasons: 1) as representatives of the Mercantile Association that sponsored the battery and 2) as concerned fathers who had sons in the unit. Vance, *Report of the Adjutant General of the State of Illinois,* vol. 8, 740-741; Cook, *Bygone Days in Chicago*, 18, 29; *Map of the Business Portion of Chicago.*

27. Private William S. Wilson was one of the earliest to enlist in the Mercantile Battery [August 5, 1862] and one of the first to be discharged [on February 16, 1863, for disability]. Vance, *Report of the Adjutant General of the State of Illinois,* vol. 8, 741.

28. Will's younger brother Lib and his regiment, the 12th Michigan Infantry, were in Bolivar, Tennessee, helping to guard the western part of that state. After his December 20 Confederate cavalry raid at Holly Springs, Earl Van Dorn led his men in an attack on a Federal post at Middleburg, Tennessee. The town was the headquarters for the 12th Michigan, which was protecting a segment of the Mississippi Central Railroad. On December 24, Lib's commander, Lieutenant Colonel William Graves, had 115 men on hand to face Van Dorn's troops. After refusing to surrender the guardhouse, he amazingly managed to keep at bay the same Confederate cavalrymen who had earlier captured 1,000 Federals at Holly Springs. It is unclear whether Lib participated in this brave stand, which earned Grant's accolades. *History of Berrien and Van Buren Counties, Michigan*, 69.

29. Henry Brown joined the army a couple weeks before Will enlisted. Henry was commissioned as 1st lieutenant under Colonel Henry C. Gilbert in the 19th Michigan Infantry. Two months before Will's letter, Henry's regiment had acted as a rear guard in Kentucky to protect Rosecrans' rail supply line against the Rebel raider John Hunt Morgan during the Battle of Stones River. In the first two months of 1863, the men in the 19th Michigan were suffering the same "Period of Despair" challenges that Will observed in his own sector of the war—including problems with desertion. Perhaps this difficult time was also magnifying the leadership deficits of Colonel Gilbert that Henry had addressed with his family. Anderson, *They Died to Make Men Free*, 119-139.

30. On February 25, the United States Congress approved the first conscription act. It was passed the day after Will's letter, on March 3, and targeted male citizens between 25 and 45. Apart from the

men who "failed to report" (i.e., deserted), Union draftees could still be considered for exemptions based on physical or mental disabilities; or for "sole means of support for a widow, an orphan sibling, a motherless child, or an indigent parent." Additionally, there was a "safety valve" whereby a conscripted man could pay either a commutation fee directly or hire someone else to become his substitute. McPherson, *Battle Cry of Freedom*, 600-601.

31. Captain Charles G. Cooley and his two remaining senior officers—1st Lieutenant Frank C. Wilson and 2nd Lieutenant Frederick B. Bickford—joined lieutenants Swan and Crego, who had resigned from the Mercantile Battery on February 6. Cooley resigned on February 24, two days after his last two lieutenants. Vance, *Report of the Adjutant General of the State of Illinois,* vol. 8, 739.

32. On February 27, 1863, Grant sent the following message to Halleck: "News just received that the *Queen of the West* and *Webb* attacked the *Indianola* about 35 miles below Vicksburg the night of the 24th, and, after an engagement of about forty minutes, captured her with most of her crew. It is said the *Indianola* afterward sank." During the next two days, the Confederates raised *Indianola,* hoping to repair her. During the night of February 26, Porter sent a fake gunboat down the river. She was an old coal barge that had been inexpensively, but realistically, disguised to look like a gunboat. But the barge's protective outer shell was wooden, as were her guns. As the Mississippi River current pushed the engine-less "gunboat" downstream, she drifted close to where the Confederates were rehabilitating *Indianola.* Alerted by the *Queen of the West* that she was one of the fearsome Union gunboats, the Confederate repairmen destroyed *Indianola.* Later, the Southerners got a close look at the $10.00 "gunboat" and discovered she was a fake. "Deluded people, cave in" was painted on one of her wooden sides. *OR* 24, pt.1, 18-19; Bearss, *The Campaign for Vicksburg,* vol. 1, 665-678; Foote, *The Civil War: A Narrative, Fredericksburg to Meridian,* 197-201; Long, *The Civil War Day by Day,* 322-324.

CHAPTER 5

1. Although Grant was notified on January 5 that Lincoln wanted him to focus on the canal project to bypass Vicksburg, he had suggested the idea first, to Halleck, five days before while in Memphis. With his characteristic tenacity, Grant worked hard toward making this strategy a success. "Break in the Levee," *Harper's Weekly,* April 4, 1863, 215; *OR* 24, pt. 1, 10, 17; John Y. Simon, ed., *The Papers of Ulysses S. Grant,* vol. 7 (Carbondale, IL, 1979), 233-234.

2. Bearss, *The Campaign for Vicksburg,* vol. 1, 449, 478, 549-591; J. F. C. Fuller, *The Generalship of Ulysses S. Grant* (New York, NY, 1991), 133; "The Outlet to the Gulf," *Harper's Weekly,* March 28, 1863, 199.

3. In the same letter in which he discussed the Chickasaw Bayou drinking water, George Throop addressed a different kind of problem with his parents: "Mrs. Livermore flatters me very much in wishing to publish my letters but if you allow her it will be with my protest." Amos G. Throop Collection, January 7, 1863 letter from son George, LOC.

4. Sarah Edwards Henshaw, *Our Branch and Its Tributaries: A History of the Work of the Northwestern Sanitary Commission* (Chicago, IL, 1868), 105; Pitts Diary, 34.

5. Pulitzer Prize-winning historian James McPherson contends that "Disease was a greater threat to the health of Civil War soldiers than enemy weapons," with two Union soldiers dying from disease for every one who was killed in battle. Soldiers in their first year of service were the most susceptible since many of them were from rural environments and had not been exposed to routine childhood diseases—like measles and mumps—let alone more exotic maladies such as typhoid, malaria, etc. Regarding the difficulties in burying the Union dead, historian Terence Winschel noted, "In the years after the winter of 1862-63, when thousands of Union soldiers died from disease and exposure in Louisiana, the annual spring rise of the river opened many of the levee graves.... In Vicksburg, it was common to see corpses or human bones floating past the city....[and] local citizens petitioned the federal government to establish a central burial location for these remains. Congress responded in December 1866 by establishing Vicksburg National Cemetery." McPherson, *Battle Cry of Freedom,* 487-488, 588; Bastian, *Grant's Canal,* 38; Rev. William Weston Patton Collection, "Mississippi

Sanitary Expedition Discourse," CHS; Terrence J. Winschel, ed., *The Civil War Diary of a Common Soldier: William Wiley of the 77th Illinois Infantry* (Baton Rouge, LA, 2001), 39.

6. On the night of March 6, the dam at the mouth of the canal across De Soto peninsula gave way, just after Grant informed Halleck the "canal is near completion." As noted by Will, the nearby soldiers' camps did not experience the full impact of the damage until March 8, when some of McClernand's troops were relocated to higher ground. While Grant doubted the likelihood that McPherson would be successful with his Lake Providence cutoff, he reported that on the other side of the Mississippi "The Yazoo Pass expedition is a much greater success." *OR* 24, pt.1, 19-20.

7. Although Will was optimistic about the prospect of launching another frontal assault against the bluffs above Vicksburg, Grant was not so sanguine. While the Union major general would not completely rule out an attack on Snyder's Bluff until the beginning of April, he was reluctant to jeopardize his men by repeating Sherman's Chickasaw Bayou strategy. Thus, he focused his attention on approaching Snyder's Bluff indirectly via the Yazoo Pass expedition. On March 11, however, Lieutenant Colonel James Wilson and his naval gunboat support met their first resistance at Fort Pemberton, a Confederate fort on the Tallahatchie River upstream from its confluence with the Yalobusha to form Yazoo River. Confederate Major General William Loring had hastily constructed fortifications near Greenwood to obstruct the Northerners' amphibious flanking operation. The Union force repeatedly tried to get past Fort Pemberton during the next several weeks, with the final retreat occurring on April 6. In mid-March, Grant launched his Steele's Bayou maneuver—through 200 miles of twisted bayous. He provided an early overview of the expedition for Halleck, writing "To hem in the enemy on the Yazoo, Admiral Porter has gone into Deer Creek by the way of Steele's Bayou and Little Black Bayou. From there he can get into the Yazoo either by running up Deer Creek to Rolling Fork, thence through the fork and down the Big Sunflower, all of which are navigable, or down Deer Creek to the Yazoo." Porter would take 11 vessels on the Steele's Bayou expedition, supported by Sherman and his infantry. Terrence J. Winschel, *Triumph & Defeat: The Vicksburg Campaign* (Mason City, IA, 1999), 20; Bearss, *The Campaign for Vicksburg*, vol.1, 519-546; *OR* 24, pt.1, 19-21.

8. The 1863 "Winter of Northern Discontent" was a dangerous time for the Mercantile Battery recruits from Chicago. Despite Will Brown's assurances to his father, there were a number of the Battery Boys who were getting sick—providing the reason that entourages from the Mercantile Association and Chicago Sanitary Commission were making trips to Vicksburg to check on their soldiers' deteriorating health. Will's continued fastidiousness kept him healthy; yet his penchant for drinking water from the Mississippi River placed him at great risk, too—albeit not as great as it would have been if he were still drinking the Yazoo "death" water.

9. With their government pay in arrears, Grant's troops grew frustrated. Visitors from Chicago reported on the troops' demoralization during this bleak period, noting the delayed payments caused the soldiers to worry about their families' financial status. Without their own spending money, Will Brown and his comrades could not buy fresh vegetables and fruit from the sutlers and local farmers to sustain a balanced diet. For this reason, the packages sent from family and friends, along with those from the Mercantile Association and the Chicago Sanitary Commission, were essential to the artillerists' well being. Representatives from the two Chicago organizations witnessed the soldiers' dreadful living conditions and raised awareness about their circumstances upon returning to the Garden City. Henshaw, *Our Branch and Its Tributaries*, 105.

10. Unable to outflank Vicksburg, Grant was allowed the luxury of stockpiling supplies for use in April, when he undertook what was to become his final, and successful, attempt to invest the hilltop fortress. On the other hand, the ongoing delay also provided Pemberton an opportunity to likewise stockpile supplies. In his landmark study *The Campaign for Vicksburg*, historian Edwin Bearss compiled remarkable statistics on the extensive supplies that the Confederates built up in Vicksburg during the spring of 1863. Bearss, *The Campaign for Vicksburg*, vol.1, 606-613.

11. Will continued to believe Vicksburg was a crucial element in the South's ability to win its independence. With his experience on Chicago's South Water Street—the hub of the Old Northwest's commercial trading—Will knew the power of restoring trade all along the Mississippi

River, which had been known as "The spinal column of America." At the start of the war, Lincoln noted, "Vicksburg is the key. The war can never be brought to a close until that key is in our pocket." A week after Will wrote his March 14, 1863 letter to his father, Halleck voiced a similar opinion to Grant, commenting, "The eyes and hopes of the whole country are now directed to your army. In my opinion, the opening of the Mississippi River will be to us of more importance than the capture of forty Richmonds." *OR* 24, pt. 1, 22; Winschel, *Triumph and Defeat*, 1-2.

12. On the Union home front, Copperheads increased their efforts to undermine Northern support for the war. During this period, another Western soldier called them the "Copperhead Butternuts." Although the soldier despised the "Peace Democrats," he surmised they were gaining ground in the North because "the army is going on at a snail's pace." Frank R. McGregor, *Dearest Susie: A Civil War Infantryman's Letters to His Sweetheart* (New York, NY, 1971), 38-39.

13. Even though Will had expressed enthusiasm about the Young's Point campground, he knew it had serious limitations: The levee was too narrow for the number of men camping on it; the land between the levee and the nearby railroad was marshy and often under water, even before the breach in the De Soto Canal; and there were not many building materials available to construct shebangs (shanties). Milliken's Bend attenuated many of these camp problems for the Mercantile Battery.

14. It is odd that the observant Will Brown did not know about the disabling and capture of *Indianola*. Either the news from below Vicksburg was slow in reaching the troops at Young's Point and Milliken's Bend, or the Union commanders were conducting damage control. Perhaps Will was simply preoccupied with other matters. Four Confederate vessels, including the captured and repaired the *Queen of the West,* attacked the *Indianola* on February 24. Its commander, George Brown, was forced to surrender the vessel, which had suffered significant damage from ram attacks. Two days later, Porter's "Black Terror" (the fake gunboat he had built for less than $10) reached the Southerners who were trying to salvage *Indianola.* Effective beyond any expectations, Porter's "Black Terror" ruse caused such an alarm that, when notified about the gunboat and its tar-burning smokestacks by the *Queen of the West,* the Confederates repairmen, who had been working to salvage *Indianola,* destroyed the warship. Long, *The Civil War Day by Day*, 322-324.

15. By the time Will wrote this letter to his father, he had heard about the Battle of Thompson's Station, which had occurred less than two weeks before. Near Spring Hill, Tennessee, Confederate cavalry, under Earl Van Dorn, overwhelmed a 2,837-man Union reconnaissance force, including the 19th Michigan Infantry, on March 4-5, 1863. During the two-day action, 173 Northerners were killed and 204 were wounded. Twelve were later listed as missing. A Union infantry brigade was compelled to surrender, and the Confederates captured 1,306 Federals. Will was anxious to learn what had happened to his brother Henry—a first lieutenant in Company I of the 19th Michigan Infantry—during this March 4-5 Union defeat. Eicher, *The Longest Night*, 437.

16. After McClernand discovered that some artillery batteries under his command had no attending physician, he arranged for his infantry regiments to share their medical personnel. Kiper, *Major General John Alexander McClernand*, 199.

17. The Chicago Sanitary Commission sent five delegations to Vicksburg in the first half of 1863. Large amounts of supplies were taken down the Mississippi for Chicago troops, including the Battery Boys. In addition to providing supplies for Illinois soldiers and monitoring their care, the Sanitary Commission delegations had another purpose, as noted by one of its leaders after the war: "The Commission resolved to send other stores under charge of committees, who should be able, on returning, to stimulate contributions, by their report, as eye witnesses, of the condition of the beleaguering army." Henshaw, Sarah Edwards. *Our Branch and Its Tributaries*, 24-27, 104-105.

18. Amos Gager Throop, along with the Mercantile Association's William E. Doggett, moved to Chicago during the 1840s and became a successful businessman. Throop was the father of the Mercantile Battery's Lieutenant George Throop. Mrs. Henrietta L. Colt also accompanied the Chicago Sanitary Commission delegation. She was the corresponding secretary of the Aid Society in Milwaukee. Although earlier delegations had found conditions in Grant's army to be "truly awful," their successors, such as this group with Mary Livermore, reported there had been dramatic improvement in the quality of care being given to Northwest soldiers. Pierce, *A History of Chicago,*

vol. 2, 202; Cook, *Bygone Days in Chicago*, 167; Henshaw, *Our Branch and Its Tributaries*, 104-105, 128; Livermore, *My Story of the War*, 282-307.

19. *Ibid.*, 303-306.

20. Since 16 of Mary Livermore's "Battery Boys" had been in her Chicago Sunday School class, it was not surprising that, during one of the evenings in a Mercantile Battery shebang, she participated in the prayer meeting. *Ibid.*, 282-283, 303-306.

21. Jane C. Hoge was born in Philadelphia. She married Alexander H. Hoge, a merchant, in Pittsburgh, where they lived until moving to Chicago in 1848. As her thirteen children grew older Jane Hoge became active in community service. At the age of 45, she helped to found the Home for the Friendless. After the war, she remained active in community work and was elected President of the Women's Board of Foreign Missions. Both Alexander and Jane Hoge died in 1890. Holmes Hoge was discharged from the CMB on May 24, 1863, to become a captain and assistant quartermaster for the Army of the Tennessee. Hoge, *The Boys in Blue*, 18, 274-275; Henry H. Forsyth, *In Memoriam* [Jane C. Hoge] (Chicago, IL, c1890), 7-12; Descriptive List and Order Book for the CMB, May 1863 Morning Reports, NARA.

22. Mark E. Neely, Jr., *The Union Divided: Party Conflict in the Civil War North* (Cambridge, MA, 2002), 40-45.

23. Simon, *The Papers of Ulysses S. Grant,* vol. 7, 533.

24. William Farwell was listed on an 1862 map of business owners as having a dry-goods store on South Water Street, where many Mercantile Association members also had their businesses. Wholesaling dry goods was a growing business in Chicago. Before the war, as one Chicago historian noted, "Twelve houses in 1859 catered to the wholesale trade alone, and within five years after that Chicago stood next to New York as the most important dry goods market in the country, with an estimated trade of $35,000,000. The cloth and sundries so distributed by Chicago merchants were imported from the East." Cooley Farwell & Co. was another prominent dry-goods company and was probably managed by John V. Farwell who, after the war, would become one of the most influential department-store owners. Because of the close-knit relationships in Chicago at that time, William Farwell's partner was either Charles G. Cooley himself, the first captain of the Mercantile Battery, or his relative. It is also likely that William and John V. Farwell were related. *Map of the Business Portion of Chicago*; Pierce, *A History of Chicago,* vol. 2, 107-109; *Chicago Daily Journal*, April 20, 1861 [advertisement].

25. About a week before Will's letter, Rear Admiral David G. Farragut sought to run the batteries at Port Hudson with a flotilla of seven warships and gunboats. Going against the strong current of the "Mighty Mississippi," made more difficult by a 100-degree turn and the narrow channel, Farragut lashed steam-powered gunboats to three of his larger warships. He took the lead in his flagship, the *Hartford*, to which was lashed the gunboat *Albatross*. Only the *Mississippi* sailed alone since her large side-paddle wheels prevented a consort. The objective of the 62-year-old naval veteran and his captains, in Bearss' words, "was to pass the batteries with the least possible damage to their vessels, so as to secure as efficient force as possible for patroling the Mississippi above." After getting underway shortly before 10 p.m. on March 14, the Union flotilla began to ease past the Port Hudson bluffs. The Confederate riverfront artillery consisted of 19 guns, including four powerful Columbiads. Alerted to the approach of Farragut's fleet, the Confederates employed calcium lights to illuminate the scene, enabling the grayclad gunners to hammer the Union ships. Only *Hartford* and *Albatross* managed to pass. The sidewheeler *Mississippi*—Commodore Matthew Perry's flagship during the opening of Japanese trade a decade before—took the worst beating, and her captain torched the wooden ship. The rest of Farragut's flotilla turned back.

On March 19, the *Hartford* and *Albatross* ran the Confederate batteries at Grand Gulf and then Warrenton, anchoring off Bedford's plantation just below Vicksburg. The next morning, Edward C. Gabaudan, Farragut's secretary, took a small boat and landed at De Soto Point to notify Grant about the availability of *Hartford* and *Albatross*. Contrary to Will Brown's report to his father, the vessels were not gunboats but a wooden steam sloop and a screw steamer. Farragut's presence on the waters from Vicksburg to Port Hudson ensured that the Confederates would soon be unable to use the Red

River and the Trans-Mississippi region to replenish their stockpile of supplies on the Mississippi's eastern shore. In addition to mentioning Farragut's run up the Mississippi, Will also referred to a Union force that had gone up the Yazoo. This was the Steele's Bayou expedition, led by Sherman and Porter (Grant was still at Young's Point). Bearss, *The Campaign for Vicksburg,* vol. 1, 679-693; Foote, *The Civil War, A Narrative: Fredericksburg to Meridian,* 212-216; James P. Duffy, *Lincoln's Admiral: The Civil War Campaigns of David Farragut* (New York, NY, 1997), 178-195.

26. With the issue of the Emancipation Proclamation, Wilbur F. Storey's *Chicago Times* began to attack Lincoln and his Republican prosecution of the war more aggressively. The Union disappointments in the 1862-1863 winter provided further ammunition for sniping at the president. As one historian wrote, "Storey's editorials influenced thousands of disaffected Democrats in the Midwest. The Democratic legislators in Illinois and Indiana called for an immediate end to the war. The *Times* went out of its way to highlight the failures of the war in an effort to sow discontent among troops and citizens alike." Karamanski, *Rally 'Round the Flag,* 191.

27. As noted by Will, the number of contrabands crossing into Union lines was growing. Lincoln's final Emancipation Proclamation, which took effect on January 1, 1863, with news of it reaching the hinterlands by March, played a major role in this increase. Some of the contrabands were being mustered into the Union army; others participated in various engineering projects, such as digging canals. Additionally, many contrabands took menial jobs as paid servants, cooks, etc., for the Union officers and soldiers. At this stage of the war, Will Brown was tolerant of blacks, although he would later develop a hostile attitude toward them when the Mercantile Battery members were forced to perform labor duties with black troops near New Orleans after the disastrous Red River Campaign. Other soldiers already openly expressed hostility toward the blacks entering the Federal camps across from Vicksburg. "The common soldiers treat the negroes badly. They insult and abuse them quite wantonly, especially regiments from Illinois," observed William Patton, a minister from Chicago visiting the troops with the Sanitary Commission in March. "They are stirred up to this moreover by the taunts of editors and politicians at home who will tell them they are fighting in a 'nigger war' to carry out the plans of the abolitionists." Rev. Wm. Weston Patton Collection, CHS.

28. While Rear Admiral David D. Porter was away on the Steele's Bayou expedition, his second-in-command at Young's Point, Captain Henry Walke, did not pass along Farragut's request to send one or two rams past the Vicksburg batteries to assist in blockading the mouth of Red River. Brigadier General Alfred W. Ellet, arriving from St. Louis, unofficially found out about Farragut's request and walked 11 miles across the De Soto peninsula to meet the renowned seafarer and victor of New Orleans. Ellet agreed to send two rams, the *Switzerland* and the *Lancaster.* His nephew, Lieutenant Colonel Charles Rivers Ellet, Jr., would command the operation. On Wednesday, March 25 at 4:30 a.m., Ellet began his dash past Vicksburg. Approximately 45 minutes later, Vicksburg's heavy guns opened fire on the rams at dawn. A plunging shot from a 10-inch Columbiad struck *Switzerland,* piercing her center boiler. The *Lancaster* fared worse, a Confederate shot slamming through her hull and sinking her. Grant was not too dismayed by the loss of the *Lancaster,* which he informed Halleck was "very rotten and worthless" and would have been a liability in future operations. Ellet was aboard the *Switzerland,* which, though badly damaged, survived, and floated downriver. Farragut's screw steamer *Albatross* towed the *Switzerland* to safety. On the day of Will's letter, March 29, *Switzerland* was being repaired to pass Warrenton and join Farragut's *Hartford* and *Albatross* as they prepared to head for the Red River. Hearn, *Ellet's Brigade,* 131-138; Bearss, *The Campaign for Vicksburg,* vol.1, 693-700; *OR* 24, pt. 1, 23.

29. There apparently were several masked batteries on the De Soto peninsula. Historian Edwin Bearss, in his classic Vicksburg study, mentioned that the Illinois Light Artillery, Battery A and Taylor's Battery at one point concealed a 30-pound rifled gun and two 20-pound Parrotts, in addition to four 6-pound smoothbore pieces, on De Soto Point "in the woods near the river downstream from the canal." In mid-April, Theodore R. Davis, a *Harper's Weekly* artist, submitted a sketch of "Our Masked Batteries Shelling Vicksburg." The Union battery Davis depicted was "a well-protected battery of heavy Parrott guns, under the superintendence of Captain Edwin D. Phillips." Bearss, *The Campaign for Vicksburg,* vol. 1, 616; "Vicksburg," *Harper's Weekly,* May 16, 1863, 312-313, 315.

30. Although Will had a good overall understanding of the power struggle going on between Grant and McClernand, his details were not entirely accurate.

31. Will thought it would be nonsensical and misleading (i.e., gammon) to portray the preponderance of cotton traders as Southerners loyal to the Union. Instead, Will characterized them as Northern agents who had gone down the Mississippi to procure lucrative cotton deals. Grant similarly held a low opinion of these cotton speculators, whom he had been battling since Memphis. In a February 8, 1863 letter to Brigadier General John McArthur, Grant wrote, "These people with the army are more damaging than the smallpox or any other epidemic." Civil War and American History Research Collection, Special Collections and Preservation Division, Ulysses S. Grant letter of February 8, 1863, to General John McArthur, manuscript Number 72.285, Chicago Public Library (hereafter cited as CPL).

32. Will continued to downplay the health risks at the Union camps extending along the west bank of the Mississippi River. On Wednesday, March 25, Will's friend Florison Pitts wrote in his diary, "A man sick with smallpox on levee in front of our camp all day. Waiting for the smallpox hospital to come along and take him off. Was vaccinated in the morning." Will and the other Battery Boys would have also been vaccinated at the same time, a precaution in case members of the Mercantile Battery had been exposed to the pox-ridden soldier lying near their camp. Pitts Diary, 34.

33. *OR* 23, pt. 1, 75, 85-93, 116-117; Anderson, *They Died to Make Men Free*, 157-201; *History of Berrien and Van Buren Counties, Michigan*, 81-82; Foote, *The Civil War, A Narrative: Fredericksburg to Meridian*, 177.

34. On March 31, Grant's men began work on a new canal that would connect Duckport Landing, above the Mississippi River mouth of the De Soto Point Canal, to Walnut Bayou and other inland waterways in Louisiana. If this latest bypass scheme were successful, Grant would use flat-bottomed boats to supply his troops on their march to New Carthage as a further step in his campaign to outflank Vicksburg. Bearss, *The Campaign for Vicksburg: Grant Strikes a Fatal Blow*, vol. 2 (Dayton, OH, 1986), 43-44.

35. In a letter to his father, Grant sought to justify his failed operations at Vicksburg and bemoaned the harsh newspaper attacks directed at him. The beleaguered major general commented he would be amenable to stepping down and taking "a less responsible position." Grant was more concerned about winning the war than reaping public accolades, noting, "I want, and will do my part towards it, to put down the rebellion in the shortest time without expecting or desiring any other recognition than a quiet approval of my course." Yet he did not want his candid views shared with anyone else, writing, "I beg that you will destroy this letter. At least do not show it." "The Hero of Fort Donelson," *Harper's Weekly*, March 8, 1862; Ulysses S. Grant letter of April 21, 1863, to his father, CPL; McPherson, *Battle Cry of Freedom*, 588.

36. Bearss, *The Campaign for Vicksburg*, vol. 2, 20, 24-25, 29-30: *OR* 24, pt. 1, 495-496; Foote, *The Civil War, A Narrative: Fredericksburg to Meridian*, 219; Winschel, *Triumph & Defeat*, 18.

37. *Ibid.*, 19-22; Edwin Cole Bearss, *The Campaign for Vicksburg*, vol. 2, 30-33; Shea and Winschel, *Vicksburg Is the Key*, 91.

38. Grant, *Personal Memoirs of U. S. Grant*, vol.1, 468-469; James Sinclair Diary, April 15-16, 1863, CHS; Samuel Rockwell Reed, *The Vicksburg Campaign and the Battles about Chattanooga under the Command of General U. S. Grant* (Cincinnati, OH, 1882), 33-42.

39. On April 4, 1863, Grant sent Halleck an overview of his plan to send troops down the western bank of the Mississippi to attack a Confederate stronghold on the other side, thereby outflanking Vicksburg: "There is a system of bayous running from Milliken's Bend, and also from near the river at this point, that are navigable for barges and small steamers passing around by Richmond to New Carthage....My expectation is for a portion of the naval fleet to run the batteries of Vicksburg, whilst the army moves through by this new [overland] route. Once there, I will move either to Warrenton or Grand Gulf; most probably the latter. From either of these points there are good roads to Vicksburg, and from Grand Gulf there is a good road to Jackson and the Black River Bridge without crossing the Black River." *OR* 24, pt.1, 25-26; James Sinclair Diary, April 29, 1863, CHS; Bearss, *The Campaign for Vicksburg,* vol. 2, 294-297; Winschel, *Triumph & Defeat*, 29-30.

40. The March 23 letter that Will received from Hiram Brown provided details about the disastrous Battle of Thompson's Station. Much of Hiram's information came from a St. Joseph newspaper article written on March 7 by the quartermaster of the 19th Michigan in Franklin, Tennessee. As the quartermaster commented, "Only 30 [members] of the 19th who went into the battle came out. . . . There is hardly enough left of the regiment to make another Company." Will's brother and his fellow officers were captured. Stripped of their overcoats, blankets, canteens, and other belongings, they were put on livestock trains. Over the next month, the officers of the 19th Michigan were transported via train from Chattanooga to Lynchburg, Virginia, and then to their final destination: Libby Prison in Richmond. "News from the 19th," *St. Joseph Traveler*, March 19, 1863; Anderson, *They Died To Make Men Free*, 196-198.

41. Reverend William W. Patton—Vice President of the Northwest Sanitary Commission who accompanied Mary Livermore on her visit to Grant's army above Vicksburg—met a surgeon from the 118th Illinois Infantry Regiment, which had gone up Yazoo River with Sherman. The doctor told Patton that there had been 800 slaves at the Hill plantation. Just before Union soldiers arrived, the owner took his healthiest and most vigorous slaves inland to protect them. The ones left were either women, children, or elderly slaves. The surgeon also told Patton one of the captured slaves said: "We were made to cut down all these trees [in Steele's Bayou], and without us the rebels would be too lazy to do it. However, we contrived to make as many as we dared fall the wrong way." Rev. William W. Patton Collection, diary, CHS.

42. Northern soldiers, such as Will, were enamored with the sight of alligators in the swamps and bayous of Mississippi and Louisiana. The alligators became a favorite object for their target practice. Some of the soldiers, in their diaries and letters, commented on seeing hundreds lying dead as the army marched through the Southern countryside.

43. Although the enlisted men of the 19th Michigan Infantry were quickly paroled, Will's brother, Henry, and the other officers remained imprisoned. Anderson, *They Died To Make Men Free*, 200.

44. As the new campaign neared, McClernand ordered that training be resumed for his troops starting on March 30. Companies such as the Mercantile Battery drilled by themselves in the morning, taking part in brigade training in the afternoon. Although there have been reports of Grant reviewing McClernand's troops at Milliken's Bend on Wednesday, April 8, the information in Will Brown's April 12 letter to his father reveals this was not the case. Will reported A. J. Smith inspected the corps on Tuesday, April 7. McClernand conducted a general inspection on Wednesday, April 8, while the "Grand review" with Grant occurred a day later—on Thursday, April 9. Will Brown's version of events is reinforced by a recently published diary from a soldier serving in the same division as the CMB. As William Wiley of the 77th Illinois Infantry wrote in his diary: "April 7th: Things began to look like business again as the regiment was ordered out to be inspected by Gen. A. J. Smith. April 8th: The XIII corps was ordered out to be reviewed by Gen Grant but Gen Grant not being present the corps was reviewed by Gen J. A. McClenard [McClernand] our corp commander. April 9th: The corps was ordered out again and reviewed by Gen Grant." Kiper, *Major General John Alexander McClernand*, 202; Bearss, *The Campaign for Vicksburg,* vol. 2, 39; Winschel, ed., *The Civil War Diary of a Common Soldier*, 41.

45. Grant continued the ongoing campaign against cotton speculators behind his own lines that he and Sherman had started the previous year in Tennessee. Brooks Simpson, *Ulysses S. Grant: Triumph over Adversity, 1822-1865* (Boston, MA, 2000), 149-150.

46. At that time, Farragut was actively employing the *Hartford, Albatross,* and *Switzerland* to wreak havoc on Confederate trade seeking to reach Vicksburg or Port Hudson via Red River. For example, on April 9, Farragut captured a Southern steamboat—the *J. D. Clark*—carrying a Confederate commissary trying to arrange shipment of Texas cattle to Vicksburg. Farragut remained at the mouth of Red River until May 4, cutting down the flow of Trans-Mississippi supplies to Vicksburg and Port Hudson. Bearss, *The Vicksburg Campaign,* vol.1, 702-703.

47. On the day of Will's letter, April 12, there was still optimism about the success of Duckport Canal. Considering the failure of other recent bypass attempts, though, it is not surprising that Will

was skeptical about its outcome. The next day, the levee at Duckport Landing was cut and the ditch began to fill. For several days, Federal engineers continued to believe that their second canal project would be successful. There was much consternation, however, when the water level in the adjacent Walnut Bayou rose too slowly. Although Grant managed to get several barges through to New Carthage (plus the tug *Victor*), he watched the Mississippi River's post-spring flood abate and, with the drop in water lavel, his hopes of relying upon Louisiana's inland waterways to support his flanking movement subsided. While he had initially thought the Duckport Canal project was essential to transport his soldiers and equipment, he learned that the overland route from Milliken's Bend to Richmond to Clear Pointe–New Carthage would suffice. Nevertheless, the Union army also had to have boats at the end of the overland march to ferry troops to the east shore of the Mississippi. This latest development compelled Grant to request that Porter attempt to get both gunboats and transports past the Vicksburg gauntlet to New Carthage. Grant made a wise decision in looking for an alternative since Federal engineers were compelled to abandon the Duckport Canal project. "Vicksburg," *Harper's Weekly*, May 16, 1863, 315; Warren E. Grabau, *Ninety-Eight Days: A Geographer's View of the Vicksburg Campaign* (Knoxville, TN, 2000), 53-54; Winschel, *Triumph & Defeat*, 20.

48. According to historian Edwin Bearss, the plantation belonged to T. C. Holmes: "Many of the Yankees mistakenly believed that Lt. Gen. Theophilus H. Holmes, the Confederate commander of the District of Arkansas, owned this plantation." Bearss, *The Campaign for Vicksburg*, vol. 2, 27.

49. On the night of April 16, an elaborate Confederate party was going on at Major Watt's house in Vicksburg. At 11:16 p.m., the night skies were illuminated as Porter's fleet ran the Confederate blockade. As historian James R. Arnold wrote, "vigilant rebel pickets had detected the fleet in motion, crossed to the shore opposite the city, and set fire to several previously prepared buildings and stacks of tar." Vicksburg's 34 heavy guns opened up on the Union flotilla. Porter was aboard the ironclad *Benton,* followed by five other ironclads—the *Lafayette, Louisville, Mound City, Pittsburg*, and *Carondelet*—and the ram *General Price*, in addition to unarmed transports. The ironclad *Tuscumbia* brought up the rear. The Union ironclads survived 47 hits during the cannonade, which lasted over two hours, and the flotilla lost one man killed and 15 wounded. James R. Arnold, *Grant Wins the War: Decision at Vicksburg* (New York, NY, 1997), 75-78.

50. On the night of Wednesday, April 22, six Union transports (the *Tigress, Anglo-Saxon, J. W. Cheeseman, Moderator, Horizon*, and *Empire City*) and 12 barges ran past Vicksburg. Although Grant was bringing his men down to New Carthage via the inland route through Louisiana, he needed boats to transport his troops across the Mississippi River to continue his flanking maneuver against Vicksburg. At 11:00 p.m., the Confederates spotted the lead boat, the *Empire City*, and fired their signal guns. With fires on shore again providing illumination, Confederate batteries blasted the Federal vessels. One transport was sunk (the *Tigress* which had carried the Mercantile Battery's recent Chicago visitors) along with six barges—but the remaining boats got through and carried supplies down to Grant's men at New Carthage, two days before Will Brown's letter. Bearss, *The Campaign for Vicksburg,* vol. 2, 74-79.

51. Four days after Will's April 25 letter, Porter launched a ferocious attack with his gunboats against a heavily reinforced Grand Gulf. The "City Series" gunboats—the *Carondelet, Louisville, Mound City*, and *Pittsburg*—each mounting 13 guns, bombarded Grand Gulf's Fort Wade, while the ironclads *Benton, Lafayette*, and *Tuscumbia* engaged Fort Cobun. For five hours, Union troops waited in vain on transports and barges to land and join in the fray. After suffering significant casualties—18 men killed and 57 wounded—Porter halted the attack. Confederate casualties were comparatively modest, with three killed and 19 wounded. Winschel, *Triumph & Defeat*, 28-30; Bearss, *The Campaign for Vicksburg,* vol. 2, 295-296.

52. Colonel Benjamin Grierson began his raid through Mississippi on April 17, his decoy cavalry force reaching Baton Rouge on May 3. *Ibid.*, 317-318; Grabau, *Ninety-Eight Days*, 143-145; Shea and Winschel, *Vicksburg Is the Key*, 93, 104-105.

53. *Ibid.*, 146-147; Bearss, *The Campaign for Vicksburg,* vol. 2, 318-319, 346.

54. Patrick H. White Collection, RBWPC; Keith Poulter, "Decision in the West: The Vicksburg Campaign, Part III," *North & South*, issue no. 4, April 1998, 77.

55. Although some historians have found no record of the Mercantile Battery crossing the Mississippi on May 1 and participating in the Battle of Port Gibson, there is evidence to show they did cross and take part in the engagement. In addition to the White memoir, the diaries of privates Florison Pitts and James Sinclair note the battery crossed in the middle of the night and marched as reinforcements—per McClernand's order—toward the battle. An article written by a reporter for the *Chicago Tribune* corroborates their diary entries.

56. Bugler Pitts noted in his diary that the battery was at the levee during the afternoon and evening of April 30; and he wrote about sleeping there in near-frigid temperatures. According to Pitts, the Mercantile Battery landed at Bruinsburg "about 2 a.m., and got unloaded at daylight to the road to Port Gibson, over bluffs and hills, through valley and dales, over ditches, bridges, and every thing else that came in our way. Had gone abt 4 miles when heavy cannonading in front caused us to move on at the double quick." The terrain was exceedingly difficult to traverse, as both White and Pitts described. Anyone traveling up the same road today still winds along an ominous route that is seemingly cut into the edge of a cliff. Edwin Bearss, who studied the topography at Port Gibson for many years while serving as historian for Vicksburg National Military Park, provided the best description of this terrain, writing, "It was a maze of ridges, each more or less flattopped and of equal height, but running in all directions, and each separated from its neighbor by a steep-sided ravine filled with an unbelievable jungle of trees, vines, and immense and almost impenetrable canebrakes....Visibility was excellent from the ridge tops, but upon descending into the ravines the jungle closed tightly about, so that each man's world became a tiny green-walled room only a few yards across." Sinclair remarked in his diary that the battery embarked on the steamer *Forest Queen* about midnight on April 30 and started for Port Gibson the next morning on the double quick. Pitts Diary, 37; James Sinclair Diary, April 30 & May 1, 1863, CHS; Bearss, *The Campaign for Vicksburg*, vol. 2, 357.

57. Sinclair reported the Mercantile Battery fired its first round at 2 p.m.; Pitts specified its position as being on the Union's extreme right. A *Chicago Tribune* correspondent reported from Rocky Springs on May 8 that, "It will gratify the friends of the Mercantile Battery to know that they performed a distinguished part in the late battle, firing over fifty rounds at the enemy. Not a man was killed or wounded. The members are in good spirits and anxious again to meet the enemy. They will give an excellent account of the Mercantile Battery." James Sinclair Diary, May 1, 1863, CHS; Pitts Diary, 38; "The Battle of Thompson's Hill: Bravery of the Mercantile Battery," *Chicago Tribune*, May 22, 1863.

58. Major General John McClernand and his 13th Corps led the Army of the Tennessee's advance from Milliken's Bend to Port Gibson. However, the 13th Corps did not take part in the May 12 battle of Raymond nor did McClernand's men participate in the subsequent assault on Jackson, the capital of Mississippi. Instead, the 13th Corps acted as Grant's rearguard. Captain White and his men would play a prominent role in the May 16 battle at Champion Hill, which many historians regard as one of the pivotal Federal victories of the Civil War. Kiper, *Major General John Alexander McClernand*, 237-239.

CHAPTER 6

1. James I Robertson, Jr., *Stonewall Jackson: The Man, the Soldier, the Legend* (New York, NY, 1997), 709-753; Ezra J. Warner, *Generals in Gray: Lives of the Confederate Commanders* (Baton Rouge, LA, 1959), 232-233.

2. Pemberton held a war council to discuss Johnston's recommendation to concentrate and meet Grant's army out in the open at Clinton and away from Vicksburg, e.g., while it was spread around the Mississippi countryside. Johnston complained Pemberton had ignored his orders over several days and had opted to implement a strategy that "his council of war opposed, and which was in violation of the orders of his commander." Bearss, *The Campaign for Vicksburg*, vol. 2, 562-567;

Joseph E. Johnston, *Narrative of Military Operations, Directed, During the Late War Between the States* (New York, NY, 1874), 176-181; Winschel, *Triumph & Defeat*, 96.

3. The Confederates' position along the Yazoo bluffs, with Snyder's Mill its outermost point, had thwarted the Union army's northern access to the Hill City for six months. Supplementing the heavy guns on the bluffs, the Southerners made good use of a log-raft dam near Snyder's Mill to obstruct the Union navy. But the raft had collapsed on April 16, due to pressure from the flooding Yazoo, giving the grayclad defenders a premonition of how they too might soon be swept away. Bearss, *The Campaign for Vicksburg*, vol. 2, 253, 267-268, 347, 399, 418-419; Shea and Winschel, *Vicksburg is the Key*, 117-118; W. H. Tunnard, *A Southern Record: The History of the Third Regiment, Louisiana Infantry* (Baton Rouge, LA, 1866), 231.

4.Pemberton's strategy once he crossed the Big Black River was haphazard and hampered by inadequate reconnaissance and communication. The general had a myopic understanding of his opponent's tactical moves at Champion Hill and poorly deployed his troops. In contrast to Pemberton, Grant's decisions were predominantly sound. Bearss, *The Campaign for Vicksburg*, vol. 2, 641-642; Winschel, *Triumph & Defeat*, 112; Shea and Winschel, *Vicksburg is the Key*, 126, 131.

5. *OR* 24, pt. 2, 31-32, 38; Bearss, *The Campaign for Vicksburg,* vol. 2, 589-590, 624-625; T. B. Marshall, *History of the Eighty-Third Ohio Volunteer Infantry: The Greyhound Regiment* (Cincinnati, OH, 1912), 78-79; Haynie, *The Nineteenth Illinois*, 60; Patrick H. White Collection, RBWPC.

6. The Confederates did not file complete casualty returns for their losses at Champion Hill. Partial records indicate there were at least 381 men killed, 1,018 wounded, and 2,441 missing, with 27 of their cannon captured. William Loring's Division never made it back to Pemberton. For the Confederates, Champion Hill was the beginning of their end: The Southerners could no longer prevent Abraham Lincoln from getting his "key" and reopening the Mississippi River to Union commerce. Bearss, *The Campaign for Vicksburg,* vol. 2, 642; Winschel, *Triumph & Defeat*, 108-111; Patrick H. White Collection, RBWPC; Terrence J. Winschel, *Vicksburg: Fall of the Confederate Gibraltar* (Abilene, TX, 1999), 78; W. E. Haseltine Papers, Wisconsin Historical Society Archives (hereafter cited as WHS); First Mississippi Light Artillery Regimental Files, James G. Spencer to Frank H. Foote, September 18, 1910, VNMP.

7. Marshall, *History of the Eighty-Third Ohio Volunteer Infantry*, 80.

8. Fuller, *The Generalship of Ulysses S. Grant*, 154; Winschel, *Triumph & Defeat*, 90-91; Bearss, *The Campaign for Vicksburg,* vol. 2, 637; Timothy J. Smith, *Champion Hill: Decisive Battle for Vicksburg* (New York, NY, 2004), 398-399.

9. Prior to the outbreak of the Civil War, Charles P. Haseltine worked in Lockport, Illinois, as an engineer and surveyor. On August 29, 1862, at the age of 26, he mustered into the CMB as a private and was later promoted to corporal. In July 1863, Haseltine, because of his professional background, was detached to work in the 13th Corps' Department of Engineers. Despite lobbying from influential friends back home—plus the endorsement of U. S. Grant—Haseltine was unable to get a permanent position as a Union engineer. In August 1864, Haseltine mustered out of the CMB at New Orleans to accept a promotion as 1st lieutenant in Company E, 97th United States Colored Troops. He mustered out of the Union army in Mobile, Alabama, on July 10, 1865. Charles P. Haseltine Compiled Military Service Records (hereafter CMSR), NARA; Charles P. Haseltine Civil War Pension File, NARA.

10. There are differing reports on the number and type of cannon that Tilghman deployed against Burbridge. This is not surprising since each Civil War battle was fluid and not a static event, akin to a modern-day video and not a snapshot. Much occurred during the course of a day's fighting, oftentimes with changing positions and armaments. According to Historian Terrence Winschel, "Tilghman's position west of the Coker house was naturally strong, being a low ridge which commanded a wide sweep of open ground. Strengthened by six guns of Capt. James J. Cowan's Company G, First Mississippi Light Artillery and two guns of Company C, Fourteenth Mississippi Artillery Battalion under Capt. Jacob Culbertson, his position was difficult to turn and would prove costly to assault." Winschel, *Triumph & Defeat*, 109.

11. Western soldiers, such as Will Brown and Charles P. Haseltine of the Mercantile Battery, appreciated "Whiskey" Smith's tough, no-nonsense approach to war. His hard drinking did not compromise his faculties on the battlefield.

12. The Mercantile Battery was positioned in front of the Coker House, not the "Champion homestead." Postwar photos of the Coker House in the Vicksburg Courthouse archives show the front yard lined with the live oak trees mentioned by Haseltine; as well as the cannon holes mentioned by T.B. Marshall of the 83rd Ohio. The Coker House is a single-story, Greek revival structure, built circa 1852 by H. B. Coker, a Mississippi farmer—or "planter" as described by Captain Pat White. It was used as a field hospital by both sides during the Civil War and today remains standing next to Highway 467. Sadly, it is now a dilapidated ramshackle, much of its original beauty having faded. Preservation groups, such as the local Jackson Civil War Round Table, have championed efforts to restore the Coker House and reopen it as a monument to the battle that swirled around it. Leonard Fullenkamp, ed., *Guide to the Vicksburg Campaign* (Lawrence, KS, 1998), 384-385; H. Grady Howell, Jr., *Hill of Death: The Battle of Champion Hill* (Madison, MS, 1993), 23.

13. Years later, Pat White recalled Haseltine's wounding in front of the Coker House: "Charlie Hazeltine thought he was killed. While he was sighting his piece, a mini ball passed by his head, so close that it broke the skin on his forehead. 'Oh! Oh! I'm killed!' he shouted over and over. This brought a laugh from Joe Day, who told him he was a very noisy dead man." Patrick H. White Collection, RBWPC.

14. Lloyd Tilghman, a graduate of West Point, settled in Kentucky after the Mexican War. In October 1861, Tilghman was commissioned brigadier general in the Confederate army. He was later entrusted with holding Fort Henry, on the Tennessee River, but Flag Officer Andrew Foote's Union gunboats overwhelmed his command. After surrendering, Tilghman was exchanged in the fall of 1862, when he returned to service in the Western Theater. At the Battle of Champion Hill, Tilghman led a brigade from Major General William Loring's Division and was killed in the action. The retreating Southerners took his corpse with them; he was buried after they reached Vicksburg the next day. Many years after the war, two of Tilghman's sons—by then successful New York businessmen—commissioned a dramatic equestrian statue at Vicksburg National Military Park to commemorate their father. There is also a stone marker where Lloyd Tilghman fell, approximately a quarter of a mile from where the Mercantile Battery fired its fatal shot. Warner, *Generals in Gray*, 306; Winschel, *Vicksburg: Fall of the Confederate Gibraltar*, 79; H. Grady Howell, Jr., *To Live and Die in Dixie* (Jackson, MS, 1991), 202-203; Kathy Witt, "General Tilghman's Place," *Civil War Times Illustrated*, December 2001, 18-20, 77-79; Fullenkamp, *Guide to the Vicksburg Campaign*, 385-386; E. Trent Eggleston, "Scenes Where General Tilghman Was Killed," *Confederate Veteran* 1, no. 10 (October 1893), 296.

15. Bearss, *The Campaign for Vicksburg*, vol. 2, 653-679.

16. *Ibid.*, 680.

17. Edwin Cole Bearss, *The Campaign for Vicksburg: Unvexed to the Sea*, vol. 3 (Dayton, OH, 1986), 743.

18. *Ibid.*, 858; Shea and Winschel, *Vicksburg is the Key*, 150-151; Patrick H. White Collection, RBWPC.

19. George Throop enlisted on August 6, 1862, among the first men to join the CMB. A 23-year-old bookkeeper—originally from Clyde, Michigan—Throop was later promoted to sergeant. During the battery's February 1863 reorganization, Patrick White approved the pending promotion of George Throop to replace one of Cooley's officers. Bearss, *The Campaign for Vicksburg*, vol. 3, 827-832; Joseph E. Chance, *The Second Texas Infantry: From Shiloh to Vicksburg* (Austin, TX, 1984), 105; Janet B. Hewitt, ed., *Supplement to the Official Records of the Union and Confederate Armies*: pt. 2, vol. 8 (Wilmington, NC, 1995), 463; Descriptive List and Order Book for the CMB, Descriptive Rolls, NARA.

20. Elizabeth Silverthorne, *Ashbel Smith of Texas: Pioneer, Patriot, Statesman, 1805-1886* (College Station, TX, 1982), 156; Alonzo L. Brown, *History of the Fourth Regiment of Minnesota Infantry Volunteers during the Great Rebellion, 1861-1865* (St. Paul, MN, 1892), 220.

21. Patrick H. White Collection, RBWPC; Amos Throop Collection, June 9, 1863, letter from son George, LOC.

22. Brigadier General Albert Lee temporarily took command of Brigadier General Peter Osterhaus' 9th Division after Osterhaus was wounded in the buttocks. Lee actually had three bridges built for Whiskey Smith's men to cross the Big Black River and move toward Vicksburg. Kiper, *Major General John McClernand*, 250; Bearss, *The Campaign for Vicksburg,* vol. 3, 743-745.

23. Warren Grabau, a geographer and historian, described the terrain the Mercantile Battery members confronted as they approached Vicksburg: "The ridgetops and many of the less precipitous side slopes were under cultivation and almost free of trees. Thus, there were unobstructed lines of sight across the ravine that fronted the Confederate defense line along almost its entire length....Since the establishment of the Vicksburg National Military Park...[most of the] area has been allowed to grow up into tall forest." Grabau, *Ninety-Eight Days*, 355.

24. Grant positioned McClernand's men on the left of his assault line. McPherson was in the center and Sherman on the right. This alignment would remain in place for the duration of the siege. On May 19, the Mercantile Battery, along with the 17th Ohio Light Artillery, supported Smith's two infantry brigades, led by Brigadier General Stephen G. Burbridge and Colonel William J. Landram. During the assault, Smith's men were unable to reach the enemy fortifications. By the end of the day, McClernand's 13th Corps, including A.J. Smith's division, held ground about 400 yards away from the Confederate works. Most of Smith's men camped that night in the Two-mile Bridge Branch lowlands. Bearss, *The Campaign for Vicksburg,* vol. 3, 757-772.

25. Colonel Ashbel Smith commanded the 2nd Texas Lunette, which guarded Baldwin's Ferry Road, one of the main approach roads to Vicksburg. His men had worked hard to strengthen the fort, adding rifle pits and clearing lines of fire by cutting down trees and burning down houses in their front. Historian Edwin Bearss commented that the 2nd Texas Lunnette "was the place of danger; the post of honor; the key to the center of the Southern lines." In describing the crescent-shaped lunette, Bearss noted its "parapet was about 4 1/2 feet high on the inside, its superior slope some 14 feet thick. It was surrounded by a ditch in front nearly 6 feet deep.... Subsequently a ditch 2 feet deep was dug on the inside of the parapet to enable the men to stand erect without being exposed to the Federals' fire." Edwin C. Bearss, "Texas at Vicksburg," September 1956, VNMP; Silverthorne, *Ashbel Smith of Texas*, 154-156.

26. For a Confederate perspective on the bitterly fought May 22 contest at the 2nd Texas Lunette, see Colonel Ashbel Smith's after-action report. In it, Smith mentioned, "One of my cannons was disabled and knocked out of battery early in the day." The Mercantile Battery cannoneers were responsible for putting this piece out of commission. Smith also noted the fort's other gun "could not be depressed so as to reach the enemy at the foot of the works." The Texans' inability to bring their remaining cannon to bear against their attackers caused them to be more creative with their explosives. As Smith wrote in his report, "To clear the outside ditch, spherical case were used as hand-grenades, and, it is believed, with good effect." *OR 24*, pt. 2, 384-389; Chance, *The Second Texas Infantry*, 106-108.

27. Due to the confusion of the assault on the 2nd Texas Lunette, which was complicated by the arrival of dusk, the companies from the 23rd Wisconsin were no longer available to help Captain White and his men take their piece back down the slope.

28. Private William G. Stephens enlisted in the Chicago Mercantile Battery on August 6, 1862, at the age of 19. A short youth—listed at 5 feet 3 1/2 inches tall—Stephens had gone to Chicago from New York and had been working as a clerk prior to the war. For his bravery at Vicksburg, William Stephens would later receive the Medal of Honor. Descriptive List and Order Book for the CMB, Descriptive Rolls, NARA.

29. No Union soldier got into the 2nd Texas Lunette during the May 22 assault. The flag Stephens mentioned, however, may have been from the 18th Indiana Infantry. As Edwin Bearss noted "50 men [from the 18th Indiana] succeeded in gaining the ditch fronting the lunette, while the remainder [of the regiment] crowded up to its edge, Sgt. Francis M. Foss planting the colors there." At the far left flank of the lunette, a color bearer from the 99th Illinois, Thomas J. Higgins, reached the fort and

tried to plant his flag on the Confederate breastworks. The Southerners were so impressed by the color bearer's bravery that they took him prisoner rather than killing him. One of the Texans recalled the "Yankee was loaded with gun powder and whiskey on the inside." Higgins, along with many other Union prisoners, was kept in the Vicksburg Court House to discourage Federal artillerists from targeting its tower. Bearss, *The Campaign for Vicksburg*, vol. 3, 829; Ralph J. Smith, *Reminiscences of the Civil War and Other Sketches* (Waco, TX, 1962), 26; Chance, *The Second Texas Infantry*, 105-106.

30. Later in the morning on May 22, Burbridge's brigade—the 18th Indiana, 83rd Ohio, 67th Indiana, and the 23rd Wisconsin infantry regiments—was trapped in the ditch in front of the 2nd Texas Lunette. The fighting between Burbridge's men and Ashbel Smith's Confederates, hunkered down within the fort, was ferocious. Some Unionists sought to climb the lunette's parapet but were thrown back into the ditch. The defenders tossed artillery shells, used as improvised hand grenades, onto them. It was during this impasse that Captain White was asked to take his cannon up the ravine to support Burbridge's men in front of the 2nd Texas Lunette. Bearss, *The Campaign for Vicksburg*, vol. 3, 829-831; *OR* 24, pt. 2, 30-35.

31. In an official report, Colonel Joshua J. Guppey, commanding the 23rd Wisconsin Infantry, summarized the role played by his men in supporting Captain White's redlegs at the 2nd Texas Lunette: "Our gallant soldiers seemed determined to get inside the fort by some means. Not being able to scale its walls, they tried to dig them down, and not succeeding in this, they hailed with cheers the cannon which had been ordered up, and two of the companies of my regiment (B and E) dragged it up the hill to the walls of the fort, where it was most vigorously served." *OR* 24, pt. 2, 39.

32. At about 5:00 p.m., Brig. Gen. Martin E. Green, with a brigade of Arkansas and Missouri troops, reinforced Ashbel Smith. *OR* 24, pt. 2, 389; Chance, *The Second Texas Infantry*, 108.

33. Union casualties for the May 22 assault—502 killed, 2,550 wounded, and 147 missing—far exceeded those of the Confederates. And Grant held McClernand accountable for a significant portion of those soldiers, who fell during the afternoon's renewed assault. Although the exact number of Confederate losses is not known, Bearss has stated it could not have totaled more than 500 men. Bearss, *The Campaign for Vicksburg*, vol. 3, 858.

34. Edwin Bearss estimated that, from the crossing of the Mississippi River at Bruinsburg through to the Battle of Big Black Bridge, the Confederates lost about 7,000 men, along with 65 cannon. Grant marched his army 200 miles in less than three weeks and won decisive victories at Port Gibson, Raymond, Jackson, Champion Hill, and Big Black Bridge. These battles were followed by two assaults against Vicksburg. Up until reaching the Vicksburg fortifications, Grant had lost about half as many men as the enemy—but his casualties roughly equaled Confederate losses by the end of May 22. *Ibid.*, 752, 773, 858.

CHAPTER 7

1. "Gallantry of the Mercantile Battery," *Chicago Tribune*, June 4, 1863.

2. In his landmark book on Civil War cannon, Warren Ripley described how to characterize light and heavy guns: "1. The size of the bore, or opening from which the projectile is ejected, 2. Type of bore, 3. Type of weapon, 4. Material, 5. Model, 6. Employment, 7. Name of inventor, 8. Method of loading, 9. Army or Navy, 10. Union or Confederate." Regarding the size of the bore—or opening of the cannon—Ripley explained that, prior to rifling, the weight designation accurately defined the gun. For example, a 32-pounder smoothbore cannon would fire solid spherical shots of a standard 6.4-inch size. However, rifling (adding grooves into a gun's bore) enabled the cannoneers to lengthen or shorten the elongated projectiles, which would affect the weight of the shot. Rifled guns typically were made of either wrought- or cast-iron and are described by the size of their bore, e.g., the Mercantile Battery's 3-inch Rodman rifle. Based on Will Brown's Vicksburg letter, the battery's 3-inch, 10-pounder Rodmans were firing 12-pound projectiles during the siege. In addition to the Rodman rifles, the Mercantile Battery was also firing 6-pounder and 12-pounder smoothbore Napoleon cannon during the Vicksburg Campaign. Most smoothbore guns, especially for the Union,

were made of bronze and often were referred to as "brass." There are very few Civil War era cannon that are maintained with this "brass" finish today since outdoor exhibits create a verdigris patina. Ripley, *Artillery and Ammunition of The Civil War*, 14-15.

3. While Will discounted the possibility of a Confederate attack, Grant and his senior commanders worried about rumors of General Joseph Johnston assembling an Army of Relief near Jackson. After their assaults on Vicksburg failed on May 19 and May 22, the Union generals knew they were in a precarious position. Grant needed to keep the pressure on Pemberton to force him to surrender. In addition to containing Pemberton's Army of Vicksburg, Federal leaders needed to protect their supply line linking them with the Yazoo River. As Grant tightened the siege, he feared that Johnston would concentrate his Army of Relief northeast of Vicksburg and drive down the Mechanicsburg Corridor between the Yazoo and Big Black rivers. From there, Johnston could roll up the Union flanks along the bluffs. Grabau, *Ninety-Eight Days*, 449-453.

4. Will referred to Union Major General Joseph Hooker's defeat at the Battle of Chancellorsville in Virginia. Robert E. Lee and Stonewall Jackson had led their troops to one of the great victories of the Civil War. Despite hearing about Fighting Joe Hooker's serious loss, rank-and-file soldiers like Will Brown continued to support him even though Lincoln would designate George Meade as his replacement some 72 hours before the Battle of Gettysburg. On May 5, 1863, Union soldiers arrested Copperhead politician Clement L. Vallandigham of Ohio. He was taken into custody to Cincinnati. An outraged mob retaliated by setting fire to a Republican newspaper in his Dayton hometown. Kennedy, *The Civil War Battlefield Guide*, 197-199; "Arrest of Vallandigham," *Harper's Weekly*, May 16, 1863, 307.

5. McClernand was so impressed by the May 22 performance of White and his Mercantile Battery that he awarded them two of the "mongrel" cannon captured at the Battle of Big Black River Bridge. Eddy, *The Patriotism of Illinois*, 469.

6. Henry Brown and the other officers of the 19th Michigan Infantry were exchanged on May 5 at City Point, Virginia, and sent to Annapolis via Fort Monroe. They traveled to Camp Chase, Ohio (near Columbus), to reunite with their enlisted men, who had been in a parole camp. There, Henry was promoted to adjutant on the staff of Colonel Henry C. Gilbert. Anderson, *They Died To Make Men Free*, 196, 201; Henry M. Brown Civil War Pension File, NARA.

7. Aside from the threat poised by Johnston, Grant had to face the possibility of General Braxton Bragg coming to Pemberton's aid. Bragg's Army of Tennessee was posted behind the Duck River, in Middle Tennessee. With Major General William Rosecrans' Federal army still dormant around Murfreesboro, Bragg ordered Major General John C. Breckinridge's 5,500-man division to reinforce Johnston in Mississippi (boosting the Confederate force to more than 28,000 soldiers). The cavalry raid through Mississippi led by Colonel Benjamin H. Grierson—from April 17 to May 2—created an invaluable diversion for Grant, enabling him to march his men down the west side of the Mississippi and cross at Bruinsburg while Pemberton was preoccupied with stopping Grierson's Raid. Grabau, *Ninety-Eight Days*, 468-469; Bearss, *The Campaign for Vicksburg*, vol. 3, 1007-1008; Foote, *The Civil War, Fredericksburg to Meridian*, 334-340.

8. On May 7, Major General Nathaniel Banks reached Alexandria, Louisiana. Banks next moved against Port Hudson, enveloping the Confederate stronghold with a multiple-pronged advance. After launching two failed assaults, Banks determined to starve the Confederates out. After Port Hudson's commander Major General Franklin Gardner heard of Vicksburg's capitulation, he surrendered on July 9. *Ibid.*, 394-395; Shea and Winschel, *Vicksburg is the Key*, 187-204; Kennedy, *The Civil War Battlefield Guide*, 181-182.

9. "Bod" was Albert H. Bodman, a correspondent for the *Chicago Tribune*. Bodman was with Colonel Charles Rivers Ellet when he lost the *Queen of the West* on the Red River. Like Ellet, Bodman escaped from the sinking *Queen of the West* on a floating bale of cotton. J. Cutler Andrews, *The North Reports The Civil War* (Pittsburgh, PA, 1955), 751; Benjamin P. Thomas, ed., *Three Years with Grant, As Recalled by War Correspondent Sylvanus Cadwallader* (Lincoln, NE, 1996), 55.

10. The day after Will sent his letter to St. Joseph, his brother Henry and the reorganized 19th Michigan marched from Camp Chase to downtown Columbus. From there, they boarded trains for

Cincinnati and headed south to try their luck again in the Confederacy. Three days before this Brown letter, a wagon showed up from Grand Gulf with the Battery Boys' personal belongings—36 days after they were left behind when the battery crossed the Mississippi River to launch Grant's rush through the countryside south and east of Vicksburg! Anderson, *They Died To Make Men Free*, 202; James Sinclair diary, June 4, 1864, CHS.

11. *History of Berrien and Van Buren Counties, Michigan*, 69-70; Grabau, *Ninety-Eight Days*, 447-453; Bearss, *The Campaign for Vicksburg,* vol.3, 979.

12. Grabau, *Ninety-Eight Days*, 455-456; Bearss, *The Campaign for Vicksburg,* vol. 3, 1023-1026; "Interesting Letter from R. B. King," *St. Joseph Traveler*, July 2, 1863.

13. *Ibid.*; Bearss, *The Campaign for Vicksburg,* vol. 3, 1026-1027; Hiram Liberty Brown Civil War Pension File, NARA.

14. Edwin Bearss, "The Mechanicsburg Expeditions," *Journal of the Illinois State Historical Society*, vol. 56, no. 2, summer 1963, 252-255.

15. James A. Gray Diary, Clay Feeter Private Collection.

16. The May 19 and May 22 assaults satisfied Grant that he could not storm Vicksburg without losing men needlessly. He opted to execute a textbook siege. According to Shelby Foote, there are "five formal stages of a siege—the investment, the artillery attack, the construction of parallels and approaches, the breaching by artillery or mines, and the final assault." A key element of Grant's siege strategy was to develop galleries under the enemy forts. He had his pioneers dig "zigzag trenches" to bring his men and equipment closer and closer to the Confederates. During this third stage of the siege, the Union army actively employed its 220 guns—some of heavy caliber—while the Confederates conserved their artillery ammunition for crucial situations. The Federals spent much effort digging trenches and mines. The Southerners, in turn, shoveled back dirt to repair damage done by the enemy's cannon—especially from the Union's heavy guns. For example, when Colonel Ashbel Smith, in the 2nd Texas Lunette, discovered 30-pound Parrott rifle shells were penetrating the 14-foot walls of his fort, he had to add another two feet to the exterior slope of his fort. The 30-pound shells were not coming from the Mercantile Battery, however, since it was firing at the 2nd Texas Lunette from Battery No. 9, positioned 400 yards away with two 10-pounder Rodman rifles and two 6-pounder smoothbores. Will and his comrades were preoccupied with avoiding Confederate sharpshooters. As Will discussed in one of his letters, the battery's flag was often the only visible object for the Southern marksmen to aim at and, consequently, it became a "bullet-plugged flag"—eventually to be put on display during the Northwest Sanitary Commission's fundraiser in Chicago at the end of October and beginning of November. Foote, *The Civil War: Fredericksburg to Meridian*, 409-410; Bearss, *The Campaign for Vicksburg,* vol. 3, 931-932.

17. Major General Ambrose Burnside had arrested Clement Vallandigham for "expressed or implied treason" and tried him in a military court. On May 18, Will's hometown newspaper reported the sentence issued by Vallandigham's court martial, which specified the Copperhead politician be imprisoned at Fort Warren in Boston Harbor. Lincoln intervened and, in the words of *Harper's Weekly*, "altered this sentence to expulsion beyond the Union lines. He was accordingly taken to General Rosecrans' army at Murfreesboro, and by him dispatched to the rebels under a strong escort of cavalry." "Vallandigham's Sentence," *St. Joseph Traveler*, May 21, 1863; "Clement L. Vallandigham," *Harper's Weekly*, June 6, 1863, 362; McPherson, *Battle Cry of Freedom*, 596-597.

18. Henry Brown and his wife Delia had just had a baby. In his August 11 letter to Henry, the new uncle wrote, "I have heard of the baby and offer you my most healthy congratulations."

19. On June 21, when Will wrote this letter to his father, Henry Brown was in Middle Tennessee at Franklin, getting ready for Rosecrans' next move against Bragg. During the upcoming Tullahoma Campaign, Henry Brown and the 19th Regiment played a peripheral role. Anderson, *They Died To Make Men Free*, 208-209.

20. Will was accurate in observing "Our right seems to be doing the main work" during the Union siege. McClernand had not made much progress on the left in advancing his trenches closer to the enemy. Two days before, on June 19, Major General E. O. C. Ord replaced McClernand as commander of the 13th Corps and was chagrined to learn McClernand's men had not advanced their

siege works very far since the May assaults. Consequently, Ord accelerated the digging of 13th Corps trenches and made rapid progress in widening and connecting them. "A. J. Smith's Approach" was the one being worked on in front of the Mercantile Battery and, as described by Bearss in this book's Foreword, was "one of the most bitterly contested by the Confederates of the thirteen Union approaches." Bearss, *The Campaign for Vicksburg,* vol. 3, 932-934.

21. An infuriated Grant decided to relieve McClernand the day after the May 22 assault. However, as reported by Charles A. Dana in a letter to Secretary of War Edwin Stanton, Grant reconsidered, deciding to wait until Vicksburg was in Union hands. At that time, Grant planned to ask McClernand to embark on a leave of absence. As usual, McClernand continued to press his luck. On May 30, he issued a general order extolling his work during the May 22 assault while castigating Sherman and McPherson. When Grant learned this, he relieved McClernand immediately. At 2:00 a.m. on June 18, James Wilson went to McClernand's headquarters, roused the general from his tent, and delivered Grant's dismissal order. Major General Edward O. C. Ord replaced the bombastic politician-general. Kiper, *Major General John Alexander McClernand,* 266-271.

22. Joe Johnston was amassing an Army of Relief to strike Grant's rear. Will Brown pointed out that if Grant "should defeat Johnston and still keep the siege, it will cap the climax." Grant was not taking Johnston's threat lightly. One of William T. Sherman's major assignments at this latter stage of the siege was to ensure Johnston did not succeed in releasing Pemberton from his Vicksburg trap. It was anticipated that Johnston would lead his troops from Jackson, cross at Big Black Bridge, and strike Grant's right flank. Sherman was ready for him, having decided to defend the high ground and roads on the western side of the Big Black River. Will correctly reported a sizable Union force was preparing for Johnston's anticipated attack, but none came. Despite their fears, Grant and Sherman were better prepared to resist a Confederate attack than Johnston was to press forward. Johnston was near Canton. The Confederate commander did not begin to advance his Army of Relief until July 1. He left the Vernon area with 32,000 men, 78 cannon, and hundreds of supply wagons. Moving at a snail-like pace through the sun-baked Mississippi farmland, Johnston's army was far too late to save Vicksburg, which surrendered on July 4. The next day, Johnston received news of Vicksburg's fall and turned his army back toward Jackson, with Sherman in pursuit. Arnold, *Grant Wins the War*, 288-291; Bearss, *The Campaign for Vicksburg,* vol. 3, 1127-1138.

23. "The recent fight at the Bend," to which Will referred, was the June 7 engagement at Milliken's Bend. While Grant surrounded Vicksburg, Major General Nathaniel Banks, commanding the Army of the Gulf, invested Port Hudson, the other Southern stronghold on the Mississippi River. Confederate authorities instructed Major General Richard Taylor to send some of his troops to attack Milliken's Bend. The assault was meant to harass Grant's supply line and take pressure off of Vicksburg. As Pemberton's army withdrew into Vicksburg, however, Grant shortened his Milliken's Bend-to-New Carthage supply line from 63 miles to 12 miles by having a road cut from Young's Point to Bower's Landing. Only a small Union force was left behind at Milliken's Bend—four regiments including new black recruits. Colonel Hermann Lieb, the commander of the 9th Louisiana Infantry (African Descent), was in charge of the Milliken's Bend post during the battle.

Taylor sent Brigadier General Henry E. McCulloch's brigade, from Major General John G. Walker's division, to capture the ground at Milliken's Bend. The brigade comprised the 16th Texas Cavalry Regiment (dismounted), in addition to the 16th, 17th and 19th Texas infantry regiments. In fierce fighting, the Texans mauled the Union troops at the Milliken's Bend levee. As Will Brown pointed out in his June 21 letter, many of the African American troops were so new they did not know how to load their muskets. The Confederates were driven back, not so much by the Union infantrymen as by the gunboat *Choctaw*, firing its heavy guns from the Mississippi (a second gunboat, the *Lexington*, arrived as the battle was ending). In the engagement at Milliken's Bend, there were 652 Union casualties versus 185 for the Confederates. This engagement became controversial when a Missouri newspaper accused the Southerners of committing atrocities against the black troops and their white commanders. The allegation was investigated but never proven. Walker's Texas troops would play a prominent role in the defeat of Banks' army at the Battle of Sabine Crossroads a year later. Terrence J. Winschel, "To Rescue Gibraltar: John G. Walker's Texas

Division and the Relief of Fortress Vicksburg," *Civil War Regiments*, vol. 3, no. 3, 33-58; Bearss, *The Campaign for Vicksburg,* vol. 3, 1168-1188; Richard Lowe, *Walker's Texas Division, C.S.A.: Greyhounds of the Trans-Mississippi* (Baton Rouge, LA, 2004), 79-101; Patrick H. White, RBWPC.

24. The siege operation Will Brown described to his father was "Logan's Approach." According to Terrence Winschel, Logan's Approach "was the most successful of the approaches dug by Federal soldiers during the siege and was carried forward along the Jackson Road." On June 25, the gallery that had been dug underneath the Confederate's 3rd Louisiana Redan—near the Shirley house landmark—was packed with 2,200 pounds of explosives and detonated. Logan's men rushed into the crater, engaging the Confederates in hand-to-hand combat. The attack continued into the next day and, after 20 hours of fighting, Grant called the operation off. Winschel, *Triumph & Defeat*, 129-137; Tunnard, *A Southern Record*, 258-259.

25. Historian Terrence Winschel's research indicates that Will Brown had an exaggerated idea of the enemy casualties Logan inflicted. Instead of the 1,000 casualties Will believed the Confederates suffered, Winschel reports the defenders of the 3rd Louisiana Redan lost only 94 men killed and wounded, while inflicting 245 Union casualties. Twenty-eight-year-old John H. White, Jr., mustered into the Mercantile Battery on August 29 during the first 1862 wave of enlistments. He was promoted from private to corporal on October 7. White was wounded June 24, 1863, at Vicksburg. Will Brown correctly predicted that White's "wound is considered a serious one"—he died in less than two weeks. Winschel, *Triumph & Defeat*, 137; John H. White, Jr. CMSR, NARA.

26. At the time of this June 28 letter from Will Brown, Banks was proceeding with his Port Hudson siege. While Port Hudson's defenders suffered severe deprivations, Banks was himself experiencing significant erosion in the morale of his troops; two failed Union frontal assaults had left a bitter taste in the soldiers' mouths and caused them to question Banks' generalship—a preview of what Banks would experience after he mismanaged the Red River Campaign in April 1864. Shea and Winschel, *Vicksburg is the Key*, 189-204. For in-depth studies of the Battle of Port Hudson, see Lawrence L. Hewitt, *Port Hudson: Confederate Bastion on the Mississippi* (Baton Rouge, LA, 1987), and Edward Cunningham, *The Port Hudson Campaign, 1862-1863* (Baton Rouge, LA, 1963).

27. Living in an era where there was no "instant communication" had its drawbacks: Will did not know his younger brother was a few miles away at Snyder's Bluff. After the fall of Vicksburg, Will learned of Lib's whereabouts and got permission to visit him.

28. Bearss, *The Campaign for Vicksburg,* vol. 3, 1279-1284; Foote, *The Civil War: Fredericksburg to Meridian*, 607-612.

29. "The Fall of Vicksburg," *Harpers Weekly*, August 1, 1863, 487; Bearss, *The Campaign for Vicksburg,* vol. 3, 1284-1295.

30. Foote, *The Civil War: Fredericksburg to Meridian*, 612-613; Sylvester Strong Letters, RBWPC; Tunnard, *A Southern Record*, 272; Walter H. Mays, "The Vicksburg Diary of M. K. Simons, 1863," Texas Military History, Spring 1965, vol. 5, no. 1, 36.

31. A civilian survivor recounted the condition around her "cave" on July 3, when Major General John Bowen passed by on his way to arrange the surrender meeting with Grant: "On the hill above us, the earth was literally covered with fragments of shell—Parrott, shrapnell, canister; besides lead in all shapes and forms, and a long kind of solid shot, shaped like a small Parrott shell. Minie balls lay in every direction, flattened, dented, and bent from contact with trees and pieces of wood in their flight. The grass seemed deadened—the ground ploughed into furrows in many places; while scattered over all, like giants' pepper, in numberless quantity, were the shrapnell balls." *My Cave Life in Vicksburg with Letters of Trial and Travel* (New York, NY, 1864), 137-138.

32. With the Tredegar Iron Works in Richmond as its only major production facility for casting big guns, the Confederacy had to rely on Great Britain for many of its heavy-caliber cannon. The Whitworth was made of steel and had unusual, hexagonal rifling. Although Will did not specify the bore size of the Whitworth—it could have been a heavy siege gun and not a field gun—one expert in Civil War artillery has written that "In tests in England, a 12-pounder delivered 2,600 yard ranges

with 5° elevation …and an unprecedented 10,000 [yards] with 35°"' which approximated the 5-mile range mentioned by Will Brown. Ripley, *Artillery and Ammunition of the Civil War*, 142-143.

33. The following list came from a Confederate source regarding the price and availability of food in Vicksburg at the end of June: "Flour was $5 a pound, or $1,000 a barrel, rebel money; meal, $140 a bushel; molasses, $10 and $12 a gallon; and beef (very often oxen killed by the national shells and picked up by butchers), was sold at $2 and $2.50 by the pound. Mule meat, sold at $1 per pound, was in great demand." Reed, *The Vicksburg Campaign*, 130.

34. When the Confederate leaders returned to Vicksburg after the debacles at Champion Hill and Big Black River, they heard wild rumors about Pemberton rampaging through their camps. Federal prisoners, captured at Champion Hill, told their captors that Pemberton had conspired to strike a deal and give Vicksburg to Grant without a fight. When Pemberton surrendered Vicksburg to Grant six weeks later, he again was accused of being in collusion with Grant. Bearss, *The Campaign for Vicksburg*, vol. 3, 747.

35. Will told his father that Lib was in good health—probably not to alarm him—but his brother had succumbed to sunstroke three weeks before, during the ill-fated Kimball "skedaddle" down the Mechanicsburg Corridor. Lib suffered permanent eye damage, which would hamper the clerical career he intended to pursue back in St. Joseph, Michigan, after the war. Hiram Liberty Brown Civil War Pension File, NARA.

36. Lieutenant Robert B. King was also from St. Joseph and was in charge of Lib's Brown's company. King wrote a letter to the *St. Joseph Traveler* July 2, 1863, describing the 12th Michigan's brutal, 70-mile march from Satartia to Snyder's Bluff. Most of the "casualties" from this march had succumbed, like Lib, to the intense Mississippi heat. Six men from the regiment died from sunstroke. "Interesting Letter from R. B. King" *St. Joseph Traveler*, July 2, 1863.

37. Will is likely referring to Captain Jay Johnston Drake of 7th Missouri Infantry, a three-year regiment organized in the summer of 1861. Jay J. Drake mustered into Company I as 2nd lieutenant on June 3, 1861, and was promoted to captain in July 1862. Drake participated in the May 22 assault on Vicksburg's Great Redoubt and was in front of the court house door when his company helped stack Confederate arms during the surrender proceedings. Drake mustered out on June 14, 1864. *U. S. Adjutant's Office, Official Army Register of the Volunteer Force of the U. S. Army, for the Years 1861-1865, Volume 7*, p. 89, MOLLUS Insignee Record Card Catalog, A-Z (2nd Lieutenant, Captain Jay Johnson Drake, 7th Missouri Regiment), Civil War and Underground Railroad Museum of Philadelphia (hereafter cited as CWURMP).

38. Port Hudson fell July 9, five days after Vicksburg's surrender. Grant's capture of Vicksburg overshadowed Nathaniel Banks' Port Hudson victory. Banks' need to obtain the national accolades he had missed in July 1863 would eventually endanger Union soldiers and jeopardize the good reputation that the Mercantile Battery gained at Vicksburg. Kennedy, *The Civil War Battlefield Guide*, 184; Shea and Winschel, *Vicksburg is the Key*, 203-204.

CHAPTER 8

1. Ord was a West Point graduate who, before the Civil War, had served against the Seminoles in Florida. In September 1861, he was promoted to brigadier general and, during the war's first winter, led a brigade on the right flank of the Washington D.C. defenses. In May 1862, he was promoted to major general and sent to the Western Theater. During the evening of July 4, 1863, Ord received orders to move his 13th Corps out of Vicksburg to join Sherman. He left with 14,400 infantrymen, 440 cavalry troopers, and 63 pieces of artillery. Sherman's General Order No. 52, issued on July 4, 1863, required that "each company should have a pack mule with a couple of small kegs, or a saddle, to which should be suspended the canteens of men." Sherman was already on the west side of Big Black River and knew from scouts that the open countryside between his expeditionary force and Jackson was suffering a drought. What he didn't know was that Johnston had cruelly exploited that lack of water. Warner, *Generals in Blue*, 350; *OR* 24, pt. 2, 574-576; *OR* 24, pt. 3, 475.

2. *Ibid.*, 461, 472; Edwin C. Bearss, *The Siege of Jackson: July 10-17, 1863* (Baltimore, MD, 1981), 55-57.

3. William J. Cooper, Jr., *Jefferson Davis, American* (New York, NY, 2000), 438-441, 449-450; E. Chris Evans, "Return to Jackson, July 5-25, 1863," *Blue & Gray Magazine*, vol.12, no. 6, 9-14; Sears, *To the Gates of Richmond*, 13-14, 65-68.

4. Pinckney S. Cone Diary, July 5-6, 1863, Abraham Lincoln Presidential Library (hereafter cited as ALPL); Bearss, *The Siege of Jackson*, 62; *OR* 24, pt. 3, 520-521.

5. Scott, *The History of the 67th Regiment Indiana Infantry Volunteers,* 41.

6. Bugler Pitts did not accompany his CMB comrades to Jackson but stayed behind to help at a hospital. In a section of his diary that was not published in the 1956 *Mid-America* issue, he wrote that the battery "had a hard time. Gus [Joseph W.] Hyde very sick . . . [and] died at 10 o clock on the morning of the 25th." Pinckney S. Cone Diary, July 7 & 11, 1863, ALPL; Bearss, *The Siege of Jackson*, 62-67; *OR* 24, pt. 2, 576; Pitts Diary, July 19, 1863, CHS; Vance, *Report of the Adjutant General of the State of Illinois,* vol. 8, 740; Descriptive List and Order Book for the CMB, June and July 1863 Morning Reports, NARA.

7. Bearss, *The Siege of Jackson*, 68-70; James Sinclair Diary, July 12, 1863, CHS; *OR* 24, pt. 2, 522-524; *OR* 24, pt. 3, 502, 510.

8. After the fall of Jackson, Sherman sent David D. Porter an update on his progress and told him he had never planned to launch a frontal assault against Johnston's fortifications. Having been with Sherman at Chickasaw Bayou, Porter could appreciate his friend's position. Sherman had bonded with Porter during their troubles with John McClernand and the Steele's Bayou Expedition, among other shared experiences. In this communication, he shared some of his thoughts about the war. On a personal note, Sherman added, "I hope soon to meet you, and that we may both live long to navigate that noble channel [Mississippi River]....I trust we may sit in the shade of the awning as the steamers ply their course, not fearing the howling shell at each bend of the river or the more fatal bullet of the guerrilla at each thicket." During the night of the July 16, Union pickets thought they heard the sound of departing Confederate wagons, as did the CMB's Pinckney Cone. Unable to confirm the evacuation from across the trenches, they had to wait until daylight. *OR* 24, pt. 2, 527; *OR* 24, pt. 3, 531; Evans, "Return to Jackson, July 5-25, 1863," *Blue & Gray Magazine*, 60-61; Cone Diary, July 17, ALPL; Shea and Winschel, *Vicksburg Is the Key*, 185.

9. A reporter for *Harper's Weekly* wrote that the retreating "rebels burned up fifty or sixty buildings on the street fronting the Capitol, on the ground of military necessity, to accomplish the destruction of large quantities of army stores which they were not able to transport in their retreat. The day was sultry, scarcely a current of fresh air being felt, and the smoke from the ruins of the fires coursed along through the principal streets, making a trip through the city decidedly uncomfortable." For a comprehensive review of the sinking—and recovery 100 years later—of the *Cairo*, see Bearss' *Hardluck Ironclad*. "The Capture of Jackson, Mississippi," *Harper's Weekly*, August 15, 1863, 524; Sears, *To the Gates of Richmond*, 66; Bearss, *The Campaign for Vicksburg,* vol. 1, 138; Sylvester Strong Letter Collection, RBWPC.

10. Amos G. Throop Collection, July 11, 1863 letter from son George to daughter Mattie, LOC.

11. Throop's letter described the Battery Boys' health problems after leaving Vicksburg. Beside Munn and the Bracketts, there were many other Chicago cannoneers listed in the Morning Reports as being ill. Descriptive List and Order Book for the CMB, July 1863 Morning Reports, NARA.

12. The other "glorious news" to which Will Brown referred was: (1) the fall of Port Hudson on July 9, (2) the Union victory at Gettysburg on July 1-3, and (3) the successful Federal defense of Helena, Arkansas, upriver from Vicksburg. At Helena on July 4, the Union garrison, with 4,129 troops, was attacked by 7,646 Confederates, led by Lieutenant General Theophilus H. Holmes and Major General Sterling Price, who belatedly sought to relieve pressure on Pemberton at Vicksburg. Major General Benjamin M. Prentiss commanded the Federals at Helena, who were reinforced by the gunboat *Tyler*. As Major General Stephen A. Hurlbut reported to Halleck, they successfully "sustained their attacks until 3 p.m., from daylight, when the rebels were repulsed at all points,

leaving 1,200 prisoners." Total Confederate losses amounted to 1,636 men. *OR* 24, pt. 3, 480; Bearss, *The Campaign for Vicksburg,* vol. 3, 1207-1238.

13. After his experience at Fort Donelson, where many Confederates escaped after the surrender, Grant assiduously made certain each prisoner in Vicksburg had to sign a parole. Before a prisoner was paroled, his name was checked against a regimental roster. The soldiers of Colonel Edward Higgins' 1,500-man River Defense command, made up predominantly of Louisianans and Alabamans, initially refused to sign paroles, preferring to go to Northern prison camps. After a period of confinement aboard river steamers, about half of these men relented, leaving 709 of their comrades to be shipped off to captivity. As the Mercantile Battery was making its way to Jackson, Pemberton and his paroled troops were also headed east. But Sherman notified Grant that he would not allow Pemberton's troops to enter Jackson during the siege. Pemberton therefore had to cross Pearl River about ten miles below Jackson. Regarding this quandary of dealing with Pemberton and his men, Sherman remarked, "I fear filling the country with paroled prisoners will do us no good, but I won't let any pass into Jackson." *OR* 24, pt. 2, 524; *OR* 24, pt. 3, 484-489; Bearss, *The Campaign for Vicksburg,* vol. 3, 1303.

14. As Sherman's noose tightened around the Jackson perimeter, Grant recognized victory was imminent and gave his friend instructions on July 13: "The object of the expedition you are commanding being to break up Johnston's army and divert it from our rear, and, if possible, to destroy the rolling stock and everything valuable for carrying on war...you may return to Vicksburg as soon as this object is accomplished." Sherman utilized his cavalry, though not as effectively as Benjamin Grierson had done two months before (which was why Sherman asked Grant to send Grierson again). Nevertheless, his cavalry, with some assistance from infantry regiments, such as the 77th Illinois, proceeded during and after the siege to destroy Confederate railroads—to distances of 40 miles to the north, 60 miles south, and 10 miles east. In addition to this damage, Sherman reported the 10 miles of tracks he destroyed to the west of Jackson in May had not been replaced by the enemy. *OR* 24, pt. 3, 507, 528-532.

15. Wiley Sword wrote that Rosecrans' Tullahoma Campaign was "one of the most brilliant strategic maneuvers of the war . . . [and] resulted in Bragg being outflanked around his heavy fortified lines." Bragg was forced to retreat to Chattanooga. Most of Tennessee was now in Union hands. While Davis and Secretary of War James A. Seddon were frustrated with Johnston's lack of action, Lincoln and Stanton were experiencing the same challenge with a hesitant Rosecrans, who was slow to follow up the Tullahoma Campaign before Bragg could be reinforced. Wiley Sword, *Mountains Touched with Fire: Chattanooga Besieged, 1863* (New York, NY, 1995), 9-10.

16. Considering Will Brown and Pinckney Cone both wrote about hearing the Confederate band playing on the night of the 16th, it is likely Joe Johnston (1) wanted the music played over more than one night so as not to arouse Union suspicions and (2) used the band to help drown out the noise of his departing army. Parke's 9th Corps conducted the July 16 reconnaissance-in-force that Will Brown mentioned; Blair was posted along the center of Sherman's line in Steele's 15th Corps. Regarding the mines mentioned by Will, historian Edwin Bearss wrote, "Last to leave Jackson were the engineers who, before putting the torch to the three bridges, planted a number of unexploded shells (the Civil War version of the 20th Century anti-personnel mine) in the roads leading to the Pearl River crossings." Bearss, *The Siege of Jackson,* 92, 94.

17. The next day, July 18, Sherman notified Grant that he had "made fine progress to-day in the work of destruction. Jackson will no longer be a point of danger. . . . The inhabitants are subjugated. They cry aloud for mercy. The land is devastated for 30 miles around." Or, as he told Porter, "the good folks of Jackson will not soon again hear the favorite locomotive whistle." Johnston had helped with the destruction of Jackson. He razed many of its buildings to either strengthen his fortifications or to eliminate shelter for the Union army on the city's outskirts. When Johnston departed, he ordered the destruction of any commissary stores that could not be carried away. Some of Sherman's men enhanced the damage by robbing (what Will called "jerking") and burning Jackson dwellings, even though guards had been posted to prevent such misbehavior. *OR* 24, pt. 2, 529, 536; *OR* 24, pt. 3, 531.

18. The capture of the Confederate band suggests it was one of the last units to leave Jackson, the musicians having stayed to mask Johnston's withdrawal, and the first to be captured. While Grant and Sherman were tempted to chase Johnston, in their typical aggressive style, they decided not to pursue him. Both Union commanders understood their men were in poor physical shape. Some were still weakened by the past six months' efforts to overcome Vicksburg; others were ailing from the heat, dust, and putrid water of the Jackson siege. On the day Sherman entered Jackson, for the second time in two months, he informed Grant that his force was much reduced by sickness. Grant replied he should pursue Johnston "as long as you have reasonable hopes of favorable results, but do not wear your men out. When you stop the pursuit, return by easy marches to the vicinity of this place." Over the next couple of days, Sherman realized he would exhaust his army if he pursued Johnston. *OR 24, pt. 2, 528; OR 24, pt. 3, 528.*

19. It was "a great victory" for Sherman and his troops. During this second Union foray to Jackson, Sherman compounded the destruction the Federals had inflicted on it in May. Central Mississippi would see the Federals return twice in 1864, one time in early February and again during the week of July 4. Total Federal casualties for the Siege of Jackson were: 129 men killed, 762 wounded, and 231 missing—about 40 percent of the casualties coming from Brigadier General Jacob Lauman's mishandled assault on July 12, for which he was dismissed. Southern casualty reports were never fully submitted, but Union records reveal the following enemy materials fell into Sherman's hands and were destroyed: two 32-pound rifled siege guns, 775 muskets, 21,000 shot and shell, 1,745 rounds of rifled-cannon ammunition, 500 rounds of smoothbore-cannon ammunition, and 850 sets of shoddy accoutrements. Additionally, 621 muskets and a 2-inch breech-loading bronze rifle were taken for the Federals' use. *OR 24,* pt. 2, 541; Bearss, *The Siege of Jackson,* 85-88, 119-129.

20. In an August 11 letter to his brother Henry, Will gave a more honest description of the siege of Jackson: "The march going and coming was an awful rough one. Almost boiling hot and dust so thick you couldn't see ten feet ahead."

21. After sheltering in their caves for the past two months, Vicksburg's merchants and entrepreneurs reemerged and pursued their passion for commerce. As historian Peter Walker wrote: "Almost like magic, signs appeared advertising fruit and candy, and, not missing a trick, metallic coffins, which were guaranteed to preserve bodies. By the first of August most of the stores were open; and, said Mary Blake, who had been without such things as coffee and tea for over a year, 'you can buy anything you want'." Walker, *Vicksburg,* 215.

22. Aside from performing his duties as a gunner and acting sergeant of his squad, Will was also handling administrative tasks for the absent quartermaster—Tallmadge—who was on his way to Chicago for a leave of absence. Descriptive List and Order Book for the CMB, July 1863 Morning Reports, NARA.

23. On July 28, the day Will sent his letter to St. Joseph, Lib Brown and the 12th Michigan were leaving for Helena, Arkansas. They would remain there until August 13, when they marched under Steele's command to Little Rock. Henry Brown and the 19th Michigan, after guarding supply wagons during Rosecrans' Tullahoma Campaign, were back in Murfreesboro on July 28, 1863. *History of Berrien & Van Buren Counties, Michigan,* 70; Anderson, *They Died To Make Men Free,* 209, 219.

24. Brigadier General Thomas E. G. Ransom, an Illinois acquaintance of Will Brown's and a fast-rising officer under whom the CMB would serve later in Louisiana, was sent with his brigade to clean up Natchez. On July 13, Ransom occupied Natchez, where cattle had been crossing the Mississippi from Louisiana, on the way to feeding the Confederacy's armies. After finding mounts for some 200 of his infantrymen, Ransom sent Union raiding parties out from the Natchez area, meeting with considerable success. Four miles away from the city, one expedition seized a herd of 5,000 cattle after chasing away its Confederate guards. Another expedition, which crossed into Louisiana, captured part of a Southern ordnance train, taking 312 Austrian-made muskets and 11 boxes of artillery ammunition, in addition to 203,000 rounds of musket cartridges. The Louisiana expedition also destroyed 268,000 rounds of musket ammunition it could not transport. Later in the

month, another of Ransom's raiding parties, composed of some 350 mounted men and an artillery piece, destroyed 5,000 bales of Confederate cotton and burned an enemy cotton factory. Among other damage, they also demolished 14 freight cars, two locomotives, two passenger coaches, and a railroad machine shop. *OR* 24, pt. 2, 680-681, 685; *OR* 24, pt. 3, 529-530; Foote, *The Civil War: Fredericksburg to Meridian*, 769-770.

25. Opening up the Mississippi River to Union commerce was a prime mission for Grant's army. Many of his soldiers came from states (e.g., Illinois, Iowa, Wisconsin) that benefited from this renewal of trade. In one of the Battery Boys' diaries that Mary Livermore quoted in her book, there is an entry for July 20, 1863, discussing St. Louis newspapers from July 12: "Counted advertisements of nineteen steamboats, soliciting passengers and freight for the lower Mississippi, including Helena, Memphis, Vicksburg, and New Orleans. The old times are coming back to us! The Mississippi is once more open to commerce! Hurrah!" Livermore, *My Story of the War*, 386.

26. As the war progressed in the West, Union soldiers became more aggressive in destroying Southern property. Some of the CMB were involved in similar incidents the previous fall (November 1863) during their march from Memphis to the Tallahatchie River in northern Mississippi. Union generals at that time, such as Morgan L. Smith, punished soldiers who were caught wantonly destroying property of Southern civilians. As the campaign in Mississippi evolved, Grant's subordinates became enraged at enemy practices like guerrilla warfare, Johnston's poison-water tactics, etc.. This led them to support soldier-initiated retribution. Grant and Sherman soon adopted the same position as their men. Pitts Collection, December 3, 1863 letter to parents, CHS.

27. Bragg was at Chattanooga awaiting Rosecrans' next move. In Charleston, the Union operation was not progressing as fast as expected. Major General David Hunter and Rear Admiral Samuel F. DuPont had launched an unsuccessful attack on Charleston's Fort Sumter and Morris Island on April 7, 1863. One Federal naval officer told a reporter that the enemy's "shot struck their vessels as fast as the ticking of a watch." One ironclad, the *Keokuk*, was sunk. The Union forces withdrew until Major General Quincy A. Gillmore and Rear Admiral John A. Dahlgren renewed the attack in mid-July. The approach this time was not to rush ships into Charleston Harbor but rather to first capture Morris Island and its forts. The army's artillery on Folly Island and nearby naval ironclads bombarded Morris Island, enabling a Federal brigade to cross Lighthouse Inlet and secure a beachhead on the southern end of the island. Fort Wagner was three miles on the far end of the island with Battery Gregg on Cummings Point. On July 11, Federal ground troops launched a futile attack against Fort Wagner. A week later, an even more ferocious Union attack began at dusk. During the assault, a black regiment, the 54th Massachusetts, performed meritoriously. Its commander, Colonel Robert Gould Shaw, was killed in the attack (the 54th Massachusetts' assault was depicted in the film "Glory"). Gillmore began a siege and brought up heavy artillery. Regarding Morgan's July 1863 raid into Indiana and Ohio, see Dee Alexander Brown, *The Bold Cavaliers: Morgan's 2d Kentucky Cavalry Raiders* (Philadelphia, PA, 1959), 177-229; "The Bombardment of Ft. Sumter," *Harper's Weekly*, May 2, 1863, 279; "The Attack on Fort Wagner," *Harper's Weekly*, August 8, 1863, 510.

28. According to historian Edwin Bearss, there were 172 Confederate cannon captured at the surrender of Vicksburg—103 field pieces and 69 siege guns—along with "38,000 projectiles (mostly fixed), 58,000 pounds of black powder, and 4,800 artillery cartridges." A CMB bugler recorded in his diary that, after the fall of Vicksburg, he "Saw a park of about 100 guns captured from the Rebs in recent operations." The Chicago cannoneers capitalized on this cache of captured Confederate cannon by trading in their "old brass 6-pdr guns" for rifles, one of which, Pitts claimed, was allegedly the well-known "Lady Price of Black River notoriety." *Whistling Dick* was the famous 18-pound Confederate rifle known because "the peculiar sound of its projectiles in flight made an unforgettable impression." The Battery Boys also named some of their guns, calling one of them "Old Abe." Bearss, *The Campaign for Vicksburg*, vol. 1, 460; Bearss, *The Campaign for Vicksburg*, vol. 3, 1301; Ripley, *Artillery and Ammunition of The Civil War*, 30-32;" Pitts Diary, 41; Livermore, *My Story of the War*, 383-384.

29. Lib Brown remained at Helena, Arkansas. Jack Vernon was Will's Chicago friend from Taylor's Battery.

30. In its collection, the Chicago Historical Society has a copy of the Vicksburg newspaper printed on wallpaper.

31. By mid-1863, much as Will observed, the quality of Confederate cannon was deteriorating. Factories in the South, like the preeminent Tredegar Iron Works in Richmond, increasingly experienced problems obtaining raw materials. Securing skilled labor was another major trouble for Southern artillery production. The lack of raw material proved the worse problem and, as noted by author Charles Dew, "Output at the Richmond plant peaked in the spring of 1862." Charles B. Dew, *Iron-maker to the Confederacy: Joseph R. Anderson* (Richmond, VA, 1999), 286-290.

32. Henry had been promoted to adjutant on Colonel Henry C. Gilbert's staff.

33. Henry's friend, Captain Jay Johnson Drake of the 7th Missouri Regiment, lived in St. Joseph, Michigan, after the war. Since Drake enlisted in the Union army at St. Louis, it is unclear how Henry knew him at the time of the Civil War (they were never stationed together). MOLLUS Insignia Record Number 15822, 2nd Lieutenant, Captain Jay Johnson Drake, 7th Missouri Regiment, CWURMP.

34. Perhaps because of his personal relationship with Pat White, Will Brown knew the battery was being prepared to transfer to the Department of the Gulf. Carrollton was a "suburb" about eight miles upriver of New Orleans and was a staging area for Banks' troops. Camp Parapet, formerly a Confederate fort known as Fort John Morgan, was located there. The fort rested against the levee on the Mississippi River and extended toward Lake Pontchartrain. Codman Parkerson, *New Orleans, America's Most Fortified City* (New Orleans, LA, 1990), 90.

35. In the 1860 presidential race, fewer Vicksburg citizens voted for the Democrat, secession-leaning candidate John C. Breckinridge than they had for the Constitutional-Unionist Party's candidate, John Bell. The conservative Constitutional-Unionist Party had sought to hold the country together, without espousing the anti-slavery position of Lincoln's Republican Party. It may not have been as difficult as Will thought for some of the Vicksburg citizens to support the Union after the city's surrender. In addition to Unionist roots, Vicksburg's commercially minded residents could see their future lay with the North—especially after Port Hudson fell and the Mississippi River was opened. *Harper's Weekly* covered the July 16 arrival in New Orleans of the steamer *Imperial*, which had come downriver from St. Louis. Vicksburg would again be a key stopping point for this renewal of Mississippi commerce. Walker, *Vicksburg*, 23-27; "Opening of the Mississippi," *Harper's Weekly*, August 8, 1863, 499-501.

36. A Union army under Major General Samuel R. Curtis captured Helena on July 12, 1862. Five months later, Frederick Steele took his division there to join Sherman's expeditionary force en route to Chickasaw Bayou. Since then, Major General Benjamin Prentiss had successfully defended Helena against a July 4 Confederate attack. Steele was only temporarily returning to Helena, preparatory to an advance on Little Rock. Mark Mayo Boatner III, *The Civil War Dictionary* (New York, NY, 1959), 392-393, 794.

37. Historian Terrence Winschel has written that the *City of Madison*, a 419-ton transport, was "Built in Madison, Ind., and launched in 1860 . . . the boat served in the campaigns against Forts Henry and Donelson, at Shiloh, and on the Mississippi River in the operations focused on Vicksburg. On August 18, 1863, while being loaded with shells, the boat was destroyed by an explosion." Pinckney Cone's August 19, 1863, diary entry verified that one of Will's CMB comrades, Al Pratt, was loading the boat but did not get hurt by the explosion. Winschel, *The Civil War Diary of a Common Soldier*, 72; Cone Diary, August 19, 1863, ALPL.

38. The lengthy list of unemployed commanders included Don Carlos Buell, Benjamin Butler, Samuel Curtis, John Fremont, Joseph Hooker, David Hunter, George McClellan, Irvin McDowell, Robert H. Milroy, and George Morell. Kiper, *Major General John Alexander McClernand*, 273-278; Livermore, *My Story of the War*, 438-439; "Army and Navy Items," *Harper's Weekly*, August 15, 1863, 515.

39. Warner, *Generals in Blue*, 17-18. See James G. Hollandsworth, Jr., *Pretense of Glory: The Life of General Nathaniel P. Banks* (Baton Rouge, LA, 1998) for details about Banks' service in the Civil War.

CHAPTER 9

1. Carrollton was a small town approximately eight miles west of New Orleans (and today a suburb of the city). When the Civil War broke out, the Confederates erected a fort to block a potential Union land attack that extended above Carrollton from the levee along the Mississippi River all the way across to Lake Ponchartrain. The Confederates called this fortification Fort John Morgan, after the Kentucky-born cavalry general. After New Orleans fell in late April 1862, the Federals occupied it and changed the name to Camp Parapet. In the letters he wrote to his father, Will Brown mentioned he was staying at "Camp of Chicago Mercantile Battery" (versus "Camp Parapet" on subsequent stays at Carrollton). Florison Pitts, during the Mercantile Battery's first visit to New Orleans, mentions going above Carrollton to see the fortifications, which would have been at Camp Parapet (the training camp for the Corps d'Afrique). Parkerson, *New Orleans, America's Most Fortified City*, 90; Pitts Diary, 42.

2. *Ibid.*, 45-46.

3. In the 1860 census, New Orleans had a population of almost 170,000, making it by far the largest city in Louisiana. Approximately half of its inhabitants were recent immigrants—many of the other residents had French or Spanish roots. The affluent city represented a quarter of the state's property value. It was also a notable commercial and banking center—with 13 banks at the outbreak of the war—and was renowned for its markets. In 1861, newspaper reporter William H. Russell wrote down his observations on the local populace and the city's entertainment opportunities: "There is an air thoroughly French about the people—cafes, restaurants, billiard-rooms abound, with oyster and lager-bier saloons interspersed." *Ibid.*, 44; Jefferson Davis Bragg, *Louisiana in the Confederacy* (Baton Rouge, LA, 1941), 34-37; William H. Russell, *My Diary North and South* (Boston, 1863), 230.

4. Pat White deeply regretted leaving Taylor's Battery, which had remained with Sherman in Mississippi. If White had stayed—and not taken command of the independent CMB company—he would have had an opportunity to replace Ezra Taylor, who became Sherman's chief of artillery. Taylor's replacement, Samuel Barrett, was quickly promoted to major in July. Israel P. Rumsey then became the newest captain of Taylor's Battery. On July 14, during the Jackson siege, Taylor sent a note to the Illinois' adjutant general (Colonel A. C. Fuller), enclosing "a communication from Capt. Patrick H. White of the Mercantile Battery to which I beg leave to call your attention in case any consolidation takes place among the companies which now comprise the [1st Illinois Light Artillery] Regiment." "General Banks at New Orleans," *Harper's Weekly*, January 10, 1863, 18; Pitts Diary, 45; Loose Papers, Muster Rolls of Volunteer Organizations: Civil War, Mexican War, Creek War, Cherokee Removal, and Other Wars, 1836-65, Records of the Adjutant General's Office, 1780's-1917, Record Group 94, Ezra Taylor's July 14, 1863 letter from Jackson, Mississippi, to Illinois' adjutant general & Ezra Taylor's July 20, 1863 order at Jackson, MS, NARA.

5. *Harper's Weekly* reported that Grant, though not fully recovered, returned to Vicksburg on September 16. Simpson, *Ulysses S. Grant*, 222-223; "Army and Navy Items," *Harper's Weekly*, October 10, 1863, 643; Pitts Diary, 43; Marshall, *History of the Eighty-Third Ohio Volunteer Infantry*, 107-108; Mark A. Snell, *From First to Last: The Life of Major General William B. Franklin* (New York, NY, 2002), 279-280.

6. Edward Bacon, *Among the Cotton Thieves* (Bossier City, LA, 1989), 132-133.

7. Will's father, Hiram Brown, worked as a young man at commission and trading houses in Syracuse, New York, and Rochester. During 1834, he entered a commercial partnership with John Griffith of Jersey City. Brown moved to St. Joseph, Michigan, taking over the forwarding and shipping business his partner had started the previous year. It was there he gained his experience in operating a warehouse. He left that business when St. Joseph experienced an economic downturn, moving his family to Chicago in 1848. Now that Hiram was back in St. Joseph, he was considering whether to get back into the warehouse business. He ultimately decided against this course, taking a job as a custom agent at the local harbor. "Hiram Brown Obituary," *St. Joseph Herald*, August 25, 1883; Coolidge, *A Twentieth Century History of Berrien County Michigan*, 176.

8. From 1853 to 1860, Pierre Gustave Toutant Beauregard—who was overseeing the Confederate defense of Charleston, South Carolina, in the summer of 1863—had been the superintending engineer of the custom house in New Orleans. When the war broke out, the building remained uncompleted. It would not be finished until 1881. While Will Brown and his cannoneer friends enjoyed seeing the custom house as part of their tour of New Orleans, they may have been unaware 250 Confederate prisoners were being held in the northern part of the building. The Southern officers had been captured at Port Hudson. T. Harry Williams, *P.G.T. Beauregard: Napoleon in Gray* (Baton Rouge, LA, 1995), 39-41; "The Rebel Prison in New Orleans," *Harper's Weekly*, August 29, 1863, 551.

9. One of the Confederacy's worst defeats was the quick loss of New Orleans. On April 18, 1862, Union Flag Officer David Glasgow Farragut's fleet, in concert with a mortar fleet led by Commander David Dixon Porter, launched an attack up the Mississippi River to capture New Orleans. Troop transports led by Major General Benjamin F. Butler accompanied the warships. Two nights later, the naval vessels breached the river obstructions the Confederates had positioned near Fort Jackson and Fort St. Philip, the backbone of the Southern defense. In an amazing accomplishment, Farragut, with his wooden fleet, ran past the Confederate forts in the early morning of April 24. They overcame the enemy warships, which included the ironclad ram *Manassas*. On April 25, Farragut anchored off New Orleans with his 11 ships and demanded the city's surrender. The next few days became a series of heated negotiations, Southern protestations, and threats of Union bombardment. On April 29, the Federals raised the United States flag above city hall and the custom house. The enraged residents had to accept the fait accompli, and, on May 1, Butler took command of the Crescent City. E. B. Long, noted chronicler of the Civil War, summarized the positive and negative aspects of Butler's administration: "Maj. Gen. Benjamin F. Butler, with his troops, officially took over in New Orleans, beginning a reign of efficiency in sanitary and other conditions, corruption in administration, and suppression of the people. Citizens of New Orleans were never to forget or forgive Butler for what were termed 'bestial acts.'" E. B. Long, *The Civil War Day By Day*, 200-206. For a detailed account of New Orleans' fall, please refer to Charles L. Dufour, *The Night the War Was Lost* (New Orleans, LA, 1991).

10. Like modern tourists, Will Brown and his comrades were intrigued with New Orleans' cemeteries, which have to be erected above ground because the city is built on a swamp that is lower than the adjacent Mississippi River.

11. Hiram B. Hoxie was Will's cousin. At this juncture of the war, he was in the 75th New York Infantry. The 75th New York was stationed in Banks' Department of the Gulf, having served at the siege of Port Hudson. When Will wrote this letter, Hiram Hoxie and the 75th New York were in Baton Rouge. On October 18, 1863, Hoxie accepted a position as 2nd lieutenant in the 17th Regiment Infantry, Corps d'Afrique, which had been organized three weeks before at Port Hudson (on September 24, 1863). On April 4, 1864, the unit's designation was changed to the 88th U.S. Colored Troops. Frederick H. Dyer, *A Compendium of the War of the Rebellion,* vol. 3 (New York, NY, 1959), 1434, 1719; U.S. Adjutant General's Office, *Official Army Register of the Volunteer Force of the U.S. Army, 1861-1865,* vol. 8, 269.

12. It is not surprising that Will Brown, as acting quartermaster, struggled to cope with bureaucratic red tape. First, any governmental activity usually requires substantial paperwork. Second, keeping track of the vast amount of government-issued supplies used in the Civil War was a horrendous undertaking. Third, as Will points out in a later letter, there was great temptation for officers and soldiers to pilfer supplies and sell them for significant profit. Few quartermaster reports exist for the Mercantile Battery. Still, many such documents have survived from another Chicago artillery unit, the Board of Trade Battery. An extensive review of them suggests the plethora of documents that Will Brown had to manage. Phrased in today's business parlance, one can broadly place many of these reports in the following categories: *Receiving* (incoming supplies); *Shipping* (outgoing and transferred supplies); *Inventory Utilization*; *Inventory Management*; *Materials Sold, Lost, Or Destroyed*; *Animals Sold, Lost, Or Destroyed*; *Services Rendered* (e.g., contrabands for

hire); etc. Usually there were separate reports for officers and soldiers. Chicago Board of Trade Collection, CHS.

13. The 6th Michigan Infantry was formed at Kalamazoo, Michigan, near St. Joseph, and it is therefore likely Will Brown knew some of the unit's soldiers. The 6th Michigan was one of the first regiments to occupy New Orleans after the city surrendered. On August 5, 1862, it was engaged at the Battle of Baton Rouge, and today a 6th Michigan "I was here" inscription remains on an arsenal wall in the city. The 6th Michigan played a prominent role in the assaults and siege of Port Hudson and received accolades from Banks for its performance in the campaign. Although Will Brown believed the 6th Michigan had been converted to a regiment of mounted infantry, Banks had transformed it into a heavy artillery regiment. The Kalamazoo unit remained at the captured Southern bastion until June 1864 when it was reassigned to serve elsewhere in Louisiana, Mississippi, Arkansas, and Alabama. Dyer, *A Compendium of the War of the Rebellion,* vol. 3, 1284.

14. After the unsuccessful attack on Forts Wagner, Gillmore and Dahlgren decided to besiege Charleston. On August 17, the combined Federal forces, utilizing their shore batteries and naval guns, attempted to reduce Fort Sumter, as well as forts Wagner and Gregg. The massive bombardment continued for many days. A Richmond newspaper reported that, on Saturday, August 22, "six hundred and four shots were fired at Sumter, of which four hundred and nineteen struck inside and outside....The fort is now a ruin." Yet, the Southerners refused to surrender. On the night of September 6-7, the Confederates evacuated Morris Island. At 1:00 a.m. on the morning of September 9, 400 marines and sailors rowed up to Fort Sumter in small boats under cover of darkness. Confederate infantry fire shredded Dahlgren's attacking force. Gillmore had been ready to launch his own attack but never initiated it. While Will Brown was optimistic about the Union prospects of capturing Charleston, the campaign was faltering. Long, *The Civil War Day By Day,* 398-407; "Charleston," *Harper's Weekly,* September 5, 1863, 563.

15. September 1863 was a time of increased concerns about foreign intervention. A primary concern was the activities of Emperor Louis Napoleon, whose invasion of Mexico violated the Monroe Doctrine. Union loyalists worried France would also recognize the Confederacy and, with a strong presence in Mexico, lend a hand to the secessionist cause. In Great Britain, word leaked out that three ironclad rams were being constructed, which were to be sold to the Confederacy. In August, a newspaper correspondent elevated the level of concern when he wrote in the *Herald* that, once the Southerners had the three ironclads, they could easily launch an attack on New York and other key Northern ports. The lead article in the September 5 issue of *Harper's Weekly* wrote a scathing accusation the that ships, "iron-plated and furnished with gun-turrets and rams," were not being built as commercial vessels and warned the British Government would jeopardize its neutrality by selling them to the Confederacy. "The Anglo-Rebel Iron-Clads" & "Foreign News," *Harper's Weekly,* September 5, 1863, 562-563; "France in Mexico," *Harper's Weekly,* September 19, 1863, 594.

16. Lib Brown's 12th Michigan was with Frederick Steele in Arkansas. Brigadier General John W. Davidson, under whom the Mercantile Battery would serve as horse artillery in December 1864, had joined his forces with Steele's army in August. Steele established a base at DeVall's Bluff. On September 1, Steele's troops marched towards Little Rock. On September 10, Steele sent a telegram to Halleck: "We have just entered Little Rock. The cavalry under General Davidson is pursuing the enemy, who are in full retreat South." Henry Brown and the 19th Michigan were still near Murfreesboro, Tennessee, and would miss the Battle of Chickamauga. Foote, *The Civil War: Fredericksburg to Meridian,* 702; "Occupation of Little Rock," *Harper's Weekly,* October 3, 1863, 627; Anderson, *They Died To Make Men Free,* 237.

17. Will was correct in stating the Federals took Morris Island along with its forts, Wagner and Gregg, which the enemy had evacuated. The Confederate commander of the Charleston defense, General P. G. T. Beauregard, decided Morris Island was expendable, having strengthened his forts at James Island (including Fort Johnson) and Sullivan's Island (Fort Moultrie) on either side of the harbor. In addition to taking these measures, Beauregard strung a line of Confederate torpedoes across Charleston Harbor, behind Fort Sumter. The Union army and navy decided not to renew a

frontal attack on Charleston. Kennedy, *The Civil War Battlefield Guide*, 193-194. For more information on the Union's unsuccessful attacks and siege against Charleston in 1863, see Robert N. Rosen, *Confederate Charleston: An Illustrated History of the City and the People during the Civil War* (Columbia, SC, 1994) and E. Milby Burton, *The Siege of Charleston, 1861-1865* (Columbia, SC, 1970).

On September 8, Braxton Bragg evacuated Chattanooga and concentrated his soldiers along with arriving reinforcements in the vicinity of Lafayette, Georgia. The next day, Rosecrans occupied Chattanooga, which had few residents but substantial strategic value due to its railroad lines. After further maneuvers, Rosecrans and Bragg joined battle on September 19, the day of Will's letter from New Orleans, near Chickamauga Creek. The word "Chickamauga" means "river of death" in Cherokee. Rosecrans' superiors had been pressuring him, after his successful Tullahoma Campaign, to drive Bragg drive out of East Tennessee. Jefferson Davis, in turn, ordered Bragg to destroy the Union army, hoping to reverse the defeats at Vicksburg and Gettysburg. Meanwhile, Burnside had entered Knoxville on September 3. D. Eicher, *The Longest Night*, 576-581; "Affairs in East Tennessee," *Harper's Weekly*, October 10, 1863, 643.

18. "Parson" William G. Brownlow was a former Methodist minister in Knoxville, Tennessee, who became editor of a pro-Union Whig newspaper. Because of his anti-Confederate declarations, Brownlow was arrested and banished to the North (setting a precedent for Lincoln to send Clement Vallandigham into exile in the South). In 1862, Brownlow wrote a political treatise entitled "Sketches of the Rise, Progress, and Decline of Secession" and went on the speaker circuit. A May 1862 speech of Brownlow's was covered by *Harper's Weekly*, which reported: "His discourse was what the audience wished—a personal narration. It is the first coherent story from a conspicuous Southern Union man of the terror which has ruled the South." In October of the same year, Brownlow spoke at Niles, Michigan, a small town near St. Joseph. Hiram Brown's local newspaper editor was at Brownlow's speech and commented that, "He was particularly severe on rebel sympathizers in the North. Said the 'men of the North, who will apologize for this damnable rebellion, ought to hang higher than Haman.'" With Brownlow's fiery propositions, Will Brown wisely raised the issue with his father as to whether the preacher-editor might be too inflammatory to effect an orderly reconstruction in East Tennessee. Brownlow got into politics after the Civil War, becoming a governor and senator from Tennessee. McPherson, *Battle Cry of Freedom*, 304; Faust, ed., *Historical Times Illustrated Encyclopedia of the Civil War*, 85; "Parson Brownlow," *Harper's Weekly*, May 31, 1862, 338-339; "Parson Brownlow," *St. Joseph Traveler*, October 22, 1862.

19. This is Will's first report on the escalating tensions between Eastern and Western troops in Banks' army. Members of Ord's 13th Corps, having served in Grant's Department of the Tennessee, were considered outsiders because of the high preponderance of well-groomed soldiers from the East Coast. With his own dapper style, Nathaniel Banks set the tone for his troops. Rear Admiral David D. Porter observed the difference between the leaders of the Department of the Gulf and the Army of the Tennessee when he first met Banks at Alexandria, Louisiana, in May 1863. Author Shelby Foote wrote, "Porter was impressed—particularly by the outward contrast between this new general and the one [Grant] he had been working alongside for the past four months around Vicksburg. 'A handsome, soldierly-looking man,' the admiral called the former Speaker of the House, 'though rather theatrical in his style of dress.'" Foote, *The Civil War: Fredericksburg to Meridian*, 393.

20. Believing his brother Henry might be involved in Union actions at Chattanooga, Will was closely monitoring the situation there. He was correct in thinking that Joseph Johnston and Robert E. Lee had sent reinforcements to Bragg. He was somewhat late in writing, on September 29, "A big battle seems impending between Rosecrans and Bragg." The "big battle" had occurred on September 18-20 near Chickamauga Creek. On the third day of the battle, Rosecrans and his commanders became confused about troop placements and mistakenly left a gap in their lines. Confederate troops came pouring into the space, routing much of the Federal army. Rosecrans and his staff joined the panicked soldiers in their flight. Meanwhile, Major General George H. Thomas, on the Union left, prevented a total disaster by holding off the Confederates and, for this gallant stand, earned the

nom-de-guerre "The Rock of Chickamauga." Thomas withdrew his men that night back to Rossville. McPherson, *Battle Cry of Freedom*, 671-674; Cozzens, *This Terrible Sound*, 511.

21. The Allegheny Arsenal in Pittsburgh, Pennsylvania, was established during the War of 1812 and remained a major U.S. military facility until 1926. One 1860 governmental report noted "the facility was active in the fabricating and repair of gun carriages, cartridge boxes, leather goods and artillery cartridges." Thomas J. Rodman was stationed at the Allegheny Arsenal prior to the Civil War and it was there that he began to experiment with his cooling process for cannon. The results of his labors, the Rodman guns, became a favorite of Civil War artillerists such as the Chicago Mercantile Battery. In August 1847, with permission from his superiors, Rodman took a patent out on his process and, subsequently, worked with the Fort Pitt Foundry to implement the casting process. The Pittsburgh foundry, one of the major foundries in the North, continued to produce Rodman guns during the Civil War, though most of them were very large bore such as 10-inch and 20-inch Rodman heavy artillery guns. Since the Fort Pitt Foundry was not far from the Allegheny Arsenal, it is may have manufactured the four new smaller-bore Rodmans about which Will Brown spoke; or they could have been made at another Pittsburgh foundry. Since the term "Rodman" was used loosely during the war, the CMB guns could also have been 3-inch rifles manufactured at the Phoenix Iron Works in Chester (outside of Philadelphia) and then shipped to the Allegheny Arsenal for outfitting. James Wudarczyk, *Pittsburgh's Forgotten Allegheny Arsenal* (Apollo, PA, 1999), preface, 17-26; Arthur Fox, *Pittsburgh During the American Civil War* (Chicora, PA, 2002), 79-80, 99-164.

22. William B. Franklin graduated first in the West Point class of 1843. Grant, his classmate, ranked 21st. Franklin served in the Mexican War and was commissioned a brigadier general soon after the Civil War erupted. He performed satisfactorily at First Manassas and in the Peninsula Campaign but not at the Battle of South Mountain, during the Antietam Campaign. In July 1862, Franklin was promoted to major general. At Fredericksburg in December, Franklin commanded the Left Grand Division of Major General Ambrose E. Burnside's army and was later made a scapegoat for the disaster. Although Burnside attempted to cashier Franklin, Lincoln would not let him. Instead, Franklin was sent to the Trans-Mississippi to command the 19th Corps under Banks. Warner, *Generals in Blue*, 159-160.

23. Regarding the Union's loss at Chickamauga two weeks before, Will wrote his father on October 5 "Rosy got whaled pretty badly but it is his turn next." Although Will was right about the extent of Rosecrans' dreadful defeat, he was wrong in thinking the Federal general would get an opportunity to redeem himself—Rosecrans' days in command of the Army of the Cumberland were numbered. He took 57,840 into the Battle of Chickamauga and lost 1,656 killed and 9,749 wounded, with 4,774 missing. The victors suffered significant losses too, though incomplete records make the exact total unknown. Bragg himself estimated that two-fifths of his roughly 68,000-man army became casualties. Peter Cozzens, *This Terrible Sound: The Battle of Chickamauga*, (Urbanna, IL, 1992), 527, 534.

24. Due to the lag in communication, Will did not know that Banks' plan to attack the Confederate strongholds on the Texas Coast had run into a snag. Sabine Pass is located at the narrow mouth of the Sabine River that separates Louisiana and Texas. Franklin was sent with 5,000 men to reduce the enemy forts there and establish a base for Banks to initiate operations against Galveston and Houston. On September 8, a combination army/navy attack failed. Four light-draft Union gunboats—the *Sachem*, *Clifton*, *Arizona*, and *Granite City*—led the way up the pass, followed by an advanced landing force of 500 infantrymen from the 19th Corps. When the Unionists discovered the marshy shore would make it difficult to land troops, their gunboats assumed responsibility for reducing the Confederate forts. Fort Griffin, manned by 20-year-old Lieutenant Dick Dowling and a handful of Southern soldiers (47 artillerists), returned fire with its six guns and disabled the *Sachem*. Next, the *Clifton* was severely hit and the commander of the fleet "loaded his after-gun with a 9-inch solid shot, and fired it through the centre of the ship, crashing the machinery in pieces and effectually destroying the vessel." The rest of the Northern flotilla turned back and ended the expedition. Besides the two lost gunboats, the Federals had 380 casualties. Banks altered his plans and sent

Franklin back to New Orleans to take an overland route into Texas. Kennedy, *The Civil War Battlefield Guide*, 232; "Repulse at Sabine Pass," *Harper's Weekly*, October 3, 1863, 627; "The Disaster at Sabine Pass," *Harper's Weekly*, October 10, 1863, 646; Richard Lowe, *The Texas Overland Expedition of 1863* (Ft. Worth, TX, 1996), 20-22.

25. With the defeat at Sabine Pass, Banks decided to try to reach Texas via an overland route. From New Orleans, Banks planned to "move westward overland by rail to Brashear City (now Morgan City), then march up Bayou Teche as they had the previous spring. Somewhere on his way up the Teche, Banks would decide either to continue northward to Alexandria and the Red River country (thereby satisfying his superior, General Halleck) or turn westward across the prairies toward Niblett Bluff on the Texas border. Once there, he could dash upon Houston and Galveston." *Ibid.*, 26.

26. There was a Private John A. Hall in the 42nd Illinois Infantry who died at the Battle of Chickamauga. Since Hall was also from Chicago, he is likely the Jack Hall whom Will mentioned to his father. The American Civil War Research Database, Historical Data Systems, Inc.

27. There was a lot of dissension among the officers of the 19th Michigan, much of it arising from the leadership style of the regiment's commander, Colonel Henry C. Gilbert. The colonel was a political appointee and "managed promotions and personnel matters much like a patronage system." As Gilbert's adjutant, Henry Brown was probably caught in the middle of the turmoil. Anderson, *They Died To Make Men Free*, 219.

CHAPTER 10

1. Hollandsworth, *Pretense of Glory*, 25-29, 62-69, 133.

2. McPherson, *Battle Cry of Freedom*, 553-553, 682-683.

3. Hollandsworth, *Pretense of Glory*, 134-138.

4. Major General Cadwallader C. Washburn took command of the 13th Corps on July 28, replacing Major General E. O. C. Ord. During the Vicksburg Campaign, Washburn had led the Yazoo Pass Expedition. His brother was Elihu Washburne (Cadwallader dropped the "e" when spelling his last name), a U.S. Congressman, who had sponsored Ulysses S. Grant's commission as brigadier general and then later as lieutenant general. Ord eventually became commander of the Army of the James and the Department of North Carolina. Lowe, *The Texas Overland Expedition of 1863*, 30, 36-39; Hollandsworth, *Pretense of Glory*, 136-137; Faust, ed., *Historical Times Illustrated Encyclopedia of the Civil War*, 547-548, 803-804; "Major-General Washburne," *Harper's Weekly*, November 11, 1863, 764; Snell, *From First to Last*, 287; Pitts Diary, 47.

5. Longfellow's epic poem about the Teche region in Louisiana was entitled: "Evangeline: A Tale of Acadie." J. D. McClatchy, ed. *Henry Wadsworth Longfellow: Poems and Other Writings* (New York, NY, 2000), 57-115.

6. David C. Edmonds, *Yankee Autumn in Acadiana* (Lafayette, LA, 1979), 18-19; Dr. Harris H. Beecher, *Record of the 114th Regiment, N.Y.S.V.* (Norwich, NY, 1866), 255.

7. As he reached the end of his journey up the Bayou Teche, Franklin's force, in the words of historian Richard Lowe, "had declined to about 24,500 men present for duty at the point of the invasion—12,200 in the Thirteenth Corps, 9,000 in the Nineteenth Corps, and 3,300 in the cavalry." Richard Taylor had 8,400 men to oppose the Union troops advancing through the Teche region. Lowe, *The Texas Overland Expedition of 1863*, 60-100; Edmonds, *Yankee Autumn in Acadiana*, 176, 272-295.

8. Hollandsworth, *Pretense of Glory*, 141; Foote, *The Civil War: Fredericksburg to Meridian*, 871; "The Texas Expedition," *Harper's Weekly*, Nov. 28, 1863; "Texas," *Harper's Weekly*, December 19, 1863, 803.

9. In a letter written after his conversation with the slave, George Throop gave his revised opinion of Franklin's white residents to his father: "I am among a set of cutthroat, rebel soldiers and spies. But they have taken the oath and we must protect them and their property. It is disgusting." Amos G. Throop Collection, October 27 letter from son George, LOC; Pitts Diary, 47-48.

10. Franklin, Louisiana, is located below Irish Bend—where Banks had a battle in the spring against Taylor's Confederates—and is the county seat for St. Mary's Parish. According to Edmonds, it was "Founded by a Pennsylvanian, Guinea Lewis, an admirer of Benjamin Franklin, it was the cultural, financial and agricultural hub of the region. This prosperous town's weekly newspaper was the *Planter's Banner* and it possessed a bank, hotels, livery stables, three churches, a courthouse, jailhouse, billiard hall and other business establishments as well as a number of fine homes. Aside from New Orleans it was the biggest, cleanest, prettiest town the troops had seen in a long time." The main duty of the 13th Corps troops at Franklin was to protect the Union steamboats transporting supplies to General Franklin's army via the Bayou Teche. Edmonds, *Yankee Autumn in Acadiana*, 38-39.

11. Henry Brown and the 19th Michigan were still in Murfreesboro at the beginning of October. In the aftermath of Chickamauga, they glimpsed the battle's carnage as Rosecrans' casualties were sent north on the Nashville & Chattanooga Railroad. The 19th Michigan was helping to guard Rosecrans' supply depot against Confederate raids. Bragg had unleashed Major General Joseph Wheeler's cavalry to harass the Union supply line to Chattanooga. In early October, after Wheeler won successes at Anderson's Crossroads and on Walden's Ridge, Northern pursuers put the Southern horsemen to flight. In an action at Farmington, Tennessee, the Federals savaged Wheeler's command. On October 9, the travel-weary, grayclad cavalrymen crossed the Tennessee River to rejoin the rest of Bragg's troops, who still had Rosecrans penned in Chattanooga. Anderson, *They Died to Make Men Free*, 237-244; Sword, *Mountains Touched with Fire*, 43-43, 68; Foote, *The Civil War: Fredericksburg to Meridian*, 761.

12. A "pickaninny" was "Used as a disparaging term for a young Black child." *The American Heritage College Dictionary, Third Edition* (Boston, MA, 1993), 1033.

13. Based on Will's description of the abundant food in Franklin, the residents of the area must have somehow thwarted Union foragers who, in the past spring, covered the Teche region like a swarm of voracious locusts. Opelousas, a town to the north of Franklin, for example, had been ruined. In Edmonds' words, "Virtually everything had been taken, including cotton, sugar, fodder, corn, livestock, implements, wagons, slaves and anything else of value." Edmonds, *Yankee Autumn in Acadiana*, 106.

14. While 1st Lieutenant Pinckney Skilton Cone was in Chicago during September 1863 on another Mercantile Battery recruiting assignment—he had also been there earlier in the spring—he was forced to enter City General Hospital for an attack of "acute dysentery." Cone had become a Chicago resident in 1854; his hometown was Wetumpka, Alabama, where he had been born on January 25, 1838. Standing 5-feet, 10-and-half inches tall, with dark hair and blue eyes, Cone enlisted in the Chicago Mercantile Battery on August 25, 1862. He had worked in Chicago as a bookkeeper and "parochial accountant." He was promoted from private to orderly sergeant. In February 1863, Cone became the battery's senior first lieutenant when Patrick White became the new captain. Pinckney S. Cone CMSR, NARA; Pinckney S. Cone Civil War Pension File, NARA.

15. The Confederate assault at Carrion Crow struck an infantry brigade from Stephen Burbridge's 4th Division of the 13th Corps—reinforced by Colonel John Fonda's cavalry brigade. The infantry regiments engaged were some of the Mercantile Battery's associates from the Vicksburg Campaign—the 60th Indiana, 67th Indiana, 83rd Ohio, 96th Ohio, and 23rd Wisconsin. Colonel Richard Owen commanded the brigade. Burbridge's force also included the 17th Ohio Battery and Nims' Battery (the 2nd Massachusetts Battery from Boston). Brigadier General Thomas Green, an aggressive Texan whom the 13th Corps would meet again six months later in the woods outside Mansfield, Louisiana, led the Confederates. Green was in charge of the cavalry division in Major General Richard Taylor's Army of Western Louisiana. During the Federal rout, Lieutenant William Marland of the 2nd Massachusetts Battery valiantly led his men in a pistol-waving charge, saving his Parrott gun and eight-horse team from capture. After the war, Marland received the Medal of Honor for his exploit at Carrion Crow. Edmonds, *Yankee Autumn in Acadiana*, 272-295; Beyer & Keydel, ed., *Deeds of Valor*, 274-275.

16. Will Brown was correct in his observation Banks was coddling secessionist planters. By October, the crafty politician-general had already sent two Southern emissaries to Richmond to explore ways to negotiate a peace settlement. Banks hoped to regain national prominence through brokering peace, a scheme that died. Hollandsworth, *Pretense of Glory*, 154-157.

17. In his Oct 25 letter, Will wrote, "Rosecrans position seems very dangerous but I think reinforcements will reach him in time." Rosecrans indeed was in danger, both militarily and politically. He had bungled the Battle of Chickamauga and now, a month later, was in dire need of supplies and trapped at Chattanooga. Influenced by a flow of damning insider reports from Rosecrans' headquarters, Lincoln and Stanton feared the general would retreat from Chattanooga. They decided to replace Rosecrans with U. S. Grant. Stanton took a train from Washington and met Grant near Louisville to provide him with the news in person. The secretary of war disliked Rosecrans and gave Grant carte blanche to replace him. Rosecrans had served under Grant before, and their relationship had been a contentious one. Grant, who reportedly claimed he could not compel Rosecrans to obey his orders, decided to remove him and place Major General George H. Thomas at the Army of the Cumberland's head. Rosecrans was back home in Ohio by the time Will Brown wrote to his father about him. Grant, still recovering from his New Orleans accident, nevertheless rode on horseback for the last two days of his journey to Chattanooga, which he reached on the evening of October 23. Braxton Bragg was now faced with a formidable adversary. Sword, *Mountains Touched with Fire*, 46-59.

18. Will Brown traveled to New Orleans with Pat White and Private Harvey Weeks. They returned via Brashear City with 10 horses they obtained from the Gulf Quartermaster Department. During the Civil War, the town was a key railroad hub for Union troops moving to and from New Orleans. "Brashear (or Morgan) City was a 'miserable dirty village of a dozen houses'," recounted historian David Edmonds, "which owed its very existence to the railroad." Where previously there were sugar cane fields now stood cattle pens and railroad facilities. The local businesses included a hotel, coffee shop, dry goods store, and a bar. The men from the 114th New York enjoyed the hospitality of the "Brashear City Hotel." The 114th New York's regimental hospital, wrote the unit's historian, "was established in a comfortable building near the railroad, that was formerly used as a store." From Brashear City to Franklin, and then on to Opelousas, there were trails that led west, which the Union army could use to reach Texas via Niblett's Bluff on the Sabine River. Major General William Franklin never moved into Texas but instead halted his soldiers and went into camp. Descriptive List and Order Book for the CMB, November 1863 Morning Report, NARA; Edmonds, *Yankee Autumn in Acadiana*, 10-13; Beecher, *Record of the 114th Regiment, N.Y.S.V.*, 119-122.

19. Although Nathaniel Banks was a strong supporter of African American regiments, he opposed placing these units under black officers and reversed Butler's policy of commissioning free blacks. Will's caution over joining the Corps d'Afrique was justified because a general impression existed that only second-rate or less competent white officers served in the Department of the Gulf's black regiments. While black soldiers in the West had acquitted themselves well at Milliken's Bend and Port Hudson, they were often disproportionately assigned to perform menial labor, such as digging latrines and ditches or building fortifications. Banks put an end to this practice when he issued General Orders No. 108 in August 1864, which ensured black and white soldiers shared equally in labor details. Blacks did most of the department's heavy physical work until that time—which posed a monumental dilemma for the Battery Boys when they returned to New Orleans after the Battle of Mansfield. Hollandsworth, *Pretense of Glory*, 144-153.

20. As evinced by Will's comments, he was, at this juncture of the war, highly tolerant of blacks serving in the army. In addition to stating "the day is not far distant when negro soldiers will be at a premium in our army," Will wrote his father he was amenable to becoming an officer in a black artillery unit. Unfortunately, Will would develop a negative (bordering on hostile) opinion of black soldiers the following year, after surviving the problems the Mercantile Battery encountered at Camp Parapet.

21. Banks' troops were universally glad the cool fall weather had attenuated their nocturnal mosquito attacks. The historian of the 114th New York Infantry eloquently recounted the tortures inflicted on his comrades during the mosquitoes' nightly feeding frenzies: "The most serious annoyance was the great number and voracity of the musquitoes. As soon as the sun had gone down, these insects would swarm from their hiding places in the swamps, and make 'night hideous' with their humming, driving away all sleep with their stings. Perpetually thirsting for Yankee blood, so large and so greedy were they, that their victims looked like small-pox patients, so pock-marked and pitted they became. The men learned a new 'manual of arms,' which consisted in certain movements of slapping and brushing the ears, face, and hands. They kept in good practice in these movements, and performed them with great precision. As a defense against this dreadful enemy, the government issued musquito bars to the troops of this Department [of the Gulf], which became a necessary part of a soldier's equipment." Beecher, *Record of the 114th Regiment, N.Y.S.V.*, 122-123.

22. William Wiley of the 77th Illinois Infantry also mentioned Madam Porter in his diary: "There was an old widow lady that lived out some distance from camp by the name of Madam Porter a war widow or otherwise. She owned a large plantation and a lot of slaves and in order to get protection for her property she was in the habit of entertaining some of our officers very nicely when they would go out to her place which they did frequently when she would get them up fine dinners etc." Winschel, *The Civil War Diary of a Common Soldier*, 79.

23. Franklin had withdrawn his men south from Opelousas and Vermillionville (today's Lafayette) to New Iberia, another strategic supply and communications link on the Bayou Teche. When Burbridge arrived at New Iberia, also the site of a salt works (the Federals had destroyed it on April 18, 1863), he decided to press gang Southern civilians into constructing fortifications. He ordered the soldiers of the 23rd Wisconsin to gather all of the town's able-bodied men and have them dig ditches. It was a humiliating situation for the residents, who found themselves laboring alongside paroled Confederate prisoners, speculators, camp followers, and slaves. One soldier in the 77th Illinois remarked that Burbridge's treatment of the civilians "pleased the boys so well that Gen Burbridge was a great favorite with them afterwards." Edmonds, *Yankee Autumn in Acadiana*, 336-338; Winschel, *The Civil War Diary of a Common Soldier*, 81; Long, *The Civil War Day by Day*, 339.

24. Banks' capture of Brownsville gave Lincoln and Stanton a political beachhead to discourage further French aggression in the area. It was also an opportunity to install a provisional "Executive Department State of Texas" under Andrew Jackson Hamilton. Hollandsworth, *Pretense of Glory*, 141-142.

25. On November 20, Union Brigadier General Albert Lee led about 5,000 horse soldiers and infantrymen—plus two batteries—on a surprise attack against approximately 150 Texans at nearby Camp Pratt on Spanish Lake. Historian David Edmonds aptly commented "The Yankees were going mouse hunting with an elephant [gun]" as they sought revenge for the defeat at Bayou Borbeau. Aside from taking about 120 prisoners, the Union attackers, in Edmonds words, "captured enough chewing tobacco to supply the entire XIII Corps for the remainder of the year." Having been outnumbered 30-to-1, the overwhelmed Texans were subjected to a short mule ride to New Iberia. There, they were paraded through the town, preceded and followed by two brigade bands playing "Yankee Doodle" and "Hail Columbia." As noted by Will Brown, the center section of the Chicago Mercantile Battery was in New Iberia for these festivities. Edmonds, *Yankee Autumn in Acadiana*, 358-362.

26. Henry Roe joined the Mercantile Battery in August 1862 at the age of 24. He was originally from New York and his occupation was listed as "Express mess." Descriptive List and Order Book for the CMB, Descriptive Rolls, NARA.

27. From November 1, 1863 to January 14, 1864, the 12th Michigan was stationed at Little Rock, Arkansas. *History of Berrien & Van Buren Counties*, Michigan, 70.

28. On October 25, the 19th Michigan arrived in McMinnville from Murfreesboro. They reached there after Wheeler's raid earlier in the month had damaged the Union supply depot. The town was located at a gap in the Cumberland Mountains, at the end of a railroad line. Henry's commander,

Colonel Henry C. Gilbert, wrote that McMinnville was in a deplorable condition, noting, "The stench along the main street is almost intolerable." One of his sergeants thought the townspeople were rough and wrote in his diary that the women there chewed snuff tobacco and drank applejack whiskey. Gilbert's first goals were to re-fortify and police the town. Anderson, *They Died To Make Men Free*, 246-247; David Coe, ed., *Mine Eyes Have Seen the Glory: Combat Diaries of Union Sergeant Hamlin Alexander Coe* (Rutherford, NJ, 1975), 90.

29. By the time of Will's letter to Henry—November 28—Grant had driven Bragg from Lookout Mountain and Missionary Ridge. The Confederates suffered 6,687 casualties, comprising 361 men killed, 2,180 wounded, and 4,146 missing. Aside from losing almost 15 percent of his army's manpower, Bragg lost 40 artillery pieces and 6,175 small arms (mostly Enfield rifled muskets). The Federal casualty list totaled 5,824 men, some 10 percent of the Union troops present for duty, with 753 soldiers killed, 4,722 wounded, and 349 missing. Bragg's demoralized army retreated to Dalton in north Georgia. Sword, *Mountains Touched with Fire*, 322.

30. When Union troops first marched through Franklin, they saw flags flying on almost every building. The Stars and Stripes was the most commonly flown flag, but the banners of England, France, Spain, and Prussia were also present, as was the white flag of surrender. By the time he wrote this letter to Henry, Will had spent enough time in Franklin to suspect that a lot of the townspeople's pro-Union expressions stemmed solely from the civilians' sense of self-preservation. Edmonds, *Yankee Autumn in Acadiana*, 39.

31. Quartermaster Sergeant Samuel L. Tallmadge was still absent.

32. The 6th Michigan Infantry was recruited near St. Joseph, Michigan.

33. An Arkansas attorney, Edward W. Gantt was elected to the United States Congress in 1861, but, due to the shifting political situation, instead wound up sitting in the Confederate congress. An ardent secessionist, Gantt decided to raise a regiment—the 12th Arkansas Infantry—and he became its colonel. He and his unit performed admirably at the Battle of Belmont in November 1861. Gantt was promoted afterward to brigadier general (a rank not confirmed by the Confederate senate) and assigned to Island No. 10, where he was part of the Confederate force that surrendered to Major General John Pope in April 1862. Gantt was exchanged in August and returned to Arkansas. Because of rumors he had been drinking to excess during the defense of Island No. 10, Gantt was not given a new command. In 1863, he underwent a political metamorphosis and turned Union loyalist, fleeing to the Northern lines. He then beseeched his fellow Southerners to end the war. His widely publicized speeches condemned Jefferson Davis, slavery, secession, and the Confederacy. An address of Gantt's was published in Little Rock on October 7, 1863; additionally, Will Brown's hometown newspaper—in its November 29, 1863 issue—commented that one of Gantt's addresses was "remarkable for the thrilling, frightful deeds of horror it recounts and hold Jeff. Davis responsible for." Bruce S. Allerdice, *More Generals in Gray* (Baton Rouge, LA, 1995), 95-96; "General Gantt's Letter," *Harper's Weekly*, November 28, 1863, 755; *St. Joseph Traveler*, November 29, 1863.

34. Banks continued his efforts along the Texas coast, intent on capturing all the ports and passes between the Rio Grande and Sabine rivers. His troops took Point Isabel, Aransas Pass, and Pass Cavallo. The Confederates, however, still held Galveston and controlled the Sabine River. As author Shelby Foote opined, "All Banks had gained for his pains these past three months, including the drubbing at Sabine Pass, was a couple of dusty border towns and a few bedraggled miles of Texas beach, mostly barren dunes, which he described as 'inclement and uncomfortable, in consequence of the sterility of the soil and the violence of the northers.'" This desolate spoil of victory was where Will Brown and the Mercantile Battery would next be heading. Hollandsworth, *Pretense of Glory*, 142-143; Foote, *The Civil War: Fredericksburg to Meridian*, 871-872.

35. Since Mary Livermore and Jane Hoge of the Northwestern Sanitary Commission—ardent supporters of Will Brown and the Battery Boys—championed the Northwestern Soldiers Fair, it is not surprising the "bullet-plugged flag" of the Chicago Mercantile Battery was prominently exhibited. The fair was held in Chicago during the last week of October and first week of November. Proceeds were devoted to the relief of sick and injured soldiers. There were Nine Classes of materials donated to raise funds. The classes included knitted products and clothing; crafts; articles from

manufacturers; agricultural and dairy products; evergreens and wreaths; fruit; flowers; and foodstuffs. The last category consisted of "Trophies, battle relics and mementoes of the war; battle-flags, rebel flags, shells, balls, guns, sabres, swords or missiles of any kind, papers and documents, accompanied by a statement of whatever gives to each its peculiar interest. These will be arranged for exhibition and sale" in Bryan Hall. Lincoln donated a signed copy of the Emancipation Proclamation that sold for $3,000. Besides the tangible items for sale at the fair, there were also many opportunities for attendees to enjoy dinners, entertainment, etc. In total, the Northwestern Soldiers' Fair raised about $80,000 to assist in caring for Union soldiers from Chicago and its surrounding areas. A follow-up fair was held in the summer of 1865, as the war was ending. *History of the North-Western Soldiers' Fair, Held in Chicago* (Chicago, IL, 1864), 3-11, 54, 184; Pierce, *A History of Chicago,* vol. 2, 453-454; Cook, *Bygone Days in Chicago,* 109-111.

36. For comprehensive studies of Grant's decisive victory against Bragg at Chattanooga, see Wiley Swords' *Mountains Touched with Fire* and Peter Cozzens, *The Shipwreck of Their Hopes: The Battles for Chattanooga* (Urbana, IL, 1994).

CHAPTER 11

1. In November 1863, Nathaniel Banks embarked on his Rio Grande Campaign. Under his leadership, the Federals captured Brazos Island and Brownsville (Nov. 2-6); Confederate batteries at the Aransas Pass to Corpus Christi Bay (Nov. 17); and Fort Esperanza on Matagorda Island (Nov. 25). On December 23, a Union brigade occupied the town of Indianola on the Texas mainland. B. P. Gallaway, ed., *Texas: The Dark Corner of the Confederacy: Comtemporary Accounts of the Lone Star State in the Civil War* (Lincoln, NE, 1994), 247-252; Hollandsworth, *Pretense of Glory*, 142-143; Lester N. Fitzhugh, "Saluria, Fort Esperanza, and Military Operations on the Texas Coast, 1861-1864," *The Southwestern Historical Quarterly*, vol. 61, 1958, 66-100.

2. Charles Beneulyn Johnson, M.D., *Muskets and Medicine or Army Life in the Sixties* (Philadelphia, PA, 1917), 156; Hollandsworth, *Pretense of Glory*, 163-164.

3. Cone Diary, December 29, 1863, ALPL; Pitts Diary, January 6-8, 1864, CHS; William H. Bentley, *History of the 77th Illinois Volunteer Infantry* (Peoria, IL, 1883), 235.

4. *OR 34,* pt. 2, 17-18.

5. The regimental history for the 77th Illinois also described the "charge" on the sheep at Matagorda Peninsula. Cone diary, December 31, 1863 & February 6, 1864, ALPL; Bentley, *History of the 77th Illinois Volunteer Infantry*, 236-237.

6. Pitts Diary, January 5-19 and February 18, 1864, CHS.

7. Many Battery Boys were avid readers. Will told his father that, while stationed at Franklin, he and others were studying school texts books. White's men were in camp for lengthy periods of time, so they read anything they could find. David Kaser, *Books and Libraries in Camp and Battle: The Civil War Experience* (Greenwood, CT, 1984). Both Cone and Florison Pitts wrote in their diaries about "Sons of Mars" meetings. Throughout the Civil War, there were many references to "Sons of Mars." The name alluded to Romulus and Remus who, according to legend, were the founders of Rome and the twin sons of Mars, the Roman God of war. Like Cone, Pitts made notes in his diary about "base ball" games played while on Matagorda Peninsula. On February 25, for example, he wrote the left section of the Mercantile Battery played ball against the right section and defeated them 16 to 4. Cone diary, February 13, 1864, ALPL; Pitts diary, February 16-25, 1864, CHS. For a study of baseball in the Civil War, please refer to Patricia Millen, *From Pastime to Passion: Baseball and the Civil War* (Bowie, MD, 2001).

8. Brigadier General Thomas Ransom had been trained as an engineer at Norwich University and, prior to the Civil War, had settled in Vandalia, Illinois, south of Springfield. In addition to working as a civil engineer, he dealt in real estate. He demonstrated his bravery early in the war. While campaigning in Missouri, in August 1861, he was wounded. He twice more suffered wounds at Fort Donelson and Shiloh. Ransom was cited for his gallantry on all three occasions. He again drew notice at Vicksburg. On July 1, 1863, the commissioned officers of Ransom's brigade expressed their

appreciation for his valiant leadership. They presented him with a $600 set of military equipment, including a new sword and a pair of revolvers. At the ceremony, Major General James B. McPherson spoke of Ransom "in terms of the very highest praise." During the Red River Campaign, Pat White was made Chief of Artillery for Ransom's 13th Corps detachment. He was responsible for overseeing the Chicago Mercantile Battery (Lieutenant Pinckney S. Cone), the 1st Missouri Light Artillery, Battery F (Captain Joseph Foust), and the 17th Ohio Battery (Captain Charles S. Rice). According to White, he also commanded the 1st Indiana Independent Light Artillery (Captain Martin Klaus). Warner, *Generals in Blue*, 389-390; *OR* 34, pt. 2, 194; *Chicago Tribune*, June 28 & July 2, 1863.

9. Kiper, *Major General John Alexander McClernand*, 278-280.

10. Lawler may have been somewhat less antagonistic towards McClernand than the other 13th Corps commanders. McClernand was the one who designated him to lead the remarkable lightening-like charge at Big Black Bridge in May 1863, from which the brigadier general gained many accolades. *Ibid.*, 278-284; *OR* 34, pt. 2, 400.

11. A member of the West Point class of 1850, Richard Arnold began his Civil War service in the East. In November 1862, he was promoted to brigadier general and made chief of artillery for Banks' Department of the Gulf. Warner, *Generals in Blue*, 10-11.

12. Washburn advanced up the Texas coast, capturing Fort Esperanza on Matagorda Island in November. *Harper's Weekly* continued to provide favorable coverage of Banks' doings, proclaiming, "The command of Matagorda Bay substantially gives us the control of the Central and Western Texas, and all the important points on the sea-coast except Galveston." Before leaving Texas, Banks installed Andrew Jackson Hamilton as leader of the Unionists there. Hamilton had been involved in Texas politics since 1846 and was serving in the United States House of Representatives when the Civil War began. A loyal Unionist, he fled Texas after the state seceded. During his exile in Washington, he lobbied for Federal troops to restore Texas to the Union. Hamilton claimed the state contained thousands of Union loyalists waiting to be liberated. Lincoln and Halleck were nevertheless unimpressed with Banks' Union-governed sliver of Texas. Local Unionists persuaded Lincoln that a strong Federal presence had to be established elsewhere in the Lone Star State. Banks had no choice but to return to New Orleans to re-examine the idea of reaching Texas through Louisiana. "Texas," *Harper's Weekly*, December 26, 1863, 819; Lowe, *The Texas Overland Expedition of 1863*, 16-19; Hollandsworth, *Pretense of Glory*, 143, 171; Foote, *The Civil War: Fredericksburg to Meridian*, 870-872.

13. Matagorda Bay is located off the central coast of Texas and is bounded by the mainland on one side and Matagorda Peninsula and Matagorda Island on the other, separating it from the Gulf of Mexico. Pass Cavallo is the entrance into Matagorda Bay between the coastal banks. During the Civil War, Saluria and Fort Esperanza were located south of Pass Cavallo on Matagorda Island. The Mercantile Battery landed on Matagorda Peninsula to the north of the pass. Fitzhugh, "Saluria, Fort Esperanza, and Military Operations on the Texas Coast, 1861-1864," *The Southwestern Historical Quarterly*, 71.

14. Forts Jackson and St. Philip guarded the entrance into New Orleans from the Mississippi River. Fort St. Philip played a key role in the War of 1812 when it withstood an attack by the British. Fort Jackson was constructed in 1832 (on the remains of old Fort Bourbon) and became a garrison for the United States Army. At the beginning of 1861, both Fort St. Philip and Fort Jackson were taken over by secessionists. Federal naval forces, in their April 1862 assault on the Crescent City, bombarded the forts and passed them. The Confederates surrendered the forts to Union forces on April 28, 1862. Parkerson, *New Orleans, America's Most Fortified City*, 31-32, 67-68.

15. Mary Livermore saw the Mercantile Battery's mascot, Doggie Doggett, while visiting her Chicago boys at Milliken's Bend during the Vicksburg Campaign. She described the mascot as "a miserable little shepherd dog." According to what the Battery Boys told Livermore, Doggie Doggett was adept at foraging, helping the soldiers track down sheep, pigs, and other animals to supplement their rations. Major General Francis J. Herron was also on board the *St. Mary's* with the Mercantile Battery. Herron was a native of Pittsburgh, Pennsylvania, who moved to Iowa prior to the Civil War.

There, he played an active role in forming the "Governor's Grays" militia, which became part of the 1st Iowa Infantry after the war's outbreak. Herron distinguished himself at the battles of Wilson's Creek, Pea Ridge, and Prairie Grove, rising from captain to brigadier general. Promoted to major general in March 1863, Herron took part in the Vicksburg siege. He was later sent to Texas, where he assumed command of the Union troops at Brownsville and along the Rio Grande. Mary Livermore, *My Story of the War*, 390-391; Warner, *Generals in Blue*, 228-229; "General Francis J. Herron," *Harper's Weekly*, February 6, 1864, 85-86.

16. At the time Will Brown was writing this letter, Galveston was the only major coastal city in Texas that the Confederates controlled. The Union navy had begun blockading it in July 1861 and captured it in October 1862. On January 1, 1863, Confederate Major General John B. Magruder overcame the Union garrison and naval flotilla at Galveston with an amphibious attack. Magruder estimated that he took some 350 prisoners, not including officers. The Confederates also captured the steamer *Harriet Lane*, as well as two barks and a schooner. According to Magruder, the Federals sank another ship to keep it from capture. In the words of historian David Eicher, "The Confederate ships were completely victorious, driving away the remaining Union ships, and Galveston was again in Southern hands and would stay that way, although blockaded, until June 1865." Long, *The Civil War Day By Day*, 91, 275; D. Eicher, *The Longest Night*, 433.

17. A soldier in the 130th Illinois reached the Matagorda Peninsula just before the Mercantile Battery arrived. In his postwar reminiscences, he described the poor sanitary conditions and lack of basic necessities he found there: "our only water for drinking and cooking was brackish; and our only available firewood was water-soaked sticks and chunks that had been washed ashore....In our front were the salt waters of Matagorda Bay; in our rear, for miles and miles, was a sandy desert; consequently there were no inhabitants from whom could be procured such articles as milk, eggs, butter and other articles of home diet." Johnson, *Muskets and Medicine or Army Life in the Sixties*, 169-170.

18. Port Lavacca was situated where Matagorda Bay juts inland, across from the outflow of the Lavacca River. From Port Lavacca, a railroad led inland to Victoria. In the summer of 1863, Magruder decided to evacuate Port Lavacca. Fitzhugh, "Saluria, Fort Esperanza, and Military Operations on the Texas Coast, 1861-1864," *The Southwestern Historical Quarterly*, 71, 89.

19. In the years before the Civil War, as the national debate over slavery became increasingly more volatile, many cotton planters from other parts of the South moved to Texas with their slaves. Alex McDow exemplified this new breed of Texas plantation owner. He was from Gainesville on the Little Tombigbee River in Sumter County, Alabama. McDow moved to LaGrange on the Colorado River and became one of its biggest cotton planters. McDow joined the Confederate army as 1st lieutenant of Company I, 16th Texas Infantry, when it was organized in March 1862. He rose quickly to captain of his company. McDow's regiment participated in the Battle of Milliken's Bend and was in Louisiana as part of Major General John G. Walker's Texas division. As part of Major General Richard Taylor's forces, Walker's command took part in opposing Banks' troops during the Red River Campaign. Captain Pat White and some of his men in the Mercantile Battery would meet Captain McDow face-to-face at the Battle of Mansfield (Sabine Crossroads). "In Memoriam: Mrs. Catherine McDow Brownson," *Confederate Veteran*, vol. 40, 1932, 402; Joseph P. Blessington, *The Campaigns of Walker's Texas Division* (New York, NY, 1875), 19-20.

20. On December 8, 1863, President Lincoln signed an amnesty proclamation. It allowed people in the Confederacy, as the proclamation phrased it, "to resume their allegiance to the United States, and to re-inaugurate loyal state governments within and for their respective States." Lincoln was willing to grant them "a full pardon" as well as "restoration of all rights of property, except as to slaves, and in property cases where the rights of third parties shall have intervened, and upon the condition that every such person shall take and subscribe an oath, and thenceforward keep and maintain said oath inviolate; and which oath shall be registered for permanent preservation." McPherson, *Battle Cry of Freedom*, 698-699; "The Proclamation of Amnesty/The Message," *Harper's Weekly*, December 26, 1863, 819.

21. Captain Pat White sent 2nd Lieutenant Henry Roe from Franklin on November 17, 1863 "to proceed to Chicago Illinois on recruiting service for the Battery and to return all stragglers as men absent from it without leave." Private Orrin W. Nash accompanied Roe on this mission to bring back "stragglers" and find new recruits—and ensure that they had enough men to avoid being reduced from a six-gun battery to a four-gun battery. White wrote a letter to Banks on January 25, 1864, to protest the reassignment of his men to other units, especially the commissioning of his artillerists as officers in the Corps de Afrique: "While I am always glad to have men promoted from my command, I do not think it just to the Mercantile Association who are using their money and doing all in their power as an individual enterprise to render the Battery effective, that so many men should be taken from this Company as to again render it ineffective. And I would respectfully ask that no more details be made from this Battery for Com [commission] in the Corps de Afrique." Apprised of the situation, Banks' chief of artillery, Richard Arnold, concurred with White. Originally from New York, Henry Roe had enlisted in the Chicago Mercantile Battery on August 8, 1862, at the age of 24; three weeks later, he was formally mustered into service. When the battery was reorganized in February 1863 outside of Vicksburg, he was promoted to junior 2nd lieutenant, replacing Frederick B. Bickford. On November 25, while the Mercantile Battery was in Louisiana, Roe returned to Chicago on a recruiting mission. Descriptive List and Order Book for the CMB, November 17, 1863 & January 25, 1864 letters, NARA.

22. It is not surprising Will and his 13th Corps comrades were suspicious about the constant leadership changes. Nothing nefarious was going on, however. Generals Ord and Washburn were apparently ill—perhaps a delayed reaction to the hardships endured during the arduous Vicksburg Campaign. In mid-January, Dana took over for Washburn who "by permission of the President, having leave of absence for sixty days." General Ord reemerged as head of the 13th Corps at about the same time and began to issue orders from his headquarters in New Orleans. *OR* 34, pt. 2, 82, 95.

23. Major General George McClellan, who no longer held a field command, was in disfavor with many Union soldiers because of his vocal support for the Democratic Party. During the October 1863 gubernatorial election in Pennsylvania, McClellan endorsed George W. Woodward, who lost to incumbent Andrew Curtin. Stephen Sears, *George B. McClellan: The Young Napoleon* (New York, NY, 1988), 344-357.

24. Five days before Will wrote this letter from Texas to his father, on January 12, 1864, members of the Democratic National Committee met in New York City to begin planning for the fall presidential campaign. These anti-Lincoln power brokers decided George McClellan was an ideal candidate. They knew the general shared their animosity toward Abraham Lincoln, who had replaced the Young Napoleon. The day before Will wrote his letter, Lincoln received Anna Dickinson at the White House. The fiery, youthful orator gave a speech that night in the Capitol, where she had been invited to speak by Congress. With Lincoln looking on from the audience, she endorsed him for reelection. Interestingly, Dickinson had been one of the keynote speakers at the recent Chicago fair conducted by the Northwest Sanitary Commission in support of Union soldiers in the West. John C. Waugh, *Reelecting Lincoln: The Battle for the 1864 Presidency* (New York, NY, 1997), 96-105.

25. Dana described Ransom's reconnaissance in a report, stating, "The enemy were closely reconnoitered at Caney Creek, 60 miles from here [Union headquarters on Matagorda Peninsula], and discovered in some force; his pickets were driven in, and although none were captured, they were compelled to abandon their horses and hide in some swamps, and their horses were captured. General Ransom saw 3,000 cavalry, 1,000 infantry, and some artillery draw up in the open ground just outside the works, preparing to repel his expected attack." Having ascertained the enemy's strength, Ransom withdrew without assaulting the enemy position. Ransom provided additional details in his own report, noting his reconnaissance force left camp at noon on February 21 with "the First Brigade, Col. W. J. Landram commanding; one gun of White's battery, and 40 men of Foust's and White's batteries as mounted infantry, Lieutenant [George] Throop commanding." Ransom told Dana he was pleased with the conduct of his troops: "Lieut. George Throop, of Mercantile Battery, and the officers and men under his command . . . deserve and receive my thanks for the efficient manner in

which they discharged the arduous duties assigned them." *OR* 34, pt. 1, 98-100; Brownson Malsch, *The Mother of Western Texas* (Austin, TX, 1988), 174.

26. *Harper's Weekly* provided national coverage of "the recent great snow-storm in the West, which covered an area of three thousand miles, and was of unparalleled severity." "The Great Storm in the West," *Harper's Weekly*, January 23, 1864, 58.

27. While the 19th Michigan Regiment was stationed at McMinnville, Tennessee, there was much internal dissension and petty jealousies, especially among the officers. Henry Brown's superior, Colonel Henry C. Gilbert, seemed to be involved in many of these internecine clashes. Anderson, *They Died To Make Men Free*, 287-297.

28. Although there was much speculation about a Union attack on Mobile (Banks numbering among the idea's supporters), Lincoln and Halleck continued to prefer a major overland campaign through Louisiana and into Texas. They were disappointed Banks had gone off on his own to seize the Texas coast. After Banks returned to New Orleans, he received numerous messages from Halleck outlining how and why a Red River Campaign was going to be the next major thrust in the Trans-Mississippi. The general-in-chief was marshaling support from Banks' colleagues. "The best military opinions of the generals in the West seem to favor operations on Red River, " he told Banks in a July 11 telegram. In addition to providing back-door access into East Texas and Houston, a movement up Red River would, in Halleck's words, "open to us the cotton and stores in Northeastern Louisiana and Southern Arkansas." Halleck wanted Banks to work closely with Major General Frederick Steele in Arkansas. Hollandsworth, *Pretense of Glory*, 134-135; *OR* 34, pt. 2, 15-16, 55-56.

29. Will continued to resent men who served as home guards in the North. A regiment of City Guards was formed in Chicago during the past summer, while Will and his comrades were risking their lives to capture the Vicksburg citadel. The City Guards held their first meeting on May 13, 1863, and sought to fill their ranks at the same time Cone was in Chicago recruiting for the Mercantile Battery. The home guard officers were supported by such influential Chicagoans as Colonel John L. Hancock, from the Board of Trade; Lieutenant Colonel E. L. Brand, from the Ellsworth Zouaves; and Captain Smith, from the Chicago Light Artillery militia (the pre-war unit in which Pat White had served). Will's animosity towards the City Guards was likely heightened by the recent Sanitary Fair in Chicago—the City Guards held a prominent place in the inauguration parade on October 26. *Chicago Tribune*, May 14, 1863; *Chicago Tribune*, October 27, 1863.

30. Will was discussing Sherman's pending Meridian Expedition. On February 3, 1864, Sherman led about 25,000 troops east from Vicksburg toward the town of Meridian, a vital railway hub. Sherman's command included divisions from McPherson's 17th Corps and Hurlbut's 16th Corps. On February 14, the day Will sent this letter to his father, Sherman's troops entered Meridian, which the Southerners had evacuated. After destroying the railroads and town, Sherman returned to Vicksburg. Unfortunately for the Union efforts in Mississippi, the Confederates rebuilt the railroads and had them functioning a month later. David S. and Jeanne T. Heidler, ed., *Encyclopedia of the Civil War: A Political, Social, and Military History* (Santa Barbara, CA, 2000), 1323-1324.

31. Sherman's "big move," the Meridian expedition, was already underway. Colonel Ezra Taylor began his Union service as captain of the 1st Illinois Light Artillery, Battery B, which subsequently became known as Taylor's Battery. Prior to the war, Ezra Taylor was in business with Gurdon S. Hubbard and was an officer in the Chicago Light Artillery. One of his officers in the local militia unit was Pat White. Battery A of the 1st Illinois Light Artillery became the first artillery unit formed in Chicago when the Civil War began. Although many of his comrades in the artillery militia joined Battery A, Ezra Taylor instead formed Battery B as a short-term state unit. On July 16, 1861, Taylor's Battery was mustered into service as a Federal three-year unit. Captain Taylor performed well at Fort Donelson and was promoted to major. Sherman was impressed with Taylor and appointed him colonel and chief of artillery prior to Vicksburg. Ezra Taylor would remain with Sherman until he was severely wounded near New Hope Church on May 30, 1864. Ezra Taylor Collection, CHS; *Illinois at Vicksburg* (Chicago, IL, 1907), 328.

32. According to the War Department's Special Orders No. 35 issued from Washington on January 23, "By direction of the President, Maj. Gen. John A. McClernand, U.S. Volunteers, will report for duty to Major-General Banks, commanding Department of the Gulf, at New Orleans, La." On February 20, again by direction of the president, McClernand was ordered to replace Ord as commander of the 13th Corps. McClernand issued an address to the corps thanking Lincoln for his restoration and complaining about Grant's mistreatment of him at Vicksburg. *OR* 34, pt. 2, 133, 378.

33. John N. (Jack) Vernon was from Chicago and mustered into Taylor's Battery for three years when it became a Federal unit. In *Reunion of Taylor's Battery*—the only quasi-regimental history for this Chicago artillery unit—one of his battery mates, Charles Turner, recalled the difficult march Jack Vernon mentioned to Will. Taylor's Battery had pushed hard to travel from Memphis to reinforce Burnside at Knoxville. Before the battery arrived, however, the cannoneers were ordered to go back through a different part of East Tennessee and on to Chattanooga. Turner recollected "we were very much short of provisions when we got within fifty miles of Chattanooga; so much so, that the horses and mules ate their own tails and manes and the overcoats belonging to the men, and when we arrived at Larkinsville we were in a rather dilapidated condition." Pierce, *Reunions of Taylor's Battery B, First Ill. Artillery*, 70, Appendix.

34. Mrs. Catherine (Katie) Seymour Bigelow would become more than "an older sister" to Will Brown; they married September 27, 1871. Marquis, *Who's Who in Chicago*, 129.

35. Will Brown was not the only one complaining about Banks' fruitless Texas strategy. Major General Napoleon J. T. Dana, in charge of Union forces at Matagorda Bay, shared similar concerns with his superior, E. O. C. Ord, in New Orleans. In a February 9 letter, Dana stated "that the results already obtained by the great outlay of this expensive expedition fall far short of satisfying the expectations of the country, and that the inactive policy which has prevailed in Texas since its occupation, both here and on the Rio Grande, has resulted in the loss of good opportunities, and tended, in some degree, to impair the impetuosity of this fine body of troops, and has decidedly increased the morals and confidence of the rebels." As Will Brown described in his February 7 letter, General Ord himself visited the Union forces along the Texas coast. Regarding the position held by Ransom and the Mercantile Battery on Matagorda Peninsula, Ord recommended to Banks' chief of staff on February 16 "that Decrow's Point be for the present abandoned." *OR* 34, pt. 2, 277, 343.

36. Lincoln and his generals were concerned about the reenlistment of veterans such as Lib Brown, who had joined the army for two-year stints that were beginning to expire. On January 11, 1864 in a telegram to Banks about the pending Red River Campaign, Halleck commented, "Re-enlistments in old regiments progressed favorably till Congress prohibited bounties; unless this resolution should be repealed, we shall get very few more old soldiers." *OR* 34, pt. 2, 55.

CHAPTER 12

1. Pitts Diary, February 27, 1864, CHS.

2. *Ibid.*

3. *Ibid.*

4. John B. Reid Collection, February 28, 1864 letter from Major Reid, 130th Illinois Infantry, to his wife, Mansfield State Historic Site.

5. Pitts Diary, February 28, 1864, CHS; Cone Diary, March 4, 1864, ALPL.

6. McClernand arrived at Matagorda Island on March 8, 1864. Although trying to make the most of his return to corps command, he did not have many military units to manage in Texas. The general found himself drawn into the local diplomatic situation, from which he characteristically tried to derive personal advancement. Citing "our delicate relations with Mexico and France," McClernand fruitlessly suggested Texas be made an independent department, with himself as its head. Kiper, *Major General John Alexander McClernand*, 284-287.

7. Gary Dillard Joiner, *One Damn Blunder from Beginning to End: The Red River Campaign of 1864* (Wilmington, DE, 2003), 36-37.

8. According to Banks' biographer, James G. Hollandsworth, Jr., the general aggressively campaigned to ensure Michael Hahn became the first governor of the Free State of Louisiana: "He ordered regimental bands to play music at Hahn rallies and made election day [Washington's birthday—February 22] a holiday. He directed all Louisiana soldiers serving in Union regiments to cast ballots, although in some cases soldiers who were not bona fide residents ended up voting. Banks also allowed Unionists who had fled from areas under Confederate control to cast their ballots in New Orleans.... The turnout was twice that required to satisfy Lincoln's 10 percent stipulation. Hahn was victorious, capturing 90 percent of the soldier vote." Hollandsworth, *Pretense of Glory*, 168-172, 175; Gerald Capers, *Occupied City: New Orleans Under the Federals 1862-1865* (Lexington, KY, 1965), 136.

9. The businessmen who accompanied Banks to Red River knew many fortunes were being made in cotton transactions during the war—often with only one major deal. The speculators could buy cotton at about $100 to $125 per bale and then sell each one for $400 to $600. The profit margins were immense. For example, an individual trader could purchase 5,000 bales of cotton and walk away with $1.5-to-$3 million in profits, with minimal risks. After the war, Kirby Smith verified these profit opportunities, commenting: "I bought cotton through my Cotton Bureau at three and four cents a pound, and sold it at fifty cents a pound in gold."

For forty years, Professor Ludwell Johnson's book on Banks' Red River Campaign was the only major study of the topic. Although other books on the campaign have recently been published, Johnson's treatise remains the definitive study of both the military campaign and the complex political machinations surrounding the quest for Southern cotton. Johnson documented the dramatic productivity decline in Northeastern cotton factories. Only 25 percent of the factories were operating when Nathaniel Banks replaced Benjamin Butler in Louisiana. Johnson's analysis of New Orleans' cotton exports showed why: "Some 27,000 bales were exported from that city in the year ending September 1, 1862, as compared to almost 2,000,000 bales the preceding year." Johnson's research also revealed that some of the Red River traders were Massachusetts acquaintances of Banks. Johnson had difficulty confirming the accusations about Banks' corrupt dealings with the speculators, including the allegation of Banks and the businessmen creating a slush fund for his presidential run. Such charges, he wrote, may have originated in "a cloud of rumors, suppositions, and second-hand stories." Ludwell H. Johnson, *Red River Campaign: Politics and Cotton in the Civil War* (Baltimore, MD, 1958), 13, 285; Capers, *Occupied City*, 166; Johnson, *Battles and Leaders of the Civil War*, vol. 4, 361, 374.

10. William Riley Brooksher wrote one of the most comprehensive reviews of the engagements leading up to the Battle of Mansfield (Sabine Crossroads) and ending at Yellow Bayou. William Riley Brooksher, *War Along the Bayous: The 1864 Red River Campaign in Louisiana* (Washington, D.C., 1998), 48-50.

11. The Confederate government had established a 10 percent tax—a tithe—on agricultural products for the previous year, payable to the Confederate Treasury Department by March 1, 1864. Confiscating Southerners' cotton along Red River had three benefits for David Dixon Porter. First, the admiral was able to thwart corrupt Union Treasury agents, whose actions helped feed Confederate guerillas. Commenting on the Treasury agents to William Sherman, Porter wrote, "A greater pack of knaves never went unhung." In addition to preempting Federal agents, Porter also had the opportunity to eradicate a source of income for the Confederate government. Perhaps most importantly, seizing cotton enriched him and his men. The navy's prize law stipulated 50 percent of the cotton sale proceeds would go to the sailors, from which the admiral would derive a five percent cut. The law decreed the remaining 50 percent be paid to a fund for disabled sailors. Bragg, *Louisiana in the Confederacy*, 203, 206; Joiner, *One Damn Blunder from Beginning to End*, 45; *OR* 31, pt. 1, 780-781; Hollandsworth, *Pretense of Glory*, 179; *Report of the Joint Committee on the Conduct of the War at the Second Session Thirty-Eighth Congress* (Washington, D.C., 1865), 272.

12. The Joint Committee on the Conduct of the War (JCCW) hearings on the failed campaign, which were held from December 1864 to April 1865, exposed the navy's seizure of cotton from Alexandria plantations. A *New York Times* reporter confirmed the sailors' role in the pillaging in the

paper's April 16, 1864 issue. Curt Anders, *Disaster in Damp Sand: The Red River Expedition* (Indianapolis, IN, 1997), 2-3; Bragg, *Louisiana in the Confederacy*, 204-205; Alonzo H. Plummer, *Confederate Victory at Mansfield* (Mansfield, LA, 1969), 45-47; Andrews, *The North Reports The Civil War*, 502-503.

13. At the Red River Congressional hearings, Porter's flagship commander, Captain K. R. Breese, provided fascinating, but largely unsubstantiated, testimony about Banks and the cotton speculators. He had witnessed the arrival of Banks' steamer, which landed near the navy's flagship at Alexandria, and saw the cotton traders disembark with their shipping materials. Additionally, Breese testified that the businessmen repeatedly approached him to offer bribes to transport cotton on their behalf. While conversing with several of these cotton speculators, Breese heard about Yates' meeting with Banks in New Orleans, as well as the alleged role of the Department of the Gulf's chief quartermaster (Colonel Samuel B. Holabird), who purportedly remained in the Crescent City as part of "the ring" to assist favored businessmen in purchasing cheap cotton. In one of Will Brown's later letters to his father, he wrote about a scandal in Banks' quartermaster department that occurred after Sabine Crossroads. By the time Richard Yates testified, however, he was no longer governor of Illinois. Instead, he had been elected to the United States Senate, and he benefited from his Congressional colleagues' goodwill during the hearing. Although Yates confirmed meeting with Banks, as mentioned by Breese, he denied having any personal discussion about the presidency— though he admitted "Something might have been said to General Banks by the other parties, not by myself, to his being a candidate for the Presidency." *Report of the JCCW*, 289-303; Johnson, *Red River Campaign*, 65, 106.

14.Wellington W. Withenbury testified at the same Congressional hearings. Withenbury was a "steamboat-man" who had operated on the Red River, during its navigable season, for 25 years. During his March 1865 testimony, he stated "I had heard the rebel General Dick Taylor say, a few days prior to his leaving Alexandria, that if the federal army respected private property he would countermand the order to burn cotton." Withenbury had been up and down Red River before and during the Union occupation and remained adamant that no cotton was burned until after Porter began to confiscate civilian cotton. He also testified to seeing Porter's men convert private cotton into government cotton, "I saw cotton taken out of warehouses in Alexandria by men who appeared to belong to the navy. That was cotton which had no mark upon either end of the bale; which had been newly baled. The letters 'C.S.A.' were marked upon one end, and the letters 'U.S.N.' marked upon the other end." Also according to Withenbury, Porter was warned Taylor and his men would retaliate and burn the remaining cotton. *Report of the JCCW*, 281-286; Bragg, *Louisiana in the Confederacy*, 202; David Ray Letters, Center for American History, University of Texas at Austin.

15. Ludwell Johnson recounted how, prior to the Red River Campaign, Banks forecasted that the Confederate government possessed about 105,000 bales of cotton from the mouth of Red River to Shreveport. Johnson also noted 50,000 to 100,000 bales of confiscated Confederate-government cotton would retail for between $30 million and $40 million. If the Confederate-government cotton was seized and sold by the Union army or navy, the entire $40 million in revenues would be profit! If Banks and his speculator companions procured 100,000 bales of civilian-owned cotton (at an average wholesale price of $100-$125), they could expect to sell each bale of cotton for at least $400—and generate profit margins of 320-to-400 percent. Often, the cotton traders were able to obtain a retail price of $500 or $600 per bale. Johnson, *Red River Campaign*, 73-76; *Report of the JCCW*, 303-304.

16. Will is referring to Major General Sherman and his February 1864 Meridian raid.

17. Second Lieutenant Henry Roe was in Chicago, with Private Orrin W. Nash, recruiting from December 1863 to the first part of February. The CMB Morning Report for February 1864 shows there were 31 new recruits (32 was crossed out). Will Brown's comrade, Thomas N. Sickels, wrote to his brother on February 19, 1864, there were 37 new additions to the battery. Sickels' number probably included the current battery members who stayed in Chicago beyond their allotted time and whom Captain Pat White had asked Roe to retrieve. Among Roe's new recruits was Nelson Smith. Smith exemplified the demographic changes among the Mercantile Battery's recruits since August

1862. At the time of the battery's organization, its recruits predominantly lived in Chicago, and the United States was their birthplace. Contrary to that profile, Nelson Smith was born in Canada and was living in Ford County, a rural area south of Chicago. Several of Roe's new recruits were also from Ford County; others came from small towns such as Lockport. (More than half of Roe's new recruits were from either Ford County or Lockport). Like Smith, many were immigrants, hailing from countries such as Ireland, England, Germany, Denmark, the Netherlands, and Scotland. When the Mercantile Battery was formed, about 10 percent of the recruits were immigrants. Since then, immigrants accounted for 40 percent of the recruits. Descriptive List and Order Book for the CMB, February 29, 1864 Morning Report, NARA; Thomas N. Sickels Letters, February 29, 1864 to brother Ed, ALPL; Descriptive List and Order Book for the CMB, Analysis of 1862-1865 Descriptive Rolls, NARA; Nelson Smith Enlistment Papers, RBWPC.

18. As an experienced politician, Banks knew the value of favorable newspaper coverage. He had encouraged three journalists to accompany him to New Orleans. Two of them—correspondents from the *New York Herald* and *Boston Traveller*—were installed as editors of the *Delta* newspaper, which was renamed *The Era*. Banks made sure *The Era* provided positive coverage of his exploits in Texas and Louisiana. Banks believed, as historian Gerald Capers wrote, "a favorable press was essential to the whole Unionization process" he was instituting. Southern-oriented papers like *The Picayune* had to be careful what they printed. The aftermath of the Red River Campaign would test Banks's ability to control the news in Louisiana. Capers, *Occupied City*, 178-179.

19. Lieutenant. Robert B. King was a friend of Will's older brother, Henry, who commanded Lib Brown's company at Vicksburg.

20. The first quartermaster sergeant for the Mercantile Battery (Edward J. Crandall) only lasted a few months and had spent much of that time on leave. Samuel H. Tallmadge replaced him on December 9, 1862 (backdated to December 1). Will Brown found himself handling many of Tallmadge's duties and complained to his father about the quartermaster's frequent absences. During the Vicksburg siege, members of the Mercantile Battery signed a petition, requesting White get rid of Tallmadge: "Experience having long since shown us that the present incumbent of the office of Commissary [Quartermaster] Sergeant of this Battery is no way fitted for the position....through his wanton neglect we are made innocent sufferers. Therefore it is our earnest request that Saml H Tallmage be, as soon as practicable, displaced from the position." They ended their petition recommending that Private John B. Kitt be Tallmadge's successor. There is no evidence Will Brown signed the petition nor is there an explanation of why White chose not to replace Tallmadge with Kitt. After the siege of Jackson, Tallmadge went on sick furlough (beginning August 15). Will continued to handle his quartermaster responsibilities and became White's administrative partner. Interestingly, Samuel Tallmadge remained with the battery until it mustered out in June of 1865. Patrick H. White Collection, June 10, 1863 petition to White, RBWPC; Descriptive List and Order Book for the CMB, Morning Reports for December 9, 1862 & August 9, 1863, NARA.

21. White was Chief of Artillery for Ransom's detachment of the 13th Corps on the Red River Campaign. Ransom's detachment included the 3rd Division, commanded by Brigadier General Robert A. Cameron, and the 4th Division, led by Colonel William J. Landram. Cameron's divisional artillery was composed of the 1st Missouri Light, Battery A (Lieutenant Elisha Cole) and the Ohio Light, 2nd Battery (Lieutenant William H. Harper). The Mercantile Battery (Lieutenant P. S. Cone) served in Landram's division, as did the Indiana Light, 1st Battery (Captain Martin Klauss). White was responsible for coordinating the batteries of both divisions. *OR* 34, pt.1, 169.

22. Will sent his father information on the March 4 gubernatorial inauguration of Michael Hahn, the politician whom Banks picked to run Louisiana. Hahn was a German immigrant who grew up in the Crescent City and had been a Stephen Douglas Democrat before the war. When Farragut and Butler captured New Orleans in 1862, Michael Hahn openly declared himself a Unionist. After Hahn's inauguration, Banks set in motion the process for electing delegates to draft a new state constitution at an April 6 convention. Electing these delegates preoccupied Banks at Alexandria and Grand Ecore. According to historian Jefferson Davis Bragg, Banks, before leaving for his Red River Campaign, issued a proclamation showing he planned "to conquer the whole state, for provision was

made for delegates from all forty-eight parishes with a total membership of 152." While the Free State of Louisiana was being created, the Confederate state government continued to operate at Shreveport with a wounded and disabled Southern veteran—Henry Watkins Allen—as its governor. This may also explain why Banks was so intent on occupying all of Louisiana. By reconstructing the entire state, and capturing its voting block for the fall 1864 presidential election, Banks would strengthen his political position as the Republican candidate. Bragg, *Louisiana in the Confederacy*, 274-289; Hollandsworth, *Pretense of Glory*, 173.

23. At the end of March, Banks and Franklin had more than 35,000 soldiers in their Red River expedition. By the time they headed toward Sabine Crossroads on April 7, they had less than 25,000 men with them. Ransom and Lee each had about 5,000 men under their command while Franklin's 19th Corps, the Corps de Afrique, and Banks' headquarters staff together provided in excess of 13,000 men. In addition to these 18,000 soldiers, there were 5,000 other men—part of the original 10,000 loaned by Sherman—under A. J. Smith who brought up the rear of the 20-mile-long Union column at Pleasant Hill. Prior to the Battle of Sabine Crossroads, Banks had lost the use of about half of Sherman's men (Major General James McPherson recalled Brigadier General Alfred Washington Ellet's 3,000-man Marine Brigade to Vicksburg while Brigadier General Thomas Kilby Smith's 2,000 men accompanied Porter's fleet up Red River). Banks himself left behind Brigadier General Cuvier Grover's 3,600-man division of the 19th Corps to guard his Alexandria supply depot, and some soldiers may also have remained at Grand Ecore to guard the transports. *OR* 34, pt. 1, 167-168; *Report of JCCW*, xxxvi; Johnson, *Red River Campaign*, 110.

24. Will referred to the easy victory Smith and Porter had won on March 14, 1864, at Fort De Russy. Cotton confiscation began there, with *Harper's Weekly* reporting 800 bales of cotton from Fort De Russy reaching the navy's headquarters at Cairo on March 17. Will was also excited about Henderson Hill. During the night of March 21, a reconnaissance force led by Brigadier Joseph A. Mower from Smith's 16th Corps—with six regiments of Sherman's infantry and a brigade of Banks' cavalry—departed Alexandria and made a 25-mile march. They surprised and captured 250 Confederate cavalrymen, 200 horses, and a four-gun battery. This loss of cavalry hindered Taylor's defensive efforts until Brigadier General Thomas Green's wild Texas horsemen showed up for the April 7 engagements at Wilson's Farm and Carroll's Mill. "Sketches of the Red River Expedition," *Harper's Weekly*, April 30, 1864, 277; *OR* 34, pt.1, 198; Johnson, *Red River Campaign*, 96-97.

25. The CMB passed through Vermillionville, a town west of New Iberia along Bayou Teche. Six months earlier, after the Battle of Carrion Crow, Northern prisoners, including men from the 67th Indiana and 23rd Wisconsin infantry regiments, were abused by the townspeople. Cone observed in his diary it was at Vermillionville (today's Lafayette) that the captured "Union soldiers were spit upon when they were prisoners by the women. I confess that the evil one prompted me to wish the town burned down." Cone's diary entry reflected the anger of Banks' soldiers, who were supposed to be on their best behavior. Some of the Northerners sought vengeance, as described by the 67th Indiana's regimental historian: "We had not been in camp but a little while when the whole prairie was lit up by a burning sugar house. Gen. Franklin immediately put our regiment and the 23d Wisconsin under arrest." Franklin released the men when no one agreed to testify against them. Cone Diary, March 19-20, 1864, ALPL; Scott, *The History of the 67th Regiment Indiana Infantry*, 69.

26. Colonel John S. Clark was Banks' aide-de-camp and had been with the general since December 1861. He estimated Taylor and his men destroyed approximately 200,000 bales of Confederate cotton between Alexandria and Shreveport. Ironically, while Clark denied that Banks or his men had engaged in cotton commerce, he himself was reported to have bought 300 bales! *Report of JCCW*, 192, 197-198, 276; Cone Diary, March 29, 1864, ALPL.

27. The men of the 77th Illinois noticed the same international pleas for mercy that Cone observed. As one member of the regiment recollected, "On some of the residences were placards bearing the inscription: 'NEUTRALITY—FRENCH PROTECTION HERE.'" Cone considered Natchitoches "seedy." A surgeon of the 114th New York Infantry found it appealing, calling it a "quaint old Spanish town, of about two thousand inhabitants." Apart from the town of Franklin, the New Yorker thought, "Natchitoches probably was the most beautiful inland town of the State.

Although its buildings are of an antique architecture, yet they bear an air of neatness and elegance. Unlike most southern villages, the houses are all painted, and have green blinds." About 25 years before the Union soldiers entered Natchitoches, the Red River channel, once running alongside the vibrant town, had shifted about five miles east. The large steamboats that once stopped at Natchitoches now bypassed it on their way up and down the Red River. With the loss of its commerce, Natchitoches became a refined resort town. William B. Jordan and William B. Jordan, Jr., ed., *The Civil War Journals of John Mead Gould, 1861-1866* (Baltimore, MD, 1997), 321; Cone Diary, April 1, 1864, ALPL; Bentley, *History of the 77th Illinois Volunteer Infantry*, 248; Beecher, *Record of the 114th Regiment, N.Y.S.V.*, 306; Daniel Graves, *Profiles of Natchitoches History*, vol. 1 (Natchitoches, LA, 1996), 2-9.

28. George Throop thought the CMB remained in Natchitoches because of a delay in the "distribution of supplies." Others believed the delay was more attributable to Banks' electioneering, as reinforced by the *Natchitoches Union's* headlines. The Battery Boys learned that Grant had been promoted to general-in-chief and was reportedly going to "transfer two or three western corps to the Army of the Potomac." They desperately hoped to be included so they could escape from the Department of the Gulf. Amos Gager Throop Collection, George Throop letters from April 3 and 5, 1864, to his sister Mattie, LOC; Steven E. Woodworth, ed. *The Musick of the Mocking Birds, the Roar of the Cannon: The Civil War Diary and Letters of William Winters* (Lincoln, NE, 1998), 121-122; November 1, 1864, issue of the *Natchitoches Union*, Watson Memorial Library, Cammie G. Henry Research Center, Northwestern State University of Louisiana.

29. Nathaniel Banks and William Franklin, along with brigadier generals William H. Emory and William Dwight, received a warmer reception from the 19th Corps on April 5 than what the 13th Corps had given them the previous day. In the regimental history of a 19th Corps unit, it was noted, "The customary salutes were given, together with three rousing cheers." Cone Diary, April 4, 1864, ALPL; Beecher, *Record of the 114th Regiment, N.Y.S.V.*, 307.

30. In his testimony at the Congressional hearing, Porter commented on the elections Banks held at Alexandria and Grand Ecore. Beside causing unnecessary delays to the campaign's progress, Porter considered Banks' political activities ridiculous, stating "the election at Grand Ecore was a perfect farce....the people were very unwilling to vote; they were very much frightened and did not want to vote. But they were impressed with the notion if they would come forward and prove their loyalty by voting they would be allowed to take their cotton and do what they pleased with it." Plummer, *Confederate Victory at Mansfield*, 48-49; *Report of the JCCW*, 280-281.

31. In his war memoir, Richard Taylor opined that if Banks had not delayed and instead "pushed to Mansfield on the 5th instead of the 8th of April, he would have met but little opposition..." and that "cotton and elections seem to have been the chief causes of delay." Taylor's men closely monitored the Federals' movements. A local legend (and one repeated in the May 1925 issue of the *Confederate Veteran*) purports that Taylor had arranged with a local doctor to send him a "signal" to reveal over which route Banks would lead his troops from Natchitoches and Grand Ecore: A plain, unbraided yellow cotton shirt signified Banks was taking the inland way to Shreveport. Regarding the continued sectional dissension in Franklin's army, some of Ransom's men believed, in the words of one Illinois veteran, the 19th Corps typically marched in "the front [of Bank's army], having every advantage of forage, and of freedom from lagging men and teams....But as soon as the sound of battle was heard, the pets were halted, and the 13th Corps was sent to the front." Richard Taylor, *Destruction and Reconstruction: Personal Experiences of the Late War* (New York, NY, 1879), 192-193; Plummer, *Confederate Victory at Mansfield*, 50-51; Bentley, *History of the 77th Illinois Volunteer Infantry*, 248-249.

32. Porter's progress was delayed because the Red River was not rising sufficiently to float his deeper-draft ironclads. A Red River pilot later verified Porter's claim about the unusual low level of the river, commenting "there had been but one year, 1855, in which the river had failed to rise; but it was rather late in the year for a rise [late March], which usually commenced in January." *Report of JCCW*, 288.

33. Colonel Thomas J. Lucas of the 16th Indiana Mounted Infantry commanded the brigade of Union horse soldiers who rode with Mower and surprised the Confederates at Henderson's Hill on March 21.

34. The $200 bounty that Lib was being offered to rejoin the army was twice the size of the one that Will received when he enlisted in August 1862—he got $25 upfront with the remaining $75 to be paid when he finished his service. William L. Brown CMSR, NARA.

CHAPTER 13

1. *OR* 34, pt.1, 447-448; *Report of the JCCW*, 188; Snell, *From First To Last*, 304.

2. John B. Reid Letters, April 2, 1864, letter from Major Reid, 130th Illinois Infantry, to his wife, Mansfield State Historic Site.

3. Educated at the Jesuit College in St. Louis, Walker was commissioned into the United States Army in 1846 and took part in the Mexican War. Having risen to the rank of captain, he resigned in July 1861 to fight for the Confederacy. Warner, *Generals in Gray,* 319-320.

4. Lowe, *Walker's Texas Division C.S.A.,* 63-64, 88-96, 135-145.

5. William Read Scurry grew up in Tennessee. After becoming a lawyer he moved to and practiced in East Texas. Scurry fought in the Mexican War and became a state legislator. During those years Sam Houston, a political opponent, gave Scurry the nickname "Dirty Neck Bill." After the outbreak of the Civil War, Scurry took part in Confederate Brigadier General Henry H. Sibley's ill-fated campaign to seize New Mexico. In September 1862, Scurry was promoted to brigadier general and enjoyed success in leading Magruder's land forces during the Confederate recapture of Galveston. Charles G. Anderson, *Confederate General William Read "Dirty Neck Bill" Scurry, 1821-1864* (Tallahassee, FL, 1999), xi-xii; Warner, *Generals in Gray*, 270-271; Blessington, *The Campaigns of Walker's Texas Division*, 163-181; Lowe, *Walker's Texas Division C.S.A.,* 173, 177-178; Joiner, *One Damn Blunder from Beginning to End*, 45-50.

6. In his memoir, Richard Taylor wrote, "My confidence of success in the impending engagement was inspired by accurate knowledge of the Federal movements. . . . On the morning of the 7th of April Admiral Porter left Grand Ecore with six gunboats and twenty transports, on which last were embarked some twenty-five hundred troops." Taylor had a good estimate of size of the army Banks was leading to Shreveport (approximately 18,000) and knew it was not concentrated. Indeed, it was strung out more than 20 miles from Mansfield to Pleasant Hill. About 5,300 of Taylor's men were infantry; 3,000 were cavalry; and the balance artillery. The cavalry fight at Wilson's Farm convinced him it was time to take a stand near Sabine Crossroads. Taylor, *Destruction and Reconstruction*, 161-162; Plummer, *Confederate Victory at Mansfield*, 14-16; *Report of the JCCW*, xli, 188.

7. A correspondent from the *Philadelphia Press* described Albert Lee, a 30-year-old former Kansas lawyer, as "a favorite of the Lieutenant-General [Grant], and with the reputation of being an efficient and active officer." Colonel John S. Clark, one of Banks' aides-de-camp, noted that "A general tone of censure at [Franklin's] headquarters regarding the cavalry. . . . [During the skirmish at Wilson's Farm] General Franklin flatly refused reinforcements, said 'he [Lee] must fight them alone—that was what he was there for.'" On the morning of the Sabine Crossroads battle, Franklin reportedly assured Banks, "There will be no fighting." Moore, *The Rebellion Record,* vol. 8, 545; *Report of the JCCW*, xxxvii, 194; *OR* 34, pt. 1, 455.

8. According to Franklin, he had about 950 wagons in his supply train, approximately 250 of which belonged to Lee's cavalry train. Lee later estimated he had 320 to 350 wagons. In response to Lee's continued requests to move the cavalry train to the rear with the army's train, Franklin refused. He had failed to grasp that since Alexandria, he was also in charge of the army's logisitics for both his infantry and Lee's cavalry. After Sabine Crossroads, Franklin admitted to keeping Lee's cavalry train far up front: "If it [the infantry column] had taken the 250 which the cavalry had and put them in front of my infantry train, my infantry wagons would never have got into camp the day of my march. The consequence would have been that the cavalry would have had their wagons up, but at the expense of the infantry. I therefore told General Lee that he must take care of his own wagons."

During the Joint Committee's investigation, Lieutenant Colonel George B. Drake, the Department of the Gulf's assistant adjutant general, stated the cumbersome cavalry train was unnecessary because Lee's "cavalry could carry three or four days' supplies about their persons and in their haversacks" to take care of their daily needs. For additional rations and forage "they could have sent up a certain number of wagons every night" from the main infantry train. Franklin's stubbornness and pettiness (1) created the obstruction that hampered his retreating army on the narrow Mansfield road and (2) reduced the number of cavalrymen available to fight in his front. Report of the JCCW, xli, 12, 47, 55-59, 66; H. L. Landers, "Wet Sand and Cotton—Banks' Red River Campaign," *Louisiana Historical Quarterly*, vol. 19, no. 1 (January 1936), 178-179.

9. Carl L. Duaine, *The Dead Men Wore Boots: An Account of the 32nd Texas Volunteer Cavalry, CSA, 1862-1865* (Austin, TX, 1966), 55.

10. During the Bayou Teche Campaign, Green led the successful surprise attack at Bayou Bourbeau. Taylor admired Green and his Texas horsemen, writing, "The men, hardy frontiersmen, excellent riders, and skilled riflemen, were fearless and self-reliant, but discharged their duty as they liked and when they liked . . . they were admirable fighters." Banks' reported losses at Wilson's Farm (14 killed, 39 wounded, and nine missing) should have alerted Franklin to the exposed condition of the Union column. Taylor, *Destruction and Reconstruction*, 150-153, 178-179; *OR* 34, pt.1, 199; Joiner, *One Damn Blunder from Beginning to End*, 103.

11. Norman D. Brown, ed., *Journey to Pleasant Hill: The Civil War Letters of Captain Elijah P. Petty, Walker's Texas Division, CSA* (San Antonio, TX, 1982), 387.

12. McDow's younger brother John was born in 1829. He graduated from Jefferson Medical Schools in Philadelphia and did postgraduate work in New Orleans. There he studied diseases related to the Southern climate, such as malaria. John McDow enlisted in Terry's Texas Rangers in 1861 but later served in an infantry brigade led by Brigadier General Camille Armand Jules Marie, prince de Polignac. "His [John McDow's] last act was to remove his overcoat to give to a sick soldier, and he thus contracted pneumonia and died among strangers." "In Memoriam: Mrs. Catherine McDow Brownson," *Confederate Veteran*, vol. 40, 1932, 402; ."In Memoriam: John Ramsey McDow, M.D.," *Confederate Veteran*, vol. 34, 1926, 330.

13. Peter W. Gravis, *Twenty-Five Years on the Outside Row of the Northwest Texas Annual Conference* (Comanche, TX, 1892), 29.

14. Edwin C. Bearss, ed., *A Louisiana Confederate: Diary of Felix Pierre Poche* (Natchitoches, LA, 1972), 105-106; Theodore P. Savas, "Col. James H. Beard and the Consolidated Crescent Regiment," *Civil War Regiments*, vol. 4, no. 2, 79-82.

15. Blessington, *The Campaigns of Walker's Texas Division*, 183; Brown, *Journey to Pleasant Hill*, 391.

16. Blessington, *The Campaigns of Walker's Texas Division*, 185-186.

17. Richard Taylor described the ground he selected for the Sabine Crossroads battlefield as "an open field eight hundred yards in width by twelve hundred in length." A contemporaneous description of the Mansfield site was published with the early Mercantile Battery accounts in the *Chicago Tribune*. It was provided by a man named A. W. Mack, who wrote in his memorandum book what he saw when the battle began at 4:00 p.m.: "The battlefield was a large, open, irregular shaped field, through about one-half of which on the right of the road a narrow belt of timber ran. . . .The road passed through the center of the field in a north-westerly direction towards Mansfield. . . .The ridge at the entrance to the field on the side of our advance was close up to the woods and commanded the whole battlefield. . . .The outer line of the field beyond the belt of timber on the right was an irregular semicircle . . . .The rebel forces, occupying a front of about one mile, were stationed under cover of the woods along the further line of these fields . . . .The main body of the rebels was evidently on the right of the road." Taylor, *Destruction and Reconstruction*, 160; "A Letter from Hon. A. W. Mack, Grand Ecore, April 11, 1864," *Chicago Tribune*, April 25, 1864; Richard B. Irwin, *History of the Nineteenth Army Corps* (Baton Rouge, LA, 1985), 301-302; Johnson, *Red River Campaign*, 127; Hollandsworth, *Pretense of Glory*, 186.

18. J. T. Woods, *Services of the Ninety-Sixth Ohio Volunteers* (Toledo, OH, 1874), 58; Charles Freeman Read Papers, 1861-1929, Mansfield State Historic Site.

19. According to witness A. W. Mack, "On the right [of the Mansfield battlefield], and in the belt of timber which separated the 1st from the 2nd field was [Colonel Thomas] Lucas' Cavalry Brigade, mostly dismounted and deployed as skirmishers, while behind and supporting this Brigade was the 4th Division, 13th Army Corps, under command of Colonel [William J.] Landram. The 23d Wisconsin, however, which occupied the left flank of this Division, was on the left of the road acting [as] a support to [Captain Ormand F.] Nims' battery. The 4th Division was composed of the following order, commencing at the right, viz.: 83d Ohio, 96th Ohio, 19th Ky., 130th Ill., 48th Ohio, 67th Ind., and [remainder of the] 23d Wisconsin. Between 83d and 96th Ohio, on the right, two small howitzers were placed. The field on the left side of the road beyond the 23d Wisconsin was occupied by Colonel [N.A.M.] Dudley's Brigade of cavalry. . . . Nims' battery, six pieces, was stationed on our extreme front, just at the point of the belt of timbers on the right. One section was on the right of the road and trained so as to fire through the woods into the field beyond. One piece was on the road and three on the left. To the left of this battery there were two small howitzers." According to Ransom's report, the 83rd Ohio was on the right of the line, with the 96th Ohio and 19th Kentucky following sequentially to its left. This accords with Mack's letter. However, Ransom reported the 48th Ohio came next in line, followed by the 130th Illinois, 77th Illinois, and 67th Indiana. As Mack noted, the 23rd Wisconsin was on the division's extreme left, where it supported Nims' guns, as did the 67th Indiana to its right. "A Letter from Hon. A. W. Mack, Grand Ecore, April 11, 1864," *Chicago Tribune*, April 25, 1864; Hollandsworth, *Pretense of Glory*, 186; *OR* 34, pt. 1, 265-266, 280.

20. Johnson, *Red River Campaign*, 134.

21. John A. Bering, *History of the Forty-Eighth Ohio Volunteer Infantry* (Hillsboro, OH, 1880), 137; Bentley, *History of the 77th Illinois Volunteer Infantry*, 251.

22. *OR* 34, pt. 1, 265, 266, 280.

23. A. W. Mack also described the Mercantile Battery's position at Sabine Crossroads after it had been brought up to reinforce the Union's sagging front lines. "The Chicago Mercantile Battery was stationed not far from the center of the first field, on the right and near a cluster of log houses, where Gen. Banks had made his headquarters. . . . About four o'clock p.m., the 4th Division was moved forward through the belt of timber and took position in line of battle behind the fence that enclosed the field beyond." "A Letter from Hon. A. W. Mack, Grand Ecore, April 11, 1864," *Chicago Tribune*, April 25, 1864.

24. Blessington, *The Campaigns of Walker's Texas Division*, 187-189.

25. Moore, *The Rebellion Record,* vol. 8, 562.

26. Blessington, *The Campaigns of Walker's Texas Division*, 187-189.

27. James K. Ewer, *The Third Massachusetts Cavalry in the War for the Union* (Maplewood, MA, 1903), 154.

28. Samuel H. Fletcher, *The History of Company A, Second Illinois Cavalry* (Chicago, IL, 1912), 139.

29. Moore, *The Rebellion Record,* vol. 8, 562; *OR* 34, pt. 1, 266-267.

30. McGregor, *Dearest Susie*, 84-85; Brooksher, *War Along the Bayous*, 99; Brown, *Journey to Pleasant Hill*, 396.

31. McGregor, *Dearest Susie*, 85; Henry Roe Collection, May 4, 1864 letter from Camp Parapet, CHS.

32. Hewitt, ed., *Supplement to the Official Records*, 2, vol. 8, 464; *OR* 34, pt. 1, 280; Winschel, ed., *The Civil War Diary of a Common Soldier*, 103-104; "The City," *Chicago Tribune*, May 2, 1862; "Captain White's Saber," Robert E. Mulligan, Jr., *Military Images*, vol. 21, no. 5, March-April 2000; Patrick White Collection, RBWPC.

33. "The Red River Expedition," *Chicago Tribune*, April 21, 1864; Livermore, *My Story of the War*, 399-400; "Excerpt from a Private Letter," *Chicago Tribune*, April 24, 1864.

34. *Report of the JCCW*, 92; Livermore, *My Story of the War*, 398, 401.

35. Johnson, *Red River Campaign*, 152-164; Henry Ward Harris, "From Comanches to Yankees," *Civil War Times Illustrated* (June 2002), 68.

36. The soldiers' contempt for Banks intensified on the retreat to Grand Ecore and lingered after the war. Sabine Crossroads survivor W. W. Warner characterized the battle as "a fiasco—a stupid affair—Banks was 'Corporal' Banks after that." "Private Letter from the Eighty-Third Ohio," Moore, *The Rebellion Record,* vol. 8, 541; Nims Battery Association Records, 1860-1914, "The Bobbin Boys Army," Massachusetts Historical Society (hereafter cited as MHS); Johnson, *Red River Campaign*, 162-164.

37. Banks and his staff were preoccupied with several pressing issues when they arrived at Grand Ecore on April 11, the day that Will and his CMB comrades wrote their scathing letters. First, they were anxiously awaiting the arrival of the rest of the retreating column, which did not arrive in Grand Ecore until noon. As noted by Lieutenant Colonel John G. Chandler, the expedition's acting chief quartermaster in the field: "Our transports were also there, from which we replenished our supplies of provisions and forage. Under the orders of Major-General Banks the command was here placed in a defensive position." Breastworks and rifle pits were hurriedly thrown up (some of which are extant today). In addition, Banks and his staff had to take care of their demoralized army, avoid a mutiny from offensive-minded commanders such as A. J. Smith, hasten the withdrawal of Thomas Kilby Smith's troops and the naval vessels north of them on the Red River, and determine whether to renew the push to Shreveport or retreat downriver to Alexandria. *OR* 34, pt. 1, 239; Moore, *Rebellion Record,* vol. 8, 542; Hollandsworth, *Pretense of Glory*, 204.

38. Will downplayed his battery's role in saving Ransom. A June article in the *Chicago Tribune* unequivocally proclaimed it was men from the Mercantile Battery who "saved that noble soldier and gallant commander, the brave and fearless Ransom. When he fell from his horse pierced by the bullets of the traitorous foe, he was caught in their arms and borne from the field of battle to a place of safety . . . they formed a living wall of brave hearts and stout arms." "The CMB: the Company Action and Arrest of the Officers," *Chicago Tribune*, June 30, 1864.

39. The CMB suffered significant losses at the Battle of Sabine Crossroads. Lieutenants Joseph W. Barr (who was already a widower and left behind an orphaned 10-year-old daughter) and George Throop were killed in action, as were Isaac Carpenter and Sergeant Leighton Dyer. Sergeant William Gardner, John F. Gruber, and John Payne suffered wounds. The list of captured men included John W. Arnold, Samuel E. Bell, Corporal Henry C. Brackett, Sergeant George E. Bryant, Amos L. Burdick, Lieutenant Pinckney S. Cone, Sergeant Joseph L. Day, Walter H. Felter, Peleg Green, Corporal Samuel Hammett, Hiland W. Hall, Lewis Mann, William Munn, Sanford L. Parker, Arthur W. Rumsey, and Captain Patrick H. White. Other soldiers, who had been detached from infantry regiments to serve with the CMB, also fell captive to the enemy. The list includes Joseph Arnold (130th Illinois), Thomas Forbes (77th Illinois), Randolph Lucky (97th Illinois), William D. McCoy (77th Illinois), and Norman D. Richards (77th Illinois). Order and Descriptive Book of the CMB, May 31, 1864, report from Orderly Sgt. Florus Meacham, NARA.

40. Contrary to Will Brown's opinion, which was no doubt shared by many of his comrades who survived Sabine Crossroads, the Union army there was not outnumbered five to one, although it probably felt that way because of Taylor's effective attack and flanking operation. While testifying before a congressional committee, Ransom provided a more accurate estimate: "I judged they had about 8,000 infantry in and about the position. Our force amounted to about 4,000 infantry and about 3,000 cavalry." For Landram's division, Ransom reported that only 2,413 infantrymen were involved in the action at the battle's outset. The Union count varies depending on the source. Ludwell Johnson and Richard Brooksher both determined the Federals had an effective fighting force of only 4,800 soldiers during first phase of the battle, far short of the 5-to-1 exaggerations. *Report of the JCCW*, 39; *OR 34*, pt. 1, 266; Johnson, *Red River Campaign*, 133, 136; Brooksher, *War Along the Bayous*, 92-93.

41. On April 14, Major Joseph L. Brent, Taylor's chief of artillery and ordnance, reported that the Southerners captured 20 cannon at Sabine Crossroads. "Inventory of Artillery captured in the Battle of Mansfield April 8th/64 by the C.S. forces, Maj Gen. Taylor com'ding: 6 rifled bronze 6-pdr guns;

8 3-inch wrought iron gun (Dyer pattern); 4 12-pdr Napoleons; 2 mountain howitzers. Sixteen caissons." In correspondence with the author, Scott Dearman, Interpretive Ranger at Mansfield State Historic Site, stated that he believes the Union artillery losses were as follows: CMB: 6; Nims' Battery: 6; Battery G, 5th U. S.: 4; 1st Indiana Light Artillery: 3; 6th Missouri Horse Artillery: 2. See also Joseph L. Brent Papers, April 14, 1864, inventory of artillery captured at Mansfield, Tulane University Manuscripts Department.

42. 2nd Lieutenant Henry Roe was the only commissioned officer left after Sabine Crossroads. Other losses are described elsewhere. Roe wrote to his brother that Ransom had "advised that we should wait untill reinforcements should come up to our assistance before advancing any further." He blamed the defeat on Banks, who "ordered an advance, in other words, ordered troops that had never known defeat before, on to be sacrificed." Henry Roe Collection, May 4, 1864 letter from Camp Parapet, CHS.

43. Will wrote that the artillery wagons during the battle were turned around in case the fighting went against Banks' army. Many of the cavalry wagons had already been turned around. Lieutenant Colonel John G. Chandler, acting chief quartermaster for the Red River expedition, reported "on reaching the advance of this [cavalry] train, I found its quartermasters turning the teams about in the road, faced to the rear, and this by direction of their superior officers, brigade or division commanders." He was concerned the wagons, which were blocking the middle of the narrow road, would obstruct the march of reinforcements to the front. Ironically, it was this premature turning to the rear that saved many of the wagons, including those overseen by Will Brown. *OR* 34, pt. 1, 238.

44. Based on his testimony to Congress, Brigadier General William Dwight was apparently involved with Banks' attempts to cover his own culpability in the failed campaign. His brother was one of Banks' key cotton speculators, representing textile interests in Massachusetts. When Banks' chief of staff, Brigadier General Charles Stone, was relieved—an easy scapegoat target because of his Ball's Bluff past—Dwight was promoted to fill the vacancy. Albert Lee also became a scapegoat for the Sabine Crossroads fiasco and was replaced by Brigadier General Richard Arnold, who had been Banks' chief of artillery. This move, Banks said, "was an act which I afterwards regretted." In his Joint Committee testimony, Dwight made many outlandish assertions about Lee's culpability that were disputed by other witnesses. Porter later accused Banks of trying to make him a scapegoat, too. *Report of the JCCW*, 17, 251, 178-192; Johnson, *Red River Campaign*, 63-67, 218-220.

45. Ransom arrived at the front around 1:30 p.m. Although he had ordered up the Mercantile Battery around that time—when he saw Captain White on his way to the front—he recalled that both the Chicago battery and the 1st Indiana Battery arrived just as the full-scale battle broke out in earnest at 4:00 p.m. "I directed him [White] to place them in an advantageous position on a ridge to the east of the road and near a house occupied as General Banks' headquarters." *OR* 34, pt.1, 265-266.

46. In his report of the battle, Nims wrote that his battery "was ordered into position on the heights [Honeycutt Hill]. Four pieces in battery to the front and two pieces in battery to the right flank within 250 yards of the woods." *OR* 34, pt.1, 462.

47. Will Brown missed the second phase of the battle during which Brigadier General Robert A. Cameron, in charge of Ransom's 3rd Division, came to the momentary rescue of Lee's cavalry and Landram's infantry. Cameron's men marched on the double quick through the mob of men, horses, and wagons clogging the road that descended from Honeycutt Hill. Constituting another undersized division of the 13th Corps, Cameron's 1,300 soldiers lined up across the road approximately one mile south of Honeycutt Hill and were joined by a 700-member remnant of the retreating front line. Author Michael J. Forsyth summarized the result of their attempted stand: "That line quickly suffered the same fate as Lee's with the Confederates curling around his flanks and rolling right over the blue line. The Confederates scooped up more guns and many prisoners with this attack, including the famous Chicago Mercantile Battery." During this second phase of the battle, Franklin was wounded in the thigh. Forsyth's book includes a comprehensive, yet succinct, chronology of major events during Banks' campaign. Michael J. Forsyth, *The Red River Campaign of 1864 and the Loss by the Confederacy of the Civil War* (Jefferson, NC, 2002), 75-76.

48. Perhaps belatedly, Franklin called for Brigadier General William H. Emory to bring up his 1st Division from the 19th Corps. These reinforcements had to march about seven miles to reach the fighting. Emory's division numbered more than 5,000 officers and men. It was as large as Ransom's two 13th Corps divisions combined. Emory reported that he received orders at 3:40 p.m. to move his troops to the front. After only moving three miles he encountered the onrush of the Union retreat and set up his line along the banks of a small creek at a place in the Pleasant Grove area. Some of Emory's men, as a veteran of the 114th New York Infantry recalled, "lay flat upon the ground, while the fugitives and skirmishers passed to the rear.... Presently, a long line of rebel infantry came out in full view, directly in front. The over-confident and undaunted enemy, flushed with the excitement of victory, advanced." Emory had to reposition his men at a right angle to prevent the Union left flank from being turned by Taylor's charging Confederates. As Emory noted, "The whole line opened on the enemy, who were driven back, and the prisoners report with great slaughter. During the fight a determined effort was made to turn the left flank, which was repulsed. Our loss in killed, wounded, and missing was 13 officers and 343 men." Since there was minimal drinking water in the area, Emory's stand along the small creek forced Taylor to take his men back toward Sabine Crossroads for the night. *OR* 34, pt. 1, 389-393; Thomas Ayres, *Dark and Bloody Ground: The Battle of Mansfield and the Forgotten Civil War in Louisiana* (Dallas, TX, 2001), 232-233; Beecher, *Record of the 114th Regiment, N.Y.V.*, 310-313.

49. By this time, Whiskey Smith only had about 5,000 troops to guard the rear of Banks' army. His men would play a pivotal role in the defensive victory at Pleasant Hill on April 9.

50. Will Brown was not the only one who was thrilled to see Whiskey Smith. Another version of the encounter between the despondent survivors of the 13th Corps and their former commander, written by a soldier who identified himself as "a Janesville boy," appeared in one of Chicago's newspapers: "We saw Gen. Smith. He was very angry and swore terribly about the way things were conducted....Oh how glad the troops were to see some one fit to command. The 3d [Division] stacked their arms and swore they would not fight under Banks, but would stay by Smith as long as a man was left." "The Retreat of the Chicago Mercantile Battery," *Chicago Tribune*, April 26, 1864.

51. Banks sent the Union supply trains ahead of the men who had fought at Pleasant Hill. These wagons arrived in Grand Ecore—about 10:00 a.m. on April 10th—just ahead of the 13th Corps' troops, which included the CMB. *OR* 34, pt. 1, 239.

52. Lieutenant Colonel John G. Chandler, the Red River expedition's acting chief quartermaster in the field, was responsible for reporting the losses of the Union's supply train, which were mainly caused by the collapse at Sabine Crossroads. He wrote that an accurate tally had been made impossible by the loss of Union records. Chandler's estimate, excluding the loss of cavalry horses, was "One hundred and seventy-five army wagons, complete [versus the 900 he claimed the army possessed at the campaign's outset]; 328 sets of wheel harness, 584 sets lead harness, 920 mules, 81 horses, 11 ambulances and sets of wheel harness. These teams when captured were variously loaded with commissary, quartermaster's, and medical supplies, with officers' and soldiers' baggage, and none of the contents were ever recovered." Ludwell Johnson thought it odd Richard Taylor reported capturing 250 wagons—versus the 175 mentioned by Chandler—and attributed the difference to wagons owned by private individuals. Regarding Will's comment about "Micawber": he was a major character in Charles Dickens' novel *David Copperfield*. Ulysses S. Grant also used Micawber to describe the overly optimistic Peace Democrats. *OR* 34, pt.1, 237, 241; Johnson, *Red River Campaign*, 141; Charles Dickens, *David Copperfield* (New York, NY, 2000); Simpson, *Ulysses S. Grant*, 374.

53. Ransom was sent to New Orleans for treatment of his severe knee wound. "We [the *Chicago Tribune*] have seen and conversed with Mr. Gooding, just from New Orleans, who accompanied General Ransom on the hospital boat *Laurel Hill* from Alexandria to New Orleans, which also had on board about four hundred wounded soldiers from the battle of Mansfield.... Our informant says the officers [on board] universally throw the blame for the disaster upon Gen. Banks....From all accounts that we receive there must have been terrible mismanagement somewhere." "General Aspects of the Battle." *Chicago Tribune,* April 24, 1864.

54. On April 8, Taylor welcomed 4,400 infantry and artillery reinforcements that arrived from Major General Sterling Price's Arkansas command. After the Unionists had retreated from Pleasant Hill to Grand Ecore, Taylor tried to press them again. Unfortunately for the Confederates, their vaunted Brigadier General Tom Green was killed at Blair's Landing on April 12 when he led his cavalry and a four-gun battery in a bizarre attack against Porter's gunboats. So fierce was this two-hour battle that one of Porter's officers, Commander Thomas O. Selfridge, described it as "the heaviest and most concentrated fire of musketry that I have ever witnessed." Green was killed when a cannonball partially decapitated him. The Union defenders reported they had inflicted between 200 and 500 casualties. Taylor, *Destruction and Reconstruction*, 162; Johnson, *Red River Campaign*, 212; Forsyth, *The Red River Campaign of 1864*, 131.

55. The Mercantile Battery portion of Pat White's memoir has never before been published. Therefore, White's account of the Battle of Sabine Crossroads has been included to augment what Will Brown described in the letters to his father. Patrick H. White Collection, RBWPC.

56. On January 11, 1864, while still on the Texas coast, Ransom assigned Pat White to join his staff as chief of artillery. In his postwar account of the Battle of Sabine Crossroads, White confirmed Albert Lee's contention that most of the Union generals expected no resistance until Shreveport. White wrongly identified Ten Mile Bayou as St. Patrick's Bayou. According to Ludwell Johnson, White was far from alone in misidentifying the stream, which flowed about seven miles from Honeycutt Hill and where the 19th Corps bivouacked early on April 8. "Of the Federals only Col. Francis Fessenden, 30th Maine, gave this stream its correct name," Johnson wrote. "All the others mistook it for Bayou San Patricio, of which Ten Mile Bayou is a tributary." Johnson, *Red River Campaign*, 128; Patrick White Memoir, General Ransom's January 11, 1864, order to Patrick White, RBWPC.

57. Captain Cyrus E. Dickey was a fellow Illinoisan whose father was a judge in Ottawa, Illinois. As Ransom's assistant adjutant general, Dickey was sent to direct Landram's troops to withdraw, but he never delivered the message because en route, he was shot in the head. "The Chicago Mercantile Battery Lose their Guns, Four Officers and Twenty-two Men," *Chicago Evening Journal*, April 19, 1864; *OR* 34, pt. 1, 266-267.

58. Although his Sabine Crossroads wound was not fully healed, Ransom went east to take part in Sherman's Atlanta Campaign. On August 2, 1864, he took command of a division in Sherman's 16th Corps. He took charge of the 16th Corps after its commander, Major General Grenville Dodge, was wounded. Ransom later led the 17th Corps, pursuing the retreating Southerners through north Georgia and into Alabama. As historian Ezra Warner wrote, "Despite illness and an aggravation of his partly healed wound, he accompanied his corps on the return from Alabama, dying near Rome, Georgia, October 29, 1864." Warner, *Generals in Blue*, 390.

59. One of the Battery Boys corroborated this incident in an article that appeared in the *Chicago Tribune*: "Some of our men saw a rebel cavalryman hold a pistol to Capt. White's head and make him surrender." "Red River Expedition," *Chicago Tribune*, April 21, 1864; Patrick White Memoir, RBWPC.

60. White wrote one of the few existing descriptions of the Union prisoners who were taken into the town of Mansfield. The courthouse that White and Cone stayed in briefly was moved after the war and a replacement built on the site. In his memoir, a soldier from the 32nd Iowa also mentioned how the Confederate guards at the Mansfield courthouse received "orders that if a man showed himself at the window he would get shot. One of the boys inadvertently exposed himself and immediately got a severe wound." John Scott, *Story of the Thirty Second Iowa Infantry Volunteers* (Nevada, IA, 1896), 362.

61. Patrick White Memoir, Alex McDow April 16, 1864, letter to his daughter Kate, RBWPC.

62. The Mercantile Association met in May and tried to get its battery refitted. "Mercantile Association," *Chicago Tribune*, May 3, 1864.

63. Although Banks had been hoping that Major General Frederick Steele's troops in Arkansas would assist in capturing Shreveport, Steele had his own reasons for not leaving the state. In a strange twist of fate, Steele's 10,000 troops faced a food shortage. The problem worsened when, on April 18,

Brigadier General John Marmaduke's troops attacked a large Union provision train at Poison Spring carrying forage back to Camden. That same day Steele received word of Banks' defeat at Sabine Crossroads. The next day, Steele learned Banks still wanted him to help overwhelm the Shreveport defenders, but Steele's lack of food compelled him to retreat from Camden to Little Rock. According to author Curt Anders, "Steele considered Banks' proposal so absurd that he did not 'entertain it for a moment.'" Halleck eventually concurred and Steele headed back to Little Rock, leaving Banks to fend for himself down in Louisiana. Anders, *Disaster in Damp Sand*, 110-115; Johnson, *Red River Campaign*, 193-194.

64. In *My Story and the War*, Mary Livermore devoted a number of pages to her "Battery Boys," including a description of their ordeal at Sabine Crossroads. She recounted the death of Lieutenant Throop, and Hugh Wilson's attempt to save him. Regarding Leighton Dyer, Livermore wrote: "Sergeant Dyer, whom I have before mentioned as a rare nurse in sickness, was shot through the lungs, and mortally wounded, while in the act of spiking his gun." Livermore's book also includes a steel engraving depicting the "Death of Sergeant Dyer while Spiking His Gun." Some 250 wounded Federals captured at Sabine Crossroads found themselves in another perilous situation the day after the Confederates retreated from Pleasant Hill. The wounded Northerners were recuperating in a Baptist church in Mansfield, which had been turned into a hospital when a delirious patient knocked a tallow candle from an attendant's hand and ignited a conflagration. A Confederate captain carried bedridden Major John B. Reid, of the 130th Illinois, to safety. Most of the other Northerners were also saved, but a few burned to death. Livermore, *My Story of the War*, 394-401; J. E. Hewitt, *Battle of Mansfield* (Mansfield, LA, 1925), 16-18.

65. By the time Chicago's Battery Boys had made their way to New Orleans, most of their comrades in Banks' army were stranded at Alexandria. Banks withdrew his troops from Grand Ecore on April 21. Pursued by Taylor, Banks' troops warded off the Confederates at the Battle of Monett's Ferry on April 23 as they barely got across the Cane River. Banks arrived back in his cotton stronghold two days before Will wrote this letter to his father (on April 25). The falling water caused much difficulty in the passage of Porter's heavy boats over the Red River shallows and rapids. The next day, April 26, the admiral was forced to abandon and scuttle his massive ironclad *Eastport*. Banks and Porter still had to get their men and ships back safely to the Mississippi River. Forsyth, *The Red River Campaign of 1864*, 131.

66. White, Cone, and their fellow prisoners from Sabine Crossroads were taken to Camp Ford Prison outside the town of Tyler in East Texas.

67. Thomas H. Bringhurst and Frank Swigart, *History of the Forty-sixth Regiment, Indiana Volunteer Infantry, September 1861-September 1865* (Loganport, IN, 1888), 117-118.

CHAPTER 14

1. Livermore, *My Story of the War*, 399.

2. According to Pitts, Sergeant Leighton Dyer was buried in a mass grave with 12 other Federal soldiers killed at Sabine Crossroads. Lieutenant Joseph Barr's body was placed in a coffin and given a separate burial. A man named Gooding reported his Sabine Crossroads experience in a *Chicago Tribune* article entitled "General Account of the Battles." Gooding traveled on the hospital transport *Laurel Hill* with Ransom, who was taken from Alexandria to New Orleans for treatment of his severe knee wound. Pitts Diary, June 17-20, 1864, CHS; *Chicago Evening Journal*, April 20, 1864; *Chicago Tribune*, April 24, 1864.

3. Regarding Mercantile Battery losses, Chase Dickinson wrote: "Our boys lost everything they had with the guns. Scarcely any of them have a change of clothing…. Universal despondency reigns. Even 'Doggett' [the CMB mascot], with drooping head and tail seems to mourn the guns he loved to follow." "A Letter to the Chicago Mercantile Association from their Battery," *Chicago Evening Journal*, April 26, 1864.

4. A number of the Battery Boys wrote angry letters to their family and friends on April 10 and 11. Many of the Mercantile Battery letters were printed in Chicago's newspapers, including those by

Will Brown, Billy Olcott (Will's friend), Chase Dickinson, Hugh Wilson, Florus Meacham, and a member who wrote under the pseudonym "Hawkeye."

5. Private Chase Dickinson was nominated by his colleagues to send a letter to the Mercantile Association, documenting that the soldiers were not responsible for the Sabine Crossroads disaster. Dickinson had mustered into the Mercantile Battery along with Will Brown and was one of the older cannoneers. He was born in Chelsea, Vermont, on December 8, 1837, and graduated from Albany Law University. He practiced law in Chicago prior to enlisting in the Mercantile Battery at the age of 25. Chase Dickinson's letter to Merrill Ladd, Secretary of the Mercantile Association, was published in its entirety in the April 26, 1864, issue of the *Evening Journal*. A *New York Daily Tribune* reporter was on the *Laurel Hill,* which was transporting Ransom and other wounded Union soldiers (along with the Mercantile Battery letters that would preempt Banks' attempts at damage control). Descriptive Roll and Order Book of the CMB, Descriptive Rolls, NARA; Chase Dickinson albumen photo inscribed with educational information, RBWPC; *Chicago Evening Journal,* April 26, 1864; Andrews, *The North Reports the Civil War*, 511; Robert U. Johnson, ed., *Battles and Leaders of the Civil War,* vol. 4 (New York, NY, 1884, 1888), 354.

6. Taylor's attack at Pleasant Hill was jeopardized by an overly complex maneuver and flawed direction from a local guide. Johnson, *Red River Campaign*, 152-164; Shelby Foote, *The Civil War, a Narrative: Red River to Appomattox* (New York, NY, 1974), 50.

7. Brooksher, *War Along the Bayous*, 152-153; Johnson, *Red River Campaign*, 214-215.

8. Whiskey Smith wanted to resume the advance on Shreveport, but could not convince Banks to do so. At the least, Smith wanted to bury the Union dead and arrange transportation for the wounded before leaving the Pleasant Hill battlefield. Banks overruled Smith, who became more incensed when he learned that during the first stage of the Federal retreat to Grand Ecore on April 9, the medical train of the 19th Corps had been mistakenly left behind. Thus, the surgeons left behind to tend to the wounded were not well equipped to do so. David Dixon Porter, *The Naval History of the Civil War* (New York, NY, 1886), 508-510; Brooksher, *War Along the Bayous*, 142-143; Snell, *From First to Last*, 313.

9. During the April 11 retreat to Grand Ecore, Banks' troops openly voiced their disdain for their leaders with vehemence at least equal to that expressed by the 13th Corps during its retreat on April 9. Many diaries and postwar recollections recount the verbal abuse of Banks. Epithets such as "Napoleon P. Banks" and "Mr. Banks" were incorporated into their improvised, sarcasm-tinged ballads, or simply blurted out when the general passed. When Grover's men reinforced the troops at Grand Ecore several days later, they found the army "greatly depressed." This was especially so among Western soldiers, such as the men of the 77th Illinois (this regiment had been with the Mercantile Battery since Vicksburg and lost almost half of its men at Sabine Crossroads). When one of Banks' staff asked a member of the 77th Illinois the name of his unit, the embittered infantryman responded, "It's-the-second-relief-of-Gen.-Banks'-slaughter-pen." According to the regiment's historian, Banks heard the soldiers calling him "Corporal Banks" and remarked, "Never mind, boys, Corporal Banks will come out all right in the end." The cynical veteran commented that Banks "did come out all right—when he came out of the Department of the Gulf, relieved of his duty." The survivors in the 77th Illinois updated a song mocking Banks when the army retreated once again, this time from Grand Ecore to Alexandria: "In eighteen hundred and sixty-four, When Banks skedaddled from Grand Ecore, We'll all drink stone blind, Johnny fill up the bowl." Johnson, *Red River Campaign*, 206, 215; Bentley, *History of the 77th Illinois Volunteer Infantry*, 277-278.

10. According to the historian of the 114th New York Infantry, Grand Ecore was "a settlement of some eight or ten houses, situated upon a high bluff on a bend of the Red River" four miles north of Natchitoches. Banks' men worked hard to erect formidable entrenchments, some of which can be seen today in the woods around Grand Ecore. Beecher, *Record of the 114th N.Y.N.*, 327; Hollandsworth, *Pretense of Glory*, 200; Johnson, *Red River Campaign*, 213-216; *OR* 34, pt. 3, 128.

11. Joiner, *One Damned Blunder from Beginning to End*, 147-148; Snell, *From First to Last*, 309.

12. After Sabine Crossroads, Banks sent his first telegram to Halleck on April 13, 1864, from Grand Ecore. In it, he misrepresented the events of the campaign. Banks claimed he had encountered

all of Kirby Smith's Trans-Mississippi forces. Rather than confronting "22,000 to 25,000" Confederate troops, Banks faced a considerably smaller force of 13,000 to 14,000. Banks also told Halleck that at Pleasant Hill, "The wounded were gathered from the battlefield, placed in comfortable hospitals. . . . The dead remaining upon the field, as far as possible, were buried during the night. The next day medical supplies and provisions, with competent attendants, were sent in." Sufficient proof emerged later from eyewitnesses, such as the outraged A. J. Smith, that the dead and wounded were abandoned at Pleasant Hill. Many of the medical supplies had already been sent back to Grand Ecore. Banks had tried to handle his defeat during the 1862 Shenandoah Valley Campaign in a similarly deceptive way. In his earlier battle report, he downplayed his calamitous losses, which is what he tried to do in 1864. *OR* 34, pt.1, 181-185; Hollandsworth, *Pretense of Glory*, 68, 204-205.

13. Banks was also coping with internal strife. According to Porter, A. J. Smith tried to convince Franklin at Pleasant Hill to take charge of the Department of the Gulf army and to "put Banks under arrest." Besides being outraged about leaving the battlefield after a hard-fought victory, Smith wanted to pursue the enemy to Shreveport by joining forces with his other soldiers, led by Kilby Smith, who were supposed to be upriver with the navy. Porter believed Whiskey Smith was a man of integrity, noting, "It was not from a spirit of insubordination that General Smith made his proposition [to Franklin], but because he thought such a course necessary for the safety of the Army." Smith's exasperation with Banks increased at Grand Ecore when the expedition commander would not send "assistance to the fleet" Porter was trying to withdraw down Red River. Smith ignored Banks and sent some soldiers to help Porter get more than 45 of his vessels to safety. Porter, *The Naval History of the Civil War*, 509-511; *OR* 34, pt. 1, 186-187.

14. Banks also misled Grant by telling him the entire 25,000 men in the Trans-Mississippi army were in front of him. *Ibid.*

15. After Banks' August 9, 1862, defeat at Cedar Mountain, Confederate Major General Jeb Stuart told Stonewall Jackson that Banks was "the best commissary and quartermaster you ever had." In contrast to Banks' humiliating defeat in the Shenandoah Valley, Jackson biographer James I. Robertson, Jr., wrote that the Federal general "had done surprisingly well at Cedar Mountain." Banks concern for his reputation after Sabine Crossroads was well founded. In May, the *Chicago Tribune* reported, "The few rebel prisoners we have are very jubilant, and say: 'Well, Gen. Banks has been the best commissary we have ever had in this Department since he has been in command. We couldn't get anything from Butler.'" Hollandsworth, *Pretense of Glory*, 80; Robertson, *Stonewall Jackson* 411, 536; "The Red River Expedition," *Chicago Tribune*, May 2, 1864. For details on the June 7 Republican convention in Baltimore, see John C. Waugh, *Reelecting Lincoln*, 187-202;

16. After Benjamin Butler took over New Orleans, he imposed rigorous censorship on the city's newspapers. "Between May 13 and November 14, Butler suppressed five New Orleans newspapers—the *Crescent*, *Bee*, *Commercial Bulletin*, *Picayune*, and *Daily Advocate*, and he seized the office of the *Delta* and operated the paper under direction of the United States authorities." Banks maintained control over the New Orleans press when he took over for Butler, especially when he created The *Era* as his personal promotional vehicle. Bragg, *Louisiana in the Confederacy*, 115-117; Andrews, *The North Reports the Civil War*, 510.

17. Brigadier General Stone was relieved at Grand Ecore on April 17. Brigadier General Lee was not replaced until April 26, when Banks got his army back to Alexandria. As more information reached Washington, officials saw through Banks' ploy to create scapegoats. A Treasury Agent in New Orleans, George S. Denison, informed his superior, Secretary of the Treasury Salmon P. Chase, that Banks had attempted "to cast blame on subordinate Generals, but without success, for they only obeyed the orders issued by Comd'g General. The army would have done better without any Commanding General." *OR* 34, pt. 3, 193, 294; Hollandsworth, *Pretense of Glory*, 204.

18. The *New York Daily Tribune* reporter, who had sailed on the *Laurel Hill* with Ransom, was disgusted that the hospital boat was so ill equipped to handle wounded soldiers. "Not one ounce of any sort of medicine was placed on board, and there was no supply of bedding, sheets, clothing, or other articles to relieve the suffering," he wrote. In a *New York Daily Tribune* article, which appeared on April 30, the outraged reporter revealed the same hospital transport—the *Laurel Hill*—had

arrived in Alexandria at the beginning of the campaign with "a plentiful supply of cotton-baling, twine, rope, and all other material necessary for the protection of cotton. What a pity the time and trouble spent in stowing away such material was not used in loading medical stores and those things requisite for a hospital boat." Andrews, *The North Reports the Civil War*, 511-512; Pitts Diary, 58.

19. *OR* 34, pt. 3, 268; Pitts Diary, 58.

20. *Ibid.*

21. Despite the poor condition of the *Kate Dale*, the Union military officials continued using the boat to transport Western troops into 1865. Johnson, *Red River Campaign*, 257; *OR* 48, pt. 1, 628.

22. The Mercantile Battery left New Orleans on April 29 and moved up to Carrollton (today a suburb of New Orleans). According to Pitts, the battery established new quarters at Camp Parapet, which was "one mile and a half above Carrollton on the river." Pitts Diary, April 29, 1864, CHS.

23. In contrast to the relaxed attitude of New Orleans' residents, Union soldiers guarding the city were in a high state of alert. Under the command of Major General Joseph J. Reynolds, there were approximately 11,000 men stationed in and around the Crescent City. Upon arriving at New Orleans on April 26 with the rest of the Mercantile Battery, Florison Pitts recorded that "No one can get in or out with out a pass." *OR* 34, pt. 3, 370; Pitts Diary, April 26, 1864, CHS.

24. The "second installment" of Mercantile Battery letters from the Red River appeared in the April 20 issue of the *Chicago Evening Journal*. The newspaper printed a lengthy, unabridged letter from one of the Chicago artillerists, followed by a three-paragraph excerpt and a one-paragraph excerpt from two other letters penned by Battery members. In the unabridged letter, the author mentions escaping from the Sabine Crossroads battlefield on a mule. In Will's April 13 letter to his father, he notes Charley Olcott made his escape on a cavalry horse. The similarity in the descriptions suggests that Olcott wrote the letter published in full length on April 20. Will was the author of one of the excerpted letters. "Additional Particulars of the Disaster to the 13th Army Corps," *Chicago Evening Journal*, April 20, 1864.

25. Willie (perhaps named after Will) was the newborn son of Will's brother Henry and his wife Delia.

26. With the addition of McClernand's troops and other soldiers from New Orleans, Banks had approximately 31,000 men at Alexandria—along with 80 guns. Nevertheless, his army was still fighting to survive while Lieutenant Colonel Joseph Bailey, an engineer on Franklin's staff, built a dam to free Porter's fleet, which was trapped by the Red River's low water. Ironically, Taylor now commanded about 6,000 Confederates. His superior, General Kirby Smith, had siphoned off troops to oppose Major General Frederick Steele's Federals in Arkansas. Johnson, *Red River Campaign*, 249-250, 254; Brooksher, *War Along the Bayous*, 209-213.

27. Taylor's troops terrorized Union boats on Red River, especially after the Mercantile Battery's *Kate Dale* had already made her way to New Orleans, where she arrived on April 26. On May 1, the Confederates captured and burned the transport *Emma*. Three days later they captured the *City Belle*, along with 300 of the 700 men of the 120th Ohio Infantry, which was on its way to reinforce Banks. On May 6, Brigadier General Daniel Ullmann wrote a summary of Banks' recent Red River losses. Besides the *Emma* and *City Belle*, the *John Warner* was attacked the day before carrying the 56th Ohio Infantry. Ullmann reported 215 of the Ohioans survived the attack by boarding the steamer *Shreveport* on her way to Port Hudson. "Two gunboats [*Covington* and *Signal*] are said to have been destroyed," Ullman noted. The Confederates had increased their pressure on Union river traffic. Will Brown and his comrades were fortunate to have gotten through the Red River gauntlet when they did. As historian Ludwell Johnson wrote, "Including the Emma and the City Belle, Banks and Porter had lost in the space of five days three transports, two gunboats, and some 600 soldiers and seamen, all at a trifling cost to the Confederates." *OR* 34, pt.1, 474-475; Johnson, *Red River Campaign*, 255-257.

28. McClernand arrived in Alexandria on April 26 with about 2,700 troops who had been stationed with him in Texas—and he must have passed the CMB, on board *Kate Dale*, on his way there. The feisty politician-general had fallen a long way from the glory days of his January 1863 victory at Arkansas Post. In Alexandria, McClernand resumed command of his battered 13th Corps remnant. Major General David Hunter, Grant's emissary to Red River, met with Banks for an all-day

conference on April 28. He immediately left to evaluate the situation at New Orleans, and reported back to Grant on May 2. *OR* 34, pt. 3, 296; Landers, "Wet Sand and Cotton—Banks' Red River Campaign," *The Louisiana Historical Quarterly*, 186; Kiper, *Major General John McClernand*, 287.

29. Major General Joseph J. Reynolds, despite his initial show of cooperation, later turned on the Mercantile Battery. Again, one wonders whether the Chicago newspaper articles (and/or verbal communication with Banks) affected his treatment of the cannoneers.

30. While the Mercantile Battery floundered without Pat White and Pinckney Cone at the helm, the 2nd Massachusetts Light Artillery was recuperating well after also losing all of its guns and equipment at Sabine Crossroads. The major reason was the Boston battery had retained its leader, Captain Ormand Nims. Despite Will's assertion that Nims' men also received muskets, there is no evidence the Bostonians served as infantrymen—especially when a plan was in place to refit Nims' Battery by July. When Lieutenant Henry Roe arrived in New Orleans with his Mercantile Battery on April 26, he was preoccupied with rebuilding the unit. That same evening, the 2nd Massachusetts Light Artillery threw a party, during which the battery's noncommissioned officers presented Ormand Nims with "a magnificent sword, sash and belt." As noted in *The Era*, "this splendid sword was manufactured by Tiffany & Co. of New York, and is one of the finest ever got up by that firm." Not to be outdone, the battery's commissioned officers got together and bought Nims an inscribed pistol. Years later, Nims recalled that he and his men had something else to celebrate: "One of my officers who was shot found the bullet that struck him reposing in his pocket, and it had the impression of an eagle, got from striking the top button of his uniform." Nims Battery Association Records, 1860-1914, "Presentation of a Sword to Captain Ormand F. Nims, 2d Massachusetts Light Horse Artillery," MHS; *The Era, New Orleans*, April 26, 1864; Caroline Whitcomb, *History of the Second Massachusetts Battery (Nims' Battery) of Light Artillery, 1861-1865* (Concord, NH, 1912), 71-74; *The Sunday Herald* [Boston], February 17, 1907.

31. Even if Banks' officers were not given specific instructions to retaliate against the CMB, they may have done so on their own initiative. After all, it was not in the best interest of their careers to be tied to an incompetent commander entangled in sordid scandals—especially as the national outcry escalated and newspapers in other major cities criticized Banks' Red River actions. Attacking the "messengers" may have been tempting, whether they were members of the Mercantile Battery or the press. Later in the month, the targets would expand to include fellow Union officers who spoke out about the cotton schemes. Andrews, *The North Reports the War*, 513-521; Capers, *Occupied City*, 179.

32. In the April 19 issue of the *Chicago Evening Journal*, there was a brief mention about the arrival of the *Luminary* in Cairo on April 18. The boat brought newspapers from New Orleans dated April 9. They carried news about the Red River expedition only up to the April 7 engagement at Wilson's farm, a day prior to the Sabine Crossroads fiasco, stating that "the army is in fine spirits, movingly steadily on Shreveport. At last account it was within a day or two's march of that place. It is thought that the enemy will retreat to Texas." The *Luminary* must have also carried the Mercantile Battery's April 11 letters. But they would have been picked up en route. If the Battery Boys' letters had gone all the way to New Orleans from Grand Ecore—and were not transferred from *Laurel Hill* to *Luminary* at the mouth of the Red River, Port Hudson, or Baton Rouge—they would have arrived later in the month (and would have been bundled with newspaper issues from a later date). "From General Banks' Army," *Chicago Evening Journal*, April 19, 1864.

33. In the same April 20 issue, the editor carried a message from the *Springfield State Journal* congratulating the *Evening Journal* for its technological advancement, which made it "the largest printed in Chicago." With the *Evening Journal* trying to strengthen its position in the Northwest, the Mercantile Battery scoop became invaluable to the upstart newspaper. *Chicago Evening Journal*, April 20, 1864.

34. "The Chicago Mercantile Battery Taken," *Chicago Tribune*, April 20, 1864.

35. *The Daily Picayune* provided a positive report on Banks' conduct: "He was everywhere in the thickest of the fight." *The Daily Picayune* was a hamstrung Confederate newspaper, while its

competitor in New Orleans, *The Era*, was an "Unconditional Union Newspaper." *The Era* oozed with its first glowing Red River reports about "the arrival of Gen. Franklin, who dashed boldly into the thickest of the fray, cap in hand and cheering on the men" to rally the Federal army and resist the Rebel attackers. According to one of *The Era's* skewed articles, "Gen. Banks, too, seemed ubiquitous, riding wherever the men wavered, and by personal example inciting them to renewed deeds of daring and reckless valor." The truth was that Banks and Franklin had lost the respect of their soldiers. It was the bellicose A. J. Smith who invigorated the army at Pleasant Hill. "Oh, how glad the troops were to see some one fit to command," rejoiced a Mercantile Battery survivor. "[Some of the soldiers] stacked their arms and swore they would not fight under Banks, but would stay by Smith as long as a man was left." In further exaggerations, *The Era* reported Banks was still moving on Shreveport and into Texas, which would have been a miraculous achievement since the Union army and navy were bottled up along the Red River. Andrews, *The North Reports the Civil War*, 510-511; "The Battle of the 'Bended Knees,'" *The Daily Picayune*, April 17, 1864; *The Era—New Orleans*, April 15, 1864; "The Retreat of the Chicago Mercantile Battery," *Chicago Tribune*, April 26, 1864.

36. "The Red River Disaster," *Chicago Tribune*, April 23, 1864.

37. *OR* 34, pt. 3, 220, 221, 235.

38. The "detailed telegraphic reports from Chicago" mentioned by Stanton in his dispatch to Grant referred to articles appearing in the April 19 issue of the *Chicago Evening Journal* and the April 20 issues of the *Chicago Evening Journal* and *Chicago Tribune*. By covering the Mercantile Battery letters, the reports perpetuated the unfair characterization that Brigadier General Stone was the major culprit for the Sabine Crossroads disaster. The only other contemporaneous source of information on the battle was the New Orleans papers, and they did not mention Stone at all.

39. On April 21, General Brayman sent Stanton a telegram reporting that Sherman's envoy, General Corse, had returned from meeting with Banks. Corse validated the Mercantile Battery newspaper accounts and disputed the positive news from Banks and his New Orleans newspapers. "Banks returned to Grand Ecore, badly injured. He refused to return Smith's command. The naval force is caught in low water, with shoals above and below." Based on this latest telegram, Grant addressed the issue with Halleck about replacing Banks. Halleck wrote back that Lincoln was not ready. "The President replied that he must delay acting on it for the present." Grant was also annoyed with Banks because (1) he could not move his troops to Mobile to draw Rebel troops away from Johnston and his Rebel army in Georgia and (2) he was not able to release A. J. Smith and Kilby Smith to reinforce Sherman. *OR* 34, pt. 3, 244, 252-253, 265.

40. Porter sent his April 14 letter from Grand Ecore to Nashville, where Sherman was planning his spring offensive into Georgia. *OR* 34, pt. 3, 153-154.

41. Grant sent his telegram from Culpeper Court House on April 25, 1864, to Halleck addressing the two Louisiana letters. On April 29, Halleck sent a message to Sherman complaining about Banks. *OR* 34, pt. 3, 279, 306-307, 332-333.

42. Major General David Hunter sent telegrams to Grant from Alexandria (April 28) and New Orleans (May 2). Grant was probably not surprised by Hunter's news that cotton businessmen were behind many of Banks' Red River problems. In January 1863, Charles A. Dana, who was accompanying Grant on Stanton's behalf, wrote from Memphis about the cotton trade's pernicious effects on the military: "[A] mania for sudden fortunes made in cotton has to an alarming extent corrupted and demoralized the army. Every colonel, captain, or quartermaster is in secret partnership with some operator in cotton; every soldier dreams of adding a bale of cotton to his monthly pay." *OR* 34, pt. 3, 316, 390; Edward A. Miller, Jr., *Lincoln's Abolitionist General: The Biography of David Hunter* (Columbia, SC, 1997), 163-164; McPherson, *Battle Cry of Freedom*, 620-621.

43. Banks (Louisiana), Steele (Arkansas), and Rosecrans (Missouri) now reported to Major General Edward S. Canby. Canby's West Mississippi Division was organized along the lines of the one Grant had commanded (i.e., the departments of Ohio, Cumberland, and Tennessee). *OR* 34, pt. 3, 490; Max L. Heyman, Jr., *Prudent Soldier: A Biography of Major General E. R. S. Canby,*

1817-1873 (Glendale, CA, 1959), 206; "General Banks' Campaign," *Harper's Weekly*, June 11, 1864, 371.

44. As the Union army prepared to cross Atchafalaya River and end the Red River Campaign, some soldiers continued hurling abuse at Banks: "The troops look dusty and worn, tired and ragged. General Banks looks dejected and worn, and is hooted at by his men," wrote one Iowa soldier. Lieutenant Colonel Joseph Bailey, under whom the Mercantile Battery would serve in Baton Rouge, was an officer on the staff of the 19th Corps who had previously created an impromptu dam at Port Hudson. He asked Franklin if he could replicate it. On April 30, Bailey's men began erecting a "tree-dam of 600 feet across the [Red] river at the lower falls" to raise the water level at least five feet so Porter's gunboats could pass. The Red River dam was completed on May 8, but additional dams had to be constructed to get all of the gunboats across the shoals on May 12-13. Bailey received a commendation from Congress and was promoted. *Ibid.*; Brooksher, *War Along the Bayous*, 213-225; Hollandsworth, *Pretense of Glory*, 203; "The Red River Campaign," *Harper's Weekly*, June 4, 1864, 355; "Porter's Gun-Boats Passing the Dam at Alexandria," *Harper's Weekly*, June 18, 1864, 395; Johnson, *Battles and Leaders of the Civil War*, vol. 4, 358-360.

45. On April 25, the *Chicago Tribune* wrote: "The subsequent reports and full details all too completely sustain the earliest rumors from that field [i.e., the first Mercantile Battery letters]." The *New York World* on May 14 typified the viewpoint of other Northern newspapers that had finally secured their own firsthand reports of the Red River expedition, calling Banks' campaign "the most complete and humiliating disaster of the whole war." The crescendo of public outrage continued and culminated in the Congressional Joint Committee on the Conduct of the War's investigation of Banks and his mismanagement of the Red River expedition. As May wore on, Grant's "On to Richmond Campaign" and Sherman's Atlanta Campaign diverted attention away from Banks' problems. "The Red River Expedition," *Chicago Tribune*, April 25, 1864; *New York Times*, April 25, 1864; *New York World*, May 14, 1864; Andrews, *The North Reports the War*, 515-516, 520, 729; Moore, *The Rebellion Record*, vol. 8, 544.

46. Will Brown was anxious because his father had not responded to his letters about the battery's Sabine Crossroads calamities (perhaps the problem was related to Banks' censorship and delay of his soldiers' mail). Will may have needed assurance that he and his comrades were not being blamed for the losses. He was also concerned about the Mercantile Battery's plight at Camp Parapet. In his June 12 letter, Will admitted that on May 15, his battery mates had signed a resolution stipulating they would not carry muskets on picket and fatigue duty and would only bear them in the city's defense. Will signed the resolution, hence his pangs of anxiety in his May 15 letter to his father.

47. Will Brown's younger brother Lib had spent the month of February in Michigan. Along with other men in the 12th Michigan who reenlisted, Lib had been given a 30-day furlough. It expired on March 4 he returned to the 12th Michigan at Little Rock. Meanwhile, Steele was short on supplies at Camden and, like Banks, was fighting for his army's survival. After losing his supply wagons at Poison Spring on April 18, his problems intensified when Kirby Smith moved from Louisiana into Arkansas with reinforcements from Taylor's army. During Steele's retreat to Little Rock, the pursuing Confederates tried to drive the Unionists into the Saline River at the Battle of Jenkins' Ferry on April 30. Aided by Kirby Smith's mismanagement, Steele extricated his army and returned to Little Rock. "At Jenkins' Ferry," concludes Edwin Bearss, "the Confederates fumbled an excellent opportunity to bag Steele's army." Steele's effort in Arkansas was no more successful than Banks' in Louisiana. Edwin C. Bearss, *Steele's Retreat from Camden and the Battle of Jenkins' Ferry* (Little Rock, AR, 1967), 161; Johnson, *Red River Campaign*, 184-188, 197-200; Liberty Brown CMSR, NARA; *History of Berrien and Van Buren Counties, Michigan*, 69.

48. By May 15, Grant and the Army of the Potomac had crossed the Rapidan River, had fought a brutal battle in the Wilderness against Robert E. Lee's Army of Northern Virginia, and was engaged at Spotsylvania Court House. For more details, see Gordon C. Rhea, *The Battle of the Wilderness, May 5-6, 1864* (Baton Rouge, LA, 1994); Gordon C. Rhea, *The Battles for Spotsylvania Court House and the Road to Yellow Tavern, May 7-12, 1864* (Baton Rouge, LA, 1997).

49. On May 2, Chase Dickinson's letter was read at the Mercantile Association monthly meeting (the letter had already been published in the *Chicago Evening Journal*). The Chicago businessmen read a letter from Brigadier General Ransom, written while recuperating in New Orleans. "The loss of the Chicago Mercantile Battery will be felt in Chicago, but it was no fault of the officers and men; they all did nobly, more than could have been expected," he wrote. The association determined to "apply to the proper authorities for permission . . . [for] the battery to return home to recruit and reorganize." "A Letter to the Mercantile Association from their Battery," *Chicago Evening Journal*, April 26, 1864; "Mercantile Association," *Chicago Tribune*, May 3, 1864.

50. By May 27, news from Grant's Overland Campaign was anything but "glorious," although his drive to Richmond continued. Will Brown was correct General Joseph Johnston and his Rebel army were outflanked and retreated from Dalton, Georgia. The Battle of Resaca along the Oostanaoula River began on May 13, and Henry Brown's regiment, part of Colonel John Coburn's brigade, spent the next two days throwing up breastworks. On May 15, the 19th Michigan charged the enemy and was heavily engaged; Henry Brown was wounded in his arm. Later that night, men from the 19th Michigan captured and dragged back four field pieces. Gordon C. Rhea, *To the North Anna River: Grant and Lee, May 13-25, 1864* (Baton Rouge, LA, 2000); Coe, *Mine Eyes Have Seen the Glory*, 130-131; *OR* 38, pt.1, 378-380; Anderson, *They Died to Make Men Free*, 325-334.

51. General McClernand fell ill in Alexandria and was temporarily replaced as the commander of the 13th Corps by Brigadier General Michael Lawler on May 10. McClernand never led his corps again because it was disbanded in June. He returned home to recuperate and resume his law practice. Kiper, *Major General John Alexander McClernand*, 289-291.

52. Some of Banks' medical personnel remained behind at Sabine Crossroads to care for the wounded, including Mercantile Battery's Sergeant William Gardner. Nearly every building, public and private, was commandeered to serve as a hospital. Hewitt, *Battle of Mansfield*, 16-18.

53. Henry Brown stayed with his regiment until May 21, when he was sent to a hospital. He returned home to recuperate. Henry Brown CMSR, NARA.

54. After the Red River failure Lincoln reduced Banks' authority in the Trans-Mississippi. On May 7, 1864, Lincoln appointed Major General Edward S. Canby to command the Division of West Mississippi. The new division included Banks' Department of the Gulf, Steele's Department of the Arkansas, and Rosecrans' Department of the Missouri. Lincoln—Banks' friend and political ally— sought a way for the disgraced general to remain active in Louisiana politics. The presidential election was only six months away, and Lincoln looked vulnerable on his reconstruction policy. Louisiana was to be the prototype for implementing his "10 percent plan" to restore a conquered Rebel state to the Union. Hollandsworth, *Pretense of Glory*, 206-207.

55. As Grant continued driving toward Richmond, Lee made a stand at the North Anna River. Stymied, Grant made another wide sweep around the Confederates' right flank. For a full account, see Rhea, *To the North Anna River*.

CHAPTER 15

1. As the company's quartermaster, Will had vital responsibilities, as specified in the "Customs of Service for Non-Commissioned Officers and Soldiers." Issuing and keeping track of "Clothing, camp and garrison equipage" and "procuring and distribution of forage" were critical duties. Additionally, "Providing fuel for the troops, especially in the winter season, is also an important duty generally intrusted to the quartermaster sergeant. . . . On the march, he attends to the loading and unloading of the wagons, and superintends the erection of tents, putting up the picket-line, &c. When property is lost or destroyed [such as at Mansfield], the sergeant should be careful to get the certificates of officers, or the affadavit of citizens or soldiers, giving the circumstances of the loss." Besides accounting for the lost equipment, Will had to re-supply the company and document every item—from cannon and wagons to horses and mules to tents and cookware. By the time he wrote this series of letters, he had handled the initial bolus of post-battle paperwork. August V. Kautz, *Customs*

of Service for Non-Commissioned Officers and Soldiers (Mechanicsburg, PA, 2001), 166-171; Chicago Board of Trade Battery Collection, quartermaster reports, CHS.

2. "Chicago Mercantile Battery," *Chicago Tribune*, June 30, 1864.

3. Men from the 22nd Iowa Infantry, who arrived from Vicksburg before the CMB, stated: "Camp Carrollton is a beautiful camping ground on the shell road. It has every convenience." It was also a vital railroad connection near the crossing of the New Orleans, Jackson & Great Northern Railroad and the Jefferson & Lake Pontchartrain Railroad. The Carrollton Railroad ran through the middle of town and down to New Orleans. The plain behind Carrollton had been the site of the "grand review of the 13th Army Corps by General Grant on September 2, 1864" (Grant was thrown from his horse). *OR* 34, pt. 4, 214; George B. Davis, *The Official Military Atlas of the Civil War* (New York, NY, 1978), Plate XC; S. C. Jones, *Reminiscences of the Twenty-Second Iowa Volunteer Infantry* (Iowa City, IA, 1907), 47-48; Henry G. Adams, Jr., *Indiana at Vicksburg* (Indianapolis, IN, 1911), 344.

4. Clark S. Willy was serving with the 15th New Hampshire Volunteers when he was assigned to Camp Parapet, from which he sent this letter on February 5, 1863. Some of the first contraband regiments were also stationed there. The Confederates named the fort after cavalryman Brigadier General John Hunt Morgan. Today, Camp Parapet's powder magazine is the only remaining fortification built in New Orleans during the Civil War. *OR* 34, pt. 4, 158; 41, pt. 2, 871; Clark S. Willy Letter, February 5, 1863, Williams Research Center of The Historic New Orleans Collection (hereafter cited as HNOC); Shannon Lee Dawdy and Christopher N. Matthews, *Final Report of Archeological and Historical Investigations of Camp Parapet, a Civil War Site in Jefferson Parish, Louisiana* (New Orleans, LA, 1998), 1-2; Parkerson, *New Orleans, America's Most Fortified City*, 90-91; Powell A. Casey, *Encyclopedia of Forts, Posts, Named Camps, and other Military Installations in Louisiana, 1700- 1981* (Baton Rouge, LA, c1983), 145-147.

5. Designated as part of Banks' Corps d'Afrique, the 14th Rhode Island became the 11th Regiment United States Colored Artillery (Heavy) on May 21, 1864. *OR* 41, pt. 2, 848; Hollandsworth, *Pretense of Glory*, 151-153.

6. Ironically, Nims lost fewer men at the Battle of Sabine Crossroads than did the CMB, even though the Bostonians were engaged first (Banks' June 1864 departmental report listed Nims as having 207 available men and the CMB 153). With both batteries back in New Orleans, Will Brown wrongly predicted the men in Nims' battery would also perform infantry duty. There is no evidence the Boston artillerists were subjected to the same indignities as the Mercantile Battery. Pitts Diary, May 28-30, 1864, CHS; Whitcomb, *History of the Second Massachusetts Battery*, 75; *OR* 34, pt. 1, 463; *OR* 34, pt. 4, 278, 322, 614.

7. "Chicago Mercantile Battery," *Chicago Tribune*, June 30, 1864.

8. Descriptive List and Order Book for the CMB, Henry Roe Court Martial, Exhibit B (May 15, 1864 Letter) & July 1864 Monthly Report, NARA.

9. After his return to Rhode Island, Nelson Viall was commissioned lieutenant colonel of the 14th Rhode Island Heavy Artillery on January 15, 1864. CMB Order and Descriptive Book, Henry Roe Court Martial, Exhibit B (Protest Resolutions), NARA; William H. Chenery, *The Fourteenth Regiment, Rhode Island Heavy Artillery (Colored) In the War to Preserve the Union, 1861-1865* (Providence, RI., 1898), 270-273.

10. Descriptive List and Order Book for the CMB, Henry Roe Court Martial, Exhibit C (Roe Testimony), NARA.

11. Colonel Robert Wilson was a successful lawyer and fire department chief who formed the 14th New Hampshire Volunteers in the fall of 1862. Wilson was commissioned its colonel and became the commander of the District of Carrollton, Louisiana, on April 20, 1864. Francis H. Buffum, *A Memorial of the Great Rebellion Being a History of the Fourteenth Regiment New Hampshire Volunteer, Covering Its Three Years of Service, with Original Sketches of Army Life, 1862-1865* (Boston, MA, 1882), 40-41.

12. Joseph Jones Reynolds graduated from West Point in the class of 1843 with Ulysses S. Grant and taught at the academy for eight years. He resigned from the army in 1857, but rejoined when the Civil War broke out. In June 1861, he was commissioned a brigadier general of United States

volunteers. After serving in West Virginia, he was forced to leave the service after the death of his brother, with whom he had been in business. He was appointed a brigadier general in September 1862, and commissioned major general two months later. Reynolds commanded a division of the 14th Corps at Chickamauga and became chief of staff for Major General George H. Thomas, Army of the Cumberland. In January 1864, Reynolds transferred to New Orleans to assume command of the city's defenses, serving under Nathaniel Banks. Warner, *Generals in Blue*, 397-398; "Chicago Mercantile Battery," *Chicago Tribune*, June 30, 1864; Descriptive List and Order Book for the CMB, Henry Roe Court Martial, Reynolds May 16, 1864 Order to Wilson, NARA.

13. Descriptive List and Order Book for the CMB, Henry Roe Court Martial, May 17, 1864 Order to arrest CMB officers, NARA. For a review of other mutinies during the Civil War, refer to Webb Garrison, *Mutiny in the Civil War* (Shippensburg, PA, 2001).

14. The member of the CMB whose letter was published on June 30 in Chicago reiterated Will Brown's assertion that the cannoneers had made a pact to refrain from writing home about the mutiny until they had some kind of resolution—an agreement many of their comrades violated. "Chicago Mercantile Battery," *Chicago Tribune*, June 30, 1864.

15. Although Will Brown signed the battery's resolution protesting its service as infantry, he was not arrested. In addition to Will, Corporal John A. Gilbert, Corporal Warren Gilmore, and Orderly Sergeant. Florus D. Meacham also signed the Mercantile Battery protest but were excluded from arrest and imprisonment. Descriptive List and Order Book for the CMB, Henry Roe Court Martial, May 15, 1864 CMB protest document (original signed version), NARA.

16. During his first two years of service, Will Brown demonstrated sympathy toward the plight of blacks in his letters. After the battery was mistreated at Camp Parapet, the tone of Will's letters dramatically changed because he associated black soldiers with the Battery Boys' problems.

17. Will's older brother Henry was back in St. Joseph recuperating from his Resaca wound. Lib's 12th Michigan Regiment was stationed in Steele's District of Little Rock. Henry Brown Civil War Pension Records, NARA; *OR* 34, pt. 4, 607.

18. Taylor delivered the speech Gardner heard on April 11, 1864 at Mansfield, Louisiana. "Never in war was a more complete victory [Mansfield] won," declared Taylor. His speech was published in its entirety in Frank Moore, ed. *The Rebellion Record: A Diary of American Events*, vol. 8 (New York, NY, 1871), 567.

19. Lieutenant Daniel J. Viall took command of the CMB on June 16. Pitts Diary, June 17, 1864, CHS; Descriptive List and Order Book for the CMB, June 1864 Report, NARA.

20. Gideon Welles, *Diary of Gideon Welles: Secretary of the Navy under Lincoln and Johnson*, vol. 2: April 1, 1864-December 31, 1866 (Boston, MA, 1911), 18-26; *OR* 34, pt. 4, 138, 241.

21. Reynolds was concerned when the War Department requested details on June 3 about the Mercantile Battery's situation. He had already ignored two previous letters from Roe (May 18 and 25) requesting clarification of his imprisonment. After Reynolds received Roe's next letter on June 14 stating his version of what had happened with Viall on May 16, Reynolds asked Viall to document that Roe had supported the CMB soldiers' mutiny and, contrary to his contention, did not ask for help with the mutiny (this would fit into the "self-protection mode" that Reynolds went into after receiving the War Department request for information on the CMB). Pitts Diary, May 18, 1864, CHS; Descriptive List and Order Book for the CMB, Henry Roe Court Martial, May 18 & May 25, 1864, letters from Roe to Reynolds (Exhibit C), June 14, 1864, letter from Roe to Reynolds, Special Orders No. 142, June 14, 1864, Reynolds to Viall request, June 16 Viall to Reynolds letter, NARA.

22. Merrill Ladd of the Mercantile Association made public a June 3 letter Congressman Isaac Newton Arnold had received from Thomas M. Vincent at the War Department regarding the CMB's situation. Vincent told Arnold "no charges relative to the said battery have been filed here" in Washington. He added it was permissible "to assign artillerists to temporary duty as infantry," but did not know any specific details about the Chicago company. "Chicago Mercantile Battery," *Chicago Tribune*, June 30, 1864.

23. On June 30, the *Chicago Tribune* carried an extensive front-page review of the entire situation. The lead article was a letter written by one of the Battery Boys: "on Wednesday an order

came from Washington, directing that all papers relative to abuses perpetrated upon the Mercantile Battery be immediately forwarded to Washington." In the same *Chicago Tribune* issue, there was a copy of the War Department letter to the Mercantile Association dated June 3. The "Wednesday," to which the CMB soldier alluded, must have been June 8. This would make sense because Reynolds issued a request the next day, June 9, for Roe's court martial to be arranged (Special Orders No. 137). *Ibid.*; Descriptive List and Order Book for the CMB, Henry Roe Court Martial, Reynolds' June 9, 1864 Special Orders No. 137, NARA.

24. *Ibid.*; Descriptive List and Order Book for the CMB, Henry Roe Court Martial Proceedings, NARA.

25. *Ibid.* (testimony of Lieutenant Colonel Nelson Viall).

26. *Ibid.* (testimony of Sergeant Florus D. Meacham, CMB).

27. *Ibid.* (testimony of Sergeant E. J. Thomas, CMB); Descriptive List and Order Book for the CMB, Henry Roe acquittal, release of Roe from Reynolds HQ, June 16, 1864, NARA.

28. Colonel Robert Wilson left New Orleans with Reynolds. On June 7, Wilson was put in charge of a brigade in the 19th Corps. "He was honorably discharged from the service on surgeon's certificate of disability, September 6, 1864." *OR* 41, pt. 2, 65; *OR* 34, pt. 4, 406; Buffum, *Fourteenth Regiment New Hampshire*, 41; Descriptive List and Order Book for the CMB, Roe Court Martial, Special Orders No. 19, NARA; Henry Roe CMSR, NARA.

29. According to Special Orders No. 219, August 16, 1864, Henry Roe was appointed to sit on the five-member "Detail of Court" for a court martial two days later in nearby Greenville. Roe had come a long way: two months earlier he was the one facing charges. Descriptive List and Order Book for the CMB, Special Orders No. 219, NARA; Henry Roe CMSR, NARA.

30. "City Matters," *Chicago Evening Journal*, May 23, 1864.

31. In February 1863, Grant had endorsed Reuben B. Hatch for promotion. A year later, Hatch was serving in Banks' quartermaster department when he tried to help the Battery Boys. Owen M. Long, Sanitary Agent of Illinois for New Orleans, sent a comprehensive letter to the *Chicago Tribune* detailing what he learned from Hatch about how Banks' subordinates mistreated the CMB. "Chicago Mercantile Battery," *Chicago Tribune*, June 30, 1864; Simon, *The Papers of Ulysses S. Grant*, vol. 7, 297-298.

32. Descriptive List and Order Book for the CMB, Henry Roe Court Martial, Special Orders No. 19, NARA; Thomas P. Lowry, information from NARA, The Index Project. For general information on Union courts martial, please refer to Thomas P. Lowry, M.D., *Tarnished Eagles: The Courts-Martial of Fifty Union Colonels and Lieutenant Colonels* (Mechanicsburg, PA, 1997).

33. Captain Ormand Nims confirmed the information in his battery's regimental history, stating that "I sent in a requisition for new guns, and seven days later I received word that they were on the way." While the veterans in Nims' battery returned to Boston, new recruits were added and the battery remained active, participating in the capture of Mobile. Ormand Nims, "Civil War Recollections" [transcript], 12 February 1910, Nims Battery Association Records, 1860-1914, MHS; Whitcomb, *History of the Second Massachusetts Battery*, 74-77; Descriptive List and Order Book for the CMB, July1864 Report, NARA.

34. Isaac N. Arnold of Chicago was elected to the United States House of Representatives on November 5, 1862. Arnold, who had also served the public as a judge, was well respected and recognized as one of the founders of Chicago. "Honorable I. N. Arnold Elected to Congress from Chicago," *St. Joseph Traveler*, November 5, 1862.

35. The Battery Boys' fortunes improved. On June 21, their officers were released from the New Orleans military prison. The next day, June 22, the cannoneers moved from Camp Parapet to the main Union camp at Carrollton. They were quartered in houses located between the levee and the Mississippi. There, they built bunks and settled in. They no longer had to perform fatigue duty. Temporary officers were announced on June 23 as noted by Florison Pitts: "Officers were detailed to the Co to day [i.e.,] Captain, 1st Lieut of Art. & 2nd Lieut of Cav." Pitts Diary, June 21-23, 1864, CHS.

36. The War Department issued General Orders No. 210 announcing that the "13th Army Corps is temporarily discontinued." It was a sad end to a corps that had reached its pinnacle of success at Vicksburg. The historian of the 77th Illinois—one of the regiments that had been with the CMB for a year and a half—lamented the disbanding of McClernand's old corps: "And so the 'Old Thirteenth' ceased to exist. . . . It was a sad day for the members of that organization. . . . 'How are the mighty fallen.'" *OR* 34, pt. 4, 304; Bentley, *History of the 77th Illinois*, 316.

37. There had been no serious Union activity against Mobile since William Sherman's Meridian expedition sputtered out in February and Farragut's demonstrations against Mobile Bay's defenses were aborted. Farragut and Canby were now making plans for an amphibious assault against the Mobile Bay forts. Among the Confederate leadership, Richard Taylor had taken a furlough in June to rest and recuperate with his family at Natchitoches. On July 18, Jefferson Davis promoted him to lieutenant general. Of the 17 Confederates who attained this rank, only Taylor, Nathan Bedford Forrest, and Wade Hampton had not graduated from West Point. Taylor was given command of the Department of Alabama, Mississippi, and East Louisiana. Although finally separated from Kirby Smith, whom Taylor despised, Smith pressed his former subordinate to take Texas troops from the Trans-Mississippi to reinforce Mobile and Atlanta. Taylor wound up crossing the Mississippi River by himself. Arthur Bergeron, Jr., *Confederate Mobile* (Jackson, MS, 1991), 130-137; T. Michael Parrish, *Richard Taylor: Soldier Prince of Dixie* (Chapel Hill, NC, 1992), 405-406.

38. Lincoln sent Major General Daniel Sickles to tour Union-held Southern territory to observe the effects of amnesty and reconstruction efforts. Will Brown's observations on Sickles demonstrated again that he was well informed about Union activities. The surgeon of the 114th New York Infantry also discussed Sickles' visit in his unit history: "Under the delightful shade of La Fayette Square, converted into a vast amphitheater, General Banks and Sickles delivered orations, and three thousand school children, aided by all the military hands of the Department, sang national airs. A couple of batteries, and the different bells of the city, were added to the chorus, by means of electrical machinery." Warner, *Generals in Blue*, 446-447; Beecher, *Record of the 114th Regiment, NYSV*, 368.

39. See Will Brown's next letter, July 17, and the role played by Hatch to exonerate the CMB.

40. Florus David Meacham and James C. Sinclair both mustered into the CMB with Will Brown on August 29, 1862. Meacham was born in Washington County, New York, on April 26, 1843. He moved to Chicago with his parents in 1857. Prior to the Civil War, Meacham worked as a clerk for the Illinois Central Railroad. At the age of 20, the 5-foot 10-inch tall Meacham joined the CMB and was promoted to orderly sergeant on July 25, 1863; and to junior 2nd lieutenant on July 9, 1864. James Sinclair's parents were two of the first settlers in Chicago (1834). He entered the CMB as a private and was promoted to sergeant on February 23, 1862. During the mutiny fiasco, Reynolds reduced him to the rank of a private on June 15, 1864. A month later, July 1864, Sinclair was promoted to take Meacham's place as orderly sergeant. *Military Order of the Loyal Legion of the United States (MOLLUS), Illinois: From January 1, 1912 to December 31, 1922* (Wilmington, NC, 1993), 460; *A History of the City of Chicago* (Chicago, IL, 1900); n.p.; Florus D. Meacham CMSR, NARA; James C. Sinclair CMSR, NARA; James C. Sinclair Diary, Family History, CHS.

41. While the veterans in the CMB still had 14 months left to fulfill their term of service, their counterparts in Nims' battery, fully re-equipped, were about to head back to Boston and muster out.

42. Owen M. Long was the "Sanitary Agent of Illinois for New Orleans" who came to the rescue of the CMB and sent their information on to the *Chicago Tribune* for publication. "Letter to the Secretary of the Mercantile Association," *Chicago Tribune*, June 30, 1864.

43. Senior 1st Lieutenant William Hunt, Jr., a member of the 17th Ohio Battery, took temporary command of the CMB. Descriptive List and Order Book for the CMB, July Monthly Report, NARA.

44. The *Kearsarge*, built at Portsmouth, New Hampshire, and launched in September 1861, was deployed to European waters to monitor and track down Confederate commerce raiders. Captain Raphael Semmes, commanding the raider *Alabama*, steamed out of Cherbourg, France, on June 19 to engage the *Kearsarge*. The *Alabama* was sunk after three hours of fighting. H. S. Hobson, *The Famous Cruise of the Kearsarge* (Bonds Village, MA, 1894), 107-119. For a comprehensive review

of the famous battle, see William Marvel, *The Alabama & the Kearsarge: The Sailor's Civil War* (Chapel Hill, NC, 1996).

45. *Florida* was one of the Confederacy's most successful commerce raiders. Commodore John N. Maffit captained the ship until the beginning of 1864 when, due to illness while in France, he gave up command. Lieutenant Charles M. Morris brought *Florida* back to the western hemisphere. The Confederate ship captured 37 more Union vessels, one of which was the Union mail steamer *Electric Spark,* as discussed by Will Brown. The U.S.S. *Wachusett* disabled *Florida* off the coast of Brazil on October 7. Faust, *Historical Times Illustrated Encyclopedia of the Civil War*, 264.

46. In an attempt to relieve Union pressure on Petersburg and Richmond, Lieutenant General Jubal Early led his Confederate troops against Washington in July 1864. On July 9, Federal Major General Lew Wallace, though significantly outnumbered, slowed Early's forces at the Battle of Monocacy, south of Frederick, Maryland. When it became clear Washington's fortifications were too strong for him to capture, Early returned to the Shenandoah Valley. D. Eicher, *The Longest Night*, 715-718. For a comprehensive study of this engagement, see B. Franklin Cooling, *Monocacy: The Battle that Saved Washington* (Shippensburg, PA, 1997).

47. Despite Will's sarcasm, Major General William B. Franklin's escape from captivity was legitimate. Major Harry Gilmor, a Confederate marauder, captured Franklin on a Federal train in Maryland during Jubal Early's July 1864 attempt to raid Washington. Gilmor left Franklin with some of his men for the night and planned to rejoin Early the next day. Gilmor showed up later and found his men asleep and the major general gone. "But we searched in vain for Franklin; he had got off safe, to my great chagrin and annoyance," Gilmor recalled. Harry Gilmor, *Four Years in the Saddle* (New York, NY, 1866), 194-203; Jubal A. Early, *Lieutenant General Jubal Anderson Early, C.S.A., Autobiographical Sketch and Narrative of the War Between the States* (Philadelphia, PA, 1912), 394. For more details on the escape, see Snell, *From First to Last*, 326-329.

48. As part of Lincoln's reconstruction of Louisiana, the state's new constitutional delegates had been meeting since April. As Will Brown noted, the convention came to be regarded as "a simple farce." Banks' most recent biographer commented: "The convention quickly gained notoriety for the lavish lifestyle its members adopted. . . . Many of the delegates took advantage of their new authority to make a run on the Free State treasury by drawing on public funds for ice, liquor, and cigars. In addition, the convention gave away gifts and lucrative contracts freely, including a $150 pen case presented to Nathaniel P. Banks after his return from the Red River Valley." The convention ended two days before Will sent his letter to Hiram Brown. Lincoln and Banks were disappointed with Hahn's lack of effectiveness in winning suffrage for blacks in Louisiana. If this had been accomplished at the convention, historian Joe G. Taylor noted, "it is very possible that so-called 'Black Reconstruction' could have been avoided" in Louisiana. Hollandsworth, *Pretense of Glory*, 207-208; Joe Gray Taylor, *Louisiana Reconstructed, 1863-1877* (Baton Rouge, LA, 1974), 42-52.

49. Henry Brown was trying to rejoin his regiment in Georgia. In September 1864, John Bennett, surgeon for the 19th Michigan, reported that Henry "returned with the wound healed, but the health otherwise not much improved. He was compelled to stop at Nashville and rest in hospital a few days on account of illness, and again at Chattanooga, and again at Kingston" before returning to his regiment on July 28. Lib was still in Arkansas. Henry Brown CMSR, NARA.

50. Will was referring to a July 1864 public-relations fiasco, instigated by outspoken New York newspaper publisher Horace Greeley, who tried to broker peace negotiations between the United States and the Confederacy. Greeley misrepresented the Confederates' position to Lincoln, i.e., that they would accept. a restoration of the Union and the abolishment of slavery. When the Confederate peace commissioners learned this, they sent the letter to Union newspapers that Will mentioned to his father. Waugh, *Reelecting Lincoln*, 246-254; "The Peace Blondins at Niagara," *Harper's Weekly*, August 6, 1864, 498.

51. Charles Smith Rice enlisted in December 1861 as a private in the 10th Ohio Light Artillery. In August 1862, he was promoted to 1st lieutenant in the 17th Ohio Light Artillery, and captain in July 1863. Rice participated in many of the Western campaigns battles in which the CMB also served: Chickasaw Bayou, Arkansas Post, Grant's final drive on Vicksburg, the siege of Jackson, and Banks'

1863 Texas Overland Campaign. MOLLUS Card Catalog Index, A-Z (Capt. Charles Smith Rice, 17th Ohio Light Artillery Regiment), CWURMP.

CHAPTER 16

1. There were many Union loyalists in Vicksburg before the war. Some converted to the secessionist cause while other sympathesizers kept a low profile. For examples, see. Peter Walker, *Vicksburg*, 24, 25, 104, 219.

2. William Husted wrote home to his mother about the St. Charles Street train and about "the considerable hard feeling between the Eastern and Western troops." He added: "The Eastern troops will, when they get home, claim that they opened the Mississippi, and of course we don't like that because Port Hudson would have fallen as soon as we took Vicksburg if Banks had not been there. But if Banks had taken Port Hudson first Vicksburg would not have fallen until we got there. Our boys tell the story that by some mistake some of the Eastern Sanitary Stores were given to the Western troop and on opening them they were found to consist entirely of 'paper collars.'" William H. Husted Letter, August 30, 1863, David Ray Private Collection; William H. Husted Letter, September 13, 1863, RBWPC.

3. In June 1864, Richard Arnold was still acting as chief of cavalry—the position he had assumed after Albert Lee was demoted after the Red River Campaign—and received permission to set up his cavalry instruction camp outside of New Orleans at Kenner, near Greenville. Federal officials believed that "The drainage is better, and . . . the health of the troops would be better. Convenient access to timber would enable all troops to cover themselves with shade." When Arnold returned to his former position as chief of artillery, he also set up his artillery camp of instruction there. Arnold sent two requests to Thomas Sherman before the Mercantile Battery was released. *OR* 34, pt. 4, 265, 308-309, 386; Descriptive List and Order Book for the CMB, July 29, 1864 letter from Richard Arnold to Thomas Sherman, NARA.

4. Getting Banks out of New Orleans served two purposes for Lincoln. First, the more-reliable Canby was in charge of the Trans-Mississippi region (after the Red River disaster, there was no support for Banks to hold any significant military position). Second, the president needed Banks' political skills and experience in Washington. Banks could help negotiate recognition of the new Louisiana constitution with Radicals in Congress and provide support in the upcoming presidential election. Since his wife and family had returned to Massachusetts, Banks did not have to hurry back to New Orleans. Ironically, the man who replaced Banks, Stephen A. Hurlbut, was also a political general. Hurlbut had served as a Republican in the Illinois state legislature prior to the war. He had been one of Lincoln's early candidates for general, along with McClernand. Hurlbut would later get into trouble for exposing the Louisiana reconstruction charade. Hollandsworth, *Pretense of Glory*, 208-215; Warner, *Generals in Blue*, 245.

5. Capers, *Occupied City*, 117-118; Jeffrey N. Lash, *A Politician Turned General: The Civil War Career of Stephen Augustus Hurlbut* (Kent, OH, 2003), 177.

6. *Ibid.*, 149.

7. *Ibid.*, 150-161.

8. *Ibid.*, 166-170.

9. On June 24, Canby assigned Brigadier General John W. Davidson to take command of his cavalry forces. Richard Arnold, who returned to his position as chief of artillery, had become familiar with the Chicago Mercantile Battery. As the 13th Corps chief of artillery, Pat White had reported to Arnold, who had seen White and his men in action at Sabine Crossroads and knew the company's losses were not the fault of the artillerists. Despite the problems encountered by the Battery Boys in New Orleans, Arnold requested in late July, and again in early August, that they be reequipped for artillery service. Subsequently, Arnold issued Special Order No. 216 on August 13: "Battery G, Fifth U.S. Artillery, is relieved from duty with the Cavalry Division and will, without delay, be reported to Brig. Gen. Richard Arnold, chief of artillery. The horses & guns will be turned over to the Chicago Mercantile Battery." After the war, Captain Nims said a foot battery's conversion to horse artillery

was "A compliment rarely given to a volunteers corps." Henry Roe was promoted from senior 2nd lieutenant to junior 1st lieutenant of the CMB in September. Descriptive List and Order Book for the CMB, Henry Roe September 1, 1864 promotion, NARA; *OR* 34, pt. 4, 531; *OR* 41, pt. 2, 682; Nims Battery Association Records, 1860-1914, Ormand Nims, presentation at the second anniversary of the Nims Battery Association, 22 February 1869, MHS.

10. On July 29, Arnold first requested that Thomas Sherman release the Mercantile Battery so the company could join his Camp of Instruction for Reserve Artillery. Sherman responded on August 1 and tried to discourage Arnold from taking back the Battery Boys. In regard to re-equipping the battery, he pretended not to know about its valiant efforts at Sabine Crossroads, writing, "Not knowing the circumstances under which they lost it, I do not know how far they are worthy of receiving another." Sherman also brought up the mutiny episode to further discourage Arnold. On August 3, Arnold replied, "I would respectfully request that all enlisted men of the Chicago Mercantile Battery now on detached service in this Department be ordered to rejoin their Command at once; this Battery is being re-equipped for Field Service, and it is essential that all its men be present with it." Descriptive List and Order Book for the CMB, July 29, August 1, & August 3, 1864 correspondence between Richard Arnold and Thomas Sherman, NARA.

11. On July 28, Arnold established "a camp of instruction for reserve artillery" at Greenville under the command of Captain Jacob T. Foster, 1st Wisconsin Battery. Other batteries encamped with the CMB included the 1st Indiana Battery, 1st Michigan Artillery, Company G; the 2nd Ohio Battery, 16th Ohio Battery; 1st Missouri Artillery, Company A; 1st Missouri Artillery, Company F; and the 2nd Illinois Light Artillery, Co. E. *OR* 41, pt. 2, 431.

12. At Mobile Bay on August 5, 1864, Rear Admiral David G. Farragut led a fleet of 14 wooden warships and four ironclad monitors past the Rebel forts and entered the bay. Fort Gaines fell on August 7, the same day Will Brown wrote about the battle to his father. He made some mistakes in his letter, such as misnaming one of the Mobile forts "Johnston" (likely confusing the name with that of Commander James D. Johnston, who was in charge of the Rebel ram *Tennessee*). Will also wrongly identified "General Morgan" as being in charge of the infantry assault during this battle. Major General Gordon Granger led the Union land forces on Canby's behalf. Long, *The Civil War Day by Day*, 551-553; Bergeron, *Confederate Mobile*, 138-146; "Rear-Admiral Farragut," *Harper's Weekly*, September 17, 1864, 597.

13. On April 16, 1862, the Confederate Congress passed what historian James McPherson called the "first conscription law in American history. It declared all able-bodied white male citizens between the ages of eighteen and thirty-five liable to service for three years." The Confederate draft had exemptions for certain professions and allowed wealthy men to hire substitutes. The hiring of substitutes was abolished in December 1863. McPherson, *Battle Cry of Freedom*, 430-432.

14. On July 30, 1864, General Sherman sent a letter to the "Agent for the Commonwealth of Massachusetts" about his distrust of "Civilian Agents," who aggressively recruited blacks and delayed the army's ability to conscript white Northern men. Sherman believed that blacks should be used as pioneers and teamsters, progressing to garrison duties, etc., before assuming a combat role. He added, "The negro is in a transition state and is not equal of the white man." John Spooner, the Massachusetts agent who was recruiting in Nashville, forwarded Sherman's letter to a newspaper, which published it. After learning of the public outcry against his views, Sherman defended himself in a letter home: "My negro letter got the Newspapers through the very man who I thought would be the last to publish it, for it was penned in haste & with some irony against a class [recruiting agents] that have done more to hurt our army than an Equal number of Enemies—men who by pay & money have filled up our Muster Rolls with names, impoverished our Treasury by high & useless bounties & brought us no men, but on the contrary cut off the only source of supply through a fair & square 'draft.'" Simpson and Berlin, ed., *Sherman's Civil War*, 677-678, 711-712.

15. Farragut, noted author Arthur W. Bergeron, "was prevented from launching a naval strike against the city of Mobile itself because the Union's land forces were still needed elsewhere." The Union army captured the last lower bay defense, Fort Morgan, on August 23, after Will sent his letter to his father regarding Mobile Bay. The Rebels retained control of the city. With the fall of the

Mobile Bay forts, Wilmington, North Carolina, became the last major port for Confederate blockade runners. Bergeron, *Confederate Mobile*, xi, 149-150; Long, *The Civil War Day by Day*, 559.

16. General John Bell Hood had replaced General Johnston as commander of the Army of Tennessee in mid-July. He evacuated his army from Atlanta on September 1. Men from Major General Henry W. Slocum's corps were first Union troops to enter the city the next day. The Democratic Convention had opened on August 29, 1864, in Chicago, with General McClellan— "Little Mac"—as the leading presidential candidate. After the recent flurry of Union victories, Democrats faced an uphill battle to rekindle interest in an aggressive anti-Lincoln platform. The presence of the incendiary Vallandigham as part of the Ohio delegation did not improve their position. Long, *The Civil War Day by Day*, 564-565; Waugh, *Reelecting Lincoln*, 280-282; Karamanski, *Rally 'Round the Flag*, 17; "The Chicago Convention," *Harper's Weekly*, September 3, 1864, 573; "The Chicago Convention," *Harper's Weekly*, September 10, 1864, 579.

17. According to his military physician, Henry Brown returned to the 19th Michigan on July 28 and "soon found it necessary to seek medical advice, and came to hospital of 3d Div. 20th A. C. on the 7th of Aug. where he remained under treatment for four weeks with but little improvement. An application for a leave of absence was again recommended, but it was disproved. He has a hereditary predisposition to tubercular consumption, and there is a strong suspicion that deposits have already taken place, but <u>conclusive</u> proof is wanting. It is my opinion that a radical change in his circumstances of living, and of diet and removal from exposure to vicissitudes of camp life are necessary for his recovery. He is at present physically unsuitable for the Veteran Reserve Corps, and his recovery is remote and uncertain. Given at Atlanta Ga. Sept. 2d 1864." Henry M. Brown CMSR, NARA.

18. General McClellan won the Democratic nomination for president on August 31. He accepted in spite of overtures from the Lincoln administration to return him to an active military command, which had been contingent on his not running for president. Lincoln and Grant had considered reappointing McClellan to command his beloved Army of the Potomac or Federal troops in the Shenandoah Valley. McClellan's chances of winning the election took a sharp downward turn on September 2 when Sherman announced the fall of Atlanta, which Lincoln and his advisors saw as crucial to the president's reelection. Sears, *George B. McClellan*, 366-377.

19. From August 14 to August 25, Grant's army tried to sever a vital section of the Weldon Railroad south of Petersburg. Will sarcastically noted that if the Rebels thought the railroad was unimportant, they would not be fighting so hard to keep control of it. For more information on this action, see John Horn, *The Destruction of the Weldon Railroad: Deep Bottom, Globe Tavern, and Reams Station, August 14-25, 1864* (Lynchburg, VA, 1991), 177, 186.

20. Brigadier General Richard L. Page was Robert E. Lee's first cousin. On March 1, 1864, Page was assigned to command the outer defenses of Mobile Bay with his headquarters at Fort Morgan. By the time he surrendered the fort on the morning of August 23, 1864, Page only had 600 men left guarding the entrance to Mobile Bay, since both Fort Powell and Fort Gaines had already fallen. Before Page turned Fort Morgan over to the Federals, he arranged for many of his remaining 46 artillery pieces to be spiked and their ammunition destroyed. As shown by Will's letter, the Union army accused Page of destroying some of his ordnance *after* he had surrendered. Page was imprisoned at Fort Delaware and released on July 24, 1865. Bergeron, *Confederate Mobile*, 81, 149-150; Warner, *Generals in Gray*, 226-227.

21. Banks accomplished the political objective Lincoln had set for him by remaining in Louisiana to implement the president's reconstruction policy. On September 5, the new Free State constitution was approved. Banks became alarmed after Canby, who had already curtailed the general's military influence in the Trans-Mississippi, eroded some of his civil powers. Banks took a leave and visited Lincoln in Washington to discuss plans for Reconstruction. Hurlbut provoked his own controversies as the commander of the department and was accused of using "his official position to further his own ends, and in so doing harassed the carpetbag government of Louisiana, much to the discomfort of Lincoln." Hollandsworth, *Pretense of Glory*, 208-215; Warner, *Generals in Blue*, 245.

22. Henry Brown received a "Surgeon's Certificate of Disability" and tendered his resignation on September 23, 1864, while he was still in Atlanta. The 19th Michigan regimental records show that he "Resigned on account of disability Oct. 4, 1864." Henry M. Brown CMSR, NARA; Brown, *Record of Service of Michigan Volunteers in the Civil War, 1861-1865,* vol.19, 17.

23. Will Brown was jubilant over Grant's progress around Petersburg, Sheridan's Shenandoah Valley victories at Winchester and Fisher's Hill, and Sherman's capture of Atlanta. Richard M. McMurry, *Atlanta 1864: Last Chance for the Confederacy* (Lincoln, NE, 2000), 172-175.

24. On September 12, 1864, General Sherman responded to a letter from Atlanta's mayor and city council members requesting he rescind an order to forcibly expel the city's inhabitants. Sherman replied he would not rescind his orders, noting, "We must have peace, not only at Atlanta, but in all America. To secure this, we must stop the war. . . . To stop war, we must defeat the rebel armies. . . . To defeat those armies, we must prepare the way to reach them in their recesses," which meant the city of Atlanta had to become a Union base of military operations in the Southeast. Sherman added, "You cannot qualify war in harsher terms than I will. War is cruelty, and you cannot refine it. . . . But you cannot have peace and a division in our country." He concluded by saying he thought it ironic the Georgians had supported the war effort from afar but, now that it was at their doorstep, they wanted relief. William Tecumseh Sherman et al, *Reply of Maj. Gen. Sherman to the Mayor of Atlanta, and Speeches of Maj. Gen. Hooker, Delivered in the Cities of Brooklyn and New York, Sept. 22, 1864. Letter of Lieut. Gen. Grant. Voices from the Army* (Washington, D.C., 1864), n.p.

25. Major General Benjamin Butler was the Union politician-general who served as the first military governor of New Orleans. Butler assumed this post after accompanying Farragut, who led his warships up the Mississippi after New Orleans surrendered on April 25, 1862. Nicknamed "Beast" by Southerners, Butler ruled over the Crescent City with the zeal and heavy-handedness of a totalitarian dictator. During his tenure he worked to break the will of New Orleans' secessionist residents. His most controversial order stipulated that any woman who openly expressed disfavor towards Union soldiers would be treated as prostitutes. As Will noted, the women of New Orleans were still incensed about it a year after the "Beast" had left. Waugh, *Reelecting Lincoln*, 108-109; Warner, *Generals in Blue*, 61; Dufour, *The Night the War Was Lost*, 299-303.

26. CSS *Tennessee* was the largest ironclad built by the Confederacy. It was captured during the Battle of Mobile Bay on August 5, 1864. Faust, ed., *Historical Times Illustrated Encyclopedia of the Civil War*, 746; "Farragut's Victory," *Harper's Weekly*, September 10, 1864, 581.

27. Lib Brown was promoted to quartermaster sergeant of the 12th Michigan Infantry on August 20, 1864. Hiram Liberty Brown CMSR, NARA.

28. James Totten graduated from West Point in 1841 and served in the Mexican War. When the Civil War began he was a lieutenant colonel in the 1st Missouri Light Artillery. He later served as chief of staff to Rosecrans and became the adjutant inspector general for Missouri. When the CMB encountered James Totten, he was a brigadier general and chief of artillery and ordnance for Canby. A Virginian, John W. Davidson also was a graduate of West Point (class of 1845) and served in the Mexican War. He was appointed brigadier general on February 3, 1862. After participating in McClellan's Peninsula Campaign, Davidson was transferred west. He led the Army of Southeast Missouri in 1863 and in 1864 commanded the Army of Arkansas before becoming Canby's chief of cavalry. Hunt & Brown, *Brevet Generals in Blue*, 621;Warner, *Generals in Blue*, 112.

29. After Banks' demoted him General Lee took charge of a cavalry division headquartered at Baton Rouge. Evidently, Lee did not fare much better under Canby, who, in February 1865, ordered him to remain in New Orleans "until further orders." Warner, *Generals in Blue*, 278.

30. Sheridan's army defeated Jubal Early's troops at the Third Battle of Winchester on September 19; Fisher's Hill on September 22; and again in a major cavalry action at Tom's Brook. The tide had completely turned in the Valley. Jeffrey D. Wert, *From Winchester to Cedar Creek: The Shenandoah Campaign of 1864* (Mechanicsburg, PA, 1997), 47-99, 108-127, 160-165.

31. In September 1864, Jefferson Davis made his third trip to visit his Western armies. "This time Davis received salutes but heard no cheers," observed biographer William Cooper. Cooper, *Jefferson Davis, American*, 415-417, 455, 489-490.

32. The men of the 114th New York Infantry believed New Orleans, with its "great number and elegance of its restaurants and drinking saloons, rivals any other city of the Union. These are thronged, night and day, by a hungry and thirsty multitude." Other soldiers were also enamored with the city. One from Maine described it in August 1863 as "the most splendid place in the U.S." He was impressed with the "side walks made of solid marble and the streets are paved through the whole city and horse cars running into every part of the city." The New Englander also noticed the beauty of "the Custom house and if it was finished it would be the most expensive building in the U.S." Beecher, *Record of the 114th Regiment, N. Y. S. V.*, 365-367; Melvan Tibbetts Letters, August 1, 1863 letter from Camp Parapet, HNOC.

33. Lake Ponchartrain was "the back door to New Orleans." The shell road was behind the Camp Parapet fortifications and ran parallel to them, leading to the lake. The cotton bale remark was in reference to the ongoing rumors that General Banks had financially benefited from his dealings with Red River cotton speculators. Dufour, *The Night the War Was Lost*, 20.

34. Lieutenant Colonel John Cowan's 19th Kentucky Infantry had marched beside the CMB through the Mississippi and Louisiana campaigns. His regiment had been eviscerated at Sabine Crossroads, losing two men killed, 18 wounded and 231 missing in action (of the 231 missing men, 229 of them ended up in prison at Camp Ford). *OR* 34, pt. 1, 259; Abstract of Units and Prisoners at Camp Ford, Smith County Historical Society Archives (hereafter cited as SCHSA).

35. Jefferson Davis and developed a new strategy to handle Sherman. Hood led his 40,000 men into North Georgia, along a similar route taken by Joseph Johnston in his retreat toward Atlanta but in the opposite direction. Hood hoped to cut his supply line and lure Sherman after him. Although he initially pursued Hood, Sherman quickly caught onto the plan and left Major General George Thomas and his 60,000 men to handle Hood. Sherman, meanwhile, with 62,000 men, embarked on his "March to the Sea," living off the land and gutting Georgia. McPherson, *Battle Cry of Freedom*, 807-809; D. Eicher, *The Longest Night*, 736-739.

36. Five enlisted men from Illinois infantry units had been detached to serve with the Mercantile Battery and were also captured at Sabine Crossroads: Joseph Arnold, 130th Illinois; Thomas Forbes, 77th Illinois; Randolph Lucky, 97th Illinois; William D. McCory, 77th Illinois; and N. D. Richards, 77th Illinois. By the time of the October exchange that Will mentioned, Walter Felter, a member of his battery, had died at Camp Ford. Descriptive List and Order Book for the CMB, May 31, 1864 and June 4, 1864 orders written by Orderly Sgt. Florus Meacham, NARA.

37. Camp Ford was named for Colonel John "Rip" Ford, a famous Texas Ranger, politician, and newspaper editor. It was initially a camp of instruction, then an "open" prison until the summer of 1863, when the stockade was constructed. Lonnie R. Speer, *Portals to Hell: Military Prisons of the Civil War* (Mechanicsburg, PA, 1997), 131-132.

38. In their memoirs, many former prisoners at Camp Ford described the stockade in detail, although estimates varied as to its acreage, wall dimensions (8-to-12 feet in height), and so forth. One thing they all agreed upon, however, was the importance of the spring to their health. Captain William May of the 23rd Connecticut recounted, "Our 'spring' is a wonderful one. It gushes out of the clay-bank cool and crystalline. . . We have several wooden reservoirs, to which the prisoners resort for washing purposes. The upper one contains our drinking water." Alfred B. Beers, Thomas Boudren, & Frank Miller, eds., *The Old Flag* (Bridgeport, CT, 1914), n.p; Alexander J. Swanger Reminiscences, photocopy in Smith County Historical Society & original in Ohio Historical Society.

39. Life at Camp Ford was especially hard on enlisted men, who lived in "dugouts" when they were unable to gain access to the scarce tools used first by the officers. "Hundreds had no home save a hole in the ground made after the manner of woodchucks and which they entered feet first, but when the rain filled the holes, of course the occupants were driven out....The sufferings experienced in facing through the long nights of a Texas Norther can never be told. Of fire we had little: being barely able with the supply of wood allowed us to cook." A popular kind of shelter was the hybrid—"a half-cave, half-cabin affair"—that was created by digging into the hillside and then building a "crudely constructed A-shaped front." Unfortunately, the prisoners' makeshift shelters provided an easy entry for scorpions and tarantulas. They called scorpions "stinging lizards" and

considered them dangerous. Tarantulas caused great concern when one of the inmates died after being bitten in the neck. Speer, *Portals to Hell*, 9-10; Livermore, *My Story of the War*, 403; F. Lee Lawrence & Robert W. Glover, *Camp Ford. C.S.A.: The Story of Union Prisoners in Texas* (Austin, TX, 1964), 11-12; Bering, *History of the Forty-Eighth Ohio Vet. Vol. Inf.* (Hillsboro, OH, 1880), 160; Beers, *The Old Flag*, n.p.; John W. Greene, *Camp Ford Prison and How I Escaped: An Incident of the Civil War* (Toledo, OH, 1893), 27; John M. Stanyan, *A History of the Eighth Regiment of New Hampshire Volunteers* (Concord, NH, 1892), 509; Augustine J. H. Duganne, *Twenty Months in the Department of the Gulf: Camps and Prisons* (New York, NY, 1865), 383.

40. Street names like Fifth Avenue, Broadway, and Park Avenue reflected the early presence of prisoners from New York City. Some of the other streets and buildings bore humorous names similar to those Will Brown found written on the hats of the exchanged prisoners. There was a Shinbone Alley, Cat Alley, Soap Street, Mule Avenue, Undaunted Hall, 42nd Massachusetts Mansion, Hawkeye Mess, etc. Bering, *History of the Forty-Eighth Ohio*, 271; Robert W. Glover, *Camp Ford: Tyler, Texas, C.S.A.* (Nacogdoches, TX, 1998), 12-13.

41. One of the early prisoners at Camp Ford recalled the men were "scarecrow figures of humanity." None of their successors, such as the soldiers captured at Sabine Crossroads, understood how the lack of clothing would also affect them if they had to spend a winter in East Texas. Henry Roe Collection, July 1864 letter from Pinckney S. Cone, CHS; Bering, *History of the Forty-Eighth Ohio*, 161, 171-174; Beers, *The Old Flag*, n.p.; Lawrence & Glover, *Camp Ford, C.S.A.*, 21.

42. Conditions deteriorated as the prison population swelled to almost 5,000 after the captured Federals from Banks' and Steele's armies arrived at Camp Ford. A colonel from the 176th New York Volunteers, who had entered the prison in 1863, commented on the camp's conditions after the Red River Campaign, calling the period "a quarter of a year of loathsome wretchedness." Additionally, a surgeon from the Chief Medical Bureau of Kirby Smith's Trans-Mississippi Department visited Camp Ford during this time and commented this "wretchedness" was worse than he had imagined (June 14, 1864 letter from Dr. F. M. Meagher). Lawrence & Glover, *Camp Ford, C.S.A.*, 24; Glover, *Camp Ford*, 16-17; Stanyan, *A History of the Eighth Regiment of New Hampshire*, 513; Charles C. Nott, *Sketches in Prison Camps: A Continuation of Sketches of the War* (New York, NY, 1865), 199.

43. Captain Joe Stevison of the 77th Illinois was in charge of doling out beef to his fellow prisoners. Since Stevison's friend Pinckney Cone assisted him, the Mercantile Battery prisoners were relatively well fed despite the severe conditions. With his experience as a butcher in Chicago, White probably also helped out. The rations were usually issued for 10 days, which created a problem for those prisoners who had nothing in which to keep the food to prevent it from getting dirty or spoiling. "There was not a box or bag or any other receptacle to put the stuff in. Some men cut off a leg of their pantaloons, some a coat-sleeve; some put it in their hats; those who could do neither dug a hole in as hard a ground as they could find, and deposited it." Once they found a way to store their food, the prisoners' next challenge was to fashion eating utensils. Livermore, *My Story of the War*, 404-405; Lawrence & Glover, *Camp Ford, C.S.A.*, 20; Glover, *Camp Ford*, 14; Swanger Reminiscences, SCHS; Bering, *History of the Forty-Eighth Ohio*, 167; Stanyan, *A History of the Eighth Regiment of New Hampshire Volunteers*, 508; *MOLLUS, Illinois*. 358.

44. According to Mary Livermore, her Boys "obtained files, and transformed the backs of their knives into saws, with which they sawed the horns of the cattle lengthwise, and then cut them into combs. These combs were commercially invaluable, and brought a good price in Confederate money. Not infrequently, rebels of high social position would come into camp, and order combs, stipulating in advance their size and the price to be paid. With the money thus earned, our boys bought sweet potatoes and other vegetables, which kept scurvy, the great foe of the camp and prison, at a distance." They also made chessmen and checkers from the cattle horns to sell. Livermore, *My Story of the War*, 404-405; Dr. Robert W. Glover & Randal B. Gilbert, *Camp Ford, Tyler, Texas: The Largest Confederate Prison Camp West of the Mississippi River* (Tyler, TX, 1989), 11; Bering, *History of the Forty-Eighth Ohio*, 166-167; Stanyan, *A History of the Eighth Regiment of New Hampshire*, 523.

45. Captain William May smuggled out the February 17, March 1, and March 13, 1864 issues of *The Old Flag*, which were later reproduced and published in Connecticut. Chicago's Battery Boys always seemed to be involved with entertaining their fellow soldiers. For example, during the 1863 Bayou Teche Campaign, a soldier from another regiment reported "a contest was then going on between a group of magicians in the Chicago Mercantile Battery and the 56th Ohio Infantry. Eating fire, swallowing swords, cart-wheeling and performing all manner of acrobats." In a few months Will Brown would tell his father about the Boys' minstrel show, which they performed for the townspeople in Baton Rouge. Thus, Cone's Camp Ford glee club fit the company's entertainment tradition. According to Livermore, Cone and his comrades also used cattle sinews to manufacture "violins of every size, and by and by organized a band, whose performances were greatly relished by their fellow-prisoners." It is likely the young men of the CMB also participated in prison baseball games, since they customarily played ball wherever they camped. Texans today believe the Camp Ford prisoners introduced baseball to the Lone Star State. Lawrence & Glover, *Camp Ford, C.S.A.*, 37; Bering, *History of the Forty-Eighth Ohio*, 156, 250, 255; Edmonds, *Yankee Autumn*, 42; Livermore, *My Story of the War*, 404; Stanyan, *A History of the Eighth Regiment of New Hampshire*, 499, 525; Glover, *Camp Ford*, 21-22.

46. *The Camp Ford News*, vol. 1, no. 1, May 1, 1865, SCHSA.

47. Politics and personal spite may have played a role in deciding whether men from particular units were exchanged. For example, some soldiers in the 130th Illinois, whose regiment had some of the highest number of prisoners in Camp Ford, believed the Confederates harbored a malicious motivation for delaying their exchange. "[T]he rebel officers were punishing them, as they said, in revenge for causing that favorite Regt of theirs [Mouton's Crescent Regiment also known as the "Flower of the South"] to suffer so" at the Battle of Sabine Crossroads. If true, the same dynamics might also have been at work with the Federals. It is possible that officials in the Department of the Gulf who resented the Mercantile Battery were not displeased that a number of the Battery Boys were languishing at Camp Ford. Speer, *Portals to Hell*, 105; Dr. Robert W. Glover & Randal B. Gilbert, "Camp Ford, Tyler, Texas, *Confederate Veteran*, vol. 5, 1996, 23-24; Lawrence & Glover, *Camp Ford, C.S.A.*, 72; H. J. Conover, *A Personal Remembrance, History and Roster of the 130th Illinois* (n.p., 1891), 5; McPherson, *Battle Cry of Freedom*, 791-793, 799.

48. After the Red River Campaign, exchange negotiations led to the release of 856 Federal prisoners on July 25, 1864. Glover & Gilbert, *Confederate Veteran*, vol. 5, 1996, 25; Bering, *History of the Forty-Eighth Ohio*, 165-166, 172-173; Glover & Gilbert, *Camp Ford, Tyler, Texas*, 17; *OR* 41, pt. 2, 380.

49. The camp's bloodhounds could follow the escapees for days, and sometimes weeks. Other factors heightened the odds against a return to Federal lines, including Confederate spies planted in the prison; the long distance that the escapees needed to travel to reach safety; having to cross treacherous swamps, etc. Lawrence & Glover, *Camp Ford, C.S.A.*, 47, 53; Nott, *Sketches in Prison Camps*, 182-183; Duganne, *Twenty Months in he Department of the Gulf*, 356; Greene, *Camp Ford Prison*, 34-35; Glover & Gilbert, *Confederate Veteran*, vol. 5, 1996, 22-23; Livermore, *My Story of the War*, 405.

50. John Arnold and Samuel Hammett both joined the Mercantile Battery with Will Brown in August 1862. Arnold was born in New York and mustered into the 4th Illinois cavalry on September 17, 1861. He was discharged for disability in Jackson, Tennessee, on August 1, 1862, but he immediately re-enlisted, this time in the CMB. At 29, Hammett was eight years older than Arnold when he joined the battery. He was from Pittsburgh, Pennsylvania, and worked in Chicago as a clerk. A diarist in the 8th New Hampshire Infantry noted on August 17, the day after Arnold and Hammett escaped, regarding some men from his own regiment: "Great rain. Seems providential, for the dogs cannot catch the scent of the escaped after such a washing." The rain continued the next day, a factor aiding the two Battery Boys in traveling such a long way before being recaptured. In his diary, John Kennedy noted, when he and John Arnold were returned to Camp Ford, they were put in jail (the "wolf pen"). Kennedy was relieved they did not "have to stump," an odd form of punishment mentioned in numerous Federal accounts of Camp Ford. According to the 8th New Hampshire

Infantry's regimental history, prisoners who were "recaptured were made to stand on stumps or barrels for days, without hats or shoes, in the boiling sun, while the guard stood over them with loaded muskets to prevent them from sitting down." John Kennedy Diary, August 16-30, 1864, SCHSA; Stanyan, *A History of the Eighth Regiment of New Hampshire*, 504; Lawrence & Glover, *Camp Ford, C.S.A.*, 60; Descriptive List and Order Book for the CMB, Descriptive Rolls, John W. Arnold and Samuel Hammett, NARA.

51. Back in prison, John Arnold fell severely ill with bladder and intestinal problems. Pinckney After the war, Pinckney Cone claimed Arnold deteriorated due to "some complications brought on while attempting to escape, being exposed for a month without any clothing and very little food. I know he was recaptured and brot back in bad condition." To pass time in prison, Arnold carved a powder horn that he used for smoking tobacco. Besides etching the scene of the guard and two dogs chasing him and his friend from Camp Ford, the imprisoned Battery Boy scratched the Union's "e pluribus unum" symbol and "Our Union Forever" on the horn. He also included the following inscription: "J. W. Arnold Chicago Mercantile Battery. Prisoner of War Tyler. Texas. Captured at Mansfield La April 8th 1864." Arnold left one of the surfaces of the powder horn empty so he could later mark down the date of his liberation. In compressed writing, Arnold later inscribed "Exchanged May 27 1865 Mouth of Red River LA." The Smith County Historical Society has several powder horns in its museum collection that were carved by Federal prisoners at Camp Ford. In its files is also a newspaper clipping, describing another powder horn found in Oregon in 1907: "Half buried in leaves and brush . . . along the Hood River. . . . Inscribed on one side is 'Camp Ford D. D. Smith, Oct. 9, 1864' . . . while at its base appears America's emblem of freedom, the spread eagle." No one has been able to trace how this powder horn got from Texas to Oregon. Kennedy Diary, SCHSA; Stanyan, *A History of the Eighth Regiment of New Hampshire*, 512; John W. Arnold Pension Files, NARA; John W. Arnold, Camp Ford Powder Horn, RBWPC; "Civil War Relic Is Found: Picked Up by Fisherman on River Bank in Oregon," *Cherokee Banner* (Jacksonville, Texas), July 29, 1907, SCHSA.

52. During the war, approximately 6,000 Northerners were imprisoned at Camp Ford. The exact number of prisoners who died there is not known, but estimates range from 232 to 286. About 183 of those deaths occurred in the summer of 1864. By contrast, 12,919 Union soldiers died at Andersonville and 4,454 Confederates perished at Camp Douglas in Chicago. Glover & Gilbert, *Confederate* Veteran, vol. 5, 1996, 12, 25; Speer, *Portals to Hell*, 218, 332, 334.

53. Benjamin Stone Roberts graduated from West Point in 1835 and later served in the Mexican War. During the Civil War, Roberts was the chief of cavalry for John Pope. After the Union disaster at the Second Battle of Bull Run, over which Pope presided, he spearheaded the attack against Fitz John Porter. Following the Porter trial, General Roberts struggled to get a meaningful command. He had been with Canby at Valverde earlier in the war, which may have helped Roberts to be assigned as his chief of cavalry for the Department of the Gulf (Davidson was the overall chief of cavalry for Canby's Military Division of West Mississippi). Warner, *Generals in Blue*, 405-406.

54. Major General Philip Sheridan—or "Wild Phil" as Will Brown called him—went to Washington to confer with Stanton and Halleck but returned to the Shenandoah Valley, stopping in Winchester on the night of October 18. His army was camped nearby along Cedar Creek, south of Middleton, Virginia. Although outnumbered, General Early launched a surprise attack October 19 in an effort to recover the initiative in the Valley. Initially successful, Early's men stopped to loot Union camps, not unlike their Western compatriots had done in April 1862 on the first day of Shiloh. Sheridan galloped to the battlefield, rallied troops, and turned a potential defeat into a stunning victory. The Confederate threat in the Shenandoah Valley was over for good. Wert, *From Winchester to Cedar Creek*, 170-238; Oscar Hinrichs Journal, October 19, 1864, RBWPC.

55. On October 7, Republicans won state elections in Ohio, Indiana, and Pennsylvania. Despite continued frustration in America's heartland over the war, the Copperheads failed to generate any appreciable support. Republicans became more optimistic about Lincoln's reelection prospects. Waugh, *Reelecting Lincoln*, 334-336.

56. Walter H. Felter was a farmer from Lockport, Illinois, whom Roe recruited at the end of 1863. Felter was only 18-years old when he mustered into the CMB on January 4, 1864. Six months later, he died of dysentery at Camp Ford (on July 14, 1864), which Will Brown mentioned in his October 30, 1864, letter. Descriptive List and Order Book for the CMB, Descriptive Rolls, Walter Felter, NARA; Vance, *Report of the Adjutant General of the State of Illinois,* vol. 8, 742.

57. During the October 23, 1864, exchange at the mouth of Red River, Captain Birchett, the Confederate assistant agent of exchange, witnessed the episode with the 48th Ohio and its hidden regimental flag. When Birchett returned to Camp Ford, he told the prisoners about the emotional event. A member of the 8th New Hampshire Volunteers mentioned Birchett's account in the regiment's history. "The rebel agent of exchange told the prisoners at Camp Ford on his return, how in his presence the flag of the Forty-eighth had been torn from its hiding place in the coat of one of the officers after the exchange, and he said that it was one of the most exciting scenes that he ever witnessed, and the regiment was deserving of great credit for preserving their 'colors.'" Stanyan, *A History of the Eighth Regiment of New Hampshire Volunteers*, 515-516.

58. In late September, Kirby Smith sent Major General Sterling Price into Missouri. Price attacked Fort Davidson at Pilot Knob and drove out the Union defenders, losing heavily in the effort. Whiskey Smith was rushed to St. Louis and helped mount a defense against Price's raid. On October 23 at the Battle of Westport, some 20,000 Federals defeated Price's command of roughly 8,000 Southerners, ending Price's gambit. McPherson, *Battle Cry of Freedom*, 786-788; D. Eicher, *The Longest Night*, 754-757; Long, *Civil War Day by Day,* 587-588.

59. Will's comrades at Camp Ford participated in a mock presidential election held on November 8. Union prisoners, organized into 13 wards, overwhelmingly voted to reelect Abraham Lincoln, who received 1,504 of their votes. McClellan garnered 687 votes. The prisoners' vote against McClellan reflected the pervasive disregard for the former Army of the Potomac commander. Bering, *History of the Forty-Eighth Ohio*, 253-254.

60. Private George Perry embodied the reason why Will Brown and the other original Battery Boys resented the new one-year recruits. Perry was from England and enlisted in the Mercantile Battery for money rather than principle. A month after he arrived in New Orleans, Perry informed his cousin "I got 575 dollars bounty . . . I thought it was a very good site to make a little money in a short time [plus] I get 100 dollars Government besides and any wages &c. The reason I enlisted was because this Battery . . . [has] not much prospect of getting in engagement for some time [since] we expect to stay here for this winter." George Perry Letters, Squire & Chester Tuttle Collection, November 17, 1864 from New Orleans, USAMHI.

61. The Mercantile Battery's beloved Thomas E. G. Ransom joined Sherman's Atlanta Campaign even though he had not fully recovered from his Sabine Crossroads' knee wound. According to Sherman, Ransom "was not well at the time we started from Atlanta, but he insisted on going along with his command. His symptoms became more aggravated on the march." Sherman visited him later and learned from his surgeon that Ransom had typhoid fever. The young general deteriorated faster than expected and died "at a farm-house by the road-side" on October 29, 1864, near Rome, Georgia. Warner, *Generals in Blue*, 390; William T. Sherman, *Memoirs of General William T. Sherman. By Himself,* vol. 2 (New York, NY, 1892), 161.

62. On Sunday, November 6, Rebels ambushed Canby while he was traveling up White River in the *Cricket*. A *New York Times'* headline pronounced: "Gen. Canby wounded . . . His Recovery Doubtful." The bullet hit Canby in the buttocks area and probably caused as much embarrassment as harm. Canby survived. Heyman, *Prudent Soldier*, 219-220; Sean Michael O'Brien, *Mobile, 1865: Last Stand of the Confederacy* (Westport, CT, 2001), 32.

CHAPTER 17

1. Wiley Sword, *Embrace an Angry Wind* (Columbus, OH, 1994), 4, 72-73; Robert C. Black, *The Railroads of the Confederacy* (Chapel Hill, NC, 1952), 263-266.

2. Sword, *Embrace an Angry Wind* 69-74.

3. Black, *The Railroads of the Confederacy*, 264; Bergeron, *Confederate Mobile*, 165.

4. Davis' division was composed of the 1st Louisiana Cavalry, 2nd New York [Veteran] Cavalry, 1st Texas Cavalry, and the Chicago Mercantile Horse Artillery. Davidson ordered his subordinates to take only one wagon for each divisional and brigade headquarters. A regiment was allocated three wagons and a battery could take two wagons. Davidson wanted his expeditionary force to travel light for maximum mobility. *OR* 41, pt. 4, 610; Descriptive List and Order Book for the CMB, Brig. Gen. John Davidson's General Orders No. 2, November 23, 1864, NARA.

5. The town of Tangipahoa was 78 miles north of New Orleans and strategically situated on the Jackson & Great Northern Railroad. Removed from the Crescent City's feverish lowlands, the small Louisiana town became a Confederate training site early in the war and was named in honor of Governor Thomas Overton Moore. The Confederates used Camp Moore throughout the next three years (including as a staging area from which Breckinridge launched his August 1862 attack on Baton Rouge). Benjamin Grierson's Federal cavalry raided it in April 1863, and the 188th Illinois Mounted Infantry struck it again in October 1864. On the morning of November 30, 1864, Davidson's troops attacked Camp Moore, scattering the conscripts stationed there. The Union cavalrymen set fire to the camp and rode off toward Franklinton. The camp did not survive its third Federal raid. Doug Gelbert, *Civil War Sites, Memorials, Museums and Library Collections* (Jefferson, NC, 1997), 76; Bragg, *Louisiana in the Confederacy*, 56-59; Samuel M. Blackwell, Jr., *In the First Line of Battle: The 12th Illinois Cavalry in the Civil War* (Dekalb, IL, 2002), 149; Casey, *Encyclopedia of Forts, Posts, Named Camps, and Other Military Installations in Louisiana, 1700-1981*, 122-124.

6. Before the war, Edmund Davis served as a district attorney and judge for the Rio Grande Valley district. In the spring of 1862, Davis traveled to Washington to meet with Lincoln and gain his support for Union loyalists residing in the Lone Star State. In October of that year, the Texan began to recruit for his 1st Texas Cavalry, which operated along the Rio Grande River until it transferred to Louisiana in June 1864. Jerry D. Thompson, *Mexican Texans in the Union Army* (El Paso, TX, 1986), 10-16, 31; Warner, *Generals in Blue*, 114-115.

7. Bergeron, *Confederate Mobile*, 166; *OR* 45, pt. 1, 788.

8. According to historian Wiley Sword, "Hood had suffered during the [Franklin and Nashville] campaign perhaps 23,500 casualties from a total strength of 38,000 men. This appalling loss of nearly two-thirds of a major American army as the result of...fighting was unprecedented. Never had there been such an overwhelming victory during the Civil War—indeed, never in American military history." To make matters worse for Hood, Benjamin H. Grierson launched a raid from his Department of the Mississippi cavalry headquarters in Memphis during the last week of December and, while inflicting more damage to the Mississippi Central Railroad, his "worst destruction had been dealt [upon] the Mobile & Ohio between Tupelo and Okalona." After Hood had escaped across the Tennessee River in the wake of his defeat at Nashville, Grierson's raid compelled him to march his retreating force by foot to Tupelo. Within six weeks, the Confederates repaired the railroad and trains and once again operated between Corinth and Mobile. *OR* 45, pt. 1, 844-847; Sword, *Embrace an Angry Wind*, 350-426; Black, *The Railroads of the Confederacy*, 266-267.

9. Will Brown's friends in the Chicago Board of Trade Battery reached Pulaski as part of the force pursuing Hood. Mobile would be the next major target for A. J. Smith whose men had become a thorn in the side of the Army of Tennessee. In referring to his soldiers' service as troubleshooters from one end of the Western Theater to the other, Whiskey Smith suggested that his troops should be called the "Lost Tribes of Israel." Dyer, *A Compendium of the War of the Rebellion*, vol. 3, 1044; "A Gallant Soldier," *New York Sun*, February 21, 1897; D. Eicher, *The Longest Night*, 706-707, 754-755, 774-778; Johnson, *Battles and Leaders*, vol. 4, 421-422; Warner, *Generals in Blue*, 454-455.

10. Florison Pitts Collection, January 4, 1863 letter, CHS; Pinckney Cone diary, December 31, 1863 & January 1, 1864, ALPL.

11. At the beginning of 1861, Baton Rouge was a vibrant city. With about 5,000 inhabitants, it was the second-largest city in Louisiana. Baton Rouge was politically and economically powerful. As the state capital, the city attracted influential decision makers, who settled in its vicinity. It was

also a center of business on the Mississippi, drawing commercial goods from the flourishing plantations in eastern Louisiana. Bragg, *Louisiana in the Confederacy*, 36, 49.

12. After accepting the surrender of Baton Rouge, Brigadier General Thomas Williams traveled with Farragut's forces upriver toward Vicksburg, anchoring below the Hill City on May 18. The local Confederate authorities refused a Federal demand to surrender, and the Union commanders decided Vicksburg was too formidable to attack. Williams and his troops returned to Baton Rouge on May 29 and received reinforcements from Butler in New Orleans. Williams started on June 20 for Vicksburg and arrived in its vicinity seven days later. He landed his troops on the Louisiana side of the river, went into camp at Young's Point, and put his troops, alongside impressed blacks, to work digging a canal cut across De Soto Point. After much travail, Williams abandoned the canal and returned to Baton Rouge. Johnson, *Battles and Leaders,* vol. 3, 582-583.

13. Breckinridge attacked Baton Rouge with approximately 4,000 men. Williams was able to deploy about 2,500 of his Union troops. Breckinridge had expected the *CSS Arkansas* to come to his aid, but the ram ran into engine trouble the next day and the crew scuttled her about eight miles above Baton Rouge. *Ibid.*, 583-585; Charles B. Johnson, *Muskets & Medicine*, 185-186; D. Eicher, *The Longest Night*, 312; Whitcomb, *History of the Second Massachusetts Battery*, 34-39.

14. Between the surrender of Baton Rouge in May 1862 and the Federal evacuation three months later, Union soldiers, as author Jefferson Davis Bragg wrote, were actively "pillaging and marauding." Before his death on August 5, Brigadier General Thomas Williams complained about his men's destructive propensities. In June, one Federal colonel, after leading an expedition into the surrounding countryside, reported his men punished local secessionists and "left nothing but the blackened chimneys as monuments." Before the Federal soldiers evacuated the city, two weeks after the Battle of Baton Rouge, Butler sanctioned more wanton destruction of property. The statue of Washington was sent to the mayor of New York and the pilfered library books were shipped and stored in New Orleans. In a letter to his wife, Butler claimed the plundering was necessary and predicted he would inflict even more damage on the Southerners. Bragg, *Louisiana in the Confederacy*, 127-129.

15. Charles F. Sherman Civil War Letters, June 11, 1862, letter from Baton Rouge, HNOC.

16. In mid-December 1862, Banks replaced Benjamin Butler and sent 10,000 troops to reoccupy Baton Rouge. The Federals maintained control of the city for the remainder of the war. A Massachusetts soldier reported to his hometown newspaper that Baton Rouge "looks ragged and desolate." Louisiana's Confederate legislature moved first to Opelousas and then Shreveport. The Union occupiers burned the state capital building in Baton Rouge. In 1869, a Union veteran and reporter returned to Baton Rouge and viewed, in his words, "the still entire walls of the beautiful State House and regretted the sacrilegious act which left them so black, dreary, and bare." The edifice was not rebuilt until 1882, when the state legislature finally returned to Baton Rouge. The Old State Capitol, as the building is now known, remains a major tourist attraction today. In addition to serving as a museum, it is used for special community activities. Public schools, for example, stage a mock electoral college there during each presidential election. Bragg, *Louisiana in the Confederacy*, 144-145, 159; Joseph C. Carter, ed., *Magnolia Journey: A Union Veteran Revisits the Former Confederate States* (University, AL, 1974), 121-122.

17. Davidson's army destroyed Camp Moore at Tangipahoa. Author Doug Gelbert noted, "This final raid ended Camp Moore as a military camp [base]." Gelbert, *Civil War Sites, Memorials, Museums and Library Collections*, 76.

18. Will Brown continued to follow the news of Grant's and Sherman's activities. For example, Will was aware of an observation Grant had made to his political friend, Congressman Elihu Washburne: "The rebels have now in their ranks their last man. . . . A man lost by them cannot be replaced. They have robbed the cradle and the grave equally to get their present force." *Ulysses S. Grant*, 373-374.

19. In June 1864, Edmund Davis and his men arrived in Louisiana to contend with enemy guerrillas around Morganza, located northeast of Baton Rouge and on the other side of the Mississippi River. On November 10, 1864, Davis was promoted to brigadier general with

responsibility for the District of Morganza. Upon returning from Davidson's raid into Mississippi, he was placed in charge of the Cavalry Brigade of Northern Louisiana. After the war, Davis served one term, from 1870 to1872, as the reconstruction governor of Texas. Joseph Bailey had been promoted to brevet brigadier general after his extraordinary engineering feat that saved Porter's fleet from its Red River trap earlier in the year. Thompson, *Mexican Texans in the Union Army*, 31-36; Warner, *Generals in Blue*, 15.

20. Canby ordered most of Davidson's cavalry back to New Orleans because he planned to use them "in a raid from Memphis against Hood's Confederate army's communications in Tennessee." Bergeron, *Confederate Mobile*, 166.

21. Historian Art Bergeron has suggested it was the wider Pascagoula River, and not the nearby Leaf River, that Davidson was unable to cross on his Mobile & Ohio raid. His research confirms the rest of Will Brown's account, including the expedition's detour to West Pascagoula. *Ibid.*; *OR* 45, pt. 1, 787-789.

22. Major General Gordon Granger was a veteran officer who had participated in many of the Union's battles in the Western Theater, including Wilson's Creek, New Madrid, Island No. 10, Chickamauga, and Chattanooga. In August 1864, Canby assigned him to support Farragut's naval attack against the Confederate fortifications guarding the entrance into Mobile Bay. With approximately 5,500 men, plus 25 cannon and 16 mortars, Granger invested Fort Morgan on Mobile Point. Outmatched, the Confederates surrendered on August 23. Historian Arthur Bergeron writes that after Davidson completed his cavalry raid, during the following December, two of his regiments were left behind in West Pascagoula in case they were needed to support Granger, who moved towards Mobile. "After landing at East Pascagoula on December 15 with three thousand infantrymen, Granger began his march toward one of the last Confederate holdouts," Bergeron wrote. From East Pascagoula there were two overland routes to the reinforced city. Twelve miles out, Granger decided to entrench and waited to see if he could draw the Confederates away from other lines of defense. Granger, in Bergeron's words, "retreated on December because of a lack of supplies." Arthur W. Bergeron, "The Battle of Mobile Bay," *Blue & Gray Magazine*, vol. 19, issue 4, April 2002, 9-10, 51; Bergeron, *Confederate Mobile*, 166-167.

23. Ship Island was nine miles long and one mile wide. It lay midway between Mobile and New Orleans, fronting Biloxi. In November 1861, the Confederates abandoned the partially fortified island after a Union warship shelled it. The Federals took over Ship Island, using it as a military base. During the spring of 1862, Farragut and Butler used Ship Island as a staging area for their amphibious assault on New Orleans. The barren island, nicknamed "Misery Island" by some soldiers, was considered an ideal location for a prison, and Federal authorities used it for this purpose. In May 1864, during the Battery Boys' mutiny ordeal, Brigadier General William Dwight had been working on behalf of Banks to send 1,300 Confederate prisoners, captured in the Red River Campaign, to Ship Island, where they would be isolated and guarded by black troops. McPherson, *Battle Cry of Freedom*, 370; Dufour, *The Night the War Was Lost*, 187-209; *OR* 34, pt. 4, 7-8.

24. With the capture of Savannah, Sherman sent the following message to Lincoln on December 22, 1864: "I beg to present to you as a Christmas-gift the city of Savannah, with one hundred and fifty heavy guns and plenty of ammunition, also about twenty-five thousand bales of cotton." Sherman, *Memoirs of Gen. W. T. Sherman,* vol. 2, 231.

25. Promoted to quartermaster sergeant, Lib Brown was at DeVall's Bluff, where the 12th Michigan had been stationed since October. The Union army in Arkansas had become an occupational force and, consequently, Lib Brown and his comrades were no longer taking part in major campaigns. Instead, they contended with local guerrillas, their regiment having been sent off in detachments to support outlying areas. The 12th Michigan's most significant action in Arkansas occurred on September 4 at Gregory's Landing. Approximately 300 to 400 Confederate ambushers fired on the regiment while it was traveling on transports. The troops were busy rounding up some of Sterling Price's men who had returned to Arkansas after their failed raid into Missouri. November 1864 had been a particularly frustrating month for Lib and the other Michigan soldiers. They had not been paid for six months—since they had re-enlisted in the spring—and the incessant rain was an

annoyance. One of Lib's comrades jokingly recounted the "mud is so deepe mules get down & you can see nothing but there eres sticking out of the mud." Greene, *The Ewing Family Civil War Letters*, 162-163; Brown, *Record of Service of Michigan Volunteers in the Civil War, 1861-1865*, vol. 2; *OR* 41, pt.1, 298-299.

26. Will Brown had made sarcastic comments about Banks' Rio Grande Campaign earlier in the year. He felt the same way about Davidson's recent raid into Mississippi, which the Union-oriented newspapers portrayed as a meaningful expedition. An orderly in the 12th Illinois Cavalry shared Will's perspective about the raid, writing, "it did very little damage and was a waste of time." Blackwell, *In the First Line of Battle*, 148.

27. Will had hoped the Battery Boys' nemesis, Brigadier General Thomas Sherman, would be gone by the time they returned to the Crescent City. Thomas Sherman would nevertheless remain, as historian Ezra Warner wrote, "in and about New Orleans until the end of the war." Warner, *Generals in Blue*, 441.

28. Will Brown's opinion of blacks, as discussed in his letters, dramatically changed after the battery's mutiny at Camp Parapet. When Will was stationed outside Vicksburg in the spring of 1863 and began to visit local plantations, he supported Lincoln's plan to provide equality for all blacks. After Camp Parapet, Will started to make disparaging comments to his father about the black troops in Louisiana, even though they were not responsible for his battery's mistreatment.

29. Will referred to Major General Joseph Reynolds. After helping Canby organize the campaign against Mobile, he took command of the Department of Arkansas in November 1864. He held the post until April 1866. J. Eicher, *Civil War High Commands*, 451; Warner, *Generals in Blue*, 397-398.

30. Catherine (Kate) Seymour Bigelow was indeed Will Brown's "best and truest friend"—he married her on September 27, 1871. Kate's father was Dr. Stephen Seymour, a "pioneer home physician of Chicago." Will and Kate remained married until her death in 1919. John W. Leonard, ed., *The Book of Chicagoans* (Chicago, IL, 1905), 88.

31. Many of the Union soldiers regarded the State Capitol building as the finest architectural masterpiece that they saw while in the state of Louisiana.

32. Will Brown continued to stay up to date on current events. "In regard to a 'Peace party' gone from Richmond to Washington," Will was referring to the trips made by Francis P. Blair. The elder Blair had been given a card signed by Lincoln on December 26, 1864, that read "Allow the bearer, F. P. Blair, Sr., to pass our lines to go south, and return." Lincoln later testified that Blair "was given no authority to speak or act for the Government." Blair nonetheless proceeded to Richmond under the auspices of trying to engage the Confederacy in a mutual strategy to expel the French from Mexico. He stayed with Robert Ould, the Rebels' commissioner for exchanging prisoners, and returned to Washington in mid-January with a letter written by Jefferson Davis. The Confederate leader had requested that a conference be held "to secure peace to the two countries." Lincoln sent Blair back to Richmond with his response that the Union government was amenable to participate in such a peace conference. Historian James McPherson writes that by publicizing the lengthy discussion with his old friend Blair, Jefferson Davis sought to rekindle Confederate support for the war. For Union soldiers like Will Brown, these diplomatic machinations, though titillating to the public, did "not affect the armies in the field." Benson J. Lossing, *Pictorial History of the Civil War in the United States* (Philadelphia, PA, 1866), 526-529; McPherson, *Battle Cry of Freedom*, 821-824; David Herbert Donald, *Lincoln* (London, 1995), 556.

33. Under Hurlbut, cotton smuggling in the Department of the Gulf became at least as bad as it was under Banks. Lincoln himself was inadvertently responsible for perpetuating the unscrupulous business climate in New Orleans after the ill-fated Red River Campaign came to an end. While a few officers may have been caught and punished, many continued, without hindrance, to take advantage of the huge financial benefits associated with illegally obtaining cotton from the Louisiana fields and selling it to the Northeast factories.

34. Davidson assigned the 118th Mounted Illinois Infantry to Edmund Davis' cavalry division on November 23, 1864, along with the Mercantile Battery. Their fellow horse soldiers in the 12th

Illinois Cavalry were predominantly from the northern part of the state. They had campaigned in both the Eastern and Western theaters. During the Antietam Campaign, the 12th Illinois was part of a cavalry force that made a famous nighttime escape from Harpers Ferry, which the Confederates had besieged. The regiment also served with Brigadier General John Buford on McPherson's Ridge at the opening of the Battle of Gettysburg, where Buford successfully held off the Confederates until Union infantry arrived. In 1864, Union military officials transferred the 12th Illinois Cavalry to Louisiana, enabling it to take part in Davidson's cavalry raid on the Mobile & Ohio Railroad. Upon returning to New Orleans, the haggard Illinois horse soldiers were shipped to Memphis and thus were not in Baton Rouge when Will outlined to his father which other units were part of the battery's brigade in January 1865. Descriptive List and Order Book for the Chicago Mercantile Battery, Brig. Gen. John Davidson, General Orders No. 2, November 23, 1864, NARA; Blackwell, *In the First Line of Battle*, 32-33, 100-101, 148-149.

35. Fort Fisher guarded the New Inlet approach to Cape Fear River and its access to Wilmington, a crucial port for Confederate blockade runners. The fort fell on January 15, 1865, after a successful Union amphibious assault. For a detailed account of how Rear Admiral David Dixon Porter and Major General Alfred Terry captured Fort Fisher, please refer to Rod Gragg, *Confederate Goliath: The Battle of Fort Fisher* (Baton Rouge, LA, 1991).

36. Jefferson Davis established a special commission to negotiate peace, consisting of Vice President Alexander Stephens, Senator Robert M. T. Hunter, and Assistant Secretary of War John A. Campbell. Lincoln designated Secretary of State William H. Seward as his representative but then decided to join him for the discussion. The conference was held on February 3, 1865, aboard the *River Queen* at Hampton Roads. McPherson, *Battle Cry of Freedom*, 822.

37. The May 14, 1864, issue of *Harper's Weekly* included a drawing and an article depicting how, for two years, "Union men have been in the [Louisiana] swamps…driven there for refuge from the [Confederate] conscription….In many cases they were hunted by dogs." "Union Refugees in the Louisiana Swamps," *Harper's Weekly,* May 14, 1864, 310, 313.

38. Richard Yates was elected senator from Illinois during Lincoln's reelection landslide. In this fortuitous position, Yates was able to avoid intense scrutiny during the ongoing Congressional investigation into the Red River Campaign. Thus, his controversial New Orleans meeting with Banks about cotton speculation and the presidential election was never closely examined. Former Major General Richard J. Oglesby replaced Yates as governor. Oglesby, a Kentuckian, had been one of the first Republican politicians in prewar Illinois. After joining the Union army he distinguished himself in Tennessee and Mississippi and was promoted to major general in March 1863, a rank he held until resigning to run for Illinois' governor in May 1864. Oglesby assumed his gubernatorial office after winning a substantial victory at the polls. After the war, he served two more terms as Illinois' governor and also became a United States senator. Warner, *Generals in Blue*, 346-347.

39. In January, Grant and Halleck began making preparations to neutralize Alabama's value to the Confederacy. Canby moved east with his troops to Mobile while, from Tennessee, Major General James H. Wilson led a large cavalry force in a raid. A major Union objective of this campaign was to eliminate the Rebel industrial capabilities at Selma and Montgomery. Bergeron, *Confederate Mobile*, 173; McPherson, *Battle Cry of Freedom*, 825.

40. There was a precedent for the Battery Boys taking on the role of entertainers in the army. The first artillery battery recruited from Chicago, the 1st Illinois Light Artillery, Battery A (Chicago Light Artillery), included professional performers, as noted by Major General Lew Wallace: "On their roster there were musicians, singers, *reconteurs*, comedians, journalists, and artists of every kind." Mary Livermore recounted the Battery Boys' Baton Rouge performances: "They found enjoyment for themselves, and helped fill their empty pockets, by a public exhibition of negro minstrelsy. They persuaded the provost-marshal to give them free use of the largest and most elegant hall in the city for several nights. There was a good deal of musical talent among the boys. They could play several instruments finely, and had often assisted us at home when we gave exhibitions of tableaux, or held festivals, with the music of an improvised band. Many of them were excellent singers; so they arranged a programme, blackened their faces, got up fantastic costumes, and for a

week gave nightly entertainments to crowded houses." Bugler Florison Pitts also mentioned the Baton Rouge performances in his diary: "I am musical director. Joseph Hennig, a violinist of this place, is leader. The troupe is composed of Brownell: tamborine; Stees: banjo; Roe: guitar an jig-dancer; Kellerman: middle man; Mendsen: tenor and triangle; Nash: basso; and Cutting: end man and Bones. Amick, treasurer. We have had quite a number of rehearsals, and the thing goes off pretty well….(Jany. 31) The first performance of the show came off tonight, to a crowded house. After paying all expenses—$25 for the hall, $55.00 that we had borrowed, and incidental expense to the amount of $10—we have $50.00 to divide, a decided success . . . (Feby. 23rd) Monday evening, the 20th, we were invited to serenade Gen. Herron."

Although the idea of minstrel shows is offensive to 21st century American sensibilities, it was a common form of entertainment during the antebellum era and picked up momentum during the 1830s. Their popularity continued to grow, and "blackface" or "burnt cork" shows became part of the 1842-1843 New York theater season. Programs included plays (e.g., Shakespeare's *Othello*), singing, dancing, skits, comedy routines, and musical renditions—all featuring white actors performing as blacks. "Two character stereotypes generally prevailed: the slave (of whom the ragamuffin Jim Crow would be the most popular example) and the dandy (Zip Coon, Jim Brown, Dandy Jim, and host of others)," wrote author Dale Cockrell. In Chicago during the Civil War, minstrel performances were held nightly in major theaters such as the Opera House and Bryan Hall (in July 1863, the "Ethiopian Iron-Clads" was performed at the latter venue). Lew Wallace, *Lew Wallace: An Autobiography,* vol. 1 (New York, NY, 1906), 349; Pitts diary, 61; Dale Cockrell, *Demons of Disorder: Early Blackface Minstrels and Their World* (Cambridge, MA, 1997), 13-27, 54, 80, 148-149; Minstrel advertisements, *Chicago Tribune,* July 2, 1863; Livermore, *My Story of the War*, 389-390.

41. Although Lincoln was opposed to negotiating for a Confederate surrender, he decided to join the peace conference anyway, which was held at Hampton Roads on February 3. During the meeting aboard the *River Queen* Lincoln made it clear that, in his words, once "the States would be immediately restored to their practical relations to the Union," he would be amenable to enter into specific negotiations. There was much discussion regarding what to do about slavery. Of the Confederates attending the meeting, Alexander Stephens, wrote years later that Lincoln was agreeable to compromise on the slavery issue. Stephens maintained that Lincoln had agreed "the [Emancipation] Proclamation was a *war measure*" and "he should leave it [slavery] to the courts to decide." Noted historian David Donald has postulated Lincoln may have been willing to adopt this seemingly contradictory stance based on the belief, in Donald's words, that "slavery was already dead." Nevertheless, Lincoln proposed to get Congress to allocate $400 million to be distributed among the Confederate states as compensation for freed slaves. On returning to Washington, Lincoln raised this topic on February 5 with his cabinet members, who pointed out the flaws in the president's desperate solution. Thus, Donald wrote," he reluctantly gave up his proposal, noting, as he folded the papers away, that they 'were drawn up and submitted to the Cabinet and unanimously disapproved by them.'" The next day Jefferson Davis spoke to the Confederate Congress, telling its members that he advocated the continuation of armed resistance and vowed never to accept the "disgrace of surrender." Donald, *Lincoln*, 557-561; McPherson, *Battle Cry of Freedom*, 822-824; Alexander H. Stephens, *Constitutional View of the War Between the States: Its Causes, Character, Conduct and Results,* vol. 2 (Philadelphia, PA, 1870), 60-61.

42. As Will wrote this letter to his father on February 12, his hero William Sherman had coiled the tail of his "Anaconda" around Atlanta and Savannah, and was now advancing its head through the heartland of South Carolina. Sherman decided to bypass Charleston—though it was the birthplace of secession and Northerners widely believed it deserved to be severely punished—and headed for the state capital, Columbia, which fell on February 17. Long, *The Civil War Day by Day*, 636-639.

43. U. S. Grant had long ago grown tired of Benjamin Butler. He had mishandled his troops in the Bermuda Hundred below Richmond, and his efforts to take Fort Fisher had been no more successful. Now that Lincoln had won his second term, Butler had outlived his political usefulness. Grant relieved him on January 8, 1865. Hurlbut also mentioned an act of chicanery Butler had committed in

New Orleans. "He took away with him a portion of the records of the headquarters of this department," Hurlbut noted. McPherson, *Battle Cry of Freedom*, 819-820; *OR* 48, pt. 1, 557.

44. After a stint commanding the13th Corps along the Texas Coast, Major General Francis J. Herron was placed in charge of the Department of Baton Rouge and Port Hudson. On February 14, 1865, Herron was assigned to command the Northern Division of Louisiana. He resigned from the army on June 27. After the war, Herron stayed in the area. Historian Ezra Warner commented, "As a carpetbag lawyer in Louisiana, its United States marshal (1867-1869), and acting secretary of state (1871-1872), his stature and fortunes steadily diminished." J. Eicher, *Civil War High Commands*, 295; Warner, *Generals in Blue*, 229; *OR* 48, pt. 1, 855.

45. A. J. Smith's troops arrived in New Orleans on February 21, camping on an old Andrew Jackson site. They had two weeks to enjoy New Orleans before moving out. Will was not the only one who recognized A. J. Smith was always "in the nick of time," making him an invaluable troubleshooter for the Union army. In a memorial article written after Smith's death in 1897, the *New York Sun* characterized the combative major general as being "in the front rank of the most distinguished commanders of the war." The paper added it was odd Smith "never appeared to be permanently attached anywhere, but…became a prime favorite for the most difficult and dangerous undertakings, and was always available. When Banks needed aid, Grant said 'Send A. J. Smith;' when Price had to be chased out of Missouri, the order came, 'Send up A. J. Smith;' after Forrest had cleaned out nearly every Union officer sent after him, Smith was put on his trail, and defeated him; when Hood sat down in front of Nashville, Thomas did not attack until Smith's veterans arrived from Missouri." O'Brien, *Mobile, 1865*, 131; "A Gallant Soldier," *New York Sun*, February 21, 1897.

46. Although Major General William Farrar "Baldy" Smith was a talented officer, his outspoken style created a series of problems for him in the Union army, especially when he criticized his superiors (e.g., Burnside after Fredericksburg, Rosecrans after Chattanooga, and Meade after Cold Harbor). His most recent episode concerned Benjamin Butler, under whom he served in the Army of the James. According to Smith, Butler was "as helpless as a child on the field of battle and as visionary as an opium eater in council." Unfortunately for Smith, he made himself vulnerable to Butler's retaliation by mishandling a surprise assault against the thinly held Rebel lines at Petersburg on June 15, 1864. Smith's delayed attack enabled the Confederates to reinforce the city's defenses. Many historians believe Smith's hesitation at Petersburg extended the war another ten months. On June 19, Baldy Smith was relieved of his 18th Corps command, apparently to satisfy Butler. Thus, Smith was available for the special assignment to investigate the quartermaster department in New Orleans. A message from Canby to his subordinates summarized Baldy Smith's role: "under authority of Executive order of December 10, and the order of the Secretary of War of December 12, 1864, Maj. Gen. W. F. Smith and Hon. Henry Stanberry [replaced in March by James T. Brady of New York] have been appointed special commissioners to inspect and report upon the condition of affairs in the Military Division of West Mississippi." The use of Baldy Smith in this manner was similar to how Grant had previously empowered David Hunter to evaluate Banks' Red River Campaign. Warner, *Generals in Blue*, 462-464; D. Eicher, *The Longest Night*, 687-689; *OR* 48, pt.1, 391, 463-464, 471, 1165-1166; *OR* 48 pt. 2, 61-62.

47. According to an article published in the *New York Sun*, "On the 6th of February, 1865, [A. J.] Smith's veterans started on their last long journey by transports via the Tennessee, Ohio, and Mississippi rivers to New Orleans, and thence by sea to Mobile." "A Gallant Soldier," *New York Sun*, February 21, 1897.

48. On February 10, 1865, 1,200 Camp Ford prisoners were exchanged but none were from the CMB. Bering, *History of the Forty-Eighth Ohio*, 261.

CHAPTER 18

1. "Babylon Is Fallen!" was a sequel to the song "Kingdom Coming." Henry C. Work, *Babylon Is Fallen!* (Chicago, IL, 1863).

2. Grant launched his 1865 spring offensives earlier than he or other Federal commanders in the East had done in the past. Irvin McDowell, for example, did not move his army out of Washington toward Richmond until July 16, 1861, and was stopped at the Battle of First Bull Run on July 21. George B. McClellan, after being prodded out of Washington by Lincoln, started embarking his army for the Virginia Peninsula on March 17, 1862. On April 5, he began the siege of Yorktown, barring the road to Richmond, and fought the Battle of Williamsburg about a month later. On April 28, 1863, Joe Hooker began to move his Army of the Potomac across the Rappahannock River. He was subsequently defeated at the Battle of Chancellorsville, after five days of hard fighting that ended on May 6. Grant himself did not embark on his 1864 Overland Campaign until May 4. He fought against Lee's Army of Northern Virginia in the Wilderness on May 5-6. Long, *The Civil War Day By Day*, 95-98, 186-207, 342-348, 492-494.

3. The Confederacy once covered a vast 750,000 square miles or "double the size of the original thirteen United States. It was now reduced to isolated pockets of resistance scattered from the East Coast to Texas; with less than 200,000 Rebel troops facing off against over a million Yankees." As 1865 began, Grant's strategy focused on subduing the remainder of Virginia, North Carolina, South Carolina, Georgia, and Alabama. Mobility would be an essential feature of his strategy, and the improved Union cavalry would play a vital role. Jay Winik, *April 1865: The Month That Saved America* (New York, NY, 2001), 73-74; Herman Hattaway and Archer Jones, *How the North Won: A Military History of the Civil War* (Urbana, IL, 1983), 663-666; Bruce Catton, *A Stillness at Appomattox* (New York, NY, 1953), 341-342; Rosen, *Confederate Charleston*, 137.

4. Stoneman left Virginia on April 9 for his second swing into North Carolina. His cavalrymen penetrated all the way to Marksville and, on April 12, occupied Salisbury on the North Carolina Railroad, inflicting considerable damage to Tarheel factories, railroad tracks, military supplies, cotton, etc. Pemberton, the former defender of Vicksburg, had helped to defend Salisbury in his role as commander of the local artillery, after he was demoted to lieutenant colonel at his own request. D. Eicher, *The Longest Night*, 836-837; Mark Bradley, *This Astounding Close: The Road to Bennett Place* (Chapel Hill, NC, 2000), 132-135.

5. Will Brown's friends in the Chicago Board of Trade Battery were with James Wilson on his raid into Alabama and Georgia. While Grant was pleased with the rapidity of Wilson's advance into central Alabama, he was annoyed at the sluggishness of Canby (as he had also been with George Thomas when Hood was at the gates of Nashville). His temper rose to the boiling point when Canby requested that he be allowed to repair the railroad from Pensacola, some 70 miles distant on the eastern side of Mobile Bay. Grant was so angry he almost replaced Canby with Sheridan. Eicher, *The Longest Night*, 837; Johnson, *Battles and Leaders,* vol. 4, 759-760; O'Brien, *Mobile, 1865*, 32-33.

6. Grant was also upset with Canby over his selection of Gordon Granger to command the reconstituted 13th Corps in the final thrust against Mobile. Grant opposed Canby's consideration of W. F. "Baldy" Smith for the Mobile Campaign because Grant wanted him to continue with the quartermaster investigation in the Department of the Gulf. Canby had been too busy to pursue the investigation himself. Many in New Orleans believed the corrupt cotton scheming had to be stopped. Fortunately for Canby, the Smith-Brady Commission Report did not discover any unseemly activity that could be conntected to either Canby or his subordinates. With Baldy Smith handling the New Orleans' investigations, Canby was able to focus on getting his troops to Mobile before Grant could replace him with Sheridan. The reconstituted 13th Corps had undergone substantial changes since Red River. Leaders such as Colonel William Jennings Landram would not take part (Landram had been a brigade and division commander in the old 13th Corps, but was mustered out on January 26, 1865). The 48th Ohio was disbanded and consolidated into the 83rd Ohio on January 8, 1865. The 130th Illinois was merged into the 77th Illinois on January 24. In addition to the reconstituted 13th Corps, many Battery Boys' acquaintances—the 6th Michigan Infantry, Nims' battery (reconstituted), 1st Indiana Light Artillery, and 17th Ohio Independent Battery, Light Artillery—were also going to Mobile. Being left behind exasperated the Chicago artillerists. Dyer, *A Compendium of the War of the Rebellion*, vol. 1, 567; vol. 2, 668; vol. 3, 1101, 1143-44, 1205, 1519; Heyman, *Prudent Soldier*, 237-249; J. Eicher, *Civil War High Commands*, 338; *OR* 48, pt 1, 455,

626, 822, 891, 939, 982, 1001-1002, 1045, 1055-1056, 1164-1165; Whitcomb, *History of the Second Massachusetts Battery*, 76-77.

7. Bergeron, *Confederate Mobile*, 166, 173-175.

8. According to author Sean Michael O'Brien, "The entire Mobile defenses were so widespread that it took several days in February 1864 for Maury, [Colonel Victor] von Sheliha, and Colonel Jeremy F. Gilmer, chief of the Confederate Corps of Engineers, to tour the entire works." In addition to the imposing outer fortifications to the west, Mobile had a series of floating batteries in its harbor created from ironclad ships, which had been rendered otherwise useless after the Battle of Mobile Bay (the Confederate vessels could no longer sail into the Gulf of Mexico). Besides Spanish Fort and Fort Blakely on the eastern shore of Mobile Bay, there were the two smaller batteries—Huger and Tracy. On December 15, 1864, Gordon Granger landed with 3,000 infantrymen at East Pascagoula while Davidson's raiders, including the CMB, were regrouping at West Pascagoula. Granger moved toward Mobile to determine its strength. He remained at East Pascagoula until Canby ordered him to withdraw on January 23 and establish garrisons in Pensacola Bay and Mobile Bay in preparation for the upcoming Mobile Campaign. Granger's reconnaissance convinced Canby to bypass the western fortifications in 1865 and launch an amphibious attack from the east side of Mobile Bay. On March 17, A. J. Smith's 23,000 men were transported on ships and boats from Fort Gaines on Dauphin Island. Granger's 9,000-man 13th Corps marched overland from Mobile Point to the rendezvous point near Fish River. With Steele's 13,000 soldiers coming in from Pensacola Bay, Canby had about 45,000 troops. On March 25, Canby and Steele moved against Spanish Fort and Fort Blakely, respectively. Over the next few days, they began their siege operations, pressing the Union lines closer to more tightly invest the enemy forts. *Ibid.*; D. Eicher, *The Longest Night*, 839; Bergeron, "The Battle of Mobile Bay," *Blue & Gray Magazine*, vol.19, issue 4, 52-53; O'Brien, *Mobile, 1865*, 13-15, 37, 61; *OR* 48, pt. 1, 618; Warner, *Generals in Gray*, 215.

9. St. John Liddell was a bellicose general who had commanded brigades at Corinth, Perryville, and Stones River, and a division at Chickamauga. After his later transfer from the Army of Tennessee to the Trans-Mississippi region, his blunt style clashed with Richard Taylor, who was equally outspoken and direct. (Liddell's quarrelsome personality led to his death after the war when he was killed in 1870 in a feud with neighbors.) Randall Lee Gibson had distinguished himself in many of the Army of Tennessee's battles, including Shiloh, Perryville, Stones River, and Chickamauga. After being promoted to brigadier general in February 1864, Gibson led his Louisiana brigade during the Atlanta Campaign and the Tennessee Campaign that followed. His depleted brigade was with him at Mobile, helping to defend Spanish Fort. Bergeron, "The Battle of Mobile Bay," *Blue & Gray Magazine*, vol.19, issue 4, 52-53; Bergeron, *Confederate Mobile*, 175; O'Brien, *Mobile, 1865*, 44-45, 68, 83-84; Warner, *Generals in Gray*, 104, 187-188; J. Eicher, *Civil War High Commands*, 523.

10. The Confederate "infernal machines" were so plentiful around Spanish Fort and Fort Blakely that, along the bank of one nearby creek alone, Canby's soldiers found 50 explosive devices. Some of the land mines were also hidden in the abatis fronting the forts. Johnson, *Battles and Leaders*, vol. 4, 412; O'Brien, *Mobile, 1865*, 144.

11. The Confederates placed a large number of "infernal machines" in the path of the Union ships. One naval historian noted, "Previous to this attack [on Spanish Fort], and while it was in progress, 150 large submerged torpedoes were removed from Blakely River and the adjacent waters by the *Metacomet.* . . . The loss of vessels during the campaign was unusually large." One of the heavy land guns defending Spanish Fort was known as "Lady Slocumb," an 8-inch Colombiad that had been moved to Mobile only a couple of months earlier from Selma. Buried under the debris of a nearby beach for the next two decades, "Lady Slocumb" was discovered in 1885 and subsequently moved to the Confederate Memorial Hall in New Orleans. Confronted with the massive forces surrounding him at Spanish Fort, and an artillery bombardment that penetrated all of the fort's deepest shelters, Gibson ordered some of his men on March 30 to construct a "narrow footpath or treadway—just 18 inches wide and about 1,200 yards long—built on pilings and running from a peninsula on the Confederate left across the swamp." Gibson and many of his men used this route through the swamp

to escape capture. Johnson, *Battles and Leaders,* vol. 4, 412; D. Eicher, *The Longest Night*, 839-840; Bergeron, *Confederate Mobile*, 179-187; Bergeron, "The Battle of Mobile Bay*," Blue & Gray Magazine,* vol.19, issue 4, 33, 36; O'Brien, *Mobile, 1865*, 155, 175.

12. D. Eicher, *The Longest Night*, 839-840; Bergeron, *Confederate Mobile*, 188-191; O'Brien, *Mobile, 1865*, 209-210.

13. The fall of Mobile would have received a lot more publicity had it not occurred when it did. In March, Sherman occupied Fayetteville, North Carolina, and was chasing Joe Johnston and his Army of Tennessee through the Tar Heel State. Before Canby overcame Spanish Fort, Sheridan broke through Lee's lines at Five Forks (April 1), Wilson defeated Nathan Bedford Forrest at Selma (April 2), Grant's army entered Petersburg and Richmond (April 3), and President Lincoln toured the fallen Confederate capital amid great fanfare (April 4). On April 9, the same day Union forces stormed Fort Blakely, Lee was surrendering to Grant at Appomattox Court House. Two days after the mayor of Mobile gave Canby the keys to the city, Abraham Lincoln was assassinated at Ford's Theatre. All this news overshadowed events at Mobile. The Mobile chapter of the war ended a month later on May 4, when Richard Taylor surrendered his army, which included Dabney Maury's remnants of the Mobile garrison, at Citronelle, Alabama. Bergeron, *Confederate Mobile*, 193; Long, *The Civil War Day by Day*, 650-675.

14. On April 2, Jefferson Davis evacuated Richmond with his cabinet and "chiefs of bureaus." They left behind most of their staffs, especially those with families in the city, and headed by train to Danville to set up the new capital. John Breckinridge, Davis' newly appointed secretary of war and a former United States vice president, supervised the removal of essential government records, the Treasury, etc. When he learned the trains were departing that night, Lieutenant General Richard Ewell authorized his soldiers to set fire to bridges across the James River, as well as to warehouses containing tobacco, cotton, and war materiel. As the soldiers left, looters emerged to ransack businesses. Men and women scooped up spilled whiskey from the gutters. City officials did not have enough fire equipment to handle the conflagration, which spread 30 blocks and continued into the next morning. A Confederate captain, one of the last soldiers to leave Richmond, described the scene on April 3: "The roaring and crackling of the burning houses . . . while the rising sun came dimly through the cloud of smoke that hung like a pall . . . a city undergoing pillage at the hands of its own mob." Union soldiers from Major General August Kautz's division marched up Main Street, astonished at the Confederate capital's immolation. On April 4, Lincoln traveled through the city to witness his army's victory firsthand. Winik, *April 1865*, 118-120; William C. Davis, *An Honorable Defeat: The Last Days of the Confederate Government* (San Diego, CA, 2001), 56-69; J. B. Jones, *A Rebel War Clerk's Diary at the Confederate States Capital*, vol. 2 (Philadelphia, PA, 1866), 466-474; A. A. & Mary Hoehling, *The Day Richmond Died* (Lanham, MD), 190-193; Nelson Lankford*, Richmond Burning: The Last Days of the Confederate Capital* (New York, NY, 2002), 98-100; George A. Bruce, *The Capture and Occupation of Richmond* (n.p., n.d.), 34-35.

15. General Braxton Bragg, sent to shore up the North Carolina coastal defenses, ordered Wilmington evacuated on February 22, 1865, in the face of a Federal assault. Major General John M. Schofield was in command of the Union land forces, acting in concert with Rear Admiral David D. Porter. The fall of Wilmington gave Sherman a secure coastal supply base for further operations, plus additional troops (a total of about 88,000 men to use against Joe Johnston's much smaller Army of Tennessee). Meanwhile, the Confederates evacuated Charleston on the night of February 17-18. A Union celebration took place on April 14 to commemorate the surrender and recapture of Fort Sumter, with Major General Robert Anderson raising the garrison flag he had been forced to haul down when he surrendered the fort exactly four years earlier. Chris E. Fonvielle, Jr.*, The Wilmington Campaign: Last Rays of Departing Hope* (Campbell, CA, 1997), 386-437; Rosen*, Confederate Charleston*, 137-150; Long, *The Civil War Day by Day*, 465.

16. Although Will exaggerated the size of Canby's force that was en route to Mobile, he was uncannily accurate in predicting that Selma, Alabama, was a more strategic target for the Union.

17. Brigadier General Joseph Bailey left Baton Rouge on March 1 with 1,200 horse soldiers, 150 artillerymen, four rifled guns, and two mountain howitzers. The objective of the Bailey expedition,

as Hurlbut explained it, was "to make as much of a demonstration as possible and give the color to the Confederates of a large expedition to be moved from that point. . . . The troops will build bridges over the Comite as if the cavalry were merely a vanguard preparing for the advance of a heavy column." This movement was a decoy, meant to distract the Confederates from Wilson's cavalry expedition to Selma and Canby's Mobile Campaign. The Mercantile Battery was left behind in the Baton Rouge garrison. *OR* 48, pt. 1, 957, 1050-1051, 1065; Eicher, *Civil War High Commands*, 112.

18. Because Cone was employed butchering cattle at Camp Ford, he was able to ensure the Battery Boys got the byproducts of his activities, such as the horns they used to make combs and tobacco pipes (e.g., like the one carved by Bugler John W. Arnold).

19. Cut off from the rest of the Confederacy, Kirby Smith was criticized in the *Richmond Whig* and in other newspapers for his inability to support Southern forces in the East. Smith was apparently more concerned about being publicly maligned—on March 9, he wrote to Jefferson Davis to defend himself against these newspaper attacks and offered his resignation—than maneuvering his Trans-Mississippi troops to strike the enemy. *OR* 48, pt.1, 1417.

20. Two cavalry divisions from Sheridan's force departed Winchester, Virginia, on February 27 and rode towards Lynchburg. Confederate Lieutenant General Jubal Early tried to stop the Union cavalry from riding south. On March 2, Sheridan's cavalry assailed the remnant of Early's army at Waynesboro. "The greater part of my command was captured, as was also the artillery, which, with five guns on the [railway] cars at Greenwood, made eleven pieces," Early admitted in his war memoir. Waynesboro was the last significant engagement in the Shenandoah Valley. Long, *The Civil War Day by Day*, 644-645; Early, *General Jubal Early*, 461-465.

21. Bailey's expedition returned to Baton Rouge on the morning of March 12. Despite being hampered by rainstorms, the cavalrymen reportedly met their objective, holding 2,500 Confederate horse soldiers in the area who might otherwise have reinforced Nathan Bedford Forrest. As for Forrest, he would soon be called on to oppose Wilson's Alabama raid. Major General Francis Herron's report of the expedition confirmed Will Brown's remark about the capture of the Federal train by the Confederate Brigadier General George Hodge. Canby ordered Bailey back to Baton Rouge so he could proceed to Mobile Bay. *OR* 48, pt.1, 128, 1118-1120; Warner, *Generals in Gray*, 138-139.

22. The steady erosion, through desertion, of the South's armies was a major factor leading to the death of the Confederacy. While many of the soldiers who survived Hood's ill-fated Middle Tennessee Campaign were deserting, they were but part of a larger trend. For example, as one military historian observed, "During the fall and early winter of 1864-1865, 40 percent of the armies east of the Mississippi deserted. The rebel soldiers, finding the cost of victory more than they wished to bear, were voting for peace with their feet." In an exhaustive review of letters and diaries from Army of Northern Virginia soldiers, historian J. Tracy Power found a myriad of reasons regarding why there was such a major increase in desertions, including "chronic shortages in food, clothing, shoes, shelter, or other necessities…and the army had not honored promises made to them concerning pay or furloughs." The Confederate soldiers were also affected by gut-wrenching reports from their families in the Southern heartland, who endured serious hardships. Archer Jones, *Civil War Command and Strategy: The Process of Victory and Defeat* (New York, NY, 1992), 218; J. Tracy Power, *Lee's Miserables: Life in the Army of Northern Virginia from the Wilderness to Appomattox* (Chapel Hill, NC, 1998), 307-309.

23. As the war moved closer to its conclusion, there was a steady flow of "Southern Refugees Flying North" as described by Will Brown. As early as September 1863, *Harper's Weekly* was reporting on the refugees who migrated from the desolated areas of the Border States: "This is a scene which may be witnessed almost daily on any highway in Tennessee, Kentucky, and Missouri." By 1865, the Deep South was experiencing the same displacement of families. "Union Refugees," *Harper's Weekly*, September 19, 1863, 603.

24. On March 11, Herron received a message ordering Brigadier General Joseph Bailey to report to Canby at Fort Gaines, outside Mobile. Edmund Davis was assigned to command Bailey's District of Baton Rouge cavalry. *OR* 48, pt. 1, 1149.

25. Edmund Davis did not like keeping his 1st Texas Cavalry inactive. "The war in Louisiana proved to be a terribly frustrating experience for the Tejanos and Mexicanos in the Union Army," wrote author Jerry Thompson. The 1st Texas Cavalry suffered a high rate of desertion. Language difficulties made interacting with English-speaking military personnel and civilians difficult for the Texas horse soldiers, many of whom spoke only Spanish. There also seemed to be many problems with "breaches of military conduct," especially when the 1st Texas horsemen went to New Orleans on leave. Thompson, *Mexican Texans in the Union Army*, 32-33.

26. Lib Brown's regiment was at DeValls Bluff, Arkansas, under the command of Lieutenant Colonel Dwight May. The 12th Michigan still served with Colonel William H. Graves, who had been promoted to command the 1st Brigade in Brigadier General Alexander Shaler's 2nd Division. *OR* 48, pt.1, 712-713, 1025.

27. No wonder Will considered the Baton Rouge command a revolving door. A week after Edmund Davis replaced Bailey, Herron ordered Davis to report to Major General Lew Wallace at Matamoras, Texas. Herron's order further stipulated, "During the absence of Brigadier-General Davis, or until further orders, Col. J. G. Fonda, One hundred and eighteenth Illinois Mounted Infantry, will, in addition to the command of the Cavalry Brigade, assume command of the District of Baton Rouge." *OR* 48, pt. 1, 1207-1208.

28. All available horses were being deployed for the Mobile Campaign.

29. On the day that Will wrote the letter to his father, March 19, Sherman was sending his men into battle against Joe Johnston, Braxton Bragg, and William Hardee at Bentonville, North Carolina. The combat lasted for three days, after which the Confederates withdrew. The aggressive Major General Joseph Mower, who had fought hard as part of A. J. Smith's attachment during the Red River Campaign, played a pivotal role during the third day's breakthrough at Bentonville. Mark L. Bradley, *Last Stand in the Carolinas: The Battle of Bentonville* (Campbell, CA, 1996), 404-406.

30. Granger's 13th Corps and A. J. Smith's 16th Corps rendezvoused at Fish River and began their advance on Spanish Fort. On the day after Will wrote this March 26 letter, in which he wondered what was going on at Mobile, some 400 Louisianans, constituting Gibson's Brigade, attacked Canby's troops as they approached Spanish Fort. Confronted by about 30,000 Northern soldiers, Gibson's men rushed back into the temporary security of their fortifications. The siege of Spanish Fort was underway. O'Brien, *Mobile, 1865*, 39.

31. Michael Kelly Lawler was a brigadier general whose Irish temper served him well on the battlefield, notably during the Vicksburg Campaign, but got him into trouble when dealing with his own men. At the beginning of the war, Lawler was brought before a court martial for using his fists to discipline his soldiers; with help from Henry Halleck he was acquitted. The Battery Boys saw a glimpse of Lawler's nasty temper in the fall of 1863, which was probably why Will was not too excited when the general assumed responsibility for the CMB at Baton Rouge. During Banks' 1863 Bayou Teche Campaign, Lawler tried to get his officers to beat an Illinois soldier who had violated a minor camp rule (i.e. taking boards from a plantation fence). When the soldier resisted, Lawler took his sword and chased him around the camp, shouting: "Kill the damned rascal!" Meanwhile, wrote one historian, "a contest was then going on between a group of magicians in the Chicago Mercantile Battery and the 56th Ohio Infantry. Eating fire, swallowing swords, cart-wheeling and performing all manner of acrobats, the entertainers had attracted a large number of onlookers with the result that Lawler's culprit soon disappeared among a sea of bluecoats. Red-faced and panting, the intemperate general soon returned to his tent." Edmonds, *Yankee Autumn in Acadia*, 42. On March 23, 1865, Herron announced that Lawler was to relieve Colonel J. G. Fonda and assume command of the District of Baton Rouge within the Northern Division of Louisiana. Warner, *Generals in Blue*, 276; *OR* 48, pt. 1, 1240.

32. Louisiana and Texas plantation owners living behind the Confederate lines may have been waiting for the war to end so they could sell their cotton on the legitimate Northern market, rather than into the existing black market. After the surrender of the Confederate Trans-Mississippi, Grant made a concerted effort to get the area's cotton backlog shipped to Northern markets.

33. On the same day (April 2) that Will wrote, "With the fall of Richmond, I look for the fall of the Confederacy," Major General Horatio Wright's 6th Corps, part of the Army of the Potomac, broke through the Confederate lines outside of Petersburg. The day before, Phil Sheridan's cavalry and the 5th Corps had routed Confederate Major General George Pickett's troops at Five Forks. During an April 2 morning service at St. Paul's Church in Richmond, Jefferson Davis received a telegram from Lee informing him of the Union breakthrough and the subsequent need to evacuate Richmond and Petersburg immediately. Davis left the church to arrange a meeting with his cabinet and Mayor John Mayo to finalize his government's abandonment of Richmond. A. Wilson Greene, *Breaking the Backbone of the Rebellion: The Final Battles of the Petersburg Campaign* (Mason City, IA, 2000), 293-328; Cooper, *Jefferson Davis*, 523.

34. During the evening of April 2, after the Union breakthrough at Petersburg, Jefferson Davis and his government officials gathered at the Richmond & Danville Railroad station. "Davis' destination was Danville, some 145 miles southwest from Richmond and just above the North Carolina line." There, it was hoped that the reestablished government could work with the combined forces of Lee and Johnston to orchestrate a Confederate resurgence. *Ibid.*; Davis, *An Honorable Defeat*, 60-69.

35. Will was correct in believing that Lee could not elude Grant's army after he got out from behind his Petersburg defenses. Lee had divided his army for the withdrawal to North Carolina, where he hoped to join forces with Joe Johnston and the Army of Tennessee. Lee's army rendezvoused on April 4 at Amelia Court House, a key communication center to the west of Petersburg. There, the Confederates expected to obtain supplies that never arrived. On April 6, a large portion of his retreating army was defeated and captured at the Battle of Sailor's Creek. The Union pursuit continued until April 9, when Lee, his army hungry and nearly surrounded, agreed to surrender terms at Appomattox Court House. Chris M. Calkins, *The Appomattox Campaign, March 29-April 9, 1865* (Conshohocken, PA, 1997), 114-127, 150-177.

36. Canby's 45,000-man army sustained 657 casualties at Spanish Fort and 775 at Fort. Blakely versus 741 and 3,700 (including 3,200 prisoners), respectively, for the Confederates. As noted by Will, James Wilson's defeat of Forrest and his capture of Selma generated a greater strategic success for the Union. Kennedy, *The Civil War Battlefield Guide, 2nd edition*, 435.

37. In charge of the Northern Division of Louisiana at Baton Rouge since February, Major General Francis Herron reassigned the musicians from the Port Hudson garrison. *OR* 48, pt. 1, 787.

38. Four days before Will's letter, on April 12, two divisions of Granger's 13th Corps approached the city of Mobile. Maury had evacuated his remaining troops from the city earlier that morning. "Using a large sheet as a flag of truce, [Mayor] Slough . . . formally surrendered to the Federals," wrote historian Arthur Bergeron. "A regiment from Granger's force occupied the town [city] during the afternoon and raised the United States flag over the courthouse." If Canby had listened to Grant and expedited his campaign, he would have received more accolades for his well-executed capture of Mobile, achieved with relatively low Federal casualties. Canby's delay enabled Wilson to reach Selma first, making the fall of Mobile anticlimactic. Bergeron, *Confederate Mobile*, 190-192.

39. Joe Johnston was near Hillsboro, North Carolina, and, though his troops were still in arms, was poised to surrender to Sherman, who was at Raleigh. Sherman wanted to end the fighting quickly to relieve the pressure on his men, many of whom had marched from Atlanta to North Carolina, and avoid the prospect of Johnston's army dispersing into guerilla bands. There was no discernible evidence that Kirby Smith was ready to surrender in the Trans- Mississippi. *OR* 47, pt. 3, 243; Shelby Foote, *The Civil War: Red River to Appomattox*, 988-989.

40. Fearing the Southern cause was about to die, actor John Wilkes Booth planned to raise the Confederate phoenix from its ashes. As historian David Donald wrote, Booth intend that: "Both Lincoln and [Vice President] Andrew Johnson would be killed. Seward would also be murdered, since, as Secretary of State, he would have the responsibility for holding new elections in the North." During the night of April 14, Booth gained entry to the presidential box at Ford's Theatre. "At a distance of about two feet, the actor pointed his derringer at the back of the President's head on the left side and pulled the trigger," Donald wrote. "It was 10:13 p.m." John Wilkes Booth then leaped

out of the presidential box onto the stage shouting "Sic semper tyrannis" (the Virginia state motto) and rushed out of the theater. The bleeding president was moved across the street to the home of William Petersen, a local tailor. Richard Oglesby, the new Illinois governor and a friend of Lincoln's, stopped by that night to see how the president was faring and discovered a deathwatch. Oglesby had visited with Lincoln earlier in the day before he left to go to Ford's Theatre. Meanwhile, one of Booth's cohorts, Lewis Powell (a.k.a. Paine), had brutally attacked and stabbed Seward. The other assailant, George Atzerodt, decided not to try and assassinate Vice President Johnson. Secretary of War Stanton took charge of the government. Powell and Atzerodt were quickly arrested. The hunt was on for Booth. At 7:22 a.m. on the morning of April 15, the physicians who were caring for Lincoln announced to Mary Todd Lincoln, "It is all over! The President is no more!" Donald, *Lincoln*, 596-599; Foote, *The Civil War: Red River to Appomattox*, 978-986.

41. As a national celebrity, John Wilkes Booth was free to enter Border States and areas of the Confederacy that the Union had occupied. In the beginning of 1864, Booth performed in St. Louis and Nashville before continuing on to New Orleans. On March 14, 1864, Henry Sampson, a member of the 67th Indiana Infantry (which had fought alongside the Mercantile Battery in many of its campaigns), wrote in his diary that he saw Booth perform in *Richard III* (the same Shakespearean play in which the future assassin had begun his acting career at the age of 17 in Baltimore) at the St. Charles Theatre. After returning from Matagorda Peninsula, Will Brown visited New Orleans to procure horses for the battery, but returned to camp at Berwick Bay a couple of days before John Wilkes Booth opened at the St. Charles Theatre.

Many Radical Republicans viewed the president's death as a blessing in disguise—as long as they could control his successor. Three hours after Lincoln died, Salmon Chase, once his secretary of the treasury and now chief justice of the Supreme Court, conducted the ceremony to install Andrew Johnson as the new president. Johnson had been a senator and, most recently before becoming vice president, military governor of Tennessee. He met the next day with some of his old Congressional friends from the Joint Committee on the Conduct of the War (upon which he had served) to discuss how to deal with the South. Andrew Johnson reiterated his viewpoint that treason was a crime of great severity and must be aggressively punished. Johnson indicated that he would be tougher than Lincoln on the secessionists. He reinforced that point by immediately issuing a proclamation offering a reward for the capture of Jefferson Davis for alleged complicity in the murder of Lincoln. Pro-Confederate Louisianans justifiably felt anxious after the death of Lincoln. Secessionists in Texas were also worried. Their initial glee at Lincoln's assassination—the April 27 and April 28 issues of the *Galveston Daily News* and the *Texas Republican*, respectively, had applauded Booth's murderous handiwork—disappeared once they realized how close the Federal government was to subjugating the Confederacy. Foote, *The Civil War: Red River to Appomattox*, 986-988; William A. Tidwell, *Come Retribution: The Confederate Secret Service and the Assassination of Lincoln* (Jackson, MS, 1988), 255, 261; Henry C. Sampson Diary and Related Papers, March 14, 1864, Williams Research Center of The Historic New Orleans Collection; Parrish, *Richard Taylor*, 437; Edward Steers, Jr., *Blood on the Moon: The Assassination of Abraham Lincoln* (Lexington, KY, 2001), 16, 95.

42. Ulysses S. Grant was supposed to attend Ford's Theatre with the president, but his wife was not fond of the volatile Mary Lincoln and asked him to decline so that they could travel by train to visit their children in New Jersey. It appears there was a delay before Stanton notified his senior commanders about Lincoln's death. Sherman did not hear about the assassination until the morning of April 17, on his way to his first meeting with Joe Johnston to discuss the Army of Tennessee's surrender. General Herron did not make his Baton Rouge announcement until April 19. Part of this lag was attributable to the slowness of 19th century communication. Aside from that, it is likely Union officials carefully planned how the news would be released so they could better manage the reaction. The Northern leaders knew the war nearly won, and did not want their troops engaging in acts of vengeance that might rally the Southerners back into the field. Steers, *Blood on the Moon*, 11-14, 96, 113-134; Sherman. *Memoirs of General W. T. Sherman*, vol. 2, 347-348.

43. John Beauchamp Jones, who kept a detailed diary during his service in the Confederate War Department, recognized the danger to him and his fellow Richmonders with the announcement of Lincoln's assassination. On April 17, Jones wrote in his diary, "I cautioned those I met to manifest no feeling, as the occurrence might be a calamity for the South; and possibly the Federal soldiers, supposing the deed to have been done by a Southern man, might become uncontrollable and perpetrate deeds of horror on the unarmed people." Jones, *A Rebel War Clerk's Diary*, vol. 2, 479; Tidwell, Hall, and Gaddy, *Come Retribution*, 3-5, 27-28; Steers, *Blood on the Moon*, 5-7, 22-26, 44-54; Duane Schultz, *The Dahlgren Affair: Terror and Conspiracy in the Civil War* (New York, NY, 1998), 142-189; Captain Thomas Nelson Conrad, *The Rebel Scout: A Thrilling History of Scouting Life in the Southern Army* (Washington, D.C., 1904), 118-125.

44. William Henry Seward lost the Republican nomination in 1860 but accepted the position of United States secretary of state after Lincoln became president. Despite his propensity for trying to upstage Lincoln, Seward collaborated with the president to help the Union through some of the war's most difficult challenges, such as the *Trent* Affair. Faust, *Historical Times Illustrated Encyclopedia of the Civil War*, 668-669.

45. Will was correct when he predicted the Confederates would have a harder time dealing with Johnson than Lincoln. Johnson was a tailor-turned-politician, a populist, and antagonist of Southern gentility. "When the war erupted, he was the only senator from a seceding state who remained loyal to the North, prompting Lincoln to reward him with the military governorship of Tennessee in 1862," wrote historian Jay Winik. The president chose Johnson as his running mate in the 1864 election. Before and immediately after Lincoln's death, Johnson claimed that the Confederates had committed treason and should be punished. As a preview of what they could expect, he stated at his swearing-in ceremony: "The duties of the office are mine, the consequences are with God." When Johnson kissed the Bible, he selected a passage from the book on the prophet Ezekiel, which dealt with retribution. No wonder the Confederates were more worried about Andrew Johnson than Lincoln. And the Radical Republicans in Congress were confident that the South would undergo aggressive reconstruction. Winik, *April 1865*, 268-273.

46. William Sherman met Joe Johnston on April 18 at the James Bennett's farmhouse in North Carolina, where they were joined by Confederate Secretary of War John C. Breckinridge. Sherman extended terms of surrender that were more lenient than Lee had obtained at Appomattox Court House. Although he was outnumbered by at least four to one, Johnston still had a viable army. As historian Mark Bradley noted, "in April 1865 the Army of Tennessee was larger, better equipped, and better supplied than has generally been thought and morale remained surprisingly good." Foote, *The Civil War: Red River to Appomattox*, 989-994; Bradley, *This Astounding Close*, xiii, 148-173.

47. On April 22, Major General Stephen Hurlbut issued General Orders, No. 41, stating, "Maj. Gen. N. P. Banks, U.S. Volunteers, resumes command of the Department of the Gulf at 12 m. of this day." Hurlbut had been planning to leave the army and submitted his resignation after Banks was announced as his replacement. One of the precipitating events that brought Banks back to New Orleans occurred on March 15, when Hurlbut sent Lincoln a comprehensive evaluation of Louisiana's Reconstruction government. Hurlbut expressed his opinion the Banks-installed government was "entirely useless, very expensive, and liable to do serious harm by its legislation." Three days after Hurlbut sent this scathing review Stanton restored Banks as the commander of the Department of the Gulf. Hurlbut's resignation was rejected. "A special commission recommended his arrest and trial for corrupt practices," wrote Ezra Warner. "General Edward R. S. Canby so ordered, but the case was hushed up and allowed to die, and as of June 20, 1865, he [Hurlbut] was 'honorably mustered out' of service." Warner, *Generals in Blue*, 245. Hurlbut was fortunate Stanton and Grant let him resign rather than face punishment for shaking down cotton traders and engaging in other dishonest activities. After witnessing Banks and Hurlbut in action, Will Brown returned home far more interested in becoming a businessman than a politician. *OR* 48, pt. 1, 1093, 1174-1176, 1206; *OR* 48, pt. 2, 156, 163.

48. Based on his monitoring of the military situation in the Trans-Mississippi region—with the April 12 surrender of Mobile and anticipated Confederate resistance concentrating in Texas—Will

correctly believed that Baton Rouge was now less significant as a garrison. The CMB would soon be redeployed to New Orleans.

49. General Herron issued General Orders No. 14 on April 19, 1865. Will Brown copied verbatim this Baton Rouge proclamation about the death of Lincoln. Herron's counterpart in New Orleans, Brigadier General Thomas Sherman, issued his order on the same day for the Southern Division of Louisiana. *OR* 48, pt. 2, 122-124.

CHAPTER 19

1. Hearing the news the Confederacy in the East was falling apart, Kirby Smith issued a message to rally his troops: "With you rests the hopes of our nation, and upon your action depends the fate of our people." Henry Watkins Allen, Louisiana's Confederate governor, also attempted to instill a spirit of resistance among his constituents. Despite such urging, neither the troops nor the civilians were optimistic that the Southern cause would survive. Smith approved Savez Read's mission with the *Webb*, in part, because he wanted to boast Louisianans' morale. Even though he was not yet 30-years old, the daring Read had much experience with Confederate naval operations. The *Webb*, a tug converted into a ram, was considered one of the fastest vessels afloat on the Western rivers; but she had been languishing on the Red River since sinking the vaunted Federal ram *Indianola,* below Vicksburg, in the spring of 1863 (the Union vessel had been commanded by another youthful daredevil, Charles Rivers Ellet, Jr.). Read's initial plan was to reach the Gulf via Atchafalaya River but, due to the *Webb's* deeper-than-expected draft, he had to go down the Mississippi, which was heavily patrolled by Union warships. Robert L. Kerby, *Kirby Smith's Confederacy: The Trans-Mississippi South, 1863-1865* (New York, NY, 1972), 412-413; Robert A. Jones, *Confederate Corsair: The Life of Lt. Charles W. "Savez" Read* (Mechanicsburg, PA, 2000), 157-159; Foote, *The Civil War: Red River to Appomattox*, 1023-1024.

2. Confederate dignitaries at the daylong Shreveport rally included Louisiana Governor Henry Allen, General Kirby Smith, Lieutenant General Simon Buckner, Major General Sterling Price, and Governor Thomas C. Reynolds of Missouri. Kerby, *Kirby Smith's Confederacy*, 413-414; Bragg, *Louisiana in the Confederacy*, 303-304.

3. As Union pressure on the Trans-Mississippi region increased in 1865, and as the Confederate losses mounted throughout the Cis-Mississippi, Canby's department began to receive more detailed intelligence reports on the Southerners' deteriorating situation, especially concerning the erosion of Rebel morale. Captain S. M. Eaton, the chief signal officer for the Military Division of West Mississippi, reported as early as January that Smith's "troops have not been paid in two years, and very much discontent exists among them." In another report, Eaton noted, "Citizens and refugees concur in stating that great discontent and insubordination exist among the rebel forces, mainly on account of lack of pay, scantiness of rations, and the destitution of the soldiers' families. Desertions occur daily. If captured the deserter is treated with vigor. Military executions take place weekly—on Fridays. Fifteen men have been shot at one time recently for desertion. One brigade at Alexandria is said to have mutinied not long since. Thirty-five of the ring-leaders were shot." No wonder Kirby Smith was having trouble maintaining troop morale after the fall of Richmond and the surrender of Lee's army. *OR* 48, pt. 1, 591, 625, 1268; Bragg, *Louisiana in the Confederacy*, 301-303.

4. Jefferson Davis was slowed down by his refusal to admit defeat and his not-very-portable Treasury, which included "gold and silver, double-eagles, Mexican dollars, some ingots, and even a fair quantity of copper pennies, totaling more than $327,000 in Confederate treasury specie, and perhaps $450,000 or more from Richmond banks . . . there was [also] some quantity of jewelry and precious stones." Davis, *An Honorable Defeat*, 74-199. Breckinridge joined Davis in Greensboro. From there, Breckinridge took a train to Hillsboro so he could accompany Joe Johnston in his negotiations with Sherman, participating as a high-ranking Confederate general and not as a member of Davis' cabinet. Meanwhile, Davis and his officials were en route to Charlotte. Breckinridge later joined Davis there and shared the tentative agreement that he and Johnston had struck with Sherman. Davis, unaware that Lincoln had been assassinated and he would become the Union's scapegoat,

stated "that the cause is not yet dead" in an impromptu speech to the soldiers who accompanied him. The situation worsened, however, when Andrew Johnson rejected Sherman's agreement. April 26 was an ugly day for the Confederacy: Joe Johnston agreed to more stringent terms (the same as those given by Grant to Lee at Appomattox Court House), and Davis and his remaining officials left Charlotte to attempt an escape to the Trans-Mississippi. Long, *The Civil War Day by Day*, 678-685.

5. Jones, *Confederate Corsair*, 161-163; Foote, *The Civil War: Red River to Appomattox*, 1024-1025; Cooper, *Jefferson Davis, American*, 528.

6. Jones, *Confederate Corsair*, 164-165.

7. *OR* 48, pt. 2, 169-172.

8. *Ibid.*, 171-172; Jones, *Confederate Corsair*, 165.

9. Two hours after the *Webb* passed New Orleans, the Confederate ram encountered the formidable 21-gun Union warship *Richmond*. The *Richmond* had been undergoing repairs but was prepared for battle when Webb approached. Worse, the blows the *Webb* received passing New Orleans had damaged its torpedo spar. Read thought about repairing the spar and ramming *Richmond* but decided instead to abandon the *Webb*. He told his crew, "The *Richmond* will drown us all, and if she does not, the forts below will . . . and they know by this time we are coming. Had we passed New Orleans without being discovered I would have cut the wires below the city and we could have reached the Gulf with little trouble. As it is, I think the only thing for us to do is to set the *Webb* on fire and blow her up." *Webb* hit bottom about 50 yards from the bank of the river. The captain and the crew poured turpentine over the vessel and, once his men had left the vessel, set fire to it and departed. Thomas Sherman sent telegrams to a captain of the 77th United States Colored Troops stationed the Crescent City: "The rebel ram Webb has been destroyed. Her crew has taken to the woods. They may attempt to come into the city through your lines. Extend your pickets to the swamp and capture them if possible." *Ibid.*, 166-167; *OR* 48, pt. 2, 172; Foote, *The Civil War: Red River to Appomattox*, 1026.

10. Banks and the other senior officers in Canby's Military Division of West Mississippi had received ongoing warnings to be on the lookout for Jefferson Davis. On April 24, Stanton sent a telegram to New Orleans outlining President Johnson's rejection of the Sherman/ Johnston truce and urging officials to be on the alert since "Jeff. Davis and his companions will no doubt take advantage of this armistice to escape with his plunder, said to be of large amount—specie [coined money]." *OR* 48, pt. 2, 167, 340; Foote, *The Civil War: Red River to Appomattox*, 1025.

11. By the time Jefferson Davis reached Georgia he knew there was virtually no chance of retoring the Confederate government. Except for Postmaster General John H. Reagan, his cabinet members said their goodbyes and left to make their own way. Federal patrols and investigators eventually caught them all except for Secretary of War John Breckinridge and Secretary of State Judah Benjamin, who headed for the Caribbean. Davis moved south, but on the morning of May 10 was captured by Federal cavalry at Irwinville, 50 miles southeast of Macon, Georgia. Davis was imprisoned at Fort Monroe on May 22. The Austrian-born ruler of Mexico who declined Kirby Smith's offer of an army already faced enough difficulty maintaining control over Mexico and did not want to get involved in a war with the United States. Maximilian's rival, Benito Juarez, eventually triumphed and executed the Austrian emperor. Eicher, *The Longest Night*, 842; *An Honorable Defeat*, 275-381; Kerby, *Kirby Smith's Confederacy*, 415; Foote, *Red River to Appomattox*, 1023.

12. For more information on Kirby Smith's surrender negotiations, see *OR* 48, pt. 1, 186-193; Kerby, *Kirby Smith's Confederacy*, 415-417; Foote, *Red River to Appomattox*, 1020; Bragg, *Louisiana in the Confederacy*, 307.

13. E. R. S. Canby had started as early as April 19 to establish some kind of settlement with Richard Taylor so he could turn his attention to the Trans-Mississippi. After the April 24th preliminary settlement between Johnston and Sherman, Taylor agreed to meet with Canby. They had "a meeting at Magee's farm, twelve miles north of Mobile" on April 29. In his memoir, Taylor drew the sharp contrast between Federal and Confederate fortunes. He and Canby met at a house along the railroad to represent their respective armies. Taylor remembered that Canby "was escorted by a

brigade with a military band, and accompanied by many officers in 'full fig'. . . . I made my appearance [with only one accompanying officer] on a hand-car, the motive power which was two negroes. . . . [we wore] our rusty suits of Confederate gray." They agreed to a truce and to meet again on May 4. Taylor, *Destruction and Reconstruction*, 222-225; Parrish, *Richard Taylor*, 438-441.

14. By the time Kirby Smith reached Houston on May 24, little remained of his army. *OR* 48, pt. 1, 193-194; Bragg, *Louisiana in the Confederacy*, 308; Kerby, *Kirby Smith's Confederacy*, 414-415, 422-424.

15. The guards at Camp Ford left on their own volition. On May 15, a Union soldier at the Tyler prison pen wrote in his diary: "Today there is much excitement. . . . The guards have all deserted." Captain Pat White, Lieutenant Pinckney Cone, and the 13 Battery Boys imprisoned with them were finally going to be reunited with the rest of their artillery comrades. They left Camp Ford two days later. On the way to Shreveport, the Union prisoners passed through Marshall. Some of the Battery Boys had previously spent time in the East Texas city as patients in a local hospital. After the war, they recalled the Marshall townspeople, including the mayor and his son, who had secretly been "avowing Union sentiments, and denouncing the war and the Confederate government." Gallaway, *Texas, the Dark Corner of the Confederacy*, 204; Bering, *History of the Forty-Eighth Ohio*, 268-269; Livermore, *My Story of the War*, 406-407; Kerby, *Kirby Smith's Confederacy*, 424.

16. Taylor, *Destruction and Reconstruction*, 226-229; Parrish, *Richard Taylor*, 442-443; Bragg, *Louisiana in the Confederacy*, 310.

17. Pitts Diary, 62.

18. D. Eicher, *The Longest Night*, 844; Kerby, *Kirby Smith's Confederacy*, 429; Bragg, *Louisiana in the Confederacy*, 311-312.

19. The day after Kirby Smith signed the capitulation document at Galveston, the rest of his Trans-Mississippi forces, except for a hard-core remnant, surrendered. The fleeing Confederates included Joseph Shelby and his troops, about 200 to 300 strong. As author Shelby Foote wrote, "Proceeding through Waco, Austin, and San Antonio, they picked up recruits along the way, together with a number of dignitaries in and out of uniform: John Magruder and Sterling Price, for instance, as well as [Governor] Henry Allen of Louisiana and Texas Governor Pendleton Murrah, who rose from his sickbed to join the horsemen riding through his capital, five hundred strong by then. Finally, beyond San Antonio, Kirby Smith himself caught up with the column. He was bound for Mexico, like all the rest." Kerby, *Kirby Smith's Confederacy*, 428; Foote, *Red River to Appomattox*, 1021-1027; *OR* 48, pt. 2, 1015.

20. Will gave his father an accurate account of the April 24 events.

21. After scuttling the *Webb*, Read divided his crew into three groups, hoping to make their capture more difficult. By April 26, Captain G.W. Curry, of the 10th Illinois Cavalry, had apprehended 26 of the *Webb's* crew. Author Robert Jones described Read's own capitulation to Federal authorities: "Not wanting to surrender to the army, Savez led his party back to the river. There he signaled a passing Union ship. Once aboard, he recognized the captain as his Annapolis classmate, Winfield S. Schley. Savez offered him his sword." *OR* 48, pt. 2, 204; Jones, *Confederate Corsair*, 167.

22. The *Webb* incident only heightened Union anxieties that Davis and his cabinet were going to succeed in crossing into the Trans-Mississippi region to unite with Kirby Smith. Will's commander at Baton Rouge, Francis Herron, was receiving urgent telegrams to "use all the means in your power to prevent the crossing of the Mississippi by Davis." In order to reduce Davis' probability of success, Herron was also notified, "That no steamers should be allowed under the present emergency, and until the escape or capture of Jeff. Davis is determined, to land between Baton Rouge and Helena [Arkansas], except at military posts or to communicate with gun-boats." *OR* 48, pt. 2, 301-302.

23. President Johnson and his cabinet were inflamed by the lenient terms Sherman offered Johnston. Unbeknownst to Sherman, Grant had been told by Stanton on March 3 "not to decide, discuss, or confer upon any political question. Such questions the President [Lincoln] holds in his own hands." Grant was sent from Washington before midnight on April 21 to remedy the situation with Sherman. He reached Raleigh at 6:00 a.m. on April 24 and met with a surprised Sherman.

Sherman and Johnston met again on April 26 at the Bennett Place and agreed on terms similar to those Grant had offered Lee. "The Bennett Place surrender was the largest of the war, embracing . . . [more than 80,000] Confederates stationed in North Carolina, South Carolina, Georgia, and Florida," wrote one historian. Sherman issued ten-day rations for Johnston's paroled soldiers in North Carolina to ensure that they would go home rather than resort to guerrilla warfare. Foote, *The Civil War: Red River to Appomattox*, 994-996; Bradley, *This Astounding Close*, 200-217.

24. Joseph Farmer Knipe was a Pennsylvanian of German ancestry. Before the Civil War he served as an enlisted man in the Regular Army and fought in the Mexican War. In August 1861, Knipe became colonel of the 46th Pennsylvania Infantry and was wounded at Cedar Mountain defeat. He was promoted to brigadier general in April 1863 after leading a brigade at Antietam. Missing Gettysburg because of his Cedar Mountain wound, Knipe served in Sherman's Atlanta Campaign and under James Wilson at Nashville, where he commanded a cavalry division. At Nashville, Historian Ezra Warner noted, Knipe was "credited with the capture of six thousand men and eight flags." In 1865, Knipe commanded a cavalry corps in Canby's Military Division of West Mississippi. Warner, *Generals in Blue*, 272-273; J. Eicher, *Civil War High Commands*, 336.

25. On May 4, Nathaniel Banks issued Special Orders No. 118: "The Chicago Mercantile Battery, now at Baton Rouge, La., will report to Brig. Gen. Joseph R. West, commanding cavalry forces in process of organization in this city, fully prepared and equipped for immediate field service." Joseph R. West was born in New Orleans. After the Mexican War he settled in California. Commissioned lieutenant colonel of the 1st California Volunteers when the war began, he later became its colonel. In October 1862 he was promoted to brigadier general. West participated in the successful Arizona and New Mexico campaigns and later served under Frederick Steele as a division commander during the Arkansas portion of the Red River Campaign. *OR* 48, pt. 2, 308; Warner, *Generals in Blue*, 552.

26. Richard Taylor surrendered to Canby on May 4 at Citronelle, Alabama, about 40 miles north of Mobile. The parole process began on May 8. In the words of historian T. Michael Parrish, Canby's officers issued paroles to "more than forty thousand men, a figure attesting to the . . . [large] number of deserters, draft evaders, chronic absentees, reserve forces, and militiamen in Taylor's department, all of whom had made little or no contribution to the war effort." Canby allowed the Confederates to keep their personal property, including horses, and officers their sidearms. All paroled Southerners received transportation home and sufficient food to sustain them. Canby was also magnanimous with Taylor personally. Having stayed behind until all his men were dismissed, Taylor had no transportation or money himself. As Taylor recounted, "Canby most considerably took me, Tom [a servant], and my two horses on his boat to New Orleans; else I must have begged my way." In New Orleans, Taylor wrote, "My estate had been confiscated and sold, and I was without a penny." He saw Canby several times and the Union general also tried to be as cooperative as possible. Parrish, *Richard Taylor*, 441-443; Taylor, *Destruction and Reconstruction*, 221-229.

27. After shooting Lincoln, John Wilkes Booth escaped to southern Maryland, where the local Confederate underground assisted him. On April 26, a detachment of New York cavalry tracked Booth down to a farm where he had been hiding and killed him there. The balance of the captured Lincoln assasination plotters were ordered to stand trial on May 10 in front of a nine-member commission presided over by Major General David Hunter, who had investigated Banks and his Red River Campaign. Lewis Powell (Seward's attacker), Mary Surratt, David Herold (Booth's guide), and George Atzerodt (Andrew Johnson's stalker who backed off at the last minute) were sentenced to death. At 1:26 p.m. on July 7 they were dropped from the execution platform at the Washington Arsenal and hanged. Four others were convicted of helping Booth and sent to prison at Fort Jefferson in the Dry Tortugas, off the Florida Keys. Steers, *Blood on the Moon*, 201-230; Foote, *The Civil War: Red River to Appomattox*, 996-997, 1032; Eicher, *The Longest Night*, 845; James L. Swanson and Daniel R. Weinberg, *Lincoln's Assassins: Their Trial and Execution* (Santa Fe, NM, 2001), 15-27.

28. On May 3, the day before the CMB was ordered to report to New Orleans, Canby sent an order to the chief engineer of his Division of West Mississippi to "prepare an expedition by sea, immediate object of which is to attack and take a fortified sea-port [e.g., Galveston]. About 15,000 infantry, with some field artillery and heavy siege train, will constitute the expedition. A sufficient number of

surf-boats will accompany the troops to land from the transports 5,000 men at once." General West, the cavalry officer to whom the Battery Boys reported in New Orleans, was organizing his horse soldiers and artillery on May 11 for the Texas expedition. On May 16, Canby telegramed Grant, stating, "The Thirteenth Corps is now concentrated at Mobile. Two divisions (13,000 strong) and 4,000 colored infantry are held in readiness for the movement against Galveston. . . . West's cavalry (2,400) is on the march from Mobile to Baton Rouge, and will be in season to co-operate with infantry from Arkansas." With Federal plans to crush Southern resistance west of the Mississippi taking shape, Will Brown and his Mercantile Battery comrades realized they might not be mustered out as soon as they thought. After Grant ordered Sheridan to take charge of the Union army's Trans-Mississippi forces, he told Canby to put his own attack plans on hold and to yield to Frederick Steele, who was to support Sheridan. *OR* 48, pt.2, 297-298, 394, 456, 476, 486-487.

29. On May 12-13 near Brownsville,Texas, Colonel John S. Ford and his Confederates defended themselves against a Federal attack at Palmito Ranch. Ford, a former Texas judge, led his men to victory in what is widely considered the final land battle of the Civil War. General Buckner, acting as Kirby Smith's chief of staff, and Major General Peter J. Osterhaus, Canby's chief of staff, signed the preliminary Trans-Mississippi surrender document on May 26. The terms were the same as those agreed to by Generals Lee, Johnston, and Taylor. When Kirby Smith approved the agreement on June 2, he tried to insert a provision that "officers observing their paroles are permitted to make their homes either in or out of the United States" since he himself was planning to go to Mexico. Canby rejected Smith's addendum stipulating that he "had no authority to determine the policy of the Government in any question of this kind." Pitts Diary, May 14, 1865, CHS; Sinclair Diary, May 28-June 2, 1865, CHS; *OR* 48, pt. 2, 600-601; Eicher, *The Longest Night*, 843.

30. Florison Pitts noted in his diary that his battery's mustering out was supposed to begin on June 4, 1865. Lieutenant James Sinclair also wrote in his diary about going home, starting with his June 7 entry. Both Pitts and Sinclair made multiple notations over the next ten days about the on-again, off-again, mustering out of the CMB. If Captain White had to take his battery to Texas, he had a full company. White also had at his disposal the battery's four 3-inch rifled guns that had remained silent, except for salutes and target practice, since taking part in the December cavalry raid that ended on the Mississippi coast. Pitts Diary, June 4-June 15, 1865, CHS; Sinclair Diary, June 7-14, 1865, CHS; Descriptive List and Order Book for the Chicago Mercantile Battery, CMB Tri-Monthly Report for June 20, 1865, NARA.

31. At the Academy of Music, Pitts wrote that he had twice seen "the Harlow Brothers in their wonderful performances on the bars in the top of the Theatre." Before the bugler left New Orleans with the Mercantile Battery, he also saw the Morningstar Minstrels, whom he commented were a "Damn poor show. All of the performers [were] drunk." Pitts Diary, May 21-June 24, 1865, CHS; Sinclair Diary, May 31-June 22, 1865, CHS.

32. Pitts Diary, 63.

33. In Roe's love poem, Jimmie mentioned that she was his "dulcinea," referring to Don Quixote's sweetheart. Regarding matrimonial "bin," Jimmie used the Latin word for "two." This poem was found in Henry Roe's file at the Chicago Historical Society. There is no available evidence documenting whether or not Roe married Jimmie. In Roe's government pension records, he was listed as having married Rosena Fisher on November 6, 1878, in Omaha, Nebraska. Henry was 37 at the time and Rosena was 19. Roe's pension records did not specify if he had previously been married. Henry Roe Collection, New Orleans poem written June 20, 1865, CHS; Henry Roe Civil War Pension Records, NARA.

34. Phil Sheridan loved a fight, but he was upset that Grant had assigned him the task of confronting Confederates west of the Mississippi River because he missed the Grand Review of the Union troops in Washington on May 23-24. Grant's order to Sheridan on May 17, 1865 stated, "Your duty is to restore Texas, and that part of Louisiana held by the enemy, to the Union in the shortest practicable time, in a way most effectual for securing permanent peace." To accomplish this, Grant assigned Sheridan approximately 25,000 of Canby's troops, along with Joseph Reynolds' 12,000 soldiers from Arkansas. Grant also gave Sheridan the 4th Corps from George Thomas' command at

Nashville and the 25th Corps from E. O. C. Ord in Virginia. Grant privately added that he wanted Sheridan to apply pressure to rid North America of the Confederate-leaning Emperor Maximilian, who still ruled in Mexico. Foote, *The Civil War: Red River to Appomattox*, 1018-1019; Philip Henry Sheridan, *Personal Memoirs of P. H. Sheridan, General, United States Army*, vol. 2 (New York, NY, 1888), 208-215; Eicher, *The Longest Night*, 843-844.

35. As Sinclair also noted in his diary, he "Went down and saw our old gun that was lost at Sabine Cross Road." Sinclair did not mention the name of the Confederate unit that had surrendered the Mercantile Battery's "old gun." It is also unclear what happened to the battery's other five 3-inch Rodman-pattern guns captured at Sabine Crossroads (Taylor's troops captured a total of eight 3-inch rifled guns that day). In Texas, at the time of this book's publication, there are allegedly two captured Union guns used by the Val Verde Artillery—one at the Confederate Reunion Grounds State Historic Park in Mexia and one located on the courthouse lawn in Fairfield. These "Twin Sisters," manufactured by the Phoenix Iron Company outside of Philadelphia, were 3-inch Ordnance Rifles given to the Val Verde Artillery after the Battle of Sabine Crossroads (the terms "Ordnance Rifles" and "Rodman rifles" were often used interchangeably during the Civil War). According to oral history, the Val Verde Artillery dismantled the guns and buried them for future recovery rather than turn them over to the Union army. As Will Brown wrote in his previous letters (October 5, 1863, and November 8-22, 1863), the Mercantile Battery took six Rodman guns to Sabine Crossroads—four new ones from the Allegheny Arsenal in Pittsburgh (likely to have been manufactured at the nearby Fort Pitt Foundry) plus a pair of older ones. Because the manufacturer of these last two guns was never specified, Phoenix Iron Company could have their maker. It is not certain, however, whether one, both, or neither of the guns on display in Texas were captured from the CMB. Patrick H. White Collection, Canby's June 22, 1865, Special Order No. 166, RBWPC; Pitts Diary, 63; Sinclair Diary, June 22-24, 1865, CHS; Joseph L. Brent Papers, "Inventory of Artillery captured in the Battle of Mansfield, April 14, 1864," Tulane University Manuscripts Department.

36. In reviewing the Battery Boys' diaries for her Civil War book, Mary Livermore was surprised to see so many entries about Doggie Doggett. Describing the dog as "a great pet," Livermore wrote that the Battery Boys were upset at his disappearance prior to their New Orleans departure. "But 'Doggie Doggett' was not to be found, and to this day no one knows his fate; but his memory is honored in the records of the battery," she concluded. Livermore also described pets other returning soldiers brought to Chicago on their way home: "One had a yellow puppy, a little barking nuisance, which nestled in his bosom. . . . Another had a shrill-voiced parrot, in a cumbersome cage—another a silken-haired spaniel—another a pet rabbit—another a kitten from Fort Sumter—another a mocking-bird." The Mercantile Battery's Doggie Doggett would have fit in well with those homecoming ceremonies in Chicago. Livermore, *My Story of the War*, 473, 390-391; Patrick H. White Collection, June 25, 1865 QM order, RBWPC; Pitts Diary, 63; Sinclair Diary, June 25, 1865, CHS.

37. As the Agent of Exchange for Canby's Military Division of West Mississippi, Colonel William M. E. Dye prepared Captain White's POW document on June 6, 1865 in New Orleans: "I certify, that P. H. White Captain of the Chicago Merc. Batty Volunteers, captured by the enemy on the 8th day of April 1864, was exchanged as a prisoner of war at Red River Landing, La., on the Twenty-Seventh of May 1865." Although Mary Livermore alludes to "the records of the battery," there is no evidence any battery history was compiled (unless it was lost in the 1871 Chicago Fire). She may have been referring to the diaries the Battery Boys gave to her. Patrick H. White Collection, Red River Parole, May 27, 1865, RBWPC; Livermore, *My Story of the War*, 390-391.

38. On June 27, the battery's boat passed Grand Gulf and stopped briefly at Vicksburg. The record of the battery's performance during the May 22, 1863, assault on the 2nd Texas Lunette at Vicksburg would eventually garner a Medal of Honor for Captain Pat White and five of his artillerists. Sinclair Diary, June 27, 1865, CHS.

39. The number of "original" Battery Boys at the Vicksburg stop was significantly reduced because of early discharges. Before leaving New Orleans, John Arnold and a majority of his fellow Camp Ford prisoners were sent home. Throughout the war, many of the other veteran Chicago artillerists had been discharged early due to illness and never recovered sufficiently to rejoin the

battery. Mary Livermore mentioned that, among the veteran Mercantile Battery soldiers who survived the war (i.e., the eight veterans from her church who returned in July 1865 plus the others who had been discharged previously for illness), few were alive when she wrote *My Story of the War* in the 1880s. George Kretsinger was a good example of someone who was discharged before the final mustering out but was left with chronic physical problems. Kretsinger was from New York and worked in Chicago as a clerk before the war (There was a Kretsinger in the Mercantile Association who was probably George's father). George Kretsinger enlisted in the battery with Will Brown and survived both the Sabine Crossroads and the Camp Parapet fiascoes. On September 19,1864, after the Battery Boys were exonerated of the mutiny charges, George was detached from the CMB to work as a clerk for Canby's chief of artillery (Totten) whose office was in New Orleans. In late January 1865, George was at work there when an ambulance driver, exposed to small pox, stopped to see the departmental surgeon who also had an office at Canby's headquarters. The driver was transporting a man with the dreaded disease and needed the surgeon to provide authorization so the patient could enter the Small Pox Hospital. Kretsinger himself contracted small pox a couple of days later and was taken to the same hospital. Florus Meacham wrote that Kretsinger "had about as hard a case of small pox as one could have and recover." The poor Battery Boy's hair and eyebrows fell out and his right eye was permanently damaged. When Kretsinger tried to return to service, his debility interfered with his artillery duties. Therefore, Lieutenant Henry Roe arranged on April 7 for him to go home. Kretsinger was honorably discharged on May 3, 1865. Vance, *Report of the Adjutant General of the State of Illinois,* vol. 8, 746; Eddy, *The Patriotism of Illinois,* vol. 2, 672; Livermore, *My Story of the War,* 407-408; George Kretsinger Civil War Pension File, NARA.

40. Descriptive List and Order Book for the Chicago Mercantile Battery, Register of Deaths & Morning Reports, NARA.

41. Sinclair Diary, June 27, 1865, CHS.

42. Will Brown wrote about the Sanitary Commission visits by Amos Throop and Mary Livermore in the March 21, 1865, letter to his father. Mary Livermore provided further details in her acclaimed book. Livermore, *My Story of the War,* 303-306, 407-408.

43. At the beginning of their march from Memphis in December 1862, the Battery Boys had been reprimanded for foraging. Sinclair Diary, June 29, 1865, CHS; Pitts Collection, December 3, 1862 letter, CHS.

44. Sinclair Diary, July 1, 1865, CHS; "Mercantile Association, Monthly Meeting: Reception of the Mercantile Battery," *Chicago Tribune,* July 4, 1865.

45. Karamanski, *Rally 'Round the Flag,* 235; Livermore, *My Story of the War,* 468; Pierce, *A History of Chicago,* vol. 2, 283.

46. Elias Colbert & Everett Chamberlin, *Chicago and the Great Conflagration* (Chicago, IL, 1872), 109.

47. Karamanski, *Rally 'Round the Flag,* 235.

48. Livermore, *My Story of the War,* 468-470.

49. Karamanski, *Rally 'Round the Flag,* 236.

50. The second Sanitary Fair in Chicago was held in massive exhibit halls built for the occasion. The central building, Union Hall, was 60 feet wide by 385 feet long. U. S. Grant donated his warhorse "Jack" to raise money and was introduced by Major General Joseph Hooker to the attendees on June 10. At the first Sanitary Fair held in 1863, Congressman Arnold arranged for his friend Lincoln to donate his original Emancipation Proclamation manuscript to raise funds (Arnold was the same man who had helped to free the Battery Boys from their mutiny quagmire in New Orleans). The death of Abraham Lincoln before the second Sanitary Fair had a profound effect on the people in Chicago. They learned of the assassination during the morning of April 15. Four days later, on the same day Lincoln's funeral service was being performed in Washington, Chicago residents put business aside to attend church. Illinois Governor Richard Oglesby had been at Lincoln's deathbed and represented Chicagoans at the Washington funeral. He was also part of the trainload of dignitaries that accompanied the president's body from Washington to Baltimore, Harrisburg, Philadelphia, New York City, Albany, and Buffalo before heading west.

The train carrying Lincoln's body arrived in Chicago on May 1. Many Chicagoans showed up to watch the funeral procession and visited the presidential remains at the courthouse rotunda. Thousands stood in the rain watching the procession go by. It was estimated that at least 125,000 Chicagoans stood in the courthouse queue to pay their respects to the slain president (in the New York area, approximately a million and a half people had similarly bid farewell). Lincoln was admired and had many supporters in the political, legal, and business communities. The president had promised to return to Chicago in May to open the Sanitary Fair but had not lived to see the occasion. The train took Lincoln's body to his final resting place in Springfield, arriving there on the morning of May 3. John McClernand, the Mercantile Battery's former corps commander, oversaw the military-dominated Order of Procession at Springfield and the final tributes to the president who had restored union to the country. *Ibid.*, 236-238, 245-249; Livermore, *My Story of the War*, 562-565, 584-585; T. M. Eddy, *The Loyal People of the North-West* (Chicago, IL, 1869), 229-274; Pierce, *A History of Chicago,* vol. 2, 283-284; Steers, *Blood on the Moon*, 102, 279-289; Scott D. Trostel, *The Lincoln Funeral Train: The Final Journey and National Funeral for Abraham Lincoln* (Fletcher, OH, 2002), 176-181.

51. The July 4, 1865 issue of the *Chicago Tribune* covered the meeting of the Mercantile Association at which the returning Battery Boys were greeted. At the end of a long article chronicling the battery's service record, the newspaper addressed the mix-up that occurred with the arrival of Will Brown and his comrades: "They arrived home from the wars yesterday morning [July 3] at seven o'clock, having left Cairo at nine a.m. Sunday . . . friends were somewhat taken by surprise owing to the failure of a telegram announcing their departure from Cairo reaching its destination. The dispatch did not reach the parties to whom it was addressed [e.g., the Mercantile Association] until after the arrival of the battery in this city. . . . Mr. Ladd, Secretary of the Association, explained the misunderstanding which had interfered with a proper reception of the battery on its arrival. He also announced that the members and ex-members honorably discharged from the battery were invited to a dinner at four o'clock this afternoon, at Union Hall [still standing after the recent Sanitary Fair], and a supper on Thursday evening at the Tremont House." The Tremont was a 260-room hotel located at the corner of Lake and Dearborn streets; its meeting rooms were often used for large gatherings and banquets. Captain Pat White gave a brief speech thanking "the Association for their kindness to the battery." The night before, White had also attended a banquet at the Revere House, honoring his former comrades in Taylor's Battery. The Mercantile Association absorbed the costs of the battery's Tuesday dinner and Thursday supper. "Mercantile Association, Monthly Meeting: Reception of the Mercantile Battery," *Chicago Tribune*, July 4, 1865; Paul Gilbert and Charles Lee Bryson, *Chicago and Its Makers* (Chicago, IL, 1929), 127.

52. No information has been found describing Will Brown's return to St. Joseph.

53. As described in the *Chicago Tribune* article, and reiterated at the Mercantile Association meeting, there was only a small group of people on hand at the train station to greet the Mercantile Battery on its return to Chicago. "Mercantile Association, Monthly Meeting: Reception of the Mercantile Battery," *Chicago Tribune*, July 4, 1865.

54. The Fred Sampson Mrs. Throop mentioned was Frederick A. Sampson, a land agent who joined the Mercantile Battery at the age of 27, with George Throop, Will Brown, and the other first-wave recruits. Sampson survived his three years of service, mustering out with the other Battery Boys on July 10. Amos Gage Throop Collection, Miscellaneous Correspondence of Members of Throop's Family, April & July 1865, LOC; Vance, *Report of the Adjutant General of the State of Illinois,* vol. 8, 741; Descriptive List and Order Book for the Chicago Mercantile Battery, Descriptive Rolls, NARA.

EPILOGUE

1. Patrick's father, Bryan White, died in 1856 and his mother, Catherine Langon White, passed away on New Year's Day, 1861. "Civil War Diary of Patrick H. White," 640; Patrick H. White Civil War Pension Records, NARA.

2. White became a naturalized citizen in either 1866 or 1867. His pension records stated that, due to lingering rheumatism and other problems associated with the harsh effects of his war duty, White was restricted to "light clerical work." *Ibid.*; "Captain White's Saber," Mulligan, *Military Images*, vol. 21 , no. 5, March-April 2000, 28; Patrick H. White Collection, November 30, 1866 document from the War Department, RBWPC.

3. According to a 1902 newspaper clipping, Pat White stopped in Chicago on his way to Vicksburg National Military Park. According to the article: "Ten or twelve years ago, when the panoramic picture of the battle of Gettysburg was opened to public view, he (White) was selected, because of his intimate knowledge, to act as lecturer and for two years told daily the story of the fight." The Battle of Gettysburg Panorama was on display in a $360,000 building located at the corner of Wabash Avenue and Hubbard Court. An 1891 Chicago publication described the experience of viewing the Cyclorama: "The visitor, though aware that he is looking at a building 134 feet in diameter and ninety-six feet high, finds himself ascending the narrow stairs in an open country, stretching many miles in every direction toward the horizon. The panorama is accurate in every detail of the landscape, and the spectator looks down upon the dreadful scenes of destruction, carnage and death of the battlefield of Gettysburg. . . . Lectures are given every hour on the picture of the battle." Newspaper clipping, "Captain Patrick H. White Is the Guest of Old Comrades," VNMP; *Chicago of To-Day: The Metropolis of the West* (Chicago, IL, 1891), 262.

4. Will's younger brother Lib did not muster out of the army until March 6, 1866. After the war Lib worked in steamboat and railway occupations. Most of his time was spent in St. Joseph except for brief stints in Illinois, Nebraska, and Kansas. From 1883 to 1920 he worked as a clerk in St. Joseph, though bothered by lingering eye problems alleged to have developed on the summer march outside Vicksburg, during which he had suffered sunstroke. After his wife Eliza died in 1924, Lib moved into the Lake View Hotel on Ship Street, located on a bluff overlooking Lake Michigan. He died on November 9, 1926, three years before his brother Will passed away, and was survived by his daughter, Mary Liston (Mrs. Arthur W. Hintze), who lived in Chicago. Hiram Liberty Brown Civil War Pension Records, NARA.

5. Hiram Brown held his position as Deputy Collector of Customs for St. Joseph from 1862 to 1883. He also worked as Justice of the Peace, City Clerk, and City Recorder. During his life, Hiram wrote numerous articles for his local newspaper and was active in Republican politics and community service. Regarding his civic activities, he was Vice President of the Berrien County Old Settlers' Association and a member of the state's "pioneer" society. After his first wife Harriet Clinton Brown died, Hiram married Jane R. Liston—the mother of Will and Lib—from nearby Niles, Michigan. She died while the family was living in Chicago and, in 1865, Hiram married his third wife, Julia M. Smith of Chicago, who survived him. Hiram Brown died in August 1883.

On September 8, 1868, Henry Brown, Will's older brother, was involved in a disaster that blemished his career as a ship captain. At the last minute before sailing, Henry was asked to command the *Hippocampus*, a steamer with which he was not familiar. The ship's hold and deck were overloaded with 7,000 boxes and baskets of fruit (mostly peaches). There were also many passengers on board. The ship encountered a storm in the middle of the night, and being top-heavy, quickly succumbed to the heavy seas. Captain Brown and his surviving crew and passengers were rescued the next day but not before 26 people died. A terse telegram was sent that night to Will Brown in Chicago: "Capt. Brown and 14 others saved. Just arrived from Saugatuck—26 lost." "Obituary: Hiram Brown," *St. Joseph Herald*, August 25, 1883; *Chicago Times*, September 13, 1868; private correspondence with Robert C. Myers.

6. Bessie Louise Pierce, *A History of Chicago*, wrote: "A group of capitalists headed by Arthur B. Meeker organized the Chicago Iron Company, whose blast furnaces, with a capacity of thirty-five to forty tons of pig iron daily, were completed in December, 1868." It is unlikely that Will Brown was one of the principle investors in this company, although he was working his way up in the business and would become Meeker's partner two years later. "Steel Trade Pioneer is Mourned," *Pasadena Star-News*, November 1, 1929; Newton Bateman and Harvey B. Hurd, ed., *Historical Encyclopedia*

of Illinois and History of Evanston, vol. 2 (Chicago, IL, 1906), 543; Bessie Louise Pierce, *A History of Chicago,* vol. 2 (Chicago, IL, 1957), vol. 2, 116.

7. *Ibid.*, 114; Pierce, *A History of Chicago,* vol. 3, (Chicago, IL, 1957), 154; William Cronon, *Nature's Metropolis: Chicago and the Great West* (New York, NY, 1991), 312.

8. "Steel Trade Pioneer is Mourned," *Pasadena Star-News*, November 1, 1929; Walter Havighurst, *Vein of Iron: The Pickands Mather Story* (Cleveland, OH, 1958), 15-16.

9. *Historical Encyclopedia of Illinois and History of Evanston*, 544.

10. The year 1883 brought both mourning and celebration for Will Brown. Though saddened at the death of his father in August, he was overjoyed at starting Pickands, Brown as a commission house or brokerage firm: "Pickands, Brown soon became the leading sales agents of pig iron, coke, and gas in the Chicago area. They were in a position to influence the purchase of coal and iron ore from Pickands Mather; at the same time Pickands Mather could refer sales business in the area to Pickands, Brown. After 1904 both companies had financial interests in the Zenith Furnace Company at Duluth; Pickands Mather furnished iron are and Pickands, Brown handled the sales of pig iron." The close connections of these businesses could also be seen in the first letterhead of Pickands, Brown, which also carried the name of Pickands Mather. In 1930, after Will Brown died, Pickands Mather acquired Pickands, Brown to sell iron ore and coke. "Obituary: Hiram Brown," *St. Joseph Herald*, August 25, 1883; "William L. Brown, Chicago Shipbuilding Magnate, Financier, Dies Here," *Pasadena Post*, November 1, 1929; Havighurst, *Vein of Iron*, 23, 154; "Steel Trade Pioneer is Mourned," *Pasadena Star-News*, November 1, 1929.

11. Miller, *City of the Century*, 241-243.

12. Pickands Mather played a prominent role in orchestrating this merger of steel companies—it had a major equity position in the Union Iron and Steel Company, and Jay Morse retained his partnership with James Pickands and Samuel Mather for the ten years he was president of Illinois Steel. This web of corporate intrigue would also include Will Brown, who served at one point as president of National Steel Company before it merged with the United States Steel Corporation. *Ibid.*, 242; Havighurst, *Vein of Iron*, 23, 43; "William L. Brown, Chicago Shipbuilding Magnate, Financier, Dies Here," *Pasadena Post*, November 1, 1929.

13. Havighurst, *Vein of Iron*, 75, 92-93; Ron Chernow, *Titan: The Life of John D. Rockefeller, Sr.* (New York, NY, 1999), 382-385.

14. Richard J. Wright, *Freshwater Whales: A History of The American Ship Building Company and Its Predecessors* (Kent, OH, 1969), 74.

15. The Babcock-Gunnell riveter and Brown Hoist traveling crane were among the Chicago Ship Building Company innovations that Brown and Babcock used to automate their new shipping business. *Ibid.*, 13-13, 74-75.

16. *Ibid.*, 75-76.

17. As author Richard J. Wright wrote, "During the last half of the decade, the company [Chicago Ship Building Company] expanded at a great rate. They enlarged their dry dock in 1897 to stay ahead of the trends in vessel construction on the Great Lakes." During 1896-1897, Brown and Babcock reached profitability. Their ongoing commitment to technological advancements expedited the construction of ships while lowering labor costs. *Ibid.*, 79-81.

18. Chernow, *Titan*, 384-388; Havighurst, *Vein of Iron*, 93-94.

19. As Wright noted, "The new corporation included the holdings of the Chicago Ship Building Company, the Cleveland Ship Building Company, the Globe Iron Works, the Ship Owners' Dry Dock Company, the Detroit Dry Dock Company, the American Steel Barge Company, the Milwaukee Dry Dock Company." Wright, *Freshwater Whales*, 136-141.

20. January 15, 1895, letter from the War Department to White, File No. 395058, Record and Pension Office, Document File, 1889-1904, Correspondence and Related Papers of the Office, 1889-1904, Records of the Adjutant General's Office, 1780's-1917, Record Group 94, NARA.

21. *Ibid.* (January 18, 1895, letter from White to the War Department).

22. *The Medal of Honor of the United States Army* (Washington, D.C., 1948), 32, 130-136.

23. In his correspondence with the War Department, White provided additional insights into the May 22 episode. Regarding his battery's voluntary support of Smith's request, he recounted, "Gen. A. J. Smith did not order me to perform this service, but merely suggested if it could be accomplished, it would greatly assist the Union forces." White also asked that "especial reference should be made of Wm Stephens who volunteered from another gun to take part in the action." In the the 1905 book *Deeds of Valor*, which describes the heroics of Civil War Medal of Honor winners, White provided more details on the May 22 assault. White's July 24, 1894 & November 5, 1894 letters, File No. 395098, Record and Pension Office, Document File, 1889-1904, NARA; Beyer & Keydel, ed., *Deeds of Valor*, 188-190; *The Medal of Honor of the United States Army*, 3. See *America's Medal of Honor Recipients* (Golden Valley, MN, 1980) regarding Medal of Honor descriptions for Dunne, Kloth, Kretsinger, McGuire, Stephens, and White.

24. Kate was born on August 20, 1846, on her father's plantation in western Alabama. Her mother, Adeline, died a year later. An only child, Kate spent a lot of time in Victoria, Texas, with her aunt, Mrs. Agnes Fleming Phillips. She later attended a girls' school in Florence, Alabama, leaving it after Union troops captured the city. In 1865, she completed college in Gainesville, Alabama. Captain Patrick H. White Collection, April 16, 1864, letter from Capt. Alex McDow to his daughter Kate, RBWPC; "In Memoriam: Mrs. Catherine McDow Brownson," *Confederate Veteran*, vol. 40, 1932, 402.

25. Albany newspaper account of May 2, 1862, sword episode (no date), mounted and encased in frame as part of Captain Patrick H. White Collection, New York State Museum.

26. Victoria's William P. Rogers Chapter of the UDC was "chartered April 6, 1896, with thirty-two members and Mrs. J. M. Brownson as the organizing president." It was one of the first UDC chapters in Texas. Kate was chairwoman of the committee that raised money to erect "The Last Stand" monument in 1912 for her chapter. For a review of Kate Brownson's role in helping to start Victoria's Bronte Club, see Leopold Morris, *Pictorial History of Victoria and Victoria County* (San Antonio, TX, 1953); Parole of Honor for Capt. McDow, Alexander McDow Civil War Military Records, Hill College Confederate Research Center & Museum; F. Lotto, *Fayette County, Her History and Her People* (Schulenburg, TX, 1902), 142, 152; Mary B. Poppenheim, *The History of the United Daughters of the Confederacy,* vol. 1 (Richmond, VA, 1938), 1-3; Jacqueline Dillard Dodge, ed., *Texas Division, United Daughters of the Confederacy, Chapter Histories* (Texas: The Division, 1990), 4-6; "The Last Stand," Monument at Victoria," *Confederate Veteran,* vol. 20, 1912, 13; Roy Grimes, ed., *300 Years in Victoria County* (Victoria, TX, 1968), 260-285, 582.

27. "Scattering," *National Tribune*, vol.15, no. 12, January 2, 1896.

28. White kept his sword in the hallway of his house, along with his coveted Medal of Honor and other memorabilia from the war. Still thrilled at having returned White's sword, Kate Brownson wrote an article about the incident, publishing it in the *Confederate Veteran* magazine. She concluded her article by reaffirming her excitement about the new Confederate publication: "I feel like taking the field and putting the Veteran in every Southern home. You may send the Veteran as long as my husband and children are alive." In 1925, in another *Confederate Veteran* article, she recounted a story from a man in Victoria whose father, Colonel C. D. Anderson, had surrendered a special presentation sword to Admiral Farragut after the Federal victory at Mobile Bay. As Brownson wrote, "Colonel Anderson, with his family, was living in Austin, Tex., when one evening a package was delivered to him. After removing many wrappings, he found, to his joy, it was his old beloved sword. A letter from the son of Admiral Farragut explained that the sword was sent by request of his father before his death, with the added inscription: 'Returned by Admiral Farragut to Col. C. D. Anderson for his gallant defense of Fort Gaines, August 8, 1864.'" Patrick White letter to Mrs. J. M. Brownson, RBWPC; *Confederate Veteran,* vol. 4, 1896, 87; "Colonel Anderson's Sword," *Confederate Veteran,* vol. 33, 1925, 288.

29. Kate was very committed to the memory of her family. In 1928, she wrote a memorial to them based on the "Old Bethel Chapel" she sponsored in Sumter County, Alabama. She arranged for five generations of her McDow and Fleming families to attend the dedication. The *Confederate Veteran* magazine noted, "The chapel is one erected by her to the memory of her father, mother, and husband

when Old Bethel Church was moved to a near-by town." "Old Bethel Chapel," *Confederate Veteran*, vol. 36, 1928, 413; Captain Patrick H. White Collection, Mrs. J. M. Brownson's January 7, 1896, letter to William H. Allanson of Charleston, Missouri (who tried to claim White's sword), RBWPC.

30. The Colorado River overflowed in 1869, destroying much property and, to a large extent, the year's crops. It was the worst overflow to ever strike the Colorado River Valley. Alex McDow's second wife, Harriet, and his brother, Arthur, who had followed him from Alabama, died in 1879 and 1884, respectively. Kate's husband John passed away in 1906—and all the local businesses, as a token of esteem, closed during the funeral. Ten years later, during WWI and in the year after Patrick White died, Mrs. Brownson sent a letter to John Boos, who was assembling the deceased Mercantile Battery captain's memorabilia. She enclosed the original copy of her father's 1864 letter and, in the correspondence, mentioned she was "engaged in Red Cross work"—an amazing endeavor for a 70-year-old woman. Yet she had more to accomplish regarding the Civil War. Before her death in 1932, Kate made a successful trip "to Columbus for the purpose of locating the grave of a young soldier from Texas who was taken prisoner at Pine Bluff and died at Camp Chase." Captain Patrick H. White Collection, January 16, 1896, letter from Mrs. J. M. Brownson to Patrick White; 1916 letter to John Boos, RBWPC; Cemetery records, Fayette Heritage Museum & Archives/Fayette Public Library; "John Milton Brownson," *Confederate Veteran*, vol. 14, 1906, 131; "A Friend in Deed," *Confederate Veteran*, vol. 34, 1926, 194.

31. The names of Illinois soldiers listed on the state's monument include 32,345 infantry, 2,391 cavalry, 1,571 artillery, 10 general officers, and 38 staff officers. To establish correct locations for the regimental monuments and markers, the Illinois commission "invited ten veterans representing the Eighth, the Eleventh, the Seventeenth, the Forty-seventh, the Ninety-ninth and One Hundred and Thirtieth Infantry and the Chicago Mercantile Battery to accompany the commission during some of its visits." *Illinois at Vicksburg*, 77, 80, 424, 446.

32. A 1902 newspaper listed the Mercantile Battery's Henry L. Bush (Board of Trade), James Dunne (Chicago & Northwestern RR), Henry C. Gray, Florus D. Meacham, Edwin S. Osgood, and Harvey T. Weeks, along with William L. Brown, as "millionaires and leaders in the commercial and financial world." Pat White had been in close contact with Meacham and sent draft maps of the battery's positions at Vicksburg for his review. On April 19, 1902, Meacham replied to his old captain, writing, "I called for several of the boys, including [James] Sinclair, [William] Brown, [Andrew J.] Howell, [William] Stephens, [Edwin S.] Osgood, [Henry L.] Bush, [Orrin W.] Nash, [John W.] Arnold and myself and we carefully examined the maps sent you as well as your plat, and after giving the subject careful consideration, we decided that your ideas were about as near correct as possible." White incorporated their comments and sent his response to Rigby. In March 1904, Meacham was appointed to the Illinois-Vicksburg Military Park Commission and served on the Committee on Locations and Inscriptions, which enabled him to ensure that White's placement of the CMB monuments and markers was properly executed. Chicago Mercantile Battery files, 1902 Chicago newspaper clipping, April 7, 1902, White letter to Rigby, & April 19, 1902, Meacham letter to White, VNMP; *Illinois at Vicksburg*, 409.

33. Captain White attended the Mercantile Battery's 20th Annual reunion in February 1882 in honor of the company's formation. A Chicago paper noted: "The members of the Chicago Mercantile Battery Association celebrated their twentieth annual reunion and revived the happy memories of the past, at the Palmer House last evening, about sixty-five members being present. . . . The annual election of officers resulted as follows: President, Wm. L. Brown; Vice Presidents, Captain P. H. White; Lieutenants, D. R. Crego. J. H. Swan, A. D. Howell, S. F. Denton, Sanford L. Parker, James Dunn [Dunne], Joshua Bell, Wm. A. Prior, R. R. Brackett; Secretary, Gardner G. Willard; Treasurer, Richard Powell; Executive Committee, J. L. Day and George Mendsen. . . . A feature of the reunion was the presence of the old commander of the battery, Captain Pat White, of Albany." "Capt. White: Famous Artillery Veteran Visits Scenes of Carnage in '63" *Vicksburg Evening Post*, September 8, 1902; "Last Night's Society," *Chicago Inter-Ocean*, February 11, 1882, page 4; Captain Patrick H. White Collection, photos of Captain White at 1906 dedication of Illinois monument at VNMP, New York State Museum.

34. On Monday March 17, 1863, the Mercantile Association held a special meeting and donated deeds at four lots in Rosehill Cemetery to bury their Battery Boys. Rosehill is the largest cemetery in Chicago (350 acres) and contains the graves of many Chicago mayors, Illinois governors, well-known businessmen, and Civil War generals (including George Thomas). By 1922, there were 24 Battery Boys buried at Rosehill Cemetery: Abram H. Bensen (died 1894), John J. Cowan (1894), Joseph L. Day (1903), Henry E. Fisk (1910), Ralph J. Gates (1882), William A. Gardner (1894), Philip Gunlock (1894), George Harper (1888), Charles Kellerman (1899), John W. Kenyon (1890), John B. Kitt (1895), William M. Knight (1905), George Kretsinger (1906), John L. Lunt (1897), Danforth Marble (1900), Florus Meacham (1918), John Mortimer (1864), Florison Pitts (1907), Charles A. D. Rogers (1900), William G. Stephens (1904), James H. Swan (1895), George Throop (1864; site 552-553 B), Lowell D. Turner (1869), and William H. Waters (1884). William L. Brown was buried in 1929 at Graceland Cemetery, regarded as the most prominent cemetery in Chicago, along with other Battery Boys such as David R. Crego, George W. Montgomery (1912), Charles Olcott (1875), Edward J. Thomas (1865), and Harvey T. Weeks (1920). Artist George Brewster designed Captain White's Vicksburg monument, which was cast and placed in 1917. *Chicago Tribune*, March 17, 1863; *The Roll of Honor, Cook County* (Chicago, 1922); correspondence with VNMP's historian, Terry Winschel.

35. In October 1967, a group of Cleveland investors, headed by George Steinbrenner III, acquired the American Ship Building Company. Steinbrenner became the company's president and expanded the business significantly, later selling it so he could pursue other interests, such as acquiring the New York Yankees baseball team. In addition to managing and directing Pickands, Brown & Company and the American Ship Building Company, William Brown held a number of other positions of responsibility during his long business career: president of the Federal Furnace Company, South Chicago Furnace Company, By-Products Coke Corporation, Calumet Transit Company, and Manitou Steamship Company. He also served as director of the Lackawanna Steel Company, Bay City Ship Building Company, Dental Protective Supply Company of the United States, Detroit Ship Building Company, Federal Steamship Company, Interlake Company, International Steamship Company, Milwaukee Dry Dock Company, Superior Ship Building Company, Zenith Furnace Company, National Safe Deposit Company, Sea & Lake Insurance Company, First National Bank of Chicago, and First Trust and Savings Bank of Chicago. Wright, *Freshwater Whales*, 157, 174, 264-266; "Steel Trade Pioneer is Mourned," *Pasadena Star-News*, November 1, 1929; John Moses, *The History of Chicago*, vol. 2 (Chicago, IL, 1895), 424; "William L. Brown, Chicago Shipbuilding Magnate, Financier, Dies Here," *Pasadena Post*, November 1, 1929; Marquis, *Who's Who in Chicago*; Bateman & Hurd, ed., *Historical Encyclopedia of Illinois and History of Evanston*, 543-544.

36. "Steel Trade Pioneer is Mourned," *Pasadena Star-News*, November 1, 1929; "William L. Brown, Chicago Shipbuilding Magnate, Financier, Dies Here," *Pasadena Post*, November 1, 1929.

37. William Brown died at the age of 87. According to his obituary, "His death was caused by heart disease complicated by natural ailments of advanced age. Active, both mentally and physically all his long life, Mr. Brown did not suffer an acute illness at the end. He just failed gradually, from day to day, and his death this morning was peaceful. He remained conscious almost to the last. His relatives observed that he began to fail immediately after returning from a trip to Chicago about two weeks ago." *Ibid.*; "Steel Trade Pioneer is Mourned," *Pasadena Star-News*, November 1, 1929.

38. *Ibid.*; "William L. Brown, Chicago Shipbuilding Magnate, Financier, Dies Here," *Pasadena Post*, November 1, 1929.

Bibliography

Newspapers

Cherokee Banner (Jacksonville, TX), 1907
Chicago Daily Journal, April 20, 1861
Chicago Evening Journal, 1862, 1864
Chicago Inter-Ocean, 1882
Chicago Times, 1868
Chicago Tribune, 1860-1865
The Daily Picayune (New Orleans), 1864
The Era (New Orleans), 1864
Harper's Weekly, 1861-1864
National Tribune, 1896
New Orleans Picayune, 1864
New York Sun, 1897
New York Times, 1864
New York World, 1864
Pasadena Post, 1929
Pasadena Star-News, 1929
St. Joseph Herald, 1883
St. Joseph Traveler, 1862, 1863
The Sun (New York), 1897
The Sunday Herald (Boston), 1907
Vicksburg Evening Post, 1902

Official Publications

Illinois Military Units in the Civil War. Springfield, IL: Civil War Centennial Commission of Illinois, 1962.
The Medal of Honor of the United States Army. Washington: U. S. Government Printing Office, 1948.
Report of the Joint Committee on The Conduct of the War at the Second Session Thirty-Eighth Congress. Washington: Government Printing Office, 1865.

The Roll of Honor, Cook County. Chicago: Public Commissioners of Cook Country, 1922.

U.S. Adjutant General's Office, *Official Army Register of the Volunteer Force of the U.S. Army, 1861-1865,* vols. 5, 7, & 8.

The War of the Rebellion: A Compilation of the Official Records of the Union and Confederate Armies. 128 vols. Washington: Government Printing Office, 1889-1901.

Manuscripts

Abraham Lincoln Presidential Library, Springfield, Illinois (ALPL)
    Pinckney S. Cone Diary
    Thomas Sickels Letters

Boston Public Library, Boston, Massachusetts, Rare Book and Manuscript Department (BPL)
    The Union Picket Guard, vol. I, no. 1 (September 14, 1861), Paducah, Kentucky; 20th.108.6

Center for American History, The University of Texas at Austin, Austin, Texas (UT)
    David Ray Letters

Chicago Historical Society, Chicago, Illinois (CHS)
    American Shipbuilding File
    William Liston Brown Letters
    Chicago Board of Trade Collection : Quartermaster reports
    Mercantile Association of Chicago Bylaws
    Rev. William Weston Patton Papers
    Florison D. Pitts Collection: Diary, Letters, William L. Brown letter to W. J. Chalmers, March 4, 1896
    Henry Roe Collection: Letter, June 20, 1865, New Orleans poem
    James Sinclair Diary & Papers
    Ezra Taylor Collection
    "Babylon Is Fallen" [sheet music] by Henry C. Work (Chicago: Root and Cady, 1863)

Civil War and American History Research Collection, Special Collections and Preservation Division, Chicago Public Library, Chicago, Illinois (CPL)
    Ulysses S. Grant Letters

Civil War and Underground Railroad Museum of Philadelphia, Philadelphia, Pennsylvania (CWURMP)
    MOLLUS Insignee Record Card Catalog and Index

Fayette Heritage Museum & Archives/Fayette Public Library, LaGrange, Texas (FHM)
   Cemetery records

Clay Feeter Private Collection
   James A. Gray Diary, 4th Iowa Cavalry

Confederate Research Center, Hill College, Hillsboro, Texas (CRC)
   Alexander McDow Civil War Compiled Military Service Records
   Alexander McDow Parole of Honor

Library of Congress, Manuscript Division, Washington, D. C. (LOC)
   Amos Gager Throop Collection. Acc. No. 21025/ MR No. 82896,
   Microfiche Sleeves 7.11.
   Correspondence of George Throop, 1863-1864. (See also The Chicago Historical
Society and California Institute of Technology.)

Thomas P. Lowry, "The Index Project"

Mansfield State Historic Site, Mansfield, Louisiana (MSHS)
   Charles Freeman Read Papers
   John B. Reid Letters

Massachusetts Historical Society, Boston, Massachusetts (MHS)
   Nims Battery Association Records, 1860-1914

Robert C. Myers Manuscript, September 1868 *Hippocampus* disaster on Lake Michigan

National Archives and Records Administration, National Archives Building,
   Washington, D.C. (NARA)
   Record Group 15, Records of the Department of Veterans Affairs, 1773-1985
      Pension and Bounty Land Application Files Based Upon Service in the
      Civil War and Spanish-American War ("Civil War and Later")
   Record Group 94, Records of the Adjutant General's Office, 1780s -1917
      Compiled Military Service Records, Civil War
      Letters Received, 1861-89; Volunteer Service Division, 1861-89
      Muster Rolls of Volunteer Organizations: Civil War, Mexican War,
         Creek War, Cherokee Removal, and Other Wars, 1836-65
      Record and Pension Office: Document File, 1889-1904;
         Correspondence and Related Papers of the Office, 1889-1904
      Regimental Bound Vols/Descriptive Books of Volunteer Organizations

New York State Museum, Albany, New York (NYSM)
   Patrick H. White Newspaper Clippings
   1906 dedication photos of Illinois monument at VNMP

Ohio Historical Society, Columbus, Ohio (OHS)
    VFM 1911 Alexander J. Swanger Reminiscences (Original)

David Ray Private Collection (DRPC)
    William Husted Letters, Chicago Mercantile Battery

Smith County Historical Society Archives, Tyler, Texas (SCHSA)
    Alexander J. Swanger Reminiscences (Photocopy)
    The Camp Ford News, vol. 1, no. 1, May 1, 1865
    John Kennedy Diary
    Abstract of Units and Prisoners at Camp Ford

Tulane University, Manuscripts Department, New Orleans, Louisiana (TU)
    Joseph L. Brent Papers

U.S. Army Military History Institute, Carlisle, Pennsylvania (USAMHI)
    Schuyler P. Coe Letter Collection—Civil War Misc Collection, Box 1
    George Perry Letters, Squire & Chester Tuttle Collection

Vicksburg National Military Park, Vicksburg, Mississippi (VNMP)
    Edwin C. Bearss, Analysis of the Battle of Chickasaw Bayou
    Edwin C. Bearss, "Texas at Vicksburg," September 1956
    James G. Spencer, Regimental Files, First Mississippi Light Artillery
    Patrick H. White, April 7, 1902 Correspondence with W. T. Rigby
    News clipping, "Captain Patrick H. White is the Guest of Old Comrades"
    Chicago Mercantile Battery Files
        "Capt. White's Bravery," 1902 Chicago news clipping
        April 7, 1902 White letter to Rigby
         1902 Meacham letter to White

Watson Memorial Library, Cammie G. Henry Research Center of Northwestern
        State University of Louisiana
    November 1, 1864, issue of the *Natchitoches Union*

Williams Research Center of the Historic New Orleans Collection, New Orleans,
        Louisiana (HNOC)
    Henry C. Sampson Diary and Related Papers
    Charles F. Sherman Civil War Letters
    Melvan Tibbetts Letters
    Clark S. Willy Letter

Richard Brady Williams Private Collection (RBWPC)
    Chase H. Dickinson Inscribed Albumen Photograph
    Oscar Hinrichs Journal

Walter Scales Letter of April 9, 1862
Nelson Smith Enlistment Papers
Sylvester Strong Letters, 20th Wisconsin Infantry
Taylor's Battery Reunion Documents
Patrick H. White Collection, Chicago Mercantile Battery
 Canby's Special Order No. 166, June 22, 1865
 Memoir
 Papers
 Patrick H. White Parole
 Quartermaster Order at New Orleans, June 25, 1865
 White's Red River Parole, May 27, 1865
 Letter from War Department, November 30, 1866
 Mrs. J. M. Brownson's January 7, 1896, letter to William H. Allanson
  of Charleston, Missouri
 January 16, 1896, letter from Mrs. J. M. Brownson to Patrick White
 1916 letter from Mrs. J. M. Brownson to John Boos

Wisconsin Historical Society Archives, Madison, Wisconsin (WHS)
 W. E. Haseltine Papers

Books

Adams, Henry G., Jr. *Indiana at Vicksburg*. Indianapolis: W. B. Buford, 1911.

Allerdice, Bruce S. *More Generals in Gray*. Baton Rouge: Louisiana State University Press, 1995.

America's Medal of Honor Recipients. Golden Valley: Highland Publishers, 1980.

Anders, Curt. *Disaster in Damp Sand: The Red River Expedition*. Indianapolis: Guild Press of Indiana, 1997.

Anderson, Charles G. *Confederate General William Read "Dirty Neck Bill" Scurry, 1821-1864*. Tallahassee: Rose Printing Company, 1999.

Anderson, William M. *They Died to Make Men Free: A History of the 19th Michigan Infantry in the Civil War*. Dayton, OH: Morningside, 1994.

Andrews, J. Cutler. *The North Reports The Civil War*. Pittsburgh: University of Pittsburgh Press, 1955.

Arnold, James R. *Grant Wins the War: Decision at Vicksburg*. New York: John Wiley & Sons, 1997.

Ayres, Thomas. *Dark and Bloody Ground: The Battle of Mansfield and the Forgotten Civil War in Louisiana*. Dallas: Taylor Trade Publishing, 2001.

Bacon, Edward. *Among the Cotton Thieves*. Bossier City, LA: The Everett Companies, 1989.

Ballard, Michael B. *Vicksburg: The Campaign That Opened the Mississippi*. Chapel Hill: The University of North Carolina Press, 2004.

Bastian, David F. *Grant's Canal: The Union's Attempt to Bypass Vicksburg*. Shippensburg: Burd Street Press, 1995.

Bateman, Newton and Paul Selby, ed. *Historical Encyclopedia of Illinois and History of Evanston*, vol. 2. Chicago: Munsell Publishing Co., 1906.

Bearss, Edwin Cole. *The Campaign for Vicksburg: Vicksburg is the Key*, vol. 1. Dayton: Morningside House, 1985.

Bearss, Edwin Cole. *The Campaign for Vicksburg: Grant Strikes a Fatal Blow*, vol. 2. Dayton: Morningside House, 1985.

Bearss, Edwin Cole. *The Campaign for Vicksburg: Unvexed to the Sea*, vol. 3. Dayton: Morningside, 1986.

Bearss, Edwin C. *Hardluck Ironclad: The Sinking and Salvage of the Cairo*. Baton Rouge: Louisiana State University Press, 1966.

Bearss, Edwin C., ed. *A Louisiana Confederate: Diary of Felix Pierre Poché*. Natchitoches: Louisiana Studies Institute, Northwestern State University, 1972.

Bearss, Edwin C. *The Siege of Jackson: July 10-17, 1863*. Baltimore: Gateway Press, 1981.

Bearss, Edwin C. *Steele's Retreat from Camden and the Battle of Jenkins' Ferry*. Little Rock: Democrat Printing, 1967.

Beecher, Dr. Harris H. *Record of the 114th Regiment, N.Y.S.V.* Norwich: J. F. Hubbard, Jr., 1866.

Beers, Alfred B., Thomas Boudren, & Frank Miller, eds. *The Old Flag*. Bridgeport: The Old Flag Publishing Co., 1914.

Bentley, William H. *History of the 77th Illinois Volunteer Infantry*. Peoria: Edward Hine, 1883.

Bergeron, Arthur W., Jr. & Lawrence L. Hewitt. *Boone's Louisiana Battery: A History and Roster*. Baton Rouge: Elliott's Bookshop Press, 1986.

Bergeron, Arthur W., Jr. *Confederate Mobile*. Jackson: University Press of Mississippi, 1991.

Bering, John A. *History of the Forty-Eighth Ohio Vet. Vol. Inf.* Hillsboro: Highland News Office, 1880.

Berrien County Historical Society. Berrien Springs: Kimball Pub. Co., 1896.

Beyer, W. F. and O. F. Keydel, ed. *Deeds of Valor: How America's Civil War Heroes Won The Congressional Medal of Honor*. 1905; New York: Smithmark Publishers, 2000.

Black, Robert C. *The Railroads of the Confederacy*. Chapel Hill: The University of North Carolina Press, 1952.

Blackwell, Samuel M., Jr. *In the First Line of Battle: The 12th Illinois Cavalry in the Civil War*. Dekalb: Northern Illinois University Press, 2002.

Blessington, Joseph P. *The Campaigns of Walker's Texas Division*. New York: Lange, Little & Co., 1875.

Boatner, Mark Mayo III. *The Civil War Dictionary* . New York: David McKay Co., 1959.

Bond, Frederic William. *A Little History of a Great City*. Chicago: privately published, 1930.

Bradley, Mark L. *Last Stand in the Carolinas: The Battle of Bentonville*. Campbell: Savas Woodbury Publishers, 1996.

Bradley, Mark. *This Astounding Close: The Road to Bennett Place*. Chapel Hill: University of North Carolina Press, 2000.

Bragg, Jefferson Davis. *Louisiana in the Confederacy*. Baton Rouge: Louisiana State Press, 1941.

Bringhurst, Thomas H. and Frank Swigart. *History of The Forty-sixth Regiment, Indiana Volunteer Infantry, September 1861–September, 1865*. Logansport: Press of Wilson, Humphreys & Co., 1888.

Brooksher, William Riley. *War Along the Bayous: The 1864 Red River Campaign in Louisiana*. Washington: Brassey's, 1998.

Brown, Alonzo L. *History of the Fourth Regiment of Minnesota Infantry Volunteers during the Great Rebellion, 1861-1865*. St. Paul: The Pioneer Press Company, 1892.

Brown, Dee Alexander. *The Bold Cavaliers: Morgan's 2nd Kentucky Cavalry Raiders*. Philadelphia: J. B. Lippincott Co., 1959.

Brown, George H. *Record of Service of Michigan Volunteers in the Civil War, 1861-1865*, vol. 12. Kalamazoo: Ihling Bros. & Everard, n.d..

Brown, George H. *Record of Service of Michigan Volunteers in the Civil War, 1861-1865*, vol. 19. Kalamazoo: Ihling Bros. & Everard, n.d..

Brown, Norman D., ed. *Journey to Pleasant Hill: The Civil War Letters of Captain Elijah P. Petty, Walker's Texas Division, CSA*. San Antonio: The University of Texas Institute of Texan Cultures, 1982.

Bruce, George A. *The Capture and Occupation of Richmond*. n.p., n.d..

Buffum, Francis H. *A Memorial of the Great Rebellion Being a History of the Fourteenth Regiment New Hampshire Volunteer, Covering Its Three Years of Service, with Original Sketches of Army Life, 1862-1865*. Boston: Rand, Avery, 1882.

Burton, E. Milby. The Siege of Charleston 1861-1865. Columbia: University of South Carolina Press, 1970.

Calkins, Chris M. *The Appomattox Campaign, March 29-April 9, 1865*. Conshohocken: Combined Books, 1997.

Capers, Gerald. *Occupied City: New Orleans Under the Federals 1862-1865*. Lexington: University of Kentucky Press, 1965.

Carroon, Robert Girard and Dana B. Shoaf. *Union Blue: The History of the Military Order of the Loyal Legion of the United States*. Shippensburg: White Mane Books, 2001.

Carter, Joseph C., ed. *Magnolia Journey: A Union Veteran Revisits the Former Confederate States*. University: The University of Alabama Press, 1974.

Casey, Powell A. *Encyclopedia of Forts, Posts, Named Camps, and other Military Installations in Louisiana, 1700-1981*. Baton Rouge: Claitor's Publishing Division, 1983.

Catton, Bruce. *The Civil War*. 1960; reprint, Boston: Houghton Mifflin Co., 1987.

Catton, Bruce. *A Stillness at Appomattox*. New York: Doubleday,1953.

Chance, Joseph E. *The Second Texas Infantry: From Shiloh to Vicksburg*. Austin: Eakin Press, 1984.

Chenery, William H. *The Fourteenth Regiment, Rhode Island Heavy Artillery (Colored) In the War to Preserve the Union, 1861-1865*. Providence: Snow & Fernham, Printers, 1898.

Chernow, Ron. *Titan: The Life of John D. Rockefeller, Sr.* New York: Vintage Books, 1999.

Chicago of To-Day: The Metropolis of the West. Chicago: Acme Publishing Company, 1891.

Cockrell, Dale. *Demons of Disorder: Early Blackface Minstrels and Their World.* Cambridge: Cambridge University Press, 1997.

Coe, David, ed. *Mine Eyes Have Seen the Glory: Combat Diaries of Union Sergeant Hamlin Alexander Coe.* Rutherford: Farleigh Dickinson University Press, 1975.

Colbert, Elias & Everett Chamberlin, *Chicago and the Great Conflagration.* Chicago: J. S. Goodman & Co., 1872.

Cole, Harry Ellsworth. *Stagecoach and Tavern Tales of the Old Northwest.* Cleveland: Arthur H. Clark Co., 1930.

Conover, H. J. *A Personal Remembrance: History and Roster of the 130th Illinois.* n.p., 1891.

Conrad, Thomas Nelson. *The Rebel Scout: A Thrilling History of Scouting Life in the Southern Army.* Washington City: The National Publishing Co., 1904.

Cook, Frederick Frances. *Bygone Days in Chicago: Recollections of the "Garden City" of the Sixties.* Chicago: A. C. McClurg, 1910.

Coolidge, Orville W. *A Twentieth Century History of Berrien County, Michigan.* Chicago: Lewis Publishing, 1906.

Cooling, Benjamin Franklin. *Forts Henry and Donelson: The Key to the Confederate Heartland.* Knoxville: The University of Tennessee Press, 1987.

Cooling, B. Franklin. *Monocacy: The Battle that Saved Washington.* Shippensburg: White Mane Publishing, 1997.

Cooper, William J., Jr. *Jefferson Davis, American.* New York: Alfred A. Knopf, 2000.

Cozzens, Peter. *The Darkness of War: The Battles of Iuka and Corinth.* Chapel Hill: The University of North Carolina Press, 1997.

Cozzens, Peter. *No Better Place to Die: The Battle of Stones River.* Urbana, IL: University of Illinois Press, 1990.

Cozzens, Peter. *The Shipwreck of Their Hopes: The Battles for Chattanooga.* Urbana: University of Illinois Press, 1994.

Cozzens, Peter. *This Terrible Sound: The Battle of Chickamauga.* Urbana: University of Illinois Press, 1992.

Cronon, William. *Nature's Metropolis: Chicago and the Great West.* New York: W. W. Norton & Company, 1991.

Cunningham, Edward. *The Port Hudson Campaign, 1862-1863.* Baton Rouge: Louisiana State University Press, 1963.

Davis, George B. *The Official Military Atlas of the Civil War.* New York: The Fairfax Press, 1978.

Davis, William C. *An Honorable Defeat: The Last Days of the Confederate Government.* San Diego: Harcourt, Inc., 2001.

Dawdy, Shannon Lee and Christopher N. Matthews. *Final Report of Archeological and Historical Investigations of Camp Parapet, a Civil War Site in Jefferson Parish, Louisiana.* New Orleans: University of New Orleans, 1998.

Dearing, Mary. *Veterans in Politics: The Story of the G.A.R.* Baton Rouge: Louisiana State University Press, 1952.

Dew, Charles B. *Ironmaker to the Confederacy: Joseph R. Anderson.* Richmond: The Library of Virginia, 1999.

Dickens, Charles. *David Copperfield.* New York: Random House, 2000.

Dodge, Jacqueline Dillard, ed. *Texas Division, United Daughters of the Confederacy, Chapter Histories.* Houston, TX, 1991.

Donald, David Herbert. *Lincoln.* London: Jonathan Cape Random House, 1995.

Duaine, Carl L. *The Dead Men Wore Boots: An Account of the 32nd Texas Volunteer Cavalry, CSA, 1862-1865.* Austin: The San Felipe Press, 1966.

Duffy, James P. *Lincoln's Admiral: The Civil War Campaigns of David Farragut.* New York: John Wiley & Sons, 1997.

Dufour, Charles L. *The Night the War Was Lost.* New Orleans: Elliot's Book Shop Press, 1991.

Duganne, A. J. H. *Twenty Months in the Department of the Gulf: Camps and Prisons.* New York: n.p., 1865.

Dyer, Frederick H. *A Compendium of the War of the Rebellion*, vol. 1. New York: Thomas Yoseloff Publisher, 1959.

Dyer, Frederick H. *A Compendium of the War of the Rebellion*, vol. 2. New York: Thomas Yoseloff Publisher, 1959.

Dyer, Frederick H. *A Compendium of the War of the Rebellion*, vol. 3. NY: Thomas Yoseloff, 1959.

Early, Jubal A. *Lieutenant General Jubal Anderson Early, C.S.A., Autobiographical Sketch and Narrative of the War Between the States.* Philadelphia: J. B. Lippincott Co., 1912.

The Echo from the Army: What Our Soldiers Say about the Copperheads. New York: Wm. C. Bryant & Co., 1863.

Eddy, T. M. *The Loyal People of the North-West.* Chicago: Church, Goodman & Donnelley, Printers, 1869.

Eddy, T. M. *The Patriotism of Illinois: A Record of the Civil and Military History of the State in the War for the Union*, vol. 2 . Chicago: Clarke & Co., 1866.

Edmonds, David C. *Yankee Autumn in Acadiana.* Lafayette: The Acadiana Press, 1979.

Eicher, David J. *The Longest Night: A Military History of the Civil War.* New York: Simon & Schuster, 2001.

Eicher, John H. and David J. *Civil War High Commands.* Stanford: Stanford University Press, 2001.

Ewer, James K. *The Third Massachusetts Cavalry in the War for the Union.* Maplewood: Historical Committee of the Regimental Association, 1903.

Faust, Patricia L., ed. *Historical Times Illustrated Encyclopedia of the Civil War.* NewYork: Harper & Row, 1991.

Fletcher, Samuel H. *The History of Company A, Second Illinois Cavalry*. Chicago: D.H. Fletcher, 1912.

Fonvielle, Chris E., Jr., *The Wilmington Campaign: Last Rays of Departing Hope*. Campbell: Savas Publishing Co., 1997.

Foote, Shelby. *The Civil War, A Narrative. Fort Sumter to Perryville*. New York: Random House, 1958.

Foote, Shelby. *The Civil War: A Narrative. Fredericksburg to Meridian*. New York: Random House, 1963.

Foote, Shelby. *The Civil War: A Narrative. Red River to Appomattox*. New York: Random House, 1974.

Forsyth, Henry. *In Memoriam* [Jane C. Hoge]. Chicago: Illinois Printing & Binding Co., c1890.

Forsyth, Michael J. *The Red River Campaign of 1864 and the Loss by the Confederacy of the Civil War*. Jefferson: McFarland & Co, 2002.

Fox, Arthur. *Pittsburgh During the American Civil War*. Chicora: Mechling Bookbindery, 2002.

Fullenkamp, Leonard, ed. *Guide to the Vicksburg Campaign*. Lawrence: University Press of Kansas, 1998.

Fuller, J. F. C. *The Generalship of Ulysses S. Grant*. New York: Da Capo Press, 1991.

Gallaway, B. P., ed. *Texas: The Dark Corner of the Confederacy. Contemporary Accounts of the Lone Star State in the Civil War*. Lincoln: University of Nebraska Press, 1994.

Garrison, Web. *The Encyclopedia of Civil War Usage: An Illustrated Compendium of the Everyday Language of Soldiers and Civilians*. Nashville: Cumberland House, 2001.

Garrison, Webb. *Mutiny in the Civil War*. Shippensburg: White Mane Books, 2001.

Gelbert, Doug. *Civil War Sites, Memorials, Museums and Library Collections: A State-by-State Guidebook to Places Open to the Public*. Jefferson: McFarland & Co., 1997.

Gibson, Charles Dana. *Assault and Logistics: Union Army Coastal and River Operations, 1861-1866*. Camden: Ensign Press, 1995.

Gilbert, Paul and Charles Lee Bryson. *Chicago and Its Makers*. Chicago: Felix Mendelsohn Publishers, 1929.

Gilmor, Harry. *Four Years in the Saddle*. New York: Harper & Bros., 1866.

Glover, Robert W. *Camp Ford: Tyler, Texas, C.S.A.*. Nacogdoches: East Texas Historical Association, 1998.

Glover, Dr. Robert W. & Randal B. Gilbert. *Camp Ford, Tyler, Texas: The Largest Confederate Prison Camp West of the Mississippi River*. Tyler: Smith Co. Historical Society, 1989.

Gosnell, H. Allen. *Guns on the Western Waters: The Story of River Gunboats in the Civil War*. Baton Rouge: Louisiana State University Press, 1949.

Goss, Thomas J. *The War within the Union High Command: Politics and Generalship during the Civil War*. Lawrence: University Press of Kansas, 2003.

Grabau, Warren E. *Ninety-Eight Days: A Geographer's View of the Vicksburg Campaign*. Knoxville: The University of Tennessee Press, 2000.

Gragg, Rod. *Confederate Goliath: The Battle of Fort Fisher*. Baton Rouge: Louisiana State University Press, 1991.

Grant, Ulysses S. *Personal Memoirs of U. S. Grant,* vol. 1. New York: Charles Webster & Co., 1885.

Graves, Daniel. *Profiles of Natchitoches History*, vol. 1. Natchitoches: The Museum of Historic Natchitoches, 1996.

Gravis, Peter W. *Twenty-Five Years on the Outside Row of the Northwest Texas Annual Conference*. Comanche: Exponent Steam Print, 1892.

Gray, Wood. *The Hidden Civil War: The Story of the Copperheads*. New York: The Viking Press, 1964.

Greene, A. Wilson. *Breaking the Backbone of the Rebellion: The Final Battles of the Petersburg Campaign*. Mason City: Savas Publishing Co., 2000.

Greene, Francis Vinton. *The Mississippi: Campaigns of the Civil War—VIII*. New York: Chas. Scribner's Sons, 1882.

Greene, John T., ed. *The Ewing Family Civil War Letters*. East Lansing: Michigan State University Press, 1994.

Greene, John W. *Camp Ford Prison and How I Escaped: An Incident of the Civil War*. Toledo: Barkdull Printing House, 1893.

Grimes, Roy, ed. *300 Years in Victoria County*. Victoria: Victoria Advocate Publishing Co., 1968.

Guyer, I. D. *History of Chicago: Commercial and Manufacturing Interests and Industry*. Chicago: Church, Goodman & Cushing, 1862.

Hattaway, Herman. *General Stephen D. Lee*. Jackson: University Press of Mississippi, 1976.

Hattaway, Herman and Archer Jones. *How the North Won: A Military History of the Civil War*. Urbana: University of Illinois Press, 1983.

Havighurst, Walter. *Vein of Iron: The Pickands Mather Story*. Cleveland: The World Publishing Company, 1958.

Haynie, J. Henry. *The Nineteenth Illinois*. Chicago: M. A. Donohue & Co., 1912.

Hearn, Chester G. *Ellet's Brigade: The Strangest Outfit of All*. Baton Rouge: Louisiana State University Press, 2000.

Hearn, Chester G. *Six Years of Hell: Harpers Ferry During the Civil War*. Baton Rouge: Louisiana State University Press, 1996.

Heidler, David S. and Jeanne T. Heidler, ed. *Encyclopedia of the Civil War: A Political, Social, and Military History*. Santa Barbara: ABC-CLIO, Inc., 2000.

Henshaw, Sarah Edwards. *Our Branch and Its Tributaries: A History of the Work of the Northwestern Sanitary Commission*. Chicago: Alfred L. Sewell, 1868.

Hewett, Janet B., ed. *Supplement to the Official Records of the Union and Confederate Armies, Part II*, vol. 8. Wilmington: Broadfoot Publishing, 1995.

Hewitt, J. E. *Battle of Mansfield*. Mansfield: Enterprise Publishing Co., 1925.

Hewitt, Lawrence L. and Edward Cunningham. *Port Hudson: Confederate Bastion on the Mississippi*. Baton Rouge: Louisiana State University Press, 1987.

Heyman, Max L., Jr. *Prudent Soldier: A Biography of Major General E. R. S. Canby, 1817-1873*. Glendale: The Arthur H. Clark Co., 1959.

Hicken, Victor. *Illinois in the Civil War*. Urbana, IL: University of Illinois Press, 1966.

Historical Sketch of the Chicago Board of Trade. Chicago: privately published, 1902.

History of Berrien and Van Buren Counties, Michigan. Philadelphia: D. W. Ensign, 1880.

A History of the City of Chicago. Chicago: Inter-Ocean, 1900.

History of the North-Western Soldiers' Fair, Held in Chicago. Chicago: Dunlop, Sewell & Spaulding, 1864.

Hobson, H. S. *The Famous Cruise of the Kearsarge*. Bonds Village: self published, 1894.

Hoehling, A. A. & Mary. *The Day Richmond Died*. Lanham: Madison Books.

Hoge, Jane. *The Boys in Blue*. New York: E. B. Treat, 1867.

Hollandsworth, James G., Jr. *Pretense of Glory: The Life of General Nathaniel P. Banks*. Baton Rouge: Louisiana State University Press, 1998.

Horn, John. *The Destruction of the Weldon Railroad: Deep Bottom, Globe Tavern, and Reams Station, August 14-25, 1864*. Lynchburg: H. E. Howard, 1991.

Howell, H. Grady, Jr. *Hill of Death: The Battle of Champion Hill*. Madison, MS: Chickasaw Bayou Press, 1993.

Howell, H. Grady, Jr. *To Live and Die in Dixie*. Jackson: Chickasaw Bayou Press, 1991.

Hughes, Nathaniel Cheairs, Jr. *The Battle of Belmont: Grant Strikes South*. Chapel Hill: University of North Carolina Press, 1991.

Hughes, Nathaniel Cheairs, Jr. *The Pride of the Confederate Artillery: The Washington Artillery in the Army of Tennessee*. Baton Rouge: Louisiana State University Press, 1991.

Hunt, Roger D. & Jack R. Brown. *Brevet Brigadier Generals in Blue*. Gaithersburg: Olde Soldier Books, 1990.

Illinois at Vicksburg. Chicago: Illinois-Vicksburg Military Park Commission. The Blakely Printing Co., 1907.

Irwin, Richard B. *History of the Nineteenth Army Corps*. 1892; reprint, Baton Rouge: Elliot's Book Shop Press, 1985.

Johnson, Charles Beneulyn, M.D. *Muskets and Medicine or Army Life in the Sixties*. Philadelphia: F. A. Davis Co., 1917.

Johnson, Ludwell H. *Red River Campaign: Politics and Cotton in the Civil War*. Kent: Kent State University Press, 1993.

Johnson, Robert U., ed. *Battles and Leaders of the Civil War*, vol. 3. New York: The Century Co., 1884,1888.

Johnson, Robert U., ed. *Battles and Leaders of the Civil War*, vol. 4. New York: The Century Co., 1884,1888.

Johnston, *Joseph E. Narrative of Military Operations, Directed, During the Late War Between the States*. New York: D. Appleton & Co., 1874.

Joiner, Gary Dillard. *One Damn Blunder from Beginning to End: The Red River Campaign of 1864*. Wilmington: Scholarly Resources Books, 2003.

Jones, Archer. *Civil War Command and Strategy: The Process of Victory and Defeat.* New York: The Free Press, 1992.

Jones, J. B. *A Rebel War Clerk's Diary at the Confederate States Capital*, vol. 2. Philadelphia: J. B. Lippincott Co., 1866.

Jones, Robert A. *Confederate Corsair: The Life of Lt. Charles W. "Savez" Read.* Mechanicsburg: Stackpole Books, 2000.

Jones, S. C. Jones. *Reminiscences of the Twenty-Second Iowa Volunteer Infantry.* Iowa City: n.p., 1907.

Jordan, William B. and William B., Jr., ed. *The Civil War Journals of John Mead Gould, 1861-1866.* Baltimore: Butternut and Blue, 1997.

Karamanski, Theodore J. *Rally 'Round the Flag: Chicago and the Civil War.* Chicago: Nelson-Hall Publishers, 1993.

Kaser, David. *Books and Libraries in Camp and Battle: The Civil War Experience.* Westport: Greenwood Press, 1984.

Kautz, August V. *Customs of Service for Non-Commissioned Officers and Soldiers.* 1865; reprint, Mechanicsburg: Stackpole Books, 2001.

Kennedy, Frances H., ed. *The Civil War Battlefield Guide, 2nd edition.* Boston: Houghton Mifflin, 1998.

Kerby, Robert L. *Kirby Smith's Confederacy: The Trans-Mississippi South, 1863-1865.* New York: Columbia University Press, 1972.

Kimball, Charles B. *History of Battery "A" First Illinois Light Artillery Volunteers.* Chicago: Cushing Printing Co., 1899.

Kiper, Richard L. *Major General John Alexander McClernand: Politician in Uniform.* Kent: The Kent State University Press, 1999.

Lankford, Nelson. *Richmond Burning: The Last Days of the Confederate Capital.* New York: Viking, 2002.

Lansden, John McMurray. *A History of the City of Cairo.* Chicago: R. R. Donnelley & Sons, 1910.

Lash, Jeffrey N. *A Politician Turned General: The Civil War Career of Stephen Augustus Hurlbut.* Kent: The Kent State University Press, 2003.

Lawrence, F. Lee & Robert W. Glover. *Camp Ford. C.S.A.: The Story of Union Prisoners in Texas.* Austin: Texas Civil War Centennial Advisory Committee, 1964.

Leonard, John W., ed. *The Book of Chicagoans.* Chicago: A. N. Marquis & Co., 1905.

Livermore, Mary. *My Story of the War: A Woman's Narrative of Four Years Personal Experience.* Hartford: A. D. Worthington, 1887.

Long, E. B. with Barbara Long. *The Civil War Day by Day: An Almanac 1861-1865.* Garden City, NY: Doubleday & Co., 1971.

Lord, Francis A. *Civil War Collector's Encyclopedia*, vol. 1. Edison: Blue & Grey Press, 1995.

Lossing, Benson J. *Pictorial History of the Civil War in the United States.* Philadelphia: David McKay, Publisher, 1866.

Lotto, F. *Fayette Country, Her History and Her People.* Schulenburg: Sticker Steam Press, 1902.

Lowe, Richard. *The Texas Overland Expedition of 1863*. Ft. Worth: Ryan Place Publishers, 1996.

Lowe, Richard. *Walker's Texas Division, C.S.A.: Greyhounds of the Trans-Mississippi*. Baton Rouge: Louisiana State University Press, 2004.

Lowry, Thomas P., M.D. *Tarnished Eagles: The Courts-Martial of Fifty Union Colonels and Lieutenant Colonels*. Mechanicsburg: Stackpole Books, 1997.

Malsch, Brownson. Indianola: *The Mother of Western Texas*. Austin: State House Press, 1988.

Map of the Business Portion of Chicago. Chicago: Edwin Whitefield, 1862.

Marquis, Albert Nelson. *Who's Who in Chicago: The Book of Chicagoans*. Chicago: A. N. Marquis, 1926.

Marshall, T. B. *History of the Eighty-Third Ohio Volunteer Infantry: The Greyhound Regiment*. Cincinnati: 83d Volunteer Infantry Assoc., 1912.

Marvel, William. *The Alabama & the Kearsarge: The Sailor's Civil War*. Chapel Hill: The University of North Carolina Press, 1996.

McClatchy, J. D., ed. *Henry Wadsworth Longfellow: Poems and Other Writings*. New York: The Library of America, 2000.

McConnell, Stuart. *Glorious Contentment: The Grand Army of the Republic, 1865-1900*. Chapel Hill: University of North Carolina Press, 1992.

McGregor, Frank R. *Dearest Susie: A Civil War Infantryman's Letters to His Sweetheart*. New York: Exposition Press, 1971.

McMurry, Richard M. *Atlanta 1864: Last Chance for the Confederacy*. Lincoln, NE: University of Nebraska Press, 2000.

McPherson, James M. *Battle Cry of Freedom: The Civil War Era*. New York: Oxford University Press, 1988.

Military Order of the Loyal Legion of the United States. MOLLUS, Illinois: From January 1, 1912 to December 31, 1922. reprint; Wilmington: Broadfoot, 1993.

Millen, Patricia. *From Pastime to Passion: Baseball and the Civil War*. Bowie, MD: Heritage Books, 2001.

Miller, Donald L. *City of the Century: The Epic of Chicago and the Making of America*. New York: Touchstone, 1997.

Miller, Edward A., Jr. *Lincoln's Abolitionist General: The Biography of David Hunter*. Columbia: University of South Carolina Press, 1997.

Milligan, John D. *Gunboats Down the Mississippi*. Annapolis: US Naval Institute, 1965.

Moore, Frank J., ed. *The Rebellion Record: A Diary of American Events*, 12 vols. New York: Van Nostrand, 1871.

Morris, Leopold. *Pictorial History of Victoria and Victoria County*. San Antonio: Clemens Printing Co., 1953.

Morton, J. S. *Reminiscences of the Lower St. Joseph River Valley*. Benton Harbor, Michigan: Federation of Women's Clubs, n.d..

Moses, John. *The History of Chicago*, vol. 2. Chicago: The Munsell Publishing Company, 1895.

My Cave Life in Vicksburg with Letters of Trial and Travel. New York: D. Appleton & Co., 1864.

The Necessity of a Ship Canal between East and West: Report of the Proceedings of the Board of Trade, The Mercantile Association, and the Business Men of Chicago, February 24, 1863. Chicago: Tribune Company, 1863.

Neely, Mark E., Jr. *The Union Divided: Party Conflict in the Civil War North.* Cambridge: Harvard Univ. Press, 2002.

Nott, Charles C. *Sketches in Prison Camps: A Continuation of Sketches of the W*ar. New York: Anson D. F. Randolph, 1865.

O'Brien, Sean Michael. *Mobile, 1865: Last Stand of the Confederacy.* Westport: Praeger, 2001.

Parkerson, Codman. *New Orleans, America's Most Fortified City.* New Orleans: The Quest, 1990.

Parrish, T. Michael. *Richard Taylor: Soldier Prince of Dixie.* Chapel Hill: The University of North Carolina Press, 1992.

Pierce, Bessie Louise. *A History of Chicago*, vol. 2. New York: Alfred A. Knopf, 1940.

Pierce, Bessie Louise. *A History of Chicago*, vol. 3. *Rise of a Modern City 1871-1893.* Chicago: The University of Chicago Press, 1957.

Pierce, Charles W. *Reunions of Taylor's Battery: 18th Anniversary of the Battle of Fort Donelson, February 14, 1880, 25th Anniversary of the Battle of Belmont, November 6, 1886.* Chicago: Craig Press, 1890.

Plummer, Alonzo H. *Confederate Victory at Mansfield.* Mansfield: United Daughters of the Confederacy No. 397, 1969.

Ponder, Jerry. *The Civil War Battle of Fredericktown, Missouri.* Independence: Two Trails Publishing, 1995.

Poppenheim, Mary B. *The History of the United Daughters of the Confederacy*, vol. 1. Richmond: Garrett and Massie, 1938.

Porter, David Dixon. *The Naval History of the Civil War.* New York: D. Appleton & Company, 1886.

Power, J. Tracy. *Lee's Miserables: Life in the Army of Northern Virginia from the Wilderness to Appomattox.* Chapel Hill: University of North Carolina Press, 1998.

Reed, Samuel Rockwell. *The Vicksburg Campaign and the Battles about Chattanooga under the Command of General U. S. Grant.* Cincinnati: Robert Clarke & Co., 1882.

Rhea, Gordon C. *The Battle of the Wilderness, May 5-6, 1864.* Baton Rouge: Louisiana State University Press, 1994.

Rhea, Gordon C. *The Battles for Spotsylvania Court House and the Road to Yellow Tavern, May 7-12, 1864.* Baton Rouge: Louisiana State University Press, 1997.

Rhea, Gordon C. *To the North Anna River: Grant and Lee, May 13-25, 1864.* Baton Rouge: Louisiana State University Press, 2000.

Ripley, Warren. *Artillery and Ammunition of The Civil War.* Charleston: The Battery Press, 1984.

Robertson, James I., Jr. *Stonewall Jackson: The Man, The Soldier, The Legend*. New York: Macmillan Publishing USA, 1997.

Rosen, Robert N. *Confederate Charleston: An Illustrated History of the City and the People during the Civil War*. Columbia: University of South Carolina Press, 1994.

Russell, William H. *My Diary North and South*. Boston, 1863.

Sandburg, Carl. *Abraham Lincoln: The War Years*, vol. 2. New York: Harcourt, Brace & Co., 1939.

Schultz, Duane. *The Dahlgren Affair: Terror and Conspiracy in the Civil War*. New York: W. W. Norton & Co., 1998.

Scott, John. *Story of the Thirty Second Iowa Infantry Volunteers*. Nevada: self published, 1896.

Scott, Reuben B. *The History of the 67th Regiment Indiana Infantry Volunteers, War of the Rebellion*. Bedford: Herald Book, 1892.

Sears, Stephen W., *George B. McClellan: The Young Napoleon*. New York: Ticknor & Fields, 1988.

Sears, Stephen W. *To the Gates of Richmond: The Peninsula Campaign*. Boston: Houghlin Mifflin, 1992.

Shea, William L. and Terrence J. Winschel. *Vicksburg Is the Key: The Struggle for the Mississippi River*. Lincoln: University of Nebraska Press, 2003.

Sheridan, Philip Henry. *Personal Memoirs of P. H. Sheridan, General, United States Army*. New York: Charles L. Webster & Co., 1888.

Sherman, William Tecumseh. *Memoirs of General W. T. Sherman*, 2 vols. New York: Charles Webster & Co., 1892.

Sherman, William Tecumseh. *Reply of Maj. Gen. Sherman to the Mayor of Atlanta, and Speeches of Maj. Gen. Hooker, Delivered in the Cities of Brooklyn and New York, Sept. 22, 1864. Letter of Lieut. Gen. Grant. Voices from the Army*. Washington, D.C.: Union Congressional Committee, 1864.

Silverthorne, Elizabeth. *Ashbel Smith of Texas: Pioneer, Patriot, Statesman, 1805-1886*. College Station: Texas A&M University Press, 1982.

Simpson, Brooks and Jean V. Berlin, ed. *Sherman's Civil War: Selected Correspondence of William T. Sherman, 1860-1865*. Chapel Hill: University of North Carolina Press, 1999.

Simpson, Brooks D. *Ulysses S. Grant: Triumph over Adversity, 1822-1865*. Boston: Houghton Mifflin Co., 2000.

Simon, John Y., ed. *The Papers of Ulysses S. Grant*, vol. 7. Carbondale: Southern Illinois University Press, 1979.

Smith, Ralph J. *Reminiscences of the Civil War and Other Sketches*. Waco: W. M. Morrison, 1962.

Smith, Timothy B. *Champion Hill: Decisive Battle for Vicksburg*. New York: Savas Beatie LLC, 2004.

Snell, Mark A. *From First to Last: The Life of Major General William B. Franklin*. New York: Fordham University Press, 2002.

Speer, Lonnie R. *Portals to Hell: Military Prisons of the Civil War*. Mechanicsburg: Stackpole Books, 1997.

Spurlin, Charles D., ed. *The Civil War Diary of Charles A. Leuschner*. Austin: Eakin Press, 1992.

Stanyan, John M. *A History of the Eighth Regiment of New Hampshire Volunteers*. Concord: I. C. Evans Printing, 1892.

Steers, Edward, Jr. *Blood on the Moon: The Assassination of Abraham Lincoln*. Lexington: University Press of Kentucky, 2001.

Stephens, Alexander H. *Constitutional View of the War Between the States: Its Causes, Character, Conduct and Results*, vol. 2. Philadelphia: National Publishing Co., 1870.

Swanson, James L. and Daniel R. Weinberg. *Lincoln's Assassins: Their Trial and Execution*. Santa Fe: Arena Editions, 2001.

Sword, Wiley. *Embrace an Angry Wind*. 1992; reprint, Columbus: The General's Books, 1994.

Sword, Wiley. *Mountains Touched with Fire: Chattanooga Besieged, 1863*. New York: St. Martin's Press, 1995.

Sword, Wiley. *Shiloh: Bloody April*. Dayton: Morningside, 2001.

Tamarkin, Bob. *The Merc: The Emergence of a Global Financial Powerhouse*. Chicago: Harper Collins Publishers, 1993.

Taylor, Joe Gray. *Louisiana Reconstructed, 1863-1877*. Baton Rouge: Louisiana State University Press, 1974.

Taylor, Richard. *Destruction and Reconstruction: Personal Experiences of the Late War*. New York: D. Appleton and Co., 1879.

Thomas, Benjamin P., ed. *Three Years with Grant, As Recalled by War Correspondent Sylvanus Cadwallader*. Lincoln: University of Nebraska Press, 1996.

Thomas, Dean S. *Cannons: An Introduction to Civil War Artillery*. Arendtsville, PA: Thomas Publications, 1985.

Thompson, Jerry D. *Mexican Texans in the Union Army*. El Paso: Texas Western Press, 1986.

Tidwell, William A. *Come Retribution: The Confederate Secret Service and the Assassination of Lincoln*. Jackson: University Press of Mississippi, 1988.

Trostel, Scott D. *The Lincoln Funeral Train: The Final Journey and National Funeral for Abraham Lincoln*. Fletcher: Cam-Tech Publishing, 2002.

Tunnard, W. H. *A Southern Record: The History of the Third Regiment, Louisiana Infantry*. Baton Rouge: Private Printing, 1866.

J. W. Vance, *Report of the Adjutant General of the State of Illinois*, vol. 8. Springfield: H. W. Rokker, 1886.

Walker, Peter J. *Vicksburg: A People at War, 1860-1865*. Chapel Hill: University of North Carolina Press, 1960.

Wallace, Lew. *Lew Wallace: An Autobiography*, vol. 1. New York: Harper & Brothers Publishers, 1906.

Warner, Ezra. *Generals in Blue: Lives of the Union Commanders*. Baton Rouge: Louisiana State University Press, 1964.

Warner, Ezra. *Generals in Gray: Lives of the Confederate Commanders*. Baton Rouge: Louisiana State University Press, 1959.

Waugh, John C. *Reelecting Lincoln: The Battle for the 1864 Presidency*. New York: Crown Publishers, Inc., 1997.

Welles, Gideon. *Diary of Gideon Welles: Secretary of the Navy Under Lincoln and Johnson*, vol. 2 (April 1, 1864-December 31, 1866). Boston: Houghton Mifflin Co., 1911.

Wert, Jeffrey D. *From Winchester to Cedar Creek: The Shenandoah Campaign of 1864*. Mechanicsburg: Stackpole Books, 1997.

Whitcomb, Caroline. *History of the Second Massachusetts Battery. Nims' Battery) of Light Artillery, 1861-1865*. Concord: The Rumford Press, 1912.

Williams, T. Harry. *P. G. T. Beauregard: Napoleon in Gray*. Baton Rouge: Louisiana State University Press, 1995.

Winik, Jay. *April 1865: The Month That Saved America*. New York: HarperCollins, 2001.

Winschel, Terrence J., ed. *The Civil War Diary of a Common Soldier: William Wiley of the 77th Illinois Infantry*. Baton Rouge: Louisiana State University Press, 2001.

Winschel, Terrence J. *Triumph & Defeat: The Vicksburg Campaign*. Mason City: Savas Publishing Co., 1999.

Winschel, Terrence J. *Vicksburg: Fall of the Confederate Gibralter*. Abilene, TX: McWhiney Foundation Press, 1999.

Woods, J. T. *Services of the Ninety-Sixth Ohio Volunteers*. Toledo: Blade Printing and Paper Co., 1874.

Woodworth, Steven E., ed. *The Musick of the Mocking Birds, the Roar of the Cannon: The Civil War Diary and Letters of William Winters*. Lincoln: University of Nebraska Press, 1998.

Wright, John D. *The Language of the Civil War*. Westport: Oryx Press, 2001.

Wright, Richard J. *Freshwater Whales: A History of The American Ship Building Company and Its Predecessors*. Kent: The Kent State University Press, 1969.

Wudarczyk, James. *Pittsburgh's Forgotten Allegheny Arsenal*. Apollo: Closson Press, 1999).

Articles

Bearss, Edwin. "The Battle of the Post of Arkansas, *Arkansas Historical Quarterly*, vol. XVIII, Autumn 1959, no. 3.

Bearss, Edwin. "The Mechanicsburg Expeditions," *Journal of the Illinois State Historical Society*, vol. 56, no. 2, summer 1963.

Bergeron, Arthur W. "The Battle of Mobile Bay," *Blue & Gray Magazine,* vol. 19, Issue 4, April 2002.

"Colonel Anderson's Sword," *Confederate Veteran,* vol.33, 1925.

Eggleston, E. Trent. "Scenes Where General Tilghman Was Killed," *Confederate Veteran* 1, no. 10 (October 1893).

Evans, E. Chris. "Return to Jackson, July 5-25, 1863," *Blue & Gray Magazine*, vol. 12, Issue 6.

Fitzhugh, Lester N. "Saluria, Fort Esperanza, and Military Operations on the Texas Coast, 1861-1864," *The Southwestern Historical Quarterly,* vol. 61 (1958).

"A Friend in Deed," *Confederate Veteran,* vol. 34, 1926, 194.

Glover, Dr. Robert W. & Randal B. Gilbert. "Camp Ford, Tyler, Texas," *Confederate Veteran,* vol. 5, 1996.

Harris, Henry War. "From Comanches to Yankees," *Civil War Times Illustrated* (June 2002).

"In Memoriam: Mrs. Catherine McDow Brownson," *Confederate Veteran,* vol. 40, 1932.

"In Memoriam: John Ramsey McDow, M.D.," *Confederate Veteran,* vol. 34, 1926.

"John Milton Brownson," *Confederate Veteran,* vol. 14, 1906, 131.

Kimmel, Ross M. "A Well-drilled Artillery Battery...," *America's Civil War*, July 2001, 12.

Landers, Col. H. L. "Wet Sand and Cotton—Banks' Red River Campaign," *The Louisiana Historical Quarterly*, vol. 19, no. 1 (January 1936).

"The Last Stand"—Monument at Victoria," *Confederate Veteran*, vol. 20, 1912.

Mays, Walter H. "The Vicksburg Diary of M. K. Simons, 1863," *Texas Military History*, Spring 1965, vol. 5, no. 1.

Mulligan, Robert E., Jr. *Military Images,* vol. 21I, no. 5, March-April 2000.

Myers, Robert C. "The Worst Colonel I Ever Saw: Francis Quinn and the Twelfth Michigan Volunteer Infantry." Western Michigan University.

"Old Bethel Chapel," *Confederate Veteran,* vol. 36, 1928.

Pitts, Florison D. "The Civil War Diary of Florison D. Pitts," *Mid-America 40,* Chicago 1958 (Pitts Diary).

Poulter, Keith. "Decision in the West: The Vicksburg Campaign, Part 3," *North & South*, Issue 4, April 1998.

Savas, Theodore P. "Col. James H. Beard and the Consolidated Crescent Regiment," *Civil War Regiments* (vol. 4, no. 2), 1994.

"Scattering," *National Tribune*, vol. 15, no. 12, January 2, 1896.

White, Patrick H. "Civil War Diary of Patrick H. White. Contributed by J. E. Boos," *Journal of the Illinois Historical Society*, October 1922-January 1923, vol.15, nos. 3-4.

Winschel, Terrence J. "To Rescue Gibralter: John G. Walker's Texas Division and the Relief of Fortress Vicksburg," *Civil War Regiments*, vol (3, no. 3), 1993.

Witt, Kathy. "General Tilghman's Place," *Civil War Times Illustrated*, December 2001.

Online Databases

Historical Data Systems, Inc., Duxbury, Massachusetts (HDS)
    The American Civil War Research Database; www.civilwardata.com

INDEX

Appendix 3

Images of Chicago's Battery Boys

Michael Graham, my great-great-grandfather, was a Battery Boy who actively served with the Chicago Mercantile Battery from the first mustering in on August 29, 1862, to the final mustering out in July 1865. While I was growing up, my grandmother told me stories about him and entrusted me as keeper of his CMB honorable discharge. My fascination with him and the Mercantile Battery continued into adulthood. In the 1990s, when I began to research the battery, I was looking for information about Michael but found very little—nothing more than his name listed on the official rosters. Although this was disappointing, the research deepened my understanding and appreciation for what the Battery Boys accomplished during their remarkable history.

It was during this time that I found Rick Williams' CMB web site. Our friendship soon began through the enthusiasm we share for the Battery Boys. As he conducted his extensive research for *Chicago's Battery Boys*, Rick occasionally contacted me with a lead or possible trail of information about my ancestor.

In December 2006, Rick contacted me when a series of CMB letters and ephemera appeared on an Internet auction site. The appearance of these items was a direct result of the increased awareness *Chicago's Battery Boys* generated for the battery. Between the two of us, we acquired most of the key correspondence, ephemera, and CDVs. To my great happiness, some of the letters and ephemera contained references to Michael Graham. Finally, a glimpse of his story as a Battery Boy emerged: his friends were some of the MOH recipients, in early June 1863 he was promoted to stable sergeant, and in the postwar years he served as a vice-president of the CMB Association.

Shortly after the December auction (and also as a result of Rick's book) an album of fifty Battery Boy CDVs appeared on the same auction site. Both Rick and I recognized this opportunity as one of great importance for the battery's legacy. The images in this appendix are from this album, assembled by Battery Boy Nelson Imus as a gift for his sister Emma. Although I have not yet found a picture of Michael Graham, or confirmed that any of the unidentified CDVs in the album depict him, I know that many of the Battery Boys appearing on these pages were his close friends.

Chicago's Battery Boys honors these soldiers, and it is appropriate they should appear for the first time in this revised edition.

David Ray, Great-great-grandson of Michael Graham.

Sgt. Nelson Imus created a Chicago Mercantile Battery photo album for his sister. The letters CMB are visible on the brim of his cap. Imus died from typhoid fever at Grand Gulf, Mississippi, on May 14, 1863.

Sgt. Joseph Hyde died of dysentery at Vicksburg on July 25, 1863.

Lt. George Throop was killed during the Red River Campaign at Mansfield on April 8, 1864.

Sgt. Edward Thomas was discharged for disability on December 5, 1864.

Private Charles Woolcott was discharged for promotion on March 11, 1864.

Pvt. Billy Sherman (left), an original Battery Boy, served through the entire war. *Private Dick Ransom* (below) was discharged for disability on March 24, 1863.

Pvt. John Lunt (below) was an original member of the Battery Boys. Note what look to be corporal chevrons on his sleeves.

Cpl. Jimmy Dunne, a Medal of Honor recipient for his bravery at Vicksburg (alias "Young Butcher"). Note the letters CMB on his cap in the enlarged center inset image.

An unspoiled image of *Capt. Patrick White* (left), a Camp Ford POW. *Pvt. George Montgomery* (below) was discharged February 9, 1863, for disability reasons.

(Above) *Alfred Barker* mustered out as an artificer (a man who maintains small arms), while *Albert Mather* (left) mustered out as a sergeant.

Original Battery Boy *Pvt. Charles Carder* served throughout the war.

Pvt. William DeGraff (left) was discharged on February 17, 1863, for disability. The CDV for *Alexander Diven* (below) indicates he was a corporal when the image was taken. He was discharged on December 11, 1862.

Orla Adams was, according to his CDV and muster rolls, an artificer. *Sgt. Warren Whitney* (center inset) was discharged for disability on March 2, 1863.

Henry Bush mustered out of Chicago's Battery Boys as a sergeant.

Pvt. William Putman (below) stands proudly to have his photograph taken. An original member of the Battery Boys, he served throughout the war.

Charles Kloth (above), an original private with the Battery Boys, was awarded the Medal of Honor for his role in attacking the 2nd Texas Lunette at Vicksburg.

2nd Lt. Henry Roe (left) commanded the Chicago Mercantile Battery from April 1864 until May of 1865. *Pvt. Edward Gooding* (above), an original Battery Boy, was discharged for promotion on August 23, 1863.

Pvt. Henry Fisk (left) was recruited into the battery on October 29, 1862. *Pvt. Philip Gunlock* (below), was an original battery member. Nicknamed the "Butcher," he mustered out as a corporal in 1865.

An original Battery Boy, *Pvt. Lewis Walton* (above) was discharged on February 16, 1865. *Pvt. Eugene Fishburn* (right) was discharged for disability on March 16, 1863. *Pvt. Eugene (or John) Gilbert* (center inset).

Two original battery members, *Pvts. Gilbert Stees* (below) and *Oliver Adams* (left).

2nd Lt David Crego (above) resigned from the battery on February 6, 1863. *2nd Lt Frederick Bickford* (right) remained with the unit only a few days longer before resigning on February 22 of the same year.